"HOW I GOT INTO SEX"

Personal Stories of

"HOW I GOT INTO SEX"

Leading Researchers, Sex Therapists,
Educators, Prostitutes,
Sex Toy Designers, Sex Surrogates,
Transsexuals, Criminologists, Clergy,
and more . . .

■

BONNIE BULLOUGH, R.N., PH.D.,
VERN L. BULLOUGH, R.N., PH.D.,
MARILYN A. FITHIAN, PH.D.,
WILLIAM E. HARTMAN, PH.D.,
& RANDY SUE KLEIN, PH.D.

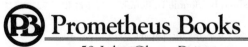
Prometheus Books
59 John Glenn Drive
Amherst, New York 14228-2197

Published 1997 by Prometheus Books

01 00 99 98 97   5 4 3 2 1

Library of Congress Cataloging-in-Publication Data

"How I got into sex" / edited by Bonnie Bullough . . . [et al.].
        p.   cm.
    ISBN 1–57392–115–7 (cloth : alk. paper)
    1. Sexology—Research. 2. Sexologists. I. Bullough, Bonnie.
HQ60.H69   1996
306.7'072—dc20   96–46523
                                                                    CIP

Printed in the United States of America on acid-free paper

The editors respectfully dedicate this volume to the memory of

Bonnie Bullough

She energetically participated in the planning, selection of invitees, and compilation and editing of this book. She died on April 12, 1996, after the manuscript had been sent to the publisher. We missed her sharp editorial skills in the final proofing. Fortunately a brief review of her significant contributions to human sexuality is included with those of her lifelong companion, and our senior editor, Vern Bullough.

Contents

Introduction

ALTHOUGH THIS BOOK has many sources, one of our editors, William Hartman, was the catalyst. He was strongly convinced that students contemplating the field of sexology, or sexual science, needed to know the people in the field and how varied their backgrounds were. He brought in his long-time collaborator, Marilyn Fithian, and also Bonnie and Vern Bullough and Randy Sue Klein. Although many others were also involved in recommending individuals for inclusion, the final decisions rested with the five of us.

The major difficulty we faced was in deciding whom to include. We wanted to have researchers, therapists, and educators, as well as individuals important in the field in other capacities. We strove to get a representative sample, and in this we succeeded since no two individuals had the same background. We also set out to obtain an age differential, ranging from those who recently entered the field to those who were pioneers. Some we asked were bound by previous contracts or could not contribute for other reasons. Generally, however, we received an overwhelmingly favorable response, although not all who agreed to contribute ended up doing so. Probably our publisher heaved a sigh of relief since the book was long enough without them, but we miss them nevertheless.

Still, we believe that we achieved what we set out to do: to show the variety of individuals who comprise today's sex and gender professionals. Most of them are academics, and they come from a variety of fields or disciplines: medicine, nursing, social work, history, law, biology, anthropology, and biochemistry, although a disproportionate number are sociologists and psychologists. Only a handful set out to be sex researchers, sex therapists, or sex educators. Instead they came to the field serendipitously. Many did so with great hesitation, unknowingly following the advice that George Corner, a professor at the University of Rochester medical school, gave to his student William Masters when Masters indicated he might want to do more sex research of the type that Corner was doing. Corner advised the young Masters to become established in another field; to marry; and then, after he had achieved a reputation in this other field, and only then, should he consider doing serious studies in sex. While none of our contributors recounted receiving any such advice, many of them entered the field with considerable hesitation, conscious of the ambivalence the public has about sex.

Some of our contributors who willingly and consciously entered the field did so in order better to understand some of their own sexual inclinations. Those that did, however, generally moved beyond this narrow focus and became interested in the field as a whole. A good example of this is found in the autobiography of Virginia Prince, a transgender person. She helped change the ideas of professionals about transgendered individuals, but she also was a major force in organizing the transgender community and encouraging it to speak for itself.

To the reader of this book it should quickly become clear that academically sexology is different from almost all other fields. It is by its nature interdisciplinary, involving biological, social, psychological, historical, and cultural factors. Thus even those who prepared themselves within their own discipline to study sex in a serious way soon found that they, too, had much to learn from their colleagues. It is this mutual learning perspective which serves to gives sexology a spirit of cohesion and support lacking in most other fields. The majority of us in the sex field are always conscious of how dependent upon others we are when we venture beyond the limits of our own discipline.

Adding to the feeling of support and collegiality that most of us have toward our fellow sexologists is the recognition that we are in what might be called a delicate field. It is one in which Congress has intervened to prevent grants, and in fact foundations that have given money for sex research have found themselves threatened with a loss of their tax-exempt status. One of the contributors indicates that he lost his security clearance because of his interest in what has come to be called "the alternate lifestyle." others have been denounced for challenging some of the popular myths about sex. The late Alfred Kinsey is currently under attack for some of the information he included in his 1948 book on the American male. Although sex sells books and newspapers, it is usually sensationalized, playing on both the general curiosity and ignorance of the public about sex. Sometimes it seems that sex raises far too many emotions for it to be discussed dispassionately. Still, people somehow or other become sex professionals in spite of all these difficulties, and this book attempts to have them explain why.

Because of the great diversity of the contributors, we found that we could not organize it around any particular theme. Many themes appeared, but none that made for major groupings. Instead we took the easy way out and listed the contributors alphabetically. We have done the same for the editors. Although some of us contributed more than others, we felt the easiest way was to list ourselves in alphabetical order. It is our hope that readers will find the brief accounts of the individuals included here as fascinating as we did. We learned a lot ourselves and hope that the reader will also.

We would also like to acknowledge with thanks the many who helped contribute to this volume, particularly Eugene O'Connor and Steven Mitchell of Prometheus Books. They have helped to make this a better book. Finally, we hope that this book will encourage others to study sexuality in a serious way. The field offers many rewards for those willing to suffer the occasional stigma of being a sexologist. We actually have come a long way in understanding sex in the past fifty years, in spite of the difficulties that many of us have faced. We certainly, as a society, look upon sex differently than we did a generation ago, and some of those in this book have been major forces in helping society to do so.

We hope you will learn from reading it.

Bonnie Bullough
Vern L. Bullough
Marilyn Fithian
William Hartman
Randy Sue Klein

1

Personal Experience Becomes Professional Involvement

Elizabeth Rice Allgeier, Ph.D.

Elizabeth Rice Allgeier, a member of the psychology department at Bowling Green State University, Ohio, is editor of the Journal of Sex Research. *Her areas of interest include societal regulation of human sexual behavior, interpersonal relations and mate selection criteria, consensual versus coercive sexual interactions, and evolutionary psychology.*

FIVE YEARS AFTER I was born in Andover, Massachusetts, my mother left my father and moved to Florida. From that time until I "ran away" from home at the age of nineteen, we moved constantly all over the country because my mother became involved with a sailor. The longest that I was in one school was two years, but there were times when I was in a given school for only six weeks or several months. This was not an optimal situation for growing up, but I attribute the constant moves to my ability to get to know people quickly and easily. I did manage to get elected "Most Likely to Succeed" by my schoolmates in the high school in Oxnard, California, where I was enrolled from the middle of my sophomore year to the middle of my senior year. I bet they would be surprised by the area in which I've enjoyed success!

We moved again—this time to San Jose, California—in early 1959 before I graduated. I was particularly upset by that move and missed my classmates very much. One evening, in my loneliness, I called a disk jockey to request a song. We got to talking, and he asked if I would like to come to the station to meet him. I did and we ended up in his apartment later that evening. I was just short of my eighteenth birthday, and he was twenty-six. It was my first coital experience. I had told him that I was a virgin, but he didn't believe me: I didn't bleed, I didn't seem to be feeling any pain, and I actually didn't feel much of anything. I was disappointed and offended that he didn't believe that I was a virgin. I never saw him again.

After graduation from high school in 1959, I had no interest in continuing my education. But I also hadn't yet learned to say no, and my mother told me that she would not allow me to date if I didn't go to college. I reluctantly enrolled at San

Jose State as a journalism/English major. I did very well in my first semester, was appointed one of the editors of the college newspaper, and won a public speaking award. However, in the middle of my second semester, I fell in "lust" with Richard, a fellow college student, quit going to classes, and spent almost all my time in his cabin.

That summer, he moved to a commune in San Francisco's Haight-Ashbury district. I lived at home and worked in my mother's real estate office that summer, but after a particularly nasty series of arguments, I ran away from home and moved into the commune with Richard. We married eighteen months later, and lived in a tiny apartment on the third floor of an old Victorian mansion, sharing the bathroom with other tenants on that floor.

One afternoon about a year after we married, Richard was downstairs in the backyard, and I was reading A. S. Neill's *Summerhill*. In one chapter Neill described how he dealt with the boys in his English boarding school when they masturbated. I had tried to masturbate a few times in the past but I didn't really know what I was doing and would always get bored before I got aroused. However, that afternoon, I idly began playing with myself while reading Neill, and I accidentally discovered my clitoris and had an orgasm! I was thrilled until I heard Richard coming up the stairs. I locked myself in the community bathroom and masturbated again, had another orgasm, and was absolutely delighted.

About eighteen months after we married, I had the first of my four children. Fourteen months after Beth was born, I had my second daughter, Sarah, which was surprising because Richard and I rarely had sex. My mother had raised me to believe that I would really enjoy sex, but her outlook was at variance with the general cultural belief system at the time, and I didn't. Although I frequently felt sexual arousal, I thought there was something wrong or animalistic about these feelings and I was afraid to initiate sex. Since Richard had been raised to believe that sex was sinful, he preferred to complete the sexual act very quickly (missionary position), early in the morning (I've never been a morning person), as and infrequently as possible. Once a month or so, we would go through this ritual, but I was always just waking up about the time he ejaculated, so that was the end of that.

Four months after Sarah's birth, I screwed up my courage to talk with Richard about our sex life. He said that he was happy, and so didn't see any need to talk. In the parlance of the 1960s, I was "the one with the problem." In desperation, I suggested that we separate for a while, thinking that this would persuade him to talk with me about our sex life. Richard was always a dreamer and thought that would be fine, because he wanted to move to Santa Barbara and start a health food store. He did, and he made a beautiful store.

I remained in San Francisco. Shortly after we separated, I became involved with Charles, one of our friends who had just gotten divorced. We lived together and then married. His attitudes about sexuality were very different from Richard's, and I thoroughly enjoyed that aspect of our relationship for the eight years that we were together. During our time in San Francisco, many of our friends were experimenting with utopian relationships, open marriage, and group marriage. The general idea was that if you really loved someone, you would want them to be happy even if it included becoming sexually involved with someone else. Jealousy was seen as a weakness stemming from our capitalistic economic system. Unfortunately, almost all of us suffered from that weakness, and many marriages and relationships ended.

In 1967, Charles was accepted by the University of Oregon's anthropology department, so we moved to Eugene, where I had my third daughter, Katy. I returned to college, and although I was very interested in psychology, the psychology department at that time was dominated by rats, Skinner boxes, and so on. I took all the non-rat courses I could, but earned my degree in a 1960s program called Community Service and Public Affairs in 1969. In my final semester, I had the good fortune—along with another undergraduate student—to be invited to a graduate level seminar called "On the Year 2000" which focused heavily on the issue of global overpopulation

That year, Charles was awarded a National Science Foundation grant to conduct his dissertation research with a preliterate, polygynous tribe in northeastern Uganda. Charles had dreamed of doing anthropological research in Africa for years. I, however, having absolutely no desire to live in a tent in Africa, suggested that he go for the year and the girls and I would be waiting for him when he came back. I wanted to enter graduate school. Despite his ardent desire to go, Charles said that he would not leave without us. I couldn't bear for him to give up his dream, so I finally agreed to go. I didn't realize it at the time, but that trip was to become my first experience with sex research.

We flew to Uganda in the summer of 1969 and spent several weeks in Kampala trying to obtain information about the Tepes (or *So*, as they called themselves), the tribe on Mount Moroto with whom we were to live for a year. Although there were a few scattered reports from missionaries, very little hard data were available. Charles's plan was to study patterns of distribution among the *So* clans during variations in availability of resources. Tribes in northeastern Uganda keep herds of cows and goats but subsist primarily on the maize and sorghum that the women grow, plus the berries and greens that they gather. There are two growing seasons each year, and typically at least one of the seasons is accompanied by drought.

Although we didn't discuss it prior to flying to Uganda, Charles expected that I would help with the interviews but that I would primarily live the role of a housewife (or, more accurately, tentwife).

I had no intention of sitting in a tent for a year. Further, I pick up languages very easily. Although Charles is extremely bright, he doesn't learn languages readily, and the *So*'s language wasn't written down until we did so and published it as part of a two-volume ethnography (Laughlin and Allgeier, 1979). Thus, for several months, Charles was dependent on me for communicating with members of the tribe, and that put quite a strain on our relationship.

Having experienced the explorations with relationship forms in San Francisco, I was extremely curious about how the *So* handled their polygynous marriages.

Were co-wives jealous of one another? At the time, I had not seen the Kinsey group's books nor did I have any training relevant to human sexuality. However, I had had several courses that dealt with research design. Shortly after we arrived, I designed a fairly lengthy questionnaire on my trusty manual Smith-Corona type-writer. I have described our initial contacts (very friendly) with the *So* elsewhere (Allgeier, 1993) when Charles, our daughters, and I trudged up the mountain where they lived when our Landrover could no longer negotiate the rough terrain.

We paid several *So* men to help build a fenced compound of limbs and thatch (*eo*) that the *So* use to surround small groups of huts (*irs*) in which we pitched our two tents. Our initial research task was to conduct a census of the entire tribe (approximately 1650 *So* lived on Mount Moroto) so that we could draw a random sample of the female-headed families. I smile as I remember having to wait for several weeks for colleagues to send us a table of random numbers that Charles claimed that we had to have to draw a random sample, but at the time, I didn't know that one could obtain a sample without that table!

While conducting the census, we also gathered genealogies. We were able to get approximate estimates of people's ages by tying their level of development (pre-pubescence, postpubescence, marriages, etc.) to significant events that had occurred in Uganda, such as the movement of the members of the King's African Rifles through northeastern Uganda, the vote for independence from Britain in 1960, and similar events. We were fascinated to learn that the *So* did not want independence from Britain, as they were a relatively poor tribe and believed that in intertribal dis-putes, the British treated them more fairly than did Ugandans from other tribes. However, members of the Ugandan army "visited" them and threatened to beat and kill them if they did not vote for independence.

After we received the table of random numbers, we selected the twenty fami-lies we intended to study in depth through observations and interviews. All agreed to participate (we paid participants a few shillings per interview) and we began the process of interviewing them in waves. It took about two weeks to complete each round of interviews.

I began my interviews with relatively innocuous questions involving gender roles, tasks expected of offspring, and so forth. Eventually, after we had become well acquainted I asked much more sensitive questions about masturbation, sexual activ-ities, feelings about co-wives, sexual orientation, and norms and expectations regarding who could have with sex with whom, in what ways and where. The women readily responded as I moved toward the more sensitive questions, but the men initially politely explained that men did not talk to women (in this case, me) about sexual matters. I said that I understood but I had no other way to learn and understand their lives, and I was willing to answer any questions they had about Europeans (whites—regardless of their birthplace—were referred to as Europeans by the *So*). I am grateful that they accepted my explanation; from that point on, all my male informants were very forthcoming.

The *So* worshiped their ancestors and some gods, the chief deity being *Akuc*.

They were unusual among the world's societies in that they claimed that no one engaged in same-gender sexual relationships. During the year we were there, we also saw no evidence of any form of relationship other than heterosexual. Initially, I had a difficult time conveying the meaning of my questions in this area because they couldn't see the point of such a relationship given that two men or two women couldn't conceive. If such an act were to occur (but they asserted that it never had), it would be evidence of possession by a hyena.

The same claim was made about adult masturbation, although some men reported that a man might stimulate himself if he was on a long hunting trip without any access to women. Women didn't understand how a woman could masturbate given that they didn't have penises. Fairly early in the series of interviews, I asked for the names of various body parts in their language. At one point I drew a picture of a vulva with a clitoris, a urethra, a vagina, and an anus. They had terms for all these body parts except for the clitoris. Although I did not conduct pelvic exams, I have no reason to believe that they were different from other women in possessing a clitoris. They were simply unaware of its existence.

In response to questions about the purpose of sexual intercourse, their response was universal: to have babies. A woman who became my *daquath* (sister) when I was inducted into the tribe late in our stay there described her first intercourse with her husband through clenched teeth. She said that it felt as if she were being burned in there and that she just kept saying to herself that she had to do this to get babies and she had to have babies to get cows. The bride price for women was (sometimes heatedly) negotiated between the fathers of the prospective couple and were in terms of the number of cows and goats the man's clan would pay to the woman's clan for him to obtain her as his wife.

Having more than one wife was an indication of the wealth (in cows and goats) of a man's clan. The largest number of wives that any one man had was four, but the majority of the men had only one—and the offspring of some of these couples actually belonged to the clan of the mother, because the father's clan hadn't paid the bride price since they were too poor. Co-wives tended to help one another and appeared to have the kind of close, affectionate relationships that exist between some adult sisters. Men also had affectionate relationships with one another, holding hands as they walked along paths together, or swinging their arms around one another's shoulders. In contrast, we never observed men and women exhibiting any affection toward one another. A few weeks after we arrived, I came out of the tent one morning to boil water for coffee. Charles came out shortly thereafter, said "Good morning," and patted me on the bottom. The *So,* who were constantly watching us for the first few months we were there, behaved the way I would expect my students to respond if I were suddenly to fart loudly while delivering a lecture. That is, there was some anxious laughter but most of them looked away and appeared to be embarrassed by this display of affection. At the time, we were puzzled by their reaction because we hadn't been there long enough to realize that we were violating a norm against public expressions of affection between heterosexual couples.

According to members of the sample, private expressions of affection were also nonexistent. Sex (*apudori,* roughly translatable as "to fuck"; they had no word for love between men and women) was carried out very efficiently. Except when it was chilly, men wore no clothes and women wore a very short apron with their buttocks bare. Breasts were not eroticized. It was taboo for women to touch men's genitals, and a man was not to touch a woman's genitals except for the accidental contact that might occur during insertion of his penis into her vagina.

Two questions came up repeatedly while we were there, and I was never able to provide a response that made sense to them. They asked, subtly at first, and then more directly, why I was not yet pregnant given that our youngest daughter was no longer breast feeding and was about two and a half. They offered to spread goat entrails on my stomach and to massage me to increase my ability to get pregnant. My consistent use of a diaphragm would have made no sense of them. I had asked what they could do if they wanted to postpone conception or have no more children. Their reaction was amazement. I might as well have asked what they would do if they wanted to be rid of their arms and legs.

The other question was based on their perception that we were wealthy (hah!): why couldn't Charles take a little wife? We explained that we would be returning in the summer of 1970 to our country, where men were not permitted to have more than one wife at a time. Nonetheless, I found myself experiencing a bit of jealousy as they suggested various young women as possible wives for Charles.

Their standards of attractiveness for a woman were based on her ability to work hard and on her having a pleasant personality. One young woman who could have readily graced the centerfold of *Playboy* based on Western standards had remained single longer than was characteristic for most women. In general, women were married, or at least engaged in an *apudori* relationship, by their mid-teens. However, this woman, in her late teens, was perceived as bitchy and lazy. Her garden was adjacent to our *eo* (house), and I watched on a number of occasions as her father chased her with a tree limb, complaining about her laziness. She had still not married at the time that we left.

Gender role expectations were, from my standpoint as an American, very rigid. Men took all the risks from the intertribal warfare, but had relatively few other day-to-day chores. Women built the huts, cultivated the gardens, and took most of the responsibility (along with older female siblings) for young offspring. Early in our stay here, they sold us several three-cornered stools that they had carved. One day while interviewing one of our informants, I made the mistake of sitting on one of the stools rather than on the ground. I was patiently informed that women were not allowed to use the stools. They were only for men. Women prepared food (except when menstruating), but ate separately from the men.

We were sad to leave the *So* in the summer of 1970. Charles obtained his first academic position at the State University of New York at Oswego, which was beginning a master's program in general experimental psychology. I applied for admission, **and** was one of eight students—and the only woman—who was accepted. I later learned that although my GRE scores, GPA, and letters of recommendation were the highest of the eight students who were admitted, I was almost turned down, not just because I was a woman, but because I had three children and there were questions as to whether I was really a serious student! I ended up being one of only two students in the history of their master's program to receive my degree with honors.

I then applied for admission to graduate school at Syracuse University in 1971. Clive Davis—who was to become one of my three most important mentors, and whose own autobiography appears later in this volume—interviewed me. Although we have had an ongoing humorous disagreement about this, in the course of the interview, he queried me about the discrepancy between my verbal (above the 90th percentile) and quantitative score (mid-50th percentile) and asked if I was brain-damaged. I explained that I had earned As in both my statistics courses in my master's program after I had taken the GREs, but had, to my detriment, avoided math at the undergraduate level. Despite my supposed "brain damage," I was admitted to the doctoral program in social psychology.

At this point, Charles objected, stating that the thirty-mile commute from Oswego to Syracuse would put a strain on our marriage. So, I contacted Syracuse and told them that I could not accept their offer. Ironically, I left Charles shortly thereafter for reasons that were unrelated to the issue of my obtaining further training. I reaccepted Syracuse's offer and moved there with my three daughters. Unfortunately, the fall that I began Clive also moved—to Uganda! There was no one else with whom I wanted to work. I had fallen in love with research while at Oswego, and wanted to continue my work on the effects of defendant characteristics on group (simulated juries) decision making. However, the climate in the social psychology program at Syracuse at that time was not particularly supportive of research. One was expected only to complete course work and produce a dissertation. During that period, I had exchanged reprint requests with an advanced graduate student at Purdue University, and we became involved in late-night phone calls about our research and other topics. One day he sent me an application for the graduate program in social and personality psychology at Purdue, writing that I might want to apply. On a whim, I did and was accepted.

In January 1973 my daughters and I moved to West Lafayette where I began training at Purdue. Within a few months, I began to work with Donn Byrne, then a professor there and a major sex researcher, who became the second of the three important mentors in my career. In a class with him, we were asked to write a research proposal. It was my first foray into sex research since the interview study that I conducted with the *So*, and it was stimulated by a combination of that experience and the emphasis on overpopulation in the seminar "On the Year 2000" that I had taken as an undergraduate. Specifically, among the *So*, your primary value as a woman was to produce as many babies as possible. I wondered if adherence to traditional gender-role expectations among American college students would be related to family-size desires. Donn loved the idea and encouraged me to conduct the study. It was my first sole-authored publication (Allgeier, 1975).

My major professor in my master's degree program encouraged me to write in the stilted fashion characteristic of so many psychologists, but I resisted this because of my early training in journalism, in which the major goal is to communicate one's ideas clearly. Donn, an absolutely wonderful writer himself, approved of my writing style and I flourished under him.

At that time (1973–1974), Purdue was the center of research on interpersonal attraction. Rick Allgeier, also a student of Donn's, had gone off on a clinical internship and didn't return until September 1973. I noticed this weird name (Allgeier) in the mail room, and was told by several students that I would have to meet Rick—that he and I would be a perfect match. I didn't think much about it. Although I was "dating," I was really taken with my budding career and had no intention of making any more long-term commitments to anyone. Shortly after Rick arrived back in West Lafayette, we were introduced. Whew! I was wearing jeans and a T-shirt. I immediately went home and changed into an outfit that left my body bare from just below my breasts to my hips and did what I later heard described as the "Parade" by Monica Moore (1985), who was involved in studying women's signaling to men. That weekend, at a pig roast attended by graduate students and some faculty, I again engaged in signaling, and Rick got the message. We've been together from that night on.

Rick defended his dissertation in the summer of 1974 and we were married a week later. He got a job at Alma College in Michigan, so we moved that fall, and I commuted weekly back and forth from Alma to West Lafayette for the next semester. I had been toying with the idea of obtaining a clinical degree (I was already minoring in clinical psychology). Fortunately, I was offered and accepted a job as Director of Advising, Counseling, and Career Development beginning in January 1975. Much of my time was spent counseling troubled college students. I would arrive at home with no energy to write, much less to interact with anyone. That experience convinced me that I did not want to go the clinical route.

Meanwhile, almost all new faculty were informed that their contracts would not be renewed because of a projected drop in enrollment at the small college. Thus, Rick went on the job market and accepted a position at a hospital for the criminally insane near Ann Arbor. I resolved to complete my prelim and dissertation, but an instructor position, teaching four courses per semester, opened at Eastern Michigan University in Ypsilanti, adjacent to Ann Arbor. I was hired and during the academic year 1975–1976, worked frantically to cover the courses (my first experience teaching human sexuality) and complete my dissertation, which involved an experimental study examining the relationship of both gender and gender-role identification on judgments of a couple having sex in the woman-above versus man-above position. I also conducted survey research examining gender-role identification and beliefs about dating, marital, sexual, and child-rearing roles.

The oral defense went well, and Donn hosted one hell of a good party for me. Rick and I staggered back to the hotel at about five in the morning. Given our hangovers, I have no idea how we did it, but later that morning, we managed to conceive. One of Rick's charms at the time we married was that he didn't want children. He changed his mind and after getting over my shock, so did I. We had both been hired to teach at the State University of New York at Fredonia in the fall of 1976. I did not realize that I was pregnant but when my cycle began to vary from its normally extremely predictable pattern, I went to the University of Michigan's emergency room. The physician conducted a pregnancy test, and informed me that the "pregnancy" was all in my head. As it turned out, the pregnancy was in my fallopian tube. I confided in one of my students at EMU whose husband was doing his residency at Wayne County Hospital. He called me, saying that I might have an ectopic pregnancy. Rick and I had already loaded the U-Haul and were planning to head from Ann Arbor to Fredonia that day. Instead, I went to the hospital where they did emergency surgery from midnight until 4 A.M. to remove the tube and part of an ovary. I spent six days in the hospital and then we lived with Rick's uncle near Ann Arbor for several weeks while I recuperated. This was a very difficult period, because I knew that having had one ectopic pregnancy, I had a 25 percent chance of having another. However, two years later, when I was thirty-seven, our son Donald was born.

We remained at Fredonia for four years. I developed a proposal for the creation of a human sexuality course which was accepted. Research activity, however, was difficult. Fredonia did not have a graduate program but I had some talented advanced undergraduates with whom I did research. However, the ethics review board would not permit them to collect data. At the time, I was interested in contraceptive attitudes and behavior (including abortion) and I had to conduct all the research myself. One well-meaning colleague suggested that I should even wear a white lab coat while collecting data!

Because I taught human sexuality, I was approached by McGraw Hill to serve as a reviewer of an initial prospectus for a sexuality text by Janet Hyde. I later was asked to serve as a primary reviewer for her text and to write the Instructor's Guide. When that task was finished, McGraw Hill asked if I would be interested in co-authoring a second edition of another text. I discussed it with Rick who suggested that he and I write a sex text. We sent our own prospectus to half a dozen publishing companies and were blessed by having the (anonymous) reviewers rave about it, and were then the beneficiaries of a bidding war. We ultimately signed with D. C. Heath, because we didn't want to have to fit into a niche between other books being marketed by the same company. Allgeier and Allgeier (1995) is now in its fourth edition.

At some point in the middle-to-late 1970s (I cannot remember exactly when), I became reconnected with Clive Davis. I had joined the Society for the Scientific Study of Sex (now Sexuality; SSSS) and Clive asked me to serve as an ad hoc reviewer of the *Journal of Sex Research* (*JSR*). I loved doing reviews and thoroughly enjoyed his appreciation of my work.

In the late 1970s, a woman whom I didn't know—Naomi McCormick—wrote me for a reprint. After exchanging reprints, Naomi asked if I would be interested in co-editing a book on the interaction of gender roles with sexual interactions. I agreed without having met her—something that I tell my graduate students is generally a very bad idea. However, our collaboration resulted in the publication of Allgeier and McCormick's (1983) *Changing Boundaries*. It could have been a disaster, but we worked very well together and still do.

In 1979, Clive approached me about accepting a nomination to be an Eastern Region Representative to SSSS. I had developed a fear of flying from an experience I had just before we left for Africa. By the time we returned, I had a full-fledged phobia about flying and hadn't gotten on a plane since. I drove or took trains. Clive was aware of my fear and pointed out that if I were elected, I would have to fly, as SSSS meetings were held all over the country. So, in 1980 when I had to fly to Dallas, I got to the airport, drank as much liquor as I could but couldn't seem to get drunk, and got on the plane.

Fortunately, I had been to one previous SSSS meeting in Philadelphia so I was not as shocked by the Dallas meeting as I might have been otherwise. The night before the board meeting, several of us were sitting in a hot tub in the SSSS suite, taking turns getting wine from the refrigerator. It was my turn and while I was bent over looking into the refrigerator for the wine, the incoming president, Ira Reiss, came into the suite. He was in quite a jovial mood and approached me in a very friendly fashion. He didn't know me, but I recognized him and suggested that he join us in the hot tub. When he saw the crowd, he declined. The next morning, as the new members of the board were being introduced, Ira smiled and said, "Gee, I didn't recognize you with your clothes on!" I thoroughly enjoyed the meeting and haven't missed an annual meeting since.

Meanwhile, I had become increasingly dissatisfied with the difficulty of doing research at Fredonia and really wanted to work with graduate students, as much as I enjoyed teaching undergraduates. Rick and I went on the job market in spring 1980 trying to find two positions near enough that we could live together. He accepted the position of clinical director of a mental health center in Lima, Ohio, and I was hired at Bowling Green State University—just a little over an hour north of Lima. Fifteen years later we are still here. I dislike the terrain and extremes of weather here, but my department has been very supportive of the research on sexuality that my graduate students and I do.

Clive Davis "promoted" me to consulting editor of *JSR* in 1981, and then to associate editor in 1983; I remained in that role until the end of Clive's tenure in 1988. I learned a great deal from him, which has been of great help to me in my current role of *JSR* editor.

In the very early 1980s, a group of us from the middle of the country began meeting informally to establish a Midcontinent Region of SSSS. At the time, SSSS was divided into the Eastern and Western Regions. I will never forget our first meeting with Barb and Howie Ruppel. We met in Chicago and Howie drove us through a driving rainstorm to Wisconsin where we met with Frank Farley, Clint Jesser, Kathryn Rindskopf Dohrman, and several other people. That was the beginning of a very strong friendship with Howie and Barb. The group, including Bob

Friar, Bob Brush, and others had several subsequent meetings at Pokagon State Park, and in 1982, the Midcontinent Region was officially approved at the SSSS meeting in San Francisco.

In 1981, I was elected secretary of SSSS at the same time that Vern Bullough was elected president. He is the third of three important mentors in my life. He promoted me within the organization and offered me a mixed blessing: the position of chair of the first annual meeting sponsored by the newly formed Midcontinent Region held in Chicago in November 1983. As any meeting chair knows, the work is extremely time-consuming for at least eighteen months prior to the event itself.

The meeting went very well, but for a few weeks following it, I experienced a strange small bout of depression which came over me suddenly. Essentially, by the late fall of 1983, I had run a successful conference, Rick's and my first edition of our sexuality text had been published, and I had been tenured and promoted to associate professor. I had been worried that because I do sex research, I would not get tenured even though there had been no overtly negative reactions and I'd consistently gotten top merit ratings on research and teaching. However, those judgments are made by an elected five-person committee, whereas tenure is decided by a vote of the entire tenured faculty. In any event, all was well, but it has been shown in research on life-change units that too many changes at once, even when they are positive, can be unnerving.

In 1986, I was selected as a G. Stanley Hall Lecturer for outstanding undergraduate teaching by my (theoretically) home organization, the American Psychological Association. I gave a two-hour lecture and wrote a chapter (Allgeier, 1987) based on the lecture. Although I was very honored by the award, I really feel much more at home with SSSS.

Thus, I was delighted at being elected to the presidency of SSSS (1985–1986). It was actually considerably less work than being SSSS secretary. After seven years on the SSSS Board, I finally resigned in 1987, but I still attend all the annual meetings and as many of the regional meetings as I can. I expect that I will do so until I can no longer walk.

My term as *JSR* editor officially began in 1993. Although we have had a few difficult authors, for the most part, it has been a very rewarding role. The workload, however, has increased each year. In 1993, we received 93 submissions, in 1994, 117, and in 1995, 163. Further, in general, the quality of the submissions has also increased. However, I hope that the quantity does not increase during the remaining two years of my terms when I will happily turn the reins over to the capable hands of John DeLamater. I have continued to do research and publish (but not in *JSR*, of course) during this period, but I am constrained by my current commitments from initiating a number of new studies that interest me. I look forward to release from the editorship so that I can pursue those ideas.

Rick, Gary Brannigan, and I have just signed a contract to edit a book on the joys and frustrations experienced by sex researchers. We are excited about this project and think that it will yield some very intriguing chapters from the contributors.

Last summer, Rick, Don, and I spent several weeks in the Netherlands (primarily Amsterdam) and Copenhagen. It was extraordinarily refreshing to spend time in cultures that are so much more positive in their sexual attitudes and norms than contemporary North America. I would dearly love to spend a sabbatical year there after finishing my term as *JSR* editor. Some of the research ideas I have involve cross-cultural comparisons. Although I have been very pleased by the supportive environment I have enjoyed at Bowling Green, Rick and I would like to relocate to a warmer climate with more contours in the terrain. If the current job market continues, such a move may not be possible until we retire. But even after we retire, I expect that we will still continue with research and writing about sexuality.

References

Allgeier, A. R., and E. R. Allgeier. 1995. *Sexual interactions.* 4th ed. Lexington, Mass.: D. C. Heath.

Allgeier, E. R. 1975. Beyond sowing and growing: The relationship of sex-typing to socialization, family plans, and future orientation. *Journal of Applied Social Psychology* 5: 217–26.

———. 1987. Coercive versus consensual sexual interactions. In *G. Stanley Hall Lecture Series*, ed. V. P. Makosky, vol. 7, pp. 9–63. Washington, D.C.: American Psychological Association.

———. 1993. So-so sexuality: Field research on gender roles with a preliterate polygynous African tribe. Invited chapter in *The undaunted psychologist: Adventures in research,* ed. G. G. Brannigan and M. R. Merrens. New York: McGraw Hill, pp. 218–34.

Allgeier, E. R., and N. B. McCormick (eds.). 1983. *Changing boundaries: Gender roles and sexual behavior.* Palo Alto, Calif.: Mayfield Publishing Company.

Laughlin, C. D., and E. R. Allgeier. 1979. *Ethnography of the So of Northeastern Uganda.* 2 volumes. New Haven, Conn.: Human Relations Area Files, Inc.

Moore, M. M. 1985. Nonverbal courtship patterns in women. *Ethnology and Sociobiology* 6: 201–202.

2

From Roman Catholicism to Sexology

Richard Allgeier, Ph.D.

Richard Allgeier, who has taught at Eastern Michigan University, Alma College, and Gannon University, is now a psychologist in private practice in Bowling Green, Ohio. His publications include studies on sex and power in the 1990s and on system and sexual abuse.

A S I PONDERED the events that influenced me to become involved in sexuality research, education, and clinical work, it is probably not surprising that my thoughts began to drift back toward my youth. The major element shaping my early views about human sexuality was my being raised and schooled in the Roman Catholic tradition. I attended a Catholic grade school and high school in Erie, Pennsylvania. The type of Catholicism that I was exposed to was peculiarly American, which, as I learned later, was quite different from its European and South American counterparts. That is, it embraced a puritanism which it shared with many Protestant fundamentalist groups. Sex was seldom mentioned in a positive manner except as something that a husband and wife needed to do in order to produce children. The allure of nonmarital sex and the dire consequences for those who might succumb to such temptation were the primary focus of my early education. My experiences in grade school and, to some extent, high school with the "fire and brimstone" for those who gave in to the temptations of flesh were the beginning of my interest in the societal regulation of sexuality, although I did not conceptualize it quite that way at the time.

I attended church regularly on Sunday and, during the Lenten season, daily, until I was approximately fourteen years old. By that time my disenchantment with Catholicism had begun to crystallize into an interest in agnosticism. Although my agnosticism was not very well developed conceptually, I knew that for me there was too much magic and irrationality in the Catholicism that I had experienced. Thinking about these issues did not consume a great amount of my time, however. I became involved, some might say obsessed, with sports and this continued into my early college years. Because of my love of sports and an embarrassing shyness, I can only recall dating four women during my high school years. None of these adventures was a rousing success. All the girls involved were Catholics and hobbled by their own inexperience. The most sexual any of these relationships ever became was an attempted kiss that resulted in our painfully bumping our foreheads.

I was the oldest of nine children. My father had been killed in World War II shortly after my birth. My mother remarried and had four more daughters and four more sons. As I was growing up I had always thought of my stepfather as my biological father until, when I was 14, my mother told me of my biological father's death. This came as quite a shock to me although I should have suspected that something was out of order from my past experience. When I was in the second grade some of the other students began to refer to me as an orphan because my last name was Allgeier and the name of my family was Scheppner. Distraught over this, I went home and reported what was taking place to my mother, who calmly said that there was no problem and that I would now use the name Scheppner from that day on. There was no legal changing of my name but all of my school records reflected the name change. As I look back I am amazed by my naivete in not wondering more about the change of names. One could probably make an argument for repression, but I think that I was basically a pretty contented and happy child for whom at the time a name change was a very peripheral issue.

Although my exposure to formal Catholicism at church and school was a negative experience, the way the religion was practiced within my family was fairly benign. We were expected to attend church weekly and to observe the basic tenets of our faith. While my parents both attended church regularly, my maternal grandmother, who lived with us most of the time when I was growing up, never went. She claimed that she had gone to church so frequently when she was younger that there was no need for her to go any longer at this stage of her life. Interestingly, my parents both stopped attending church after their youngest child graduated from high school. To my knowledge, they never set foot in a church again unless it was for a wedding or a funeral.

After graduating from high school I received a football scholarship to Xavier University in Cincinnati, Ohio. In my sophomore year, after becoming embroiled with the head football coach on the practice field over what I perceived to be his authoritarian manner, I quit the team and left school. I worked the following year for the New York Central Railroad as a welder. During this time I began to read Sigmund Freud's work voraciously. His ideas helped me to realize that one might be able to develop a rational system for understanding humans and their sexuality. Thus buoyed, I returned to college in my hometown and eventually graduated with a bachelor's degree in psychology from Gannon University. During my senior year I also married Cathy Beal, who was an interior designer. She had graduated from the Pratt Institute in Brooklyn and espoused many ideas that seemed radical to me but were reflective of the times. This was the mid-sixties and protest against the

Vietnam War was becoming more intense. It was a heady time in which some of the more radical students and intellectuals on the left felt that it was possible to overthrow a system that they perceived to be fascist. Experimentation with drugs and sex was common and I lost my inhibitions. During my senior year, Cathy and I and several others formed a chapter of Students for a Democratic Society (SDS). At that time, it was a peaceful organization but elements of it would turn violent a few years later. We held meetings, organized protests, handed out literature "to educate the people," and marched in street demonstrations. During this time I received my summons to report for a physical examination pursuant to being drafted into the army upon my graduation. By this time I was so fervently against the war in Vietnam that I could not consider serving in the armed forces even though I could not be sent into combat as the only surviving son of a soldier killed in action.

I decided to register as a conscientious objector even though I was not truly a pacifist. My views then were as they are today, in that I would do almost anything to avoid violence or killing. However, I could envision myself engaging in violence and even killing if my life or the life of a friend or family member were threatened and there appeared to be no other alternative to physical aggression. As I battled with the draft board over what looked like a losing battle for conscientious objector status, we considered fleeing to Canada, an option that was becoming increasingly popular among those who opposed the war. My war status became irrelevant in the summer of 1967 when I was involved in a near-fatal industrial accident. I crushed and severed my left forearm in a mishap on an outdoor crane. Doctors were able to reattach my arm and sew together pieces of bone that had splintered. I spent the next two months in a hospital undergoing a series of surgeries. During this time the war lingered on and I began to think about leaving the country for a while. Both Cathy and I were interested in traveling abroad and this, combined with our frustration over the continuing war, led me to apply to the master's program in psychology at the American University of Beirut in Lebanon. I was accepted into the program and after being reassured that the continuing surgeries I would need on my arm could be done at the University Hospital left for Beirut in the winter of 1968. On our way to Beirut we stopped in London, Paris, Madrid, and Rome. This was my first experience with other cultures and the beginning of my fascination with cross-cultural psychology.

Beirut in 1968 was still considered the "Switzerland of the Middle East." It had been a year since the 1967 war with Israel which left Beirut's status as the financial capital of the Middle East relatively unscathed. With its large diplomatic and business community as well as the university students, Beirut was a cosmopolis of myriad nationalities living together in a cultural blend of Western and Eastern influences. The rift, however, between Christian and Muslim was obvious to anyone who listened to the conversations at the outdoor cafes, and one could sense the potential explosion that was to come later with the Lebanese civil war.

The American University of Beirut had a beautiful campus overlooking the Mediterranean Sea. Its students came from all parts of the world. Besides the

Lebanese there were students from northeast Africa, other parts of the Middle East, Iran, and Europe. The language of instruction was English, so I had little trouble adapting to my graduate courses. My first semester was difficult because I had to have a series of surgeries which involved lengthy stays in the hospital. Luckily I had a skillful surgeon, Suhail Boulos, and flexible professors who allowed me to make up work I had missed. I eventually received my master's degree in psychology in 1969 but that was only half of my education in Beirut. From my interactions with university students and myriad other Lebanese, my interest in the social regulation of sexuality began to coalesce. Many experiences contributed to this development. One that comes to mind is the high price that the Lebanese put on female virginity, particularly in the villages. A fellow graduate student informed me that in her village there had been a long tradition that involved a "virginity check" on the newlywed couple's first night together. This usually consisted of a female relative checking the nuptial sheets for blood stains after the couple had left the room. The sheets would then be presented to the relatives as an indicator of whether the woman was actually a virgin. Given that some women may have very thin hymens and will produce no bleeding when ruptured or that the hymen may be broken through some types of exercise or in an accident, it would put young women at risk of being ostracized by relatives, of having their marriage annulled, or, in rarer cases, being killed by relatives for bringing shame on the family. Therefore, it came as no surprise that the village women had developed a safeguard. This consisted of taking a small vial of lamb's blood with them to the nuptial bed and pouring it onto the sheets when their husbands' attention was directed elsewhere.

At the university I took a course from Harry Lindgren, on leave from San Francisco State University, in social psychology. He encouraged my writing and also urged me to go on for my Ph.D. Harry was a friend and colleague of Donn Byrne, with whom he had co-authored an introductory textbook on psychology. I was aware of Byrne's work on attraction and found the idea of studying with him to be quite compelling. My entry into a Ph.D. program, however, was put on hold for a year. Cathy had worked as an interior designer while I was attending school. It was now her turn to go for her master's degree, so I took a position as an instructor in psychology at Gannon. During my year there, I applied for graduate school at Purdue University where Donn Byrne served on the faculty. Cathy continued to work on her master's. We were, however, beginning to move in different directions in terms of our interests and career goals. As the academic year ended, we decided to separate, with Cathy taking a position at Colorado State University and me accepting a graduate assistantship at Purdue. Although we would continue to see each other in a long-distance relationship, we gradually grew apart and eventually she filed for an uncontested divorce.

My first two years at Purdue were hectic and busy. Donn had a productive group of graduate students who were churning out research on attraction guided by the reinforcement model he had developed. I became part of that group and my first two publications were in the area of attraction. I had also been taking courses in clinical psychology; for my third year I applied for clinical internships and was eventually accepted an internship at Crownsville State Hospital. My internship was a relatively uneventful experience and I returned to Purdue to finish my dissertation. While I was on internship there, I met Betsy Laughlin, a new graduate student who had started in the Ph.D. program, at a graduate student party and it was lust/love at first or maybe second sight. I quickly learned that she had been previously married to an anthropologist, and had spent a year studying a preliterate tribe in Uganda, had three young daughters, and was interested in psychology and the law. Eventually I moved in with them and after much discussion we all agreed that marriage might be a good thing. I was finishing up my dissertation on talkativeness and interpersonal attraction and had accepted a job in the psychology department at Alma College. We decided to go back to Betsy's parents' home in North Andover, Massachusetts, with the girls and get married there. We then moved to Alma, Michigan, and Betsy commuted back to Purdue as she worked on finishing her dissertation.

After Betsy recovered from her ectopic pregnancy (see chapter 1), we moved to Fredonia, where we went about our teaching duties and began a series of studies on attitudes toward abortion. This research would eventually cause me problems when I applied for staff privileges at a hospital affiliated with the Catholic Church. Basically what we found was that emotion had more of an effect than knowledge on judgments about abortion. The ecological validity of this was borne out when my application for admission to the Catholic hospital previously mentioned was blocked for a time because, in looking at my résumé, they thought that these studies indicated that I was condoning abortion. As far as I can tell, none of the membership committee had ever read the articles.

As Betsy has already indicated, while at Fredonia, we decided to write our own book and began the task in 1978, a significant date since our son Donald was born that year. The task turned out to be much more time-consuming than we had envisaged. Our goal was to integrate the literature from anthropology, biology, history, psychology, and sociology to show how they interact in affecting human sexual behavior, hence the title *Sexual Interactions*. Evenings and weekends became dominated by the "book." Luckily we had very supportive editors, George Abbott and Nancy Osman, who softened the hard edges of producing a college textbook. Finally, in October of 1983, *Sexual Interactions* rolled off the press. As of this writing, the book is in its fourth edition. One of the unexpected results of publishing a sexuality textbook, was that we became "experts." Lawyers, journalists, and various and sundry people from all walks of life consulted us on topics ranging from abortion to witchcraft. Often we referred them to other "experts" with more knowledge than we had on the subject.

In the midst of writing the first edition, we moved to Bowling Green, Ohio, in 1980. Betsy joined the faculty at Bowling Green State University and I accepted a job as a clinical psychologist at the Northwest Center for Human Resources in Lima, Ohio, about sixty-five miles south of Bowling Green. For the next three years

I primarily engaged in clinical work and eventually became Clinical Director of Northwest. In 1983, I accepted a position as Clinical Director at Wood County Mental Health Clinic in Bowling Green, Ohio. I left two years later to go into private practice. But I continued to teach as an adjunct professor at Bowling Green because I enjoyed teaching and wanted to keep in touch with students for whom our textbook was targeted.

My clinical practice is a general one, although I am referred a good number of clients for sex therapy. By not specializing in sexual difficulties, I see a wider variety of problems such as anxiety and depressive disorders. What is common to almost all of the difficulties I have encountered is that they are enmeshed in relationship problems of one sort or another. Depression is often related to a romantic relationship that is under duress or has ended. It is more likely to occur in females because they have been socialized to take responsibility for the emotional aspects of a relationship. If the relationship encounters difficulties, she is the one who usually internalizes the problems as somehow being her fault. Depression often ensues particularly if her partner sees her change in affect—crying, emotional outbursts—as a sign of mental illness rather than a reflection of an inequitable relationship. Obviously this type of dynamic affects a couple's sexual interaction, usually negatively, and reflects an interesting phenomenon. Sexual interactions are the most accurate predictors of how two people relate to each other in the nonsexual areas of their relationship. Withholding sex, pursuing sex, acquiescing to sex, playing with sex often mirror how couples deal with financial issues, household chores, and parental decisions.

Relationships are as much about power as they are about love. By power I mean the ability to affect the outcome of interactions. When power is tilted toward one partner, problems ensue. In this culture, power has usually accrued to the male, although this dynamic is slowly changing. As relationships become more equitable, the disparity between rates of depression for men and women should be greatly reduced.

Finally, I should mention a major influence in my life, the Society for the Scientific Study of Sexuality (SSSS). I joined SSSS in 1977 and began presenting papers at their conferences. It was a group of people that was unlike any group I had run into at psychology conferences. Most of the individuals I have met through SSSS have been extremely open and honest about their personal, research, educational, and clinical lives. It was and is a support group for most of us who found that many of the colleagues whom we worked with on a daily basis viewed us as odd, aberrant, or not "real" scientists, educators, or clinicians because of the subject matter that we were interested in. Betsy eventually joined SSSS and we have both been very involved with the society and will continue to be so. It gave us the opportunity to meet many of the shining lights of the emerging field of sexual science. Vern and Bonnie Bullough, Ira Reiss, Clive Davis, Bill Masters and Ginny Johnson, Wardell Pomeroy, Paul Gebhard, Howie and Barb Ruppel, and Charlene Muehlenhard are just a few of those whom I found to be of great value in their support, advice, and friendship.

In looking back and looking ahead, I continue to be optimistic that we can move toward a sane and rational sexual environment. Myth, prejudice, ignorance, and fear still dominate the sexual landscape in the United States. For those who wish to pursue a career in clinical work, research, and/or education there are daunting challenges. Specializing in sexuality can impede career paths and raise suspicions among colleagues. I have encountered little overt resistance to advancing my ideas about sexuality in the many settings in which I have worked, but suspect that there has been covert opposition. On the other hand, there has been the delight of seeing a student's eyes light up when introduced to a new idea or a different way of seeing things, the look of gratitude of a client or student when their fears are dispelled with accurate information, and finally the intellectual challenge and satisfaction that comes from trying to unravel the complexities of human sexuality.

3

Cop, Call Girl, and COYOTE Activist

Norma Jean Almodovar

Norma Jean Almodovar is active in COYOTE (Call Off Your Old Tired Ethics), the organization of sex workers. She is also an author, a former member of the Los Angeles Police Department, a convicted felon, and at one time contemplated a career as a missionary.

I F YOU, THE reader, had met eighteen-year-old Norma Jean Wright in the summer of 1969, you'd never in a million years imagine that someday she/I would become a notorious prostitute and political activist. There was just nothing in my background to suggest that I would or could actualize a 180-degree turn from an ultra-conservative, religious upbringing to make a dramatic metamorphosis into a whore—societally unacceptable and a pariah among "good" women. If you had even suggested the possibility existed, I would have gladly and righteously condemned you to hell for blasphemy. After all, that June, I enrolled in the Philadelphia College of the Bible, and was preparing for the fall classes with the lifelong dream of becoming a Christian missionary to save the lost souls in Puerto Rico.

Perhaps the missionary urge never left me and that is what compelled me to make the choice to become an advocate for prostitutes' rights. Certainly there are strong similarities between preaching hell fire and damnation to the heathen and standing on my soap box to preach the gospel of personal and sexual freedom to the morally uptight. Still, it is difficult for many to fathom the progress I made from the ultra-shy, innocent, and godly girl that I was to the outspoken convicted felon prostitute that I became.

I'll start at the beginning. I was the first daughter born to Mr. and Mrs. Harold Wright of Binghamton, New York, in what ultimately became a family of six girls and eight boys. My mother, the former Helen Ruth Doolittle, was one of four daughters of Arthur and Clara (Chauncey) Doolittle. My grandmother, Clara Chauncey, came from a long and impressive line of ministers going back to the Rev-

34

erend Charles Chauncey, the president of Harvard University from 1654 to 1672. It is well documented that Reverend Chauncey was a direct descendent of King Henry I of France, who, in turn, was a direct descendent of Charlemagne (who was noted for, among other things, his sadistic persecution of prostitutes). Additionally, my grandmother was a direct descendent of John Howland of the Mayflower. The two family lines joined through marriage sometime in the 1800s, and consequently, my siblings and I share the distinction of having the direct ancestry of Mayflower passengers, ministers, and kings.

Of course, none of this mattered to me during my childhood. There was no money to go with the blue-blooded pedigree, and besides, my mother's conversion from her liberal Presbyterian upbringing to the more strictly fundamentalist Baptist doctrines ensured that she would raise us to believe that such things were irrelevant.

She also believed that the mind-numbing destitution into which she brought her fourteen children was important to secure her place in heaven. From the day I was born until I left home at eighteen, I was instilled with the conviction that it was God's will that my family suffer and do without the bare necessities and luxuries that my friends and their families enjoyed. I admit that despite my firm beliefs, as each new addition to my family stretched the few dollars available, I suffered pangs of discontent and developed a loathing of poverty and our unstable financial condition.

In addition to her lectures on the virtues of poverty, there was thorough indoctrination with the fundamentalist convictions that sex, especially outside of marriage, was grievously sinful. Even sexual longings fell into that unholy category, and I learned at a very early age that evil women who provoked men to lust were called whores and would undoubtedly suffer the worst of God's punitive wrath. The wearing of seductive clothing such as short-sleeved blouses or the use of any cosmetics put a good girl at risk of being mistaken for a prostitute! I was torn between the desire to be like my school friends who wore mascara, lipstick, and short-sleeved clothing, and the equally strong yearning to be a good, pure Christian girl far removed from worldly temptations.

Despite the unrelenting condemnation of sex and all things sexual that my parents attempted to embed in my developing mind, I experienced the pesky phenomenon of biological urges, raging hormones, and passionate, lust-inspired girlhood crushes on the opposite sex. No amount of prayer seemed able to squelch my budding libido. I had learned at a very early age to enjoy my sensual nature, because my father frequently gave into temptations of the devil and sexually fondled me.

I don't believe that it was the sexual fondling at an early age that was the most emotionally damaging to me. I think my confusion, pain, and anger sprang from the conflicting messages about the evils of this activity and the instillation of guilt in me, my father's apparent inability to conquer the desires of the flesh, and my own positive reaction to being sexually stimulated. I'm not saying that incest and child abuse should be tolerated, but should the child be inflicted with a sense of wrongdoing because of the molester's guilt? Further, I think it's appalling that when the "victims" of incest reach adulthood, they are disallowed the memories of pleasure that the intimacy perhaps gave them as a child.

It is aggravating that people speculate that my childhood experience with my father led to my adult decision to become a prostitute. Perhaps it could be surmised that I chose my law enforcement career for the same reason, The one unfortunate consequence truly attributable to those experiences was the weight I gained and maintained until my early twenties. Throughout my junior and senior years in high school, I hid behind a thick pair of glasses and a seriously overweight body, hoping to avoid any unwanted attention being paid to my female attributes. I was the quintessential wallflower—overly bright, ultra-religious, fat, poor, and plain. No one ever mistook me for a sex object. All the guys ever wanted from *me* was my mind, they wanted me to give them the answers to the test questions. I aced all my foreign language classes, English, literature, art and science. I hated math, but I was good at it.

The heavenly minded teen that I was felt smug and superior to my classmates because I knew that my future held great things, and I would change the world for God. The earth-bound girl suffered teenage angst, jealousy, and rejection. There was un-Christian-like envy in my heart when I looked at the well-dressed, petite, pretty, and very popular girls in my class. Perhaps within that envy lay the seed of latent sexuality that one day allowed me to blossom into the whore instead of the missionary. And that is the only connection between the childhood sexual intimacy with my father and the empowered, exultant, sex-positive, politically active prostitute that I am.

By the time I was ready to enter Philadelphia College of the Bible in the fall of 1969, I was already undergoing internal transformation. Heretical doubts about God himself filled my mind. Certainly I questioned the rationality of a belief system that espoused the notion that one could get pregnant merely by attending a movie . . . alone! Before I left home that summer to go to New York City to work at my friend's uncle's bookstore, my mother made sure that I understood the consequences of "going out into the world." She handed me several religious tracts which admonished young women to stay out of movie theaters at all costs, or we would "get pregnant in technicolor." Other tracts contained dire warnings of the evils of big cities and how to avoid temptation. The theme of all the tracts was sex, sex, and more sex. No useful facts about birth control, just a tirade of irrational, anti-sex platitudes that couldn't convince me the authors had a grasp on reality.

By the end of that summer, I had a new job working at the Empire State Building and decided to postpone my first semester in college until the following year. The exposure to new concepts, interesting people, and my personal discovery of cognitive thinking demanded that I examine and overhaul if necessary my cherished convictions. By the first of the new year, I abandoned all the religious values that had no foundation in reason. If I was not yet a confirmed atheist, certainly I was an agnostic,

January 1970 was a bitterly cold month. One of my Puerto Rican friends, Lourdes, from the Christian summer camp I used to attend, had just moved to Los Angeles. She returned for a brief visit to her family and invited me to have lunch with her. We went to the nearby Woolworth's luncheonette on 34th and 6th Ave., where she enticed me with stories about the beauty of L.A. and its warm weather. And by the way, she said, she was involved with this marvelous "local church" group, and wouldn't I like to come out and meet these wonderful people? They were nothing like the Christians we grew up with, she explained when she saw the skepticism on my face.

Not long afterward, my father's sister Rusty, who lived in California, invited me for a visit. As she was my favorite aunt, I could hardly refuse. Whenever she stopped at our house on one of her cross-country trips, she always seemed so glamorous, sophisticated, and rich! My mother could barely conceal her disdain for this worldly heathen called a sister-in-law. Aunt Rusty's outrageously interesting costumes mesmerized me and I am sure her flaming red hair inspired me to be a redhead. She never failed to bring me little presents of silk scarves and tiny perfume samples which I treasured and carefully hid from my nosy sisters. Surely her phone call to me that January 1970 was a sign that I was meant to go to California.

On January 17, when I boarded a plane and headed west, it was 18 degrees below zero in New York City. In contrast, when I landed at Los Angeles International Airport, it was a balmy 62 degrees and clear skies. What's not to fall in love with? It didn't take much convincing for me to decide to stay in L.A. rather than return to New York.

Lourdes had made me promise to visit her while I was in California. I called her one evening, and she and her church friends drove to my aunt's house to pick me up. To make a long story short, my friend and her "sisters" from the church made it impossible for me to ever be alone at any time; they overwhelmed me with their "Christian love" and quickly prevailed over my agnosticism. In no time at all I was sucked in, praising the Lord with the rest of them. I became deeply immersed in this religious cult.

During the early spring of 1970, Lourdes's cousin Al came to visit her. Just as I had been powerless against the force of a thousand happy people strangling me with "love," so was he. Like flies drawn to the sugary sweetness on a fly trap, we found ourselves stuck in something neither of us had the strength to leave.

Al was everything I thought I wanted in a man. He was tall and big, dark and handsome, and now he was a member of the "church." He was eligible marrying material, and I made certain he knew I was available, too. I still wore a size sixteen, but in the local church, it was acceptable to use minimum makeup, so I tested the limits. By now I wore contact lenses, and eagerly applied mascara to my big green eyes, which I batted at Al every time I saw him. For the first time in my life, a man responded to me as a woman, and, oh, how I loved it!

We began dating under the supervision of other married "brothers" and "sisters." It wasn't long before we were sneaking up to the rooftop of his apartment building all by ourselves. Passionate kissing gave way to heavy petting, and my panties were soaked as I experienced desire. Soon I was as unable to control my lust as he was, and on those warm summer nights up on the rooftop under the stars, we tried everything with each other but intercourse. Once I had bitten the apple, I was hooked. I wanted to be with Al all the time, and I wanted him to do those things to me, things like my father had done. My roommates suspected that something was happening, but I refused to answer their pointed questions.

Unfortunately, the more intense our relationship became, the guiltier I felt about it. Whatever we were doing, it was still a sin because we weren't married. Finally my conscience got the better of me, and one afternoon I sought the advice of one of the elders' wives, who was one of my close friends in the church. Big mistake. After I left her that afternoon, she went directly to her husband, and then to the other elders. Al was called before them and accused of fornication. He was told that he must marry me immediately or leave the church. After the evening service that night, he pulled me aside and told me we had to talk. His ashen face warned me that something was wrong.

We drove in his old Volkswagen to MacArthur Park near downtown L.A. As we sat on a park bench, he held my hand and asked me why I thought it was necessary to tell anyone about our rooftop activities. I was shocked, My friend must have betrayed me! I got up and walked toward the lake, and Al followed. He insisted that he wasn't angry with me, but he didn't understand why I told anyone. When I didn't reply, he took me by the shoulders and turned me around. He told me the ultimatum the elders gave us— get married or leave, those were our only choices. And so we were married, although we were not permitted to have a church ceremony, because we had sinned and didn't deserve the church's blessing.

Many church members were moving out to the San Fernando Valley, where another branch of the church was forming. We moved out there, too, in order to start out with a new group of "brothers" and "sisters" who didn't know our sorry past. Al had a job as a construction worker, and there was plenty of construction in the valley.

After we moved away from the close-knit unit of church members, we began skipping meetings. Brothers and sisters would call on us and inquire why we were not at the church every night. The pressure became unbearable and irritating, and eventually we stopped going altogether.

Before we moved to the valley, Al had filled out an application for work on the Los Angeles Police Department. He had been a military cop when he was in the air force, and his background made him ideally suited for the job. By the time the police department sent him the paperwork to complete before taking the written tests, he was happy with his construction work and didn't want to leave it. Without his knowledge, I filled out the paperwork and returned it. Being a bored housewife did not suit me, and besides, for many reasons I was contemplating leaving Al. We did not have anything in common other than the church, and at times he was physically rough with me—although compared to the spousal abuse that other women suffer, he was a gentleman. In addition, he had slept with my sixteen-year-old sister who was living with us, and I wasn't enlightened enough then to be understanding.

In August 1972 I entered the civilian police academy and in three months became a traffic officer with the LAPD. I felt privileged to be one of the few women hired by the LAPD to work in the male-dominated field of traffic enforcement. At five feet four inches, I didn't meet the five-feet-eight-inch height requirement to be a police woman. But then a police woman's job was boring because at the time, women were not being hired to work in patrol cars as police officers as it was considered too dangerous. Police women could only work day shifts, always indoors, and were assigned to menial tasks like answering phones and filing reports. I, on the other hand, was assigned to the night watch and given a patrol car to drive. I had no gun, and usually no backup partner when answering traffic-related radio calls from 6:00 P.M. until the wee hours of the morning in some of the most dangerous parts of the city.

By the time I graduated from the academy and "hit the streets" of Hollywood, I had left Al, filed for divorce, and moved into a bachelorette apartment in Hollywood. I had lost a lot of weight and now was a cute, perky, little red-haired girl in a uniform, on a job with few other women, and ogled by every male officer in the division. I had learned in high school that most guys don't fancy brains in a woman, especially if they want to sleep with her. Therefore, out of self-preservation, I made it a point to conceal my intelligence by adopting the mannerisms of a bimbo. With my happy-go-lucky attitude, basically sunny disposition, and deliberate masking of any intelligence, I made those cops feel comfortable around me.

When I walked into the Hollywood station to go to work, I wore a skintight T-shirt with no bra. It didn't take me long to catch up with my former high school classmates who knew the power of their femininity. It absolutely astounded me that men were so, well, easy. A little light flirtation, a wiggle of my firm, round butt, a giggle and a sigh, and guys seemed totally helpless. I had my pick of those handsome cops, and developed an appetite for the attention they paid me.

So I dated many of them, often ending up in bed after a first date. I knew that many of them were married, but I didn't care, since my divorce wasn't final anyway. In the early seventies, macho cops subscribed to the philosophy that any woman who enjoyed sex must be a whore. Above all else, I didn't want them to think I was one of *those,* so I felt that as long as I didn't ask for my own pleasure, they would respect me. So as much as I wanted and needed sexual gratification, I preferred to maintain the illusion that I was a good girl, even as the cops marveled at what an "easy lay" I was. With few exceptions, they didn't bother to inquire if I had had an orgasm. My pretending that I was a "good" girl absolved them of any responsibility to reciprocate sexual favors. Years later on the "Joan Rivers Show," I sarcastically explained my multiple liaisons with cops—that I was trying to find a cop who knew how to make love, but unfortunately, most cops think making love is like using their gun and all they have to do is take aim and shoot, but most of them can't get it out of the holster before it goes off.

All those years of religious indoctrination were difficult to shed and so my own hang-ups left me sexually frustrated. I was doing a fine job of behaving like a "slut," but I wasn't enjoying it at all because I could and would not admit to myself that I was *that* kind of woman who enjoyed sex, the kind that was called a *whore.*

Then in January of 1976, my life changed forever. Victor, the man who is my husband, lover, and best friend, entered my life and transformed my way of thinking, or more accurately, made me return to my interrupted teenage days of objective thinking.

Victor was older than I, and at first I thought of him as a wonderful older man who would be perfect for my recently separated mother. He didn't ask her out on a date when I brought her to meet him and didn't seem very pleased that I had. Nevertheless, I found him intriguing and agreed to go out with him on Valentine's Day eve.

Victor was unlike any other man I ever dated. He was cultured, well educated, and during the first six months that he took me out, he never made a pass at me—never tried to get me into bed. He took me to the theater and other places I didn't know existed. How could I? There was never a time in my young life that I had the opportunity to discover this other world. He was such a gentleman, so suave, and so different from the cops I dated that I thought he was gay. I didn't care if he was, because I enjoyed his company so much. Even more, I enjoyed the respect he showed me. Perhaps because I thought he was gay and therefore not interested in me sexually, I didn't behave like an airhead. He listened to what I had to say and treated me as an intelligent adult.

Six months into our relationship, he phoned me and explained that as much as he cared about me, his feelings for me were not merely Platonic and it would be impossible for him to continue seeing me on that basis. I was speechless! I stammered something unintelligible and hung up. That night, I thought about him in an entirely different way. I admitted to myself that I *was* very attracted to him physically but I never explored those feelings out of respect for his supposed sexual preferences. The next day, I returned his call and invited him to dinner. After dinner, we each tore off the other's clothes and discovered new facets of each other. We made love for hours, and I didn't want him to stop whatever he was doing to me

Even as I was basking in Victor's attentions, I was mortified by my reaction. The good girl me disappeared and a woman I had never seen and didn't know at all came forth moaning and groaning and orgasming like the whore from hell. Try as I might, the genie was out of the bottle and it was hopeless to pretend it hadn't happened.

For the sake of brevity, I will condense the story of my incredible relationship with Victor. Do the expressions "grand passion" or "love of my life" help you understand what he became and still is to me? We spent six months getting to know each other on so many levels that when sex was added to the equation, I fell deeply and passionately in love with him. With him, I never needed to hide behind a silly, shallow facade. He encouraged me to use my mind, to learn and grow, and he made me realize I could do anything I wanted to. When I told him I had always wanted to write, he didn't laugh. He believed in me and made me believe in myself.

In our sex life, I went from being embarrassed by my wetness in response to my feelings for him, to exalting in and embracing my sexuality. There were no taboos in our bedroom, and he encouraged me to share with him all my wildest fantasies. Any time my childhood hang ups prevented me from being completely open with him, he always asked one question that he insisted I answer—"why?" Victor compelled me explore the answer to its root, and if there was no rational foundation for my trepidation, he challenged me to shed the inconsistent beliefs.

We saw each other only on our days off, but more and more, those days we spent together were the only oasis I had. My job was quickly becoming a nightmare as the reverence I once held for the LAPD disintegrated in light of the multitude of cop scandals that were no longer possible to ignore. I had become what the captain called a "borderline insubordinate," and I couldn't keep my big mouth shut when I observed unacceptable conduct by my supervisors and peers.

The first few years with the LAPD were enlightening to me in so many ways. I came to the job so naive, so innocent, that it was impossible for me to believe that there could be bad cops on *my* police department. I manifested the same self-righteous attitude toward anyone who dared to criticize the LAPD that I had when someone questioned the word of God. The cops were my heroes and they could do no wrong. And God help me, I defended them even when I knew the truth. (Is an atheist permitted to say that?)

Being the only woman assigned to the night watch for a number of years, I saw a side of law enforcement invisible to most. My idealism faded after I witnessed police abuse, corruption, and inhumanity beyond comprehension. Some of the cops said and did things in my presence that made me realize that the vacuous pose that I had adopted in the beginning of my career gave them a false sense of security around me. Unbeknownst to them, I began keeping notes about what I saw and overheard, which I intended to turn into a book someday. Among other things, I wanted to expose the hypocrisy in police abuse of prostitutes. Prostitutes were treated in an atrociously degrading manner by the very agents of the law who were supposed to protect them, but the cops' abuse of public trust, property, and human life caused far more harm than commercial sex activity ever could. Observing this and other forms of the LAPD's state-sanctioned violence against unarmed citizens seriously damaged my emotional health as the years passed.

I was disgusted to see how the police officers treated street prostitutes. In the nightly roll call, the male officers laughingly described how they rounded up prostitutes, using what they called the "whore car" to collect these hapless working women and bring them to the police station for booking. Their methods for determining who would be arrested that evening were appalling. Often, the women were rounded up like cattle and forced to entertain the officers by running a foot race on the street after they removed their high heels. The women who finished last were then arrested and dragged to the police station, booked, fined, and permitted to return to the street early enough to ensure that they could make the money to pay the fine. The women became so immune to this abuse that they, too, began thinking of this violation of their rights as a game—they laughed with the officers when they were tagged for the night.

There was one pregnant, fifteen-year-old prostitute with a broken arm whom the cops arrested every night for a week. Night after night when I returned to the police station to do my paperwork, she would be there, shackled to the bench at the rear of the station, begging to be allowed to use the women's bathroom. (Pregnancy makes a woman need to urinate more frequently.) Since there were no police women around to take her into the ladies' room and I wasn't allowed to, she was told that she would just have to "wet her pants." The poor pregnant teenager, with a cast on her arm and tears smearing her mascara, did just that, and soon a puddle of liquid trickled down the hall from where she sat on the bench. I never spoke to her, but I wondered if this pathetic woman-child, sitting there embarrassed, frightened, and lonely, actually believed that this treatment was supposed to teach her that she was in a degrading profession and that the police were actually doing this to her for her own good. They were, after all, "rescuing" her from a big, mean pimp who didn't care anything about her, and from life on the street. I was outraged at the way they treated her, but what could I do?

My rage continued to boil as the nefarious activities of the cops were exposed. Not too many years earlier, there had been a sex scandal involving some of the male police officers and the teenage female explorer scouts (a branch of the Boy and Girl Scouts of America) who worked out of Hollywood Station. Although convictions for statutory rape by non-police officers resulted in sometimes lengthy prison terms, the law-breaking officers were only suspended or, at worst, fired. In 1982, one of the officers who had been caught the first time but only suspended was caught again. This time the officer was accused of being sexually involved with a fifteen-year-old girl over a five-year period, commencing when she was only ten years old. Fired from his job, he chose to plead guilty rather than stand trial, and he was given a two-year-probation sentence.

Due to internal problems at work, I felt completely overwhelmed, psychologically battered, bruised, and incapable of controlling my emotions. The rage, humiliation, pain, and indignation welled up inside and left me without the capacity to cope with stress. Every incident now reduced me to tears. I could not communicate with anyone, even Victor, without breaking down, and I was embarrassed. This was just not like me—I had survived other formidable situations in my life and had shown great strength. Indeed, I had always been regarded as independent, determined, strong, and capable, not a psychologically weak and helpless victim.

By April 1982, after ten years on the force, I was completely burnt out. I knew it was time for me to leave the safe harbor of a well-paying public service job with its health benefits and special privileges to go out on my own, but what was I going to do? Whatever new job I chose, it had to allow me the time to write—the only catharsis against the crippling anger within me. Realistically, I had no prospects for any other kind of work that would give me either the money or benefits I had earned with the LAPD. What work could I do that would almost guarantee me a public forum to get people to listen to what I had to say about the police department? Though I'd never thought of myself as an outspoken person before I joined the LAPD, now I was determined to find a way to publicly speak out about my experiences with as impassioned a voice as I would have had, had I become a missionary years before.

I entertained thoughts about working as a prostitute. Playing a call girl was my favorite fantasy. It was wildly provocative and stimulating to imagine myself as the most desirable sex goddess, whom men would pay large sums of money to have for one night. Was it a stretch to think I could actually become a call girl in order to earn a living?

I was intrigued by a call girl I had met, who lived in a beautiful house, drove an expensive car, wore nice clothes, and seemed to have plenty of self-esteem. Contrary to stereotypes, she was no air-headed bimbo, and she wasn't angry and burnt out as I was. She also liked her work, something that I no longer did, even though I had a job that society approved of and she was an outcast.

While I grappled with my conscience which insisted that I quit my job, fate intervened. On April 18, 1982, as I was patrolling Hollywood Boulevard (again), my police car was struck by a drunk driver. As his car rear-ended mine, I sighed with relief, "Well, that's it! This is the end of the line for me with the LAPD. Bless that man, whoever he is!"

At three in the morning, after my release from the hospital and filling out the mountains of paperwork required for workman's compensation benefits, I went home and, as a symbolic gesture, tore up my uniform and cut up my shoes. It would be far too expensive to replace them, and I didn't want to be tempted to change my mind. That was the last day I would ever work in any capacity for the Los Angeles Police Department. While I was not seriously injured physically, emotionally I was damaged almost beyond repair. I was determined never to return to my job no matter how much pressure the captain put on me. It was time to heal my soul.

After I had spent several months on disability leave, the city informed me that my benefits had run out and that I would have to return to duty. I opted not to go back to work, filed a lawsuit against the department, and eventually won a small disability pension. It was then I resolved to contact the call girl I knew and possibly seek employment in her profession while I wrote my exposé of the police department. After a long talk with her one afternoon, I decided that I could earn a living by selling the one favor that I freely and foolishly gave away to the many cops I dated before I met Victor.

The decision to become a prostitute wasn't easy. Was I prepared to be considered an "outlaw" and be disowned by my family and friends and society? The cops had an ambiguous attitude toward call girls, but others might not be so understanding. They might not get the statement I wanted to make, that I would rather be an honest whore than work for the LAPD in any capacity. So many things to consider, including discussing it with Victor, because whatever choice I made would also affect his life.

When I approached Victor with my plan, I told him that this was something I had to do, and I would understand if he chose to leave me, but I hoped he wouldn't. As we usually did when we discussed important issues, he made me work through my reasoning until he was certain that I knew what I was doing and why. In the end, he could find no objection to my decision, because I had carefully examined every motive and consequence before I went to him. There was no jealousy issue because he knew how much he meant to me and that would never be jeopardized. His only concern was that I not become "hard and jaded" by a career in prostitution. I reasoned, how could the act of giving people pleasure—for money—affect me that way if ten years of seeing the worst side of humanity hadn't resulted in my becoming bitter, "hard and jaded"?

Regardless of my laissez-faire philosophy of sex, in the beginning I feared that I would not enjoy the work as a prostitute, that it would be nothing like the fantasy experience with Victor, but I didn't care. My sole aim was to get people's attention, and perhaps persuade them to take more responsibility for their police department. When I discovered that I was born to be a "whore," I felt an immense sense of relief and liberation. It was wonderful that I enjoyed the work which subsidized my writing career!

One of the consequences of prostitution was the possibility of arrest. I knew that even though the cops seldom bothered call girls, what I was doing *was* illegal. The legislators claimed that the laws existed to protect women from exploitation. I knew that I had made the choice as an adult, and didn't feel legislators had any business making choices for me, but nevertheless prostitution was a misdemeanor and I could get arrested. It was ethically necessary to tell my friends and family that I was a prostitute before they heard it on the evening news, if my public battle with the LAPD led to my arrest. I was prepared to lose their affection and support, but was delighted that instead of rejecting me, they all chose to stand by me.

Not long after I began working, I had my first opportunity to explore my commitment to "the cause." In August 1982, the vice squad conducted a sting operation that resulted in the arrests of two of Los Angeles's most important madams and some of their girls, including me. During the sting the police learned I was writing an exposé about them and they unsuccessfully attempted to confiscate my manuscript.

The arrest both startled and terrified me. I wasn't prepared for the extreme emotional distress that I felt in the custody of the same men I used to sleep with for free. The old feelings of helplessness and rage returned and left me temporarily incapacitated. For a time, I was certain that I was under constant police surveillance and couldn't eat, sleep, or work. Eventually that feeling passed, and I resumed all my activities—including writing the book that would eventually cost me eighteen months of freedom.

It turns out I wasn't being paranoid, because the police really wanted my manuscript. Nearly a year later, I did what I thought was a good deed for an unattractive, overweight, and middle-aged former female friend of mine from the department, and in so doing, I handed the cops the opportunity to arrest me and confiscate my book. The charge was pandering, an activity that, in 1983, the legislators had decreed a felony with a mandatory three- to six-year prison sentence upon conviction. The law took effect without any public comment, so there was no way for me to know of it when I was calculating the risks I would be taking.

On Saturday, September 17, 1983, seven cops burst into my home with their guns drawn, charged me with one count of pandering, and seized my unfinished manuscript. This was before I had a computer and I had only one copy. I knew if they took it I would never see it again, as there was no way I could prove it ever existed. I demanded to be given a receipt for the material that Fred Clapp, the vice cop in charge, was stuffing into a paper bag. He handed me a property report which described the four-inch stack of pages representing years of work—my notes and research—as "miscellaneous typed notations in a manila envelope." I told him he must be kidding and I insisted that he document my manuscript completely. He refused to answer as he handcuffed me in front of Victor and led me away. Victor was furious, of course, and demanded to know what crime they were charging me with and why they were taking my manuscript. The cops told him that he could bail me out within a few hours, at which time I would tell him what crime I had committed. They told him that they needed the manuscript as "evidence" of my criminal activities,

I was all too familiar with the games the cops played with those they wanted to keep in custody, and I knew they didn't intend to release me until sometime the following week. Sure enough, the cops "lost the paperwork" after I was processed into county jail, the "computer broke down," and later the excuse was that the release processing officer had gone home for the night. It wasn't until two days later, when Victor contacted a friend of ours who was a district attorney, that I was finally released.

The first defense attorney I chose delivered a message from the cops and the D.A.'s office that the whole thing could be resolved if I would plead guilty and would not sue them for stealing my manuscript. They would impose probation rather than the mandatory three-year prison sentence. I declined their offer and insisted that they return my manuscript, which they continued to deny having taken when talking to the press. However, during the preliminary hearing, the vice cop admitted that he had indeed appropriated my manuscript, and that while it wasn't the only reason for my arrest, it was one of the reasons.

My attorney filed claim after claim in state and federal court to force the cops to return the manuscript, but they stalled even after they were ordered to do so. Finally, under threat of contempt of court charges, the prosecutor handed my attorney a small sheaf of papers copied from the original. The one-inch stack was incomplete and uncollated, hardly the four inches of material that they had taken. It was unusable and I had to rewrite my book from scratch.

A year later, I went to trial. By this time, I had to replace my attorney because he had a scheduling conflict. The new attorney waived the opening statement, and when the "victim" admitted on the stand that the reason she set me up was to "stop me from writing an exposé on Los Angeles Police," he did not cross-examine her or demand that the case be dismissed because it was clear that the police had intended to violate my First Amendment rights from the beginning.

After the prosecution rested, my attorney did not present any defense, did not permit me to state my case to the jury as I had insisted I wanted to do, and made no closing arguments. Without hearing my side to controvert the perjured testimony of the cops and the "victim," the jury had no choice but to convict me. Some members of the jury later told the press they felt I had been set up because of my book, but the lack of any testimony from me or on my behalf left them without the option to vote for "reasonable doubt." I sued the attorney for malpractice and incompetence, and years later won the case.

Meanwhile, the judge did not want to impose the mandatory minimum three-year sentence because the First Amendment issue really bothered him. But the law obliged him to do something once I was convicted, so he chose to send me to state prison for a ninety-day psychiatric evaluation, known as a 12.03.03 diagnostic study. He gave me a week to put my affairs in order, and directed me to return to court the day before Thanksgiving 1984, to be remanded to custody. During that time, we learned that Victor would not be permitted to visit me unless we were married, so we tied the knot the night before I was due back before the judge. It was a hell of a honeymoon knowing I was going to prison in the morning!

As I was taken into custody, the good judge explained that he wanted to give me a taste of prison and determine if I posed a "danger to society." After he read the evaluation report, he would decide whether or not to impose the mandatory prison term.

Because of my law enforcement background, I was held in solitary confinement "for my own protection." Each time I was marched across the prison yard for the interviews with the psychiatrists, I was shackled to myself and to two guards. When I was occasionally permitted out of my cell to take a shower, which was ten feet away from my room, I was given a body cavity search. Worst of all, even though Victor and I had married in compliance with the prison requirements, he was not permitted to visit me on Christmas Day as he had been promised. The guards were masters at playing mind games, as I knew they would be, but that knowledge didn't prevent me from succumbing to the pain they inflicted.

Finally the ordeal was over. The evaluation had taken a mere three hours of interviews and testing, but I had been kept in custody fifty days. The report was delivered to the judge and I was sentenced to three years' probation and released from prison.

The incarceration experience had exactly the opposite effect on me than what the judge, D.A., and cops intended. It did not convince me to shut up and go away; rather I became more determined than ever to expose the cops and the system. Now I could add charges of First Amendment violations to the list of grievances, and I truly believed the American public would not tolerate government censorship of an individual who was trying to expose police corruption. I was wrong. No one seemed to care at all.

As I predicted, the media were more than happy to obtain ratings by giving a platform to a former traffic cop turned convicted prostitute, and I was invited to speak on numerous radio and television shows. My actions were not well received by the District Attorney, who took the unprecedented measure of filing an appeal of my probation sentence on December 9, 1985, eleven months after my release from prison. In the petition to the appellate court asking to overturn my probation, the D.A. made fifty-seven references to my book and the harm it would cause to society if it was ever published.

Everyone who read the D.A.'s appellate brief was incensed at the blatant attempt to censor me, and all assured me that there was no possibility of such an appeal being granted. I wanted to believe them but I knew that I was fighting a hopeless battle, although there was no way I was going to stop trying.

I was frequently asked to share my story with many local California libertarian groups, and as I was a long-time libertarian, someone thought it was a good idea for me to run for office in 1986. I took the challenge and campaigned for the office of lieutenant governor. I never expected to win, I just wanted to have the opportunity to reach more people with my message. My candidacy gave me the platform to be heard and it seems some people were listening because I received over one hundred thousand votes. Unfortunately, all the publicity in the world did not help me win the appeal. In March 1987, the California Appellate Court agreed with the D.A. that just because no one else went to prison under the mandatory law was no reason I shouldn't. Three of the four justices determined that three years in prison for my "crime" did not constitute cruel and unusual punishment and they overturned my probation sentence. The judge ordered me to return to court for re-sentencing.

In late June of 1987, the producer of the "Donahue Show" called and invited me to appear on the show one more time. The show would be taped and aired only if I went to prison. Victor and I contemplated fleeing the country via New York to avoid prosecution and more jail time. I flew to New York and taped the show. That evening I called Victor and he told me he had just spoken to our attorney, Larry Teeter, who insisted I was not going to prison at all. With time served under the original sentence, the two years and seven months on probation, plus the fifty days in solitary confinement, there would be no new time to serve. The judge must give me credit for time served to any new sentence he imposed.

Was I skeptical? You bet I was! Victor met me at the airport back in L.A., and we drove home in silence. The night before I had to return to court for re-sentencing was the second worst night of my life, the first being the night before I went to prison in 1984.

The next morning we took a cab to the courthouse downtown. Within a few minutes, my case was called before Judge Munoz, and without listening to any of my attorney's arguments, the judge sent me away for three years. I was not even permitted to say goodbye to Victor.

The prison experience is the subject of yet another book that I am writing, and undoubtedly that one will get me into as much trouble as the first one did. Fortunately I did survive, although Victor almost didn't make it. He was in a serious automobile accident while I was away, which nearly cost him his life. Throughout my incarceration, Victor stood beside me, fully supporting my decision to continue pursuing the publication of my book when I was released, During my time in prison, I was interviewed by Mr. Ed Bradley for a segment of the "60 Minutes" program. It aired twice during my incarceration, but it did nothing to bring about an early release.

Prisoners in California are given a day-for-day credit for good behavior, and as long as one abides by the arbitrary rules set by the guards and changed day to day, one could be released after serving half of one's sentence. I was released from prison and work furlough on December 14, 1988, and then I was required to serve an additional three years on parole. So, for the crime of trying to fulfill my friend's fantasy, I paid with nearly seven years of my life.

This ordeal taught me that I was much stronger than I thought, and certainly I was much more stubborn than the cops realized. I had been involved in the prostitute's rights movement from the beginning of my career change, so after I was released from prison, I received permission from Margo St. James to form a Los Angeles chapter of COYOTE.

As I had done after the first prison experience, I resumed my campaign against the LAPD, and soon began receiving invitations to lecture at colleges and universities across the country. I continued to rewrite my manuscript and searched for a brave publisher, but the first few years out of prison I was not successful. It was disheartening. Then came the Rodney King incident, and for the first time in years, people were openly discussing police brutality, racism, and corruption. At long last, my book was relevant, and in 1992, an editor at Simon and Schuster decided to take a chance and publish it. In May 1993, my ten-year dream became a reality.

My work was not done, though, because as long as the prohibition against prostitution remains, the police are free to abuse the law and the women they are entrusted to protect. In the years following the publication of my book, even more repressive legislation has been enacted, which gives the police unparalleled power to violate our constitutionally protected rights. Arrests for prostitution now carry mandatory jail sentences, and as of January 1, 1996, cops can arrest people who they say possess the mere intent to commit prostitution. A man or woman can be in their car, driving down the street and the police can stop and charge them with thought crimes! I truly believe it is only a matter of time before the cops realize they can use that law to harass me. But no amount of punishment or threat of punishment has or ever will convince me that prostitution is wrong, that sex is evil, and that sexual women like me belong behind bars. The genie is out of the bottle, and I will not be silenced.

4

Sex and Serendipity

Lonnie Barbach, Ph.D.

Lonnie Barbach is a psychologist and sex therapist. She originated the preorgasmic women's group program and went on to write a number of best-sellers on sex and relationships. She continues to write and lecture and remains active as a therapist.

T HE DAY I stumbled upon my life's work I was teaching a seminar for Planned Parenthood personnel on pregnancy and abortion counseling. I had been doing research and counseling for Planned Parenthood while studying for my doctorate in psychology at the Wright Institute in Berkeley, California. My course work and internships were finished and I was looking for a dissertation topic. Struggling financially, I was hoping to find a job that would enable me to keep my head above water. Being paid to do therapy seemed like a dream.

It was 5:00 P.M. and I was hanging around the podium after finishing the workshop on counseling skills I had been giving when Leah Potts, who had been a sex therapist at the University of California Student Health Center, came up to me and invited me to apply for the job she was leaving. She liked my work, she said; it didn't matter that I knew nothing about doing sex therapy. Although I couldn't believe that I might actually get paid for doing psychotherapy before getting my Ph.D., I applied for the job.

Of course, few therapists knew anything about sex therapy back in 1972. Harvey Caplan, Rebecca Black, and David Geisinger, however, were reputed to be the local experts. Harvey and Rebecca were co-directors of clinical training at the sex therapy program at the University of California Medical School in San Francisco. David was co-director of the Behavior Therapy Institute in Sausalito. I read Masters's and Johnson's *Human Sexual Inadequacy* and made appointments to pick Harvey's, Rebecca's, and David's brains.

I then convinced my fellow graduate student, Bob Cantor, to interview for the job with me since, at the time, you could only conduct sex therapy as a male/female team of therapists. Somehow we must have managed to convince the interviewers that we knew what we were doing, because we got the job. Starting fall quarter 1972, Bob and I would be employed by the UC Berkeley's Student Health Service in Berkeley to do couple's sex therapy.

Fast forward to September and picture Bob telling me that he wouldn't be able to keep his commitment because he was too overwhelmed by course work, dissertation, and his job as a dentist (he was switching careers). I was devastated. I not only would have to forego this exciting new position, but I would have no income. I was desperate, and I got lucky. Six women who didn't have partners or whose partners refused to go into sex therapy with them had called the UC program requesting help. None of them was orgasmic. They didn't have partners to attend therapy, I didn't have a partner to conduct the therapy—maybe I could make this work yet.

During the previous year I had been in a women's consciousness group—all the rage in the late sixties and early seventies. I had also led a half dozen personal encounter groups and had completed courses in group psychotherapy. I got creative. I convinced the powers that be to allow me to run a ten-session women's group program focused on orgasm. A colleague agreed to co-lead the group with me; we used Charles Lobitz's and Joe LoPiccolo's ten-step masturbation program[1] for our homework progression and began meeting twice a week so that we could complete the group before final exams.

During our hour-and-a-half meetings, we laughed; we cried; we sent women home with mirrors to discover their clitorises and we busily shifted the didactic content to fit the pace of the group. Masturbation and other sexual assignments were completed at home. Because I was no expert, I listened carefully to each woman's story. I quickly became educated. It became obvious that every woman was unique and that what worked for one woman wouldn't work for another—a perspective that has formed my entire orientation to sex therapy.

At the end of the ten sessions, all the women had become orgasmic with masturbation and a few had begun to experience orgasm with their partners. Bringing in a bottle of champagne to celebrate, Nancy and I confessed that it was the first group of this kind ever to be run. After recovering from the shock, the women thanked us for not divulging this information earlier. They then offered to come and talk to future groups as testimonials to the program's success. They wanted to inspire others to achieve what they had achieved. With great enthusiasm, one woman announced, "We were not frigid; we were not nonorgasmic; we were just preorgasmic. Everyone is preorgasmic at some time." The positive, nondysfunctional label stuck and the preorgasmic women's group process had been born.

While ecstatic about our success, I wasn't exactly sure how or why the program worked. So I decided to research the preorgasmic women's groups for my doctoral thesis. Immediately upon making this decision, I had to face the obvious criticism: you could get students at Berkeley to participate in a group therapy program without their partners, but it would never work with middle-class housewives. I needed access to a different population of women.

With the success of the pilot group in hand, I went back to the Human Sexuality Program at the medical school. Harvey Caplan and Rebecca Black arranged for me to be interviewed by the director of the program, Jay Mann. Jay loved the women's group idea, but had no money to fund another therapist, not even very part-time. I thought that the money the women paid for the groups could support my minuscule living expenses. What I required in order to start such a program was credibility, and the university certainly provided that, so I offered to rent space from the Human Sexuality Program to run the groups as long as I could use the university's name in promotion and could charge the participants for therapy. Jay, bless his heart, agreed. I was off and running—except for the minor fact that I had no clients.

At the time, Don Chamberland was hosting a very popular radio talk show called "California Girls." Relationship and sexual issues were among the most common concerns of the women who called in. When Don learned that a treatment program for women with orgasm problems would be run under the auspices of the medical school at the university, he was only too happy to refer his listeners. I don't know how many times he mentioned the women's groups on the air, but within six weeks, we had over one hundred women on a waiting list. I had created a monster. Now I had to figure out a way to respond to the needs of all the women who were waiting. I immediately began training sex therapy interns at the Human Sexuality Program to run the groups with me. We also instituted evening educational programs to provide women with information as well as a preview of the preorgasmic group program.

The women's group programs were so financially successful and were being so well received by the community that the Human Sexuality Program deemed that it was more financially viable to hire me to train their trainees and lecture to the medical students than to charge me rent. I had a part-time job and I could also begin accumulating more predoctoral hours for my psychologist's license: a win-win situation all around.

Lecturing came easy to me—plus, I had a mission. I could not believe the number of women who were either embarrassed, inhibited, or disgusted when it came to sex. I was appalled by the culture, religion, or parents responsible for creating such negativity about sex that women were rendered unable to enjoy the pleasurable sensations their bodies naturally held. I was a feminist—it was the sexual revolution, and I was living and working in San Francisco. It was the time and place to be doing this work.

The preorgasmic groups were incredibly powerful, even groups that were being run by trainees had more than a 90 percent success rate in terms of the attendees becoming orgasmic. I had no idea that on the East Coast I was considered a heretic and our work was being mocked. The belief at the time was that you had to work with both partners if you wanted to make an impact on the couple's sexual relationship. Luckily, ignorance was bliss because, had I known the opinions of those more experienced than myself, I might never have attempted a group program in the first place. With no one to tell me why it wouldn't work, I was free to see if it would.

My newest problem was time. Being recently divorced required me to work long hours to support myself. The group program was booming and I had been gathering my data, but I had no time to write my dissertation. Again, Jay Mann came to the rescue, this time by suggesting that I write a self-help book on the pre-orgasmic process—a book to help women who could not join groups to become orgasmic. I thought he was crazy. Me, write a book? Besides, didn't everyone already know this information? Jay convinced me it was needed and that my per-spective was unique. So, I sat down and wrote two twenty-five-page proposals: one for a popular book which ultimately became *For Yourself: The Fulfillment of Female Sexuality*, and a second geared to professionals as a guide to running the preorgas-mic groups, *Women Discover Orgasm: A Therapist's Guide to a New Treatment Approach.* I sent the proposals to Jay's friend's agent who wasn't interested, but who sent it on to a colleague of hers, a woman just entering the agenting business. I also sent the proposal to three publishers and went to New York City to meet with the editors, all of whom were interested. I was overwhelmed. As they queried me on such details as how many pages the book would be, whether I would need an index, or how much of an advance I required, I realized I was out of my league and signed on with Rhoda Weyr, who has continued as my literary agent to this day.

The next step was fun for Rhoda and horrifying for me. The publishers were bidding against each other. That meant I would actually have to write the book. I won't go into details about my writer's block and all that, but the good news was that I would be able to write the popular book and then live off the advance while I wrote my dissertation. I wouldn't have to work twenty-four hours a day trying to write and support myself simultaneously.

I took a leave from the university and wrote *For Yourself* in six months. In preparation for the dissertation, I had been writing down anecdotes on index cards and I had filled hundreds of cards from which the book just naturally flowed. How-ever, I was neither a very experienced nor a very good writer. I needed help. As luck would have it again, Jay Mann, who was an exceptional writer and editor, got phlebitis and was home-bound. But ever energetic, Jay couldn't sit still and appre-ciated having my book to work on. With unbelievable acumen, he edited *For Your-self* in about five days and was responsible, in large part, for making the book the classic it has become today.

For Yourself established me in the sexuality field and it also started what later developed into somewhat of an addiction to writing. In addition to a sequel to *For Yourself,* I wrote a book titled *For Each Other: Sharing Yourself,* designed to deal with lack of orgasm with a partner as well as lack of sexual desire. Then I joined with Linda Levine to co-author *Shared Intimacies* and *The Intimate Male,* the result of inter-views with hundreds of men and women who didn't have sexual problems, but who felt good about their sexuality.

During all this time I had a secret desire: to publish erotica written by women. I felt that the absence of sexually explicit material written by and for women was noteworthy: it helped promote the belief that women were asexual beings. But I was afraid to take on the task and worried about losing my credibility. I was younger than the other experts in the field and my work was more nontraditional than most. I didn't dare cross the line any further. At last, by the mid-eighties, I felt secure enough professionally to create *Pleasures: Women Write Erotica,* a compilation of real sexual experiences written by talented women writers. I must have waited too long because other than a lot of "finally"s, it hardly created a stir.

As I look back, I see that over the years, I have endeavored to learn about as many facets of human sexuality as possible. Then I have taken what I have learned and presented it in a variety of forms: as lecture material, books, video, or audio-tapes. Each has provided me with a new challenge—a way to take the material I know and fashion it into yet another form. This inherent variety has kept my work ever interesting and exciting.

My career has also had a profound effect upon my personal sexuality. I didn't get into the field, as many do, because of a sexual dysfunction. I didn't actually know that much about sex when I started, but I hadn't received many negative messages in my childhood that I had to overcome. My parents were rather open and nonjudgmental, so I found it easy to talk to people about a subject that almost nobody talked about. In the early 1970s, this alone was sufficient to make me an "instant expert," even without any formal education in the area of sexuality. Talking to so many people with so many different ideas, interests, or unique sexual responses enabled me to truly accept my own sexuality. The side benefit is that I've never felt any pressure to measure up to someone else's idea of good sex. I've also felt enormous freedom to explore and experiment. Being in Berkeley at the height of the sexual liberation movement didn't hurt either. There was permission to engage in sexual activities that would have never crossed my path during any other time in history. This fundamental acceptance of the vastness of human sexuality has generally enabled me to have wonderfully satisfying sexual relationships.

The drawback occurred when I was unattached. I couldn't describe my career to most of the men I dated because of their inevitable responses. Men either leered at me and began to deal with me as a sex object or they got intimidated, felt inadequate, and dropped me like a hot potato. Sex without the intimacy of the relationship didn't mean much to me so I ended up dating very few people—only men who felt secure enough and sufficiently centered in their sexuality, as well as in other aspects of their lives, to take me on as a respected equal. Once I got over the hurdles and found an intimate partner, the sex was terrific. And the deeper the relationship the more profound the sexuality. The idea that a sexual relationship could get better over time seemed like a theoretical abstract—something you intellectually believe is possible, but don't see realized very often. My eleven years with my husband, David Geisinger, have concretized and made quite real the abstract belief. The relationship requires attention and energy, but of the most pleasurable kind, and if the relationship is infused daily with caring and love, the sex goes places that are truly cosmic.

Revisiting my extended family's response to my visibility in the sex field amuses me. At first, they didn't seem to take much notice of my accomplishments. I had to ask my father to read *For Yourself* three times before he finally did. (He kept claiming it was for women.) After he had completed it I asked for his evaluation, to which he replied, "I don't want to talk about it." And we never have, even though on numerous occasions he has driven me to radio and television interviews.

I think my mother was less embarrassed than my father about having a daughter who was an expert on sex. I remember a party I gave for the publication of *Pleasures* at which my parents were present. One guest went up to my mother and asked her how she felt about her daughter compiling a book of erotic writings. Wasn't she a bit shocked? What did her friends think? My mother replied, "We're no longer shocked by anything she does. We've had a lot of time to get used to the whole thing." But it wasn't until I was on the "Alan Burke Show" out of Miami that my extended family acknowledged my expertise. Most of my family live in southern Florida and the whole lot of them joined me to be in the audience. Alan Burke had the reputation for being very tough, confrontational, and downright nasty to guests, often undermining them or putting them down. I remember centering myself for the onslaught, but the onslaught never came. Burke was positive and supportive, agreeing with me on almost every topic. What was more amazing was that his validation of my work led to my entire family's acceptance of me as an authority. When the program was over we gathered for coffee and cake at an aunt's house. During the evening, my relatives lined up, practically taking numbers, so they could talk to me about their personal sexual problems and concerns. Until that moment, I think I had underestimated the power of television. I got more credibility from appearing on one television show than I had received from writing a half dozen books.

Were I to choose a profession all over again, I would take the same path. I have found my work doing couple's therapy and sex therapy—as well as writing and lecturing—both exciting and valuable. I can't think of another area in psychology that offers equal challenges and equal rewards. My day is made when a marriage is saved or a couple is able to reach levels of sexual pleasure never before considered—not just because their sexual problems have been ameliorated, but because they are able to attain a level of intimacy with their mate that had before been unattainable. Best of all, I have been able to apply all of this learning and experience to my own personal life and feel blessed to have the partner, child, and family I enjoy today.

Note

1. W. C. Lobitz and J. P. LoPiccolo, "New Methods in the Behavioral Treatment of Sexual Dysfunction," *Journal of Behavioral Therapy and Experimental Psychiatry* 3 (1972): 265–71.

5

How We Got into Sex

Bonnie Bullough, R.N., Ph.D.,
and Vern Bullough, R.N., Ph.D.,

Bonnie and Vern Bullough have authored, co-authored, or edited over fifty books on sexuality. Bonnie Bullough received her doctorate in sociology and was dean of the nursing school at the State University of New York at Buffalo. She died as this book was going to press. Vern Bullough, also a nurse, and a historian, is distinguished professor emeritus at the State University College at Buffalo, where he was the dean of natural and social sciences. He is currently on the faculty of the University of Southern California and has served two terms as president of the Society for the Scientific Study of Sexuality.

WHILE MOST OF the accounts in this book are of individuals, much of our work has been as a team. One of the difficulties with working as a team in academia is that promotion and tenure committees tend to emphasize the contribution of the other member and indicate that the person they are evaluating is being carried by his or her spouse. This was particularly true of Bonnie who became an academic somewhat later than Vern, although we both suffered from it. Nevertheless, it became important for each of us to occasionally venture out on our own, if only to emphasize that we could do it. Occasionally also we disagreed with each other and Bonnie once refused to allow her name to go on a book because she felt her ideas were not forcibly enough expressed in it. On another occasion, this time on an article, and not one dealing with sex, we disagreed so vehemently that we ended up with two endings, one by Bonnie and one by Vern, and the journal published both of them.

Perhaps one of the reasons we have been able to collaborate so well, however, is that we, in a sense, grew up together. We were the mythical teenage high school sweethearts who married, settled down, and lived happily ever after. Reality, however, is different from the myth, and we were lucky that our interests grew and developed along the same lines, although we both worked hard to make this happen.

First a little of our background. We are both natives of Utah, but our family backgrounds were radically different. Bonnie's family had come to Utah pushing a handcart and settled in Manti, Utah, although Bonnie herself was born in Delta. Her mother was somewhat of a rebel from Mormonism and during her middle teens she became pregnant. She and the teenage father were forced to confess their sins publicly in church and to marry, a remedy which did not work. Bonnie's father immediately moved to California to start a new life, leaving his wife behind to cope as best she could. Shortly after Bonnie was born, her parents were divorced, and her grandmother stepped in to take care of her for a couple of years until her mother remarried; Bonnie moved with her mother and stepfather to Indiana and spent a few years living on a farm. When she was nearly four, she was sent out on Halloween with a candle-lit pumpkin without adult supervision. The jack o'lantern came in contact with her costume, burning her severely and leaving scars on her face, arms, and legs, which required operations over many summers to make her more presentable.

Later, in the depths of the Depression, the family moved back to Utah, where in spite of the birth of a brother and sister, the marriage began to fall apart. Neither parent could afford to get divorced from the other and both spent much of their energy trying to get enough money to support themselves and their children. One year, they even lived in a tent home. Much of Bonnie's time was spent with her grandmother and her unmarried uncles and aunts, several of whom were not much older than she. By the end of the thirties, the country's economy was picking up and the family moved to Salt Lake City, where both parents managed to get jobs in the rapidly expanding war industries, although both had long commutes to work and in opposite directions.

Meanwhile, Vern was growing up in Salt Lake City surrounded by relatives. In his early childhood he had ten cousins within a block of where he lived and dozens more not too far away. The closest cousins were all children of his mother's brothers and sisters, and the whole family was presided over by his immigrant grandfather and grandmother in an area heavily peopled by other immigrants. Although all the uncles and aunts had been born in this country, they had not spoken English until they went to school. Vern's grandmother never did speak very good English. His father's family was more scattered and had long been residents of Utah; one of the Bullough ancestors had accompanied Brigham Young westward. When Vern was eleven, his father, mother, and twin brothers moved to the rural outskirts of Salt Lake City where they could keep pigs and cows, and grow much of their own food to supplement the family income from his father's job; soon after his mother sought part-time work on her own in the booming wartime economy. Although bettering the economic condition of the family was perhaps the major reason for the move, a strong secondary reason in the mind of Vern's father was to escape the confinement of his wife's family.

The move for Vern was enlightening, since no farm child can be entirely ignorant of sex when surrounded by it. Bonnie had this same experience. Moreover, the new neighborhood included a number of Japanese, Mexicans, and even one family of blacks; the junior high school Vern attended was tremendously mixed racially although for the most part not economically. Families were at best working class and many were below that. While he was in junior high, Vern's mother became pregnant; this late pregnancy and the birth of a sister were subjects of considerable discussion among family gatherings, and served as a good sex education for him.

It was in high school that Bonnie and Vern met, although she was a year ahead of him. We were both good students: each held student body offices and each was a commencement speaker. Vern also played football, and although in spring practice he was not particularly good, the first string was drafted before the season began, and he ended up playing every minute in every game of the official season. Vern tended to be a kind of cutup, and few knew that he was a good student since among his peer group this was not the thing to be. We met in the debate club and confirmed our mutual interests when we also found we were both members of an off-campus interracial group; soon afterward we found ourselves together in a politically aware organization that included both high school and college students.

We were both working part-time to support ourselves, something each of us had done since we could remember. Vern had helped his father install furnaces from the age of five, at twelve he had a paper route on his own, and by fourteen had two employees under him. At fifteen he became an apprentice baker, then successively an ice puller (when most ice came from commercial ice houses), a ditch digger for the gas company, a mosquito abatement worker, a warehouse stacker, and finally a newspaper reporter, all the while attending high school. He also played in a dance band on weekend nights and played the organ in a church on Sunday. During the summers, he often worked sixty-hour weeks, something possible during the worker shortage caused by the war. Bonnie worked as a waitress, then in a hospital cafeteria, and also as a correspondent for a local newspaper, a job which she passed on to Vern when she graduated. This served as Vern's entry into the newspaper business, which evolved into a full-time summer job where his speed in typing (he could do about 120 words a minute at that time) made him a valuable addition to the rewrite desk. The shortage of good reporters had forced the newspapers to put their best reporters on the beat; they then telephoned in their stories, dictating them to this sixteen-year-old typist, who then edited their copy and handed it in to the city desk.

Probably the thing that made Bonnie initially so interesting to Vern were the complications in her family life. Between junior high and high school, she had legally changed her name, as she was adopted by a bachelor uncle (a career army man who then could give her an allotment to help her grandmother support her). The name change had caused a lot of talk and had helped make her a mysterious figure to the naive high school students. But the real story is one of sadness and tragedy, which helped direct both of us into furtive studies in human sexuality. Perhaps Bonnie was interested in Vern because his life seemed comparatively stable.

The events in Bonnie's life require some explanation. When her mother and father finally got good jobs, they realized that they no longer had to stick together. Since her stepfather had a job fifty miles or so west of Salt Lake, he moved there, coming home only occasionally. Bonnie's mother also went to work, leaving Bonnie in charge of her sister and brother until she returned in the evening. Then one day her mother did not come home. Bonnie stepped into the breach and ran the family on the money her stepfather sent; she did so for several months until the school authorities found she had been signing her sister's report card. Welfare swooped in, and her father, on an emergency trip home, made some temporary arrangements with a neighborhood woman to move in and take care of the children.

It was several months before Bonnie found out that her mother had been taken in by another woman and had entered into a lesbian relationship with her. This relationship lasted until her mother's partner died some thirty years later. In the subsequent divorce, Bonnie's stepfather took her brother and sister, while her uncle adopted Bonnie and she went to live with her grandmother and a maiden aunt.

Vern only gradually learned the full story, but the experience helped cement their commitment to social concerns, and to further investigation into sexual matters. Our career choices, however, were not so easily made. Bonnie went into nursing, in part because she had spent so much of her life in a hospital, and in part because the Cadet Nurse Program (a wartime effort to build the supply of nurses) paid for nursing school, including room and board. Vern graduated from high school the following year and began college, but he ran into financial difficulty which working two jobs did not solve.

Both Vern and Bonnie continued to date but nursing school allowed only one late night out a week at best, and in the nursing home for three hundred young women, there were only two telephones and so communication was not easy in between dates. One had to be in by midnight at the latest. Although we engaged in petting (the term then in use to describe the groping and pawing teenagers engage in), we both believed that having sex before marriage was not quite right. Moreover, several of Bonnie's classmates had to drop out of nursing school because they became pregnant, a fear we also had, since she wanted to finish school. Even after World War II ended, the military was still drafting. Military service seemed not unattractive to Vern in large part because of the enactment of the GI Bill. This seemed a way to help solve both our financial difficulties and our moral dilemmas. The upshot was that Vern went into the army, and as soon as Bonnie finished nursing school (in 1947), they were married. Vern had just turned nineteen.

After returning to Utah in 1948 to complete Vern's education at the University of Utah, Vern and Bonnie spent many hours with Bonnie's mother and her lover, Barrie, renewing acquaintances and trying to make peace with her. Both of us became fascinated by the topic of homosexuality and lesbianism. Vern, who had spent part of his army free time trying to decide what he wanted to do with the rest of his life, had decided to major in history instead of the pre-med that he had originally decided upon. While at the university Vern also spent time in the library surreptitiously studying homosexuality and lesbianism, aided also by some books in Barrie's library.

Note the surreptitiousness of our approach to sexuality. From our cautious approaches to professors, it appeared clear that sex was a forbidden research topic, and we did not want to be labeled, although Vern did several term papers on the topic. He went on to the University of Chicago to continue his studies in history, particularly in the history of science and medicine in the medieval and early modern period. Bonnie worked at the University of Chicago and later for the Chicago

Public Health department and we continued our political activism, helping to form an organization that later became the Medical Committee for Human Rights.

By the time Vern got his Ph.D. degree in 1954 (at twenty-six), there were no college teaching jobs. The postwar enrollment of GIs had disappeared, and the baby-boom generation would not reach college age until 1959. Vern had accepted a job with the mayor's Commission on Human Relations in Chicago, when a friend from Youngstown University called to say there was a job open there. We went, but it was not what Vern had expected. Rather than history, he ended up teaching social science courses: sociology, political science, economics, psychology, anthropology, and even geography at a college level. The one history course he taught was American history, a subject he had avoided in college. The result was a comprehensive reading program, tremendously broadening, trying to keep two or three lectures ahead of the students, and becoming exhausted in the process. Since Bonnie helped Vern survive the ordeal, doing some reading for him, we both gained a wide-ranging background. We had also started our family and had two boys. Bonnie began working only part-time in order to take the two semesters she needed to get her bachelor's degree. Vern was doing freelance writing for various magazines to pick up a little extra money and a lot of free books. One of the books he reviewed was on the Wolfenden Report, a British Parliamentary report dealing with prostitution and homosexuality.

A publisher who happened to read the review wrote that he thought it was a very perceptive review and he wondered whether Vern would want to write a book on either prostitution or homosexuality. This led to a detailed family conference. In 1959 we moved to Los Angeles where Vern was now at California State University, Northridge, and Bonnie soon after enrolled in a master's program in nursing at UCLA (she later went on to get a second master's and a Ph.D. in sociology). We had also adopted two children to make four in our family (and we later adopted a third child after our eldest son was killed), and we were both fearful of how doing sex research would affect us. We were early members of the Society for the Scientific Study of Sexuality (SSSS), but Vern's colleagues were in the process of getting rid of a colleague because of his open homosexuality, and Vern was fearful of how he might be treated. We did decide to accept a contract from the publisher but on prostitution rather than on homosexuality, perhaps because Vern was fearful of being labeled a homosexual, something he was not yet secure enough to tolerate. We also covered ourselves by doing books on nursing, and by writing numerous scholarly articles on nonsexual topics as well as an occasional freelance popular article. The prostitution book eventually appeared and although there was a great deal of joking about the topic, and the reviewer in the *American Historical Review,* treated it is an aberration for a serious historian, it otherwise did not affect our career or marriage in any way. In the meantime we both had become active in One Inc., an early homosexual rights organization, and wrote for *One* magazine and for the *Ladder,* the publication of the Daughters of Bilitis. Vern also published some scholarly articles on prostitution and received a rather large grant to do a study of military deterrence. By this time Bonnie had finished her Ph.D., and had joined the faculty at UCLA. Vern had run for political office (state assembly) and lost, and been investigated by the FBI for, among other things, advocating the abolition of the Mann Act, enforced by the FBI and originally conceived as a method of preventing women from being forced into prostitution by being taken across state lines.

Vern gradually emerged from the closet of sex research, and became bolder in his scholarly writing on sexual topics. He also began to teach a course on women (what now would be called a course on sex and gender), and Bonnie was willing to spend more time on such topics as she, too, moved up the academic ladder. One of the contacts we made through our study of prostitution was with Evelyn Hooker, who had become chair of a task force in the National Institutes of Mental Health (NIMH), to make recommendations about research into homosexuality. Vern, who was invited to be the historian of the group, was already committed for the period to another research project on intellectual and creative achievement, and so had to decline. The group turned for a brief historical overview to Jonathan Katz, who later went on to study the topic more seriously. Vern was invited to apply to the NIMH for a grant as soon as he was able but by that time the project had lost its funding. Failing to get support from the NIMH, Vern was offered support by the Erickson Educational Foundation.

In the late 1960s, we both emerged as key researchers into the study of human sexuality, although most of our books on the subject did not begin to appear until the 1970s. As we became more open, we found all kinds of support for what we were doing. Vern wrote an ACLU policy statement advocating legal action on behalf of gays and lesbians and had become chair of a committee in that organization to deal with sexual issues. Both of us spoke widely on sexual topics and the law to a variety of groups, from swinging singles to service clubs to church groups. We helped found the original Parents and Friends of Gays in Los Angeles, and became active supporters of COYOTE and other groups of advocates for women in the sex industry. When we first moved to Los Angeles, we made contact with Virginia Prince and the emerging transvestite movement and spoke at a number of clubs. As we explored the varieties of sexual behavior, we felt that we could not regard the people with stigmatized sexual practices as subjects or clients, but rather simply as people; we felt it essential to help fight their battles when we could or were asked to do so. Otherwise, we simply stood in the background giving moral and scholarly support. We were very political in various sexual causes and were among the founders of Californians for Therapeutic Abortion, and all kinds of local groups, trying to disseminate more accurate information about sexuality. California State University was supportive of our efforts and Vern was given the title of Outstanding Professor. He also joined with several colleagues in other disciplines to found the Center for Sex Research, and served as its first chair and director.

As he moved more into the sex field, Vern felt a need to have more clinical hands-on experience than his social science and history background gave him, so he went back to school to gain a nursing degree. Interestingly, where we had once hesitated to make our sex research public for fear of damaging our academic careers, once we made a decision to move full speed ahead on our research, our careers blossomed. One study led to another, and one project to another, although we both continued to publish more specialized monographs and even books in other areas of history, sociology, and nursing. We felt that this helped keep us honest, since much of sex research at that time was not of the quality that existed in some other areas of our expertise, and by being able to get good peer review and input in the other areas, we felt we could feel comfortable with our standards in sex research field. We explored all kinds of sexual topics, one of the more interesting being of Bonnie's mother and her partner. Barrie had done an earlier study of lesbians, which we knew about, but it was incomplete, and she had filed it away. When she died, the material came to us and we wrote it up for a scholarly journal, identifying ourselves with our subjects.

Bonnie in the meantime had been experimenting with academic administration. She had left UCLA to coordinate a consortium of programs involving, among others, Long Beach State and the University of California, Irvine. As a result of this experience, she decided she might like to become a dean of nursing, a job which would entail a willingness to leave the Los Angeles area where we were well entrenched. Since she had moved from northern California (where we lived when we were first married) to Salt Lake to Chicago to Youngstown to Los Angeles on behalf of Vern's career goals, it would only seem logical that Vern should be willing to move. He had also joined with Bonnie in writing about discrimination against women and the need to break the glass ceiling. Still, you might describe him as a reluctant mover, one who recognized the legitimacy of Bonnie's career aspirations, but was also somewhat fearful of what would happen to his own. When Bonnie went on the job market, she was swamped with offers and interviews, and Vern accompanied her on many of them. The problem of what to do with the spouse of a female candidate was a new kind of thing to most institutions, although many half-heartedly offered to make some sort of job for Vern in order to get Bonnie. Eventually, Bonnie decided to accept the offer from the State University of New York at Buffalo, and Vern began exploring the job situation there. He found there was a deanship opening at a nearby SUNY campus and applied for it. Soon after Bonnie moved to Buffalo as a dean, Vern, after taking the state boards for nursing registration, followed her as Dean of Natural and Social Sciences at SUNY College, Buffalo. It is interesting that what once had been regarded as a handicap to academic advancement, Vern's study of sexuality, was welcomed by Buffalo, and in fact the rather large committee set up to examine candidates had some who were gay men or lesbians themselves, although only one was out of the closet.

While in Buffalo, even though we were administrators, both of us continued to do research into human sexuality. In fact, we became more active in the professional sex organizations, all of which were then stronger in the East than in the West. We were also invited to speak widely around the country on sexual topics. Vern served as dean for nearly ten years before resigning to become a SUNY Distinguished Professor. Bonnie remained on as dean for another year, and then, after returning to the faculty for a year or so, retired. We then moved back to Los Angeles where we picked up on old research projects and explored new ones.

In looking back at our careers, it seems obvious that we were always interested in sex research and in extending the rights of those stigmatized by society for their sex, their sexual persuasion, their race, their gender, or even their physical appearance. The fears we had about openly exploring various aspects of human sexuality might well have had a basis in reality, but much of it was our own lack of self-confidence and our own anxieties about being labeled. Once we confronted our own sexuality in order for us to continue research, it was easy to overcome our anxieties about being labeled. Occasionally, we still get letters labeling us as perverts, but they are much easier to ignore than they once were. We were always surprised at the reactions of some of our acquaintances and colleagues when they found out about our major research interest, of which they had previously been unaware. Most were surprised because in so many ways we seemed to be such squares. We looked and acted like an old married couple; we also looked and acted like academics. In short, sex for us proved to be a rewarding research field, one that was slow to open up to modern research methodologies. It has made for an interesting and fulfilling life and we have encouraged others who are interested to pursue it. Actually doing sex research was a nice way to grow old and in our case even respectable, and Vern still carries on with the work after Bonnie's death.

6

How I Came to Be a Sexology Journalist

Jan Morris Dailey

Jan Morris Dailey came to sexology journalism in middle age. Her academic background in human physiology led to publication of sexual issues in popular magazines, and strong advocacy of better sex education.

ENTERED THE field of sexology fairly late in life. I characterize my early years as being erotophobic, that is, I had a fear or hatred of sex. I learned such attitudes from my mother who in turn had learned them from her grandfather's housekeeper. My grandmother had died when my mother was ten and her father had never remarried. The task of mothering his children was turned over to an unmarried housekeeper who was hostile to all things sexual. So fearful was my own mother that she never even told me how babies came about until I was twelve.

I grew up thinking sex should be secret. Erotophobia to me is catching and it can be transmitted like an epidemic. In college I majored in physiology, and went on for a master's degree in it. During my graduate studies, I served as a teaching assistant, so that in terms of anatomy and physiology of sex, I became well prepared, although even this was not enough to overcome some of my childhood attitudes. While in college, I also minored in journalism. One of my early articles, about my experience in learning to fly, won an award. I was the first woman enrolled in the wartime pilot training program preparing college women to ferry planes overseas.

When I married, nature asserted itself and for a time my erotophobia was given short shrift. I settled down to raising a family and painting portraits to earn extra money. Increasingly, however, sex took a back seat, particularly while I was fighting the city of Los Angeles over the expansion of what was to become Los Angeles International Airport. I was a leader in a prolonged political and legal struggle which went on for nearly a decade. I was almost totally engrossed in meetings, talking on the telephone for hours, sending my children out as late as 11:00 P.M. to deliver flyers door to door, and seeking support for the "cause." When I went to bed exhausted, sex was forgotten. Although we eventually won our case, the battle ruined our family life. My husband said that he had seriously considered divorce. I suddenly became aware of how a neglected mate might well desire to take another partner, although he never did, and we celebrated our fifty-fifth wedding anniversary in 1995.

After the trial was over in the mid-1950s I realized that I needed to know much more about sexuality, particularly since one of the factors in the favorable ruling by the judge was that the noise of the planes flying ever overhead was potentially damaging to the litigants' sex life. In fact I received five hundred dollars from the court as damages for this particular factor. By this time, I was in my fifties, with time now to devote to a program of self-study of human sexuality, calling and talking with local "sex" experts and reading what I could find. Although I learned more about the nature of human sexuality, I did not progress fast enough to suit myself. Fortuitously, in 1972 I received an announcement of a twentieth anniversary meeting in Las Vegas of the Society for the Scientific Study of Sexuality (SSSS). I had never heard of such a group, but apparently one of the contacts whom I had pumped for information had put me on a list to receive invitations.

I believed that this meeting gave me a great opportunity to learn more about sex from the experts, and all I needed to do was attend. My husband agreed, and more or less pushed me out of the door and onto a plane for what I regarded as "Sin City." Since I had not made any reservations, I found on arriving that I could not get a room in the convention hotel. While wandering through the registration area, I met a woman who agreed to share her room, and we became roommates, although I no longer remember her name. The woman herself had taken as her mission in life the protection and defense of those who were sexually different.

I was fascinated by some of the people I met, such as Virginia Prince, whose autobiography is also in this volume. Almost everyone I met impressed me with his or her compassion, knowledgeability, and jovial good humor. Particularly important to my budding new career was Barbara Schrank, the editor of *Sexology* magazine. She was struck both by the new-found interest about sex in a fifty-year-old woman and my ability to communicate about the importance of sexuality with others. She had been searching for someone just like me to give the magazine a new slant, and I was in her mind the perfect candidate. Soon after, she appointed me the "West Coast Editor" of *Sexology*. It was not a high-paying position: I received only a hundred dollars a month plus an additional amount for every article I wrote. But the position gave me entry into a new and different world. It was as a journalist writing about sex that I began to really understand sexuality.

My position was particularly important to me because it enabled me to correspond with many of the leading sexologists. I came to know many of them well, not only the researchers and therapists, but transsexuals, gays, lesbians, transvestites, porn stars, sexual surrogates, and what have you. I came to realize that there are many faces to sexuality. I enjoyed the friends I made and my library on sex grew, many of the books autographed copies by my new-found friends.

One of the things I became interested in was sexual humor, a field which I felt had been neglected. Over the years I collected a number of what might be called sex jokes including limericks. The collection has continued to grow as friends and acquaintances add to it. I am particularly fond of what I call the two-liners:

Question: What is better than roses on your piano?
Answer: Tulips on your organ!

or

Question: Why did the rubber fly across the room?
Answer: It got pissed off!

In short, I became fascinated with the language of love and sex. I have often thought that my mother would have been horrified at the terms I learned, although I am not certain she would understand many of them. I became a walking encyclopedia on sexual positions, on masturbation, on how to make an orgasm last longer, and all sorts of interesting information, much of which I wrote about in the pages of *Sexology* or other publications.

Now, in my late seventies, I think I have conquered the old demon erotophobia, although I probably never will completely, since it is difficult to unlearn lifelong prejudices and assumptions, and I started much too late in life to do so completely. Sex, however, has proved to be fascinating to me, and in my retirement years, it still retains my interest.

7

Cultural Psychologist to Sexologist

Clive M. Davis, Ph.D.

Clive Davis started out as a cultural psychologist and spent some years in Uganda. When he was no longer able to return there he broadened his scope to include sexuality. He became editor of the Journal of Sex Research *and served in that capacity for ten years, making it into a first-class journal.*

HOW DID I become a sexologist, or a social psychologist whose primary topic of substantive interest is sexualities? Most readers of these autobiographical comments are no doubt familiar with the fact that when adolescents who have experienced nonmarital coitus are asked how the first act came about, they often reply that it "just happened." As I pondered how I became a sexologist, my initial reaction was much the same: "It just happened."

Of course, it did not "just happen," either for the adolescent or for me. If we probe, it is usually possible to obtain a reasonably clear picture of how the confluence of the individual's beliefs and attitudes, the residuals of his or her previous behavior, and the situational factors of the moment led to the seemingly unplanned outcome. There is one difference in this comparison: There was no defining moment or event when I "became a sexologist." But, having said that, maybe there was. Here is my story.

When I try to sum it all up, to capture the essence of the forces leading to it "just happening," the words *curiosity* and *independence* stand out, but the word *opportunity* is every bit as important. It is as simple and as complicated as that. I brought some things to the "table" that were critical to the choices I made, but the situations in which I found myself were at least equally influential to the outcome. I know that sounds a lot like a social psychologist talking, but, what can you expect, after all? That is my training. In any event, although the developments were logical and are understandable, at least in retrospect, they certainly were not actively planned out, with the goal being that of becoming a sexologist.

Although there may be no truly defining event, I can date my more formal entry into sexology to 1971, because it was during the spring semester of that year when I taught my first seminar on the topic. I had no idea what would come of that; that twenty-five years later a significant part of my identity and certainly my career would be defined by that interest. From one perspective, it could be argued that moving into this unorthodox, even unacceptable, field was a gross departure from the conventional paths my life and career had taken to that date. Yet, from another perspective, I think it makes perfect sense. It was a nexus of my childhood and adolescent socialization with regard to sexuality; my formal educational experiences, particularly from high school through graduate school; my personal sexual experience during young adulthood; and my professional experience as a young social psychologist. Let me try to reconstruct that history.

I'll start toward the middle. In 1958, I left my rural home state of Maine to attend a small liberal arts college in Lamoni, Iowa: Graceland College. Graceland is a church-owned college (the Reorganized Church of Jesus Christ of Latterday Saints [RLDS]).[1] At that time, the overwhelming majority of the eight hundred or so students were members of the RLDS church, and the ethos, as well as the rules, was traditional and restrictive, even in comparison to the conservative larger American culture of the day. For example, smoking and the consumption of alcoholic beverages were not permitted. There was no dancing. Women were restricted to their dormitories after 9:00 P.M. on weeknights. Except for the latter rule (and perhaps not even that), these were not burdensome restrictions because most students did not smoke or drink, and few relied on dancing as a major recreational activity. Most of us were active churchgoers, and there were ample recreational and entertainment opportunities at the school, in spite of the fact that the town was remotely located on the Iowa-Missouri border, nearly two hours from Des Moines, and almost three from Kansas City.

I did not feel isolated or deprived. Rather, I felt privileged to be sharing my life and education with those of like faith. And I was, in almost all respects, the ultimate conformer. I did it all "by the book." In my small high school, I had been on the starting teams in baseball, basketball, football, and track. I was valedictorian of my class. I was involved in every activity going. I just didn't know any better. I thought that was what one was supposed to do. It was all very challenging, great fun, and enormously rewarding.

It was the same at Graceland, except for the sports. It was now time to become a "serious student," so active participation in sports was put aside (being only 5′8″ and 130 pounds may have had something to do with it, too, as I think back). Although I was an A student, I was still involved in many extracurricular activities,

---

1. The RLDS church is one of several, most notably the Church of Jesus Christ of Latter-Day Saints (Mormons), that can trace its roots to upstate New York and Joseph Smith, Jr. Smith founded the LDS church in 1830. When he was assassinated in Nauvoo, Illinois, in 1844, one group, under the leadership of Brigham Young, moved to Utah. In 1860, the RLDS church emerged under the leadership of Joseph Smith III.

including student government, the drama group, and editing the yearbook. I was the loyal employee, too, working about twenty hours a week, mostly in the campus post office and taking tickets at sporting events, so I got to know virtually every student by name.

I was also very active in the church. The priesthood of the RLDS church is mostly a lay priesthood, with a small number of members "called" from the ranks to serve as full-time missionaries. I had been "called" to the priesthood while in high school, and there was some expectation back home that I would eventually be among those "promoted" to full-time status. It is difficult to recall whether I really ever expected that to happen, but I did take the priesthood responsibility very seriously, actively fulfilling my role in many ways.

Thus, during high school and college, I pretty much walked the straight and narrow, conforming to the rules and demonstrating very little independence, let alone rebelliousness. Consider—I would probably have voted for Richard Nixon in 1960 had I been old enough to vote. But the seeds of that curiosity and independence had been nourished at home and in school for many years and were about to sprout.

Although Graceland was primarily a junior college in those days, it had begun adding B.A. programs, the first of which in religion. I decided to pursue that major, partly because doing so would allow me to stay at Graceland two more years and partly because I had no other clear goal in mind. I began thinking that I might go on to graduate school in philosophy.

During my junior year, two developments occurred that made a huge difference: I took my first courses in social and personality psychology, and I met the woman who became my first coital partner and my wife. In the classroom, I was being exposed to theories about human nature and research about social behavior. In life, I was trying to figure out who I was, what I wanted to do with my life; grappling with the romantic feelings and sexual urges that I was experiencing in a way that was different from any previous relationship. It was fortuitous that these two experiences occurred at the same time, but I think it was important, ultimately. It was also the case that the religion and philosophy courses were having an impact: I was being asked to think, to ask questions, to challenge the status quo. It was not long before my thinking about religion and the RLDS church took a radical turn.

During my senior year, Sandra and I decided to marry following graduation. She was only a sophomore, but marrying at such a young age was not at all uncommon in those days, particularly for women. Having done well in school, and encouraged by several faculty members, I decided to pursue graduate study. Psychology, particularly social psychology, had captured my interest as a career possibility. By this time, I did not see a future for myself in the full-time ministry, but there was still a strong "do good works" mentality pushing me forward. I did not, however, see that desire fulfilled in becoming a clinical psychologist. Having had several professors I admired greatly, the role of college professor increasingly seemed to be an attractive option. But I also liked journalism and public relations. I had been editor of the yearbook in my junior year, and I had worked in the public relations office for a year as well and done some writing in that capacity.

Not having any idea how I would fare in my effort to be accepted in a graduate program, I visited and applied to the two nearby universities with supposedly good programs in both areas (the University of Iowa and the University of Missouri). I was accepted in all four programs.

The time came to make a choice. Practical person that I was, and with marriage approaching, I accepted the offer of the psychology department at the University of Iowa, mostly because it offered the most financial assistance (a $2,000 stipend was a lot of money in those days) and the clearest (or shortest) track to the Ph.D. Supposedly, with the proffered fellowship, I could finish in three years. I could and I did, still "playing by the rules," almost to the letter. During that time, I took the standard fare of substantive courses in social and experimental psychology, research methods, statistics, and so forth. I do not recall the words *sex* (except for its use in relation to male-female, or sex differences) or *sexuality* (except in relation to the mounting behavior of the rats used in some of the laboratory work and in the personality courses in conjunction with Freud) being mentioned once in any coursework during the entire three years. It simply was not a part of the subject matter of social psychology in those days.

While in Iowa City, we continued active involvement with the church. It was comprised of a sizable group of students attending the university and a group of older local residents. For the most part, the two groups interacted well, but I (and a couple of others who had been religion majors at Graceland) had become very liberal, theologically and politically, and were on a mission of revolution designed to bring our group and the larger church into our vision of the "RLDS church of the twentieth century," whether they were ready or not. Some folks, and the church itself, were not ready.

As the final year of my graduate program approached, it came time to think about "what next?" My advisor suggested I apply for a postdoctoral fellowship and follow up on some of his work in East Africa. This too was a rather radical departure from the straight and narrow path of professional development, although I did not realize it at the time. A "postdoc" was not that unusual, but moving into cross-cultural studies certainly was. There was only a handful of social psychologists doing cross-cultural work in those days.

I received the fellowship. We spent a semester at Syracuse University in the East African Studies Program preparing for the trip and the next eighteen months in Uganda, conducting research and teaching part-time at Makerere University. These were wonderful times, except for the political instability of the country. We were continually exposed to new things: people, customs, foods, and more, including sexual practices and what was, for us, sexuality-relevant behavior, such as women not wearing clothing over their breasts, men wearing only a loin cloth, and men walking hand in hand. I was not doing sexuality research, and I knew only a little about varying sexual practices across cultures, although I had read some of

Margaret Mead's work. While these variations piqued my curiosity somewhat, they did so no more than the many other variations, and less than some. To explain why they were no more provocative, let me turn back the clock and describe a couple of key factors in my childhood and adolescence.

My family is of middle-class roots. Although only one of ten children (an aunt) in my parent's generation had attended college, mostly because of lack of finances, education was valued in both families, and particularly valued by my parents. The importance of doing well in school was instilled in us (my brother, who is three years younger, and me) from the very beginning as the key to the "good life." I am not sure why they felt so strongly about this, but I think it had a lot to do with my father's experiences, beginning with his travels as a seaman. Right out of high school he served on merchant ships (his father was the captain of one) and traveled the East Coast, visiting every port from New England to the Gulf. Then, as a member of the Merchant Marines during World War II, he traveled widely, regularly going back and forth from the United States to either Europe or the Pacific. My father saw a lot of the world in those years. He told few "war stories," but he was fascinated by the places and peoples he visited. After the war, he returned to the civilian sea life for several years, mostly along the East Coast, but occasionally reaching the West Coast also. Again, the stories he brought home were of the peoples and places. Although he was promoted through the ranks to the point of becoming eligible to captain his own ship, he left the sea to spend more time with his family. He became a salesman and during most of my youth, he traveled back and forth across the state of Maine as the representative of a national manufacturer of large appliances. Once again, it was people and places, whether in the stories he brought home, or when we occasionally traveled with him.

Out of all of this came, for me, an openness to "new" and "different," be it food or customs or religion. It was more than openness, actually; it was an appreciation for the differences. I recall an incident when I was nine or ten in which children in the neighborhood were picking on some new "kids on the block." They were Chinese, and some of the "picking" was directed toward their race or ethnicity. I am quite sure I was not among the guilty parties, but when my parents learned that this was going on, we were strongly lectured in matters of equality and individuality. Peoples of all races and cultures were to be accepted and valued as individuals; racism was totally unacceptable. Over the years, there were many other instances of my parents modeling openness to new experience and appreciation for diversity. I think this background made the prospect of traveling and living abroad appealing when the time came to consider the African experience. People have often asked, in amazement, "and you took your young children with you?"[2] We thought nothing of it.

There was another aspect of my childhood socialization that is even more directly relevant to my previous comment about not being particularly curious about

---

2. Our son had been born in the middle of the second year of the graduate school years (1963), and our daughter was four when we returned to Uganda in 1972.

the diversity in sexual practices we noted in Africa. It reflects how unusual my family situation actually was, given its geographic locale, educational level, religion, and social-class situation. And to this day, I do not understand how this came to be. My parents were not only very open about their own sensuality and sexuality, they taught and modeled a positive attitude toward one's body and toward sexuality.

Nudity was never flaunted, but it was perfectly natural to observe both my mother and father nude if they were changing clothes or coming from the shower. My parents were very openly affectionate to one another, including the occasional squeeze of the breast or pat on the bottom. Our bedroom was a few steps from my parents'. About the only time the bedroom door was closed was on those occasions when, for several minutes after they went to bed, the light was still on and the bed was squeaking. When it stopped, there was a short visit to the bathroom and things settled down. Early on, I understood what went on "behind closed doors." They made no effort to hide that "perfectly normal" activity, although it was kept as private as possible under the conditions. We learned it was what parents who loved each other did. As we grew older, and as appropriate occasions arose, during the family discussion that always took place in conjunction with evening dinner, we were told about aspects of sexuality, such was women's menstruation, nocturnal emissions, and even masturbation. These periods of instruction were not long, drawn-out lectures, but just another topic among the many that were a part of these discussions. We were always told that if we had questions that we should ask. I do not really recall doing much asking about sexuality, but I did know that I could, without being turned away or chastised for doing so. More generally, asking questions and discussing issues were a regular part of the menu of our lives.

Thus, I came to my adolescence with a generally erotophilic or positive view of sexuality. It was okay to have sexual thoughts and to be a sexual person. Nonetheless, I was not immune from the more sex-negative attitudes of my culture. Masturbation, for example, was certainly not a topic for discussion with my peers, or anyone else for that matter. Although there was a part of me that understood it was all right, I also felt very guilty about doing it. "Heavy petting" was very stimulating, but coitus "had" to wait until marriage. In a sense, I am glad I held that attitude for as long as I did. Condoms were not available without asking the pharmacist for them, à la the scene in the movie *The Summer of '42,* and I am not sure I could have done that. It might well have been easier to risk pregnancy, but it was not really an issue during my high school days. Of course I did not make it to marriage before changing my attitude, or at least my behavior, but being in love and engaged sort of legitimized the behavior when it finally occurred.

Returning to the thread about the diverse sexual practices in Africa, I think the "sex-positive" background led me to simply accept the diversity of sexual practices I saw there as normal, just as the diversity of foods, music, and other customs was normal. I certainly was not offended by these differences, and I was not even especially interested in them.

In 1967 I returned to Syracuse University as a member of the faculty. In 1969 we were scheduled to return to Uganda for another year of teaching and research, but we never got there. Political conflict between the Ugandan government and Syracuse University put our program on hold for nearly a year. Although I enjoyed the cross-cultural work I was doing, the thought began to emerge that these kinds of conflict might not only continue but even worsen. Funding to do research in Africa and access to do the research, even when funded, were certainly going to be major considerations. Furthermore, the political stability of the East African countries left a lot to be desired. I began to wonder if I could make this work my career. I began to ask myself what other aspects of social behavior piqued my curiosity.

This is the point at which all of the pieces of the puzzle start to come together, and I developed that first seminar. Allow me to go back to the Graceland days for just a moment. Probably the single most important aspect of that experience was that I had been encouraged by some inspiring faculty members to really think, to ask questions, to challenge, and to be independent; to be willing to take the path less traveled. As a result, the conformist began to rebel, at least in some ways. When the opportunity for the post-doc in Africa came, it was not difficult to accept the challenge and try something different from my peers. When "the church" 's answers to my theological questions were not adequate, it was not difficult to argue that it was the church that was wrong and should change, rather than me. When I saw it would not and that basically good people were being unnecessarily dragged into my personal conflicts, it was not difficult to become inactive. When I reached the point of realizing that a career as a cross-cultural social psychologist was filled with mine fields, I began to explore alternatives with a "what can I do that is different from everyone else?" mentality.

I looked at the literature of the field (the textbooks and the journals), and I asked myself questions: what aspect of social behavior interested me *and* was not being studied much by other social psychologists? The one topic that met both criteria was sexualities. Recall that this was during the time of the so-called sexual revolution. The challenges to the traditional sexual standards were abundant. There were lots of obvious questions to ask about why we think, feel, and act as we do, sexually. At a personal level, I was asking about my own standards and behavior. At a societal level, I was observing the changing standards and behavior of the culture. At a professional level, I was asking why some of these standards existed in the first place, and why people were so intolerant of diversity. I began looking for "what do we know about this" answers to the many questions about variations in sexual attitudes and behavior.

To my surprise, I realized that there was virtually no coverage of the most intimate of social behaviors in the social psychology texts.[3] With a rare exception, the social psychology journals did not report research about sexual behavior, or the social influences thereon. I wondered why, or why not. I began to search and to read what I found. My interest grew, and my knowledge of what we knew and did not

---

3. I believe it was 1972 before a basic text contained a chapter devoted to sexualities.

know accumulated, eventually to the point of feeling that I was ready to "go public" and to offer the seminar mentioned at the outset. This is not, however, the end of the story of my becoming a sexologist.

We did go back to Uganda for eighteen months, beginning in the summer of 1972. Idi Amin was the president. In early 1973 he began his outrageous reign of terror, expelling one group after another from the country, fostering intertribal conflict and ultimately war within the country and between countries. The last nine months became increasingly difficult, to the point that we made plans to get the children out of the country quickly if things deteriorated further. The most important point of all of this is that when we left Uganda in December, it was with a heavy heart as well as with the knowledge that the country and people we loved were in for some very difficult days, and that we might never get back there again. But there was also a sense of relief. We were free and safe. We had survived, literally, when friends and acquaintances had not. There was a bitter taste, too. We were very angry, having witnessed such intolerance and inhumanity. All of this made it much easier to move away from that painful experience and on to sexology.

The transition period was from 1974 to 1976. I believe I joined the Society for the Scientific Study of Sex (now Sexuality; SSSS) in 1974, and I know I attended my first annual meeting of SSSS in 1975. In 1976, the SSSS meeting was held in conjunction with the international meeting in Montreal. Curious about the organization and interested in governance, as I had been from my high school and college days of involvement with student government, I attended the business meeting. Held at 8:30 A.M., attendance by SSSS members, other than the board members required to be there, was sparse. I happened to sit next to Tina Wheeler, who was, I believe, secretary at the time. Before the meeting began, I introduced myself and we chatted. When time came for nominations to the board for the following year, she asked me if I would be willing to be nominated. Somewhat taken aback, but also flattered, I agreed. Little did I know then what an impact that would have on my life and my career. That one, almost impulsive, "yes" is the fortuitous opportunity that clinched the "decision" to become a sexologist. I had sealed my fate, almost by accident. It had "just happened."

I was elected to the SSSS board of directors, and I served on it for the next ten years. In the spring of 1977 I was asked to become acting editor of the *Journal of Sex Research,* and then formally elected to two five-year terms thereafter. In 1984 I served as president of SSSS, in 1985 I became the founding president of the Foundation for the Scientific Study of Sexuality. These and a number of related activities and roles have dominated my professional life, along with my teaching and research related to sexualities, since that time in the mid-1970s.

There are a lot of things about this career "choice" that reflect the characteristic of independence that I mentioned at the outset. I did not want to do what everyone else was doing; to follow the crowd. I guess I have not, and from the standpoint of personal satisfaction, I have been amply rewarded. It has been challenging, interesting, and rewarding. I trust I have made some modest contribution along the way. It has also certainly been a plus that Sandra has worked with me so closely, first as an assistant with the *Journal of Sex Research,* and then in many other capacities, developing her own role and identity, particularly in connection with the foundation.

I do have a few regrets. I have paid a price for my rebelliousness. I could have done it, played the game, better. During those years of intense involvement with SSSS and as editor, I did very little writing of my own. I worked with my graduate students and facilitated their research, and I helped dozens of people get their research into shape for publication. I did not, however, devote enough time to my own research program. In a system that rewards people almost solely on personal research productivity, and in a department and college (or perhaps more accurately, with a chairperson and dean) that viewed sexuality research, at best, with suspicion and as not very valuable, I paid a price for deviance from the narrow path. If I could have those ten to twelve years back, I would certainly be a bit more selfish and a bit more conforming. The effort would be rewarded with merit salary raises and promotion, and that work would be satisfying, too. Yet, having said what I would have done if I could do it over again, I recently chose to write an advanced-level textbook focusing on social influences of human sexual behavior rather than devote that time to individual research investigations. The book project has consumed me now for two years and will continue to do so for at least another couple.

I have made the decision to take early retirement from Syracuse University in 1998. I trust that I will be able to continue teaching part time, and the teaching priority for me is, of course, my sexualities courses. I also hope the freedom will allow me to do some other writing, editing, and consulting. Perhaps I will even take up some offers to become a visiting professor for a semester or a year, consulting with other sexologists and students preparing for a career in the field. It is these things that challenge me and motivate me now as I become a more senior member of the field. I certainly do not plan to really retire. Nonetheless, a little more time for recreational activities at the cabin in Maine and on the beach (or in the water) in Hawaii will not be all that bad either.

8

Coming of Age in the Land of Two Genders[1]

Dallas Denny, M.A.

Dallas Denny, a male-to-female transsexual, is the founder and director of the Atlanta Educational Gender Information Service (AEGIS). She has written some seventy-five articles on transsexualism for magazines, newsletters, and professional journals, and is the author of two books on the subject.

I AM HONORED to be asked to contribute to this book of personal histories of sexologists. I consider it a milestone not only in my own life, but also in the history of transsexual people, for until recently, no matter what our credentials or talents, we were too marginalized to be considered anything more than curiosities. We had no significance beyond the fact of our transsexualism. I have great respect for Vern and Bonnie Bullough for their ability to see me as a professional first, and as transsexual second.

In order to do my story justice, it was necessary to provide it with a political and historical framework. Thus, the chapter moves from the general to the specific, from a description of the marginalization of transsexual people to an explanation of the work I do, and how I came to do it.

Part I: Gender Politics

Until recently, all major theoretical papers, all of the descriptive studies, and all of the textbooks about transsexualism were written by nontranssexual persons. This situation is analogous to the study of black history and identity without the

---

1. Portions of this chapter have already appeared in *The News* (Atlanta, Ga.) and *Empathy: An Interdisciplinary Journal for Persons Working to End Oppression on the Basis of Sexual Identities,* and are reprinted with permission.

involvement of black scholars, or of gay and lesbian history and identity without gay and lesbian scholars.

The problem was not that transsexual persons are unable to write. Indeed, some of our most talented and beloved authors, including Carson McCullers, Daphne Du Maurier, and Ernest Hemingway,[2] seem to have had significant transgender tendencies (it's often impossible to tell, because transgender status is so often a well-kept secret). No, the problem was that those of us who were out—that is, who were honest and open about our transsexualism—were marginalized. We were kept so busy with our struggle to understand and cope with our condition, and with defending ourselves against those who acted with hysteria and malice to us when we dared to disclose our transsexual natures (often our own family members as well as the professionals to whom we had turned for help), that we had little time or energy to expend on anything more than simple survival. What we have published has been, until late, because of our curiosity value (the ubiquitous transsexual autobiography), or materials distributed more often than not at our own expense in order to help other transsexual people through the very difficult process of self-discovery and self-invention.

From the late 1960s until the mid-1980s, most transsexual people—that is, men and women who wished to change their bodies to more closely resemble those of the other sex—knocked on the doors of gender clinics that offered a one-stop, one-size-fits-all approach which was nevertheless very obstructionistic; only those transsexual people who fit the clinics' frequently inaccurate and sexist notions of what they should be like were provided with services, and then only by jumping a rigorous set of hurdles designed to discourage them or turn them into highly stereotyped caricatures of nontransgendered men and women (Bolin, 1988; Denny, 1992; Kessler and McKenna, 1978).

Many clinics, citing confidentiality restrictions, actively discouraged transsexual people from interacting with each other. Except for brief and usually anonymous contact with others in therapist-led support groups, transsexual people were isolated, unable to communicate with each other, and forced by the clinics and by societal and peer pressure to assimilate as "normal" men and women in the larger world. This prevented the formation of any type of community. The insistence of the clinics upon assimilation—putting one's transsexualism "behind oneself" after transition—was an additional factor in preventing community.

---

2. In *No Man's Land: The Place of the Woman Writer in the Twentieth Century*, Gilbert and Gubar discuss the extensive erotic transgender imagery in Hemingway's *Garden of Eden*. Garber (1991) notes that as a child, Ernest Hemingway was cross-dressed by his mother, and that apparently this went somewhat beyond the custom of the times (for instance, Garber describes a photo of Hemingway at nearly two years of age which bears the title "Summer Girl").

According to Margaret Forster, a biographer of Daphne Du Maurier who had the cooperation of her children and full access to the author's unpublished works, Du Maurier, who was intensely homophobic, had private fantasies of being emotionally a male. Similarly, Virginia Carr, a biographer of Carson McCullers, concluded that like the somewhat transgendered main character in McCullers's *A Member of the Wedding*, McCullers desired to be a man.

In 1979, the Gender Identity Clinic at the Johns Hopkins University, which had taken the lead in the study and treatment of transsexual persons since its inception in 1967, abruptly shut down as the result of a scheme concocted by psychiatrist Paul McHugh (McHugh, 1993) and carried out by Jon Meyer, the head of the clinic, who submitted a study of the effectiveness of transsexual surgery to the journal *Archives of General Psychiatry* (Meyer and Reter, 1979). Meyer called a press conference to announce the findings, namely, that surgery made little difference in transsexuals' lives, which was conveniently timed so that psychologist John Money, the primary power behind the clinic, was out of the country (Ogas, 1994). This study was immediately and soundly criticized on a number of fronts, but had its intended effect; the clinic was closed due to political pressures brought as a result of the publicity campaign mounted by Meyer.[3]

The closing of the prestigious Johns Hopkins clinic had a domino-like effect on university-affiliated gender clinics. By 1991, of the more than forty programs in the United States, all but two had closed their doors (Denny, 1992). However, market pressures brought to bear by thousands of men and women seeking sex reassignment led to the development of a transsexual grapevine which channeled those who wanted sex reassignment to private practitioners willing to provide services.

Riding piggyback on the support network that had arisen for heterosexual cross-dressers, or attending one of a very few support groups for transsexual people which had sprung up across the country, transsexuals began to come into contact with one another in the early 1980s. Most, however, remained firmly in the closet of assimilation. In 1986, Merissa Sherrill Lynn founded the International Foundation for Gender Education (IFGE). Although Lynn frequently and loudly proclaimed that IFGE was not an umbrella organization, it served admirably as such, bringing into frequent and often conflict-ridden contact with one another both cross-dressers and transsexual people, and a newly emerging class of people who did not fit either category—transgenderists, who lived full-time as the opposite sex, but without genital surgery.

To the consternation of Virginia Prince, who had coined the word "transgenderist" to refer to people like herself, who lived across genders without genital surgery, "transgender" soon came into use as a global term for the entire community. It has recently gained wide recognition in the gay/lesbian/bisexual press, largely because of the activities of activists like Riki Anne Wilchins and Phyllis Randolph Frye. Transsexual and transgendered persons are now officially included in the mission statements and names of many organizations which once actively excluded us. Incidentally, many transsexual persons do *not* identify as transgendered, but simply as men or women. However, the term transgender, especially when considered to be shorthand for "transgressively gendered" (Bornstein, 1994),

---

3. There is no doubt there was a conspiracy. In a 1993 article in *American Scholar,* McHugh noted that his intention upon coming to Hopkins in the mid-1970s was to terminate that institution's participation in sex reassignment. See Ogas (1994) for the story of the closing of the Johns Hopkins clinic, and Blanchard and Sheridan (1990) for a devastating critique of Meyer and Reter (1979).

is the term most widely used to describe the wide range of transsexual people, trans-genderists, cross-dressers, drag kings and queens, stone butches, passing women and men, and gender blenders who challenge binary gender norms.

As part of the increasingly recognized community of transgendered persons, transsexual and transgendered scholars and authors are at long last coming into prominence. Kate Bornstein and Martine Rothblatt, both of whom are postopera-tive transsexuals, have written books for general audiences (Bornstein, 1994; Roth-blatt, 1994) which were released by mainstream publishing houses. Leslie Feinberg, who once identified as transsexual and now considers herself to be a transgenderist, has found enormous grassroots popularity with her semi-autobiographical novel *Stone Butch Blues* (Feinberg, 1993). When the president of Bradford College recently vetoed Feinberg as keynote speaker at graduation, angry students took over the administration building; after renegotiation, Feinberg spoke after all.

Transsexual scholars have been writing and presenting papers at scientific con-ferences for some years, but the first published contribution to the academic litera-ture by an acknowledged transsexual person, so far as I have been able to tell, was an essay by Sandy Stone in Epstein and Straub's 1991 book *Body Guards: The Cul-tural Politics of Gender Ambiguity.* Stone pointed out some of the many ways in which transsexual people had been misapprehended and maligned by nontranssexual writ-ers. Her essay, "The Empire Strikes Back: A Posttranssexual Manifesto," immedi-ately achieved legendary status among the scholars of the transgender community.

So far as I know, the first submission by an admitted transsexual published in a psychological journal or book (excluding "what it's like to be transsexual" articles) was a letter I wrote to the editor of *Archives of Sexual Behavior,* which was published in that journal in 1993.[4] However, one of the authors in Blanchard and Steiner's (eds.) 1990 *Clinical Management of Gender Identity Disorders in Children and Adults* was written by Maxine Petersen, a transsexual woman, under her former name (Clemmensen, 1990). Recently (1995), Petersen used her new name as co-author of an article in a peer-review journal which frequently publishes articles about trans-sexualism (Petersen & Dickey, 1995).[5]

My work for Garland Press, *Gender Dysphoria: A Guide to Research,* is, so far as I know, the first academic book-length contribution by an out transsexual author. It

---

4. Previously, the label of transsexual had been the cause of immediate rejection. As a single illus-tration of this, Bolin (personal communication, 1994) told me that when a rejected manuscript was returned to her, one of the reviewers had penciled "Obviously a transsexual" on his copy. The reviewer had apparently felt that no transsexual could possibly have anything relevant to say about transsexualism!

Bolin is not transsexual, but she has been outspoken in her criticism of the medicalization of transsexual persons. In this instance, challenging the orthodoxy of the literature got her branded as transsexual and silenced.

5. It's ironic, but hardly surprising, that those most attracted to the field of transgender studies have frequently had their own unacknowledged issues with gender and/or sexuality. There's no telling how many authors have been secret cross-dressers, or secretly transsexual, or secretly or openly gay or les-bian. And there's little doubt, at least in my mind, that many clinicians and researchers are in the field because they are morbidly fascinated with or sexually attracted to transgendered and transsexual persons.

is a voluminous (over 650 pages) annotated bibliography of the literature of transsexualism and cross-dressing, published at the suggestion of Vern Bullough, one of the editors of this book (Denny, 1994a). However, even though I am extremely visible, both locally and nationally, as a transsexual woman, I did not mention my transsexualism in the book. I *am* planning to discuss it in my forthcoming edited text for Garland, *Current Concepts in Transgender Identity: Towards a New Synthesis* (Denny, in press).

The year 1995 was a watershed year in the emergence of transsexual scholars. In February, a historic conference took place in Van Nuys, California. The International Congress on Cross-Dressing, Gender, and Sex Issues, hosted by the Department of Sex Research at the University of California at Northridge, was attended by more than three hundred scholars, transgendered (many of them transsexual) and nontransgendered alike. For the first time, transgender credentials were as important as academic credentials. I was proud, at a workshop I gave on the first day of the conference, to proclaim that my *first* credential was as a transsexual woman.

It was something I could never have done before.

Part II: My Work, in Brief

Although I have worked in the helping professions since 1971, I had no notion that I would end up doing sexological work. However, as I went about the business of confronting my gender identity issue, I was struck by the astounding amount of misinformation about transsexualism and a concomitant lack of support for transsexual persons. Perhaps that would have been enough to eventually draw me into my present activities, but I'll never know, for I was drafted. In the fall of 1989, as I was preparing to live full-time as a woman, Lynn and Jerry Montgomery, who had been running a support group in the Atlanta area, convinced me to direct the group. I reluctantly accepted, and did so for a year. In 1990, I founded Atlanta Educational Gender Information Service, Inc., which quickly took on a national prominence and a new name: American Educational Gender Information Service (AEGIS).

AEGIS is a national clearinghouse for information on transsexual and transgender issues. We operate a help line which receives calls from transsexual and transgendered people of all ages, races, and social classes; parents and children of transsexual people; employers; journalists; and helping professionals who have transsexual clients. AEGIS publishes *Chrysalis: The Journal of Transgressive Gender Identities* and a newsletter, maintains the National Transgender Library and Archive, and advocates for common sense and reason in the medical and psychological treatment of transsexual people. In 1995 we published our first book, *Recommended Guidelines for Transgender Care,* by Gianna E. Israel and Donald Tarver, M.D.

In addition to full-time employment as a behavior specialist in a day program for adults with developmental disabilities, I am executive director of AEGIS, which keeps me very busy. I've been active on a local level as well. In early 1991, I founded, and remain active in, the Atlanta Gender Explorations (AGE) support group, which currently has about forty members, most of whom identify as transsexual. In 1994, I was appointed a senior advisor on Gay, Lesbian, Bisexual, and Transgender Affairs to Atlanta mayor Bill Campbell. Also in 1994, I became a member of Atlanta Pride, an event equivalent to Gay Pride Day, and serve as its secretary.

AEGIS has given me an autonomy that I could never have had in an academic setting. Because my salary is not dependent upon people being pleased with what I have to say; because I am a competent writer, and a prolific one; and because I have had sufficient determination and energy to address a lot of envelopes and lick a lot of stamps, I have been able to speak my mind and make myself heard, and I am proud to be a small part of the current reappraisal of what gender means in our society.

Much of my work has been geared toward reforming the professional literature of transsexualism. I've taken delight in pointing out the literature's many shortcomings, especially the ways in which clinicians' and researchers' naive notions caused them to make assumptions and ask research questions which nowadays seem silly enough to render much of their research irrelevant. I must confess that it has given me some delight to do so, especially since such "research" was once used by a gender clinic to deny me medical services which would have helped me to feminize my body; I was judged and found wanting because I was not dysfunctional enough to be transsexual (i.e., transsexual people are pathetic and marginal creatures, and I was employed and well educated; therefore, I could not possibly be transsexual). The truth was that the literature reflected research done only on those "transsexuals" who had been selected by gender clinics because they were severely dysfunctional; therefore, the research population was not reflective of transsexuals in general (Bolin, 1988; Denny, 1992; Kessler and McKenna, 1978). Unfortunately, in an age in which many transsexual people are physicians, physicists, airline pilots, attorneys, computer programmers, army officers, politicians, policemen, and college professors, we are left with dozens of such studies that will prove to be ultimately worthless.

Indeed, I have come to object to the term "disorder," as it seems to me, after living with and studying transsexualism for so many years, that it is more a blessing than a curse—at least it has been for me. It makes much more sense, and is much less stigmatizing, to view traits like left-handedness, transsexualism, and homosexuality as natural ways of being human, and not as unfortunate traits which should be eradicated. We no longer tie the hands of left-handed children behind their backs, and homosexuality is no longer listed in the American Psychiatric Association's *Diagnostic and Statistical Manual* (DSM). Why, then, should transsexualism continue to be considered a disorder?

Part III: My Personal History

The way I came to be involved in this field is simple: when I turned twelve (and a very naive twelve, at that), I found myself compelled to wear women's clothes.

There I was, an iron filing in the electromagnetic field of life, with a very strong magnet only yards away in my mother's room. When she was away, I would go through her lingerie drawer, silently memorizing the position of each guiltily borrowed garment so that I could fit it back in place like a piece from a nylon jigsaw puzzle. I had no idea why I, a boy of the highest ideals and purest character, who had always been strong of heart and unlined of brow, suddenly found myself drawn so powerfully to women's apparel, but I did know that I was possessed of something far stronger than I. Something had wakened in me, and it *would* have its way. I considered very briefly trying to fight it, but deep in my bones I knew that it would destroy me if I did. But I also knew that to share this desire with an unaccepting world would be disastrous (it was, after all, the South of the 1960s); my parents, with every good intention, would take me to be "fixed," and would damage or destroy me in the process, or I would destroy myself by internalizing the struggle. My solution was not to fight the temptation, but to yield to it secretly. I thought at the time that it was a purely hedonistic decision, but today, thirty years later, having seen the scars on many of my fellow transsexuals who did wage such an internal struggle, I realize now how very wise or lucky I was to reach the decision that I did at such a tender age.

On the infrequent occasions when I was alone in the house, I would slip on my mother's panties; tuck myself into a girdle that was already too small; pull on nylons, fastening them, in those pre-pantyhose days, to the girdle's dangling rubber thongs; struggle to snap a bra (the mechanics of which, I discovered, I had no inherent knowledge of); and cover it all with a slip and a dress.

I very quickly discovered that women's clothing were but a means to an end: it was necessary in order to build the disguise of myself-as-woman. I remember well the day, when I was about fifteen, that the gas gauge of my gender identity leapt for the first time out of the "M" zone and strayed defiantly into "F." The rest of the family had gone for a Sunday drive, and I made an excuse not to go. I was sitting on the floor of the living room, wearing a purple dress (I had gotten my own by that time), experimenting with my face and hair. And for the first time, I got it right. Looking in the mirror, I would ordinarily see a boy, and only a boy, with a mandatory short-on-the-sides haircut. In that dress, with Cover Girl skin and Maybelline eyes, my hair blended into a fall, I saw a very pretty, an almost beautiful girl. I didn't—and this is important—see a boy dressed as a girl. I saw a *girl*. I remember thinking in awe, "This is who I want to be. This is who I probably should have been." But I also remember thinking that it couldn't be. It wasn't possible. I was looking at a fiction, a fabrication, a creature created out of cosmetics and cloth. The girl in the mirror was a fantasy, and I could see no way to make her real. She had no name. In the end, she wound up in a paper sack which I hid under a loose board in the summer-hot attic.

Few secrets can be kept in a small house with six people living in it, and the girl with no name was soon discovered. In no uncertain terms, I was let to know how scandalous, how perverse, how ugly she was. Despite my decision to give in to my urges, I had been having real problems dealing with what I considered to be the unnatural need of an all-American boy. The revulsion of my mother, who caught me flat-footed (but not flat-chested), did not help, nor did my father's disgust, when he was told. This was the man who had once jumped on me with both feet (figuratively; he was not a violent man) for talking like the cartoon character Snagglepuss the Lion. Heavens to Murgatroyd! I didn't understand what the problem was until later, when I realized that he thought it sounded effeminate. Now, his son revealed as a boy who dressed up like a girl, he threatened to make me walk the long five miles into town in women's clothing, as he followed in the car.

Would that he had, for I would have been "out," and perhaps it would not have taken me another ten years to come to some resolution about my cross-dressing and my life. Instead, the clothes were disposed of and the girl with no name was dismembered as effectively as if we had cut her up and thrown her chunk by bleeding chunk from a speeding car on a moonless summer night.

My parents took me to a psychiatrist. In my shame and denial, I led him to think that the cross-dressing was not very important, had just been an experiment. And he went for it, telling my parents that I was "just going through a phase." It's a "phase" that's still going on, now, more than thirty years later.

I had not been very successful in my quest for information about gender dysphoria—it was not, after all, something I felt comfortable approaching authority figures about, and the few books on the subject in the public library were often checked out or stolen by people much like me. But in the late 1960s, I heard the news that the Johns Hopkins University was opening a sex reassignment clinic, and that they would evaluate two people a month. Two people a month in a country with a population of hundreds of millions! What chance would a girl with no name have? She was, after all, a lie, a wraith, a sometimes creature. Surely Hopkins would take those boys who were lucky enough to naturally look like girls without having to work at it, those with ambiguous genitalia, whose parents had more money than mine. And how would my parents take it, my father who thought that Snagglepuss was a faggot, and a mother who thought that Miss Jane Hathaway on "The Beverly Hillbillies" was played by Christine Jorgensen? "I just thought I would try it," I told the shrink. "It's not that important."

It was three or four years later. The girl with no name was back, spending most of her time hanging in a wardrobe in the Ross Fireproof Hotel in downtown Nashville. I had graduated from high school and been summarily ejected from my parents' house due to a combination of bad attitude and parental defiance. I had found a job as a busboy, and, as I had no car, I would ride the city bus to work and back. In the evenings and on my day off, the girl with no name would come out of the closet and wander around downtown, shopping at Belk's and Cain-Sloan and Harvey's, Nashville's three big department stores; going to the movies; visiting the library; eating in restaurants; hoping desperately to spot someone like herself so that she could at long last share her feelings with someone. She never managed to do so. Men in cars would whistle and slow down and try to convince me to get in beside them, and I would ignore them, always. But then one day something happened. I—or rather, the girl with no name, for I would never have done such a thing—found herself in a lip-lock with a cab driver. I had never been kissed before, had never masturbated, had never even touched my privates except to wash them, or to push them up inside me so I could pretend they weren't there, and here I was in an embrace that was growing more passionate by the moment. I was struggling to keep his hands out from under my skirt (a mini—it was the sixties, after all), struggling with my self-identity. Here I was being kissed by a man, and I damn well knew that underneath the clothing I was a boy, after all, and I reasoned that I couldn't be gay, for I had no interest in men as a man. Here I was, with a gender identity which had suddenly slammed itself firmly against the "F" peg and would never again wander into the "M" zone. Here I was with an awakening awareness of my genitals—genitals I was wholeheartedly wishing were "innies" instead of "outies" so that I could go to bed with this man like any other woman. Here I was, wondering if I would be killed and decapitated if this heterosexual man were to discover that his girlfriend was really a boy.

I managed to call a halt to proceedings just shy of blastoff, and a little short of discovery. The man pleaded with me to be his girlfriend, and asked me to go with him to meet his friends—but I refused, and did not see him again.

During those days at the Ross Fireproof Hotel, the girl with no name would plot and scheme, trying to figure out how to find a job (short of prostitution, which I was sure would get me killed) that would allow her to stay out of the closet forever. But she was fighting Mother Nature, and she knew it. She, who had years earlier found a single hair on her face and shuddered, had been only too correct in her prediction that it was but an advance scout for a full beard. Every day, there was more hair on her face, and less on her head. She could *feel* the testosterone in her body, and she hated it and the gonads which produced it—but she, being ignorant about hormonal therapy, could think of nothing to do about it, short of self-castration, which she seriously considered, but eventually decided against.

I did consider becoming involved with the gay community, where I thought that there might be a place for me, but as I was no less homophobic than the rest of the populace, I could never quite bring myself to do it. Nashville had a gay bar of legendary fame, Juanita's, but in my mind's eye, it was a seedy little place where older gay men cruised each other. When, years later, having gotten to actually know some gay people and begun to work through my prejudices and stereotypes, I finally got around to visiting Juanita's, and discovered that it *was* indeed a wrinkle room. No, I didn't go to the gay bars, and there was no transgender community. There was nowhere else *to* go except out into the greater heterosexual world, where I had to pass or die (or so I thought).

The testosterone marched on: I entered adulthood as a man instead of as a woman, and the straight world instead of the gay. I married a woman, grew a beard, went to college. I got weak in the knees every time I saw a pretty girl, because I wanted to *be* her so much. I got divorced (for reasons not having to do with transsexualism).

It was 1978. Single again, I had moved back to Nashville after completing a master's program at the University of Tennessee in Knoxville. The beard of seven years was gone, and the girl with no name was back, even if she was not passing so well because of testosterone poisoning. I was going to the gay bars, having sex with men in parking lots, facing a lifetime of looking increasingly more bizarre in a dress, becoming increasingly dysphoric about my body. I was finding it more and more difficult to think of myself as the girl with no name, for I was starting to see in the mirror not the girl, and not the woman she should have become, but a man in a dress. My dysphoria, which had always been present, was becoming overwhelming. One fine day, I told myself that whatever was going on with me wasn't going to go away, that it was time to stop hiding the girl with no name in the closet, and to integrate her into my life, doing away with the butch-femme extremes to see who I really was.

I started by acknowledging that I was at the very least a cross-dresser. I quit worrying that my pumps or wig would be seen, or that I would be spotted wearing them. One by one, I told my friends and acquaintances. Step one.

Those were the days of Jan Morris and Renée Richards; gender reassignment, while still scandalous, was at least thinkable. Step two was to ask myself whether I wanted to be a woman. The answer to that was, of course, yes.

Step three was to take an honest look at myself, to determine if it would be possible, via surgery, electrolysis, and better living through chemistry, to ever pass convincingly as a female. I refused to be a man in a dress. I took careful stock of my body. I didn't at all like what I saw. My body had moved in undesirable directions since that day when I found that single hair growing on my face. I was too hairy. Too big. Too this, not enough that. I made a list, and then scratched off things that could be changed through hard work, hormones, electrolysis, surgery. I looked at what was left and thought "Just maybe . . ."

And so I took myself to the gender clinic at Vanderbilt University, where I gave them some money and told them about the girl with no name and took a battery of psychological tests that I had been trained to administer. After a time they got back to me, saying that they had made a decision about my gender. *They* had made the decision! And no, it wasn't the one I wanted. Because I was not so dysphoric that I was dysfunctional as a man, they would not offer me feminizing procedures like hormonal therapy or surgery. They would, however, offer me counseling to help me in my life as a man. Thank you very much. Fuck you. I didn't go back.

I began to haunt the library at Vanderbilt University Medical School, reading books and articles about transsexualism. They confirmed what I had been told at Vanderbilt—that transsexual people were marginal, maladjusted creatures. Since I did not fit the stereotype: since I was not a sex worker; since I did not hate my genitals, but only thought them the wrong ones; since I had not wanted to be a girl from earliest memory, but only since age twelve; since I had never seriously considered suicide, I thought that I could not possible be what was considered transsexual. I was simply a man who desperately wanted to be a woman.

Vanderbilt's refusal to give me female hormones cued me about what I needed to do to pursue physical change. I visited a number of physicians, asking for hormones, but was refused. The easygoing manner of the doctors would change when I explained my situation. They would exit in confusion, and return a few minutes later to tell me no and give me their bill. Finally, in frustration, while waiting alone in an examination room, I tore a dozen sheets from a prescription pad and put them in my purse. Later, at home, I studied the *Physicians Desk Reference,* looking for a suitable estrogen, and forged a prescription at what I hoped was the proper dose. Later that same day, trembling, I stopped at a drug store and left with a bottle of diethylstilbestrol tablets (a synthetic preparation possessing estrogenic properties, but more effective than natural estrogen).

That simple act of defiance, illegal as it might have been, changed my life. Had I not started a regimen of hormones at age twenty-nine, my body would have continued to masculinize. Instead, it started to feminize. The physical changes were subtle at first, but cumulative. The ultimate consequence of that act was that ten years later, I did not look like a thirty-nine-year-old man, but like a thirty-nine-year-old woman, which made transition from the male role to the female role easy, in a physical sense. But the emotional consequences were devastating.

During this ten-year period, I obtained a license to practice psychology, took a job in a remote corner of the state, began a very tumultuous eight-year relationship with a man which was simultaneously the most satisfying and most frustrating experience of my life, and went once again to graduate school. In the fall of 1988, after I had given up hope of the relationship ever improving, I began to quietly prepare myself for transition. I underwent a course of electrolysis, located a support group, and began seeing a therapist (who gave me a referral to an endocrinologist, legitimizing, at long last, my hormonal therapy).

In December 1989, I resigned from my civil service position as a psychological examiner in Tennessee and moved to Georgia with everything I owned in a U-Haul truck. I was sure it would take years to find an equivalent position, but to my surprise, I found one immediately; as I write, I am in my sixth year of employment there.

I would like to assure the readers of this book, many of whom are undoubtedly therapists, that my use of third-person pronouns in referring to "the girl with no-name" is a convenient literary device, and has no clinical significance. We have come to a time in which the "psychopathology" of transsexual people must be readdressed. Certainly, I have never felt very impaired by being transsexual; any confusion, guilt, or indecision I felt while trying to sort myself out was much more the effect of a nonunderstanding society than the result of my transsexualism. I realize that societal reaction to transsexualism does traumatize some of us, but it did not do so to me, and I will continue to fight against those few and unenlightened who still tar us all with the brush of psychopathology.

References

Bolin, A. 1988. *In search of Eve: Transsexual rites of passage.* South Hadley, Mass.: Bergin & Garvey Publishers, Inc.

Blanchard, R., and P. M. Sheridan. 1990. Gender reorientation and psychosocial adjustment. In *Clinical management of gender identity disorders in children and adults,* ed. R. Blanchard and B. W. Steiner, pp. 159–89. Washington, D.C.: American Psychiatric Press.

Bornstein, K. 1994. *Gender outlaw: On men, women, and the rest of us.* New York: Routledge.

Carr, V. 1975. *The lonely hunter: A biography of Carson McCullers.* New York: Carroll & Graff.

Clemmensen, L. H. 1990. The "real-life test" for surgical candidates. In *Clinical management of gender identity disorders in children and adults,* ed. R. Blanchard and B. W. Steiner, pp. 119–35. Washington, D.C.: American Psychiatric Press.

Denny, D. 1992. The politics of diagnosis and a diagnosis of politics: The university-affiliated gender clinics, and how they failed to meet the needs of transsexual people. *Chrysalis Quarterly* 1 (3): 9–20.

——. 1993. Letter to the editor: Response to Charles Mate-Kole's review of *In search of Eve: Transsexual rites of passage* by Anne Bolin (South Hadley, Mass.: Bergin & Garvey). *Archives of Sexual Behavior* 22 (2): 167–69.

——. 1994a. *Gender dysphoria: A guide to research.* New York: Garland Publishers.

——. 1994b. *Identity management in transsexualism: Negotiating the paper trail.* King of Prussia, Pa.: Creative Design Services.

——, ed. In press. *Current concepts in transgender identity: Towards a new synthesis.* New York: Garland Publishers.

Feinberg, L. 1993. *Stone butch blues.* New York: Firebrand Books.

Forster, M. 1993. *Daphne Du Maurier: The secret life of the renowned storyteller.* New York: Doubleday.

Garber, M. 1991. *Vested interests: Cross-dressing and cultural anxiety.* New York: Routledge.

Gilbert, S. M., and S. Gubar. 1989. *No man's land: The place of the woman writer in the twentieth century.* Volume 2: *Sexchanges.* New Haven: Yale University Press.

Hemingway, E. 1986. *The Garden of Eden.* New York: Scribner's.

Kessler, S. J., and W. McKenna. 1978. *Gender: An ethnomethodological approach.* New York: John Wiley & Sons. Reprinted in 1985 by The University of Chicago Press.

McHugh, P. R. 1992. Psychiatric misadventures. *American Scholar* 61 (4): 497–510.

Mate-Kole, C. 1992. Review of A. Bolin, *In search of Eve: Transsexual rites of passage. Archives of Sexual Behavior* 21 (2): 207–10.

Meyer, J. K., and D. Reter. 1979. Sex reassignment: Followup. *Archives of General Psychiatry* 36 (9): 1010–15.

Ogas, O. 1994. Spare parts: New information reignites a controversy surrounding the Hopkins gender identity clinic. *City Paper* (Baltimore), March 9: cover, 10–15.

Petersen, M. A., and R. Dickey. 1995. Surgical sex reassignment: A comparative survey of international centers. *Archives of Sexual Behavior* 24 (2): 135–56.

Rothblatt, M. 1994. *The apartheid of sex: A manifesto on the freedom of gender.* New York: Crown Publishers.

Stone, S. 1991. The empire strikes back: A posttranssexual manifesto. In *Body guards: The cultural politics of gender ambiguity,* ed. J. Epstein and K. Straub, pp. 280–304. New York: Routledge.

9

How I Became a Sexologist

Holly Devor, Ph.D.

Holly Devor, a Canadian sexologist, is both a feminist and a lesbian. Over the years her interests have broadened to include a variety of sexual topics, although gender issues remain at the core of her studies.

I T WASN'T EASY to be a gay teenager in the 1960s. Just being a lesbian and under the age of twenty-one made me a criminal, a juvenile delinquent who could be locked up or sent off for mandatory psychiatric treatment at the whim of others. My older lovers were guilty of an even greater crime, punishable by imprisonment, simply for the act of sexually loving me. When I read in my parents' *Reader's Digest* a statement by the then head of the FBI, J. Edgar Hoover, that "Any citizen of these United States who is not involved in some illegal activity has nothing to fear whatsoever," I laughed ruefully and clipped it out to post on my door. I knew that something was very wrong. Luckily for me, having been raised Jewish in a society recovering from the holocaust of World War II, I was more inclined to think that the problem lay with those who hated than with those who loved.

That was the beginning of my quest to understand sexuality and how it is shaped and controlled by social forces. I knew that I had done nothing wrong by loving women but that I was, nonetheless, engaged in stigmatized and criminal activities. Back then, when we were called "queer," it was said with a sneer. There was no pride or rebellion in that term. It was just that we butches were weird sickos.

When the Gay Liberation Front appeared after Stonewall, I was eager to join the fray. When I read *Notes from the Second Year*[1] of the women's liberation movement, I was eager to join up. I wanted to be able to live as I was, without fear of incarceration, without social rejection. When I found both fledgling movements in my adopted home of Canada, I became a political activist on both fronts. I spent the early years of the 1970s working full-time to improve the social conditions of women, lesbians, and gays.

As I did so, I read everything that I could (and at that time you could pretty well keep up with things) which might shed some light on why we were the way we were. That is, why we women, lesbians, and gays were the way we were; and why we, as a society, were the way we were. Why did some people have the right to deride other people for being women, butches, queens, lesbians, gays, etc., and why were some people "queer"? These were political questions for me; these were vital questions for me. If I wanted to change the world, I had to know how it was put together. If I wanted to reconstruct, I needed to learn how to deconstruct. Thus, I began my journey into sexological theory.

Having been raised within a society which taught me from a very early age to think about sex, gender, and sexuality in entirely biologically deterministic ways, not to do so required some intellectual effort from me. That effort, however, was one that I was more than willing to undertake in the early 1970s, when I was energetically engaged in the gay and women's liberation movements. I had been taught that women were born to be inferior to men and I saw it as in my best interests to reject that proposition. Instead, I adopted Simone de Beauvoir's dictum that "one is not born a woman, but rather becomes a woman."[2] In so doing, I was throwing my weight in with a group whom I was later to learn to call *social constructionists*. Over the years, I came to temper that position somewhat, although I still retain very strong leanings in that direction. Indeed, as I now conceptually separate sex and gender, I still agree that women are made, not born. However, I would argue that most females are born and that women are generally made from females.

By the end of the 1970s, I was getting pretty hungry being an activist, so I decided to try working for a living. I soon found that my mind also needed more nutrition and I went back to school. After floundering for a few years in a physics program, I decided to work from my strengths. I began tutoring in a women's studies program, and decided to enter a graduate program in communications. In order to become a graduate student, I had to have a thesis proposal. I asked myself what I thought could hold my interest for a few years. Well, sex and gender had already held my interest for a few years, so I figured that it would probably continue to do so for a few more. That became the subject matter of my M.A. in communications at Simon Fraser University in Vancouver.

I chose as my thesis topic a question which had been personally vexing to me during the previous few years. I, and several women I knew, were feminist butch women who were disinclined to obey patriarchal expectations of femininity. We thought of ourselves as "woman-identified women,"[3] but other people who didn't know us at all seemed to just as often think that we were men. Here we were trying to be really good feminists and really woman-identified and other people thought that we were men. How ironic! That apparent contradiction became my thesis topic. I named us *gender-blending females* and investigated the phenomenon through indepth interviews with fifteen women who had had extensive experience of that type.

That work brought me into contact with a lot of important new (to me) ideas. Although when I had returned to school to pursue graduate studies I did not have any mentors who specialized in the study of sexuality, I did get some very useful guidance and a lot of wholehearted support for what I was doing. One of my supervisors guided me to the works of symbolic interactionists and ethnomethodologists, while another of them sent me off to read about the psychology and biology of sex and gender differences. I found the ideas of George Herbert Mead, Erving Goffman, and Harold Garfinkel to be particularly stimulating.[4] I also read with enthusiasm from Money and Ehrhardt, Nancy Chodorow, Carol Gilligan, Sandra Bem, and Suzanne Kessler and Wendy Mckenna.[5] I learned from these scholars that I need not think of sex and gender as interchangeable concepts and that all meanings which people give to human interactions are socially negotiated within the framework of various sets of social contexts.

I also learned to look at the world around me on several different levels at one time. I learned that although genetics and other contributions from our physiological realities may provide some bottom-line limitations on who and what we might be or become, just about everything can be negotiated or manipulated by individuals and/or by social forces. When it comes to sex, gender, and sexuality, one particular quote from Kessler and McKenna pithily sums up one of the important lessons I learned during that stage of my studies. They noted that, "Beards, breasts, and other gender characteristics can be bought in a store."[6] In other words, in terms of everyday life, as I had learned some years before from the dykes, queens, and transsexuals whom I had known in my gay liberation activist days: gender is a performance, whether individual social actors realize it or not. Furthermore, it is one that can be consciously manipulated and controlled by social actors who understand the rules in their social environments and are sufficiently skillful to effectively present their desired images. I also picked up the concomitant idea that if gender is a performance and can thus become divorced from physiological qualifications, then sex and gender must be related, but distinct, social categories. As Virginia Prince so aptly explained: "Sex is between the legs; gender is between the ears."[7] However, they do tend to mesh well most of the time.

In the process of finishing off my M.A. thesis, I started to realize that sexuality was very much a part of the equation. However, it wasn't until I had done some more teaching that I really started to make the connection between sexuality and gender, in particular, when I taught introductory women's studies courses to male inmates in Canadian federal penitentiaries as part of an in-house university education program for prisoners. The men I met there made it perfectly clear to me that they when they thought about women, they thought about sexuality; and that when they thought about themselves as men, they thought about sexuality. Furthermore, I also taught similar university and nonuniversity introductory women's studies courses to classes composed entirely of convicted male sex offenders. These courses focused specifically on those men's understandings of the interactions between their ideas about sexuality, their thoughts and actions concerning women, and their conceptualizations of themselves as men.

If I hadn't gotten the message before, it came through loud and clear then. As Catherine MacKinnon said, "sexuality is gendered as gender is sexualized."[8] If I wanted to understand issues of gender, I needed to consider their intersection with issues of sexuality. If I wanted to understand sexuality, I needed to look at how gender shapes sexuality. In trying to help those men better to understand women and themselves, I had to talk with them about many of the basic issues of social life. Sexuality and power were of the greatest interest to them and were indivisible from questions of gender.[9]

Around the same time as I was teaching these courses, I was reworking my M.A. thesis to turn it into my first book, *Gender Blending: Confronting the Limits of Duality*. Taking my new understandings to heart, I added a chapter on sexuality to *Gender Blending*. I was clearly becoming a sexologist, but I did not yet know the term. Intellectually, I still housed myself under the rubrics of feminism and women's studies. When I wrote papers, I presented them at feminist conferences and submitted them to feminist journals. My work was well received. People were interested in what I was doing but, in those arenas, I seemed to be the only one doing them. I felt as though I was always starting at the beginning when I talked or wrote about the things that captivated my interest.

Shortly before the publication of *Gender Blending*, I applied for my first tenure-track academic appointment at the University of Victoria, British Columbia. For personal reasons, there was really only one job open at the time in which I was seriously interested. The department to which I applied had never previously had any faculty who specialized in sex, gender, and sexuality. Indeed, the entire university was pretty much devoid of such research. I applied for the job on the strength of my work in the field of sex, gender, and sexuality and, interestingly, no one seemed to object to my obvious interest in lesbianism, feminism, or sexuality. Rather, they seemed to have been blinded to my enthusiasm for such topics by the stellar reference letter I received from one of the top academic statisticians in the United States. Thus, I must say that my interest in sexuality research seemed to have been a moot point at the initiation of my academic career. However, it has been absolutely central to my advancement since that time.

When *Gender Blending* came out, it received almost entirely positive reviews in both academic and popular journals. However, I soon discovered that when one writes about topics of sex, gender, and sexuality, readers can take it very much to heart. When discussions of sexuality, sex, and gender are combined with feminism, people can react with a lot of heat. Whereas one reviewer took me to task for being too feminist, another criticized me for not being feminist enough. In the more critical of these two reviews, the reviewer's assumptions about my own sexuality seemed to color her ability to understand and interpret my comments about sexuality. Another ironic twist: I had refrained from writing about my own experiences as a gender-blending female or a butch lesbian because of fears that, at such an early stage of my career, such disclosures might stymie my advancement. Having made that defensive choice, I subsequently found myself assumed to have written *Gender*

Blending as a hypercritical outsider rather than as a sympathetic and insightful participant observer. Happily, the tone of critical response to *Gender Blending* was overwhelmingly and enthusiastically positive.

While working on a related topic for my Ph.D. in sociology, I began working on my second book, *FTM: Female-to-Male Transsexuals in Society*.[10] By this time, it was entirely clear to me that I could not study issues of sex and gender identity without also studying sexuality. In my mind, the three were inextricably mixed. However, it wasn't until I attended the Tenth World Congress on Sexuality in Amsterdam in the summer of 1991 that I began to think of myself as a sexologist. Finally, I was among the people whose works I had been reading for years. Finally, I did not have to start my discussions at step one. We could debate and discuss, argue and engage. Here were people from whom I could learn. I had found my niche.

From that point onward, I have focused my energies in the community of scholars known as sexologists. I have attended other World Association of Sexology conferences, become a member of the Society for the Scientific Study of Sexuality, the Harry Benjamin International Gender Dysphoria Association, and the International Academy of Sex Researchers. As I have continued my sexological research, there have been certain general principles which have guided me in my intellectual life and work. Most of them are moral and political in nature, and a few are more abstract intellectual ideas which have inspired my thoughts as a sexologist. Either way, they have been my working principles as a researcher, as a teacher, and as a citizen.

To begin with, feminist values inform my work. To me, that means a number of things about how I conduct research, about how I write about what I do, and how I disseminate the knowledge which I acquire. It means that generally I do what Glaser and Strauss called *grounded theory*.[11] I assume that the best experts on any subject are those who know about it from the inside out. When I want to understand something, I start by going to the people who live it and finding out from them how they understand their experiences. My insights are built on theirs.

Thus, when I try to trace my intellectual roots, I come up with mentors from "the field" as often as I find them among my professional peers. When I think back to moments of epiphany which mark times when theoretical vistas started to open up for me, the ones that stand out most prominently for me are experiential ones. Meeting Merissa Sheryl Lynn, Yvonne Cook-Riley, Ari Kane, Sheila Kirk, Virginia Prince, and Dallas Denny at my first IFGE (International Foundation for Gender Education)[12] convention are such markers for me. Debating sex, gender, and sexuality with them; working on the board of directors of the IFGE with them; partying in the wee hours of the morning with them, all taught me as much or more about sex, gender, and sexuality than could innumerable academic treatises. Making the acquaintance of many female-to-male people who took me into their confidence and showed me some of their secrets, and becoming friends with Jason Cromwell, Rupert Raj, and James Green have enriched my life first as a human being and second as a researcher. These people have taught me about their lives by taking me into their worlds and letting me live among them for a little while, as I have shared some of my life with them.

My feminist principles also show up in my assumption that I have substantial obligations to the people who have been generous enough to help me with my explorations. I try directly to give them voice in what I write and say about their lives. I write in language which I hope will be accessible to most of the people in the communities who were the subjects of my research, and I try to publish some of my work in outlets which might reach those whose interest in it is personal. I quote the people who have helped me as often and as completely as I am able. I take what I write to members of the communities who have helped me and ask for their advice and as much approval as they can offer. I count their endorsement as ultimately more important than those of other "professionals" and "experts."

One result of having such policies is that it forces me to be as scrupulous and as thorough in my research as possible. There are always people among those who participate in my research who become my friends, and other people whose paths I cross in other capacities. I have to face these people again. I know that I have the power to define their lives in print. I take that power seriously and do my best to be as accurate and as respectful as I can be. I know that I will have to answer for what I say for years to come. I try to do it in such a way that I will able to make those answers while looking real people in the eye.

I also feel a more tangible obligation to repay the people who open their lives to me. I do what work I can as an advocate for the interests of those people whom I study. In particular, I have served for three years on the board of directors of IFGE. During this time, I have worked in conjunction with the IFGE and leaders of the female-to-male transsexual community to establish representative participation by female-to-male persons in the IFGE and to build political ties between male-to-female and female-to-male communities. Within professional organizations, in my writing for professionals, in my public speaking, and in my contacts with the mass media, I try to build empathetic understanding of the lives of the people whom I study. I try to advocate for their rights, and to make my peers and the general public see our human similarities and honor our very important differences. My work is empty unless it helps to improve the lives of those who made it possible. In the final analysis I see no other legitimate reason for it.

On a more abstract intellectual level, there have been a few ideas which have informed almost all the work I have done. As I, and my work, have matured, they have become more clear to me and more pronounced in how I conduct and write about my research. The idea that social meanings are negotiated on an ongoing basis at all levels of social interaction continues to be one of my basic intellectual assumptions. I owe a debt to symbolic interactionists and ethnomethodologists for these ideas and also to historians of sexuality such as Lacqueur, Foucault, and Weeks.[13]

Another important idea that has been part of my thinking is that sex, gender, and sexuality are best understood as three distinct, but related, phenomena.

Although this thought is certainly not new to me, I have become an ardent advocate of it. On an academic level, Money and Ehrhardt first alerted me to the conceptual distinction between sex and gender[14] (although the male-to-female transsexuals and drag queens whom I had known in the early 1970s certainly demonstrated the idea clearly enough in their everyday lives). The work of Kessler and McKenna and David Grimm, among others, further drove home this point.[15]

However, it was not until I met a couple named Josephine and Linda at an IFGE convention that the whole thing started to really fall into place for me. Josephine and Linda were two people who had male bodies but who lived full-time as women. They lived together as lovers and considered themselves to be lesbian women. In the discussions which I had with them, and with Virginia Prince, I started to see more clearly that sexuality seems to be more intrinsically tied to persons' gender identities than to their sex identities; and that there are often gaps between persons' own identities and the attributions made about them by other people. Josephine and Linda maintained that they were lesbian women, many of their women friends thought of them as lesbian women, Virginia Prince and some lesbian women called them homosexual males.

These discussions led to my work on *gendered sexuality,* wherein I argue against simplistic assumptions that sex, gender, and sexuality will always align as per the dictates of dominant gender schema. Rather, it is my contention that thoroughgoing understandings of sexuality require that sex, gender, and sexual identities and attributions must all be taken into account, along with considerations of actual and attributed sexual fantasies, desires, and practices.[16]

It was in my work with female-to-male people that I became most completely convinced of the necessity to approach sexuality in this way. What I learned from female-to-male transsexual persons convinced me that, to paraphrase Woody Allen, the brain is the largest sex organ in the body.[17] The stories which female-to-male people told me about their own and their partners' sexuality demonstrated to me that sexuality is far more intricately tied to issues of gender identity and attribution than it is to questions of bodily sex. The female-to-male people whom I have known have made it clear to me that it is far more important that genders and sexualities fit together comfortably than that particular body parts be present or absent from sexual encounters.[18]

Thus, once again, I found that people negotiate their meanings within the limits of their own imaginations and within the contexts of their social environments. As I had learned from my study of gender-blending females, I again found that, in social relations, physical bodies are symbolic markers which can be called upon to confirm or invalidate genders, or which can be made subservient to other social cues. Thus, I had come full circle. I began by studying gender identity and attribution. In the course of doing so, I came to see that gender cannot be understood without delving into sexuality, and that interpersonal sexuality cannot be played out without being imbedded within a framework of gender identities and attributions. Sexualities may be enacted using sexed body parts, but sexualities are created by gendered selves.

❈   ❈   ❈

As I go on with my work, and as I look back upon the steps which brought me to this point of my career, I count myself as very lucky to have become a sexologist when and where I have. I have benefited greatly from having had the opportunity to spend years of my life studying questions which are personally important to me and whose elucidation has the potential to improve the lives of other people. I have been fortunate to work in Canada during a time when sex research has not been held in disrepute.[19] In Victoria, I have enjoyed the mixed blessing of relative isolation from other scholars with similar interests. My location has permitted me to feel especially free from peer pressures and fads, and to think independently, while I still have been able to attend important meetings and to stay in touch through phone, fax, and e-mail.

In addition to all of this, I have had the pleasure to see my years of contribution to political activism bear fruit in the form of a social and intellectual climate in which I not only could research sexuality, but I could do so as an open lesbian and an avowed feminist. In such a climate, I have been able to fully enjoy the benefit of a wise and loving partner who has intellectually and emotionally supported me in my work. Furthermore, I have been able to take my interest in sexology into my classrooms and develop and teach curricula on human sexuality, and on gay, lesbian, bisexual, and transgendered people. My study and teaching of sexology have therefore been deeply gratifying to me by giving me the tools, and the opportunity, to liberate a few more minds from prejudice and shame, and to inspire a few more budding young sexologists to join me in the work of sexology. The rewards have been great.

Notes

1. *Notes from the Second Year* (1970), Archives, June Mazer Lesbian Collection, West Hollywood, Calif.

2. Simone de Beauvoir, *The Second Sex* (New York: Bantam, 1952).

3. Radicalesbians, "The Woman Identified Woman," in *Radical Feminism,* ed. Anne Koedt, Ellen Levine, and Rita Rapone (New York: Quadrangle Books, 1970), pp. 240–45.

4. Anselm Strauss, ed., *The Social Psychology of George Herbert Mead* (Chicago: University of Chicago, 1962); Erving Goffman, *The Presentation of Self in Everyday Life* (New York: Doubleday, 1959); Erving Goffman, *Stigma: Notes on Management of a Spoiled Identity* (Englewood Cliffs, N.J.: Prentice Hall, 1963); Erving Goffman, *Behavior in Public Places: Notes on the Social Organization of Gatherings* (New York: Free Press, 1963); Erving Goffman, *Gender Advertisements* (London: Macmillan, 1978); Harold Garfinkel, *Studies in Ethnomethodology* (Englewood Cliffs, N.J.: Prentice Hall, 1967).

5. John Money and Anke Ehrhardt, *Man and Woman, Boy and Girl: The Differentiation and Dimorphism of Gender Identity from Conception to Maturity* (Baltimore: Johns Hopkins University Press, 1972); Nancy Chodorow, *The Reproduction of Mothering: Psychoanalysis and the*

Sociology of Gender (Berkeley and Los Angeles: University of California Press, 1978); Carol Gilligan, *In a Different Voice: Psychological Theory and Women's Development* (Cambridge, Mass.: Harvard University Press, 1982); Suzanne Kessler and Wendy McKenna, *Gender: An Ethnomethodological Approach* (New York: John Wiley & Sons, 1978); Sandra L. Bem, "Gender Schematic Theory and Its Implications for Child Development: Raising Gender-Aschematic Children in a Gender-Schematic Society," *Signs: Journal of Women in Culture and Society* 8 (1983): 598–616; Sandra L. Bem, "Gender Schema Theory: A Cognitive Account of Sex Typing," *Psychological Review* 88 (1981), 155–62.

6. Kessler and McKenna, *Gender: An Ethnomethodological Approach*, p. 68.

7. Virginia Prince, "Sex versus Gender," *Proceedings of the 2nd Interdisciplinary Symposium on Gender Dysphoria Syndrome* (Stanford, Calif., 1973), pp. 20–24.

8. Catherine MacKinnon, "Feminism, Marxism, Method and the State: Toward a Feminist Jurisprudence," *Signs* 8 (1983): 635–58, p. 635.

9. For more about this work, see Holly Devor, "Teaching Women's Studies to Male Inmates," *Women's Studies International Forum* 11 (1988): 235–44; Holly Devor, "Teaching Women's Studies to Convicted Sex Offenders," *The Yearbook of Correctional Education* 1 (1989): 129–54.

10. Holly Devor, *FTM: Female-to-Male Transsexuals in Society* (Bloomington: Indiana University Press, forthcoming).

11. Barney Glaser and Anselm Strauss, *The Discovery of Grounded Theory: Strategies for Qualitative Research* (Chicago: Aldine, 1967).

12. The International Foundation for Gender Education, P.O. Box 229, Waltham, Mass., 02154–0229.

13. Thomas Lacqueur, *Making Sex: Body and Gender from the Greeks to Freud* (Cambridge, Mass.: Harvard University Press, 1990); Michel Foucault, *The History of Sexuality*, trans. Robert Hurley (New York: Pantheon, 1978); Jeffrey Weeks, *Sex, Politics and Society: The Regulation of Sexuality Since 1800,* 2d ed. (London: Longman, 1989).

14. Money and Ehrhardt, *Man and Woman, Boy and Girl.*

15. Kessler and McKenna, *Gender: An Ethnomethodological Approach*; David Grimm, "Toward a Theory of Gender: Transsexualism, Gender, Sexuality, and Relationships," *The American Behavioral Scientist* 31 (1987): 66–85.

16. For a discussion of the idea of gendered sexuality see Holly Devor, "Toward a Taxonomy of Gendered Sexuality," *Journal of Psychology and Human Sexuality* 6, no. 1 (1993): 23–55. For a discussion of the dominant gender schema see Holly Devor, *Gender Blending: Confronting the Limits of Duality* (Bloomington: Indiana University Press, 1989).

17. In the film *Sleeper,* Woody Allen said: "My brain, it's my second favorite organ."

18. See Holly Devor, *FTM*; Holly Devor, "Sexual Orientation Identities, Attractions and Practices of Female-to-Male Transsexuals," *Journal of Sex Research* 30 (1993): 303–15.

19. The Social Sciences and Humanities Research Council of Canada has been especially generous in supporting my sexological research.

10

The Road to Paradise

Milton Diamond, Ph.D.

Milton Diamond, an internationally renowned sexologist, teaches and researches at the University of Hawaii: his interests include the combined effect of genetics and environment on sexual behavior and development. Dr. Diamond has led a series of popular workshops on human sexuality in both the United States and Asia, and was an early outspoken advocate of AIDS education and prevention.

A S A STAUNCH believer in the interaction of both nature and environment in shaping one's sexual development, I see its parallel in how I ended up teaching and researching sexuality in the State of Hawaii. My path was shaped by a combination of a wide-ranging curiosity, some ability, sheer chance, and luck. The convoluted road here also speaks to the strong influence of certain individuals.

I was born in the Bronx in 1934 in an area then a neighborhood of Eastern European Jewish immigrants who had worked themselves out of the ghetto of the Lower East Side. My father and mother owned a small corner grocery store. While I was still a preschooler, my parents began to change one store for another in seeking better business locations. So, too, did we often move. My father was excellent at taking stores that were failing, building them up, and then reselling them and moving on. It was the classic mode of buying low and selling high, with my parent's sweat equity (and our—my brother's, sister's, and my—added labors) making the difference. Unfortunately, these failing stores waiting to be revitalized were often in neighborhoods where academics or "neighborliness" were not rated highly by all. Some of my earliest recollections of elementary school times were of having rumbles or other "street adventures" not of my making.

My second year of junior high school found us moving to upper Manhattan. Here the majority of my peers belonged to street gangs and thought school a waste of time and gang fights a sanctioned team sport. Fortunately, except for an occasional "zip gun," firearms were rare. But knives were not and any excuse seemed good enough for someone to pick a fight. Although I had enjoyed school until then, and had skipped a grade in my junior high freshman year while living in the Bronx, I now tried to avoid fights and whatever else I found negative at school and the school yard. I would regularly play hooky. School had become an aversive location. I would usually go to the park and read, walk the streets, or visit a museum. The advice and aspirations of my immigrant parents, "Get a good education. We were denied the opportunities to go to school in Ukraine and in America education will be your vehicle to whatever you want," didn't seem to make much sense at the time.

An accidental academic break came when some friends told me they were taking a test to enter a special high school. Since it meant another day off from school I decided to take this legitimate opportunity to be away from class and take the test. I had no idea of what was on offer. From this test followed a major positive turning point in my scholastic life. I was admitted to the Bronx High School of Science. Although it meant travel from Manhattan to the Bronx every day, it was well worth while. School now became enjoyable and a valued adventure in learning. My peers here looked forward to school and camaraderie replaced combativeness. We competed in fun for who knew more trivia while keeping up with the adult world, sports, and other extracurricular activities. While I would return home to the "gang" neighborhood to work in the family store and get in my homework, it was now school that provided relief. My Bronx High School of Science experience convinced me that my future would be in science and teaching would be my preferred occupation.

My choice for a college was uncomplicated. From a poor family, the only possibility I could realistically consider was the subsidized City College of New York (CCNY). I was admitted to the college and enrolled as a physics major. As I hadn't fully appreciated the high school I was choosing before my experience there, the same was true for CCNY. Nevertheless, I came to relish my college experiences.

My physics major courses were stimulating and engrossing. To this day I fondly recall some of the challenging questions posed and the theoretical discussions. But the university, as most, required taking courses outside one's major area. This included biology courses and nonphysics electives. As I passed beyond the basic biology courses into more electives such as genetics and comparative anatomy, I found the area fascinatingly stimulating and realized I wanted somehow to integrate biology into my physics interest. I switched my major to biophysics and, as far as I am aware, was the first student to graduate from CCNY with that as an undergraduate major. An undergraduate research project on the lethal effects of heat on living organisms helped earn me a scholarship in marine biology at Woods Hole. But here again was another serendipitous occurrence that shifted my direction.

I entered college in January 1951 when the possibility of being drafted for the Korean War was a reality all male college students faced. Joining the ROTC (Reserve Officers Training Corps) offered a way to stay in school and also get the small stipend it provided to help pay tuition. (I supported myself all through college and looked forward to the promised GI Bill to help finance graduate studies.) While I finished all required courses and was eligible for graduation in January

1955, I was not yet twenty-one, the minimum age to be commissioned. Since the ROTC would pay for any further schooling, I remained in school an additional semester so I would be of age when I was graduated and could receive my second lieutenant's bars. This was consequential for my academic direction. In this last "extra" semester I took two additional biology electives: endocrinology and animal behavior. The teacher for both courses was William Etkin.

Etkin was one of those fabled teachers who could inspire and weave knowledge, learning, and research into a fascinating fabric. His own area of expertise was evolution and metamorphosis and some of his publications are as valuable today as they were then. His knowledge of both endocrinology and behavior was extensive. I loved the courses and subject matter; our in-class and after-class discussions led to our becoming good friends. Now I thought to myself, "This is the direction I want to go. I want to understand behavior and its underlying mechanisms." But before I could pursue this area I had an obligation to Uncle Sam. While this precluded going to Woods Hole, it proved a substitute stroke of fortune.

My assignment in Japan was as a topographic engineering officer involved in the analysis and the production of maps. (Being a biophysics major I had the unique opportunity as an ROTC cadet to choose whether I wanted to be in the infantry or engineers. It was standard that for the third and subsequent years of ROTC training and active military duty, all biology majors were assigned to the infantry and all physics majors were assigned as military engineers. Given a choice, I made a decision that probably took all of about three seconds.)

My outfit was stationed outside Tokyo. My wife and I (we married just prior to coming to Japan) lived off base in a typical Japanese neighborhood and loved our Japanese experiences so much I renewed my two-year military contract for an additional year. I was even, for a while, seriously considering making the topographic service my career. The work was interesting and allowed me the opportunity to travel to many Asian countries. My first professional publications were on cartography and mapping. While in Japan, however, I established relationships with Japanese animal behavior researchers at Tokyo Kyoiku Daigako (Tokyo Teacher's College) and met with them regularly. These experiences in Japan would later prove quite significant.

While living in Japan I asked Professor Etkin to recommend for me graduate schools in which to pursue the interface of behavior and its hormones. In the old-school manner he recommended not schools, but individuals with whom to study: Frank A. Beach at UC Berkeley, Charles H. Sawyer at UCLA, and William C. Young at the University of Kansas. I applied to all three without any real preference. I only knew these individuals from some of their writings but trusted Etkin completely. I didn't apply to any other schools. As things were done in those days, graduate school training was to start in the summer or fall and applications and acceptances were to be finalized the preceding April. Chance again intervened. Acceptance from Young arrived by airmail, and came before the cutoff dates. The acceptances from Sawyer and Beach came via sea mail and arrived afterward. I responded to the offer of studying with Young. The joke at home was our life itinerary would read: New York, N.Y., to Tokyo, Japan, to Lawrence, Kansas. The sequence, going from the sophisticated, urban areas of New York and Tokyo to rural Lawrence, seemed ludicrous. The joke was on us. We loved Lawrence for what it had to offer as we had loved New York and Tokyo for other reasons. With Etkin I did one of my first behavior publications. It was a movie describing a colony of Japanese macaques and some of their socially transmitted behaviors (Etkin and Diamond, 1961).

A certain naiveté must be admitted to at this time. Attending only to the individuals with whom I might work, I gave little real thought to what academic department I would be in nor how that might influence my future. I had no idea of what it meant to be associated with an anatomy department and that is the department to which I was admitted. Both Young and Sawyer were anatomists. In retrospect, at the time I would have preferred to major in a psychology or a zoology department. However, I guess if Young were in a nutrition department I might have gotten my degree in that field. Similarly, I had no real preference as to which behaviors I might study. My thinking on the issue was quite global. At the time, I didn't realize that the only behaviors with which Young was interested were those associated with reproduction.[1] Indeed, at that time it was probably the area of reproductive behavior in which underlying mechanisms were better understood than for any other aspect of behavior. And actually all three, Beach, Sawyer, and Young were researching different endocrinological aspects of sexual behavior. It is also well to appreciate that until the 1970s, *reproductive behavior* was easily understood to incorporate all aspects of *sexual behavior*.[2] That part of my graduate training now seemed fixed without any real choice of my own.

A minor area of study was required by the graduate school requirements of the University of Kansas. Against Young's advice—who preferred I minor in biochemistry—I chose experimental psychology, where I came under the wing of Professor Ed Wike. He too became a friend and mentor. The combination of anatomy, endocrinology, and experimental psychology I found very enjoyable and beneficial.

At the time I was at Kansas (1958–1962), another configuration of fate was to my benefit. Working with Young at the time were Robert (Bob) W. Goy, Charles (Charley) H. Phoenix, and Arnold (Arnie) A. Gerall. I couldn't imagine a better graduate school research environment in which to cut my teeth. Later fellow graduate students Ken Grady and Harvey Feder joined the mix. It was ideal. Research

1. It was Young and colleagues N. W. Dempsey, R. Hertz, and H. I. Myers who first established the linkage of ovulation and estrus which is now taken for granted (Dempsey, Hertz, and Young, 1936; Myers, Young, and Dempsey, 1936; Young, Dempsey, and Myers, 1935; Young, Myers, and Dempsey, 1933). It also can be kept in mind that almost all research on reproductive behavior until the 1960s was located in anatomy departments. This was due to the interest of anatomists in the structure and function of the endocrine and reproductive systems and their interest in fertility and embryology. Also, experimental psychologists, under the sway of leaders like B. F. Skinner, C. L. Hull, and K. W. Spence, were looking into the basic behavioral constructs and theories of hunger, learning, reward, and motivation.

2. Masters and Johnson, when first starting their research on human sexuality, identified their organization as the Reproductive Biology Research Foundation.

was in the air and one could go to the old wooden-shack lab at any time of day or night, seven days a week, to find one or more of the group. Everyday discussions typically revolved around one aspect or another of sexual behavior and its associated reproductive and endocrinal mechanisms. Interest in different theories, research attempts, failures and successes was not something affected but part of the intellectual juices and mental challenges that gave us all pleasure. It was a wonderfully cooperative and mutually supportive group. We became more than colleagues; I consider them all friends and respect them, each in his own way, as having influenced me.

Certainly the hot topic at the lab at the time was trying to understand sexual development. Using guinea pigs and rats as primary models, research focused on prenatal influences on the developing individual. Out of this work came the now-classic study that showed how early androgen administration can masculinize the female fetus, the *Endocrinology* paper of Phoenix, Goy, Gerall, and Young (1959). The significance of the work was apparent to all. And each of us, in his own way, saw this as the springboard to many other lines of research to be pursued. As a graduate student my first thesis attempt in this vein was to see if estrogens could feminize male fetuses as androgens masculinized females. My injections of estrogens into pregnant guinea pigs invariably resulted in fetal death. This was a great disappointment to me since it's hard to study behavior that way. Had I or others at the lab been thinking along different lines at the time, however, we would have recognized this now-understood phenomenon and touted my findings as a simple and safe abortifacient or "day-after" pill.

While injecting the guinea pigs in the lab in an attempts to induce masculinization of the fetuses, I noticed that the pregnant females into which the testosterone was injected did not themselves masculinize. In contrast, those that aborted did. My final thesis research looked into the mechanism of this maternal protection. It led to one of the early descriptions of the protection offered by pregnancy (Diamond and Young, 1963). Several years later, this line of research with Ulrich Westphal (Diamond, Rust, and Westphal, 1969) brought to light specific testosterone and progesterone binders particularly available during pregnancy. This route became for him and others a major direction of biochemical study. I preferred to focus again on behavior.

It is relevant to recall that in the 1950s and early 1960s funds for graduate research were scarce. Such money came from the university departments themselves and grants were uncommon. Funds for graduate students were also uncommon. Most of us earned our income, if we could get it, as teaching or research assistants. I assisted in teaching neuroanatomy to the medical students and teaching gross anatomy for the university athletes majoring in physical education.[3] I also earned money as a research assistant. Injecting and testing guinea pigs for the lab became a seven-day-a-week routine.

---

3. Congress, for the interim period just before I left the military until after I left graduate school, did away with the GI Bill. Again I had to fully subsidize my education without outside resources.

Consideration of funding is pertinent since the opportunity appeared to apply for a graduate research stipend from the National Academy of Sciences, National Science Foundation (NSF), Committee for Research in Problems of Sex. It was the first time such NSF funds were available for graduate students. One of the requirements for the award was that a research paper be submitted. For my application I prepared an analysis of how I saw humans fitting into a paradigm of having their adult sexual behavior biased by prenatal events. This analysis and critique of the then-prevalent theory of John Money and his colleagues that humans were independent of such influences (Money, Hampson, and Hampson, 1955a; Money, Hampson, and Hampson, 1955b; Money, Hampson, and Hampson, 1957) helped earn me the award. The critique, eventually published in the *Quarterly Review of Biology* (Diamond, 1965), basically proposed and defended the then-novel theory of a biased interaction of nature and nurture working together to forge an individual's sexual behavior. While there were those who continued to do so, no longer could one rationally argue that human psychosexual behaviors, such as those related to sexual orientation and identity, were the exclusive result of nature *or* nurture. From that period on, while continuing experimental work with animals, I was simultaneously interested in human physical and psychological sexual development. Intersexuality of all sorts and sexual variations of all stripes became grist for the mill.

I received my doctorate in 1962 and went to teach at the University of Louisville. One of the attractions to that university was the agreement that I would be able to simultaneously attend classes to obtain a medical degree. It wasn't that I wanted to practice medicine but I wanted better access to patients with whom I could more closely study human sexual development and intersexuality. Now, while a member of the faculty, I initiated a seminar on sexual behavior for medical and graduate students. It quickly became clear that the faculty and student interest was more on humans than on other animals. My teaching and research, too, expanded to encompass human subjects as well as animals. During my stay at Louisville, William C. Young died. In his honor I edited a festschrift volume of the *Anatomical Record* (Diamond, 1967).

As things developed, life at the University of Louisville was, unfortunately, not up to my experiences at Kansas. Nor was it to my wife's liking. While I was fortunately able to pursue my research and scholastic interests, and able to begin research on intersexed individuals (Diamond, 1968), we began to look for new opportunities. Chance again took center stage. Vincent J. DeFeo and Robert W. Noyes from Vanderbilt University, both well reputed for their works on reproduction and fertility, were heading to Hawaii to help start a new medical school. It was their idea to start a program that would cover all aspects of reproduction throughout the life cycle. In their minds this would include sexual behavior from puberty through fertile years, pregnancies, and so on. They invited me to join them in starting this new type of department: one that would combine teaching and research in both basic and clinical sciences and concentrate on all aspects of reproduction. It was to be called the Department of Anatomy and Reproductive Biology. Bob Noyes, an obstetrician-gynecologist, was to be the department chair and assistant dean. By then I had completed my basic medical science boards and I was also offered the opportunity to complete my medical degree while on the faculty. After considering other possibilities, I agreed to come to Hawaii. My primary responsibility was to teach neuroanatomy and sexuality to the medical students. My research was to be on topics at the interface of reproductive biology and sexual behavior. My wife and I also thought Hawaii would be an ideal place to raise our children. We now had four daughters. The year was 1967.

Here again was a wonderful and fruitful research environment. Along with Noyes and DeFeo was Ryuzo Yanagimachi, world renowned for his work on fertilization. The four of us forged a strong academic and animal research environment. My research focused on endocrine and behavioral parameters of reproduction. Now, some thirty years later, three of us are still together. The medical school welcomed my offering an elective course in human sexuality to the medical and nursing students which I started in 1968. Along with this, in 1968, without any fanfare or objection, I became faculty advisor to a gay student organization. "The Gay Student O'hana (family)," believed to be perhaps the first college-sanctioned gay organization in the country, is still in existence.

Perhaps more importantly for the nation as a whole, and surely influential for furthering my career in human research, in 1968 the state began to discuss the possibility of legalizing abortion. As related to reproductive biology and sexual behavior, I and colleagues from the departments of sociology and maternal and child health began to simultaneously look into the scientific aspects of the matter and consult for the state legislature. In 1970 Hawaii became the first state in the union to permit legal abortions and, with state and federal funding, we began to do in-depth studies of abortion-related behaviors. These writings were among the first to offer abortion data not only from matched cohorts but also from a total population. Along with these major human studies, basic research on sexual behavior in animals continued apace. But the work on humans began to take a major share of my time. It included defending the biased nature-nurture interaction in transsexualism and intersexuality (Diamond, 1974).

My professional and personal life took another series of major steps in the 1970s. They were each unique and had a significant effect on my research and academic direction. The first event was catastrophic when, in 1970, my wife became seriously ill with a disease that would affect our lives until she died in 1989. Among other things it precluded my being able to finish my medical degree.

A good turn occurred in 1973. In that year, in collaboration with Public Television Station (PBS) KHET-TV and the University of Hawaii educational extension program, I was asked to offer a human sexuality television series. It was the first such television series on sexuality in the country that went beyond the so-called talking heads. Until then people only discussed sexual matters. This series, in contrast, took viewers to the action, whether it was to a transvestite bar, a nudist beach, or a demonstration of a breast or prostate examination. The series, with additional requirements and a final test, was also used as an extension credit course by the University of Hawaii and other colleges around the country. Although it was extremely low budget, it showed and discussed a wide gamut of subjects, controversial and mundane. It covered topics from many angles. The series was quite popular and went on for thirty one-hour programs. It was rebroadcast several times and, surprisingly, received few complaints while dealing with all the politically sensitive issues our field has to offer. In 1973 the series won the National University Extension Association "Creative Programming Award" for Arts and Sciences. Most listeners found it refreshing and informative as well as entertaining.

The success of the television series led to my being requested to offer an American Association for the Advancement of Science–National Science Foundation Chautauqua series of short courses for college teachers. Four weeks a year, from 1974 to 1977, I traveled around the country teaching hundreds of teachers how to teach: "Human Sexuality: Psychological, Biological and Social Aspects."

Meanwhile my thesis of a biased interaction of nature and nurture for human psychosexual development as presented in the *Quarterly Review of Biology* paper seemed to be catching on and I was invited to spend a 1974 sabbatical at Oxford's Children's Hospital to work with Christopher Ounsted and David Taylor investigating human psychosexual development. This was a wonderful opportunity to learn firsthand of some of the research going on in Britain and to meet John Bancroft, now director of the Kinsey Institute, and others.

Two additional events added to this exciting period. On my return from England I was invited to join the Human Sexuality Graduate and Psychiatry Residency Training Program headed by Richard Green at the State University of New York at Stony Brook. I readily accepted this opportunity and for three years held, along with my position in Hawaii, a joint appointment at the department of psychiatry at SUNY. Richard and I became close friends and I found it an extraordinary occasion to interact with Joseph LoPicollo, Julia Hymen, Diane Fordney-Settlage, and others. The staff and postdoctoral candidates offered a wonderful, calm intellectual atmosphere. Several joint works resulted from these associations, particularly in the developing area of video education for physicians. The second event was an invitation to offer a workshop for Japanese sex educators of the same type I was offering for Americans. This started a string of invited lectures and workshops both in Hawaii and Japan that continues to this day. Obviously while I still did animal research, my medical school human sexuality teaching as well as my human research activities and publications began to increase in salience.

Many of my ideas and syntheses from the decade of the 1970s and before were introduced in a text and teachers' manual published in 1980 with Arno Karlen (Diamond and Karlen, 1980a, b). Candidly it must be said that appreciation of my work on human sexuality outside of Hawaii was not mirrored by the feelings of all my medical school colleagues at home. Several new department members and other faculty of the developing medical school were not as broad-minded or visionary as the school's founders. They thought animal research associated with reproduction appropriate while investigation of human sexuality "a little far out" and perhaps actually inappropriate. Thank goodness for tenure.

The 1980s brought with them additional involvement in teaching sex to professionals. The decade started off with my being contracted by the United States Agency for International Development (US-AID) to do a two-week workshop in Thailand, to be attended by professional population experts and ministers from throughout Asia. The workshop was organized, at their request, to teach family-planning workers how to integrate sex education and sexuality concerns into their population control programs. Amusingly, since US-AID didn't want to use the word "sex" in the workshop in fear it might offend someone, they gave the workshop the longest title they ever used: "The International Workshop on Training of Trainers in Family Life Education Relative to Family Planning."

This experience was coupled with a mini-sabbatical in Japan and Hong Kong to learn more of cultural components of sexuality and to collaborate with colleagues in those countries. The sabbatical time was also used to complete two chapters for the American Medical Association medical handbook *Sexual Problems in Medical Practice* (Diamond and Karlen, 1981a, b). The first chapter was on the sexual response cycle. Our second chapter, on sexually transmitted diseases (STDs), was one disease too short. Completed in the late 1970s and reviewed by James W. Curran, who would later come to head the Centers for Disease Control HIV/AIDS investigation program, the chapter contained nothing on this scourge.

HIV/AIDS most prominently began to penetrate into our lives and consciousness in the early 1980s. With the increasing number of cases of this strange infection primarily touching the lives of homosexuals and heroin addicts along with Haitians, hemophiliacs, and harlots (the disease's victims were then best identified by the mnemonic string of "h"s), it seemed natural for me, both as a sexologist and as a medical school faculty member, to turn attention to the topic. In the early 1980s I saw this disease developing as had the "great pox" of syphilis of the fifteenth century: a mysteriously spreading sexually transmitted disease that had no cure. I started to lecture and speak wherever I could warning about AIDS and the future as I saw it. At first only a minority of individuals, heterosexual or homosexual, academic or lay persons, politicians or businessmen, would listen. Even my dean thought I was making too much of the issue and thereby calling undue attention to the medical school. Indeed, he objected to my identifying my early AIDS work with the medical school.

In a more general mode I also published a synthesis of my accumulating ideas on sex in general with a cross-cultural perspective (Diamond, 1984). This book, *SexWatching*, following in the mode of Desmond Morris's *Man Watching* with many illustrations, was highly popular and reprinted in the United States, the Netherlands, Japan, and elsewhere. Along with these human-related activities, research continued on animal sexual behavior in many species, including hamsters and rabbits. I still loved the intellectual challenge of experimental animal research.

But without doubt my attention was turning to the developing social impact of AIDS. The evolving situation appeared too serious to avoid. In 1985 I co-founded the Hawaii AIDS Task Group (HATG), one of the first community-wide organizations of its kind. Acceptable to both the straight and gay populations, the HATG fostered the start of many city, county, and state government and nongovernment groups and projects dedicated to all aspects of dealing with HIV/AIDS. Until disbanding in 1995, after having served its purpose, the HATG was the only statewide nongovernmental organization known in the country which was able to amicably bring together diverse political, educational, and administrative factions to work for the common good. While serving as director of the HATG I started to simultaneously do research on HIV/AIDS. Considering the potential pandemic effect of HIV in Asia, I also authored a book *AIDS: Love, Sex, Disease* (Diamond, Ikegami, and Thorne, 1988). Originally prepared primarily for a Japanese audience, the book has since been reprinted in Chinese in Hong Kong and Taiwan and is now being prepared by the Chinese government for educational distribution throughout the People's Republic of China.

During the second half of the 1980s, in addition to working with HIV/AIDS, I returned to research sexual orientation and identity (e.g., Diamond, 1989), and turned to new interests in pornography, cross-cultural aspects of sexuality, and the esoteric topic of asphyxiophilia, or erotic self-strangulation. In the latter study I had the good fortune of working with two Swedish students from the department of psychology at Göteborg, Sweden, Sune Innala and Kurt Ernulf, and their professor, Lars Gösta Dahlöf. I also began to establish links with the national AIDS programs of the Netherlands. Some of these European links are still maintained.

The decade of the 1990s has continued to focus my research increasingly on human sexual issues, several occurrences of which I am particularly proud occurred early in this decade. The first was an invitation to Europe, initially to do an "outside" review of the HIV/AIDS prevention, research, and educational program for the Dutch Ministry of Health and Culture and then to deliver the Magnus Hirschfeld memorial lecture held at the Reichstag at the historic Third International Berlin Conference for Sexology. The first and second such Berlin conferences were held before World War II and this meeting, organized by Erwin Haeberle and Rolf Gindorf, also served to honor the rejoining of the previously divided Berlin. I spoke on "Bisexuality: Biological Aspects" (Diamond, 1994). Research on the development of sexual orientation and identity among different populations was again occupying my attention.

Animal research, while still of interest, has taken a back seat to my human interests, which continue to expand. In addition to ongoing research on pornography and sexual aspects of body modification (tattooing, piercing, etc.), future subjects look ever interesting. This is said in full awareness of the censorious nature of the times and the increasingly loud call for measures against sex education, sex research, and sexual pleasures. On the other hand, during my professional lifetime majestic changes have occurred in the sexual world in which we live. These offer reason for optimism. Thirty years ago in the United States it would have been unthinkable to imagine the wide availability of contraceptives, abortion as a legal choice, the availability of a simple abortion "pill," no-fault divorces, and the relative availability of sexually explicit material. Most dramatically, these last thirty years have seen major steps forward in the rights of and protections for women, the wide acceptance of domestic partnerships, the abolition of anti-homosexual laws in many states, and even the consideration of same-sex marriages. Certainly there are backlashes and jeremiads against such changes, but I think despite such retrogressive calls and forces, the field of sexology and the accompanying adjustments of society will proceed apace. I trust my research will augment and document some of the future changes. From a school dropout to a perpetual student and from physics to sex—now if those sorts of changes can be bridged there is no telling what is possible.

References

Dempsey, E. W., R. Hertz, and W. C. Young. 1936. The experimental induction of oestrus (sexual receptivity) in the normal and ovariectomized guinea pig. *American Journal of Physiology* 116: 201–209.

Diamond, M. 1965. A critical evaluation of the ontogeny of human sexual behavior. *Quarterly Review of Biology* 40: 147–75.

———. 1968. Genetic-endocrine interaction and human psychosexuality. In *Perspectives in reproduction and sexual behavior,* ed. M. Diamond, pp. 417–43. Bloomington: Indiana University Press.

———. 1974. Transsexualism. *Medical Journal of Australia* (January 12): 51.

———. 1984. *Sexwatching: The world of sexual behaviour.* London: Macdonald/Multimedia.

———. 1989. Foreword: When husbands come out of the closet. In *When husbands come out of the closet,* ed. J. S. Gochros. New York: Haworth Press.

———. 1994. Bisexualität aus biologischer Sicht [Bisexuality: Biological Aspects]. In *Bisexualitäten: Ideologie und Praxis des Sexualkontaktes mit beiden Geschlechtern [Bisexualities: Ideology and Practices of Sexual Contact with Both Sexes],* ed. E. J. Haeberle and R. Gindorf, pp. 41–68. Stuttgart: Gustav Fischer Verlag.

———, ed. 1967. *Anatomical record: William C. Young memorial volume,* vol. 157. Philadelphia: Wistar Institute.

Diamond, M., and A. Karlen. 1980a. *Sexual Decisions.* Boston: Little, Brown.

———. 1980b. *Sexual decisions: Instructor's manual.* Boston: Little, Brown.

———. 1981a. The sexual response cycle. In *Sexual problems in medical practice.,* ed. H. Lief, pp. 37–51. Chicago: American Medical Association Press.

———. 1981b. Sexually transmitted diseases. In *Sexual problems in medical practice.,* ed. H. Lief, pp. 307–22. Chicago: American Medical Association Press.

Diamond, M., and W. C. Young. 1963. Differential responsiveness of pregnant and non-pregnant guinea pigs to the masculinizing action of testosterone propionate. *Endocrinology* 72: 429–38.

Diamond, M., C. Ikegami, and D. Thorne. 1988. *AIDS: Sex, love, disease.* Tokyo: Gendai Shokan.

Diamond, M., N. Rust, and U. Westphal. 1969. High-affinity binding of progesterone, testosterone and cortisol in normal and androgen treated guinea pigs during various reproductive stages: Relationship to masculinization. *Endocrinology* 84: 1143–51.

Etkin, W., and M. Diamond. 1961. The Japanese monkey center. *American Zoologist* 447.

Money, J., J. G. Hampson, and J. L. Hampson. 1955a. An examination of some basic sexual concepts: The evidence of human hermaphroditism. *Bulletin of the Johns Hopkins Hospital* 97: 301–19.

———. 1955b. Recommendations concerning assignment of sex, change of sex and psychological management. *Bulletin of the Johns Hopkins Hospital* 97: 284–300.

———. 1957. Imprinting and the establishment of gender role. *Archives of Neurology & Psychiatry* 77: 333–36.

Myers, H. I., W. C. Young, and E. W. Dempsey. 1936. Graffian follicle development throughout the reproductive cycle in the guinea pig with especial reference to changes during oestrus (sexual receptivity). *Anatomical Record* 65: 381–401.

Phoenix, C. H., R. W. Goy, A. A. Gerall, and W. C. Young. 1959. Organizing action of prenatally administered testosterone propionate on the tissues mediating mating behavior in the female guinea pig. *Endocrinology* 65: 369–82.

Young, W. C., E. W. Dempsey, and H. I. Myers. 1935. Cyclic reproductive behavior in the female guinea pig. *Journal of Comparative Psychology* 19: 313–35.

Young, W. C., H. I. Myers, and E. W. Dempsey. 1933. Some data from a correlated anatomical, physiological and behavioristic study of the reproductive cycle of the female guinea pig. *American Journal of Physiology* 105: 393–98.

11

Our Accidental Entry into Sex

Dwight Dixon, J.D., Ph.D., and
Joan R. Dixon, Ph.D.

*Dwight and Joan Dixon are a husband-and-wife team.
Dwight is a quadriplegic who earned a law degree and
for a time practiced law in Hawaii, and it was there
they were married. Although they have also explored
many other topics, they became particularly interested in
the sexual problems of those who are physically impaired.*

THE PLUSH LOBBY of the hotel ballroom pulsated with an energy force one could actually feel coming from the milling throng of excited, hyped-up, and turned-on humanity that filled it to overflowing. Sheets of brown paper had been taped over the glass doors of the entry that faced the street. Arriving guests entered instead from an interior courtyard of the hotel. The scene inside the building that evening was not to be shared with (or imposed upon) passersby or the merely curious.

The event was the Erotic Masquerade Ball at the 1995 Lifestyles Convention being held in San Diego. That evening's festivities culminated the twenty-second annual gathering of people from throughout the United States and abroad who espoused the belief that sexual activities between consenting adults can be enjoyed as a social recreation. The entire hotel had been reserved for the three-day gathering of some three thousand guests.

Dressed in string bikinis, sheer tops, the briefest of shorts, and an assortment of similar garb the attendees spent their days socializing around the pools, browsing the exhibits, and attending several dozen presentations ranging from health care to censorship issues to how to better bind, gag, and whip your submissive partner. Many had spent their evenings (and a few of their days, too) involved in a series of sexual liaisons in their bedrooms with a revolving assortment of partners.

We had been invited to give a presentation titled "Mid-Life and Beyond: Crisis or Pleasure?" in which we discussed how one can take steps to maintain one's health as aging progresses, and translate a healthy physical and emotional state into a pleasurable sexual life throughout one's later years. Our presentation had been given the morning of the masquerade ball, which allowed us admission to the ball that evening.

Each of us is an inveterate people watcher. We study people like an astronomer studying stars or an ornithologist in a bird blind. So there we were, having arrived early, both of us dressed in an innocuous fashion involving black leather, black this, black that—admittedly conservative by the standards of the evening, but comfortable. We bought a drink at the lobby bar and situated ourselves at a convenient position to observe the amazing array of visions that appeared before our eyes for the next few hours.

To get a flavor of the scene, one need imagine several thousand adults—most in their twenties and thirties but some eighty or more, handsome or plain—arriving two by two for an evening of unabashed sensual dancing and socializing dressed in every type of erotic getup imaginable. Most would top off the evening at a swinging sex party or two.

In the throng were members of most every profession and most of the status levels of society, from struggling college students and starving artists to multimillionaires and clergy. Some were almost totally nude except for a daub of body paint or a glued-on feather here and there. Perhaps a narrow strip of cloth covered a nipple and the crotch or a fake two-foot-long penis extended from a man wearing a priest's garb or a husband and wife, her very large breasts bare, sported matching white diapers fastened by a giant safety pin. On and on they came. Many went into the ballroom to dance to the throbbing music. Hundreds mixed socially in the lobby—our laboratory.

Of course we were constantly commenting to each other about the fascinating kaleidoscope of scenery parading before us, including some of our professional colleagues and friends.

It was in the midst of this melange of sights and sounds that Dwight happened to think about this autobiography that we had been asked to prepare and asked Joan, half jokingly, "How did we get here?" Knowing the implications of the question and that a real answer was not required at that moment she nodded, laughed, and simply said, "Yeah." Both of us knew so well the very long road we had traveled to be there at that moment.

This brief and somewhat narrowly focused account of two lives is not being written as a joint autobiography merely because we have existed on this planet longer as a couple than as single persons, which is true, but, more importantly, because we have so thoroughly intertwined and integrated our personal and professional lives that, beginning soon after our marriage in 1964, a recitation of the events of one of our lives becomes a near-identical rendition of the other's.

In the interest of fair disclosure, we feel we should admit at this point that when we were invited to contribute an account of our lives to this volume, each of us was reluctant because neither feels that we have attained the status or accomplishments in life that we associate with a "person of note." Having agreed at the outset that we are indeed not persons of note, why did we write this?

We did it in the hope that this exposure of our lives and our work, modest though they are, will somehow spur others to truly open their eyes to the reality *we* see, and to take up the challenges of making this a better world in which all women and all men will be free to express their sexuality in any way they choose if they do not harm anyone else.

That pretty much states our ideal philosophy of sex (and of life, actually). Naturally, we realize ideals don't always wash in a real world—there are some competing needs of society, some obligations to others, and so forth. But our philosophy is that individual freedoms are the starting point, the bedrock of society. After all, people normally take certain individual rights with them when they go from state to state and country to country. Even our U.S. Constitution recognizes that the individual possesses autonomous rights and powers and that the states and federal government only possess the powers granted by the people, with all residual or unspecifically conferred rights residing with the people. The free spirits at the Lifestyles Convention were expressing those individual rights.

That evening, in the midst of the bedlam, Dwight's mind kept flashing back to various stages of his and Joan's lives, searching for an answer to that question: How did we get here? Hawaii kept popping into focus. Dwight was about a month short of his thirtieth birthday when he arrived in Honolulu in June of 1963. He had just completed his studies at the University of Miami Law School and had agreed to foot the roundtrip bill if a friend of his would accompany him from Miami to Honolulu and help him get situated there.

Dwight needed some help in picking up and moving like that because he is a quadriplegic. He has no use of his legs; very little use of his arms; no use of his wrist, hand, or finger muscles; no bladder or bowel control. He cannot dress or bathe himself, cannot get into or out of a bed or his wheelchair by himself or perform any of a number of other personal chores necessary to ordinary daily living.

Dwight had never been to Hawaii and knew no one there. His friend could stay only three or four days. But Dwight was determined that Honolulu was to be his new home, so in those few days he had to solve his transportation, housing, and personal help needs.

It's five months later, November 1963; Dwight has a rented house on a hillside overlooking a beautiful palm-tree-lined lagoon and the Pacific in a suburb of Honolulu, a new van in which he can ride in his wheelchair, live-in help, and a junior executive job at a venerable old-line financial institution. It's undeniably beautiful there. But paradise can also be lonely. Dwight places a call to an old school buddy, Joan Kendall, who's then living and working near Los Angeles.

Joan had been an undergraduate phenomenon at the University of Miami School of Business which she and Dwight had attended and graduated from together. She had blazed through and finished summa cum laude, top student in their class. Upon graduation she had gone to work in the then-fledgling missile industry at Cape Canaveral. Dwight lucked into a law scholarship. Joan became a part (albeit an admittedly small one) of the incredible government and industrial machine that helped establish the early U.S. space program from the cape. Joan's subsequent moves had taken her to California by November 1963.

We had been good friends at that time for almost seven years but had never dated. During our undergraduate days we would often spend an hour or more in conversation on a whole gamut of topics, usually on the phone late at night. We had thoroughly discussed and knew each other's thoughts about such things as religion, interpersonal relationships, integrity, philosophy of life, economics, personal finances, work ethics, children, marriage, politics, lifestyles, and ambitions. We had not talked much about sex, just some joking around about it a few times. Neither of us wanted or were ready for that complication in a very good and valued friendship.

During the phone call from Hawaii Joan revealed she was to be free over the Thanksgiving weekend, so it was agreed that she would fly to Hawaii and spend a few days at Dwight's house. She arrived two days after President Kennedy was killed. Hawaii, then a heavily Democratic state, was thrown into deep mourning. But out of the tragic mood came our personal silver lining. We discovered during those few days that we really did want to take our friendship to a new and much deeper level, that we were going to try marriage and see how it worked out. Practical souls that we were, we knew full well that making a marriage work under the circumstances of Dwight's physical disability would be very difficult, so we agreed at the beginning that we would take it from month to month and year to year. We agreed that marriage in general was full of pluses and minuses and that if either of us ever came to seriously feel that the minuses outweighed the pluses to such an extent that it wasn't worth going on as a couple, then both of us would simply and amicably call it off. Even looking back after thirty-one years of experience, we still don't think either of us would have been willing to proceed at the time without that kind of mutual understanding. The potential problems to be faced in a marriage with a quadriplegic are enormous. Obviously it's possible for it to work out. In our case and in many others it has.

Dwight had already been stung by the opposite experience. Raised the seventh and youngest child of a typically hard-working middle-class family, Dwight took part-time jobs from the time he was old enough to cut grass. It was instilled in him to be responsible for some of his own expenses such as clothes and lunch money. While still a junior in high school, and even though holding three part-time jobs, Dwight joined the Florida National Guard. It meant a few extra bucks income and only took one Monday evening a month of his time.

Within a year the Korean War began, and in early 1951 Dwight and his unit were activated—one month prior to his high school graduation. At this crucial time he was in a serious relationship with a classmate which involved talk of their probable future marriage. Those plans materialized in their hastily arranged marriage a few months later. Within a year their son was born. Dwight had been promoted and was serving in the military police at a busy but now abandoned army fort in New Jersey when he dove into the ocean one hot June afternoon. He slammed head first into a large water-soaked piece of timber that was floating just below the surface.

After floating face down in the water for several minutes he was dragged ashore unconscious by two men whose identity he has never discovered. When Dwight awoke in an army hospital several days later he was in a crude, plaster body cast from his waist to the top of his head. Surgical steel pins were screwed into his skull with steel weights attached to them so as to stretch his vertebrae. The only muscles he could move were in his face. He had been married less than ten months. His son was less than a month old. And Dwight was only eighteen years of age.

Sex had been an important part of his life and marriage up to then. Now it was too painful a subject even to think about for a while. By today's standards, medical care for quadriplegics in those days was crude, rehabilitation all but nonexistent, hope for the future close to zero. Dwight was told to expect no more than five years' survival. As months passed the cast wore away the flesh from his bones. He would lie in pools of pus and blood that oozed from the openings in the cast. For over three months he lay in a bed while developing pressure sores that reached to the bone on his ankles, sacrum, spine, and shoulder blades. It was discovered that his left hip had ossified to the point of being unbendable. There had been no physical therapy on his legs. In order to enable him to sit, Dwight's hip joint was surgically destroyed.

In an army hospital communal ward with some thirty or so other such patients there was no conjugal privacy except a flimsy curtain to be partially drawn, to say nothing of any possibility of private sexual intimacy even if it had been physically possible. Lying on a narrow tubular steel frame, with no power to move except for a few neck and shoulder muscles, no skin sensation below mid-chest, with a rubber catheter protruding from his penis, no encouragement at all from any of the hospital staff about his future, all hope of a cure shattered, told only that his life expectancy might not extend to his son's first day in school, and seeing his beautiful nineteen-year-old wife aging as if weeks were years, fretting about her and their son's bleak future, Dwight was as low as he could get.

A transfer to a Veterans Administration hospital produced only a different communal ward with thirty or so different men mostly vegetating. Some lay in bed drugged continuously, some stayed drunk when they could, others were in various states of mental dissociation with reality without any outside help. The career civil service aides did as little as they could get by with, the career administrators made do, and the patients drifted for better or worse from day to day. There was no counseling, not one professional would discuss sex, no career guidance for a brighter tomorrow, no independent living encouragement or training, almost no physical therapy. For most there was simply no serious thought of planning for a life outside of that little institutional space. A few tried it, mostly paraplegics. They could pretty much meet their own personal care needs. Many quadriplegics who tried life on the outside did poorly or failed, some badly. Family members often couldn't handle all that was involved with a quad. Almost every marriage that existed when a veteran became a quadriplegic failed after a short while. Dwight's was no exception.

It was mutually agreed. Dwight's wife and son would take up a new life, hopefully a much brighter life full of happiness and hope for an ever better future. There was no anger, no hate, no blame—just painful mutual recognition of and resignation before what at the time seemed the only hope for a real life for his wife and baby son. Now alone, Dwight sank into a very dark place.

Enormous amounts of alcohol served to deaden everyday reality. It was as if he had joined some nonexistent "me too" club of men around him who just wished to speed up the inevitable. Strangely, though, just as the darkest gloom descended some spark of survival appeared deep in his consciousness, so faintly as to be almost unnoticeable. It struggled to the surface of his thoughts and fought against being summarily disregarded and beaten down. "Survival," he thought, "Who would want that—like *this*?" "No," he answered himself, "No way!" And the internal battle went on. Long days, nights, and months went by.

The tiny spark did grow and it did win. By then Dwight's former wife had settled with his son, a new husband, and a new daughter a thousand miles away. Dwight arranged to travel to Miami from the hospital in Richmond, Virginia, and with hired help, lived with his parents until he could settle in a place of his own. The place he found happened by pure chance to be only a few blocks from the campus of the University of Miami. At that time, no one in Dwight's family had ever gotten a college education, and Dwight himself had never seriously thought about going to college even before his accident. He had been awarded his high school diploma, having had enough credits to graduate even without the last semester which the army interrupted. In the army he had done well enough on various tests to qualify to take the Officers' Candidate School test but had not done so. Still he was far from sure that he was smart enough to succeed at the college level. But that spark that had been so successfully nurtured up to that point was then fueling a burning desire to do more than survive; it had kindled a desire to grow and expand, to learn, and to be able to give rather than just take.

The very first day of his first college class, Dwight met eighteen-year-old Joan Kendall.

Joan's life to that point couldn't have been any more different in some ways than Dwight's had been. As the only child of a college professor father, whose two doctorates included one from Harvard, and a registered nurse mother who wished she could have been a physician and who placed enormous value on academic achievement, Joan had excelled in both public and private schools, graduating at the top of her class at a prestigious girl's school in New York. Her father had been instrumental in establishing and operating the air force's flight physiology program during and after the Second World War and was called back to active duty during the Korean War. As a result of the many changes of assignment stations that work entailed, between periods teaching college, the family had moved fourteen times by the time of Joan's senior year in high school.

Even having moved and changed schools that many times to be with her father, Joan and her mother had long periods of time when they lived alone together. Her mother believed firmly in a woman being self-reliant. She not only wanted to raise a cultured and well-educated daughter, she also wanted to send a young Renaissance woman out into the world. Horseback riding, ballet, music, and sewing lessons were joined by practical work in auto, home electrical, plumbing, and woodworking repair. Joan learned from her mother how to lay concrete block, paint a house, catch and clean a fish, row a boat, cook meals, design and make a dress, stand up for her rights, diagnose and treat many illnesses, deal with boys and men, and generally meet life head on. Sex was another matter. There the "Renaissance girl" was directed to her father's medical physiology and anatomy books and a dictionary. The maternal drive to teach what, how, and why evaporated. Joan entered college armed in sexual matters with mostly a reliance on a little basic body knowledge and her own common sense. Among the other things given to her by her mother she also had a powerful sense of being able to handle situations that came her way, a strong sense of self-confidence. That was still somewhat rare for young women her age in the 1950s. It was probably that enormous personal strength and self-confidence that led them both to think that she could handle the multitude of problems that faced a wife of a quadriplegic. Still largely ignorant of what sex together would be like or, for that matter, what kind of sex with each other would even be possible, we were nevertheless determined to give marriage a good ol' college try.

By the end of that first Thanksgiving holiday visit in Honolulu we had decided to marry—almost seven years after first meeting.

Joan began teaching at a business college in Honolulu while Dwight studied to take the Hawaii bar exam. When he passed we faced the next dilemma. Despite his academic record, related work experience, and civic organization leadership (he had been state president of a veterans' organization), he could not find a job as a lawyer. He even offered to work for the local legal aid organization for free, but to no avail. Dwight's perceived disability overshadowed his obvious competency. Ironically, at the trust company he had worked on legal matters with many of the law firms that could find no place for him. There were other obstacles to a legal career. Most of the courtrooms were upstairs, as was the law library, the entire state supreme court, and some administrative offices. Moreover, there was no elevator in the main courthouse downtown. And some Honolulu courts were scattered throughout the Island of Oahu.

The only alternative was almost unthinkable—start a solo practice. The details are too many to go into here, so suffice it to simply say the almost impossible was indeed accomplished. With some very long work days we had Dwight's law practice up and running within a few months and soon had more legal work than we should have taken on. The fear of failure is a jealous mistress. Dwight turned away no one.

Joan quit her teaching job and devoted all her time to the project. Their office was located in Kailua on the so-called windward side of the island from Honolulu proper. Tens of thousands of people resided in and around Kailua and commuted to work daily in Honolulu town. At that time relatively few wives worked outside the home. Thus, Kailua was mainly a residential community in the traditional sense of being principally composed of households with working husbands and at-home housewives.

With Joan busy operating the office, typing reams of documents, doing all the book work, and driving Dwight to court and other offices, the midnight oil burned and the practice took off like a jet fighter. Before long Dwight had represented most of the businesses in the area; had been appointed to a special assignment by the state attorney general's office; regularly represented clients of a foreign consulate; had established a steady work flow from the state's largest bank; and had handled cases in bankruptcy, real estate, adoption, divorce, collections, negligence, felon and misdemeanor defense, wills and trusts, contract disputes, zoning, taxation, partnership and corporate matters, and many other areas too numerous to mention. He served on the board of directors of several corporations and became general counsel of a small airline and a flight school. He literally became "the" town lawyer. The Kailua area then had about sixty thousand inhabitants, and there were only two other lawyers with an office in the area. One was ill and soon died. The other became a part-time judge and thus only a part-time lawyer.

Partly due to the peculiar "bedroom community" aspect of Kailua and probably partly due to his growing reputation in such matters, Dwight's practice in domestic relations disputes grew in a few years to the point that it was said he probably had the second largest domestic relations practice in the state. It also helped the feelings of many domestic relations clients (who were mostly female) to know (which most of them did) that ours was a husband/wife office. Confidences were kept "in house," as it were. And in such a small town with many well-connected people, there were a lot of very explosive confidences. We both worked hard to put people at ease during such a very difficult time in their lives.

It was during in-depth talking, listening, and gentle counseling of clients whose domestic lives were coming apart and often shattering their world that it became clear to both of us how vitally and centrally important sex was in the equation that had gone awry. It was in some form a pivotal factor in almost every domestic relations case Dwight handled. The unfortunate part was that neither of us knew a whole lot about sex in general. With a lot of experimentation in our own sex life (stories about which have made many college sex ed classes we held howl with laughter in later years), a generous supply of good humor, and a genuine love for each other, we had developed a good personal sex life. But Dwight felt, rightly so, woefully inadequate to properly deal with the sexual aspect of other people's lives. And we knew no one to ask about sex counseling.

Then one day in 1966 one of us read a brief news item about a new book on the market by someone named Masters and Johnson. No copies being available in the local bookstore, we had to order one. When it arrived, a very embarrassed bookstore clerk handed it, wrapped and sealed in plain brown paper, to Joan. We quickly read it out loud to each other and discussed it from beginning to end. When we had finished we felt as if we knew a little more about sex than previously, but so many questions remained concerning the practical problems presented by many of Dwight's clients that we still felt quite inadequate to deal with many of them effectively.

We both sensed a growing level of frustration. We knew that far too many families were falling apart and too many lives were being effectively but needlessly crushed—all because of people dealing inadequately with their and their mate's sexual or intimacy problems through simple ignorance, theirs, ours, and that of every other professional we knew.

As we said earlier, we were in an era of wives who were homemakers, not career women. Few of Dwight's women clients or the wives of his male clients had much work experience outside of the home nor did many have much advanced education. In those days when a typical marriage came apart, everyone—husband, wife, and children—suffered the constraint of one pay check being divided between two households.

Whether the woman in a divorce case was a client or the wife of a client, we both always felt great empathy for what she and her husband were about to face. This was a time of very little gender equality in our society. We knew about that firsthand. Even with Joan's undergraduate academic honors, on graduation she could not get one of the available scholarships to graduate business school at our alma mater because she was a woman. Attempting to use her aviation administration major to find a job after graduation, she could find work only as a secretary. She knew well what problems those divorcing women faced.

We had become very sensitive to the justice inherent in equal opportunity for the genders. Even though Dwight served as chairman of a Democratic mayor's committee and served on a Democratic governor's committee, in 1968 he was asked and agreed to be campaign treasurer for the first woman to run for and to be elected to the Honolulu City Council. She was a Republican. On an earlier date, when he had attended with Joan his first meeting of the local junior Chamber of Commerce as a new member, Dwight was informed that women were not allowed to attend the meeting and that Joan would have to be asked to leave. Instead, Dwight resigned on the spot and we both left. Dwight then applied for membership in the local senior Chamber of Commerce and within a year was elected to be its next president—with Joan attending all meetings.

Nineteen sixty-eight was a pivotal year for us in many ways. The workload had gotten unbearable. We were sleeping sometimes only three or four hours a night and seven-day work weeks had been routine for several years. We had taken on the legal work of almost a whole town. To top it off Dwight had that year been hired by a group of local citizens to establish a new political party in the state in time to get George Wallace's candidacy for president on the upcoming ballot. Time was short. Dwight felt he had an obligation to help them even though we strongly disagreed with the candidate's policies. He cleared it with his Republican City Council candidate and we launched into the monumental task in addition to all our other work. The American Independent Party of Hawaii was drafted, organized, and took its first breath in our tiny office. After several hectic months necessary official approvals were granted and George Wallace's name appeared on the November ballot in Hawaii (as well as each of the other forty-nine states). It was indeed ironic that in but a few years George Wallace would himself become a quadriplegic, in his case as the result of a would-be assassin's bullet.

It was obvious we could not keep up this workload. Dwight cast about for a partner, but everyone wanted to be located downtown where all of the "real action" was. However a young associate of one firm offered to buy the assets of Dwight's practice and take it over himself as a solo practice. We were so worn out by then we agreed to do it. After all, we thought, after a good long rest we can start again somewhere.

In the spring of 1969 as our plane winged across the continental United States to our temporary destination in Washington, D.C., the horrors of the Vietnam War and the resulting societal paroxysms that engulfed our nation were in full force. Our country seemed to be on the edge of some massive cultural change. Up to then we had been so busy with the problems of individuals that we had been less aware of the cultural shocks that we saw so vividly now that we were able to take the time to really look and listen. We decided then and there to find out more about our world and its people.

After a brief stay in Washington, we set out in a new motor home specially adapted to accommodate our unusual requirements to see and really experience our culture. We lived in that motor home for the next four years, traveling through each of the forty-eight contiguous states, almost all of Canada, and much of Mexico. We talked with and listened to as many people from all areas and all walks of life as we could. We were like blotters soaking up ideas and an endless variety of experiences, some good, some bad, some inspiring, some sorrowful.

It was the height of the sixties phenomenon. We witnessed its many manifestations throughout our land and were constantly amazed. It happened that our travels brought us to the San Francisco/Berkeley scene in late 1969 as flower power thoroughly gripped the area. The sexual revolution was on. What a dramatic difference in mass behavior and tolerance of different moral choices we found between them and the more traditional lives that had characterized our clients, colleagues, and acquaintances in Hawaii.

Intrigued by the new sexual dimensions we found, we determined to learn as much about them as we could. We found so many options for sexual expression that could have helped so many of our clients had we only known of them and understood them. It pained us that we had labored in such a vacuum of knowledge concerning so important a force in people's lives.

After steeping ourselves in the various cultures we encountered in the United States and our nearby neighbors we decided to expand our horizon. We shipped our motor home to Europe and traveled through it for several years to see the world from other perspectives.

From many of the people we met in the dozen countries we visited, we gained a breadth of human understanding and appreciation of diversity that we couldn't have gotten in any other way. Finally we felt it was time to return to the United States.

Settling in California, we found the sexual revolution in full bloom. Laws in many states regulating and criminalizing some sexual activities were being repealed. Publications, television, and movies were being liberalized. More and more people were seeking to enhance their sexual relationships, to become more easily and more fully or more frequently sexually aroused, or to be aroused for the first time. The repression and ignorance of the past are deeply rooted in our cultural and individual psyches. This we knew in good measure from our legal practice days. We also knew how much injury and misery such repression and ignorance causes and were determined to do what we could to help dispel some of those problems.

We were being asked to speak to different groups of people and some college classes. Knowing all too well the ravages of sexual ignorance on the disabled, Dwight initiated, and for the next four years wrote as a volunteer for, a national magazine for the disabled, a monthly column on sexual issues specifically directed to disabled readers. And we began lecturing at no charge to any group of disabled people who would ask us. After becoming volunteer on-air readers for the blind on a local public radio station, we created, produced, hosted, and edited a weekly one-hour taped program called "Sex and the Disabled Amateur," directed to sexual matters of concern to the disabled listener. We interviewed experts (or so we thought) on a wide variety of issues, one topic per program. The show was later picked up by National Public Radio and aired by a number of NPR stations across the country.

Knowing we needed more knowledge about sex (the more we learned the more we knew we didn't know), we joined a new group formed of people with a health-care-professional interest in human sexuality. No one in the group had any formal training in the subject. Some of our members were therapists of various persuasions, some were writers, a few were doing sex research, and some were just interested in the subject. Once a month we drove 150 miles each way to the meetings and always left feeling good in the knowledge that we had been in the company of like-minded, serious people who were striving as we were to learn more about human sexual behavior.

With the societal expansion of what was considered permissible sexual behavior, we also began to see an increase in the activity of those who wished to impose more restrictions on what people could legally do sexually, not only as to engaging in various sexual acts themselves but also writing about sex, filming it, possessing erotic art, and so on. In order to maintain personal freedoms and responsibilities in sexual matters we helped found an organization in San Diego which was dedicated to the defense of individual freedoms as expressed in the U.S. Constitution, in particular the Bill of Rights. We joined and began contributing to a growing number of similar groups, such as the ACLU and some newer organizations supporting greater equality for women, including their reproductive rights.

It was clear to us that freedom of the woman to prevent or abort her pregnancy as she chose was an essential key to being in control of her own sexuality. And it was equally clear to us that the people who wished to control the sexuality of women (and men) also recognized that connection, and that the real battle was about who was going to control the sexuality of the individual—the individual her/himself or some group. To help protect other personal rights we joined with some other interested people and helped form a Southern California coalition of individuals and organizations against censorship. Dwight headed the San Diego chapter. And at every opportunity we accepted offers to speak on those topics to other groups and to write to politicians, journalists, editors, broadcasters, and corporation executives.

Although practically everything we were doing in the sex field we were doing as unpaid volunteers, it became obvious to us at some point that for greater credibility some professional credentials would be very useful. And just about that time the leadership of the National Sex Forum in San Francisco opened a unique school, the Institute for Advanced Study of Human Sexuality. It offered California state-approved courses leading to several different advanced degrees in human sexuality—just what we wanted. We enrolled immediately.

In all of the organizations and other personal contacts we had had up to then with people involved in the vanguard of personal sexual rights we had found comrades in spirit with similar ideas regarding most issues we felt were important. From our first day at "the Institute," as it is usually referred to by its friends, we felt a wonderful sense of having come to the right place.

From the beginning of our work in the sex information field we continually came in contact with a wide range of fascinating people whose interests and experiences represented a large variety of sexual behaviors. We became friends with male and female homosexuals and bisexuals; transvestites; transsexuals; exotic dancers; writers, actors, and producers of erotic art and media; prostitutes; swingers with a wide range of sexual interests; and heterosexuals with interests and experiences in a variety of sexual variations. We attended scores of parties and other encounters where the primary or sole purpose was some form of sexual interaction. The encounters ranged from just one other person to very large orgies. As observers we witnessed up to that time approximately three thousand different people engaging in several times that number of sexual acts. In our travels we visited several dozen nudist camps and resorts in seven countries in which we observed or socialized with many thousands of nude people ranging from an international jewel thief to a Catholic bishop, Crown Prince Peter of Denmark, and the deputy assistant to the then-president of France—as they recreated and relaxed in the altogether. Thus the free-flowing intellectual examination of the broad varieties of sexual behavior we found at the Institute was exactly what we were looking for. As we interacted with faculty, students, and guest lecturers, and studied the large number of books and other sources we were assigned, we often reflected on our struggles with so many of Dwight's clients who had so desperately needed access to the knowledge and sexual wisdom we were acquiring.

In the course of writing his magazine column on disability-related sex issues Dwight was contacted by a female amputee with problems concerning her love for a man who was interested in her because she was an amputee. This contact led to our publishing an article in a sex and disability journal on the subject of a sexual attraction to amputees, several paper presentations at sexology conferences, and our establishment of a newsletter and worldwide organization for both amputees and persons attracted to them. Since turning the organization and newsletter over to an amputee lady to run, the organization has developed into a large, active international group which holds conferences in various cities and has produced several marriages and a great improvement in many lives. It educates and makes people understand themselves and others and learn to feel good about themselves.

A couple of years after graduation from the Institute we joined with a few other alumni and formed an alumni association. Dwight drew up the papers, and got it approved as an official California charitable corporation and secured its federal tax-free status. He also served as its first president for six years; Joan succeeded him in that office, and later served as treasurer and as board member for eleven years. An association-endowed fund we started awards three scholarships a year to promising graduate sexology students.

Our early explorations and work in the field of human sexual behavior had taken place during an era mainly characterized by the movement to enrich, develop, expand, explore, and enjoy one's sexuality to the fullest extent reasonably and morally possible. Almost without exception the individuals and organizations with whom we had socialized and labored could be correctly described as pro-sex, pro-individual development and expansion. We imagined ourselves to be secure in our belief that we were surrounding ourselves with kindred spirits in the noble cause of individual freedom and sexual development. In that important cause we were willing to expend enormous amounts of personal effort, finances, and time.

That was the mood and background from which we emerged as we entered the sexology profession and the inappropriately named, in our opinion, field of sexual "science." Unfortunately, disillusionment was waiting for us. The time was the early eighties. President Jimmy Carter had presided over the death throes of a time of expanding personal freedoms. The ascent of Ronald Reagan promised an impending harsh brand of extreme societal control and restriction of those freedoms. A mysterious and terrible malady (AIDS), with roots in certain sexual behaviors, suddenly, as it were, became ever more evident, along with the attendant pall it cast on the whole notion of sexual liaisons and carefree sexual behaviors. The rate of proliferation in the number of sex education courses from grammar school to medical school began to reverse. Local and national organizations (such as some feminist groups) that sought to expand the rights and freedoms of women began to concentrate much of their efforts on trying to accomplish those worthy goals by inducing society to restrict and punish a wide range of behaviors (by both women and men) that had heretofore been permitted or tolerated as legal or overlooked, as the case may be. As is well known, the eventual result of that massive effort to societal controls has been the passage of a series of wide-ranging laws that seek to regulate much of what happens in personal relationships ranging from the intimate behavior of lovers and spouses to employment, housing, leisure, and the merely public interactions of strangers.

This was the watershed time in which we entered "the profession." Wishing to be able at last to channel our efforts from within a fold of fellow professionals who shared our desire to bring the "good news" of sexual knowledge and personal expansion to everyone, we eagerly joined local and national organizations of fellow professionals dedicated to sex education, research, and therapy, or various combinations thereof. Not wishing to discuss particular organizations here, let us say merely that we immediately threw ourselves into the work of each. We quickly volunteered for and were appointed or elected to committees and offices, in various cases conference chair and president. As a result it is no exaggeration to say that for several years following our entering the work on a professional level the great bulk of our daily lives was devoted to a massive load of volunteer work for several professional organizations.

As we immersed ourselves in the internal workings of these organizations, we became aware of a dynamic that seemed to be common to each in varying degrees. At first we were completely mystified. That feeling later evolved through greater and greater degrees of concern and disappointment which we were experiencing to some extent in each organization. We had anticipated that in our professional associations we would be in the comfortable midst of empowered peers who were as singleminded and dedicated as we were to the empowerment of others through the enhancement of the sexual knowledge and the growth of personal inner strength through the unshackling of inappropriate societal constraints. We had looked forward with great expectations to the symbiotic effect of combining our zeal and efforts with a whole group of like-minded professionals.

But what we began to find was a diverse combination of different agendas. To our increasing dismay we discovered that these agendas ranged from the mere achievement of personal glory and academic career enhancement (which, though unfortunate, was the least troubling to us), to the wholehearted dedication by some to enhance the powers of one class of individuals primarily by restricting the power and punishing the actions of another. This philosophy was not only gripping society at large but was also quickly gaining substantial currency in each of the professional groups in which we then toiled. We began to find that we were often (or so it seemed to us) an alien camp in our own committees or organizations.

Fate of a different kind stepped in at that moment in our lives, for we found that Dwight's health had seriously deteriorated in many ways; not the least of his problems was that he had bladder cancer. Rightly or wrongly, admirably or not, our response was eventually to withdraw and conserve our energy. We dropped out or cut back on all of our activities in the sex field. After treatments, operations, and a lot of recovery-directed efforts by both of us Dwight's health has significantly improved.

At this stage in our lives we are contenting ourselves with working quietly on a few research projects involving untraditional sexual behaviors, doing a small amount of writing and lecturing, and giving an occasional paper at a professional conference.

Long ago our family and friends came to grips—as have we—with our strange journey from the hallowed halls of law courts to the quirky, musky netherworld of mankind's most feared, loved, detested, desired, thought about, undiscussable, pervasive, punished, misunderstood behavior—sex. It's been a serendipitous path filled with fascinating surprises every step of the way, and we are a long way from finding the end of it. We certainly have no regrets, and are more in love with each other than ever.

12

How I Became the Guru of Female Sexual Liberation[1]

Betty Dodson, Ph.D.

Betty Dodson is a pioneering feminist who in 1973 began running physical and sexual consciousness-raising groups for women. She believes that women's liberation not only required economic and social liberation but sexual liberation as well.

WHEN I FIRST began thinking about teaching sex to women, I knew it had to be experiential. As an art student, I had learned by doing. In fact, every time I learned something new that involved my body—a sport or the latest dance steps—I didn't just sit in a classroom thinking and talking about how to make the moves. Actually, sex, sports, and dance have a lot in common: rhythm, movement, form, content, and aesthetics. But how on earth could I teach sex by doing sex, short of staging sex parties? That would restrict the number of interested women, and I was aiming for every feminist in America. That was my dilemma in the early seventies when I was bicoastal and the women's movement was no longer on the launching pad waiting for liftoff. In New York City and San Francisco thousands of us were orbiting the planet with ideas about how to achieve more equality between women and men. This energy was contagious because everything seemed possible. And each woman's history became her agenda for change once we learned that the personal is political.

After thoughtful analysis of my own sex history and subsequent sex experiences in the late sixties, I came to the conclusion that sexuality was as critical as economics to women's quest for equality. All my cherished romantic illusions had either mystified my lack of orgasm or aggrandized my dependent orgasms as I searched for financial security through love and marriage. As long as women remained blinded by love and bound by an invisible sexual and financial double standard, feminism

---

1. This autobiography is condensed and printed with permission from Kenneth Ray Stubbs, *Women of the Light* (Larkspur, Calif.: Secret Garden, 1994).

would never pose any real threat to our present authoritarian system. Once I became committed to the women's movement, it didn't take me long to discover that my idea of liberating masturbation was too shocking for most feminists. Few were interested in becoming responsible for creating their own orgasms, alone or with a partner. Most women wanted just a little bit of freedom: equal pay, child care, access to the political process. But when it came to sex, they still wanted to find Mr. or Ms. Right who'd provide them with love, orgasms, and security forever.

At first I was devastated and hurt, and then I became furious. Turning my anger into energy I resolved to go it alone, the artist's fierce stance of individualism. The conservative, mainstream feminists could fight the good fight for the Equal Rights Amendment while I would storm the barricades waving my banner for the Equal Orgasm Amendment.

In 1973 I began running physical and sexual consciousness-raising groups, which turned into the sexuality seminars that I run to this day. Since I was an artist, not a therapist, I felt free to break all the rules, especially to avoid the role of being an "expert" who knows all the answers. First-person sharing of our sexual experiences seemed the best way to learn about sex. I shared what I'd learned about sex from several sources: my own sex history, reading extensively about sex, drawing sex, having three one-woman exhibitions of erotic art where I talked to hundreds of people about their sex lives, and gathering a wealth of firsthand sexual experience by participating in group-sex parties.

My first approach to teaching was demonstrating manual sex, showing the use of electric massagers and dildos, and encouraging everyone to develop a repertoire of sexual fantasies as a way to focus their minds on sex instead of drifting off into compiling a grocery list. I also acted out a range of orgasms from mild to intense, giving women in the groups a visual image that was worth a thousand words. Later they practiced masturbating at home with followup discussions in the next group session.

Over several years, the workshops developed a basic pattern. The two main subjects were healing our body and genital imagery, and learning the basis of orgasmic release through masturbation. The only requirement for attending a group was agreeing to nudity. We all benefited from seeing natural bodies instead of constantly comparing ourselves to fashion models and centerfold nudes. There was no doubt in my mind that self-love started with loving our physical selves.

Originating with my own self-therapy, I'd already developed a method for confronting women's negative genital imagery. In 1965, shortly after my divorce, a lover had shown me magazine photos of women exposing their genitals because I'd confessed mine were deformed. Until that moment, I'd thought my inner lips had been stretched from childhood masturbation! To share this healing experience with other women, I created a slide show of one hundred beautiful color photographs of friends' genitals that premiered at the historic 1973 Women's Sexuality Conference sponsored by the National Organization for Women (NOW). The presentation was titled "Creating an Aesthetic for the Female Genitals." Afterward, I was given a standing ovation that sent shock waves of compassion and excitement through me.

Providing positive genital imagery became an essential ingredient of the workshops. At first, showing the slides to each group was sufficient until I realized that looking at ourselves directly would have an even more profound impact. One by one, starting with me, we took turns under a spotlight in front of a free-standing mirror displaying the exquisite shapes and colors of our vulvas. My fine art background was perfect for showing each woman how to "see" her unique beauty, shape, and form. We were also getting an important lesson in comparative anatomy by viewing a range of genital appearance. This single process transformed a multitude of women's sex lives by dispelling myths and filling in information about our clitorises, vaginal lips, strange little bumps and tags at the vaginal opening, secretions, the urethra, the PC muscle, different colorations, scars from episiotomy, and the interesting range of pubic hair.[2]

The "Genital Show and Tell" breakthrough gave me the courage to propose to one group that we actually share orgasms in the workshop. To my amazement, they all said yes! In those early days, the group masturbation was informal, with everyone lying down, using their electric massagers, doing their own thing. Most of the women kept their eyes closed, but they could hear the sounds of breathing with a few audible orgasms, and they could sense the energy in the room.

Eventually, I got the inspiration to lead the group in a guided masturbation celebration. Sounding like an enthusiastic gym teacher, I started with the group standing in the circle with our massagers on and our eyes wide open. Sometimes I was a rock star playing my massager like a bass guitar; other times I was a top sergeant barking out a cadence. There was always great humor and bawdy comments with lots of healing laughter. We were more outrageous than I ever expected! For the first thirty minutes, I led the group through different sexual positions: standing, kneeling, doggie style, and lying down with different leg positions. We varied our pelvic thrusting while breathing out loud to increase sexual pleasure. I showed them how to do slow pelvic rocking with a fast massager, or the reverse, fast pelvic movements with a stationary massager. We practiced slow, sensual penetration with cucumbers or zucchinis and coordinated our breathing with tightening the PC muscle while rocking our hips forward and back. What I said, I did, modeling each concept with a live, visual image.

Our masturbation celebration ended with an erotic recess. Everyone was shown how to keep going after her first orgasm by putting her hand over her clitoris to soften the vibrations until the hypersensitivity passed. In moments she could continue into another sexual buildup. Having many orgasms was easier and more natural than most expected, and pushing at our sexual boundaries was exhilarating with group support. Most women were spending only ten to twenty minutes on self-loving, and here we were, masturbating together for nearly two hours and having a great time.

Teaching sex by doing sex was the most logical thing in the world. Everyone

---

2. The pubococcygeus (PC) muscle in males and females extends across the pelvis from the os pubis in front to the coccyx in the rear. Episiotomy is the incision of the perineum to facilitate delivery and avoid laceration.

got to see a range of sexual arousal and orgasmic responses. Right before our eyes we witnessed the huge variation in women's sexual patterns. Some women had many little orgasms with quick buildups in between. Others took thirty minutes to an hour to have one big orgasm, and there were a few who could have several fairly big orgasms, each with a visible buildup. There were also those women who were having little spasms that they did not label "orgasm" because of their expectations. Unable to identify the beginning of their orgasmic response cycle, they couldn't create more sexual pleasure.

Clearly, masturbation was the key for sexual growth. It gave each woman a chance to focus totally on herself instead of being concerned about pleasing a partner. She could take as long as she wished, try all sorts of different things, and experiment with creating new fantasies. From self-love and sexual self-knowledge, I reasoned, healthier and happier relationships would naturally follow. And for women who wanted to be on their own for a while, they could be their own lovers.

It took several years, but after I got over my concerns and fears of teaching sex with this logical but unheard-of method, I began having some of my best orgasms in the workshops. The combination of playing teacher, being a voyeur of the erotic sights, exhibiting my sexuality in a group, and getting paid to masturbate to orgasm was hedonistic heaven.

The concept of teaching sex by doing sex will be perceived by many as a kind of prostitution. The minute a woman accepts money or favors for sex, she is flirting with the world's oldest profession. On the other hand, if a wife receives money or a new fur coat for sexual favors from her husband, it's viewed as normal. A sex worker[3] friend liked to point out that marriage was legalized prostitution with one difference: a wife sold her body permanently, while a sex worker only rented hers. Most women will smile knowingly at this kind of remark because we sense the primal connection between sex and money though it's seldom discussed.

If I'm getting paid to have orgasms with women who are also having orgasms, does that make me a sex worker? Is masturbating with my students considered "having sex" with them? Does watching another person masturbate count as "having sex"? What about viewing sex for research purposes as Masters and Johnson did? How does anyone do legitimate sex research if she follows all the rules? Denying educators and researchers the right to participate in a range of sexual activities results in a lack of valid and complete information for textbooks. Too many sex teachers are ineffectual because they don't know enough about real, live sex. They have not had sufficient experience to even identify their own sexual problems.

Most of our contemporary images of sex are based on what we see in the movies or on television. Often we get kissing as a stand-in for sex. The alternative is lovers frantically ripping off each other's clothes with mouths glued together until they fall onto a bed, still half dressed. We seldom get to see scenes of slow, sensuous sex.

---

3. I define a sex worker as one who provides sex for a fee. This would include activities ranging from nude dancing to telephone sex to actual intercourse.

Instead, we're bombarded with images of sexual urgency, desperate grabbing with mouth mauling, and compulsive kissing. When passion equals urgency sex becomes a rush to the finish line. For those of us who rent R-rated videos, images of sex aren't much better. To create more drama, most porn directors encourage faked female orgasms with screaming and bucking. Male orgasm is presented with ejaculations flying through the air, often landing on some part of a woman's body. Nothing like a big glob of jism pooling in the corner of a heavily massacred eye to turn most women off porn. Maybe coming on a woman's face is revenge for all the times we've said, "Careful, don't mess up my makeup." Or from some men's point of view, perhaps it's a symbolic way of making a woman more of a participant in the sexual action instead of remaining a passive sleeping beauty.

When I turned sixty, after I had described my workshops a million times to prospective participants, reporters, TV talk show hosts, teachers, students, and strangers at parties, I finally decided to make a videotape that shows what I'd been doing all those years. At every turn, the problems seemed to be insurmountable. Wasn't it enough that I'd written about my personal sex life for thousands of people to read? I was having a monumental struggle with the idea of being nude at my age, displaying my genitals, and mass-marketing my orgasm for the all the world to see. Clearly one of the biggest challenges of my life was at hand.

The entire production was handled by my partner Samantha and me. The shooting was the easy part. To my amazement, all the women were willing to participate. The tough part was the endless hours we spent in the editing room with me looking at my sixty-year-old body. I, "the Queen of Selflove and Body Acceptance," sat there day after day passing critical judgment on how I looked. I wanted less of me, more of the women, and I sounded like a parrot who kept repeating, "Cut, cut, cut." After weeks of carrying on like that, one day Samantha turned to me and asked, "Could you please get over yourself so we can move along?" I got it and shut up. The final outcome was a one-hour video titled *Selfloving: Video Portrait of a Women's Sexuality Seminar.*

After twenty years of hearing myself and listening to women share their sex lives, I found that one of our most consistent problems is the constant power struggle going on inside each of us: good girl versus bad girl. The morality that's been shoved down our throats from religion, government, school, and the family has conditioned us to be divided within ourselves. I no longer have any illusions that masturbating to orgasm will eliminate this conflict, but having an orgasm with ourselves is at least a moment of getting in touch with our bodies and senses that just might support individual choice over all those conditioned responses.

Another barrier to becoming fully sexual is most women's insistence on having romantic love and passionate sex with some mythical, perfect lover. By constantly being focused on finding fulfillment "out there," we never have a chance to look within, to develop the ability to fantasize, or to create new erotic images that would consistently charge our sexual desire and arousal. Instead we are stuck with our repetitious dreams of romance.

People use the word *romance* to mean many things. However, my dictionary said it quite well: *"A fictitious tale of wonderful and extraordinary events, characterized by much imagination and idealization."* If this were a definition of sexual fantasy, it would work. But confusing "fictitious tales" with reality causes some serious problems. When lovers turn into ordinary persons with blemishes and flaws, when the burden of trying endlessly to sustain sexual passion through increasingly artificial means finally fails, we fall out of love, only to repeat the pattern with someone else.

These romantic images feed our notion of what sex *should* be like. As a teenager, I remember longing for a penis inside my vagina with my "true love," knowing the experience would produce an orgasm that would be far and beyond anything I'd ever experienced from masturbation, including all the orgasms from hand-jobs with my teenage boyfriend. Ironically, in my second year of marriage, I was secretly masturbating to memories of those hot, high-school hand-jobs. Contrary to much of the available romantic literature, an orgasm is not always a grand mal seizure, especially when a woman is first learning about sex alone, with a new lover, or with her husband. Even simple, basic skills require learning how to make the moves, something I can teach, by showing them while wearing a lubricated latex glove.

The idea of touching a client is severely frowned upon in most therapeutic circles. Perhaps the reason for this was to protect clients from sexual advances by therapists. While this might present a problem for some, I personally have never felt any overt sexual desire in a teaching context. For me, the laying on of hands is an integral part of any healing process. Rather than calling myself a "therapist," I see myself more as an "orgasm coach" who helps clients change their behavior. That doesn't mean I don't include some standard therapeutic processes, such as listening to a person's problems, verbal probing, and gentle guidance that will lead to insights. We need to take advantage of every possible approach in helping people to discover sexual pleasure.

Although most of my work has been around female sexuality, I have done a few workshops and some private counseling with men. Some middle-aged men have come to see me just for the thrill of sharing masturbation with an interested woman who won't be judgmental. Most of the older men have problems with erections, and they're convinced their sex lives are over unless I can give them some magic trick to restore their *potency.* Yes, you guessed it, masturbation to the rescue.

Using the same techniques I teach women, I have them use an electric massager, assuring them they can have an orgasm without a hard-on. At first, most men complain about not liking the sensation of an "electrical appliance," but I ignore their complaint and keep talking. "Just keep breathing, rock your pelvis, squeeze the PC, and fantasize I'm Marilyn Monroe." Usually I can see the moment they let go of their resistance, get into the good sensations, and finally come all over the "electrical appliance" with a soft-on. They admit the orgasm felt great, but want to know how they can have sex with a woman without a hard-on. I list the ways they can be good lovers, including massage, manual sex, oral sex, either partner strapping on a dildo for vaginal or anal sex, using other sex toys for penetration, using one massager for two, and sharing masturbation where both people have their own massagers.

The other big problem for men is ejaculating too soon, becoming flaccid, and believing in the arbitrary thirty-minute refractory[4] period that ends the sexual exchange. I believe the lack of erections and premature ejaculation is the counter-part of women not coming at all. These men are "preorgasmic," although we never use that term when we're talking about male sexuality. The solution for both pre-orgasmic women and men is basically the same: masturbate, and train your body to respond to sexual stimulation. Men can learn to control the urge to ejaculate by con-tracting their PC muscle and squeezing the penile glands before they reach the point of no return. The erection will subside a bit, but with continued stimulation, it comes back for more. Men also need to be encouraged to use lots of sensuous mas-sage oil when they masturbate, especially if they are circumcised.

Teaching sex by doing sex hasn't always been an erotic bowl of cherries. Aware that I was treading on dangerous ground, I learned to walk softly. Always mindful of the defenders of the status quo, I knew religious fanatics, right-wing politicians, and anti-sex feminists were all capable of violence. However most of the attacks on me and my work came in the form of name calling that was meant to degrade me per-sonally or to demean my words and art.

One of the first labels hurled at me was "pornographer." Lacking any experi-ence with the word, I was angry and hurt. "How could anyone find my beautiful drawings pornographic?" But soon I learned that name calling was at the heart of all censorship. The real issue at stake was freedom to think, to fantasize, to imag-ine the unimaginable—in short, the freedom to be creative. My healing came when I stopped defending myself and embraced the label. "Yes, I'm a feminist pornogra-pher who believes in First Amendment rights and artistic freedom." Next came the pejorative hiss, "lesbian!" which was supposed to intimidate me back into passive female conformity. "Yes, I'm a lesbian feminist who loves both women and men." When the ultimate degradation, "Whore!" was hurled at me, I welcomed that label, too. "Yes, I'm a whore, a sacred prostitute, an ancient temple priestess who serves the goddess of love." Taking on all the labels allowed me to claim my power.

My sexual evolution has been an integral part of my spiritual growth. Once I understood that masturbation was a meditation on self-love, my sexuality and spir-ituality grew closer together. When I think about my other spiritual practices, I put art near the top of the list. Drawing was a beautiful meditation, and mastering the nude was an excellent discipline. The creative process and developing a sense for aesthetics, the search for beauty—its sources, forms, and effects—will always be a profound spiritual consideration for me.

Although I came from the Bible Belt in Wichita, Kansas, my parents were not reli-gious people. Mother thought the Bible was a collection of fairy tales, and that only ignorant people believed it was the word of God. My dad was an atheist. With no reli-

---

4. Refractory refers to a period of erectile incompetence following ejaculation.

gious pressure, I naturally wanted to join a church. So Mother took me to a Methodist church to be baptized at twelve. After a few months of boring Sunday School and a brief stint of singing in the choir, I got over wanting to belong to an organized religion. But I kept searching for something outside myself to give life a special meaning.

My spiritual quest has been very eclectic because I explored each new teacher, group, or process that intrigued me. First I was into psychiatry and group therapy. Next it was general semantics and non-Aristotelian (nonlogical) thought, followed by a new mystical model of the universe that led to study of the teachings of Gurdjieff, which was basically a form of esoteric Christianity for a chosen few. After that I got involved with the twelve-step programs that opened their doors to everyone who had a desire to stop using their drug of choice. I began studying and practicing yoga. I took Tantra workshops. For a while I worshiped group sex as the highest Tantra ritual. I learned Transcendental Meditation. Becoming a vegetarian, I turned health into a religion. I went on retreats, I fasted, I got colonics (enemas). I became a feminist and turned that into a religion. There were many psychic readings where I learned about my guardian angels, spirit guides, and past lives. I studied metaphysics. I got Rolfed (deep-tissue massage), rebirthed, and had foot reflexology. My horoscope was done; I used the Tarot cards and then the I Ching. I worshiped the goddess and made up my own rituals. I joined a lesbian SM[5] support group and so forth. I continue to practice my sexual meditation with masturbation.

Every teacher, each discipline, and all these groups taught me something about myself—a stepping stone along a winding path. But the struggle between "turning my life over to a power outside myself" and "being committed to questioning all authority" always bailed me out. My need to be an individual on my own terms would pull me back into the mundane world to grapple once more with my divided self: good girl versus bad girl.

Maybe it was because my initials spelled B.A.D. that I tried so hard to be good. But in the end, the juiciest bit of wisdom I gleaned was that I was both good and bad in an imperfect society. As I continue along my spiritual path, one thing is sure: I know the path will never remain the same.

Every time we follow gurus or teachers we adore, they become authority figures and we end up surrendering our power to them. Although I might be addicted to being adored, I have never wanted to perpetuate that kind of authoritarian control, especially over women who took my workshops. I used to call myself "a one-night-stand guru." With each passing year, I realize more and more the importance of designing a method of teaching that required women to take only one, or maybe two, workshops. After that, there was nothing to join and no way to see me on an ongoing basis. The antithesis of sexual freedom would be creating thousands of little Bettys who were all having orgasms just like me.

---

5. SM and S&M as used here are terms referring to forms of erotic expression usually employing the consensual playing of *dominant* and *submissive* roles along with activities resulting in intense sensations which a nonparticipant might label pain.

While I personally believe my sexuality and spirituality are closely connected, I don't want to go overboard by turning sex into a religious practice. And I certainly don't want all of my orgasms to be sacred, ecstatic, ritualized communions with some divine purpose. There are times I just want a quickie with a scuzzy fantasy of being tied down and fucked by a sadistic scoutmaster and his entire Boy Scout troop.

Now that we are in the nineties, I'm still perceived by some people as "weird" to be sure, but I have also been acknowledged by many wonderful people who respect my simple message: "Self-sexuality is the ongoing love affair that each of us has with ourselves throughout our lifetime." Teaching masturbation by masturbating has kept me fairly honest, not that I don't still lie to myself occasionally, but when you see your teacher *playing with herself*, it's difficult to turn her into someone who is more than human or larger than life.

Given the current political power trip of the Christian Coalition, with its agenda to gain control over the way people worship, live, and love, it's surprising that I have received such a small amount of hate mail. Instead, the file folder marked "love letters" fills up several times each year. I've heard from educators, clergy, doctors, lawyers, lesbians, mothers, housewives, soldiers, prisoners, nurses, healers, therapists, nuns, priests, bankers, artists, executives, writers, entertainers, and other folks who didn't identify themselves. It's very much like the women who take my groups: a cross-section of America in all its glorious diversity Their common interest is a desire to know more about human sexuality, especially self-sexuality.

I have always been excited by the possibility of change for every woman who has taken a workshop. Sometimes the change takes place before my eyes; other times I get the feedback later on. Getting a first orgasm is thrilling. Some younger women with new lovers have told me they're beginning to explore what turns them both on with a more open dialogue about sex. Married women have said that sharing their sexual self-knowledge with their husbands has charged a flagging sex life. Mothers have talked with me about not interfering with their children's natural sexual exploration with masturbation. More women are dispelling myths about romantic love. They're no longer confusing good sex with love. Some are questioning the ideal of monogamy when they know it rarely exists. Couples who do choose to be monogamous are agreeing to a single standard. Women are also taking a hard look at jealousy and possessiveness as an unhealthy way to express a loving posture.

Today I believe sex energy is not only the life force, but also the source of all creativity. Each orgasm is a precious moment of joy. Sex quiets the mind; deep breathing brings oxygen into the bloodstream; the heart is exercised as it pumps blood through the veins; hormones and endorphins are released; the skin sweats, muscular tension is heightened and then drained, followed by deep relaxation and a sense of well-being and contentment through an intimate encounter with ourselves or another person. As we awaken our bodies through the senses, we awaken our minds to the knowledge that we are all connected.

13

How I Became Interested in Sexology and Sex Therapy

Albert Ellis, Ph.D.

Albert Ellis was one of the founders of the Society for the Scientific Study of Sex and its first president. He is also the founder of the Institute for Rational Emotive Therapy in New York City and is the best-known practitioner of Rational-Emotive Therapy (RET), a form of cognitive behavior therapy.

MY KEEN INTEREST in sex began, at the very latest, at the age of five, when I was caught by my parents trying to pour some milk through a funnel into the vagina of Mary J., a blonde and blue-eyed five-year-old bombshell with whom I was madly in love. I don't remember that I considered this act sexual. But both our sets of parents certainly did! So Mary, my beloved and my friend, was abruptly whisked out of my life.

I continued sexual—or at least nude—exploration at the age of seven when I spent ten months with nephritis in New York's Presbyterian Hospital and used a flashlight to reveal the nude bodies of the other children in my ward—and to let them see how scrumptiously I was hung. Still curiosity—no real sex.

However, I soon graduated, and just about got my first degree in sexual pleasure, when I discovered that if I pressed my genitals against the rails of my hospital crib, I could get a semi-orgasm—a real sexy thrill. So I made myself slightly addicted to crib-rail sex. Later on, when I went back to school, I found that climbing ropes in gym could also lead to genital joy. So, though I generally hated gym, I became quite a rope climber!

My first feeling of shame about sex was at the age of twelve, when I found that I had an almost constant erection, and was afraid that other people—especially the girls in my class whom I obsessively loved—would notice it and despise me. Oddly enough, however, I was still so ignorant about sex that I didn't start to control my perpetual erections by masturbating until I was fifteen. Then I really went to town!

I masturbated twice daily and wasn't guilty about that until I figured that

131

maybe I was too uncontrolled. So I rushed to the public library—to which I was also addicted—and found a few books that said that masturbation was okay, even when frequent. Pretty good books for the 1920s!

From the age of sixteen onward (in 1929), I read many books by Freud and his followers, but I could see that Freud was especially obsessed with the sexual "origins" of disturbance, especially with the ubiquitousness of the Oedipus complex. I could also see that he was an overgeneralizer and a dogmatist, and therefore a poor scientist. But I was helped by psychoanalytic details about sex to loosen up and to consider practically all forms of noncoercive sex permissible. In fact, at the age of fifteen, I had my first and only homosexual episode—with my thirteen-year-old brother no less! I saw that I could easily come to orgasm in that way, too, and didn't feel one bit guilty. Realizing, however, that to seek out gay sex would probably get me into trouble—especially in *those* days!—I thereafter continued to obsess about and to try to have sex only with women. That was a little easier and safer.

Sidelight: When Alfred Kinsey, about fifteen years later, interviewed me for his first report and discovered that I was highly heterosexual, he seemed delighted to find that I also had had an early homosexual encounter. I think that he was determined to discover that a large percentage of males had at least one homosexual episode in their lives. So fortunately I fulfilled this quota!

My accompanying obsession to sex was writing. At the age of twelve, I decided I would mainly be a writer; and between my eighteenth and twenty-eighth years I wrote no fewer than twenty book-length manuscripts—novels, plays, poems, and nonfiction works. Many of them, especially my novels, were very sexy. In fact, probably too sexy to be published—for I described sex play as few published writers other than James Joyce had previously done.

No dice. I got a number of fine rejection letters, and some near-publications, but no real hits. So at the age of twenty-six I decided that nonfiction writing on sex, love, and marriage would be my best bet. Why? Because I was quite interested in these related fields; and presumably because those areas sold well.

As usual, I went to the New York Public Library, and to two special private libraries I was a member of. Between all three, I could borrow ten books every day. So I did—well, at least five days a week. On Saturdays and Sundays I went to the main reading room at the 42nd Street Public Library, and devoured from thirty to fifty books each day.

Thirty to fifty? Yes, indeed. I am a fast reader. Without having taken any Evelyn Woods courses, I skim magnificently. Especially when all the books are on sex, love, and marriage, and most of them nauseatingly repetitive.

For two years I read hundreds of books and thousands of articles and began writing my "masterpiece": a thousand-page single-spaced tome titled "The Case for Promiscuity." Did I get any publication offers on it? Not one. Some great feedback from editors, but the unanimous view was that it was just too liberal for the early 1940s. Years later, I published the first volume of it (Ellis, 1965).

My notable library endeavors, however, catapulted me into becoming a sexologist and a sex therapist. My friends and relatives, hearing that I was studying sex, love, and marriage so intently, started to ask me how they could deal with their personal problems in these important areas. To my surprise, I was able to give them some good answers. In one or a few (unpaid) sessions of avid and often highly intimate conversation, I dispelled their ignorance, gave them realistic suggestions, relieved their anxiety, and helped a number of them to lead happier sex, love, and marital lives.

My subjects and I both benefited. I discovered much additional sex-love information. And I greatly *enjoyed* doing this kind of counseling, so much so that at twenty-seven I funded the Love and Marriage Problems (LAMP) Institute, devoted to helping and to doing research in sex, love, and marriage.

Great! But I had no status in the field, and my lawyer for my first divorce strongly advised me to get some. At that time, graduate schooling in sex therapy and even in marriage and family therapy did not exist. The closest thing to it was a Ph.D. degree in clinical psychology. So I applied for that.

Because my bachelor's degree was in business administration—which I really took to make money and support myself as a writer—I had trouble getting into graduate school at NYU and Columbia. But I did so well in taking three trial courses during the summer term at Columbia that they broke down and let me enroll in the clinical psychology program at Teachers College for the fall of 1942.

A piece of cake! Within a year, by *not* letting Teachers College know that I was working full-time, I received my M.A. with honors and was soon matriculated for a Ph.D. degree.

Came, however, a hitch! When it was time to work on my doctoral dissertation, I had the good sense to avoid doing one on any overtly sexual subject. That would have been verboten. So I thought I skirted this ticklish issue by doing one on *The Love Emotions of College-Level Women*. Everything at first went well and I was about to write up my interesting data on this subject when—wham!—Teachers College, Columbia, most unusually forced me to hold a special seminar to decide whether my topic was kosher.

Whereupon all thirteen members of the clinical psychology department got together with the provost of the college. The provost? I didn't realize that we even had one, until my main advisor told me that we definitely did—for administrative and not academic purposes. He never sat in on a thesis seminar. But this time he had heard about my topic, was afraid that the Hearst newspapers would make a federal case of it, and called this special seminar to see if I was to be allowed to polish it off.

Nothing daunted, I presented my research to the assembled professors and the provost, they politely listened, and then voted twelve to two in my favor. They agreed that I had a great topic, that I was a fine person and a scholar, and that I was proceeding scientifically with my study. Marvelous! But, as my advisor, Professor Goodwin Watson, sadly told me, the two (anonymous) dissenters were going to adamantly oppose this and *any* dissertation on love that I could come up with. They would be sure to show up at my final thesis orals and knock me for a loop, no matter *what* I did.

Well, that ended that. Not being a whiner, and wanting my degree, I picked another topic that had nothing to do with love, sex, or marriage, and quickly polished off a safe, highly statistical dissertation, *A Comparison of the Use of Direct and Indirect Phrasing in Personality Questionnaires* (Ellis, 1947a), which was nicely accepted. My poor orphaned thesis on love? I turned it into seven pioneering articles on the subject which I published in several psychological and sociological journals. So I fixed Teachers College, Columbia (Ellis, 1947b, 1948, 1949a, 1949b, 1949c, 1950, 1953d).

Soon after this, I began writing on sex with a vengeance; by 1954 I had published no fewer than forty-six articles on sex, love, and marriage, in addition to two book (Ellis, 1951, 1954a) and two anthologies (Ellis, 1954c; Pillay and Ellis, 1953). I was also the American editor of the pioneering journal the *International Journal of Sexology*. I had a wide psychotherapy practice and specialized in seeing hundreds of clients with sex, love, and marital problems.

Although I was well known in the psychology profession as a sexologist in the 1950s, my public fame mushroomed in the early 1960s when several of my books appeared in paperback form and became best-sellers. Thus, millions of copies were sold—and more millions borrowed from libraries—of my books *Sex without Guilt* (Ellis, 1958), *The Art and Science of Love* (Ellis, 1960a), *The Intelligent Woman's Guide to Man-Hunting* (Ellis, 1963a), *Sex and the Single Man* (Ellis, 1963b), and *Nymphomania: A Study of the Oversexed Woman* (Ellis and Sagarin, 1964). Although at this time my name was not exactly, like Kinsey's, a household word, his books were widely bought and not read while mine were avidly read as well as bought. I still, thirty years later, meet many individuals who enthusiastically tell me that they were first catapulted into enjoyable and guiltless sex by reading my books. I think that I can say without immodesty that the sexual revolution of that decade was largely sparked by the writings of Kinsey and Ellis.

All this notoriety at first did me little good professionally. To be sure, I received many referrals for sex therapy from psychologists and sexologists whom I had never met and who knew about me only from my publications. But I also received much opposition from professionals who were against popular writings by psychologists and who therefore hated my guts.

Professional journals and other publications have actually censored some of my sex writings. Thus, the *International Journal of Sexology* refused to publish my article "New Light on Masturbation" (Ellis, 1956a) because it would offend certain members of sectarian groups if Dr. Pillay, the editor, published it in India. The *Journal of Social Therapy* also refused to publish my article on masturbation among prisoners. The editors of the book *Sexual Behavior in American Society* refused to republish a pro-Kinsey article of mine that they had already published in the journal *Social Problems*.

For many years national popular magazines, such as *Redbook* and the *Ladies*

Home Journal, asked me to do articles on sex; but when I sent them outlines or actual articles, they found them "too unrealistic," "too bold for our readers," or "too controversial." *Esquire* accepted one of my articles, "A Case for Polygamy" (Ellis, 1960b), and paid me well for it. But one of their chief editors later found it "too strong" and refused to publish it.

In 1958, after I published the first edition of *Sex without Guilt,* I appeared on many radio and TV shows, but also ran into considerable censorship. Although many of my Long John Nebel radio shows were very popular and were recorded and often rebroadcasted, the show that I did on *Sex without Guilt,* in which I specifically mentioned masturbation and fornication as desirable acts, was forbidden to be rebroadcast by the management of radio station WOR.

I have had many other brushes with censorship and with being first invited, and then uninvited, to appear on popular radio and TV shows. Twice the Federal Communications Commission took the programs in which I was appearing temporarily off the air because of my espousal of premarital sex relations. On David Susskind's "Open End" TV show I appeared with Max Lerner, Hugh Hefner, Ralph Ginzburg, Maxine Davis, and Reverend Arthur Kinsolving for a two-hour presentation, "The Sex Revolution." But when Susskind asked me on the air what I would do if I had a teenage daughter who insisted on having premarital sex and I replied, "I would fit her up with a diaphragm or birth control pills and tell her to have fun," the tape that we made was banned from the air and never played anywhere. Ironically enough, Max Lerner, on this same show, had previously remarked that the mere fact that we were doing this program that night showed how liberal TV was becoming in its attitudes toward sex!

Several of my books have been banned here and abroad, especially *Sex without Guilt* whose sale was prohibited in a county of southern California. The opposition to my work as a sexologist also spilled over significantly into my reputation as a theorist and practitioner of psychotherapy. In 1955 I started to do rational emotive behavior therapy (REBT, later RET), the pioneering form of cognitive-behavior therapy, and since that time I have spent by far most of my time as a therapist, writer, and workshop presenter dealing with general psychotherapy, not just with sex therapy. But my reputation as a sexologist followed me into the general field of therapy, too; I have often been savagely criticized for my "controversial"—meaning, largely sexual—positions.

Even friends and associates of mine who follow much of my therapeutic teachings have often tried to induce me to tone down my sexual writings and presentations. Thus, Rollo May, who used to send me his "difficult clients" for RET when he practiced in New York in the 1950s and 1960s, opposed my becoming president of the American Academy of Psychotherapists because I was "too controversial." And many other "respectable" psychologists have used my therapeutic teachings without giving me due credit, or even going out of their way to criticize me, largely because of my reputation as a liberal sexologist.

Some other prominent sexologists have also vigorously opposed my sexual liberalism and my widespread popular publications on sex. My good friend Hans Lehfeldt, who helped me found the Society for the Scientific Study of Sex in the 1950s, opposed my being nominated as its first president because he felt that, once again, I was "too controversial." Fortunately for me, the other members of our board of directors, including Harry Benjamin and Henry Guze, did not go along with Hans. So I was renominated and elected.

In spite of this kind of opposition, I continued to absorb myself in the field of sexology as well as psychotherapy, largely because I took my own counsel as a therapist and firmly taught myself that it is great to be loved and approved by other people, including members of one's own profession, but that it is far from *necessary*. This is one of the main tenets of RET. Without following it myself, I might well have given up being a sexologist and merely have stayed with the safer aspects of psychotherapy and counseling. On the other hand, clinical sexology definitely has its rewarding aspects which kept me interested in working within it despite the disadvantages that it also entailed. Let me mention some of the rewards that I have found in being absorbed in it for over half a century.

First, sexology is the science of sexuality. I greatly enjoy the *discovery* aspect of science. Thus, in 1943 I was doing a term paper for a clinical psychology class on the various "causes" of homosexual behavior, when I accidentally discovered that most hermaphrodites whose libidinous direction was known were heterosexual in spite of their physiological and hormonal anomalies. This led me to publish my first scientific paper, "The Sexual Psychology of Human Hermaphrodites" (Ellis, 1945), which appeared in *Psychosomatic Medicine* and created quite a stir. It showed that although the power or strength of the human sex drive is strongly influenced by biological factors, its direction is largely influenced by familial and cultural teachings.

This was a very exciting discovery; I enjoyed the article's being cited in a great many articles and books and its influencing the work of some other outstanding sexologists, such as Harry Benjamin and John Money. Almost any kind of discovery—including artistic, political, and economic findings—can be uplifting. This, of course, also goes for sexological discovery.

Second, I have always found that my absorption in clinical sexology has important practical aspects. From my earliest consultations with my friends and relatives to my later sessions with thousands of clients and my writings for therapists and for the public, I have apparently helped almost innumerable people with their sex, love, marriage, and general problems. This has been, and still is, most gratifying. The hundreds of voluntary endorsements that I have received from readers in every major country in the world have been especially satisfying. Conveying my knowledge to these people has often produced splendid results.

Third, I have naturally benefited myself from my sexological findings. Not only, as noted above, did I overcome my own guilt and shame about sex largely as a result of my reading—and not from conversations with mentors or therapists—but I also tackled some of my own problems, such as the fast ejaculation that I was plagued with early in my life, and significantly helped myself by my sex researches.

In addition, I helped quite a number of my sex and love partners to decrease their anxiety and increase their pleasure. And that has been great!

If I had my life to live over again, would I still choose the field of sexology as one of my major pursuits? Definitely. I have always disagreed with Freud (1965) that sex problems, including incestuous thoughts and actions, are the major causes of general emotional problems, such as anxiety, depression, self-deprecation, and rage. One of the causes or contributions, yes, but hardly the only one. On the contrary, as I have said for several decades, general human disturbance is much more likely to lead to sex disturbance than vice versa. Actually, the two tend to be interactional.

Humans, as I keep preaching in RET, are both born and reared to be easily disturbable; and their emotional and behavioral disorders are both nonsexual and sexual. The solutions to their problems, moreover, are complex and involve a number of important cognitive, emotive, and behavioral insights and methods (Ellis, 1957, 1962, 1988, 1994, 1996). But sex is an exceptionally important aspect; and anything that we can do to minimize its disorders and enhance its fulfillment is meaningful and of great consequence.

The twentieth century has so far been the outstanding period of general psychotherapy and of sex therapy. In the latter area we have the pioneering findings and ideas of a number of unusual scholars and clinicians, including Havelock Ellis (1936), Alfred Kinsey and his associates (Kinsey, Pomeroy, and Martin, 1948; Kinsey, Pomeroy, Martin, and Gebhard, 1953), William Masters and Virginia Johnson (1960, 1970), Joseph LoPiccolo (LoPiccolo, Stewart, and Watkins, 1972; LoPiccolo and LoPiccolo, 1978), and many others. I am delighted to have been one who was friendly with and who worked with these pioneering sexologists and to have made some significant contributions myself.

Shall I risk mentioning what I consider my main contributions to the field of sex, love, and marriage? Why not? Here are some of them:

1. I was probably the first prominent psychologist to unequivocally point out that masturbation is not only not harmful and shameful, but that it is also actually beneficial for most people (Ellis, 1951a, 1952a, 1954a, 1955a, 1956a, 1958).

2. I was one of the few psychologists in the 1940s and 1950s who told my clients and members of the public that mutual consenting premarital sex relations for adults, when engaged in with proper sexually transmitted disease and pregnancy precautions, are not necessarily bad or immoral and can enhance one's sexual and general life (Ellis, 1951a, 1953a, 1954a, 1955a, 1956b, 1958, 1963a, 1963b, 1965, 1976; Ellis and Harper, 1961, 1975).

3. I vigorously opposed the idea that unconventional sex behavior is perverse or deviational and proposed that sexual "abnormality" is usually a myth (Ellis, 1951a, 1952b, 1952c, 1954a, 1954c, 1958, 1963a, 1963b).

4. I was a pioneering feminist and particularly showed women how they could be assertive and not aggressive (Ellis, 1954a, 1954c, 1955b, 1960a, 1963a, 1963b).

5. I was one of the few psychologists who strongly advocated gay liberation in the early 1950s and was made an honorary member of the Mattachine Society (Ellis, 1951a, 1951b, 1952c, 1954a).

6. Along with Kinsey and against Freud and his orthodox followers, I disputed the sacredness of the so-called vaginal orgasm in women and showed both sexes how women could achieve satisfactory noncoital orgasm and still be very healthy and "normal" (Ellis, 1951a, 1951b, 1953a, 1953b, 1953c, 1954a, 1954b).

7. I originated the idea of establishing the Society for the Scientific Study of Sexuality in 1950, but at first failed to enlist enough support for it. Persisting, and with the aid of Hans Lehfeldt, Robert Sherwin, Harry Benjamin, and Henry Guze, I actually got it going a few years later. It now flourishes.

I am proud of these sexological advocacies and accomplishments. But I was hardly alone in fighting for them, as I had other solid sexologists with me—such as Harry Benjamin (1966; Benjamin and Ellis, 1954), Kelly (1953), and Alfred Kinsey (Kinsey, Pomeroy, and Martin, 1948; Kinsey, Pomeroy, Martin, and Gebhard, 1953). All of us, and many other researchers and clinicians, are steadily making the field of sexology a highly vital and respectable area of science. Let us continue our healthy efforts!

References

Benjamin, H. 1966. *The transsexual phenomenon*. New York: Julian.
Benjamin, H., and A. Ellis. 1954. An objective examination of prostitution. *International Journal of Sexology* 8: 100–105.
Ellis, A. 1945. The sexual psychology of human hermaphrodites. *Psychosomatic Medicine* 7: 108–25.
———. 1947a. A comparison of the use of direct and indirect phrasing in personality questionnaires. *Psychological Monographs* 61: 1–41.
———. 1947b. Questionnaire versus interview methods in the study of human love relationships. *American Sociological Review* 12: 541–43.
———. 1948. Questionnaire versus interview methods in the study of human love relationships. II. Uncategorized responses. *American Sociological Review* 13: 62–65.
———. 1949a. Some significant correlations of love and family behavior. *Journal of Social Psychology* 15: 61–76.
———. 1949b. A study of human love relationships. *Journal of Genetic Psychology* 15: 61–76.
———. 1949c. A study of the love emotions of American college girls. *International Journal of Sexology* 3: 15–21.
———. 1950. Love and family relationships of American college girls. *American Journal of Sociology* 55: 550–58.
———. 1951a. *The folklore of sex*. New York: Boni/Doubleday.
———. 1951b. Introduction to D. W. Cory, *The homosexual in America*, pp. ix–xi. New York: Greenberg.

Ellis, A. 1952a. Applications of clinical psychology to sexual disorders. In *Progress in clinical psychology,* ed. D. Brower and L. A. Abt, vol. 1, pp. 467–80. New York: Gruwe & Stratton.

———. 1952b. Perversions and neurosis. *International Journal of Sexology* 6: 232–33.

———. 1952c. What is normal sex behavior? *Complex* 8: 41–51.

———. 1953a. Discussion of W. Stokes and D. Mace, "Premarital sexual behavior." *Marriage and Family Living* 15: 248–49.

———. 1953b. Is the vaginal orgasm a myth? In *Sex, society and the individual,* ed. A. P. Pillay and A. Ellis, pp. 155–62. Bombay: International Journal of Sexology Press.

———. 1953c. Marriage counseling with couples indicating sexual incompatibility. *Marriage and Family Living* 13: 53–59.

———. 1953d. Recent studies on the sex and love relations of young girls. *International Journal of Sexology* 6: 161–63.

———. 1954a. *The American sexual tragedy.* New York: Twayne. Rev. ed. New York: Lyle Stuart and Grove Press, 1962.

———. 1954b. Psychosexual and marital problems. In *An introduction to clinical psychology,* ed. L. A. Pennington and I. A. Berg, pp. 264–83. New York: Ronald.

———, ed.. 1954c. *Sex life of the American and the Kinsey report.* New York: Greenberg.

———. 1955a. Masturbation. *Journal of Social Therapy* 1, no. 3: 141–43.

———. 1955b. Woman as sex aggressor. *Best Years* 1, no. 3: 25–29.

———. 1956a. New light on masturbation. *The Independent,* Issue 51, 4.

———. 1956b. On premarital sex relations. *The Independent,* Issue 58, 6.

———. 1957. *How to live with a neurotic: At home and at work.* New York: Crown. Rev. ed. Hollywood, Calif.: Wilshire Books, 1975.

———. 1958. *Sex without guilt.* New York: Lyle Stuart and Grove Press. Rev. ed., 1966.

———. 1960a. *The art and science of love.* New York: Lyle Stuart and Dell.

———. 1960b. A case for polygamy. *Nugget* 5, no. 1: 19, 24, 26.

———. 1962. *Reason and emotion in psychotherapy.* Secaucus, N.J.: Citadel.

———. 1963a. *The intelligent woman's guide to manhunting.* New York: Lyle Stuart and Dell Publishing. Rev. ed. *The intelligent woman's guide to dating and mating.* Secaucus, N.J.: Lyle Stuart, 1979.

———. 1963b. *Sex and the single man.* New York: Lyle Stuart and Dell.

———. 1965. *The case for sexual liberty.* Tucson, Ariz.: Seymour Press.

———. 1976. *Sex and the liberated man.* Secaucus, N.J.: Lyle Stuart.

———. 1988. *How to stubbornly refuse to make yourself miserable about anything—yes, anything!* Secaucus, N.J.: Lyle Stuart.

———. 1991. Achieving self-actualization. *Journal of Social Behavior and Personality* 6, no. 5: 1–18. Reprint New York: Institute for Rational-Emotive Therapy.

———. 1994. *Reason and emotion in psychotherapy.* Revised and updated. New York: Birch Lane Press.

———. 1996. *Better, deeper and more enduring brief therapy.* New York: Brunner/Mazel.

Ellis, A., and R. A. Harper. 1961. *A guide to successful marriage.* North Hollywood, Calif: Wilshire Books.

———. 1975. *A new guide to rational living.* North Hollywood, Calif.: Wilshire Books.

Ellis, A., R. A. Harper, S. Dyer, R. Timmons, R. Hill, and N. Kavinoky. 1952. Premarital sex relations. *Marriage and Family Living* 14: 229–36.

Ellis, A., and E. Sagarin. 1964. *Nymphomania: A study of the oversexed woman*. New York: Gilbert Press and MacFadden-Bartell.

Ellis, H. 1936. *Studies in the psychology of sex*. 2 vols. New York: Random House.

Freud, S. 1965. *Standard edition of the complete psychological works of Sigmund Freud*. New York: Basic Books.

Kelly, G. L. 1953. *Sex manual for those married or about to be*. Augusta, Ga.: Southern Medical Supply Company.

Kinsey, A. C., W. B. Pomeroy, and C. E. Martin. 1948. *Sexual behavior in the human male*. Philadelphia: Saunders.

Kinsey, A. C., W. B. Pomeroy, C. E. Martin, and P. H. Gebhard. 1953. *Sexual behavior in the human female*. Philadelphia: Saunders.

LoPiccolo, J., R. Stewart, and B. Watkins. 1972. Treatment of erectile failure and ejaculatory incompetence with homosexual etiology. *Behavior Therapy* 3: 1–4.

LoPiccolo, J., and L. LoPiccolo, eds. 1978. *Handbook of sex therapy*. New York: Plenum.

Masters, W. H., and V. E. Johnson. 1966. *Human sexual response*. Boston: Little, Brown.

———. 1970. *Human sexual inadequacy*. Boston: Little, Brown.

Pillay, A. P., and A. Ellis. 1953. *Sex, society and the individual*. Bombay: International Journal of Sexology.

14

The Sex History of an Average American Housewife

Marilyn A. Fithian, Ph.D.

Marilyn A. Fithian spent much of her early married life as a housewife. She, however, read widely about the current research in sexuality, and when she returned to college she continued her studies, and soon began to collaborate with William Hartman in doing both sex therapy and sex research.

NLIKE MOST OF my colleagues, I knew very early in my life that I wanted to be a sexologist. I didn't know what it was called then. Just as the little boy wanted to grow up to be a fireman or a policeman, and little girls wanted to be a nurse, I knew that I wanted to do sex research. The following is how I see the evolution of my life's work. My reaction and feelings about these events were important factors in my early and continued interest in the field. Once my youngest child entered kindergarten I went back to school. I obtained my degree and eventually became a licensed marriage, family, child therapist. Eventually, I earned a Ph.D. in sexology.

Where does one's experience and views of one's own sexuality begin? How is it molded and developed? What are the components that make up the sexuality of an individual? What are the experiences and events that shape how one views, acts, and reacts to sexual events? This is how I see it developing for me.

For many years I was the only grandchild in a relatively large family. I lived in an adult world where I was picked up, hugged, kissed, read to, and fussed over. At the same time, I was expected to be an adult. All of my role models were adults. My contact with other children was very limited and more by appointment only than "going out to play."

I lived at either one of my grandparents' homes for most of my childhood, until I was about thirteen. There were intermittent times when my parents lived elsewhere, but again, it involved few people my own age. This, however, did not preclude early sexual experiences. The first occurred when I was between eighteen months and three years old. We had come to California from my father's family ranch in Oregon when I was eighteen months old. My father was looking for a job in California.

We were living with my mother's stepfather and her mother in a house always filled with young adults, aunts, uncles, and cousins. It was a two-bedroom house and relatives slept on pallets in the hall or on the couch. There was always room for one more. I slept on two large overstuffed chairs pushed together. I was too little to climb out of bed myself; someone had to pick me up to take me out of bed.

On this particular early morning a cousin was sleeping on the couch. I thought of him as an adult although he must have been only a teenager, which gives me a different perspective on his behavior. He was at an age where there were raging hormones at work and not really anywhere to go or do much about them. This was in the early 1920s and one did not have the options that are available today.

What happened? Nothing, really. He picked me up and put me in bed with him. He placed my very small hand on this big hard thing and tried to get me to move my hand back and forth with his hand. I did absolutely nothing. I kept my hand limp and if he didn't move it then it just lay there on what I was later to learn was called a penis. At about two, I didn't know what it was. My thoughts were, "there must be something wrong with this because it has never happened to me with my father or my grandfather." They were my role models and the ones who oriented me in what to do and not to do regarding males. When I could, I slipped off the couch and went into the bedroom where my father picked me up and put me in bed between him and my mother. There I felt safe.

Later, when I started school, I was flashed a couple of times. But since I had been told what to do in such a situation by my mother, I reported it when I arrived at school and apparently the men were caught. My mother and grandparents talked about this when I was older. I mention these incidents because I don't remember them but my relatives knew. I wondered, as an adult, if I didn't remember because they knew? Most of the events that I remember my parents knew nothing about.

I remember playing on the bars at an older girl's home when I was about six. I noticed blood on her bloomers (we wore bloomers back then), and asked her if she had hurt herself. She became hysterical and went into the house crying. When I went home and told my grandmother about it, she explained menstruation to me. I felt bad for my friend since no one had ever told her anything about menstruation.

My mother and I spent summers down at the beach with one of her sorority sisters and her two daughters. There was a playhouse out in back where we would go to play. One day, we decided we would play Jesus Christ being crucified. That meant off with the clothes. He, of course, was flagellated as he walked to the cross. I don't even remember what we used to flagellate each other in turn as we played the role. I never thought of the experience as being sexual at the time, but of course it was. We did get pretty excited but lashing each other as we played the crucifixion scene was the extent of it. I probably recall the incident because a neighbor boy peeked in the window and saw us. We obviously felt we were doing something we should not be doing since we were concerned he would tell our parents. We were all scared but nothing happened.

I was never into sexual explorations although the two sisters involved in the above incident were involved in some sort of sex play with each other. I was invited to participate but was never really interested. Why would anyone want to put a pencil up their vagina? That was my reaction to it. As an adult it made more sense when I found I could not put a tampon in. That scared me because my friends all wore them and I couldn't push it in. I talked to a doctor friend of my parents who explained to me about a hymen. Later, I had several students when I taught at the university who came in to talk to me about this same experience. They were afraid something was wrong with them.

My aunt lived in Hollywood. She had a nightly radio show. (This was long before TV.) She knew quite a few movie stars and had an apartment behind Wallace Beery's home. She spent her free time at grandmother's so we always heard the latest Hollywood gossip. Sex was talked about indirectly in the home since dinner conversations often included parents or grandparents talking about who was sleeping with whom, who had a new homosexual lover, and so on.

My grandparents went to the Klondike during the gold rush in 1898. My grandfather was the district attorney of Nome and my grandmother became the social leader. She often talked about her experiences at that time. One of the most often told stories was the one where a smallpox epidemic decimated the population. There were few women. In fact, wives and prostitutes were the only females, and most of the men had no one to care for them. Grandmother took over a warehouse as a makeshift hospital. Since none of the wives would help nurse all the sick, the town prostitutes took over the care of the men. This was when her attitude about prostitutes changed. Their willingness to take care of the sick and the dying and to spend long hours without respite impressed Grandmother. She was very negative about the local housewives who refused to help in any way. Grandmother always viewed prostitutes in a positive light as a result of this experience. I never heard the negative things that other children were exposed to about prostitution. In my household they were looked upon as worthwhile human beings.

My parents led an active social life and had many friends who were sorority sisters or fraternity brothers. They were professionals who were said to be more liberal sexually than less educated people. I suspect they were just more open about it. When I married into a middle-class situation, I found just as much sexual activity but much less talk about it. People were more judgmental and much more uptight. Lots of denial but plenty of activity and a great deal of guilt.

I was married and a mother by the time I was nineteen. By the time I was twenty-two, I had read everything available in the public library related to sex. Mainly the works of Havelock Ellis, Sigmund Freud, and that group of people. The book on Ellis from his childhood sexual experiences to his adult impotency was fascinating. His account of marriage to a lesbian and his later relationships with other women was insightful.

Several things occurred that were important to me in reinforcing my decision to work in the sexual field when I could. They did not relate to me directly but affected me emotionally. Friends jumped off refrigerators or used coat hangers to terminate pregnancies. A friend's husband killed her when he caught her with another man. Friends were having affairs. Leaving a spouse for someone else. Becoming pregnant by someone other than their husband. Suicides related to sexual behavior were causing problems. I was often the one consulted about what to do, but I felt totally unqualified.

I lived a fairly normal middle-class life with four children. I became the mother of three boys and a girl in that order, active in PTA, scouting (where I received the Scouters Award for my services), church and recreational activities. I lived in a rural dairy community of 7,500 people close to a large metropolitan area. I certainly would consider it a typical small-town community. My classmates ran the full spectrum of social class: some dropped out and others became millionaires, so it seemed to be fairly representative of the culture at large.

Not only were a number of male homosexuals and lesbians among the people I knew but also couples where the male was bisexual. This was long before such behavior was openly talked about or admitted.

One woman friend talked about coming home to find her husband dressed in her full-length girdle with his best male friend in the bedroom. Her concern was "it was the middle of the day, what if the kids had come home." Or the husband caught in a compromising situation at work with one of the men he supervised. The threat to the job and family security was of great concern to the wife. Another was involved sexually with his young daughter. These men had intercourse several times a week with their spouses. They also were involved as well with other women. The wives wanted to know what to do and how to handle the situation, but I really couldn't tell them. Their only solution was divorce since there was no such thing as sex therapy back then. These events further motivated me to alleviate in some way the problems my friends faced.

When the youngest of my four children entered kindergarten I returned to school. I was uncertain about a major since I wanted to do sex research, but such a program was unavailable. A close friend said I should major in sociology. He felt it would better serve my interest than psychology.

At that time there were no courses in human sexuality and what was available was often inaccurate information. My health science teacher informed the class that masturbation caused insanity. I couldn't believe an educated man knew so little about sexuality. To give that information to students, some of whom obviously were involved in masturbation, was unconscionable.

Classes in anthropology were interesting in relation to sexual behaviors in primitive and other cultures. Often, extra reading assignments gave a great deal of background information in the sex field. Cross-cultural studies and sexual behavior among primitive people were all important to my future understanding of sexuality. Later papers such as the symbolic meaning of sex, the meaning of sexuality, sexuality and race, and so on, all were beneficial.

Where there were no courses in sexuality I made my own. Sociology classes allowed me to investigate various areas of sexuality as part of my class assignments. As a result, I read and wrote reports and papers on topics such as incest, homosexuality, birth control, sexual symbolism, art and sex, sexual behavior and social class, prostitution and women's issues, to name a few. All of this information has helped me in my later work in the sexual field.

As a student, I found a place to buy banned books. As an avid reader I purchased many used books. When as a college student I needed reference books on sex little was available. I asked the man at the Acres of Books in Long Beach, which I often frequented, if he had any books on sex I could use for my research papers. I followed him to a secret room about six feet long and five feet wide with stacks of books on the floor and up all the walls for about ten feet, with a ladder to reach those books higher up. I was locked in and he came and checked on me from time to time. I visited this room regularly over the years as each paper was researched. I never left without a large shopping bag full of sex books. My recurring fantasy was that there would be a major earthquake while I was in there and I would be inundated with sex books.

Later, when I taught, I aided in the selection of books for the university library from that bookshop. I was I infuriated when I found the school library put them in a locked cage. The only way you could get to them was if someone went in there with you. They stood by you until you were finished looking for what you wanted. I thought it was humiliating for students to have to be put through this. When I questioned the librarians about this objectionable practice, they said "students tore the pictures out of the books." Few of the books even had pictures.

As a junior, I read an ad in the *American Sociological Journal* about a new organization called the Society for the Scientific Study of Sex. You had to have a master's degree to join, which I didn't have. I asked my advisor if she thought they would accept me. I was anxious to receive the journal since it was in my area of interest. She said, "I am sure if you send your money they will accept it." They did. I have been on the national board of the organization several times and a Western Regional Officer a number of times. Twice I was president of the Western Region. I am still a member on a retired status. Later, when it formed, I joined the Association of Sex Educator, Counselors, and Therapists and was a member for many years. Both organizations have honored me for work in the sex field.

In my senior class in Research Methodology, I worked up a sexual research questionnaire projected for women magazines like *Cosmopolitan* or *Ladies Home Journal*. My instructor was very impressed with it but said "such a thing would never happen." It would be another fifteen years before such a project did appear in *Cosmopolitan*. Other magazines have also done sex surveys.

My papers in the sexual area interested some of my teachers and resulted in my being asked to teach classes at the university. A female faculty member became ill and asked me to teach her class in deviant behavior. A cross-cultural study of prostitution resulted in being asked to teach a comparative literature class in the English department.

When my husband and I were trying to work our marriage out, we went to the Counseling Center at the university. After a few sessions my husband quit going, but I continued on a while. I was then asked if I would be interested in doing counseling at the center. It gave me some formal counseling experience for which I was grateful. Since there was internal political conflict between the sociology department and a member of the counseling department, I was asked by the sociology department to make a choice between working there or teaching. I chose the latter. I also did library research for two professors in the sociology department who were working on a paper on marriage and the family. I gathered a great deal of information for them on sexual behavior.

My thirteen years of teaching at California State University at Long Beach was an important adjunct to my sex education. First, I was a moderator in a marriage class in which students talked about their fears, anxieties, and stress related to marriage and sex. Here I learned about the myths and misconceptions that young people had. One young woman said, "I could never ever have sex with a man. I have never ever let anyone see me nude." She had managed to go all the way through high school and college gym classes without ever having taken a shower with other girls. She had never been nude in front of any member of her family since she was a small child. In later therapy we experienced such cases and by then I knew how to deal with them.

My years as an instructor in folklore and mythology in first the English department then in the comparative literature department were probably the most productive. I usually team taught although I also had classes on my own. When I team taught I dealt exclusively with the sexual aspects of folklore and mythology. In class we discussed ritual circumcision among males and females and the ramifications of this, various love philters and potions, the *Malleus Maleficarum* and its description of impotence brought on by a witch placing a spell on a man, witchcraft in general and its relationship to sexuality—everything from Comstock to corn flakes. Research on the poltergeist and its relationship to puberty was of considerable interest to students. Some had experienced sexual frustration in their relationships and interesting things were happening to them. There were open discussions and each student kept a journal that was turned in each week. Also, students had to have two counseling appointments a semester to come in and talk. Some of these private discussions on their sexuality were most interesting. I learned a lot about what people think, believe, and do sexually. Later, I taught human sexuality in the psychology department.

A study of social nudism conducted by Dr. Hartman done in the mid-sixties included questions about sexual behavior at my suggestion. We did an in-depth study of social nudism together, resulting in a book, *Nudist Society*, a biological, psychological, social approach. Later we did a study of nonorgasmic women together. Dr. Hartman had started it and when he came back from a session of putting women on pelvic exercises, I asked him how he knew the original condition of the pelvis and the changes that occurred with exercises. We then had a long discussion which resulted in our doing a three-year study of nonorgasmic women. We examined the vaginas of the women before the pelvic exercises on a monthly basis up through their becoming orgasmic. As these women become orgasmic new women were added to the study.

I was never adverse to doing research on myself if I was curious about something. I noticed that when angry I seemed to have pelvic congestion. I took a measurement shortly after a disagreement with someone and found that there was considerable vasocongestion[1] in the pelvis. As a sample of one it didn't mean much but when we did some thermography we further explored this phenomenon and found again that with anger or fighting what might be considered sexual arousal occurred. This was important in working with couples where there was fighting going on. It became obvious that the fighting was foreplay to their sexual activities. The literature had indicated that in therapy with a couple who fought, when you changed that behavior they often divorced. That would explain what was happening. If you took away the foreplay and didn't replace it, their sex life might deteriorate. It also explained why some people would not press changes against a partner when fighting occurred and the police were called.

About 1966, when Dr. Hartman asked me to open the Center for Marital and Sexual Studies with him, I was reluctant. Both our research studies had gone well and we had no problems working together. I had been separated from my husband since the late fifties and Dr. Hartman was still attempting to resolve marital problems of his own. I felt that working in a situation where we would be seeing each other daily for long periods of time might cause him problems, and I was concerned about that.

Also, his main interest was in doing sex therapy; while mine was in sex research. After considerable discussion we decided we could each do what we were mainly interested in doing. We wrote two books, *Treatment of Sexual Dysfunction* in 1972, on sex therapy, and *Any Man Can* in 1984, based on our research findings on multiply orgasmic men.

Where I personally have not had what I would consider problems concerning my work, I can't say this for my family. During the Vietnam War, both my oldest son and my son-in-law each spent a couple of days being grilled on my work and what I did. There was a question about whether they should get a top-security clearance. They did receive it, but they felt uncomfortable about the experience and wrote me about it.

When a younger son questioned me about my work, I talked to my children about it, and how I was still their mom; but I had gone to school to be trained so I could support myself and what I was doing was professional. There have been no problems since. They save articles for me, tell others about what I do, and let me know when a program on sex is on TV. They borrow books for friends who have sexual problems. They read what I write and certainly some of them practice what they

---

1. Vasocongestion is the increase in the amount of blood concentrated in certain body tissues. It is the primary physiological response to sexual stimulation.

read. When a grandson lost one of my books in a recent move he immediately wanted to know if he could have another one. All my grandchildren have helped on various of my numerous writing projects, for which I am very grateful. I have not had the problems some of my colleagues have apparently had with their families.

While I am semi-retired, I am still involved in writing and an occasional intensive sex therapy case and some individual therapy cases. With a new computer in the office, I hope to be able to do research on all of the data that has been collected over the years, much of which has never been analyzed. Some of this material is interesting and may be beneficial in enhancing sexual knowledge once it is made available.

I find in therapy and among friends that there is still a lack of information as well as a lack of funding for sex research. This is a loss for everyone. Sex affects all of us in one way or another, not only those who don't have any sexual conflicts but those who have many. As we learn more about these extremes and everything in between, the healthier and happier a nation we will be.

I recently read books on two murders which might have resulted in no conviction in one case and a better understanding in the second if the lawyers, judges, juries, and people generally had known more about sexuality. Obviously the lack of knowledge affects society in many ways.

I was really glad when women could go to a physician for an unwanted pregnancy. Although I am opposed to abortion, I feel women should have a choice. I now feel the procedure is greatly overused, however; women resort to abortion rather than contraception. I still hear women say, "The pill is unsafe and if I get pregnant I will have an abortion." The pill is much safer than an abortion.

Something happened to me as I was writing this that was important and meaningful to me. We get cards at Christmas, letters, baby pictures, and wedding and birth announcements from former clients. And often they come and visit or call us. But as I was preparing dinner recently, the telephone rang. A man's voice said: "This is ———. You may not remember me but you changed my life. I was a student thirty years ago at the university. I worked with you and Dr. Hartman on your nudist research data. You gave me the self-confidence and self-concept needed to be successful in life. I was out in California and I wanted to look you up. I would like to come and see you if I can. I may not get to see you but I wanted you to know how much what you said meant to me. You didn't know I was gay because I hadn't come out yet and was fairly secretive back then about it. We were talking and sex and homosexuality came up, and you said homosexuals have a right for a good life and good sex with loving and caring relationships. Those things are important for people. I have kept track of you and your work for the last thirty years." The conversation lasted for several more minutes. He said he was out with a friend with AIDS who was in a hospice, and he himself had been HIV-positive for twelve years. My former student was in good health and taking care of himself. In fact, he was able to visit and we had a good chat. He had led a very productive and interesting life and was a well-known professional in his field.

One of the questions asked of me is how working in the sex field affected my own sex life. I would say not at all. Most of what I learned, I learned before becoming a professional. Observing over a thousand people copulating or masturbating, seeing many porno films and live shows as a professional had little influence on my sexuality. To my knowledge, I never became aroused but stayed strictly in a professional observer role. I never personalized the experiences. I must say, however, that recently I attended a movie in a nonprofessional capacity and I found about a quarter of the way through that my body had a great deal of tension. I realized it was sexual, so I relaxed and enjoyed it. I thought it was one of the best movies I had seen in a long time, although it was severely criticized by the reviewers. I wondered if their criticism was based on their own unwelcome reaction to the film. I would love to have had the audience hooked up to measure their sexual arousal. We have investigated buying the film, so who knows, that might be a future research project.

I have found the field of human sexuality to be rewarding and interesting. Rewarding in the sense that I am able to impart information to people that has helped them be more accepting of themselves and their own sexuality. I know from my own life experiences that there is much more to sex than sex. Many things pertaining to sexuality occurred throughout my life that continued to keep me interested and focused on the area of sexual behavior.

15

From Theology to Evolution to Embryology to Sex: The Making of One Sexologist

Robert T. Francoeur, Ph.D.

Robert T. Francoeur, a biologist as well as a married Catholic priest, has taught a course on human sexuality at Fairleigh Dickinson University in New Jersey since 1972. A prolific author for both the popular and academic media, he recently edited The Complete Dictionary of Sexology *and the multi-volume* International Encyclopedia of Sexuality.

IN 1945, INSPIRED by two wonderful nuns, my seventh- and eighth-grade teachers, I moved from a Catholic elementary school in Detroit to the minor seminary and studied to become a priest. In the next eight years of high school and college, sex would be explicitly mentioned only once. I don't recall what the priest told us about sex in my sophomore year of high school, but it couldn't have been very detailed—probably only a tiny diagram of the male drawn on the board and the implication that a male somehow used his anatomy in some combination with a women to make a baby. Somewhere in my high school years my father took me into our basement and offered to explain "the facts of life." He was greatly relieved and stopped the moment I told him Fr. Majewski had told us "all about that."

I don't recall the seminary's spiritual director ever talking directly and candidly about sex proper but we did hear a lot about the evils of "self-abuse" and "particular friendships." We were never told explicitly what a "particular friendship" was or why it was so dangerous, but maybe I was just too naive to understand. (I had only recently discovered the superficial anatomical differences between men and women in the *National Geographic* articles on ancient Greece and Egypt, which my uncle always hid when my cousins and I visited for holiday celebrations.) We were told that if we walked around the athletic field with the same classmate more than twice in a week we had a "particular friendship" and had to break it off. I had no idea why. It was impossible to imagine two males doing anything sexually when I didn't even have a clear idea of what a male and female did with their different anatomies.

Besides I had a more pressing, recurring problem. Those pictures of nude Grecian and Egyptian maidens fueled too many troubling, obviously sinful, fantasies. Frequent confession with renewed consecrations to the Virgin Mary as taught by St. Louis de Montfort were little help in nightly battles to fall asleep without the relaxation of self-abuse. At one point in college, my battle with recurring temptations brought on by surging adolescent hormones resulted in vasocongestion that made walking painful. My spiritual director sent me to a Catholic urologist who gave me a complete physical and pronounced me perfectly normal and healthy. Being a good Catholic, he never explained the cause of my pain or its obvious solution!

When I graduated tied for last place in my college class I was told I was not bright enough and too much of a nonconformist to advance to the major seminary and four years of theology. (Sacred Heart Seminary had a very Prussian regimentation, using the bell-and-rote memory approach to education that just didn't engage me.)

That crushing blow to my future was the start of my redemption and salvation. I still desperately wanted to become a priest, so I found a job teaching biology and physics in a Catholic high school, replacing a sick nun. I had flunked college physics and "aced" my high school biology course, but it was a job and allowed me to take some graduate courses in education and biology with the Jesuits at the University of Detroit while I looked for a new bishop and diocese to sponsor my studies. At U. of D. a marvelous lay professor engaged my curiosity about sex by introducing me to the wonders of embryology and evolution that have enthralled me ever since.

A year later the bishop of Steubenville, Ohio, agreed to let me study for the priesthood in his diocese. I left for St. Vincent's, a hundred-year-old Benedictine monastery, college, and major seminary in the Blue Ridge Mountains just east of Pittsburgh. I still keep in touch with some of the monks who led me into the riches of Catholic theology and biblical studies. These men were also warm and open. They treated us like young men, not robots responding to bells and punished with work-crew assignments when our response was tardy. St. Vincent's was a creative, growth-inspiring environment.

Knowing that I would be expected to teach in one of the diocesan high schools after ordination, I continued my graduate studies in biology during summers at home in Detroit. My interest in biology and the open atmosphere at St. Vincent's led me into the biology labs over in the college where I was immediately charmed by the two biologists I met there, Fr. Edward and Fr. Maximilian. Fr. Ed had his doctorate in embryology from Columbia, and Fr. Max was a renowned arctic botanist. Both were enthusiastic evolutionists who had long argued that Catholic theology and evolution were compatible. Their tales of pioneering, heroic theologians and scientists who found no conflict between their faith and their science were irresistible. They encouraged and supported my summer work in biology and urged me to work on a master's degree in theology at St. Vincent's.

One day while talking about possible thesis subjects, one of my classmates, Bernie, suggested I read Lecomte du Nouy's best-seller *Human Destiny* and use his attempted synthesis of theology and evolution for my thesis. I read *Human Destiny* and quickly decided I had the perfect subject. One day, while pursuing my research in the library, the librarian came over to tell me one of the monks had left an issue of *Cross Currents,* a liberal intellectual Catholic quarterly, for me. To this day I have no idea who that monk was, but the article he wanted me to read changed my life and gave me a worldview, a *Weltanschauung,* that has guided my work in sexology and my daily living every day since.

The article was a summary by a French cleric and theologian of the evolutionary synthesis of Pierre Teilhard de Chardin. Teilhard was a French Jesuit paleontologist, poet, visionary, and theologian who in the 1920s had so upset the orthodox Vatican he was exiled to the Gobi Desert of Outer Mongolia. Teilhard gained worldwide fame as one of the discoverers of the fossil Peking Man, but it was his many unpublished essays describing an evolutionary process worldview, a cosmogenesis, a synthesis of the best of liberal cutting-edge Catholic theology with modern paleontology and evolutionary science, that inspired me and countless others. My introduction to Teilhard came a year after he died, but it quickly led me to bold and impassioned correspondence with his many friends in France, and years later to found the American Teilhard de Chardin Association. Teilhard's ideas went far beyond LeComte du Nouy's and were quickly incorporated into my master's thesis. My thesis mentor, Fr. Demetrius, had studied at École Biblique in Jerusalem, and so I was fortunate to have his support and encouragement to pursue Teilhard's revolutionary synthesis.

My memories of St. Vincent's include getting my hands on a little pamphlet titled *Happiness in Marriage.* Published with the endorsement of the Canadian bishops, it had been banned in the United States. Bernie and I decided to type out the whole pamphlet on our manual typewriters and make carbon copies for our twenty-two classmates. We read this tame description of marital—that's sexual—intercourse over and over. The pamphlet had no anatomical diagrams, those we got out of my biology texts. The monks knew about our effort, but never interfered with our brazen curiosity. They never showed any of the obsessiveness with sex, "self-abuse," and "particular friendships" I almost drowned in at Sacred Heart.

Another early sexological venture that is very vivid for me came two weeks before ordination when my good friend and classmate Skippy dropped by to ask my help. We were studying for a final exam in canon law, and he just could not understand what Fr. Matthew had said about impotence being an impediment to marriage. The two-inch diagrams of male and female anatomy Fr. Matthew put on the board were not all that clear from thirty feet away! Skip just couldn't understand why a man couldn't have an erection any time he wanted one. The more I explained the more confused Skippy became, and the more frustrated I got. Finally, I challenged Skip when he said he could have an erection any time he wanted. "Show me!" He did—sticking his tongue out. I slumped in my chair, realizing I had assumed too much. Off my shelf came a biology text with line drawings of a penis and vagina. Skip left with accurate information about impotence, oral sex, and vaginal intercourse. When two other classmates came by with the same question and demonstrated their "erectile" ability, I panicked, realizing the twenty-four of us would be heading out into parishes to do marriage counseling in a few weeks. Down in the smoker that evening, I went around asking my classmates if they would like to join me and Fr. Ed over in the biology lab the next day to watch a movie on sex education the monks used in the prep school. "Sure! What time? I'll be there!" Three weeks later we were ordained and went off to counsel our parishioners about their marriage problems.

In 1958, with my master's degree in biology almost finished and my master's degree in theology in hand, I headed off to Steubenville, where for three years I was a parish priest and taught biology and religion in Steubenville Catholic Central. Despite this being my first full-time teaching experience, Sister Joan of Arc and I agreed we wanted to include some elementary sex education in our four sections of sophomore biology. I even encouraged some of the science club members to do projects related to reproduction, making models of chromosome meiosis in egg and sperm production with fetal pictures from my embryology textbook. This daring venture soon brought down the wrath of the principal, Fr. Kramer, who decided Sister Joan of Arc should teach the girls and I should teach the boys. In a large coed school, separating the boys and girls in biology was like plastering a red CENSORED-FORBIDDEN sign on the door of our classroom, and the students responded with appropriate giggles and sly looks anytime we mentioned anything remotely connected with "that subject." Twenty years later, after I had married with the Vatican's permission, I heard that Sister Joan of Arc had left the convent and was happily married in Texas.

In the parish and high school, I was oblivious of situations which in hindsight I know involved a few of my fellow priests in sexual relations with the altar boys or older women parishioners. Although there was an occasional gossipy allusion to such situations, I never heard any overt mention. Still totally inexperienced sexually and a virgin at thirty, I protected my abiding interest in questions sexological by hiding them within my more legitimate interest in biology (embryology), evolution, and Teilhard.

My interest in Teilhard and my bishop's encouragement to go for a doctorate in biology took me to Johns Hopkins University in 1963. During my year at Hopkins I was chaplain and taught biology at Mount St. Agnes, a small women's college. Some of the nuns said I should use an embryology text that did not show the male anatomy and dissect only female cats in the anatomy lab. I ordered male, female, and pregnant cats for dissection. Meanwhile, Sister Faith and I arranged to leave our office doors and windows unlocked as a convenient way for "the girls" to slip out of the fourth-floor dormitory and out the back door for a few post-curfew hours with their boyfriends. We sadly joked about "the girls" being handed a thick telephone book as they headed out for a date (to protect them against pregnancy in case they sat on the boyfriend's lap), and tried to calm the occasional student denounced for wearing skirts and shiny leather shoes.

My bishop fully supported me when my first book, *The World of Teilhard de*

Chardin, was banned by the Vatican before it was published. He also fully supported my publishing several articles defending the morality of Catholic married couples using the birth control pill or other artificial contraceptives according to their conscience. This was the era of the Second Vatican Council and Pope John XXIII was throwing open the windows to change. Teilhard was "in" and my articles advocating the acceptance of artificial birth control appeared on the front page of many diocesan and national Catholic publications.

In 1962 I returned to Steubenville for a year and then headed off to finish my doctorate in embryology at Fordham University. Two years at Fordham and I was ready to look for a full-time teaching position. My bishop cautioned me not to apply to any Catholic college. With my interest in evolution, process theology, and, yes, sex, he thought I would be safer and more comfortable in a non-church-affiliated institution. A final year at the University of Delaware to finish my research in experimental embryology, and I joined the faculty at Fairleigh Dickinson University in Madison, New Jersey. Thirty-one years later I'm still at this private university where I have taught undergraduate and graduate sexuality courses since 1971 with only one or two minor problems. (Bishop Mussio's sensitive, commonsense advice and support worked.)

Before delving into my career in sexology at Fairleigh, I need to insert a brief diversion. While at Fordham in 1963–64, Vinny, my lab partner and buddy, was trying to convince his parents it was okay for him to marry his girlfriend, Kathy. Vinny's Irish Catholic parents expected him to become the doctor and his brother the priest. Being from divorced parents in Minnesota, Kathy didn't meet their expectations. Vinny decided to invite Kathy to visit and I would join them on a date to "pass inspection on Kathy" and, as the all-knowing priest, persuade Vinny's parents she was okay. The other fellows in the lab thought this was crazy and persuaded Vinny to find me a blind date and not tell Kathy I was a priest. Vinny finally married Kathy, and I informed my bishop I wanted to marry my blind date, Anna, and remain functioning as a Catholic priest teaching biology and embryology at Fairleigh Dickinson. Unexpectedly my bishop found no problem with my outrageous proposal. Twice he wrote to Rome endorsing my radical request to marry and remain functional as a priest. Twice we were turned down. Finally we sent a civil marriage certificate with a third request to Rome. By accident, they gave rubber-stamp approval to my request, leaving me in a legal no-man's land, a validly married priest who was never forbidden to function. Three years later, when Anna and I visited my bishop with our first daughter, I was a nervous wreck as Nicole ran around the bishop's art- and antique-filled home. Bishop Mussio laughed and handed her a giant red strawberry.

In 1970, my friend and biology colleague Ruth Elsasser took a sabbatical to develop a program for respiratory therapists, radiographers, and physical therapy assistants. Ruth asked me to develop and teach courses in death and dying, medical ethics, and sexuality. I had just published a book on new trends in human reproduction, *Utopian Motherhood,* and started research for *Eve's New Rib,* which would examine the social implications and impact of artificial insemination, artificial wombs, embryo transplants, and surrogate mothers on our experience of being male and female, on marriage and family.

At a meeting in Toronto of the National Council on Family Relations, I met Dick Price, one of the early producers of sexually explicit education films. Dick invited me to watch a film of John Money he had produced. I sweated and squirmed in a corner chair as I watched the table top projector show a couple naked in bed, with a giant vibrator, and talking about having sex as they "did it." I had never seen anything like this, but I couldn't leave because Lester Kirkendall, Wardell Pomeroy, and Paul Gebhard were between me and the door. I survived my embarrassment, and was soon relaxed enough to joke and chat with Kirk, Paul, Wardell, and Dick.

Returning to Fairleigh, I couldn't resist telling my advanced embryology students about my experience. "Hey, Doc, how about getting those films and showing them to us?" "That might be possible. This fellow Price has his office next door to our Teaneck campus." I called Dick and he was delighted. Friday morning Dick and I arrived for class with my eleven biology major seniors. The noise grew louder as we approached my classroom, and then I saw two hundred or more students milling around the door. Panic.

After sending everyone but my eleven students back to the dormitories, I tried to introduce Dick. My panic had not subsided and I did a good bit of stammering before Dick stepped forward to suggest I sit down and relax while he introduced himself and showed his films.

I didn't get fired. In fact, after I told Ruth Elsasser about my experience, my dean and the former biology chairman offered me two thousand dollars to buy some of these new sexually explicit education films and start a proper course on human sexuality.

Dick Price quickly became a good friend and advisor. Early on, he took me to one of the monthly meetings of the Society for the Scientific Study of Sex at the Barbizon Plaza Hotel in midtown Manhattan. As we entered, Dick cornered John Money and Wardell Pomeroy, and told them they would be endorsing my membership application. In subsequent years, I served as president of the society's eastern region and enjoyed many years of work with dear friends in the society, and in the American Association of Sex Educators, Counselors and Therapists, the Groves Conference on Marriage and the Family, and other sexological organizations.

By the late 1970s, we were offering three or four sections of human sexuality both fall and spring semesters, and a couple of sections in the summer. From the start, we had "Sex Saturday/Sunday," a one- or two-day Sexual Attitude Reassessment (SAR) multimedia marathon of films and small-group discussions. On the fifth weekend of the course, up to three hundred students and their Significant Others (SOs), including parents; siblings; boy and girlfriends; favorite rabbi, nun, or priest; grandparents; and supportive hand-holding friends, would stagger out of the dormitories and parking lots to find their way to the main auditorium. As they walked in, they found the walls covered with poster boards filled with male and female centerfolds. Experimentation and student feedback led us eventually to a nine-hour Sex Saturday with three film sessions followed by small-group discussions. My group leaders were enthusiastic volunteers, sex-positive teachers from high schools and colleges in Jersey and New York City. Some leaders even brought their own students and SOs from Montclair State College, Rutgers University, the doctoral program in sexuality at New York University, and elsewhere.

After more than fifty SARs and something like six thousand participants, Saturday became an institution on our conservative campus. Students delighted in trying to embarrass me in front of faculty and administrators by asking a friend if they "had had sex with Francoeur," or "been to Bob's Sex Saturday?" as they passed by me talking with a colleague.

Only once did Sex Saturday encounter a problem. I always covered my back when we got a new dean by scheduling a brief meeting to let her or him know about my unusual course, and the sexually explicit films I used. This way, if a complaint came in, they would not be caught unprepared. One new dean asked if he could attend, and said his psychologist wife might be interested in working as a group leader. Both showed up, and so did a reporter from the *New York Times.* The reporter stayed for the whole nine hours, and interviewed students, parents, and, of course, the new dean. "Fairleigh is a liberal arts college, and a liberal arts education has to be a balance between the intellectual and the emotional. Bob's sex course is one of the few courses that deals with both the emotional and the cognitive. It's a great educational experience."

When a fair and balanced long article on our SAR appeared on the front page of the Family Section of the *New York Times* a few days later, the headline was something else: "New Jersey College Uses Porn Films in Sex Education Course." The telephones in the dean's and president's offices rang off the hook for several days. Morality in Media wanted to send observers to my class, maintaining that any frontal nudity was obscene and pornographic. I was fortunate that my alerting the administrators to what I was doing in my course and the education philosophy behind it gave them the information they needed to defend me and my course. The furor died down in a week or so, and we all had a good laugh after I stopped sweating.

From the beginning, my friends and faculty colleagues have enjoyed telling outsiders in my presence about the course I teach and the fact that I have been a long-time contributor to *Forum* magazine published by *Penthouse.* But only because I take their comments as compliments and they know I will not be embarrassed by anything they say. Since the early 1970s, I have published popular but solid articles on sexual issues in *Forum* and a wide variety of popular magazines, including many Protestant, Catholic, and Jewish publications. Even when I published *Hot and Cool Sex: Cultures in Conflict* with a description of my several visits to Sandstone, an experimental sexually open community outside Los Angeles, and a detailed theology and sociology of sexually open marriages, I encountered no problems from my university colleagues. Any time my visits to Sandstone were mentioned, the comment was always added that I was there, of course, only as a scientific observer.

I never expected any problem or negative reaction when I published a *Complete Dictionary of Sexology* or a multivolume *International Encyclopedia of Sexuality*. But I have been pleased that my colleagues and university administrators seem to accept my appearances with transsexuals and transvestites on the outrageous "Morton Downey, Jr., Show" or with an allegedly pregnant male-to-female transsexual on the "Joan Rivers Show" as something they can be proud of because it says their university and mine is a liberal, progressive school that is not afraid of being on the cutting edge.

Looking back to my childhood, and especially the past thirty or so years I have taught, lectured, and published on sexuality, I believe the reason I have had such a smooth path is that I had some very good advice from now long-time friends like Dick Price, Wardell Pomeroy, John Money, and others. In essence, what these friends told me years ago was this: Know what you want to do, and why you want to do it. Be clear, honest, and in no way defensive when you explain to chairpersons, deans, administrators, or the public what you are doing, or what you want to do. Present a solid, positive philosophical position for your work. You may get some negative reactions behind your back, but up front very few will want to appear reactionary or anti-sex. Faculty and administrators like to appear progressive and open to new ideas, even when they are not. They will go along with you as long as you appear to know what you are doing and present strong arguments that let them know you have done your homework, are quite knowledgeable, and have talked with and are supported by experts with a solid reputation in the field.

As I look over the past I marvel at my good fortune. As I look to the future, I am not optimistic. I have watched several friends retire and seen their popular and still much-needed courses in human sexuality disappear from the course offerings. Talking with my chairman about my concerns, I'm not encouraged. I know there will be no one to take my place, not even a part-timer, despite the cost effectiveness of paying a part-timer the tuition of two students and leaving the income from thirty-three others for the university coffers. You can forget about the needs of the students in this era of bottom-line academic planning.

For me, as for many others, life has been a long and ongoing quest for understanding my own sexuality and human sexuality in general. For years I have tried to analyze, understand, and anticipate where our current rapidly changing society and culture is headed. I've long been fascinated with what the future may hold for us as we try to meet our needs for intimacy, nurturance, and love. My work in sexology has always had a very practical and personal dimension and root because it involves me, my family—wife, daughters, and brother—and a flowing network of friends who play and will play important, vital, and unique roles in my life-long quest to become as fully sexual a person as I can. Throughout my adventure in sexology, the link between sexuality and spirituality has always been an obsession.

16

The Evolution of a Sex Researcher

Paul H. Gebhard, Ph.D.

Paul Gebhard, an anthropologist, was a member of the Kinsey research team. After the death of Alfred Kinsey he became the director of the Institute for Sex Research at the University of Indiana in Bloomington, a position he held until his retirement.

L IKE MANY BOYS I liked to collect interesting things: rocks, fossils, insects, arrowheads, bird's nests, and so forth. While I did live in a city, I was on the outskirts so that open land was within walking distance and the neighborhood always had a few vacant lots where one could turn over stones and rummage around. My parents, other relatives, and their friends knew of my interests and sometimes gave me items. By age seven my father had built shelves around the walls of a basement room for my collections; I produced a sign (crayon on cardboard) "Gebhard Museum 1924" and attached it above the door. Since my family was well-to-do we always took an annual vacation, driving to most of the parks and other scenic places west of the Mississippi, and these travels allowed me to collect even more, for example, fragments from the Petrified Forest, some orange-red earth from Bryce Canyon, and a few potsherds from Mesa Verde.

As one might expect, I was very fond of museums and spent much time at the Colorado Museum of Natural History, a haven which I could easily reach by bicycle. While most of the staff were too busy to spend time with a preteenager, I did find several elderly men who, I now realize, must have been lonely. One in particular, a mineralogist, spent hours identifying minerals from my collection which by this time had been enormously enhanced by my grandfather's mineral collection which I discovered in the attic of my grandparent's mansion (along with a stamp collection and other goodies). This friendly reception emboldened me to apply for work at the museum in a letter dated December 1927. I quote it verbatim below:

Pres. of the Colorado Museum:

I am Paul Gebhard a boy of 10 but I have a good museum, it consists of a fine collection of minerals gotten from my grandpa. A miner owed him money so he paid it in minerals. Also some peculer shells found in Santigo Calf. Some stamps which a relative had been saving for 20 years a pheasant plume, hair ball, Indian bow, cigar bands some 14 years old, sparrow nest, gold, some rare agate, sugar beet, and a pack rat in a box with artifishel [*sic*] rocks, and background, with dirt on bottom. I also have some Dinasour shavings from my best friend Mr. Homer of the Ft. Collins Museum. You must excuse my writing for I did it by night by a bad light. If you want a map of my museum ask the man that checks your hat and coat. I wanted to know if you would let me have a job, dusting of the glasses or picking up papers for 2 cents per week my address is 617 Adams St. Denver Colo I wish you would drop in for a while to see my museum.

> Yours truly
> Paul Gebhard

(P.S.) I am a good artist and take lessons so my map will be good.

While this did not result in immediate employment, I was still welcome in the museum where I was tolerated in shops and offices forbidden to the general public. The director of the museum, Dr. Figgins, the archaeologist who discovered the famous Folsom point, gave me a few minutes and then ushered me out of his office for good.

When I was thirteen or fourteen my parents moved temporarily to San Diego for most of a year so that my mother could visit relatives, and I gravitated to the seashore to collect marine life and shells and to Balboa Park where there were museums. There I encountered an elderly paleontologist, Sternberg, who was famous for his early work around the turn of the century. He had a workplace where he was removing fossil bones from their matrix, restoring them, and piecing them together. He was a widower and I never knew if he had any relatives in the area, but he was quite lonely. He taught me about fossils, allowed me to help a bit, and as his reward had me listen to him loudly recite his poems which were dramatic and Miltonesque. They dealt with geological events and the mighty extinct fauna. He met my father and they took a liking to one another as they talked of the old days in the western states. Sternberg also accompanied me to some marine fossil sites I had discovered in a ravine and pronounced them as Pliocene. Out of affection for the old man my father purchased his Pliocene and Pleistocene marine fossils and donated them to the Colorado Museum. This gift had more effect on my employability than had my earlier letter; after we returned to Denver the museum allowed me to work gratis in the paleontology workshop under an old German, Reinheimer, who assigned me to less valuable fossils. The following summer I was taken on an expedition to an area around Torrington, Wyoming, where we recovered Eocene fossils. While I received no salary, I did get room (tent) and board. My parents did not learn until after the expedition that the area was in the throes of an epidemic of

Rocky Mountain spotted fever which had a mortality rate of over 50 percent. Knowing this we inspected ourselves and one another diligently.

As I got more into high school my interests shifted from paleontology to archaeology. I began visiting Dr. Renaud, the archaeologist at Denver University. When he discovered that I owned a model A Ford (he didn't drive) he enlisted me as one of his helpers on surface survey expeditions in New Mexico and southern Colorado. The other helpers were his college students. This reinforced my interest and I decided to become an archaeologist, a choice which disappointed my father who had hoped that I would go into business, preferably the cattle business which had occupied the entire Gebhard family ever since Henry Gebhard, my grandfather, had settled in Colorado in 1869.

When I graduated from high school I applied for admission to the University of Arizona which had a good archaeology department headed by an old reformed pothunter, Dean Byron Cummings. I was admitted and thereby became the first member of the family on my father's side to attend college. My maternal uncles had college educations; my mother had one year and would have continued had her father not died. Consequently, she was not dismayed by my choice of career. While at Arizona I participated in the excavation of some Hohokam sites, did a little searching around in Sonora, and put in one summer excavating the pueblo site of Kinishba. This all came to an end during my junior year. The university had compulsory ROTC, a fact of which I had been aware, but I was informed that it was a cavalry unit and I envisioned spending the time riding. In actuality I found myself in a scratchy, hot, khaki uniform with high-laced boots marching around on a baking dusty field. Consequently, I inquired of my fraternity brothers how many drills I could skip without being kicked out of the university and I skipped them in my sophomore year. Every year the ROTC collected the records and sorted them into three categories: good students who attended all or most drills and who were therefore promoted to sergeant, mediocre students who were promoted to corporal, and wretched students who were to remain privates. One of my fraternity brothers who assisted in this process noted my wretched record and, without ever telling me, inserted it into the pile of good records. Having been promoted to sergeant, I assumed that I could cut even more drills and risk nothing more than a demotion, and I did so. However, my unearned promotion eventually came to official attention; I was abruptly suspended from the university and told that I could remain only if I took the entire ROTC program over again. This did not appeal to me, so I departed Arizona and enrolled in Denver University and, at about the same time, applied to Harvard. I could not have chosen a better time to do so: Harvard's President Conant was trying to diversify the student body and I was one of the few applicants from Arizona and Colorado with a decent scholastic record. My departure from Arizona actually worked in my favor, for the admissions people at Harvard thought that I was some species of conscientious objector, and in their letter of acceptance they made some remarks about valuing young people who acted according to their convictions.

My stay at Denver University was to be brief. I heard that the Smithsonian was arranging an archaeological expedition to the Aleutian islands with Dr. Ales Hrdlicka as the leader; I applied and was accepted. Therefore in the spring of 1937 I found myself in the Aleutians and ultimately in the Commander Islands owned by the USSR. The group consisted of Hrdlicka and half a dozen volunteers, all young except for one man. While we were not paid, we did receive board, room, and marine transportation. This expedition reinforced my love of archaeology.

In the fall of 1937 I entered Harvard, the first time I had been east of the Mississippi except for Chicago. I arrived at Harvard Square wearing my blue jeans, a green velveteen Navajo shirt, a Navajo bracelet, and high-heeled Mexican shoes, and struck out on my own and soon discovered a clump of academic buildings, one of which I entered to ask where I could register. The lady I addressed gently told me that I could not register in Radcliffe and suggested I go across the street to Harvard. Culture shock was immediate and my velveteen shirt and jeans were first to go. In a cafeteria, as I reached for my plate, the counterman noted my bracelet and queried, "What are you, a fag?" Exit the bracelet. The high-heeled shoes were last to go, when two old ladies sitting across from me in the subway began remarking how tragic it was to see young people with deformed feet. Soon I conformed with a sober suit, a tie, a hat, and the standard green bookbag.

Harvard more than lived up to my expectations, but it refused to recognize Arizona as an equal and hence I had to enter as a sophomore. I majored in anthropology with an emphasis on archaeology and was taught by excellent professors, some of whom were famous, such as Ernest A. Hooton, Clyde Kluckhohn, Carlton Coon, and Lester W. Ward. I graduated cum laude (an honor given to about one-third of the graduates) in 1940, but my degree was B.S. rather than B.A. because I had no college Latin or Greek.

I went directly into graduate school with scholarships covering my tuition and the competition was even more fierce. Summers I spent in archaeology in Colorado and Mississippi with expenses covered but no salary. Most of one year I dropped out and worked as a WPA archaeologist to earn extra funds, and I treasure my resignation document from that organization which states as my reason for leaving "to return to Harvard." This WPA job educated me as to the sexual behavior and mores of the lower socioeconomic stratum. I was in charge of a crew of six men, all of them my seniors and several old enough to be my father. We worked outdoors and my crew talked a great deal about sex . The picture that emerged was stereotypical. All men and most women had premarital intercourse, the men relying frequently on prostitutes. During this period they all drank heavily on weekends. Eventually the men fell in love and/or got a woman pregnant and subsequently married. Their premarital lifestyle carried over into the first years of marriage when they had extramarital coitus, but later the men settled down and abandoned their extramarital activity and stopped, or reduced, their alcohol intake. Nevertheless, some marriages failed and abandonment was as common as divorce. Sexual techniques were recounted and while fellatio by a female was acceptable or even laudable ("She could suck the chrome off a trailer hitch"), the men were reluctant to admit to cunnilingus although they talked and joked about it. Homosexuality was considered a perversion if one received a penis in one's mouth or anus, but there was only a small stigma attached to being fellated by a "fairy" or "queer" during periods when females were not available. I found all of this interesting and felt like an anthropologist in a strange culture. Knowledge of this pattern served me well during my years as a Kinsey interviewer.

When World War II began I anticipated being drafted; so when I learned that the navy wanted anthropologists for military government, I volunteered immediately. During the examination and questioning they learned that I had been diagnosed as having had lymphatic tuberculosis. This didn't bother them as they were used to ranch and farm boys with essentially the same thing: bovine tuberculosis, and Colorado was accustomed to "lungers" who had been coming there for decades. Consequently I passed the physical examination and looked forward to being taken on as an ensign. This expectation was later rudely dashed when I was told that I was too young, by one year, for military government duties. Now convinced that I would be drafted, I returned to Cambridge and waited while continuing my studies. Finally, I was summoned for the draft physical examination and when tuberculosis was mentioned, they threw me out with a 4F rating and probably mopped the floor where I had stood with Lysol. During the war years I worked as an interviewer for Massachusetts General Hospital, helped with gas mask measurements for the army, interviewed Air Corps applicants, assisted Hooton in measurements for railroad coach seats, and even put in a few weeks as a salesman in a liquor store (until I forgot to lower the awning and the bottles in the display window exploded). In summary it took me an eternity to reach the Ph.D., finishing the requirements in 1946 and being awarded the degree in 1947.

Turning now to the primary subject of this treatise, sex, I should say I was a fairly typical upper-middle-class case: puberty at twelve, ushered in by "wet dreams." An older boy had unsuccessfully tried to prepare me for this event by saying, "Some morning you will wake up with some slimy stuff in your bed and that will mean you are grown up." This struck me as utter nonsense. Masturbation soon began and occasioned the usual guilt in the sense both of sin and of fear of physical consequences. I should interject at this point my parents never gave me any sexual information. I had heard that saltpeter quelled sexual impulses so I repaired to my small chemistry lab (an adjunct to my museum) and dosed myself with potassium nitrate for several nights. It had absolutely no effect, not even a placebo effect. Then I tried putting a padlock around the offending organ, but nocturnal tumescence made that too painful a remedy. This whole affair began making me question why a god would give me these impulses and then condemn me for them. I was already leaning toward agnosticism, having caused trouble in Sunday School by asking why Jesus was a blue-eyed blond when he was a Jew and asking questions about Lot and his daughters and why weren't the children of Adam and Eve indulging in incest. Fortunately, our local lending library had a few books which mollified my fears about physical consequences.

Petting began at age fourteen and became a pleasurable, if often frustrating, game to see how far one could go before being stopped. By around sixteen there was petting to orgasm, fairly common for me, but less common for my partners since not all of them allowed their genitalia to be manipulated. Despite desire and effort, I never succeeded in achieving coitus. Sometimes I went with friends to brothels, but never indulged because of a justifiable fear of venereal disease. Indeed, one of my slightly older friends did contract syphilis which settled in his finger joints and put an end to his vision of becoming a professional violinist. While I was in Arizona a few friends and I used to drive to Nogales, Mexico, and sometimes while there visit a brothel a few miles south of town named "Ranchita de las Muchachas." As usual I did not partake of sex, but it was a lively place with a bar and dance floor. I sometimes danced with the girls and bought drinks. I quit playing cards with them and some males (relatives and perhaps pimps) when I found I was out of my league, but I did play chess with one man. I discovered that the cribs were actually small apartments with the sexual activity confined to the front room, the remaining rooms being filled with parents, siblings, husbands, and children. It dawned on me that these prostitutes were not fallen women, but the family breadwinners. During one visit one of the girls announced that she had found my sister in a brothel in Nogales or, if not my actual sister, someone who looked very like me. Bets were taken, but not by me since I did look a bit Mongoloid like many Indians and Mexicans. Indeed, my college nickname in Arizona was "Chan." Finally, to settle the matter we took a cab (actually the cabs there were pickup trucks with two benches in the truck bed) to the brothel in question. My "sister" really did look very much like me facially except her moustache was fainter than mine. We had a drink together, but she didn't approach me sexually, saying it would be too much like incest.

I had no homosexual experience, but became much more tolerant of it in high school when I learned that one of my best friends was gay. My peer group was, as one might expect, extremely intolerant and my reputation was slightly tarnished because I refused to avoid my friend. Even in my twenties at Harvard I was incredibly naive about homosexuality. Two friends, who I now realize were homosexual, took me to a bath where I soaked in several pools of water of different temperatures, had a massage, and was finally put in a small cubicle with a bed. Men kept opening the door and I would smile and say, "Sorry, this room is occupied," and they would depart with a puzzled look. Afterward my friends realized that I hadn't any idea that I had been in a gay bath.

Sometime in mid-high school I learned of female homosexuality. Of course I had heard of it, but had only a vague idea and had never known any lesbians. At this time I had a female friend with whom I had a Platonic relationship. She developed a relationship with a woman artist perhaps ten years her senior. When I visited my friend this older woman was often there and they would kiss and pet in my presence, becoming visibly aroused. When the petting verged on the genital I would (as earlier requested) recall some appointment elsewhere and leave. This lesbian relationship ended tragically. My friend's father discovered it, took her to psychiatrists who pronounced her mentally ill, and tricked her into going on some pretext to the mental ward of a hospital where she was incarcerated against her will. I used to fantasize about rescuing her. Shortly thereafter I left for college and never saw her again. I was later told that she was bitterly alienated from her father (her mother was dead) and that when she was released from the hospital, she left home for good.

The bottom line is that I had known various homosexuals, had become tolerant, but never understood why these friends and peers were gay, and I remained quite curious.

Premarital coitus finally began shortly after I entered Harvard. My sole partner, a Radcliffe girl also in anthropology, ultimately became my wife not long before my twenty-first birthday. Our sexual adjustment was reasonably good, but she did not always achieve orgasm in coitus, so I consulted a physician who suggested that as part of precoital play I "blow" her. He became embarrassed when I asked him what he meant and simply repeated his suggestion. Thereafter I blew vigorously on my wife's genitalia which proved only mildly pleasant.

Marriage satisfied me physically, but intensified my curiosity about sex. I was becoming aware of how little I knew about it and sought to remedy my ignorance through reading books such as those of Havelock Ellis, Theodore H. Van deVelde, and some marriage manuals. A somewhat older friend, Frederick "Eric" Douglas of the Denver Art Museum, had quite a library on sex and loaned me his volumes freely. Of course I also read what was available in the anthropological literature, but this didn't amount to much quantitatively and qualitatively. By 1946 one could say that I had an academic (but not very experiential) knowledge of sex, and that I was aware of how little I and science knew.

Upon having completed requirements for my doctorate except for a thesis examination (nobody had ever failed one), I managed to obtain a job as an archaeologist in Nebraska beginning in September. Since it was now June I looked forward to a summer of complete indolence and relaxation after the grind of graduate work. However, fate stepped into my life in the form of Professor Clyde Kluckhohn, a brilliant workaholic. He encountered me one afternoon outside the Peabody Museum and began admonishing me. It seems that he recognized serious "lacunae" in my "academic armamentarium" as he put it. To illustrate his point he asked what I knew about symbolic logic and I had to admit I knew essentially nothing and, seeing what was coming, I took out my notebook and pencil. He advised me to read Korzybski and some others. Next he asked what I knew of the work of Alfred Kinsey. Again I knew nothing and when I asked what I should read, Kluckhohn informed me that Kinsey had not as yet published the research Kluckhohn had in mind. Then he said that social scientists were so concerned with detail that we couldn't see the forest for the trees, that we fiddled with minutiae and dared not look for the big picture, and that we were buried in the complexity of numerous different cultures. He followed by saying, however, that Kinsey was dealing with a simple, but vital matter common to all mankind so that it lent itself wonderfully to cross-cultural study and to related fields such as psychology. He concluded by saying if anyone found some basic laws of human behavior, Kinsey would probably be the one, and that every anthropologist should become aware of Kinsey's work. When I inquired what this great matter was, he replied "sex" and immediately had my full attention. Kluckhohn gave me Kinsey's address and suggested that I write to him and arrange an appointment in New York City, which Kinsey often visited, to learn more of the research work. I later discovered how it was that Kluckhohn was so fully informed about Kinsey: he was on the National Research Council Committee for Research in Problems of Sex, an organization which had been funding Kinsey since 1941.

I wrote to Kinsey and in a week or two received a favorable reply with the stipulation that I contribute my own case history. I met him in the evening at the Hotel Astor and contributed my case history which didn't take much time. I was greatly impressed by Kinsey's interviewing techniques. I had done a fair amount of interviewing, but had been taught to deal with touchy subjects with euphemisms and circumlocution. Kinsey never resorted to such tactics; he was straightforward and worded his questions plainly. (This is no place to describe his interviewing technique so I shall desist.) After the interview we asked one another questions, I about his research and he about my knowledge and attitudes. When Kinsey asked me what I thought was the incidence of male homosexuality, I replied 1 or 2 percent. He paused for a moment and then asked me to describe in detail how I got to New York (I had told him I visited often) and what I did upon arrival. I said I got off the train at Grand Central Station, went to the restroom downstairs, urinated, and came back up to call a cab to my destination. He nodded and said, "Come with me." We left the hotel, walked to Grand Central and to the head of the broad stair which led to the restroom. At this strategic point which gave a view of the room below, Kinsey asked me how long it would take a man to urinate, zip up, and wash his hands. I estimated one to two minutes. Kinsey made some remark about how anthropologists were supposed to be observant and suggested I watch. Soon I realized that the room contained at least half a dozen men who stood before the urinals glancing from side to side and after a time leaving to wash their hands at the lavatory bowls only to return to the urinals. This behavior would be repeated until, finally, the man would climb the stairs leading out of the restroom and stop at the top, or a few feet into the station lobby, and pause. Soon another man would come up and join him and the two would walk off together. I had been utterly oblivious to this cruising. Kinsey and I then walked back to the hotel and as we passed through Times Square he pointed out where the female prostitutes congregated and where the male hustlers had their territory. We watched their operations for a bit and then, because it was now early morning, returned to the Astor where I suddenly realized that I had not made hotel reservations. Kinsey pointed out that he had an extra bed and that I was welcome to sleep in it if I would promise to be out of the room by 8:00 A.M. since he had scheduled an interview for nine. I fell into bed, and what seemed moments later was awakened by Kinsey shaking my shoulder and announcing it was eight o'clock. I returned to Cambridge much impressed.

About two weeks later I received a letter from Kinsey saying that he thought that I might be suitable as a member of his team; he invited my wife and me to visit Bloomington at his expense. I had not anticipated this, but accepted the invitation, arriving in Bloomington in early July. There for perhaps three days we were interrogated almost continually about our attitudes, experiences, political and religious views, and so on, and my wife contributed her case history. This interrogation was done by Kinsey, Pomeroy, and Martin, and we also met and spoke with their wives (being married was a sine qua non for a team member). A tour of the beautiful campus was included. At the conclusion of all this Kinsey asked me what my Nebraska job was paying and I proudly said, "Four thousand dollars." He replied, "I'll give you $4,500" and I promptly accepted. My wife and I had earlier agreed that I should accept an offer if one was made.

My wife and I returned to Cambridge and shortly thereafter left for our planned vacation in a cabin her mother owned in Maine. I soon learned Kinsey had little time for trivia such as vacations, for he began sending messages (we had no telephone) urging me to begin work. Soon I said a temporary farewell to my wife and son and arrived in Bloomington in mid-August.

My arrival there was serendipitous: a department of anthropology was in the process of formation and when Carl Voegelin, soon to be its chairman, learned of my presence, I was invited to join him, Georg Neumann, and Glenn Black. The next year, 1947, the four of us constituted the faculty of the new department. In the beginning my salary came wholly from Kinsey's grant, and he was generous enough to allow me some time to teach. This was not easy since the Kinsey team traveled a great deal and hence my teaching had to be compressed into the time I was between trips, but this arrangement was satisfactory to the university, the department, and Kinsey. I began as an instructor and slowly started my way up the academic ladder; meanwhile, the university began paying a small part of my salary. This piece of academic biography is not irrelevant to our main topic of sex, for in the midst of my career I found that sex research carries penalties. A dean of the college of arts and sciences discovered that I, an assistant professor by now, was on the verge of completing my seventh year of service and hence entitled to tenure. He announced that this was impossible, that I had been picked by Kinsey rather than by the normal university procedures, and that sex research was not a recognized basis for advancement. Indeed, Pomeroy and Martin had been denied university titles (they lacked Ph.D.s at that time), but had been granted faculty privileges. He said I should be denied tenure and relabeled as lecturer. I responded that lecturer was a good title if one were at Oxford, but Indiana University wasn't Oxford, and I wanted to retain my rung on the ladder. Fortunately, Kinsey and Voegelin came to my defense and a unique compromise was finally agreed upon: I could remain on the academic ladder with the usual titles. While I would waive ordinary tenure, I would be given "research tenure" meaning that I was tenured with the Kinsey research. This compromise was also advocated by the zoology department which had a woman in exactly my position: hired by a famous biologist and on grant monies for almost seven years of service. Ultimately she, too, was given this new form of tenure. I didn't mind giving up real tenure because I felt I would not want to stay in a university if it didn't want me, and consequently I never brought the matter up again. Many years later, when I was being promoted to full professor, I was given normal tenure.

I am sorry to add that this bias against sex research was not confined to my experience of more than forty years ago, but surfaced again in the 1970s and 80s when my institute colleagues Weinberg and Williams found their numerous publications in sex research journals and their sex research books somehow didn't carry much weight with university promotion committees.

Although a few of my professors told me they were sorry to see me essentially abandon archaeology, virtually all the other anthropologists accepted my choice of specialization since both they and I considered I would be doing anthropological research, studying our own culture rather than others. This acceptance was to be expected since anthropologists often worked in peripheral fields: studying work behavior in factories, running archaeological rescues ahead of the bulldozers, doing military government, being forensic scientists, et cetera. An occasional peer would view me ambiguously, on one hand thinking sex research was not quite kosher, but on the other envying me my interesting job. Older anthropologists from the era when the discipline was really sex shy (it was born in Victorian times) and who regarded Malinowski and Mead as scandalous were polite to me, but clearly indicated that I was in something like a lunatic fringe. This I expected since I had often looked up "sex" in the indices of anthropological tomes only to find it missing or referred to as "sex: *see* division of labor." One such professor, Alfred Tozzer, when I told him of my job with Kinsey, said, "Well, you always were interested in that sort of thing, weren't you?"

My career put my relatives in an awkward situation because while they wanted to announce that their son with the Ph.D. was employed at a university, they did not want to specify the specialization. Therefore they always said I was hired by a university as an anthropologist to study human behavior; quite true, but a bit evasive. Of course the proverbial cat was out of the bag with the publication in 1953 of *Sexual Behavior in the Human Female*. Since their son/nephew was co-author of a famous best-seller the book had to be on display in the living room, but I imagine they suffered when guests inquired about me. Bless them, they never chided me, but I know they would have preferred that I be in a more respectable job.

When I first entered the field of sex research I was disappointed to find that Kinsey did not want me as a professional anthropologist, but as an interviewer, Hollerith card puncher, calculation checker, index compiler, photographer, and general factotum. He discouraged me from theorizing; to him "theory" and "philosophy" were bad words meaning armchair speculation. My suggestion that we have an introductory chapter explaining our presuppositions, assumptions, and theoretical stance (as Kluckhohn would have desired) was dismissed as wasteful introspection. Indeed, Kinsey felt that one should enter a new field without first formulating

hypotheses since these could well trap one into old patterns of thought. This same
danger he believed lay in reviewing all the literature in a field before entering it.
His credo was first, do a lot of fieldwork and only then is one in a position to make
hypotheses and evaluate the literature. Consequently, he viewed me in the beginning as an assistant, not a colleague, a status I shared with Pomeroy and Martin.
Nevertheless, when he decided that our research group should become an independent not-for-profit corporation, he made all four of us the sole trustees of the new
corporation when it formed in 1947. There were three reasons for our incorporation.
First, we wanted to legally own the case histories and other confidential material so
that no one could have access without our permission. Second, we wanted to ensure
that any book royalties and lecture fees would go to the new institute. The third
reason was that of the university: it wanted us autonomous so that if we became a
public scandal, it was not their fault or responsibility. This precaution, authored by
President Wells, proved politically valuable later.

While I chafed for a time, I got over it as the research became more engrossing
and rewarding, and with the passage of time I rose in Kinsey's esteem and was
assigned various projects with a considerable degree of autonomy. Thus, for example, I was supposed to cover the literature on anthropology, physiology, and neurology. He even sent me on side ventures such as reading the relevant books of the
Talmud so that I became an educated goy. I might add that now I see why so many
lawyers are Jewish. In addition, it was easy to persuade Kinsey, a natural collector,
that the products of a culture gave one insight into its sexual attitudes and possibly even behavior. Consequently, he had me visit museums to ascertain what, if any,
erotic objects they had. Thus, for example, I found that Margaret Mead had relevant sculptures from Bali, which she was good enough to let me photograph, and
my continual discovery of erotic Mochica ceramics ultimately led to an institute
trip to Peru where Kinsey, Dellenback (our photographer), and I examined all of the
major archaeological collections and photographed all erotic material.

My increased status resulted in an understandable, but still rather irritating,
showmanship. When Kinsey would be conducting visitors on one of the frequent tours
of the institute he would, without warning, fling open the door of my office and, as
the visitors gaped, announce, "And this is our anthropologist, Dr. Gebhard" and close
the door. I seriously considered putting up a sign "Do not feed the animals." Another
result of promotion was an increased responsibility bearing with it added stress. At
first Kinsey would have all staff members read his rough draft and make comments
and suggestions. This democratic process resulted in interminable sessions lasting well
beyond normal working hours and, ultimately, beyond Kinsey's patience. Consequently, he solved his problem by making me middle man: the staff's criticisms and
suggestions were given to me and I presented them to Kinsey. While this was more
efficient, I was in the unenviable position of passing on criticism and unacceptable
suggestions to the boss and arguing for some of these. In retrospect, he was tough, but
fair. If we could present a solid case he would accept it; otherwise he would consider
the matter and then say, "Pass on," meaning forget this and go on to the next issue.

After 1953 we all faced the fact that we were, because of our subject matter, in grave peril. A subcommittee of the United States Congress had excoriated us, U.S. Customs was confiscating our imports, and our major financial backer, the Rockefeller Foundation, had ceased funding us. Indeed, aside from the university, our only income was from book royalties, lecture fees, and a small stipend from the National Research Council. Kinsey, at the height of his fame, couldn't raise a dime. The heads of foundations greeted him cordially, praised his research, and gently propelled him toward the door while giving excuses for their inability to help. Joseph McCarthy was in his heyday and the institute had been publicly accused of destroying American morality, weakening the family, insulting womanhood, and making it easier for a Communist takeover. Kinsey, then in ill health, was embittered and terribly stressed, but he continued his vain efforts up to his premature death in 1956 at sixty-three.

After Kinsey's death the institute was in even more precarious straits. Our savings (all royalties and fees reverted to the institute) were rapidly being exhausted and there were no funding agencies on the horizon. We were paying the penalty for being highly controversial. No new best-seller was in the pipeline since Kinsey had devoted his last years almost solely to research and fund seeking. Our case versus U.S. Customs threatened to bankrupt us (fortunately our attorneys later halved their fee). Pomeroy, Martin, and I were not established scholars; we were commonly known as "Kinsey's boys." While I had been made director of the institute, I had the terrible feeling that I had been promoted to the captaincy of the *Titanic.* Shortly after Kinsey died I telephoned an order to the university for some chairs and was told, "Why do you need more chairs? You are not going to be in business for long." *Sic transit gloria mundi.*

The institute's ultimate recovery thanks to the support of President Herman Wells and later the National Institutes of Mental Health (NIMH) need not be described in detail here. Suffice it to say that McCarthy was discredited and out of the picture, funding agencies were recovering their bravery, and a couple of people at NIMH were bold enough to give us grants to salvage our great backlog of unanalyzed and unpublished data. Lastly, the university increasingly picked up staff salaries during the golden years of the 1960s when we obtained multiple grants from several federal agencies. We had four faculty members on our staff with salaries paid by their departments although they devoted half their time or more to the institute. Our basic staff of librarians, an administrative assistant, a bookkeeper, a computer operator, a photographer, and clericals was augmented by numerous work-study students. When fieldwork was in progress we also hired and trained interviewers. The university provided ample accommodations. However, this happy and productive situation was not destined to last indefinitely.

During the 1970s, with the increasing influence of the Moral Majority, the John Birch society, the Citizens for Decent Literature, and similar right-wing religious organizations, the funding situation became increasingly austere, especially for sex research. Even Masters and Johnson could not receive government support:

some of the NIMH review committee members (all elderly M.D.s from the East Coast) visited the Kinsey institute after having been at Masters, and they made it plain that his work was entirely too controversial. We at our institute survived with grants with innocuous titles and with laudable goals such as conducting educational sessions, converting our data onto computer tape, establishing an information service, and so on, but the handwriting on the wall was clear: all sex research was being discriminated against. Meanwhile I was finding life progressively less pleasant. Before one project was completed I had to start writing a grant proposal for another, and the knowledge that the sizable staff was depending on our obtaining grants was a heavy burden. I did less research and scholarly writing and became a bureaucratic paper shuffler signing requisitions, account forms, and reports. There was also occasional friction between staff which required my intervention, and there were times when I was less than popular. When I retired as director at age sixty-five, in keeping with university policy, I frankly felt great relief at giving up an increasingly difficult and stressful task.

In retrospect it is somewhat disconcerting to realize how much in human life hinges on chance. My early life seemed to lead me to a career in anthropology with emphasis on archaeology, but Clyde Kluckhohn appeared as a deus ex machina and threw a switch which turned my track to sex research. In my case I can say that despite the difficulties and tensions of fieldwork and administration, I found it ultimately rewarding and satisfying: I can look back and say that I helped keep the institute alive, productive, and honest, and that we contributed importantly to society and science.

17

Homophobia and My Career in Sex

Kenneth D. George, Ph.D.

Kenneth George is a professor at the University of Penn-sylvania in Philadelphia. He founded the graduate degree program in human sexuality at the university, one of only three Ph.D. programs in the country.

WHEN DID MY interest in human sexuality begin? That is a very difficult question. I have always believed that we enter this field because of our own personal agenda. Something about ourselves that we wish to explore. What was my agenda? Did it start with my interest in my own sexuality? The issues surrounding homo-phobia—my own as well as society's? My loving relationships? My first teaching experience? The experiences with my mentors? The various people I met along the way? My mid-life crisis? I believe my interest in human sexuality is an integration of all of these elements. But how did it begin?

The Beginning

Perhaps my interest in human sexuality began when I entered the seventh grade. It was my first day in a new school, a Chicago junior high school, where I didn't know anyone. I had to choose a locker partner. I turned to the boy sitting next to me, who didn't know anyone either. His name was Fred. I asked him if he wanted to share a locker. The answer was yes and that began a relationship that lasted through college.

I never knew I wasn't supposed to be attracted to another boy. I just was. Fred and I shared all classes. We studied together. We ate lunch together every day. We talked on the phone every night. We had dinner with each other's family on Sun-day. We started to have sex together.

When we went to high school, we continued as locker partners, shared classes, studied together, talked on the phone every night, had dinner on Sundays, and continued to have sex with each other. We were always together. We also knew we were supposed to date girls, so we double-dated all the time. After our dates we would go back to one of our homes to spend the night together. We would have sex with each other, but it was more than just a sexual relationship. We were in love with each other. Neither one of our parents told us that this was "wrong"; in fact, they encouraged our relationship. At some level they had to know we were more than friends.

But something changed when we began senior high school. The other male students made fun of us. They called us fairies and sissies. They imitated the way we talked and walked. With their continued torments, we withdrew more into each other. It then became us against them. We did not know why we were being picked on.

Fred and I did not have a label for our relationship. We did not know the words "homosexual," or "gay." We both felt isolated. It seemed to us that we were in a hostile world that neither one of us understood.

Then one day when I was about fourteen, I read a magazine called *Confidential*. It talked about men who had sex with other men. These men were called "homosexuals": they had sex with each other at a place called "Fire Island." The article described how the police came in and arrested them all for having sex with each other. I was terrified. Could I be arrested? Could Fred? Could we be arrested for having sex with each other? Was something wrong with us? I did not discuss the article with anyone—not even Fred. I couldn't go to my parents. I couldn't go to my teachers. This was my "horrible secret." I felt all alone.

But as all bright students do, I went to the school library looking for books to read. There was nothing in the library that included the word "homosexual." I don't believe there were any books that had anything to do with human sexuality. I had no school counselors or teachers who would understand. There was no one and nothing for boys who loved other boys. I learned about sexuality education from the other boys in the gymnasium locker room. They talked about sex with girls and told "homo" jokes. That was the extent of my sexuality education.

During my high school days, my favorite subject was biology. I was passionate about the study of plants and animals. They had a sex life. Through the study of biology, I hoped that I would find out more about my own sexuality. I believe that this was the beginning of my interest in human sexuality education (although this was not a recognized field then). Fred and I graduated from high school in 1951. We both knew we were going to college and both decided to go to the University of Illinois at Urbana. My declared major was biology.

Undergraduate and Graduate Training

At the University of Illinois, Fred and I were roommates. We took classes together. We studied together, ate together, talked together, slept together, and we continued to have sex together. Nothing changed. We continued to be "best friends."

Then one day during my sophomore year in college, I had lunch with Bob, another student. As we walked into the cafeteria he looked at another boy and said, "Isn't he cute?" Fred and I had never talked about other boys being cute. We never talked about sex—we just did it.

Life has never been the same since I had lunch with Bob. We both talked about finding other boys attractive. He told me that we were gay and that there was a whole world of gay men on campus. I now had a label for who I was—I knew I was gay (which sounded so much better than homosexual).

I went home and told Fred; for the first time I talked about being attracted to men. Fred never said a word. He never talked about it. But I felt good about what I had learned.

I started meeting other gay men and going to gay parties. I finally belonged to a group. I finally became popular and had fun. There was a whole world of people who were like me and I enjoyed being with them.

I also learned that being attracted to other men was not "acceptable." I found out that other male students were being expelled from the university for being gay. I was an excellent student, but again I felt fear as I had when reading *Confidential* magazine, fear that I would be discovered as being gay and that I could be expelled. I realized that being gay was wrong and that part of me had to be kept a secret.

For some reason, Fred always kept his sexuality a secret. He never joined me at any gay gathering or talked about being gay. Fred did not accept this part of his life. Fred decided he no longer wanted to be roommates with me and joined a fraternity. We stopped having sex, although we continued being best friends until he committed suicide thirty years later. I wish I could have helped him. I wish he could have found someone to help him. He survived the sexual revolution and Stonewall, but he never resolved his homophobia. In some ways Fred's history has been important to me in making some of the decisions about what I was going to do with my life. I have tried to help other young people who needed to look at their own issues regarding their sexuality. I have spent most of my career on issues of homophobia. But more of this later.

During my senior year, I found my first mentor, Dr. John Renner. John had just completed his doctorate and was teaching an "education" course. He was dynamic. He talked about teaching. I decided I wanted to be a teacher and to work with children and adolescents.

I received my student teaching assignment: a "rough" Chicago high school. I didn't do too well. I was a feminine male. John probably suspected that I was gay and advised me not to be a teacher. However, the more he tried to discourage me, the more determined I became. John gave me a low grade for student teaching. But when I graduated with a degree in liberal arts, with a major in biology, I also received my teaching certificate.

I wasn't quite ready to leave the university. It felt safer to stay there with all my friends. I didn't want to go back to my parent's home. I wasn't sure where I wanted to live. I stayed another year at the university and graduated with both a B.S. and an M.S. in 1956.

❊   ❊   ❊

After graduation, I obtained a position at a junior high school in the Chicago suburban area teaching science, mathematics, and sex education. I knew a lot about science and math. But what did I know about sex education? I knew all about the sexual "plumbing"—after all I was a biology major. Plants and animals were easy to understand. But what about human sexuality? I knew how to do it—with men. But could I teach human sexuality to junior high school girls and boys?

When in doubt, I did what I always did—I went to the library and looked for books about sex. There were at least a few books, as compared to my junior high school days. The sex books all had something in common: they were boring and dull.

I made my science and math classes come alive. I was a good teacher. But how could I make sex come alive for twelve-, thirteen-, and fourteen-year-olds? Could I teach about homosexuality and masturbation? I discussed these ideas with my principal. The answer was NO. I could teach the sexual plumbing—menstruation, pregnancy, fertilization, anatomy, and so on. Sexuality education was going to be dull. I had no choice.

My sexuality education classes were divided by gender. My career as a sex educator for the girls lasted two weeks. Their mothers came in to see the principal and demanded a female teacher for their daughters, who went to the music teacher. I continued being a sexuality education teacher for the boys for four more years. I loved it, but I never did make it an exciting class. We never covered masturbation, love, relationships, or homosexuality.

I also began living a double life: a school teacher during the week and a gay man on the weekends. I knew the two couldn't be blended. I learned that the first week of class. I bought my first car, a blue convertible. The superintendent called me into his office and told me that a convertible was an "inappropriate" car for a teacher in his district. I learned that I should not be "inappropriate."

I knew I had to stay in the closet while being a teacher. That was the "norm" in those days. However, soon after I started to teach, I had to make a decision about that closet. In those days, young men were drafted into the armed services. I was exempt while a college student, but I was no longer a student. Shortly after starting to teach, I received a letter informing me that I had to report for an army physical.

One of the questions I would be asked would involve my sexual behavior with other men. I knew that because homosexuals were not drafted into the armed services. Other friends had taken their physical and told me that they lied about their homosexuality. Some were drafted and later received dishonorable discharges when it was discovered that they were gay. Fred also took his army physical and was drafted. He never was discovered—his homophobia had protected him. The decision to answer that question honestly was very difficult for me to make. I was concerned that my answer would affect my teaching career. I didn't know who had access to my file. But I knew I had to be honest in my answer.

The day of my army physical arrived and the first thing I had to do was to complete a questionnaire that included the question, "Have you ever had a sexual experience with another man?" I answered the question "yes." I returned my questionnaire to the sergeant on duty. He reviewed it and after he reached the "sex" question he stared at me. From his actions, I don't think he ever encountered someone who answered that question with a "yes." He looked at me with disgust, and shouted to a fellow armed service person, "I have a homo here." Needless to say, all eyes were on me.

I went through the remainder of the physical examination. I then reached the psychiatrist who asked me if I ever had sex with another man while an adult. I answered that I had. That is all he asked me. I finished my physical and returned to the sergeant on duty. The psychiatrist had indicated (I assume by mistake) that I was eligible for active duty in the armed services. The sergeant was shocked when he saw this. He again shouted as loudly as he could, "Send the homo through again, someone made a mistake." I returned to the psychiatrist who changed whatever he wrote on my medical record. I returned to the sergeant who looked relieved. A short time later I received my draft card—I was "4F," ineligible for service in the Armed Forces of the United States. I have never regretted that decision.

During my four years as a junior high school teacher, I reaffirmed my love of teaching. I worked hard and wrote lesson plans that other teachers would borrow and use for their own classes. I was offered National Science Foundation summer fellowships every year. During these summers, I developed curricula to be used with my students. I learned about Piaget. I met my next mentor, Dr. J. Myron (Mike) Atkin at the University of Illinois, through whom I developed skills of inquiry teaching. I wrote books for children that emphasized inquiry learning. I started a Piaget club in my school district. With other teachers, we developed inquiry methods of presenting abstract learning to our students.

During my fourth year as a teacher, someone in the Illinois Office of Public Instruction heard about my curricula in inquiry teaching. I was asked to teach workshops for other teachers around the state. I did this and enjoyed this type of work. In 1960 I accepted a position with the Illinois Office of Public Instruction. Through the National Education Defense Act, I was paid to develop curricula for teachers that utilized inquiry teaching methods. I asked my two previous mentors—Dr. John Renner and Dr. J. Myron Atkin—to help me to develop programs that encouraged children to use inquiry skills. I loved my work. We worked as a team, writing books and developing curricular guides. My mentors also talked about my continuing my education—to get a doctorate and to teach at a university.

I wanted to continue studying inquiry-teaching methodologies. I looked at various universities and decided the best new mentor for me was at the University of Kansas, where I was accepted in the doctoral program. I was going to have a new mentor who was well known in the field of inquiry education; however, two months before I was to start graduate work at Kansas he resigned.

At that point, Dr. Kenneth Anderson, the dean of the School of Education asked me to come to the campus for a visit. During that visit, the dean offered me a position on the faculty to take the place of the person who had resigned. The dean also offered to become my doctoral advisor. I accepted his offer and resigned from the Illinois Office of Public Instruction in 1962 to study for my doctorate with a new mentor.

Being both a faculty member and a student at the University of Kansas was a very difficult experience. It was hard being friends with colleagues who were on the faculty when I was also one of their students. It was also hard being friends with the students when I was also faculty. I was gay as well—and being gay in Kansas was not the most acceptable lifestyle. I did meet other gay men, but there wasn't too much socializing. They were very closeted, but I was also in the closet. This was the "norm." However, being in the closet was soon to change.

During my first year at the university, I returned to Chicago during our spring break to visit with friends. I remember the evening quite well. It was Good Friday and we had all agreed to meet at a gay bar in the southernmost part of Chicago. I had been away since the previous August and I was looking forward to seeing everyone.

As we sat and talked, the front door flew open and the police came in along with a television crew, floodlights, and newspaper reporters. One of the policemen shouted, "All right 'girls,' face the wall and put your hands up." Of course there wasn't a "girl" in the bar! We were all searched—I don't know what they were looking for—as we all faced the wall with our hands up in the air. Then we were marched outside and placed in a police van to be taken downtown to the Chicago police headquarters.

I sat next to my best friend, Chuck, who was also a graduate student. We knew our graduate careers would soon be over. We opened our wallets, tore up all of our school identification cards, and then swallowed them. I would leave no evidence of my connection to the University of Kansas. Many of my gay friends whom I had graduated with from the University of Illinois had been arrested in Chicago police raids. They were all teachers who lost their teaching positions after the newspaper reports came out. My future was doomed since I was going to have a police record.

Why did we predict this horrible future? Because the Chicago police were notorious for raiding gay bars, after which all the men were booked for "illicit conduct." The next day, all the Chicago newspapers would carry coverage of the police raid and give the names and occupations of everyone arrested.

The police interrogated me. Why was I in Chicago? (I had a Kansas driver's license.) What was I doing in that bar? Did I know any of these other people? After all of us were interrogated, we had to post bail. Luckily Chuck and I had enough money. They let us out of jail at six the next morning. We were in downtown Chicago and our cars were in the parking lot at the gay bar on the south side. Since most of our money had been used to pay our bail, we took buses and walked. We finally got back to our cars around 10 A.M.

I went to my parents' home. I had not been to bed and I was completely exhausted. However, I could not go to sleep. The only thing I wanted to do was to read about my arrest in the morning paper. But I was too scared. I got into my car and drove all the way back to the University of Kansas. Without sleep, I arrived about twelve hours later. I called Chuck as soon as I got into my apartment. What did the newspapers say? I was safe! It mentioned only that the police had raided a gay bar on the south side of Chicago. No names were given. To this day, I do not know why we were not mentioned by name.

However, there was a trial for all of us who were arrested. I chose not to appear, so I never got my bail money back. However, the judge tossed the case out of court. Was this a sympathetic judge or was there no evidence of "illicit conduct"? We were all young men whose only "offense" was being gay and sitting in a bar that was gay owned. That arrest, however, changed my life. Ever since that day of my army physical, I never really felt as if I were in the closet. Being gay was part of my "official record." I was comfortable being gay and accepted that as being "normal." However, I had never discussed being gay at college or at work. After being arrested, I decided I would never be in the closet again. My career closet door was not blown open, but it could have been. I could have lost everything. I was never going to hide my gay identity again.

The University of Kansas was outstanding; however, it was not a socially stimulating environment for a young gay man. I wanted to leave Kansas and go somewhere more "gay" friendly in the East or West. But I knew I couldn't leave until I had finished my degree and obtained a position at another university. During the summer of 1963, I talked with my advisor (also dissertation chair and dean) about completing my degree within a year. Although he didn't think I could do it, he gave me the go ahead to attempt "the impossible."

Doing a literature review was so difficult in 1963. We did not have computers to do library searches. I remember spending time that summer in various libraries, none of which was air-conditioned. (If you have ever spent the summer in Kansas you can imagine what that was like.) I had to review bibliographies of bibliographies, compile hundreds of index cards, review articles after hand-searches through hundreds of journals. I completed the literature review. I was on schedule for completing my dissertation.

In September I started my actual research. I was examining the effect of abstract activities on the critical thinking ability of adolescents (such as the effect of pregnancy on teenagers). I traveled extensively visiting high schools and testing hundreds of adolescents. I collected data. During the spring of 1964, I started my analyses. I was still on schedule. Data were analyzed on a hand calculator. Hours and hours were spent doing analysis of variance and covariance. The cutoff date for completion of my dissertation for that academic year was July 31. More analyses. Rushing to the typist. Proofreading—there was no spell check. I turned in the completed copies to my dissertation committee. I scheduled the defense for July 31, 1964. I did it! I held my defense and completed my degree right on my schedule. But I still couldn't leave Kansas since I didn't have another position. I had been too busy writing my dissertation to be actively involved in a job search. So I agreed to continue on the faculty at Kansas, where I was promoted from instructor to assistant professor of education. But I still wanted to leave Kansas.

In December of that year, I received a notice of a job at the University of Pennsylvania. I wrote a letter of interest and then left for Acapulco for a winter break vacation. Upon my return to Kansas, an invitation was waiting for an interview at Penn. It proved successful.

The University of Pennsylvania: The Beginning Years

In July 1965, I arrived in Philadelphia with my cat, a car, and a few suitcases. My office at Penn was in an attic and my classroom was in the school cafeteria of an old elementary school. The new office and classroom I had been promised in a new building would not be ready until the following year. I spent the month of August getting the office and classroom ready for occupancy. I met my colleagues and got to know my surroundings. The dean's secretary reviewed the "do's and don't's" of being a Penn professor. Though she knew I was gay, she recommended that I not go to gay bars. Penn professors did not go to gay bars. "This is an Ivy League university." But at least I wasn't in the closet. I was also assigned my first research/ teaching assistant, Sister Lizette. Sister's "office" was an orange crate and a stool next to my desk. I was still trying to figure out "the honor" of being at an Ivy League university.

I spent that academic year (1965–1966) teaching, writing, publishing, getting grant money, and meeting people. At the end of the year, we moved to our new building. The dean raised $50,000 from the alumni to build me a laboratory. I had a nice office. Sister Lizette had her own office and I hired my first secretary, Mrs. Ida Kerns. Things finally felt like an Ivy League university.

Dr. Morris S. Viteles, the cold and distant dean who had initially interviewed me for the job, began to become warm (not with everyone, but with me). I was invited to his and his wife's home for dinner. Mrs. Viteles was a warm and kind person who made me feel as if I were part of the family. I invited Dr. and Mrs. Viteles to dinner. Dr. Viteles became my mentor, advising me and guiding my career. He encouraged my research, my writing, and my teaching. Dr. Viteles appointed me to the executive committee. Academically things couldn't be better.

During that year, I also met a man my age who had just graduated from medical school. We dated for a year. We fell in love. His name was Lynn Possinger. Lynn and I purchased a condominium and moved into it together. He started a private practice.

During my fifth year at Penn, I asked for an early academic review and was promoted to an associate professor with tenure. Lynn's practice flourished. We purchased a house on the Mainline, in Gladwynn. Dr. Viteles had retired and his and his wife's home was near ours. We visited and spent time together. We had faculty parties. We were viewed as a couple by everyone at Penn.

One summer, I taught a short course at East Stroudsburg University in the Pocono

Mountains. I loved it up there and so did Lynn, so we both decided to buy a weekend getaway house in the Poconos. I had forgotten about homophobia. This was 1971 and we were simply two men looking to buy a house together in a rural area. We didn't realize this until the real estate agent called us one day and told us he found the perfect spot for us: five acres on which we could build a house. We loved the property, purchased it, and contracted with a builder. Construction began on our house on an isolated road on the side of a mountain. There were only four other houses on the road.

One weekend one of the neighbors called and invited us to stop by. On the roof was a man fixing the television antenna and in the kitchen was another man cooking. Lynn and I looked at each other. They were gay—another male couple. They told us that they had been concerned about who their new neighbor was going to be. They immediately invited the people in the other three houses over for a visit— two other male couples and a female couple. We found a new group of friends and our social life focused around the weekends in the Pocono Mountains.

Sister Lizette, who had by then changed her name to Sister Maureen Dietz, also spent many weekends with us. She had finished her doctorate and had accepted a position as an assistant professor at the University of Maryland. We used the mountain house as a place where Sister and I wrote two books. Lynn, Maureen, and I spent more and more time in the Poconos writing and socializing with our neighbors.

In 1972, I became associate dean of the graduate school of education, which meant less teaching and more administrative work. However, my research continued and the two books I had written with Maureen were published. In 1974 I was promoted to full professor.

Career Shift: Human Sexuality Education

In September 1972, there was a young man waiting to see me. I asked this particular young man (having nothing to do with his being cute) what he needed. He told me he wanted permission to take an independent study course in human sexuality with Harold Lief, a psychiatrist and chairman of the Marriage Council of Philadelphia (which is a part of the department of psychiatry at Penn's medical school). His request made sense and I signed his permission slip. The student's name was Andrew E. Behrendt. This meeting changed my life and my career. Neither one of us knew that chance meeting would be so significant, indeed the beginning of what has become a significant relationship for both of us.

Andy was a research assistant at Marriage Council and was completing his master's degree in statistics and educational research at the graduate school of education. After our initial meeting, he stopped in my office frequently to talk about his independent study with Harold and his work at Marriage Council. He was enthusiastic about the field of human sexuality. As we talked, I became more interested and excited about his work and the work being done at Marriage Council.

During the following semester, Andy registered for an independent study with me. He wanted to do an in-depth study in human sexuality. I did not know that much about the field, except for my undergraduate work in biology and my experience at teaching sexuality education with junior high school students. Of course, not too many other faculty members at Penn knew that much about human sexuality either. Andy and I spent much time together in the library and developing our knowledge about the field. Of course I was the professor and he was the student, but we were more colleagues working together. We were developing a common interest in an exciting field. We were also becoming friends.

During the 1975–1976 academic year, Andy and I went to our first American Association of Sex Educators, Counselors, and Therapists (AASECT) meeting, and we took a workshop with Bill Stayton (who was also on the faculty at Marriage Council) at the American University in Washington, D.C. Andy completed his M.S. degree. He wanted to continue graduate study and obtain a Ph.D. in the field of human sexuality, but there was no such field of study available at Penn. We did, however, have a special category called an "independent major," which required three faculty members to agree to serve as advisors and to plan an approved program of study. Of course I was willing, and Harold and Bill were willing to serve as the other two members of this special Ph.D. program of study.

Andy was on his way, but I was beginning to wonder where I was going. By 1975, I was a full professor, had written books and articles, was an associate dean, had two beautiful homes, and I was in a relatively happy relationship. But all of a sudden I began to wonder what career accomplishments were left for me to accomplish. Had I done it all? What else was left to do? Is this what I wanted to do for the rest of my life? Was this what was called a mid-life crisis?

I also began to wonder where I was going with my personal life. I was not happy living in Gladwynn. I loved the Poconos on the weekends, but during the week I wanted to be closer to the university and the city. Lynn and I also started to have separate interests. Busy with his private practice, he was hardly ever at home. When he did arrive home, he simply worked some more and went to bed. On weekends, he would arrive late Friday night in the Poconos and sleep most of Saturday. Eventually there was not even enough time for him to get away on weekends. We were a successful couple (before the term "yuppie" was coined) in terms of career success and money, but there was no time left for each other. Lynn was spending more and more time at work and I was spending more and more time at Penn—working with Andy and developing my new interest in human sexuality.

I talked with Lynn about my "crisis." I wanted to move back into Center City Philadelphia. He was not too excited about the idea—he loved the Mainline. But he agreed to move into the city. I also talked with him about my new interest in human sexuality and wanting to be a couple therapist. I volunteered at a newly formed counseling center for gay and lesbian people. I started developing an interest in male couples in conflict. I began seeing male couples at the counseling center. I met new people. I was again getting involved in the gay and lesbian community. I started to see a new beginning (but there were also the ties to the past).

Lynn and I bought a house in Center City Philadelphia with space for him to have an office. When it came time to move, Lynn did not want to go. We agreed I would move to the new house. Lynn would have his office in the new house and continue to live in Gladwynn. We decided on a separation so that I could pursue my new career interests. I spent the weekends in the Poconos, weekdays working at Penn as associate dean and with Andy in the field of human sexuality, and evenings at the counseling center.

I applied for a year's sabbatical from the university and for a postdoctorate year of study at Marriage Council. Marriage Council was also interested in offering a Ph.D., through an academic school within the university. In my application of study for Marriage Council and in my request for a year's sabbatical, I stated that I wanted to develop a graduate program of study in human sexuality education at the graduate school of education. My sabbatical was approved and of course I was accepted as a postdoctoral fellow at Marriage Council. (How could they turn down a Penn professor and associate dean?)

In August 1976, I resigned as associate dean and as a volunteer at the counseling center and started a year of study at Marriage Council. I was living in Center City by myself, learning to be a couple therapist, seeing male couples as part of my internship at Marriage Council, and developing a new graduate program in human sexuality education in cooperation with the Marriage Council. My life was turning in a new direction.

Human Sexuality Education at the University of Pennsylvania

In September 1977, I proposed to the faculty of the graduate school of education a new area of specialization—human sexuality education—which would offer an M.S. and a Ph.D. The program would be in cooperation with the Marriage Council.

The faculty asked questions: What would you teach about masturbation or homosexuality? I was prepared for their questions. Kinsey was right: to be successful in the area of human sexuality you need to be established, with tenure. My reaction to the questions was that I was already a tenured professor and human sexuality was the new direction for my research and writing.

The dean also asked why the graduate school of education should have a program in human sexuality. I should add to Kinsey's comments about being established and tenured, that you need to do your homework and to be politically prepared. As you may recall, my proposed plan in my request for a sabbatical leave was to develop a graduate program in human sexuality education. This plan had been approved by the newly appointed dean (one of his first acts), the provost of the university, and by the board of trustees. I informed the dean that if the proposed program was not to have his approval, he should have informed me prior to my leave since I had taken a year off in order to prepare this program. The graduate program was finally approved by both the faculty and the dean.

We began admitting students. At that point, it became clear that the combined program with Marriage Council was not working. These students were more interested in becoming clinicians. A Ph.D. program at Penn is a research degree that prepares university scholars. The students were not interested in research seminars. The faculty was not interested in clinical studies regarding a patient population. During the second year of the program, we dissolved the cooperative relationship with Marriage Council. The graduate program, however, would continue within the graduate school of education.

Since the combined program with Marriage Council had been dissolved, we had to look for faculty members. The school then made a major decision—the majority of the faculty appointed to the program would be part-time. We wanted a variety of faculty with very specific credentials. This decision had both positive and negative aspects: positive in that we would have a large faculty with diverse interests and abilities, negative in that I was the only full-time tenured faculty member in the program. So we began the process of adding part-time faculty.

The program started with Andy Behrendt and me. We taught the introductory courses and the research seminars. In 1977, there was an approved major in human sexuality education in the graduate school of education. Andy finished his Ph.D. and was the first person appointed as a lecturer in human sexuality education. Andy is an expert in gender identity, children's learning about sexuality and sex, relationships, including nonsexual relationships with companion animals, and HIV infection and control.

William Stayton, a member of Marriage Council when the program started and active in planning it, was appointed an adjunct professor. Bill is a relationship and family therapist, specializing in human sexuality issues from treating sexual dysfunctions to working with persons and families with differences. Konstance McCaffree then joined the faculty as a lecturer. Konnie is an expert in adolescent sexuality issues, elementary and secondary school sexuality education, resources for use in sexuality education, affective sexuality education methodologies, developmental issues, and teacher training. She is a secondary-school human sexuality educator and consultant for parent, religious, community, and other professional groups. Ryda Rose has been a lecturer at Penn for twenty-five years. She is an expert in research methodologies.

Richard A. Friend was one of our first doctoral students. After he completed his degree, he joined the faculty. Richard is an expert in issues of equity, such as sexism and heterosexism, as well as affective sexuality education methodologies, homophobia, gender identity, and the sociopolitical aspects of sexuality education. Also joining the faculty after they completed their degrees were Loretta Sweet Jemmott and Ernie Green. Loretta is an expert on HIV education with African American adolescents and is also a tenured professor in the school of nursing. Ernie, who also teaches at Lehigh University, is an expert on gender role development, especially in men.

All the faculty have been active in the major organizations in the field: SSSS

(Society for the Scientific Study of Sex; now Sexuality), AASECT (American Association of Sex Educators, Counselors, and Therapists), and SIECUS (Sex Education and Information Council of the United States). Andy has been the editor of the *Society Newsletter* (SSSS), a member of the board of directors, an officer of the Eastern Region, and a recipient of the Outstanding Service Award. Bill has been the president and a member of the board of directors of SIECUS and president of AASECT. Konnie has been a member of the board of directors of SSSS, an officer of the society, and the president of the Eastern Region of SSSS. Richard has been a member of the board of directors of SSSS as well as an officer of the society.

When Andy and I attended our first AASECT meeting in Washington, D.C., everyone was housed on the same floor. I think the hotel was nervous with all these people interested in sex and decided to keep us all together. Our hotel room was next to Lester Kirkendahl's, who was sharing his room with Ron Moglia. I had known Ron since the sixties when he participated in a two-year program that I conducted at the University for Philadelphia elementary school teachers. Ron went on to get his doctorate at Temple University with Eugene Abraham, who received his doctorate under my supervision at Penn. At times this field seems very incestuous. Which is one of the exciting aspects of being in a relatively small field.

The AASECT meeting was very interesting to me coming from a more cognitive academic field. One day Andy and I got into the hotel elevator where two AASECT members (both women) were discussing the size of the penises they had performed oral sex on the evening before. I was surprised at the openness of their discussion. I was not yet ready for the affective aspects of this field.

I chose to become more active in SSSS. I attended the first Eastern Region meeting in Atlantic City in 1977. When I attended my second Eastern Region meeting in Philadelphia, John Sumerlin (who was then president of the Eastern Region) asked me to become secretary. With that invitation I began a relationship of many years with the Eastern Region, ending as president. From that position, I became a member of the board of directors of the society and then the president. I have served on many committees and have been involved in a variety of roles. One of the most exciting duties was that of meeting chair of the annual meeting in Atlanta.

SSSS has also become part of my family. The people I have met have contributed so much to my personal and professional growth and development. That relationship has been very rewarding.

A few years ago, the human sexuality education program at Penn formed a joint relationship with SIECUS which provides opportunities for both to continue research and to have joint funding in common areas of interest. Bill Stayton and Konnie McCaffree serve on the board of SIECUS.

All of these relationships have been significant and rewarding in my development. There have also been some hassles As all of us in the field know, we are not immune to others who view this field as threatening. University programs in human sexuality are just as vulnerable as those in public schools. As part of my development I have learned that power is essential in maintaining a successful program in this field. As I mentioned earlier, having in writing the purpose of my sabbatical was a key factor in obtaining administrative support for the program. Very few administrators read carefully the purpose of a sabbatical, but that purpose was what I later implemented.

Money is also power. The University of Pennsylvania works on a budget system that is quite unique. Any undergraduate student who takes a course in human sexuality education in the graduate school of education has a part of his or her tuition transferred to the school. Our faculty are great teachers and our courses grew increasingly larger in the number of students enrolled. More and more tuition money was transferred to the graduate school of education. The dean began to rely on this income. The dean needed us.

I also know that being involved within the university means power. I wanted to keep the program alive and well. I wanted the program to grow and the faculty to feel safe. I joined powerful committees at Penn: the university senate executive committee, university steering committee, university council, university grievance committee (chair), and the president's committee on affirmative action, to name just a few. This took much time and effort.

However, it paid off. Two examples will illustrate the necessity of being powerful rather than vulnerable when you are at a university that believes the only "legitimate" field is one that can be defined by *the* scientific method. In our introductory course in human sexuality education, there are a large number of undergraduates. In keeping with our philosophy that small-group discussions are essential for sensitive topics, the course uses eight teaching assistants. These assistants also meet with students individually to help them with their papers and other assignments. This extra help is provided until the students have achieved their maximum potential—which usually means they get grades of A or B. One day my dean received a letter from the provost indicating that there were too many high grades in the human sexuality course. According to the provost, it was necessary for an Ivy League university to maintain academic standards, and unless this course was graded on the "normal curve" it would no longer receive undergraduate credit (since we are a graduate school, the undergraduate students are not under our control).

For me this was a violation of my academic freedom. I sent copies of the provost's letter and my response to the senate executive committee (of which I was a member). I also mentioned his letter at the next steering committee meeting (which was advisory to the president and consisted of a few faculty members, the president, and the provost). I kept raising issues of academic freedom. The normal curve requirement was soon dropped. If the provost had been successful, there would have been a distribution of grades that also included Ds and Fs, which would have not been consistent with our philosophy of working individually with our students. It would also have lowered enrollments, which would have reduced the income to my school. In this issue, the dean was very supportive.

Another example of power being helpful to the maintenance of the program was when I was asked to provide a copy of my course syllabus to an undergraduate curriculum committee. Since I was not a member of an undergraduate school, this seemed like a strange request. But it was one that I knew had to be threatening to the maintenance of the introductory course. I again raised this as an issue of academic freedom and harassment at a grievance hearing (I was a member of the grievance commission). I could prove this was harassment if I was the only graduate professor who received such a request (many professors teach undergraduate students in their graduate-level courses). The request for my syllabus was dropped.

All of us in the field of sexuality education have experienced some type of hassle. Public school teachers have hassles from certain elements in their community. University professors are under less pressure from the "fringe" elements, but hassles do exist: criticism of our research, our teaching, and, for those who are not tenured, denial of tenure. But, for me, it is worth it. This field has been a joy. The letters I have received over the years from previous students saying that the course they took with me in human sexuality has been one of the best and most influential course they have ever taken; the students who wait to talk with me after class, who call me at home, who applaud me at their graduation, and who stand up during the last day of class and cheer—all these accolades tell me that I have had an effect on many lives.

My Ph.D. students who are now in the field tell me I made a difference. I will not identify them for the list is too long. Some of their students are now doing a Ph.D. with me. I have become a mentor to my students' students. This is an example of Erik Erikson's stage of generativity and a successful conclusion.

The End—The Beginning

In 1994 we inaugurated a new president. We have a new provost. This year we have a new dean who is very supportive of the program. She has also asked me to (re)accept the position of associate dean for academic affairs.

The role of associate dean is quite demanding; however, I did not want to give up teaching, which is a major love of my life. The dean agreed to change the status of Andy Behrendt from part-time lecturer in human sexuality education to a full-time tenure-track position. Andy is now more involved in the running of the program which has given me some of the time I need to cover the duties of associate dean.

I am now completing my thirtieth year at the university. This past year, the university eliminated its early retirement program (it is age discriminatory). All of us who have been at Penn as long as I have been had to decide to accept early retirement or forever lose that option. I did not choose to retire early. I have decided that being a part of the human sexuality education program is too much fun to ever stop doing. But I also know that if I retired the program in human sexuality education would not survive. The program means too much to me and to the other faculty members who have worked together all these years. We have created something that we are all proud to be associated with for many more years. "It's a wonderful life!"

18

Psychiatry, Sexology, and the Law

Richard Green, M.D., J.D.

Richard Green is a psychiatrist and sex researcher-turned lawyer who has fought for greater freedom of sexual expression and the rights of sexual minorities. He was influential in having homosexuality removed from the American Psychiatric Association's catalogue of mental illnesses.

ALWAYS WANTED to be a sexologist. But why? Two early childhood and one teenage event set the stage.

I am about three or four years of age and outdoors on Carroll Street in Brooklyn where I lived from birth to high school. My mother is there and I think another mother or two and kids. I start to push a child's baby carriage. My mother says "No, that's for girls." She could have said, "No, it's not yours." One of many similar incidents shaping early gender identity?

I am the same age. We are in our three-room apartment. My mother, naked at least from the waist down, is walking from the bathroom toward the bedroom. I am aware of her hips and buttocks. I must have said something about that because my father says, "He's starting early." Good for them for encouraging childhood sexuality.

It is December 1952; I am sixteen. The front page of the tabloid *New York Daily News* boldly headlines "Ex-GI Becomes Blond Beauty," with pictures of George and Christine Jorgensen. Everyone is fascinated by Christine, not just the would-be transsexuals for whom she became a leader. I ask my father, "Why can someone else's hobby become one person's career?" To his credit and my destiny, he answers: "Why not?"

Growing up middle class in an upwardly mobile inner-city Jewish family, a child is repeatedly asked the question, "What will you be when you grow up?" with the inevitable hope being "my son the doctor."

As a pre-med in college, I majored in psychology, not zoology, because my best friend in the freshman dorm was a psych major. I did not know much about psychology but wanted to share classes with someone who made me laugh a lot. His name was Richard Dolinsky, a professor now, too.

In college, I also had a fantasy of being an actor. At the end of my fourth year a fraternity brother with whom I had double-dated was going off to do summer stock. I decided to go along as an apprentice making sets and playing bit parts. Before then I only knew in the abstract that there were homosexuals. But summer theater was stocked, including my fraternity brother and another who was a married man. The mystery of sexual orientation intrigued me.

Beating their 10 percent Jewish quota, I became the first Syracuse University student accepted at Johns Hopkins University medical school. I was thrust into gross anatomy, dissecting a human cadaver, mindlessly memorizing every artery, nerve, and bone bump. With sex on my mind, when given the opportunity to choose a topic for the term paper in the class, I selected hermaphroditism.

With my goal of being a psychiatrist and sex researcher, when it was time to chose a topic for my elective quarter research, I climbed the stairs to the psychiatry department to see the professor in charge, John Hampson. When he asked if I had ever done research, I told him that I had just written a paper on hermaphroditism. He informed me that the man down the hall and he had just completed a study on that topic. Through his secretary he made an appointment for me to see John Money. The reason for the indirect communication was that the two collaborators who had co-authored the now classic 1950s papers on hermaphroditism were no longer speaking to each other.

Studying sex and gender did not offer the professional promise of alternative careers such as cancer research or the biochemistry of mental disorder. Those were hot with a long-shot chance to make that big breakthrough and garner the scientist's Oscar—the Nobel Prize. Psychosexual development was not mainstream science, not mainstream psychiatry. But my dad had said, "Why not?"

My fate was sealed when I selected UCLA for psychiatry training based solely on its climate. In residence there, however, was Robert Stoller, the only other medical school researcher of gender identity in the country, a fact unbeknownst to me until I arrived.

Set on the course I wanted to take, I was stimulated by two mentors who could not have been more different in their training, personal style, or sexual style: John Money and Bob Stoller. The medical psychologist versus the psychoanalyst, the confrontational versus the ambassadorial, the ghetto dweller versus the estate owner, the bachelor sexual explorer versus the monogamous family man. But they shared their compelling interest in gender identity and in me, nurturing me, giving me the opportunity to demonstrate what I could do.

The UCLA and later the SUNY Stony Brook years were the halcyon days of recreational sex and sex research. The pill was there; HIV was not. Masters and Johnson authored best-sellers. I was on a National Institutes of Mental Health (NIMH) study section that funded sex research projects throughout the country. Our postdoctoral training program at Stony Brook with Joseph LoPiccolo and Julia

Heiman, and later Milton Diamond and Richard Whalen, had nine postdoctoral fellows for five years.

Then, after twenty years with about 150 papers, chapters, and books behind me, and my twenty-five-year study of prehomosexual boys dispatched to Yale University Press, I took my leave from medicine for law. One reason that I applied to law school was that years of expert witness work convinced me that I could do better than most lawyers I had worked with. Another was that I had no one to support financially but me. A third was that my father had graduated from law school, but for him it was the Depression and he did have others to support—a young son and a wife. So he got a job and never practiced law.

I went to Yale Law School to work at the same topic—human sexuality. My first case as a trial lawyer was the "gay Boy Scout case," in which a homosexual Eagle Scout was suing the Boy Scouts for refusing to let him be a scout leader. The Boy Scouts for their part were arguing that the scout oath containing the phrase "morally straight" meant "sexually straight." The Boy Scouts did not change their policy.

On reflection, have these hours upon the stage been gratifying?

Jousting with windmills has been. The first joust dealt with transsexual surgery, with established medicine refusing to recognize the legitimate plight of the transsexual. When I began seeing transsexuals with Harry Benjamin, the father of the transsexual movement, in his New York office in the mid-1960s, no American medical center was performing sex change surgery. At the time I wrote my first letter endorsing surgery for one of his patients to be done in Europe, I was only partway through my residency training. In retrospect this might not have been a wise political move to foster a new career.

The second windmill was the designation by the American Psychiatric Association that homosexuality was invariably a mental disorder. I wrote a paper in about 1970 challenging that assumption, and when I showed it to John Money, he suggested that I put it away in a desk drawer. Publishing it would hinder my budding career. Not always listening to those who should know better, I did publish it in 1972. One result was being appointed to the APA subcommittee on sexual disorders. The committee challenged the equation that homosexuality equaled mental illness. With the help of others, notably Judd Marmor, who was my first witness to be examined in a court of law, a major windmill toppled when homosexuality *per se* was removed from the American Psychiatric Association's catalogue of mental disorders.

A third windmill still turns but is listing and should topple. It is the notion that hordes of children were sexually abused year after year, often by parents in satanic cults, and then repressed all memory of the horrors for twenty to thirty years until recovering it in psychotherapy. This just made no sense. In 1992, I was one of the less than a handful of psychiatrists agreeing to be named to the scientific advisory board of the new False Memory Syndrome Foundation. The vitriol of those who believe in the historic validity of these "recovered" memories has been greater than those condemning sex change surgery or indicting homosexuals as invariably sick. But again, the tide of professional and public judgment is turning. Not all will become convinced, but then not all splinters from the first two demolished windmills have been swept away either.

Has it been gratifying? I have testified against filmmakers being jailed for sending pornographic films to consenting undercover postal workers, for lesbian mothers trying for a level playing field against heterosexual ex-husbands suing for child custody, and on behalf of transsexuals just wanting to visit their children. Often I lose. Then, pondering the ruling by the court against my testimony, I despair. But believing I am right and knowing that without my testimony these sexual and gender pariahs will lose by default recharges my battery for the next joust.

Part of the appeal of defending the sexually disenfranchised has been their stigmatized minority status. Growing up Jewish in a Christian country, only a few streets from where the "wait till next year" Brooklyn Dodgers baseball team played and lost, I had to root for the underdog.

As one ages and the road ahead shortens, one looks back at the distance traveled. What will be the legacy?

Research papers in journals are often outdated at publication. Books initially read by few remain on library shelves, later to provide quaint reading for the curious browser.

Two accomplishments are my professional legacies. One is the journal *Archives of Sexual Behavior.* I was asked to be founding editor in 1970 by Seymour Weingarten at Plenum Publishing at the suggestion of Bob Stoller. Seymour, who had been Bob's editor for *Sex and Gender,* sensed the void in academic journals for sex research. There are no books about how to start a journal, but it seems that you need an editorial board and you need manuscripts. I carved a solid board by asking respected friends and colleagues to join me. I then solicited manuscripts from them. I assured publication of not just one issue—before the first was published, the second was ready. Over a quarter century we have remained one issue ahead. *Archives* has lived up to its ambitious name.

The second professional legacy is the International Academy of Sex Research. In 1972 there were not select international organizations for sex researchers. With early help from Paul Gebhard, I formed the core of a new group from the new editorial board of *Archives.* Then I set about planning its first meeting. It came off with two glitches, only one of which I could have prevented. I neglected to see that the auditorium at Stony Brook for the paper presentations would be unlocked on a Saturday morning. The second was the torrential rain that rounded all attendees into my house one evening, pinning a damp Bill Masters and others against the wall, instead of allowing them to mill about comfortably at an outdoor barbecue. Over a quarter century, the Academy, too, has lived up to its ambitious name.

All fades in the shadow of the third legacy. It is Sunday and my son is doing his second-grade homework next to me. He asks what this is. I tell him that it's about my life. He pleads, "Put my name in it, yes yes yes." That's what it's all about, Adam.

19

Penis Power

Gary Griffin

Gary Griffin (a pseudonym), a former Mormon mission-
ary, established a special niche for himself in the sex field
as the popular expert on penises. He worked with medical
professionals, encouraging more research on the topic, and
established a publishing company to disseminate informa-
tion. While this book was in production, Gary Griffin
died of AIDS.

MY FATHER WAS outside washing the car when my mother's water broke. This was a particularly difficult pregnancy, and my parents knew that it would be their last. My mother had already given birth to six other children (including three miscarriages) and this pregnancy was extremely onerous—-with devastating episodes of morning sickness, anemia, and spotting. Nevertheless, I was wanted (I must have felt this even in the womb) and my parents took special precautions to ensure that I was born healthy.

My father tucked Mother into the front seat of the car and flew to the hospital with soapsuds flying off the fenders. Since he was a meticulous, organized man, it was uncharacteristic for my father to leave a job half done, but when my mother went into labor, he knew that he had to get her to the hospital immediately—even if it meant that there was no time to rinse the suds off the car.

At the hospital, the situation turned critical. My mother began to hemorrhage, and a bevy of medical professionals gathered around her to stop the bleeding while trying to deliver the child safely. At 6:18 P.M. on a warm and sunny Sunday evening of September 18, 1955, I was delivered—a healthy and whole baby boy. The doctors stabilized my mother, and although she was weak from the loss of blood, she was delighted to have delivered her third son. My father undoubtedly beamed with pride and joy. They decided to name me Gary, allegedly after the box office star, Gary Cooper. I've always liked that name and feel that it suits me well.

For the first two years of my life, we lived in a newly constructed tract home in a suburban neighborhood in Cupertino, California, surrounded by plum groves and poppy fields. In 1957, my father, a banker, received a transfer to Salt Lake City, and our family, being devout Mormons, gladly moved.

My earliest recollections are of the dark-bricked home with the huge front porch on Boulevard Gardens. This was one of the country's most unusual streets, for it wasn't a street at all. Instead of a paved avenue running down the front of our property, a wide expanse of well-manicured grass stretched an entire block (automobile access was made via an alleyway behind the houses). This block-long swath of lawn was the ideal playing ground for children, and as most of the twenty homes on this unusual "street" were occupied by families, there were always games and laughter abounding in the front.

Most of our social lives centered around church. Virtually all of our neighbors were also Mormon, so we saw each other regularly. Mormonism is a particularly active religion, with various meetings occurring virtually every day of the week. For the children, there was primary on Wednesdays; for teenagers, "Mutual" (short for Mutual Improvement Association) on Thursday evenings; and for the parents, Relief Society for the women and Priesthood meeting for the men. Church was an integral part of my life and I was instructed in goodness and morality from an early age. Mormonism teaches that this life is a "testing ground" of sorts—that we are to strive for perfection. If we adhere to the laws that God has set for us and get married in the temple (for time and eternity), then we can achieve the highest level in the afterlife—the Celestial Kingdom. From my earliest years, my parent instilled in me the need to "obey the commandments" so that our family could live together in the Celestial Kingdom one day.

Good I was. I was the kind of child that any family would have loved. I was achievement oriented, loving (although intensely stubborn), and obedient. I was also gay before I had any clue as to what that meant. I was six or seven years old when I was caught flinging a pencil eraser at Gail Smith during Sunday school class. My teacher, tired of my antics, called Brother Birmingham up to our class to take care of me. A loving and gentle man who lived just three houses down from us, he sat on a chair in the front of the classroom and made me sit on his lap. This tactic I'm sure was to embarrass me in front of my ten Sunday school classmates. But I liked it. I remember feeling his long, flaccid penis under my buttocks and imagined it snaking its way up through my thighs. I also knew that such thoughts were "bad."

One day in the early sixties, my next-door neighbor took several of us neighbor kids to a nearby park that featured an outdoor pool. The locker room was located next to the pool, and we entered to change into our bathing suits. I was fascinated by the dozens of glorious male bodies in various stages of undress. I watched transfixed as several fathers showered nearby with their sons. The penis was an object of wonderment, joy, and fascination, and I stared unabashedly. My neighbor had to shake me from my reverie and remind me that we were there to swim.

My fascination for men and their penises continued to grow, but instinctively, I knew it was "wrong" so I simply kept my thoughts to myself. Nevertheless, I always sought out opportunities to be around men and boys in locker room or restroom situations where I might sneak a glance at their genitals.

Interestingly, my playmates were almost exclusively female. I enjoyed playing with girls and got along with them famously. Gail, Joni, and Kathy were my most frequent playmates, and I had no compunction about playing "house" while my peers were tossing footballs or playing catch. I never was athletic, so such pursuits were of little interest to me. However, I did develop a few friendships with other boys in grade school, and in traditional childhood sexual experimentation, I ended up awkwardly attempting fellatio with three or four of them by second grade. I knew it was "wrong" but I enjoyed it immensely.

I always had girlfriends, and never lacked for female company. At the age of eight, I was caught by my brother kissing Joni on the lips behind her garage. I genuinely felt a strong puppy love for this girl (whom I always prayed at night that I would eventually marry) and nurtured a strong affection for her throughout my childhood. But my sexual fantasies were always focused on men.

When I was ten, my father was offered an attractive job promotion in San Diego. This was a major move for our family, leaving the familiar behind and moving to a city with comparatively few Mormons. Nevertheless, the charm, warmth, and beauty of Southern California beckoned, and we made the move. I entered the fifth grade in 1965 and was placed in a split class—half fifth grade and half sixth. My teacher, Mr. Robison, was a dashing, handsome single man in his thirties. He sported a full head of wavy black hair, a megawatt smile, a lean, muscled body, and a genuine love for children. I was strongly attracted to this man and did all I could to curry his favor. I excelled so strongly that within three months, he decided that I should "skip" a grade and move to the sixth grade side of the class. Of course, skipping a grade required additional tutoring to get me up to speed, so I spent time after school being privately coached by him. There was never anything untoward in his behavior, yet there was always a sexual component on my part. Secretly, I wanted to sit on his lap and feel his genitals against my buttocks. But naturally, I never mentioned this to anyone.

The following year, I enrolled in junior high. This is always a big move for children—what with lockers, teenagers, and six teachers and classrooms instead of one. Most horrifying, though, was P.E. class. We actually had to undress and shower in front of every one. I'm sure the first few times were just as terrifying for the other boys, who were schooled in the fine art of modesty. Within a few weeks, however, most of us had lost our inhibitions and took to the showers naturally. I found it a wonderful voyeur's paradise. I came to know all of my classmates' penises by heart: who was uncircumcised (I thought foreskin was a genetic defect for a long time), who had long penises, and who sported large testicles. Naturally, I was attracted to the well-endowed boys.

I had my first teenage sexual experience during Boy Scout campouts. Generally, our scoutmaster would pile eight or nine of us pubescent scouts into his roomy VW van and ferry us up into the Cuyamca Mountains in eastern San Diego County.

We learned the basics of outdoor cooking, knot-tying, first aid, and survival. At the end of the day, we pitched our pup tents and paired off. During my two to three years in the scouts, I attended a couple of dozen campouts and was able to bunk with most of the guys in the troop. I "fooled around" with at least six of them before going to sleep. Our experimentation was truly quite innocent, and consisted mostly of mutual masturbation and awkward attempts at fellatio. It quickly became known that I had the largest penis in the troop, and the other boys often fought over who would be my tentmate at night. During one particular moonless night, three of us decided to dispense with the tent and sleep under the stars. We zipped our three sleeping bags together to make one spacious bag, and began mutual body exploration. Because I had the largest penis, the other two boys disappeared under the covers and proceeded to have fun with my genitals. I remember lying there, counting the stars with a grin on my face while I was brought to a delicious orgasm by two horny Boy Scouts.

I began dating at age fourteen. Each year, I seemed to have a different girlfriend. It was customary to "go steady" back in the sixties, and this generally consisted of presenting a St. Christopher's medallion (worn around the neck) to one's girl. I had no idea of the significance of the medal, being Mormon. I simply accepted the fact that this was a token of fidelity between steadies. Patti was my girl in seventh grade, Mary in eighth, and Karen in ninth. I was never an affectionate or doting boyfriend, and in retrospect, I now know why these girls broke up with me. I was expected to hold hands, kiss, and neck on a regular basis, yet this was slightly abhorrent to me. When we would go to the movies, I would offer the obligatory smooch or two, but never had any interest in going beyond these simply juvenile moves. Never once did I participate in necking, petting (those words have since gone out of favor), or body exploration, and to this day I can safely say that I have never felt the female breast (nor do I have any desire to do so).

A few years before, at age twelve, I had secured a paper route which included a three-block strip of commercial businesses. I arose every morning at 4:30 A.M. to fold and deliver my papers on bicycle. I noticed one day late in 1969 that an adult bookstore had opened for business on my route. The establishment was located in a small building nestled between a restaurant and TV repair shop. A large picture window was partially painted over to discourage furtive viewing of the merchandise. I was immediately curious. One morning, I arose around 3:00 A.M. with the objective of finishing my paper route early and exploring the premises of this adult bookstore. At four, I was finished with my rounds. The streets were empty and quiet, and I was ready. The picture window in front of the adult bookstore featured a ledge or sill, which was barely three feet off the ground. I leapt up on the sill and was tall enough to peer in the upper part of the window that hadn't been painted over. Spying racks of magazines full of naked men and women, I was fascinated.

Each morning, I arose a little bit earlier so that I could spend time peering in the window at the nude bodies that paraded in front of me. In fact, I made a habit of carrying a pair of pocket-sized, fold-up binoculars. This brought the magazines into full view and I was able to see adult genitals close up for the first time. One morning, I had finished my route before five, and pedaled over for my daily viewing session. When I arrived, I noticed that someone had smashed a hole through the front window. Shards of glass lay on the sidewalk. I don't know if the motive was vandalism, theft, or revenge by angry neighbors who didn't want such filth in their neighborhood; but regardless, I took advantage of the opportunity and reached in the hole, extracting dozens of magazines and stuffing them in my empty canvas paper bags. I returned those featuring naked females as they were of no interest to me. Loaded with sexual booty, I pedaled home and stashed the magazines under my bed. Several times a day I would retrieve a magazine and masturbate while fantasizing about those huge adult penises. I had to be careful, as I shared the room with my brother. One day, he saw a corner of one magazine protruding beneath the dust ruffle. I guess I had carelessly tossed it under the bed without making sure that it was well-hidden. He took the magazine and showed it to my parents. My father quickly came in and lectured me on the evils of homosexuality. I cried. I was confused. I began to feel that my predilection for the other men was evil and that I was condemned to hell if I didn't change.

I seriously tried to change. One day, while I was home alone, I tossed my porn magazines into an aluminum trashcan and set them all on fire. Half-way through the inferno, I had a change of heart and quickly put out the flames. I was able to retrieve a portion of the magazines that hadn't gone up in smoke. Some of my favorite big-dick photos were partially charred, and I lovingly flicked off the ashes from those that could be salvaged. This time I made sure that they were kept in a safe and secure place where they couldn't be discovered by my nosy brother or anyone else. For over a year, these pictures became my regular masturbation material and possibly set the tone for the type of man I would be attracted to later on.

I went through various episodes of repentance and regression. For weeks at a time, I would repent of my sins and stop masturbating (our church bishop had made it clear that masturbation was evil), then sexual desires would well up like pressurized lava ready to explode from a volcanic vent, and I would resume masturbating several times a day. The guilt would hit once more and I would repent again.

During my high school days, I began to excel academically, although in retrospect, I didn't apply myself as much as I should have. I enjoyed P.E. class, but was never truly athletic. While the "jocks" went out for track, wrestling, or football, I was content to collect my B grade and concentrate on getting As in my other classes. Nevertheless, I relished shower time, in which I could get an eyeful of the other boys. In particular, I always made sure that I showered next to Ray B., who sported a thickly veined, pendulously long penis that seemed to reach halfway to his knees. Visions of this manhood trophy penetrated my thought several times a day, and I sincerely wanted to experience sex with this guy; but at age sixteen, I knew that if rebuffed, I would be branded a "faggot" and would soon become a campus pariah. I couldn't chance it. During my adolescence, I had several of my buddies sleep over, and during this time, I came to love, understand, and appreciate the beauty of the male body. We engaged in mutual masturbation, oral sex, and frottage. And by fourteen, I had learned the joys of anal sex. I was a full-fledged homosexual. My favorite partners were a pair of fraternal twins with large penises who loved to play "Lucky Pierre"—a sexual game of group anal sex in which I was the middle of the sandwich—with one twin in front and one behind.

I had always wondered why I was attracted to men. My parents, siblings, church leaders, teachers, and friends were all (allegedly) straight; yet I had absolutely no attraction to the opposite sex. Over time, I began to accept the fact that my sexuality was genetic. There was no way that it could be conditioned as I knew no gay individuals in my childhood. All of my role models, teachers, church leaders, and friends were heterosexual, yet by some quirk of nature, I turned out differently. This anomaly, coupled with the extreme guilt that religion places on homosexuals, affected every aspect of my life, and I faced years of sincere attempts at reforming myself.

During my senior year of high school, I developed a friendship with my Spanish teacher. In tenth grade, I had become attracted to Steve S. who taught fourth-year Spanish. He was in his late twenties, of medium stature, with short brown hair, a slim build, and *very* hirsute (I've always been attracted to hairy men). I was always a good student of Spanish, but never outstanding—that is, until he became my teacher. I wanted him to notice me and soon I began to study and apply myself. By the end of the year, I was one of the top students. I continued on with Spanish the next year, making sure that he was my teacher. I learned that his hobby was archery, so I took up the sport as well. One day, he invited me on a deer hunting trip to the San Bernardino Mountains behind San Dimas which I readily accepted. I arose at 5 A.M. and drove to his house. It was a two-hour drive to San Dimas, and during that time, we talked about school, archery, and hunting. My heart palpitated at an accelerated pace during the entire trip, and my penis was certainly erect with adolescent excitement.

Steve (married with two small children) and I quickly became friends as well as hunting partners, and began to enjoy monthly trips together. By my senior year, he asked me to be his "teacher's aide" for first-year Spanish class. We spent three years together in the classroom, and although nothing sexual ever developed between us, I could sense his attraction for me, while mine for him was nothing short of obvious. In retrospect, I'm glad that nothing transpired as I now understand the danger of student/teacher entanglements. My attraction to Steve was instrumental in my development of love for language from my experience as a senior aide and has largely shaped my academic and social life to this day.

During my senior year, I was accepted to Brigham Young University. There was never any question about where I would go, BYU was the natural choice. I lived in the dorms, and enjoyed intense friendships with a series of roommates. I was very chaste during this period, concentrating on my spiritual and academic development. I started out with a pre-med major, but organic chemistry quickly changed my mind. I decided to concentrate on subjects that were truly interesting to me: I focused my studies on geography and languages, studying Russian, Spanish, and Italian.

By age eighteen, it became time to seriously think about going on a mission—a tacit obligation of young Mormon men. I was actively involved in Army ROTC, quickly establishing myself as one of the top cadets, and I fancied a military career. This was an ironic move for me, considering the fact that I had never been involved in any of the traditional male endeavors such as athletics, but I became fascinated by the disciplined, masculine nature of the military. I loved wearing the uniform and liked the way I looked in it. I also got a lot of looks of admiration from the coeds on campus. Equally important, I loved the looks of the other cadets in uniform. Although sexually tempted, I never made a move on a fellow cadet, as I knew that homosexuality was ground for immediate dismissal.

Although I was certain that I would pursue a successful military career, there was always a nagging voice in my head that told me I should go on a mission. For months I conveniently ignored that prompting. Finally, one evening as I said my nightly prayers, I casually asked my Heavenly Father if I should go on a mission. I wasn't expecting an answer, yet I got one the next day. I felt a warm glowing sensation through my body which told me that it was the right decision. It was as if I had a complete change of heart. I *knew* I had to go on a mission and I was delighted with my choice. In October 1974, I concluded my interviews with my bishop and Stake President and submitted my papers. Ten days later, I received my call. It was a cold Saturday morning in October and I was dressed in full-dress military gear. I had attended the BYU/Wyoming football game and had raised the flag prior to kickoff. I remembered shivering during the game from the bitter north wind that delivered snow later in the day. Immediately after the game (we lost), I rushed back to the dorm and headed straight to my mail box. I immediately recognized the large, white envelope. The next two years of my life were contained in that letter.

A flood of emotions poured through my mind. Where would I go? Finland? Italy? Argentina? I figured that since I had already studied in several European languages, I would be headed East across the Atlantic. Anywhere but the Orient, I said. Please don't send me there. With trembling hands and racing heart, I ripped open the envelope and read the words: "Dear Elder Griffin, You have been called by the Lord to serve in the Bangkok, Thailand, mission." Without bothering to read the rest of the letter, I ran throughout the dorm, excitedly shouting my news to all my dormmates. I was elated. I wasn't really excited about going to the Orient, but my disappointment quickly disappeared. I was going to one of the most exotic spots on the planet, and I was elated. I was to report to the Language Training Mission in Laie, Hawaii, in less than two months!

For the next eight weeks, I mentally prepared myself by studying scriptures, trying to teach myself the rudiments of the Thai language, and praying. I was determined to expunge my homosexual feelings and become the ideal missionary. I was certain that if I served the Lord diligently, that he would change my evil nature and turn me into a heterosexual. Believing in miracles, I knew that this change was a bonafide possibility.

In January, I flew to Hawaii and endured two months of mentally draining language boot camp in Laie, on the north coast of Oahu. Forget the gorgeous scenery, the sandy beaches, and the perfumed air. We didn't have time to enjoy any of that. Our days were occupied from 6:00 A.M. to 10:00 P.M. with language study and memorizing the "discussions" in Thai that we would deliver to interested "investigators" in Thailand. The language, based on a series of five tones, was diabolically difficult, and I cried myself to sleep many nights. I already spoke fluent Spanish and Italian, but this was another matter altogether. In retrospect, what we accomplished in that two-month period was nothing short of miraculous. We memorized the equivalent of seventy pages of Thai dialogue (with scarcely a clue as to what we were committing to memory), and were speaking rudimentary Thai within eight weeks.

On March 17, 1975, I and my seven fellow "elders" (as Mormon missionaries are called) flew to Bangkok to begin our missions. I was assigned as junior companion to the Branch President in Bangkok. I was disappointed as I wanted to go to the North where I would be able to pedal my bike through the jungle. Instead, I was relegated to this crowded, polluted, stinking metropolis. Elder Koniuszy, the Branch President, was assigned as my companion. He was a twenty-seven-year-old, barrel-chested, beefy military-type man who reminded me of Yogi Bear. We were two different men from two different backgrounds. We never got along and spent two difficult months together. Despite our disparate backgrounds and compatibility, I found myself secretly attracted to him. Physically, he was my ideal. Every night (as instructed) we kneeled down to say our prayers together. Dressed only in our religious underwear, I was able to see him from the rear—a well-built, hirsute man, who also sported a large penis. I often went to sleep fantasizing about him— and although our personalities clashed, I was attracted to him like a moth to a flame. However, I knew that if I ever acted on my desires, I would quickly be excommunicated and sent home in disgrace. I couldn't risk such humiliation and degradation. I kept my fantasies to myself—and felt terribly guilty for them.

My mission was a success. By my eighth month, I was told that if I were placed behind a sheet the natives would not be able to tell that I wasn't Thai. I excelled in the language (I spent two hours a day memorizing words from the dictionary) and was soon speaking it fluently. This got me past many doors and I found myself coming out of my shell. Before my mission, I was a shy, reticent boy who steered away from strangers. However, in this exotic land, I soon became a star. A handsome, blond "farang" (Thai slang for Caucasian) who spoke their language fluently, I attracted attention wherever I went. When assigned to rural outposts, I used to pedal my bike through the jungle with my companion and come across Thais who had never before seen a white person. They were fascinated by our appearance and listened in rapt attention as we spoke their language. I loved to watch the mouths drop as I spoke. I became very attached to two of my companions in particular, and we shared tearful farewells when one of us was transferred to another city. By the time my mission concluded two years later, I had served in four cities and had mastered several dialects. I came home a different person in 1977.

I quickly resumed my studies at Brigham Young University where I moved back into the dorms. Within weeks I was called to serve in the Elder's Quorum Presidency in my branch (Mormon diocese). I became quite popular and was involved in a number of school- and church-related activities. In September 1977, I met the girl who I hoped would one day become my wife. Vicki was an eighteen-year-old freshman with a myriad of talents. She was a mathematician who played concert violin and spoke German. She was a fresh-faced blond, blue-eyed Scandinavian girl whom I quickly fell in love with. I knew we would make beautiful children together. I asked her to marry me and she quickly accepted (much to my surprise). Then I got terrified. I was in one of the most confusing aspects of my life. I was supposed to marry, but I had no sexual inclination.

At this time, I became increasingly attracted to men, yet I continued to deny my feelings. I took up an interest in racquetball and played several times a week at the Richards P.E. building on campus. At the conclusion of the game, I usually put my street clothes back on without showering for fear that I would get an erection while watching other men in the nude. Finally, I decided that I was going to go into the sauna and shower. This required a great deal of bravery on my part and it became a pivotal point in my life. For the first time in my life, I was sitting next to five to six gorgeous students, all enjoying the sanctuary of the heated sauna in the nude. I was fascinated. I often brought in the *Daily Universe* (the campus newspaper) and pretended to read it, all the while peering secretively over the top of the page while spying the penises seated opposite me. One man, a 6'10" basketball player, caught my eye. He smiled sheepishly, then proceeded to "nod" his penis up and down. It must have been a foot long, and I developed an immediate erection. I had to wad up my towel and place it over my genitals so that my other sauna mates wouldn't notice. I finally summoned enough courage to begin a conversation. He introduced himself as Lee and said that he was just a few months away from his Ph.D. We quickly became friends and after a few "dates" became sexually active. This was my first sexual experience with an adult male, and I was transfixed. Never before had such an experience been so fulfilling or so powerful. We took long walks up into secluded Rock Canyon, holding hands, embracing, and kissing. The sensations were galvanic, and I figured that this must be how it feels for heterosexual boys when they begin to date girls. I loved Lee and wanted to spend every free moment with him. He was a great kisser, having learned how from his wife, from whom he was divorced. With each passing day, our emotional attachment increased. Yet I was engaged to be married. I wanted Lee, but knew I was to marry Vicki. After a few months of sterile, clinical dating, Vicki sensed a calm emotional withdrawal on my part and called off the wedding. I was devastated and relieved at the same time.

As my sexual experimentation increased, so did my distance from the church. I knew that I was transgressing, and if caught, would be excommunicated; so rather than risk punitive action for my homosexuality, I simply distanced myself from the religion. I graduated in 1979 and moved to Salt Lake, where I became very sexually active, meeting men in the parks and at the baths. My motives were always the same—to look for love. I sincerely wanted to find a man whom I could love and live with, but such a partner proved elusive. I was invariably attracted to clean-cut, successful, married Mormon men (usually twenty years my senior) and quickly learned that such liaisons pointed to dead ends. I had relationships with a series of men, including one polygamist who had four wives—and me. I asked him what his secret was. He said he consumed copious quantities of the herb damiana, which kept his libido up. Damiana, by the way, was once colloquially known as "Mormon Wafer" as it was a popular folk tonic among the early polygamists to keep their lustful fires burning.

In 1980, I had my first true relationship. I fell madly in love with a successful, married, forty-seven-year-old Harvard-trained attorney I met in a San Diego bathhouse. He was called to start a new office in Los Angeles, so he temporarily left his family behind in La Jolla for a year. We rented an apartment and set up housekeeping. Fortunately, he went back to his home on the weekends, so we never had to worry about surprise visits from his wife. I was madly in love with Ken, and every waking moment was spent thinking about him. He was my idol—successful, wealthy, handsome, and sexual. I worshiped this man and finally knew what it meant to be truly and completely in love. But this blissful experience proved short-lived. Once his L.A. tenure was up, he had to return to La Jolla to work and family and we ceased living together. My world was crushed and I went through a major depression. Nevertheless, I knew I wanted to be like him, and the only way was through advanced education.

I soon enrolled in the M.B.A. program at UCLA and spent the next two years in intense study. During the summer of 1982, I was hired to fill an internship at Atari in Sunnyvale, California. At the time, Atari was one of the nation's hot companies, with dozens of popular videogames and home computer systems on the market. I had a dream job, marketing the computer systems to the European market, while jetting on weekends to Zermatt and St. Moritz to conduct international Pac-Man competitions. At the opening of the opera season in San Francisco, I ran into the company chairman at a gala black tie affair. I introduced myself as one of his thousands of employees. His eyes caught mine, and one thing led to another. We ended up having an affair until I had to return to L.A. to complete the final year of my M.B.A. program, receiving my degree in 1983. I went through a series of marketing jobs in the pharmaceuticals and computer industries, as well as through a parade of lovers—always in search of that elusive man to replace Ken.

In 1989, I had landed a wonderful job making $50,000 a year (a lot of money for a single man back then) as a marketing manager for an international software firm. I had a great boss, a terrific lady, who doted over my every idea and achievement. We made a great team. Then she became pregnant and decided to take a two years off to raise her child. She was replaced by a megalomaniacal tyrant who quickly assumed that I must be gay, considering that I was thirty-three and unmarried. He trumped up an excuse that financial troubles necessitated my dismissal, but I later learned that he harbored an immense hatred of Jews, gays, and Asians.

There was one of each of us on his staff, and within a month, all three of us had been fired. That was the first time that I had ever witnessed such blatant discrimination based on sexual preference, but I had no concrete proof to pursue legal action, so I simply went on my way.

I vowed that I would never again be the victim of the pink slip (or of anti-gay discrimination) and decided that my future lay in self-employment. I had no idea which skills could propel me into my own business, but decided to write a book—quite on a lark. I knew that some of my greatest interests lay in the field of sexuality, and so I proceeded to write on the subject of penis enlargement. Why such a salacious and controversial topic? I guess because the subject fascinated me and I knew that there were thousands of others who shared my interest. When I began my research, I learned that there was precious little original material on the subject, but nevertheless, I compiled enough to result in a thin fifty-page booklet. I used the last of my savings to have five hundred copies printed. I proceeded to advertise it in a couple of gay publications. The orders began to trickle in. As more advertising was placed, more orders arrived. By the end of 1990, the book had sold out and I went to press with a second edition.

The success of this book inspired me to write a followup title, *The Art of Auto Fellatio* and a third, *Penis Power—A Complete Guide to Potency Restoration.* Soon, I developed a loyal audience who hounded me for more titles. During the next couple of years, I cranked out an entire series of books on the subject of male sexuality, including *Testicles—The Ball Book, The Vacuum Pumper's Handbook, The Horsemen's Club, The Condom Encyclopedia, Aphrodisiacs for Men, The History of Men's Underwear, Decircumcision, Straight Talk about Surgical Penis Enlargement, Sex for One—The Art of Male Masturbation,* and *The Legendary Endowment Project.* I also developed a newsletter, *Penis Power Quarterly,* which featured the latest developments in penis enlargement, surgical genital enhancement, potency restoration, aphrodisiacs, and HIV breakthroughs. Within a year I had several thousand subscribers and had been the subject of stories in *Penthouse, GQ,* and *Esquire* magazines.

With each new book, I developed an increasingly loyal reader base who eagerly awaited the next in the series. I had stumbled on this niche market quite by accident, and quickly realized that there were millions of men who wanted reliable information about their sexuality, but who had nowhere to turn. I decided to become the expert and to research every aspect of this area in order to provide, fun, entertainment, and reliable information to my readers. By 1994, I was considered by many to be one of the "experts" in my field. *Muscular Development* magazine contacted me and asked me to write a monthly column titled "Sexual Performance." Almost overnight, my sales doubled, and immediately I attracted tens of thousands of male heterosexual readers—many of whom purchased my books. I soon discovered that the fascination with the male body is shared by both gay and straight men. I sought to improve the quality of my writing and the quality of my books to present a more professional image, while retaining the erotic and alluring nature of their presentation.

In 1993, the medical world discovered penis enlargement, and within a month, dozens of surgeons began offering phalloplasty augmentation to their male patients. For several thousand dollars a man could undergo a fairly simple surgical procedure and have his penis lengthened and thickened. This new field fascinated me and I proceeded to meet all of the doctors involved in this burgeoning enterprise. After I wrote my book on surgical penis enlargement, I invited a number of the doctors to attend a meeting in Palm Springs. I wanted to bring them together so that they could network and exchange ideas. Doctors are notoriously jealous, protective, and egotistical. While they are willing to openly discuss their procedures with me, they are quite reticent about opening up to other doctors—who may learn their surgical secrets. I wanted to break down this barrier and get a dialogue started between them so that they could be mutually supportive and learn new techniques that would benefit the patients.

My meeting was a success, and the doctors encouraged me to arrange a followup. By our fourth meeting in Palm Springs, in 1995, there were more than thirty doctors in attendance and a number of friendships had developed between them. Dr. Robert Safford, a prominent Colorado urologist, approached me with the idea of formally organizing an official medical academy. He wrote up a series of bylaws and asked me to nominate a president, secretary, and treasurer to launch our association. At our June 1995 meeting at the Westin Mission Hills resort in Rancho Mirage, we formally organized. An impressive group of urologists and plastic surgeons from around the world attended. Much to my surprise, they nominated me as the executive director—the only nonsurgeon in the bunch. I was honored beyond words.

Today, I am busy conducting more research into my beloved field of male sexuality, in the process of writing my fourteenth and fifteenth books (*Sexual Performance Secrets* and *Hair Restoration Breakthroughs*) and have just celebrated the third year of my successful publication, *Penis Power Quarterly*. I'm proud to say that this publication is read by a number of doctors, professionals, and sex researchers around the world. Over the past two years, I have been the guest on over one hundred radio and television talk shows, and must give my personal thanks to John Bobbitt. Before his penis amputation by his ex-wife, Lorena, we were unable to mention the word "penis" in polite company. Now it has become a hot topic in the media, and the related interest has translated into explosive sales of my books. My flagship book, *Penis Enlargement Methods—Fact & Phallusy,* is now going into its ninth edition, and a slightly sanitized version is now mass-marketed in the major bookstore chains, including B. Dalton, Crown, and Barnes & Noble. Who would have thought that a penis book would make it to the mainstream just five years age? A Portuguese edition will shortly be available in Brazil.

In addition to my research in male sexuality, I have become increasingly involved in HIV research. I am tired of seeing thousands of my brothers and sisters succumb to one of the most devastating diseases known to man. This plague must have an end. Various new treatments and alternative methods of dealing with AIDS are evolving. I intently investigate all of these areas and hope to be able to direct my readers to promising therapies in the near future. This is my mission in life.

In addition, I still harbor my love of languages. I am in the process of writing my magnum opus—a compendium titled *The World's Top 100 Languages—from Albanian to Zulu*. This will be a fun, informative book that explores the nuances of each of the world's major languages. A followup, *The World's Most Unusual Languages* will be my next project. It will be co-authored by my former linguistics professor at BYU and will be accompanied by a CD which features snippets from such unusual languages as Hopi, Inuit (Eskimo), Ainu, Neo-Melanesian, Lappish, aboriginal tongues, and others. It will be a fun project.

It took thirty-five years for me to reconcile my sexuality. Ever since I first realized that I harbored lustful feelings for members of the same sex, I felt guilt and shame. I believed the church doctrine that homosexuality was evil and that God would ultimately punish me. I assumed that I was already damned and adopted a devil-may-care attitude in my early twenties which resulted in careless sexual experimentation and promiscuity. Fortunately, I completely avoided alcohol and recreational drugs. By 1983, when HIV hit full force, I realized that I had to settle down and met my current lover at the Rose Tattoo restaurant in West Hollywood. In 1994, I began some serious self-exploration, and with months of serious prayer and meditation, received a strong feeling that I was loved and accepted by God the way I was. This self-acceptance allowed me to reveal my sexuality to my family and friends. In my wildest dreams, I never thought that I would be able to admit my homosexuality to those close to me, but once I did, I felt a strong sense of liberation. I no longer had to lie or hide. Fortunately, I had surrounded myself by honest, loving, and loyal friends and not a single one among them abandoned me for my sexuality. In fact, the revelation brought most of us closer.

My mother cried for three days when I told her I was gay. My father accepted the revelation calmly, as did my siblings. It was a difficult admission, but I assured my parents that I was the same, loving, compassionate son. My sexuality was not a choice. God knows, for thirty years I tried *not* to be gay. But despite my fasting, prayers, and devotion to my church, God never sought fit to change my sexuality. I finally realized that he had no intention of doing so. Once I came to a quiet acceptance of my gayness, I began to grow spiritually. Religion was no longer a factor in my life, but true spirituality and inner growth became the hallmarks of my existence. Through my study, I came to realize that the purpose of life is twofold—to gain knowledge and to learn to love. I've dedicated my life to helping others, and part of that dedication comes through my writings in male sexuality. Through my publications and phone consultations, I've been able to help thousands of men with various sexual problems who had nowhere else to turn.

Shortly, I will relocate to the White Mountains of Arizona. Having lived in Palm Springs for five years, I have grown to love this desert paradise, but realize that I am sitting on top of a seismically volatile area. My dream is to live in a spacious five-bedroom ranchette where I can establish my publishing business and write in a quiet, natural environment. I will have ample acreage in which to cultivate wildflowers and a flourishing vegetable garden. And let's not forget my dogs.

My most faithful companions will be rewarded with frolicking squirrels, falling pine cones, books, and fresh alpine air.

I have major plans for my business, Added Dimensions Publishing. I look to have my flagship book translated into German and French and will continue to research and write new titles that are of interest to my readers. I will shortly launch a magazine of high-quality photos of nude bodybuilders taken in the 1950s and 60s. I recently inherited thousands of negatives of photos that would have been banned when first taken. These are beautiful art photos and merit publication. The magazine will be titled *Adonis Classic.*

Ultimately, I have discrimination to thank for getting me into my line of work. I truly turned a difficult situation into an advantage. Had I not been let go by a homophobic boss, I never would have had the courage to venture into the uncharted waters of male sexuality.

20

Life as a Sexologist

William E. Hartman, Ph.D.

William E. Hartman, who set this book project in motion, began as a marriage and family counselor and then with Marilyn A. Fithian became a sex therapist and researcher. Two of the pioneers in sex therapy, he and Fithian traveled the country offering seminars to those interested in learning more about the field. Like William Masters and Virginia Johnson, though unlike most therapists, they conducted major research on orgasms and other physiological aspects of human sexuality.

MY INTEREST IN human sexuality began as a family sociologist teaching courses in marriage and family relations. The reproductive function of the family theoretically included all socially approved sexual function.

As a marriage counselor, I saw many serious problems related to sexuality contributing to a rapidly rising divorce rate. In an effort to help couples with their marital and sexual problems, I asked Marilyn Fithian to assist me in opening the Center for Marital and Sexual Studies in 1968.

A brief history will summarize my activities prior to the establishment of the center.

I was born in Meadville, Pennsylvania, in 1919, the eldest of four children. My parents had met in Meadville as students at Allegheny College. My father was a Methodist minister.

In June 1944, I married Iva Decker of Mesa, Arizona. The first of our seven children was born in June 1945. We were divorced in 1980. My children and grandchildren have always been a source of great joy.

Following the war, we purchased a home in Los Angeles. I enrolled at the University of Southern California and completed three degrees, including the Ph.D. in sociology, by 1950.

Following receipt of my M.A. degree in 1948 I began part-time practice as a marriage counselor/psychotherapist. My interest in human sexuality began in these professional clinical settings. Resolving nonsexual problems was more easily accomplished than dealing with sexual issues.

I didn't recall any sexual activities during my childhood until I began working in the area of human sexuality. By my taking histories of people in therapy, my memories resurfaced. Three minor events come to mind. First of these was a small group of preadolescent youngsters, including myself, showing each other our genitalia, without the knowledge of our parents. The second event involved a carpenter doing repair work a few houses from home. To the best of my memory, I think he had me and possibly another youngster involved in some kind of oral stimulation. No one was ever told about the event, hence nothing was ever said or done about it. I had forgotten all about it and it made little impression on me, then or now. The last event was the beginning of adolescence. Our parents were away and a babysitter taking care of my sister Jane and me exposed her breasts. I thought this was a good lesson in sex education. I'm sure my babysitter's and my parents would have questioned the wisdom of that, had they been aware of it at the time.

I taught one year at El Camino College after receiving my Ph.D. I then taught twenty-nine years at California State University at Long Beach, chairing the sociology and social welfare department from 1960 to 1963. I taught courses in marriage, family, criminology, juvenile delinquency, and small groups. In the mid-1960s, I introduced a course in the sociology of sexual behavior. The students were like dry sponges with a few drops of moisture in the form of being able to listen to lectures about human sexuality and writing their midterm papers which included an analysis of their own sexuality. Students in the marriage course wrote autobiographies of which sexuality was a part. Maybe it's only fair now that I'm doing a brief analysis of my own sexuality.

My sabbatical leave in 1959 proved to be a significant turning point in my professional career. Teaching criminology and juvenile delinquency suggested the wisdom of researching the basic causes of aberrant and antisocial behavior. I proposed spending a semester in New York City and Boston. The university sabbatical leave committee agreed.

In New York, I was referred to postal inspectors who saw pornography as causing crime. Basically, they felt nudist magazines were suspect, noting that many pictures came from nudist parks in California. I had never heard of nudism or nudist parks before. Returning home, the challenge of researching social nudism remained a possibility sometime in the future. Little did I realize what hornets' nests would be stirred up at home and in the church and community.

It seemed the better part of wisdom to ask respected colleagues at the university about the judiciousness of proposing funding for a project on social nudism. Their reply was "only if you are a full professor and have tenure." Since both conditions were met, I made a proposal and received modest funding during the 1963–1964 academic year. The only restriction was that the university president did not want a car owned by the university being driven in and out of nudist parks.

I constructed a simple one-page questionnaire. A leading nudist who was a well-known writer was asked to make contact for visits. He had also written on nudism, but under a pseudonym. I've since wondered what would have happened if

I had done the same thing. At that time being up front about my identity, the proposal, and research seemed the only way to go. It still does. Living daily under the possibility of exposure was not a viable alternative for me.

Data gathering began immediately and cooperation in getting the one-page questionnaire completed was superb. One woman, however, hesitated to cooperate, stating "I'm not a nudist." I soon learned that she was typical of many nudist participants who could not risk official membership records which might be exposed to reveal their participation. Teachers, ministers, and priests seemed largely to comprise this group. My definition of a nudist evolved very quickly—anyone nude in a nudist park was a nudist. In all, I visited some twenty-five nudist parks.

After I had several hundred completed questionnaires, the next problem was how to get the data analyzed. I asked one of my students, Marilyn Fithian. She responded positively and never balked when the initial two hundred respondents increased almost sevenfold to one thousand three hundred eighty-eight.

One gentleman, upon completion of his questionnaire, informed me that my research had a serious limitation. Since no woman was involved in the project, the public would regard me as just another dirty old man in a nudist park. This was quickly and easily remedied by offering Marilyn Fithian co-authorship of the next in-depth questionnaire. We constructed one of six pages. In addition, we administered the Minnesota Multiphasic Personality Inventory (MMPI) which comprises 566 individual questions. We received 432 completed questionnaires. About half that number took the MMPI. The personality test data were so pro-nudist we asked MMPI experts at the University of Minnesota to evaluate it. Nudist women must be one of the most normal groups ever evaluated, according to the results of the MMPI ("normal" meaning absence of psychopathology). The findings of our research, *Nudist Society*, were published by Crown Publishers in 1970 and reprinted by Elysium Growth Press in 1991. The book concerns personal, family, church, and other reactions to this research. One sentence from the introduction illustrates the appeal of the subject: "Our culture makes nudism a fascinating social and sexual phenomenon."

All my sex research and therapy activities were as a member of a dual-sex therapy team. Marilyn Fithian was a full partner, present in all activities. Neither of us could have done the research, treatment, training, and filming alone. Two heads are better than one, and in some creative aspects of these activities hers was better than mine.

Our next project in the mid-1960s was on nonorgasmic women. A leading Los Angeles OB/GYN physician, Kenneth Morgan, M.D., said he would cooperate with us if I had some training. Who would provide it? He suggested Dr. Arnold Kegel, who agreed and turned out to be a superb teacher. He sat me down in Los Angeles County General Hospital and taught me the female pelvis. First in words, then in the examining room. This was a wonderful opportunity for a nonphysician to work in the clinic.

One day during our weekly training sessions Dr. Kegel directed me to examine a forty-five-year-old female patient whose history reflected extensive experience with alcohol and sex. My hand not involved in the pelvis was on her knee. Dr.

Kegel, sensing something awry, approached her and asked, "What is wrong?" She replied, "His hand is on my knee." I removed it, said nothing, completed the exam, and gave the matter considerable thought. It was all right to have my finger in her vagina but a hand on a knee was too familiar. Thirty years later women often comment positively about a warm hand upon a foot during a sexological examination. I now stay away from the knee.

In working with nonorgasmic women in Dr. Morgan's office we needed a psychophysiological procedure to help women become orgasmic during coitus, one that could not be claimed by the medical board as a medical procedure. To fill this need we created the sexological examination. Everyone is entitled to choose to be examined as a sexual being. This is a physiological-psychological exam evaluating feeling, perception, and response of the genitalia. We developed this procedure which Dr. Morgan agreed was nonmedical in nature. All clients/patients sign a release acknowledging such and noting the need for routine medical examinations as a separate issue. Some two hundred fifty pages of unpublished manuscript recorded the result of our nonorgasmic women study. We noted the significance of pelvic exercises in enhancing sexual response for all women. Later we learned the same to be true for men.

Our three-year study of nonorgasmic women numbered eight-six subjects. Seven were habitually orgasmic with penile-vaginal intercourse and thus represented a control group. Two-thirds of the women became orgasmic with penile-vaginal stimulation during the course of the study. Others responded with clitoral stimulation only.

Major findings were the significance of motivation, attitude, and self-concept. The successful women reflected their motivation by keeping appointments, doing their assigned PC (pubococcygeus) exercises, and completing personality tests. They developed more positive attitudes toward their sexuality as they felt better about their identity and self-concept. Obviously, progress in therapy contributed to these changes. The last notable finding was that three husbands became impotent when the wife became orgasmic. This emphasized the importance of treating couples in sex therapy. I felt this study helped me understand female sexual function much better.

The key to my therapeutic interests has always been the enhancement of relationships. In all our sex therapy, we have required the participation of both partners. Our policy has been not to supply replacement partners (surrogates) for married clients. The most difficult case had one partner trying to place the entire blame on the partner beginning with the intake interview.

We developed a thirty-four-step treatment process for couples in sex therapy which we published it in 1972 as *Treatment of Sexual Dysfunction* (Jason Aronson; reprint 1974). Significant inclusions were the sexological examinations and body image work from our nudist research findings. It helped us evaluate the self-concept of the individual. Films were made of couples functioning effectively from which our dysfunctional couples could learn.

During the study of nonorgasmic women a rare event occurred. A twenty-one-year-old university student reported frequent urinary stress so that no social activity could be planned unless a restroom were immediately available, and that her boyfriend could not penetrate her vaginally. Examination revealed that a full bowel made vaginal penetration impossible. I would never have realized this could be a problem unless I had encountered it during the research.

Many anorgasmic women had bowel contents preventing penile contact with vaginal sexual segments at four and eight o'clock. Changing habits of elimination often produced much greater female response. Along with women becoming orgasmic, we found that many who had stress incontinence problems resolved them by pelvic exercises.

In the mid-1960s I saw a tremendous challenge in doing research and therapy in human sexuality. I was, and am, a great admirer of the seminal research of Kinsey and Masters and Johnson. For me, it provided the scientific basis for a discipline to be properly called sexology. I felt that what Dr. Masters was doing could profitably have a similar West Coast base of operation. I visited the Kinsey Institute on the campus of Indiana University where I was able to visit their film library. Some films made me uncomfortable at the time. We are a no-look, no-touch culture and those taboos needed to be worked through to work effectively in the sexual area.

When our nudist research was completed and ready for publication, I thought it time to consider specifically what to do in the area of sexuality. At this time, Marilyn was a full-time research partner and I asked if she would be interested in establishing a center where we could do research and therapy in human sexuality. She hesitated at first, sensing opposition would come from the Mormon church (to which I belonged), family, and, possibly to some extent, the community. Finally she agreed, and we sought an advisory board of professional people who would advise and stand with us in this venture.

There were several significant factors contributing to my entrance into the field of human sexuality. Beginning in 1948, when I became a therapist, many referrals were made to physicians for physical examinations. Presenting sexual problems suggested the wisdom of doing so. No sexual problems were resolved by these referrals.

University students flooded to courses in human sexuality. They wanted to know what science knew about the subject. As a sociologist teaching marriage and the family, I saw the divorce rate climb. Since many of these divorces were related to unsolved sexual problems, I wanted to see if this trend could be reduced.

Reaction to nudist research indicated a hard core in our society regarded nudity and sexuality as unresearchable. My church felt these areas should be illegal for practice as well as study. Receipt of religious tracts reflected the public call to repentance. Church authorities threatened disciplinary action should I conduct any research similar to Masters and Johnson. Part of my response reflected these threats. Something that can't be done is always a challenge. I didn't realize at the time the effect it would have on my children. Although I felt bad about that, the rewards of doing this work and seeing the positive results made it worthwhile.

I became a sexologist primarily because of the challenge of working in an area so many regard as taboo. Large numbers of Americans want and need help with their sexuality. Our sex-negative culture tends to dissuade professional help in terms of basic research and action-oriented therapy.

I have remained a sexologist for over twenty-eight years of full-time work because the results of therapy are so rewarding. The treatment process, based on our research, produces results our clients, and we, are pleased with. We note the same needs in Europe, Asia, and Africa. I doubt in our lifetime we can analyze all the research date we have collected.

When the center opened in 1968, we set up a special laboratory for physiological research. We followed the advice of Berry Campbell, Ph.D., professor of physiology at the University of California, Irvine, medical school. During our first ten years, we each worked more than ten thousand hours in the laboratory. We recorded, on a Beckman R411 Dynograph, masturbatory and coital activities of 751 research volunteers (469 women and 282 men). A research volunteer myself, I found it to be a significant experience in being comfortable with my own sexuality. I believe anyone doing sex research should be a subject. This helps them better understand how others may feel in the research laboratory. Some research volunteers were monitored in twenty-five different sessions. We learned that:

1. Pelvic muscles contract across the floor of the vagina, uterus, and anus.

2. It is impossible to tell male orgasms from female orgasms. Both have similar patterns.

3. In females anal and pelvic contractions match. This allows comparison of male and female physiological responses.

4. Cardiac data most accurately indicate orgasmic response. Heart rates of 120 for women and 155 for men are typical at orgasm.

5. Respiration is not a significant determinant of orgasm. Changing respiratory patterns, however, are the most effective approach to helping female subjects reach orgasm.

6. Twenty nonorgasmic women were monitored. Three-fourths were orgasmic with low intensity ratings (i.e., one, two, or three on a scale of ten). Changing breathing patterns intensifies orgasm, and reaching orgasm.

7. There is a "fingerprinting" effect of orgasm. Each individual has a unique pattern. Male and female patterns cannot be differentiated.

8. No research volunteer monitored by us reported a negative laboratory experience. Most volunteered for repeat sessions indicating satisfaction that science had confirmed their sexual function. A few subjects appeared to volunteer as "free therapy." They expected researcher's suggestions to improve their functioning.

9. We learned that men had the capacity to become multiply orgasmic. We included them in our physiological research protocol. The thirty-three multiple orgasmic men represented 12 percent of our male research population.

After laboratory documentation of this phenomenon we wrote *Any Man Can* (St. Martin's Press, 1984). Male orgasm and ejaculation can be separate events. Controlling ejaculation makes possible the occurrence of orgasm without ejaculation. Male PC muscle training is the ideal way for motivated men to become multiorgasmic. For immediate results the squeeze technique and/or stop/start stimulation may be preferable.

In the late 1960s, we had a couple in treatment with claims of serious sexual problems. The wife reported never having vaginal lubrication or orgasm, even with extended foreplay. My associate and I decided we should check this complaint at the conclusion of a body caress she and her husband completed in the laboratory.

She reclined on an examining table in an adjacent room. I checked for vaginal lubrication. Immediately she had an intense orgasm. Following Marilyn's suggestion, I continued checking. Abundant lubrication was present. I looked into the client's eyes and during concentrated eye contact she had another intense orgasm. This seemed to represent to her an intimate relationship. Her therapy group had suggested she have an affair outside her marriage to work out her sexual problems. One final intense orgasm occurred and Marilyn signaled the conclusion of the examination. I felt comfortable and professional and in no way sexually aroused.

Was I ever sexually aroused during therapy or research? Twice in fifteen years I noticed an emotional reaction to breathing patterns of couples copulating. There was no erective reaction. Falling asleep, particularly late at night, was a much more common response for me. When we were doing these observations, Marilyn Fithian and I had to nudge each other when one of us would begin nodding off.

I became a therapist before the days of state licensing in California. I was grandfathered in as a marriage, family and child counselor, and I had to take an examination to be a licensed psychologist. This I passed in 1968. Gradually professional influence and control has decreased, to be replaced by legal influence and control.

My most dramatic experience with this phenomenon occurred when I was national president of a learned society. I had informed the board of the society of the serious problems existing with our only paid employee, our executive director. She resigned and sued for purported character assassination. The case was tried in federal court in New York since she resided on the East Coast. She won the case and a one-dollar settlement. No possible professional solution was ever mentioned such as the ethics committee of the society. Although my malpractice insurance company paid for the legal expenses, I had to spend a lot of my own time and money traveling back and forth. Still, reflecting on whether I would pursue human sexuality again, I would answer yes. Many supportive professionals made our success possible. Our advisory board would be number one on the list. Ed Brecher, a writer and encourager, introduced us to Berry Campbell, our physiologist.

Some clients taught us that there is much more to sex than sex. These clients taught us about intimacy. They were supposed to rate the success of their treatment program on a scale of zero to one hundred. When asked to explain their rating of one hundred fifty they indicated what they thought was an intractable problem: a penis that wouldn't get erect, a vagina that didn't lubricate, or lack of orgasm. These problems were fairly easily resolved. The couples found and reported a great depth of mutually satisfying feeling never before experienced in their relationship. Physical and emotional intimacy were typical results of our form of sex therapy. They never were presenting symptoms, which tended to be impotency and physical problems such as anorgasmia.

Our clients' rating of their success in therapy averaged 92 percent. We didn't include in the average those reporting a figure of more than one hundred. Outside evaluation was done by a psychologist at a major university, which confirmed this figure.

Results of our sex therapy were uniformly high, ranging far above those noted in marriage counseling or individual psychotherapy. Economic rewards are another matter. Jim Young, our audio/visual coordinator at the center, hit the nail on the head when he informed me, "You have an expensive hobby." No one should expect sex therapy to be economically profitable. It needs to be combined with teaching or other therapy for a reasonable economic return.

Our seminars for professionals around the country supported our physiological research. We terminated these due to the outlay and concern that the income received would no longer cover the expense of doing them.

A male research subject, whom we had monitored a number of times, asked if we would like to see what he really did at home. He demonstrated his masturbatory pattern during which he energetically spanked himself which was a part of the routine. His whole session was worked from cue cards. Berry and his wife left stating the subject was "sick." We thought the routine unusual but normal for this subject. His MMPI showed him to be normal and our interaction over the months confirmed this assessment. This indicates normal people sometimes do interesting things.

We recorded 134 orgasms during a fifty-minute research session with a female volunteer. Upon studying the chart our physiologist was unconvinced that so many separate orgasms had been recorded. He reevaluated the chart and changed his mind after three other subjects had a similar pattern. Did she have 134 separate orgasms with 134 contractions? This is our current thinking, but future research might well define and monitor status orgasmus as well. This refers to subjects entering and remaining in a state of orgasm for extended periods of time.

Pelvic contractions of subjects are not easily monitored since some start contractions easily and stop after orgasm. Others begin when the orgasm reaches a high degree of intensity but continue on long after the cardiac data indicate that orgasm is technically over. Some subjects tighten their muscles to bring on the orgasm so contractions occur on a tightened muscle. In all these situations a sharp, clear pattern of contractions is not present.

Perhaps the most revealing aspect of working in the field of human sexuality concerned physicians. Shortly after opening the center in 1968, two physicians contacted us concerning opportunities for research to be conducted in our laboratory. In one instance, we cooperated in establishing a research protocol to monitor masturbatory and coital activity. The equipment was procured and set up and our first research subject was available.

I received a phone call from a physician heading a large medical complex. He inquired whether a young associate was included in doing research with us. I confirmed that he was which elicited the statement, "He'll have to choose between medicine and sex." We never heard from our collaborator again. This was received more than twenty-five years ago.

A similar incident occurred at approximately the same time. Another physician from a large medical school approached us about physiological research. Part was to be conducted in our lab and the remainder in the medical school. He phoned to report that when requesting approval from his dean he was told to make a choice between medicine and sex research. Regretfully, that was our last conversation.

We did have physicians in the lab with us. We did conduct research in physicians' offices though organized medicine seemed at the time and still seems reluctant to include sexuality as part of any core curriculum. I recall lecturing at a medical school in the Midwest in the 1970s. During a break in an all-day lecture, one senior medical student informed me that there were no sexual problems for physicians to be concerned about except those caused by people, like myself, going around talking about sex.

During sex therapy, we teach the male how to caress his wife's vagina with his index finger. One gynecologist refused to insert his finger without a glove. We had to convince him that his wife was different from his patients. Another distinguished gentleman was assigned to caress his wife's vagina in their motel room following a body-and-genital caress. The next day in the office we inquired about his success with this assignment; he replied, "I failed—my finger lost its erection."

We insisted researchers use gloves to insert transducers into vaginal and/or anal orifices. Even though he had been carefully instructed and the procedure had been agreed upon, one senior researcher contracted gonorrhea in the eye.

An ongoing challenge is responding to letters and phone calls, not just the routine but also the frantic. "My relationship will terminate if I don't get an immediate reply." Problem: "I don't ejaculate." My problem: "What's the problem?"

Long-distance calls from Europe had supposed life-and-death implications. "I'll kill myself if I can't get it up," or "I can't satisfy her." These allegedly successful professional men had to be helped to calm down, evaluate alternatives, and obtain professional help to move from life-and-death sex situations to relaxed encounters with fun.

In 1970, we first used a female surrogate. The forty-eight-year-old male client was a virgin referred by his psychiatrist. Socially and sexually inept as he was, professionally he was a very successful educator. Following the favorable termination of a two-week treatment program, he was asked to write a review of his progress. Part of his reply included the statement, "This is the first time in my life I ever felt love for anyone."

In the busy mid-1970s, time became a very rare commodity. Teaching full-time at the university and working full-time at the center left little time for anything else. Professionals wanted to visit. Sexuality classes wanted to tour our offices and laboratory.

Having visitors come to lunch solved most problems. Answering questions, posing for pictures, touring facilities, and signing books were an almost daily routine. Most memorable was a gentleman from Los Angeles who wanted to be hired on the spot. During lunch he expounded his sexual exploits, insisting he could "go either way," and wanted to start working for us following lunch. We kept him in mind but never found use for his services.

One secretary we hired didn't last an hour. Since she had been married five times, she thought working for us would benefit her. We agreed her typing skills could prove very useful. She was given some of our research material to type. When she encountered the word "masturbation" she was too upset to continue and quit immediately. This uptightness on her part may have had something to do with divorce.

Several years ago, a series of telephone death threats was received. The calls came on three successive nights: a male voice with a distinct foreign accent intoned, "You will die." No mention was made of sex or working in human sexuality. It would be interesting to know whether a female answering the phone would have received the same message. Female secretaries and my female associate received calls where the male caller apparently masturbated while speaking to a woman. These averaged four or five yearly, before and after the mid-1970s. During our peak years, the average rose four- or fivefold.

One female caller apparently masturbated while emoting with a male answering evening and late-night calls. What was an appropriate response to such calls? Suggestions for an office appointment to see a therapist were never accepted. Finally, after successive calls on the same evening, Marilyn picked up the phone. This terminated further calls.

A final source of late-night calls came once every few months from exuberant participants at Saturday night parties. One could hear raucous laughter in the background while a male voice requested treatment advice for a male or female sexual dysfunction. Installation of an answering machine solved virtually all such problems, though a few such calls and cries for help are still recorded.

We opened the center on the fifth floor of a bank building in 1968. Several years later the building was sold. As the director of the center, I was called to a meeting with a representative of the new owners, who would not permit our office to continue to be listed on the ground floor directory as "Center for Marital and Sexual Studies." What was the objection? The word "sexual" could not be listed in the directory. I responded that it was already so listed. In addition, it was the legal name of our nonprofit California corporation. It remained unchanged for the fourteen years we had offices in that building.

A fire marshal came to the office one day and wanted to "see it." The "it" was apparently the research laboratory and the bed in it. His appeared to be more curiosity than fire concern. During our book tour for *Any Man Can,* there evolved some interesting sexual phenomena. Male television and radio talk show hosts confided to me privately that they were multi-orgasmic. They voted in staff meetings to have our book discussed on their programs. They never felt it appropriate, however, to ever reveal their multi-orgasmic sexual function.

Once, I confided to fellow airplane passengers the nature of my business on a book tour trip. They asked to see the book. The others in my row acted like a group of adolescents discussing pornography. It was a good illustration of why it's safer to discuss sexuality on radio and television than it is in semi-public or social situations.

Rarely is it appropriate to answer "sex therapist" when questioned in a social situation about my occupation or profession. Sometimes a host or hostess will blow my cover. Otherwise, wisdom suggests caution in revealing my sex research and therapy experiences in social situations.

Times have changed. In the late 1960s we were involved in TV talk shows about sexuality where we were told we couldn't say "penis" or "vagina." How one is to explain about sex without mentioning either of these areas of the anatomy was not quite clear. We said impossible. So they had gofers running back and forth between us and lawyers for the television station to find out if what we were saying was okay.

Our work has taken us to many parts of the world to lecture, which has been most rewarding. We have been identified in airports after we appeared on television. While we were lecturing in Israel at a kibbutz, one of the people there said, "I saw your picture in a news magazine six months ago."

A few years ago a close friend, a physician who was dying of cancer, invited us to say goodbye. He had hoped to live to age seventy. Now, a few months shy, he knew it was not to be. His sense of humor was remarkable, always with a joke to tell. His last words were, "It's been a great trip." I agree. I've already had eight more years of life and health than he had. I've never missed a day for illness. Cataracts removed from my eyes have improved my vision. Hopefully our research, writing, and therapy will contribute to the quality of life of our fellow human beings. Work is a blessing. Economic rewards satisfy my needs. Love of and from God, family, and significant others has indeed made my life a "great trip." Researching human sexual function and treating sexual dysfunction have been a challenging and rewarding part of that trip.

21

Second Generation

Janet Shibley Hyde, Ph.D.

Janet Shibley Hyde, a second-generation sexologist, is the author of one of the most popular texts on human sexuality. She is a psychologist who has specialized in gender studies.

BELIEVE THAT I am only one of a few persons, perhaps the only one, in the field of sexology today who can claim to be a second-generation sex educator, because my father taught high school sex education classes. Today I function primarily in two capacities: sex educator at the college level, and sex researcher. Although my Ph.D. is in psychology, I am not a clinical psychologist, and I therefore do not practice sex therapy. But let me begin at the beginning.

I was born in 1948, an only child. My mother was a piano teacher and my father, at different times, taught high school or worked as a safety engineer for the National Safety Council. I was a "cuddler," and I remember receiving lots of cuddling as a child.

Although my father taught sex education classes, my own sex education was pretty inadequate. My father always told me to ask any questions I had, but I was so naive that I didn't know what questions to ask. My father did not volunteer information about sex to me, perhaps because he felt uncomfortable talking about it with his own child (even though he was comfortable talking to a classful of students), and perhaps especially with a girl child. My mother was not sex-negative, but rather was part of a generation and a family tradition that held that polite people did not talk about sex. She gave me good, factual information about menstruation, but that was the extent of her educational efforts. Other messages were conveyed less directly. Good girls did not engage in premarital sex. I should not marry or have children until I graduated from college, because a college education was essential to my future—not such a bad message for a girl to hear.

My early family experiences, then, while not pro-sex, were certainly not anti-sex either. I never learned that sex was a nasty thing. Although my parents never engaged in public displays of affection with each other, I received a great deal of love and felt comfortable with my body. All this has bearing on my later career in sex education, because the topic always seemed comfortable to me although, paradoxically, I was extraordinarily naive about it. This deep-down, gut-level comfort with sex was, I think, crucial to my success when I later became interested in teaching about sexuality.

My public school sex education did little to fill in the knowledge gaps. I remember a ninth-grade biology class in which we discussed the union of the sperm and the egg. The only problem was that I didn't have a clue about how the sperm got to the egg. I spent quite a bit of time puzzling about it, but wasn't able to come up with a good answer. I was too polite to ask the question in class, of course. I experienced the usual sixth-grade ritual of a one-hour session on menstruation, girls only, with the boys taken off somewhere else to talk about something else. I actually learned most from the English teacher my senior year in high school, whose forte was instruction in the sexual symbolism in novels. Before her, I had thought a motorcycle was a motorcycle.

My naiveté continued unabated. I arrived at college, an eager freshman, to learn that I was in the class of 1969. All my classmates were making jokes about being the class of '69, but I didn't understand what they meant. I quietly asked my roommate, who was worldlier than I was.

I took abnormal psychology during my junior year. The professor took some time to educate us about homosexuality, including playing a tape-recorded interview between him and a gay student at our college who was "out," quite a daring thing in 1968, even at liberal Oberlin College. My reaction at the time was a measure of my naiveté—I had truly not known that homosexuality existed before these educational classes.

My naiveté may become a bit tiresome to the reader. I detail it because it is crucial to understanding that I truly did "bumble" into my career in sex research and sex education. But there are a few more elements to fill in before I get to the moment of the bumbling.

I began college as a chemistry major. I had done well in it in high school, and it clearly was my father's choice for my major. This by itself shows the extent to which my family was not gender stereotyped in many ways. I am sure that it helped my cause that I was an only child, so that my father could not direct his desires for a chemist offspring toward a son. Nonetheless, he had me, and he encouraged me in science. By the end of my sophomore year, when I had to declare a major, it was clear to me that chemistry wasn't going to work. I did well enough in the class work, but my lab technique was a disaster. I swallowed sulfuric acid while pipetting, and often came out with answers for analyses of unknowns that were off by a factor of 2 or 3. I declared a mathematics major; I was quite successful in my math classes, and there was no lab work!

Not until I was a junior did I take my first psychology course. Within a few weeks, I was in love with it and knew it was the career for me. By that time, it was too late to finish a psychology major, so I completed the math major and took as many psychology courses as I could in the time that remained. I decided to go to graduate school, because I wanted to teach psychology at the college level. Fortunately, none of the graduate schools seemed to mind that I didn't have a psychology major as long as I had a math major. (People are always unduly impressed by mathematics majors.) It is worth noting that no undergraduate sexuality course was available to me, as was probably true at virtually all colleges in the country at that time.

I headed off to graduate school at Berkeley in the fall of 1969, the height of the Vietnam War. I planned to specialize in mathematical psychology, applied statistics (capitalizing on my math background), and mouse behavior genetics, which I had learned about while working in Norm Henderson's lab at Oberlin. I dropped the mathematical psychology part because I found it dull and my instinct was that it was not going to be a productive research area. I finished a dissertation on the genetics of learning ability in mice.

Continuing on the bumbling theme, it is worth noting that I earned my Ph.D. in precisely the same department where the faculty included Frank Beach, certainly one of the great sex researchers of this century, a specialist in animal sexual behavior. I never had a course with him. He never offered a graduate seminar in sex research, nor did he offer a regular undergraduate course. On one occasion he did offer a small, undergraduate sexuality course, limited to twenty-five or so students. I remember seeing the long line of students at his door, waiting to be interviewed to see if they would be admitted. It sounded interesting to me but as a graduate student I was ineligible. He and I passed like the proverbial two ships in the night.

Although I have been focusing on academics, there was, of course, a personal side to my life, which certainly affected my approach to sex education and research. I will spare the reader the details of my sex life, but will mention a few highlights that seem relevant to my entry into the sex field. My first real boyfriend, my senior year in high school, was a lovely, pleasant boy. He was very affectionate, and we spent many hours "parking" and experiencing heady sexual arousal. I am grateful that my first postpubertal sexual encounters were so pleasant. The conditioning was definitely in the positive direction. And again, my comfort with sex increased.

At the beginning of the second semester of my freshman year in college (after a couple of disastrous short romances with men I would now call "jerks"), I met the man who would become my first husband. Clark Hyde and I had a nice, secure relationship through the rest of college and married the day we graduated. We went off together to Berkeley, he to attend seminary to become an Episcopal priest, and I to earn my Ph.D. in psychology. He and I later collaborated on some writing together, especially on the topics of ethics, religion, and sexuality. Perhaps even more relevant to my career, he was not a person who advocated traditional gender roles. We had a very egalitarian marriage and he was very supportive of my career. In particular, he had no problem with my pursuing research in either of my two areas, feminist psychology or sex. In fact, he thought that both were pretty fascinating.

The three years we spent in graduate school in Berkeley were during the height of the Vietnam War protests, but also the height of the sexual revolution, and Berkeley was certainly one of the places where a lot of the revolution was occurring. I was comfortably married and cannot claim to have participated in exciting sexual exploits at the time, but I certainly observed others with interest and learned a lot. I could go to Grace Cathedral and see an obvious male cross-dresser parade up the aisle for communion. In the apartment building next to ours, there was a group that engaged in wife-swapping, as it was called then—and this was seminary housing! It was a time when one could read a lot about sex, talk about it, and observe interesting others. I soaked it up like a sponge.

Three years later we emerged, my husband with his seminary degree and I with my Ph.D. We faced the problem that all two-career couples face: how to secure positions for both of us in the same area. We made a decision—again, thanks to the fact that neither of us advocated traditional gender roles—that whoever got the best job first would take it and the other would follow and find something. He was offered a mediocre job as assistant in an Episcopal church in Eureka, California, and I was offered a tenure-track position as assistant professor of psychology at Bowling Green State University. It was clear which was the better position, so we packed our boxes for Ohio.

It was at Bowling Green that I bumbled into sex education and research, but even then through an indirect route, the psychology of women. In 1972 as I was finishing my Doctor of Philosophy degree, I began to read some of the feminist literature that was proliferating at the time—what we now call the beginning of the Second Wave. Two influential books for me were Kate Millett's *Sexual Politics* and Germaine Greer's *The Female Eunuch.* I had actually already converted to feminism during graduate school, spurred by one single influential event. A Committee on the Status of Women had been formed, headed by Susan Ervin-Tripp. When they issued their final report, I was shocked. The psychology department was singled out as among those with the worst record at Berkeley on hiring women. There was not a single woman among the forty-five or so faculty members. To make matters worse, the last time they had hired a woman was in 1928. It wasn't as though good women were not available. Jeanne Block worked in one research institute and Ravenna Helson in another. I actually had not noticed that all the faculty were men, because that was just the way faculties were in those days. But the day I read the report, I became a feminist. I was completely disillusioned with the male faculty members who were so self-righteously radical over the Vietnam War but who, I now realized, treated the women in their own backyard abysmally.

My first year as a faculty member at Bowling Green (1972–1973), I busily offered the courses I was trained for: behavior genetics and statistics. But feminist issues were burning in my head and heart, and I was reading the rich intellectual offerings of scholars like Millett and Greer. I decided to offer a psychology of women course and the "guys" in the department tolerantly let me do, even though they told me the topic was a passing fad. The course was a first at that university, and among the first in the nation. Only one textbook, by Judith Bardwick, was available and it was clearly a first attempt in a very new field. Basically I was constructing the syllabus and the curriculum as I went.

Based on my reading of feminist works, I knew that sexuality was one of the key elements on the feminist agenda and so, in the middle of the term, I did a one-week unit on sexuality. Masters and Johnson's work was available to me, as well as some of Bardwick's writing. The classic by the Boston Women's Health Book Collective, *Our Bodies, Ourselves*, was also newly available. Those were my resources for the unit. I simply taught it, as I had all the other units. Halfway through it occurred to me that I was talking about sex in front of approximately thirty people and perhaps I should be embarrassed. But I didn't feel that way, and the students were obviously eager—an understatement—to learn the material. I could tell that I had a winner, and I happily proceeded. That is how I first stumbled into teaching sexuality.

About two years later, my department faced an FTE (full-time equivalent) crisis. The college of education was doing away with its requirements that all their students take a statistics course in the psychology department. That meant an enormous loss of FTEs, with the ugly possibility of then having to reduce the number of faculty. I had an idea. I went to the department chair and argued that if we offered a large-lecture human sexuality course, we could easily get large registrations from it, equal to those we were losing in statistics. The department chair liked the idea. I went off that summer to the Kinsey Institute at Indiana University for their two-week human sexuality training session. That was the extent of my preparation. I returned and taught the course for the first time in the fall of 1974.

Initially I insisted on team-teaching the course because it is so broad and interdisciplinary in content. My first team members were Neil Kirshner, a clinical psychologist who was interested in sex therapy, and Don Ragusa, a biological psychologist. In later years, Neil left and Howie Markman replaced him as the clinician on the team. I am grateful to have worked with these excellent colleagues; I learned a lot from them and continue many of the ideas I learned from them in the course I teach today.

It was clear from the first time we offered the course that we had a winner, so again I had stumbled into teaching sexuality, this time in an extensive way, and again everything seemed to be a smashing success. I've offered the course at least once every year since then and I've loved it every time.

When I began teaching the course in 1974, only two undergraduate textbooks were available. One seemed to have been written for medical students, using lots of forbidding Latin terms that undergraduates seemed intimidated by. The other was by James Leslie McCary, a psychologist. It was quite accessible, but it had a not-too-subtle undercurrent of sexism and a paternalistic tone that grated on my feminist sensibilities. I had just finished writing one textbook, *Half the Human Experience: The Psychology of Women*. I decided to write an undergraduate human sexuality textbook. *Understanding Human Sexuality* appeared in 1979.

Writing the sexuality textbook gave me the time to read sex research both deeply and broadly. Textbook writing gives authors unique visions of where the gaps are in research. We are often brought up short, wanting to fill in a particular piece of information and finding that no one has done the necessary study.

By 1978 my research interests were shifting. I had earned tenure based on a program of research in mouse behavior genetics. Never forgetting my feminist perspectives, I had conducted a program of selective breeding for aggressiveness in female mice. But as the years passed, I became less interested in animal behavior genetics, partly because I saw the next advances needing to be made in physiological research, an area in which I was not well trained. Two other forces led to my waning interest in mouse behavior genetics: I was increasingly interested in research on the psychology of women; and I left my job at Bowling Green because my husband took a new job—now his turn, in our egalitarian marriage, to find a good job—at a church near Columbus, Ohio. I found a new position in the psychology department at Denison University, a purely undergraduate liberal arts college with no graduate students and limited animal lab facilities—it would have been difficult for me to maintain an animal lab. So my gradual shift to research on psychology of women became complete after moving to Denison.

As I left mouse behavior genetics, I considered quite deliberately whether to specialize primarily in psychology of women research or in sex research. I decided to specialize in the former and pursue the latter secondarily. Again, I can claim no inspired vision behind this decision; it was based mainly on pragmatic considerations. Psychology of women research was quite feasible in a liberal arts college setting. To my mind, both at that time and to the present day, good sex research is a much more ambitious undertaking. The two models before me were Kinsey and Masters and Johnson. I was well aware of the persecution Kinsey had faced for his research, which I admired greatly (the research, not the persecution). Although I had always managed to teach the human sexuality course without incident—I have never had a complaint from a parent, for example—I had no confidence that I could undertake anything like a major sex survey and keep my life relatively peaceful. Masters and Johnson's research seemed to have brought them nothing but fame and fortune, but they did it in a medical school setting, very much within a medical model, and that was not my situation. With my interests in developmental psychology, I would have loved to interview children about their interests in sexuality or their sexual behavior, but it didn't take much thought to realize that the schools would never grant permission for such research, nor would parents. In short, I concluded that it wasn't feasible to do sex research that would make a major contribution, so I settled on psychology of women and gender research, which I knew was quite feasible, and where I thought I could have some impact.

In retrospect, I may have made the wrong decision. Clearly many of my colleagues, over the last two decades, have successfully conducted sex research. A few of them, however, have suffered persecution; I think especially about Elaine Hatfield having been the object of Senator William Proxmire's Golden Fleece Award (given for the "most silly" grants) for her research on love. But she was right—the topic is important and researchable—and he was wrong, and all researchers in the field today know it. Many sex researchers in the last two decades have done ambitious studies that have truly advanced our knowledge of human sexuality. Nonetheless, I cannot help but ponder how much more would be known today, scientifically, about sex if the obstacles to being a sex researcher were not so great.

From then until the present, I have spent most of my time doing research on the psychology of women and gender. Trying to capitalize on my expertise in statistics, I have done a number of meta-analyses of research on psychological gender differences. These studies have had an impact. One, for example, showed that gender differences in mathematics performance are small, overturning a longstanding belief in male superiority in mathematics. Research on the psychology of women and gender satisfies me intellectually, but it also satisfies my moral commitment to pursue research that may in some ways benefit women.

In 1986 I moved to the University of Wisconsin to accept a position jointly as professor of psychology and director of the Women's Studies Research Center. My husband had decided that he wanted to pursue a Ph.D. in theology at Marquette University, the goal being to become a seminary professor, so the joint move made sense for both of us.

Adding to my focus on the psychology of women and gender, and keeping sex research secondary, is the fact that at Wisconsin I am generally overwhelmed with prospective graduate students wanting to study the psychology of women with me, whereas those wanting to pursue sex research are rare. Perhaps they, too, have gotten the message that it is tough to pursue a career in sex research.

I do sex research when I can. Because of my program of meta-analytic (broad-scaled) studies, I wanted to do a meta-analysis of research on gender differences in sexuality. When a graduate student (at the time), Mary Beth Oliver, approached me saying that she wanted to do just that, I agreed immediately and we had a marvelous collaboration that resulted in an article in *Psychological Bulletin* in 1993. Since 1988, motivated by my interest in psychology of women and public policy, I have been involved in a long-term, large-scale project on women and maternity leave. Funded by the National Institutes of Mental Health (NIMH), we have followed a sample of more than five hundred women and their families from pregnancy, initially through a year after the birth, and now with new funding, through five years after the birth. My goal in the project has been to look at the impact of maternity leave (length of leave, going back to work full-time or part-time, and so on) on women's mental health. Although it was not at all the main point of the study, there is a series of questions about sexuality administered to both wives and husbands. I recently wrote an article on sexuality during pregnancy and the year postpartum based on those data, which appeared in the *Journal of Sex Research* in 1996.

Sometimes sex research—like the meta-analysis of gender differences in sexuality—has gone easily and smoothly. More of the time, there have been obstacles, some of them merely irritating, others insurmountable. There are always obstacles in research, of course, but these occur because sex is the topic of the research. An example comes from a dissertation done by a graduate student of mine, Rose Jadack. Together we generated a fascinating topic for her dissertation. We realized that often, situations concerning sexually transmitted diseases (STDs) are moral dilemmas. For example, if a woman has genital herpes, but is not currently having an outbreak, and is contemplating engaging in intercourse with a new partner, should she tell him? Does she have a right to keep this information private, if she believes there is little actual risk to him (which is probably not the case, given what we now know about asymptomatic viral shedding)? Or does she have an absolute obligation to inform him, thereby possibly risking rejection? Rose and I generated a set of STD moral dilemmas of this sort. We then wanted to conduct a cross-sectional developmental study, to see how adolescents and young adults think about these ideas, believing that understanding their moral reasoning might be of great value in STD prevention efforts. We therefore needed a high school sample, preferably ninth and twelfth graders, and a college sample. After two rounds of pleading with school officials in Madison, we were denied permission to do the research. They were quite honest that the denial had to do with the topic being sex. Ironically, it was about as low risk a sex study as one could imagine. We weren't asking students at all about their own sexual behavior or even attitudes. We just wanted to learn their judgments about fictitious characters in moral dilemmas. We tried several other local school districts and received the same message in each place. The lesson was clear: It is impossible to do sex research in the public schools, even innocuous research with high school students and even in a liberal community like Madison.

Over the years, my colleagues' reactions to my sex research have been mixed. In some sense it is difficult to sort out exactly what they are reacting to, because I work in two marginalized areas, feminist psychology and sexuality. If anything, I think that I have received more negative reactions about the feminist psychology part than the sexuality part, no doubt because some people feel threatened by feminism, and because women's studies and feminist psychology are highly critical of traditional research in psychology. Even then, I generally have not been overwhelmed by negative reactions. My colleagues privately may have their doubts and think the field is flaky or lame-brained, but if they do, they have the courtesy not to share those thoughts with me, which I appreciate. I have always believed that it has helped that I have heavy-duty expertise in multivariate statistics, which gains respect and probably makes colleagues more likely to tolerate my other interests. The reactions to my sex research have generally not been negative, but could rather be described as titillation. People get a bit giggly when I talk about some new sex study I'm doing, and they always want to know the results.

Returning to my personal life, my first husband died at forty in 1989, certainly not something either of us had envisioned in our current life plans. The loss was very difficult for me, as well as for our children Margaret (age ten at the time) and Luke (age seven). I never felt so grateful to have tenure as then; I knew that I had a secure income, and that we wouldn't have further upheavals in our life. I could, for example, afford to keep us in the same house we had been living in.

In a true sex researchers' romance, I "met" my next husband in 1992 at a convention of the Society for the Scientific Study of Sexuality (SSSS). I put "met" in quotes because I actually knew him slightly already. He—John DeLamater—is a professor in the sociology department at the University of Wisconsin; but given the size of that mega-university, we bumped into each other casually about once a year. And we were both teaching undergraduate sexuality courses, he in sociology and I in psychology. At those meetings in 1992, we noticed each other for the first time, and discovered that both of us were single, he having been recently divorced. Upon returning to Madison, he carried out an old-fashioned, romantic courtship, which delighted me, and we were married in 1993.

It's great being married to another sex researcher. As of this writing, we have collaborated on a book chapter and a journal article and he has become a co-author of my human sexuality text. We worked on the newest, sixth edition, in 1995 and nearly burned ourselves. I have no idea how I would have done the revision of the entire book rather than half of it. Our collaboration works well because we have some overlap of academic expertise—he trained as a social psychologist, so we speak the same language—while at the same time we have different areas that we cover.

That brings me to the present time. I continue on the faculty at the University of Wisconsin, teaching a large undergraduate human sexuality course once a year. The course is always fun and satisfying. I do a lot of research on the psychology of women and gender, and some sex research.

Conclusion

This has not been the tale of someone who decided, at age sixteen, that she wanted to devote her life to sex research, and then planfully climbed each ladder that had to be climbed to reach that goal. My story, rather, is one of stumbling into sex research. The tale, I hope, is reassuring to undergraduates who are having trouble deciding on a major, because I tried several fields before I found the one that was perfect for me. Other persons might have had the opportunities to venture into sex research that I had and not taken the bait. I believe that I did so partly because, on a personal level, I feel very comfortable with sex. I also find it extraordinarily interesting and I think most other people do. I've always had a strong preference for teaching courses that undergraduates find fascinating, and sexuality definitely fits the bill.

Many years ago, when my first husband was serving as the Episcopal priest for a small, rural congregation in northwest Ohio and I was playing the role of priest's wife, someone asked me if it didn't create a lot of trouble for myself teaching a sexuality course, given my husband's occupation. They also wondered how I, as a Christian, could even do such a thing. I replied that the congregation didn't seem to mind, and that I actually felt I was doing good deeds by teaching the course. If things were going as I hoped, I was providing students with a lot of knowledge that might save them from contracting a disease, or help them have more satisfying sex lives or better marriages. I feel privileged to work in a field in which I can do such good and helpful things for others.

Selected Bibliography

Hyde, J. 1976, 1980, 1985. *Half the Human Experience: The Psychology of Women.* Lexington, Mass.: Heath.

———. 1979, 1982, 1986, 1993, 1997. *Understanding Human Sexuality.* New York: McGraw Hill.

———. 1986. *The Psychology of Gender.* Baltimore: Johns Hopkins University Press.

———. 1996. "Sexuality during Pregnancy and Postpartum." *Journal of Sex Research* 30, no. 21: 143–51.

22

Early Transgenderist

Ariadne Kane, M.A.

Ariadne Kane is the founder of Fantasia Fair, a living and learning center for cross-dressers. Ari came to sexology after varied careers in teaching, administration, and real estate. She is an outspoken advocate of greater openness and diversity of sexual lifestyles, and has appeared on many local and national talk shows.

THE FIRST FIVE years of my life were basically blissful. The first-born male in my family, I began life in a cold-water brownstone house in New York City. Apparently, there were some serious economic problems at the time, so I was sent to stay with relatives during most of my first three and a half years, growing up with my dad's parents and his younger sisters and brother. I was the "golden light" of the household and showered with much love and affection by all (save my dad). One of the traditions of my family was the Saturday night home party. The entire family, including cousins who lived in the neighborhood, would come to grandpa's house to eat and dance and play. There would be platters of homemade traditional Greek specialties made by grandma and my aunts. There was lots of traditional dancing, singing, and storytelling about life in the remote region of Greece, where my grandparents came from. I can remember being carried on the shoulders of my uncle, who led a traditional group folk dance, and receiving gobs of wonderful attention.

I slept in the bed of one of my aunts or uncles. I can remember arguments about who Ari would sleep with tonight. I once slept with an aunt who put one of her cotton nighties on me. It felt warm and was another form of love that this aunt showed me. My grandfather had scenes from his village painted on the walls of the bedrooms: lots of blue sky, a green mountainside, a shepherd tending his flock of sheep. It left a deep impression on me. I was bathed with much love, attention, and affection by my dad's parents and family. But it was not so for me with my mom and dad.

At about age five, I had the first adventure that I can remember. We were living in a flat in another part of New York City. Having been given a tricycle as a

225

birthday gift, I decided to take a trip and headed straight away from my local area. Soon I found myself in the countryside where there were some small farms and no clearly marked sidewalks. It was a pleasant day and I was totally unaware of where I was or how far from home I had traveled. I stopped at one of the farms to ask the lady there if I could have a drink of water. It was getting dark and I began to think about my return home, but I could not remember the route. Fortunately the farm lady called the local police station, who got word to the police station in my neighborhood, and they came and took me back home. My parents were very angry about what I had done. As punishment they took the bike from me and I received a thrashing from Dad.

It was in those early years that I began to wear feminine apparel and accessories. Always curious about why girls and women wore different types of clothing, I decided to secretly try on some items of my mother's apparel. I can remember as a prepubertal putting on a pair of her high-heeled blue suede pumps when no one was home. Her shoes fit my feet, although I felt funny when I tried to walk in them. Later on, I got bolder. I tried on other items of Mother's and found some of them to feel silky smooth and comfortable. I liked the feeling and vowed that one day I would dress up completely; I fantasized about what it would be like to be dressed as a woman all the time. My mother was very attractive, with good taste in clothes and accessories. In a way I thought I was emulating her by dressing in her clothes. It also served as a means of being close to her spiritually. The question was when could I get the opportunity to explore this fantasy without being discovered since we were then living in a railroad-style tenement where there was not much privacy. Finally, when I was eleven years old an opportunity opened up. My folks announced that they were going to be away all day Saturday for some important social event and would be returning home in the evening. My sister was away staying with a friend for the weekend. When I finished up my household chores I thought about the exciting afternoon I was going to have dressing in Mom's clothes. I selected an outfit from her wardrobe: a pair of panties, a garter belt, a slip, a pair of nylons, a blue crepe dress, and matching pumps. I was extremely careful to note the place where all these items were found so that I could return them exactly as I had found them. Remembering the process I had seen when I watched my aunts or my mother dress, I laid the chosen items on my bed and began the process of dressing. I recall thinking about what to insert in the bra to make the right shape for the upper part of the dress. I ended up using a pair of heavy socks in each cup. Since I had no experience with makeup I decided to explore this aspect of "womanhood" at another time. It took about twenty minutes to dress from the skin out. Once satisfied that I had all the items correctly in place (including the seams of the stockings), I walked up and down the length of the flat. On each pass by the full-length mirrors in the master bedroom, I stopped, gazed at the image, smiled, and told myself that I was a very attractive "woman."

After about two hours of this activity, I made some tea and sat in a living room chair and read. It was approaching mid-afternoon and I thought I would spend a few more hours "dressed" since my parents were not expected to be home until about seven o'clock, and I felt there would be enough time to change and return Mom's clothes to their proper places. About 4:00 P.M., I heard the jingling of keys in the door of the flat. I panicked, not knowing who it could be. I timidly asked who was there and heard Mom's voice. Quickly, just like Superman, I dashed into my bedroom, latched the door, and ripped off all of the clothes, stuffed them under my bed, and dove under the bed covers, frightened, sweaty, and stark naked. I waited until I heard my father yelling to unlatch the door or he would break it down. I put on my bathrobe, unhooked the latch, and quickly returned to my bed, pulling the covers up to my neck. My parents entered the room demanding to know why I had latched the door and why I was in bed. I told them that I was feeling chilled and ill and wanted a warm place to rest. As my father came closer to examine me, he noticed a piece of blue cloth sticking out from under my bed. "What's this?" he asked in an angry voice as he pulled out my mother's clothing. I was tongue-tied but he demanded an answer. Not saying another word, he undid the belt from his trousers and I knew that I was going to get the beating of my life. My mother, although she was also upset, calmed him down somewhat and they began to argue about whether or not to punish me with a beating. In the meantime I was crying profusely. Finally, Mom suggested that I should see our family doctor to get his opinion about my behavior. Perhaps I needed medical help. When I agreed to see the doctor, Father calmed down and returned his belt to his pants, still very angry about his son's crazy behavior. Mom was relieved that a major family feud had been averted, at least for the moment.

My appointment with the doctor was arranged for early Monday morning. I stayed in bed all day Sunday, nervous and not wanting to eat. My father did not talk to me at all. I timidly apologized to Mom for ripping one of her dresses. I went by trolley car to the doctor's office alone, because both Mom and Dad had to work that day. After his examination of me the doctor said that physically I was fine, but he was less certain about my cross-dressing. He said that he had had another case with the same behavior several years before and that it turned out to be nothing serious. He reminded me of my enviable status in a good neighborhood and admonished me to "never do that crazy stuff again." He told my parents that I had a moment of idle fantasy, common among bright young boys at that age, and not to worry about it recurring. I was so relieved about the entire outcome that I vowed never to experiment with wearing women's clothes again. Mom was pleased to hear the doctor's opinion, but my dad thought that the doctor was favoring me. He perceived my behavior as reason enough to be sent to an "insane asylum," although he took no steps to have me committed. The storm having passed, it would be four years before I considered cross-dressing again.

I set out to explore both places and things. Many of those places were associated with my discovering the natural world and my relationship with it. As a Boy Scout I learned many survival skills and developed a sense of self-worth and self-reliance. Those outdoor experiences helped me in my personal odyssey of river travel, mountain climbing, visiting remote areas of the world, and meeting people whose lives were vastly different from my own. I had some exciting experiences in the area of river travel, being the first American to single kayak the length of the Tiber River from its source in the Apennine mountains to the city of Rome, a distance of about three hundred kilometers. I was a part of a small international group of "river rats" consisting of four Germans, two Frenchmen, seven Italians, and myself. The earlier sections of the river were characterized by moderate rapids and called for skills with the paddle and reading the signs of a changed contour of the river. As we continued the trip, the river calmed down and we could enjoy the scenery. The adventure ended with our "grand" entrance into Rome amid crowds of spectators waving pennants and throwing flowers.

In other river trips down the Rio Grande and the Black Water River in British Columbia, I was personally challenged to use my body, mind, and spirit in some harmonious combination. My sense of autonomy and use of inner resources came from these types of experiences. This same core system of challenges was part of other adventures in mountain climbing, underwater diving, and trekking in the northern Sahara Desert.

The opportunity to develop my leadership potential came when I was in college majoring in education and was asked by the student body president to organize and supervise the college prom. My role included negotiating with the hotel for the ballroom at a fair price, scheduling Charlie Spivack and his orchestra for the main attraction, ticket sales, security, and all the other associated chores. The prom was a social and financial success. I made lots of friend, and it was the first time I was actively engaged in directing others. From this beginning I took on other leadership opportunities during my undergraduate years.

I got married right after college. I had met Cindi during my senior year and become infatuated with her. She was attractive and very bright. While we had our differences we also had a core of common interests. Cindi had been accepted for a graduate program at a university in New York City and I had a prospect of starting my career as a management trainee with a major company there. Within two weeks after our marriage, having completed the tedious process of interviewing with officials on several different levels of the company, I was informed that because of the current recession they would delay my training for an indefinite period of time. So I was now out in the job market looking for a position commensurate with my academic training and leadership skills. I found several opportunities during the next three years, but these jobs did not challenge my intellectual interests and curiosity, so I decided to seek training in biophysics. Cindi was proceeding well with her graduate program, getting enough scholarship funding to pay for school and also allow us to live, albeit frugally.

Our marriage during this three-year period was not doing well, however. Our differences became greater and our interests less common. I applied to and was accepted at a graduate program in biophysics at a major university in Western New York, which meant that we had to separate. We agreed that being apart for three months would give us both a chance to review our relationship and decide if we wanted to divorce or stay together. Within a month after starting my program, I received divorce papers from Cindi's attorney. Emotionally devastated, I found myself unable to concentrate on my work. When I returned to New York City to confront her about her decision, I found the apartment empty. Eventually I did see Cindi and found out that she was living with a colleague from her program.

The breakup made me realize how emotionally vulnerable I was. I was challenged to rethink a set of traditional values I had clung to and thought were immutable. I experienced, for the first time in my life, deep depression, with no immediate relief in sight. I began to cross-dress again, as a means of forgetting the pain of the past three years. After a month of deep depression I found the courage to call a friend, Bill, in Boston. He came to stay with me for the weekend and it was the best solution I could have had. Within a week after his visit, the depression subsided and I was able to continue my graduate studies. Bill was later to become my best friend and roommate when I relocated to Boston one year later.

As I examined the values in my life, I began to look at my career objective, that of being a laboratory scientist. I decided that it would not work for me; I needed the social interactions with other people in a professional setting where I could make a difference. I decided I would prefer teaching mathematics and science rather than spending a lifetime in laboratory. My first position was at a private school in the Boston area. A subsequent position was at a Swiss teaching academy which specialized in English for adolescents whose families were living in Europe or North Africa. The art of teaching came naturally to me and I enjoyed the experience immensely. I participated in a UNESCO study comparing the teaching syllabi for mathematics courses in European and American high schools. After this project, I decided to become entrepreneurial, establishing two small teaching projects. One was a private tutorial service for American children who needed coaching for admission into the American university system, the other was a technical translation service for European firms seeking funds from English-speaking contracting firms. These were all successful projects which taught me more about my talent and creativity. In all I spent four years working and living in Europe before returning to New England.

With the knowledge gained from these experiences, I founded my own educational consulting service. Since the methodologies of teaching mathematics and science were changing, I wanted to offer new ways to present traditional material. Therefore, I developed several creative modules for teaching geometry and offered some new ways to view important ideas in science. One of these modules used the geometry of cityscapes and skylines to illustrate Euclidian concepts. Another focused on the theory of relativity. I visited the heads of high school mathematics and science departments, demonstrating my teaching tools, hoping for a contract to incorporate these methodologies into their current curricula. My firm, called Educational Dynamics, also developed a model for international student travel-educational exchange. It was hard work and did not yield very much money, but it was an exciting period of creativity and learning about the pedagogical aspects of the profession.

The scars of my first marriage made me very cautious about entering into any long-term relationships with other women. I became a strong advocate of long-term semicommitted coupling but not marriage. I had several such relationships over the next decade, until Nina, whom I met on one of the many hiking trips I led for my outing club. She was a lover of the outdoors, of teaching music, and of kids. We courted each other for over seven years before I felt comfortable enough to propose marriage. We have been together for over twenty years and I feel it has been one of the better decisions I made in my life.

After closing down my company I searched for a position that could fully use my talent, creativity, and experience. I finally found what I thought would be the best job for me, an assistant hospital administrator for medical research at one of the teaching hospitals in the greater Boston area. There were many challenges associated with the position, foremost among them being the political intrigues and jealousies between hospital administrators and the research associates. I spent two years with this job and decided that I didn't feel I could make any real difference in the way hospital clinical research was managed. So I resigned and tried selling and managing real estate, with little success.

Since my departure from graduate school, I had learned to modulate and control my cross-dressing behavior. I shared this secret with Bill when we were rooming together. My interest was in wearing female clothes and props and fantasizing about what it might be like to be a "true woman."

I knew there was a cross-dressers' (CD) club in the Boston area, but I harbored such fear about the type of individual I would be talking with when I phoned that on several occasions prior to establishing voice contact, I actually hung up as soon as I heard a voice at the other end of the line. Finally, I managed enough courage to hang on and actually speak to the other person. She sounded warm and reassuring about the club, explaining how they screen prospective members, and emphasizing the importance of feeling secure in the meeting place and the peace of mind one could get by knowing that there are other males who cross-dressed. I made an appointment to be interviewed, soon after which I was invited to attend one of their meetings. Following two more months of putting off the decision, I went to my first CD Club meeting at the duplex apartment of the club coordinator. It was an awesome experience. I came early, so that I could meet some of the veteran club members. I remember guys coming in dressed in masculine garb, carrying a suitcase, going upstairs, and returning after about an hour dressed as women. There was all manner of cross-dressers: Some wore elegant dresses with all the appropriate accessories, full makeup, and wig, while others chose to dress in the casual woman's fashions of the period. I did not dress at that first meeting since I was not sure if the kind of wardrobe I had would be suitable. In addition, I had never used female wigs or learned how to apply makeup to create an attractive, feminine-looking face. I was struck not only by the diversity of clothing the club members wore but also by their friendliness and sincere desire to make me feel comfortable. They readily answered the many questions I had. I had been alerted by the club coordinator not to ask the legal names of members or what kind of work they did or where. The name I chose for myself was Ariadne. In short, it was a memorable evening for a "closet case" who was leaving that dark and lonely place. From that time on, I began to get my "act" together so that I could dress at the club. I purchased my first wig and bought a kit full of cosmetic items and practiced how to use them. I quickly became adept enough at performing this transformation from he to (s)he that I could do it in about forty-five minutes. The discovery of the CD social contact group was the catalyst that allowed me to recognize the femme person inside my psyche. It also served as a staging area to ask questions about cross-dressing and cross-gender behaviors and to clarify some of the critical issues, both generally and personally.

One year after my becoming an active member of this club, the club leader announced that (s)he would be going for sex reassignment surgery and that it was no longer possible for her apartment to be used for weekly club meetings. Having become an advocate of the concept of a CD club to learn and be more comfortable with the behavior, I organized a house search committee and located a new meeting place in Boston proper. With that the Cherrystone CD group was created. It was at this time I thought I should share my new experiences with cross-dressing with Nina. Having given serious time to how best to tell her, I developed a strategy of gently relating my story to her over a romantic dinner. The outcome was positive and somewhat supportive. In fact, within a week after I told her, she wanted to meet Ariadne. I was a little apprehensive about this so I waited for more than a month for that important meeting. When Nina did finally meet "her" it was at my apartment. We both had a good laugh about how funny I looked, as my wardrobe and accessories were not coordinated. Nina then offered to help me with style selection and coordination of the other props of femme gender wear. It was exciting and fun to have some much needed assistance from a loving partner.

From these initial beginnings, I rapidly became a leading spokesperson on the subject, both in guest lectures to psychology and criminology classes at colleges and universities and on regional radio and TV talk shows. In 1979 1 received an invitation to be a guest on the Phil Donahue show. This presented me with a dilemma: Do I go national with my lifestyle and expose myself to millions of Americans, possibly including friends and family who might recognize me? I talked it over with Nina, and after much deliberation made the decision to accept the invitation. It was a one-hour program with just me and a professional sex educator presenting before a live audience. I received over eight thousand pieces of mail from people who saw the program, and who for the most part were complimentary and positive. Only ten of the letters were hostile.

After that breakthrough, I was invited to be on many other regional and national talk shows. One of these was the David Susskind program on PBS. The significance of this appearance was that it was viewed by a more knowledgeable viewer audience which allowed for an in-depth dialogue about the issues. Another important outcome of these nationwide video appearances was the awareness that I had reached many cross-dressers who were very much in the closet. Indirectly, we got some promotion for Fantasia Fair, a living and learning center for cross-dressers that I had established.

My educational efforts with this "paraculture" as it was called by some of the sex educators, counselors, and therapists led me to become a member of the Society for the Study of Sexuality (SSSS) and the American Association of Sex Educators, Counselors and Therapists. I began doing workshops and giving papers at both the regional meetings. I was invited to be a presenter at the first International Androgyny Conference held in San Diego. With all of this activity, I developed an identity as a sexuality and gender specialist, and this became my new career. I was invited to join the staff of Sexuality Health Center of New England to provide counseling services to clients who came in with some type of gender conflict. In addition to creating Fantasia Fair and other programs for the cross-dressing and cross-gender population, I also saw the need to provide education and training for health care providers addressing the specific issues of gender diversity and expression. To make this all possible and obtain a measure of professional credibility, I founded the Outreach Institute of Gender Studies. It has become a major resource for sexologists, counselors, therapists, nurses, physicians, and educators. The institute is incorporated and is managed by a board of directors. It has been, for me, a true labor of love, as well an area of personal and professional growth.

I am looking forward to a future which truly appreciates a diversity of lifestyles and activities, even in this rigid society. I hope for a world in which the individual self and mutual respect are the fundamental blocks of loving and caring for others.

23

A Student's Perspective

Randy Sue Klein, Ph.D.

Randy Sue Klein, a co-editor of this book, is the youngest contributor and a recent Ph.D. She offers a doctoral student's perspective on sexology as a concentration (focal point) for therapy and research.

WHEN IT WAS suggested to me that I contribute my autobiography as it relates to sexology, I was shocked to say the least. I am twenty-seven years old and feel like there is an enormous amount of fate guiding me toward a meaningful direction in life. I feel as if I am being carried on a magic carpet representing sexology. The carpet may land numerous times throughout my life, in many interesting places, and each experience will thrive off of my expertise and energetic, accepting attitude. I find it thrilling that sexology has led me to influence a vast array of people and in turn has allowed me to be influenced by amazing people.

I was born in 1969, the Year of the Cock, according to the Chinese calendar. What a coincidence! My mother named me Randy after a vivacious, beautiful friend they adored. Nobody remembers if her name was spelled with a "y" or an "i." My mother spelled my name with a "y."

While I was a preteen at summer camp for the first time, I was introduced to a camp counselor from England. I remember thinking he was pretty cute. I courteously stuck out my hand and said, "Hi, I'm Randy!" He laughed in my face. Once the hysterics ended, he apologized and said, "I'm sorry. Do you know what your name means?" I had no idea. In front of a roomful of campers and counselors, he proclaimed that "randy" means "horny." I was not embarrassed, even though I probably should have been, as I was a little too young to understand what this all meant. Do you still think this is all a coincidence?

The dictionary actually describes "randy" as a horny, shrewd woman. Terrific! I have since given my parents little digs about not looking "randy" up in the dictionary before naming me. I tease them that they are the reason for my becoming a sexologist. I am not shy about what my name means, given the fact that any well-read person has seen it used over and over again. Granted, it is most commonly used in trashy romance or Victorian novels.

I have also been plagued by "Randy" being a boy's name on the West Coast and a girl's name on the East Coast. I was born in Montreal and moved to Los Angeles when I was six months old. My junk mail always reads "*Mr.* Randy Klein" which is less than amusing.

Years ago I began to appreciate the wide range of opportunities open to some-one who is not bound by an effeminate or strictly gender-specific name. I would have been an awful Jennifer or Michelle. I was a tomboy and always will be. I have always felt that I was responsible for creating the ideal male-female personality that fits me, Randy. I have decided that when I have kids someday I am going to name them something that could go either way, a name that doesn't fit any particular mold. I treasure the unique aspect of my name.

I grew up in a sexually positive home environment which allowed me to become a self-confident, touchy-feely teenager. I am the oldest of three very differ-ent but closely bonded siblings. Our parents treasured, encouraged, and supported our style and independence throughout our lives.

As a family we shared our feelings with the initial guidance of Jewish Family Enrichment, a branch of Jewish Marriage Encounter. The whole point was to open up and share without fear of being judged. My brother, Bram, was too young to write all of his feelings on paper so he would draw pictures and then describe them during sharing time. We all shared deeply creating a family bond that could never be broken.

My sister, Tam, and I shared a huge bedroom. We were best friends so every night was a slumber party. At times I would make Tam hold my hand while we slept. I still haven't met anybody who will let me do that. Oh, well.

Tam is proud that I found my perfect career, but less than amused about hav-ing to tell her colleagues, lawyers and businessmen and women, that her sister is a sexologist. At one point in my life, I considered playing golf professionally. Tam was behind me 100 percent. She thought that would be interesting and much eas-ier to explain.

A good part of my interest in sex derives from my elders. Sixty years ago, my paternal grandfather was a pharmacist/chemist who created a new drug for male sexual vigor called Testprosterone. Now at ninety years old, he and my grand-mother, eighty-six, are still sexually active on a consistent basis. We hear stories through the family grapevine. For my grandfather's ninetieth birthday, I gave him a couple of books on sex. He was so excited, he showed all his friends down in Leisure World.

My maternal grandparents believe that sex makes up to 90 percent of their marriage. This was uncovered by interviewing them separately for a project I had to do for a Marriage and Family Relations class in college. We had to interview couples we knew had been together for over twenty years and find out what kept them together. I only had to interview one couple but I couldn't resist finding out about my parents and both sets of grandparents.

My parents and I had many discussions while I was growing up that related to me their deep love for one another, enriched with mutual powerful sexual drives. My father would tease me that sex was the greatest form of exercise. As a smart-mouthed teenager, I couldn't help but ask if I should quit softball and weight training and just concentrate on getting a "real" workout.

When I got my driver's license, my father was ecstatic. On Sunday mornings, he would come in the kitchen and approach me with a plan. He would give me money and tell me to take my sister and brother out to breakfast, a movie, lunch, another movie, whatever we wanted, but just stay away from the house for the day. I knew exactly what he meant, and in a flash we were gone. As a teenager, I found it refreshing to recognize and support my parent's sexuality.

When asked, my parents used to say that when I turned eighteen I would be old enough to have sex. When I actually did turn eighteen, they were hoping to adjust the age to twenty-one. No luck. When I wanted to go away with my boyfriend after the prom, I let my mom hold one of our newborn puppies and told her I was on birth control. I wanted to make sure she was calm and couldn't lunge at me. I knew I was being responsible without divulging too much information. When I look back on it now, I made my teenage years quite easy for my parents. They gave me my independence, but taught me to take responsibility or accept the consequences.

In my family, sex was a celebration of love that people did responsibly for fun, pleasure, and exercise. My parents and grandparents had shared openly about their birth control methods which eliminated the mystery, but focused on responsibility.

My experiences and perspectives on sexology may appeal to future students who do not know where to start. My first piece of advice would be to get involved and saturated as soon as you realize that you want sexology to be a major part of your life. When I was in high school, I did not know what I wanted to do. With the promise of a new car, I decided to attend a local university, California State University, Northridge.

When I started college, I joined a sorority hoping to create close friendships with women. I have always been a tomboy, and as such I had mostly male friends. I was not sure I could ever find other women like me. In the sorority, I developed some amazing friendships. Through sports, dating, and parties, I created close-knit bonds.

During my second year of college, I took a class titled Human Pregnancy and Embryology which inspired me to consider becoming a geneticist. I was interested in genetic counseling for couples who would use chemistry to defy their odds of having an unhealthy child. The next semester I enrolled in human sexuality taught by Dr. James Elias. Career-wise Dr. Elias seemed to me to be extremely well balanced. He was teaching interesting classes on sex, practicing sex therapy, and conducting research on sociosexual issues. Finding my ultimate profession took merely finding someone who was living my dream.

After taking human sexuality, I decided to become a sexologist. I realized that I had always been able to talk about sex easily, openly, and without the moral objectives that often accompany the topic. Luckily, Cal State Northridge was one of the few schools that offered human sexuality as a minor. I was able to take a wide variety of classes that stimulated and encouraged my interests.

I had a purpose in the sorority. My sorority sisters needed solid advice and a good sexual guidance counselor. I made the subject of sex fun. Some sisters hated condoms so I had them play with them as if they were balloons and enjoy the feel. When a sister would have her first orgasm, I arranged private "Big-O" parties in celebration and affirmation of her sexuality.

Some people despised the idea of a teenager being so open about sexuality. My sorority's alumnae advisors were adamant about suppressing my ideas and philosophies relating to sex. They perceived "sorority" as pure—never did they have the inclination to explore the nature and beauty of sex. No matter what I did, the sorority alumnae did not appreciate it. I was frequently called in to face their accusations. They were always amusing yet hurtful. They assumed that if I was so open about sex that I must be promiscuous.

I quickly learned that "promiscuous" actually meant that I was having sex more than they were. I assumed they were jealous. Although I have some understanding about their attitudes toward sex, I cannot forgive them for leaving a tidal wave of sexual negativity within my memories of my college years. But rather than become frustrated with what I perceived to be ignorance, I channeled my energies in a positive direction. They did not know my tolerance for judgmental, coxcombical, asexual people.

As a junior, I joined the AIDS Speaker's Bureau which was part of the university's health services. I started meeting interesting people who could also talk openly about sex. The AIDS Speaker's Bureau went to all types of classes and gave speeches about safe sex, condoms, and sexually transmitted diseases. The energy we had resulted in classes full of attention, responses, and even participation. I felt electrified each time I went in front of a group. We used props, skits, jokes, and anything else to get our word across. It was our peers that we were helping.

One day, I found a glow-in-the-dark condom at a store in Hollywood. The next day it was included in our skit. As the responsible female who always has one in her purse, I would take out the condom and suggest we use it. My teammate would read the caption aloud that said, "for novelty use only, does not protect from sexually transmitted diseases." I had so many people come up to me later and tell me that they had had no idea. They thought a condom was a condom. I knew I was making a difference in my little corner of the world.

The AIDS Speaker's Bureau also had special events around Valentine's Day and the AIDS Walk Los Angeles. As a group we would pass out condoms around campus and ask people if they wanted a condom. I decided that I could pass out a lot more condoms if I were on rollerblades. Rollerblading was not really allowed on campus but I wasn't worried about being caught. I couldn't picture the campus cops not allowing me to pass out condoms. I flew around campus for two days personally handing out more condoms than ever before. I was not shy as I gave them to people to use. If they said they didn't need one, I insisted they give it to a friend who did or hide it away until they did need it. Everybody got a condom or two. People who were sincere when they asked for a second or third always got them.

For the next year or so, people around campus would stop or chase me and ask for condoms. The demand was crazy on the days I wore my rollerblades. Some students actually stopped me to tell me how beneficial their relationship had become since they heard me speak. I felt like a firefly, glowing brighter and brighter each time I helped someone. The benefits of sexology were paying off.

I realized that I, too, wanted to become a sexologist like Dr. Elias, so I scheduled a conference with him. I was graduating Cal State Northridge with a bachelor of arts in psychology and a minor in human sexuality. I was not interested in studying lots of excess material that would not be directly related to sex therapy and sex research. Dr. Elias told me about the Institute for the Advanced Study of Human Sexuality in San Francisco where he had received a doctorate years before.

I gathered all the information about the school and applied. I did not want to apply anywhere else. My sister thought I was crazy, but I was confident. I was going to the institute. I am glad that I didn't know at the time that I was about to be the youngest person they ever accepted into the doctoral program. Most of the students there were on second careers or using the sexology program as an addition to their current practices. I had a lot of energy and enthusiasm to devote to sexology, along with strong support from Dr. Elias.

My parents came with me to San Francisco to check out the institute. We understood that this was not going to be a traditional graduate program. The day I interviewed, my father came along. His interest in sex and my career was obvious to all. He was enthralled by the institute and all it had to offer. We met with Maggi Rubenstein, the dean of students, and the three of us talked for a long time about expectations and course requirements. When we left, I was ecstatic. As my dad and I walked back to our hotel, we were walking on air. I was going to start the institute about one month after I graduated from Northridge in December 1991.

I had just turned twenty-three when classes began. I had no idea what to expect but I was open to anything. There were only two other new students because it was the spring quarter. Heidi and Harry were my new partners in mischief, sort of. Heidi, five years older than I, was from Vancouver, British Colombia, and an expert in media, computers, and much more. Other than sex, we didn't have much in common, but we became close friends during the two years I spent in San Francisco. Harry was a whole different story: a sixty-something-year-old Roman Catholic priest, who had recently left his parish in Minnesota to learn about sexuality, something which he felt was desperately lacking in the Church.

Being a semi-innocent Jewish woman, I had no preconceived notions about how to act in front of a priest. I knew that I could laugh and joke with my rabbi at home and assumed no difference. Harry was a blank slate when it came to many aspects of sexology. The second day of classes Heidi and I took Harry to Good Vibrations, an all-encompassing store for everything sexual. None of us had been there before but we were informed by other, more experienced students what we *needed* to have. The three of us checked out the whole store, bought our "necessities," and headed back to class. From then on, Harry would tease me by saying that he was going to write his dissertation on the relationship between Jewish women and vibrators. I'm sure the Church would have loved that idea.

I had fun teasing Harry also. One time during class, we were instructed to conduct a touch exercise. I used my nails and lightly scratched Harry's forearm. Hours later his arm was still tingling and having contractions.

During my two years of classes at the institute I got a certificate of erotology which means I am an expert in anything erotic, mostly media. I had to watch a hundred hours of erotic films that covered every time period, country, and sexual act. When friends or strangers try to get me to shock them, images from these films usually appear in my head.

My personal eroticism is artistically displayed mostly in stone or in clay. I have sculpted the human form in all its glory. I love to sculpt what turns me on or sexual positions that stand out in my memory. Artistic expression is an important aspect of my life. I even used clay to honor a foot fetishist we studied in class who had recently died of AIDS-related complications.

The classes at the institute brought the students and the professors quite close. During my first summer in Sam Francisco, I took the required Sexual Attitude Restructuring (SAR) class which covers all aspects of sexology, with emphasis on personal feelings, body imagery, and acceptance. There had been so much mystery and hype surrounding the class that I couldn't wait for it to start. The third day of this seven-day class was spent at the Gay, Lesbian and Bisexual parade. I decided to rollerblade because I figured I would be sitting along the parade route all day. To my surprise, San Francisco was wall-to-wall people. I quickly got separated from our group and headed down Market Street by myself.

I ran into a woman with whom I had played softball in high school. She was surprised to see me and I was caught in a weird situation. I figured she was lesbian or bisexual because she awkwardly introduced me to her "roommate." She wanted to know what I was doing there. I had to admit, shyly, that it was for school and not because I was gay. We exchanged numbers and off I went. I felt embarrassed that I was straight.

As I rollerbladed aimlessly along the parade route, I saw banners that read "Straights for Gay Rights." As they came closer, I noticed some of my professors and fellow students. I jumped up and bladed out to meet them in the middle of the street. They were just as excited to see me as I was to see them. The next few hours were simply breathtaking. I never realized how much appreciation and love could be expressed through equality. There were approximately twenty of us who walked the route. We got a standing ovation coupled with hand signs saying "peace" and "I love you." I kept thinking to myself that this is absurd. We are just people who are walking for the rights of other people. Millions of people fall into the category of straights for gay rights. Why were we getting such love and attention? When the day was over and I was heading back to school I kept thinking to myself that this had been one of the most life-affirming and special days of my life. SAR was filled with days that were simply magical and transforming for everybody in the group. I treasured the experience so much that the next year I asked to lead one of the groups and help teach some of the classes.

On my own, I decided to become a hypnotherapist. I went to the Hypnosis Training Institute that is based out of Santa Clara where I learned many beneficial tools that I use in sex therapy and competitive athletics. I currently train in Olympic-style weightlifting six days a week. Both the snatch and the clean and jerk take amazing visualization and concentration skills. The skills I learned continue to help my teammates and me enormously.

I had never been hypnotized before I took the class. I found out that I am a somnambulist, meaning I go into a very deep trance. I don't hear anything but I am listening. During group hypnosis sessions, I found myself drifting in and out of the suggestions as I felt they applied to me. I could not seem to find any negative childhood memories to explore so my mind went back to my personal peaceful settings in my parent's backyard or on the beach.

One of the requirements at the institute was to conduct a hundred-person research project using a given questionnaire. I chose to use the men and women who go to Mark groups as my sample. Mark groups meet every week as a division of a sexually oriented, communal housing organization called More University. During Mark groups, the participants play games to get to know each other, then explore feelings and attitudes through a question-and-answer period where one person is on the "hot seat." Everybody is quite social and sexual in their responses. Heidi and I went together to our first Mark group and took everybody by storm. We had several surprising answers and quick remarks that brought us a lot of attention. This study increased my interest in sex research.

When I was in San Francisco, I joined the alumnae group of my college sorority. It wasn't something I was going to do at first but I was far from Los Angeles and figured it couldn't hurt that badly. I was straightforward about who I was and what my career goals were. During my second meeting, the president announced that the Berkeley chapter was having a career night and was asking for volunteers. I volunteered as a joke. The whole group loved it and thought I would be perfect. I felt like screaming, "Hey, do you remember? I'm the sexologist."

On the following Monday night, I met a roomful of bright-eyed collegiates hanging on our every word. I had a lot of fun with my talk. One very pregnant alumna in the back of the room raised her hand, trying to be serious, and asked if I knew how she could not end up like this any longer. We were all cracking up. It felt so refreshing to be in a town that had a long history of sexual openness and acceptance.

Getting involved with sexology takes some time and dedication. I heard about the Society for the Scientific Study of Sexuality (Quad S or SSSS) and the American Association of Sex Educators, Counselors and Therapists (AASECT). I plunged in quite quickly by going to the national meetings of both SSSS and AASECT in my first year. The conversations were always interesting and the lectures were inspiring. I met a wide range of people in all fields who consider themselves sexologists. The beauty of sexology is that it incorporates all aspects of life that deal in any way with sex and sexualities. I have been getting more involved each year with SSSS on a local, regional, and national level.

After two years in San Francisco, my parents decided that they could use my help in Los Angeles. I had finished all my classes, so with a little fuss, I moved back to L.A.

My next project was to pick a dissertation topic. Many people had warned me to make sure I picked something that really interested me. That is more difficult than it sounds. A dissertation is a compilation of research that has never been studied before. Before I had made a final decision and got full approval from my committee, I was on my third proposal. My first proposal had been a study of sexual practices and guidelines concerning Orthodox Jews—a good idea if I were a rabbinical student and not a sexologist.

Around this time I got a call from Ted McIlvenna, the president of the institute who said that he had talked to Dr. William Hartman and Dr. Marilyn Fithian from Long Beach about me. He definitely had my attention. They wanted to know if Ted knew anybody who would be willing to work with them doing sex therapy. When Ted called me, I thought he was kidding. I had had some experience and training, but nothing too extensive.

We discussed their expectations and my desire and need for training. They were working with a man in his thirties who needed help and encouragement socially from a young fireball like me. Marilyn and Bill had been retired for years but were accepting mostly referral cases. They had not done any dual-sex team training sessions in quite a while. As you can imagine, they were not expecting to do much training with me. We agreed that in exchange for hours of work with their client, they would train me in sex therapy and much more. The arrangement has worked out well for both sides.

One of the highlights was working with my ex-boyfriend as if we were clients. Bill and Marilyn guided us through hand, foot, face, hair, and body caress activities. Understanding how clients feel is a major part of becoming a great sex therapist. I had never been to therapy before so I treasured each step of the process. I have been working with Bill and Marilyn since May 1994 as their sole intern. We get along quite well and I keep them fired up about life, fast cars, and sexology, not exactly in that order.

My second dissertation proposal was developed after extensive study of laboratory work done at the Center for Marital and Sexual Studies. I was interested in anal eroticism in men. Better measuring tools must be created before data can be accurately compiled. Time to move on to another topic.

Bill and Marilyn introduced me to a urologist who asked me if I wanted to watch him perform a penile augmentation. I had never seen a real live surgery so I agreed. He answered all my questions and made sure that I could see every step of the surgery up close. He was interested in having me research the men who were undergoing an elective penile enlargement.

I talked it over with Bill and Marilyn (aka George and George) and we decided that this would make an interesting dissertation topic. I created a pretest questionnaire that would ultimately become a nine-page fully investigative research tool to understand men who have had penile augmentation surgery. Sixty-five questionnaires were returned, uncovering interesting results and trends. I am proud of the final draft of my doctoral dissertation that has recently been turned in to my committee. By the time this book is published, I will be a full-fledged Doctor of Philosophy.

Looking over this autobiography, I can see that my interest in sex as a science has been long developed. I am confident that both my studies and experiences will benefit those who choose to share my knowledge. Sex is not an isolated subject; it cannot be studied without incorporating life. That's why I'm here. My life incorporates sex, and sex is part of me. If there is any truth that everyone has a destiny, I am sure that I have found mine. Sexology is an art and a way of life. Behind all the value judgments, moral hang-ups, and repression lies the essence of our being. It defines who we are. My job, then, is to help others reach this same realization. Sex is a thing of beauty and a source of pleasure.

24

From Design to Sexology

Ronald R. McAllister, Ph.D.

Ronald R. McAllister, after devoting twenty years to research and education, is now the leading designer and developer of sexual enhancers.

M Y POSITION IN the sex industry as one of the top designers of sex toys in the 1990s is a far cry from my adolescence in the mountains of California. I grew up relentlessly normal in a small resort town in the High Sierras. Much of my earnest approach to life and my early beliefs that everything is possible for those who work hard came from my mother and the college education she afforded me.

My father passed away suddenly when I was still a toddler from malignant hypertension, a disease that is hereditary although it can skip a generation. Hence, I never had children of my own. My mother, younger brother, and I moved to my grandparents' in San Bernardino where we lived in harmony, lacking only in outwardly affection. Needless to say, the subject of the "birds and the bees" was never discussed in our home. My mother expressed feelings that she had a hard time accepting sex as pleasurable in a day-to-day setting. Sex for procreation was the only acceptable answer. In view of this and my respect for her, when she died April 1995, she did not know what I did for a living. The only sex education during these early years was the sharing of lies and tall tales interspersed with minimal truths in the playground. The social structure at the time was very unbending when it came to sexual experimentation and education. A double standard being the rule, it was okay for boys to be promiscuous, but not girls, thus placing a lot of guilt and anxiety on any sexual relationship.

My first innocent, yet highly stimulating, sexual experience was at age nine with a neighbor of approximately the same age. She and I continued our exploration with such antics as "doctor and nurse" for quite some time thereafter. Armed with this new sexual experience and not knowing any better, I found sex satisfying but not necessarily fulfilling.

At twelve, I was delighted to have my first experience with sexual intercourse with a girl of the same age and soon realized that I had a remarkable addiction to sex. I earned myself a reputation in school for being too sexual. Any new girl would be well warned about the sexually focused person that I had become! I, however, thought it was rather macho and cool. In junior high and high school I found girls older than I more attractive than girls my own age. This continued into my college years.

In the early sixties I moved to Hollywood. My mother and her new husband offered me the opportunity to enroll in a design and business college in Los Angeles. My uncle had the largest furniture store in San Bernardino and he greatly influenced my career choices. To supplement my college education, I worked as an interior designer's assistant and sold furniture.

No longer considered an outcast or sexual degenerate in college, I blended in with other sexually open students who enjoyed experimentation and promiscuity. A number of my sex partners were interested in varying and different areas of sexual activities, foreplay, intercourse, exhibitionism, control, and experimentation from aggressive to submissive. Photography gave me immense pleasure as a hobby, especially whenever I could use nude women as my subjects.

I graduated from college with a bachelor of professional arts degree which provided me with a professional background in conceptual design as well as with a practical application in graphic layout and three-dimensional art. The more I pursued the arts the more I found a growing passion and appreciation for erotic art, both in print and sculpture. I started collecting and creating my own erotic paintings and sculptures. My fascination with erotic and sexual art translated into a need to design and fulfill fantasy with real products designed to stimulate those fantasies. As a ferocious collector I had flat and three-dimensional art, old T. J. Bibles (sexual comic books, which I donated to the Institute for Advanced Study of Human Sexuality), old 16 mm film, hardbound books, and photographs. In collecting old erotic literature it was interesting to note that even the Greek comic playwright Aristophanes, writing in the fifth century B.C.E., refers to dildos in his plays[1]; in the *Arabian Nights* (tenth century) it is written, "O bananas, of soft and smooth skins which dilate the eyes of young girls . . . you alone among fruits are endowed with a pitying heart, O consolers of widows and divorced women." In China of the Ming Dynasty (1368–1644) a "pearl" on a ring was designed to stimulate the clitoris and lateral wings, emanating from a dragon, the "pearl" was designed to stimulate the labia. Rings made of jade and ivory were placed over the penis to prolong erection and to stimulate the woman. In Japan, a device used hundreds of years ago was the

---

1. In ancient Greece, Rome, and during virtually all eras of humankind in the Western and Eastern worlds, dildos were made of a variety of materials, including gold, silver, ivory, ebony, animal horns, glass, wax, stuffed leather, and wood. Most dildos made prior to the 1960s were *hard* and made of materials such as leather, metal, and rigid plastics. Today's products are firm yet soft and flexible.

precursor to the vibrator: "Rin-No-Tama" or "Ben Wa" balls, as we know them today, were usually two hollow metal balls, one empty and the other small and solid or filled with mercury or small pieces of lead. Both balls were placed in the vagina, and with the vagina blocked they would be set in motion by rocking the hips. The Chuckchee of Siberia used a dildo made of the dried calf muscle of a reindeer. The Azande of Afnea used wooden dildos, but if caught by their husband they were beaten. The Lesu of New Ireland (South Pacific) sat in a position with their heel pressing up against their vulva and rocked back and forth. These were just a few of the historic and cross-cultural anecdotes I came across and found fascinating.

I realized that lust was wonderful but lasted only six months or so, and I wanted to learn and create something that could continue that kind of excitement. I read as much as possible on sexuality. One drawback was that I had to carefully choose to share my interests with only a select group of friends. My family was not included.

In the late sixties I took a design position with a manufacturer of window and door geared and locking devices for commercial, residential, and recreational window and door manufacturers. As a 360-degree visionary, I needed to make my audacious dreams a reality, so after five years I started my own freelance design company. I went back to the drawing board and used my associations and design experience to create new products. For capital I designed a number of prototype security devices for the residential marketplace and sold the manufacturing rights to the designs.

A girlfriend of mine told me that a friend starting an adult product distribution company needed someone part-time to help create a new numbering system for wholesale price list and inventory control, along with sales flyers highlighting special sale items and the introduction of new products. Coincidental with the sexual revolution of the 1960s was an ever-increasing demand for sex toys and other aids for sexual enhancement, impotence, and masturbatory fantasy fulfillment. I must admit that I have always been drawn toward challenges, and with my curiosity for the adult industry, I agreed to do it.

Having a multitude of adult toys available and being allowed to try anything in stock created all sorts of wild fantasies, I could share with partners that newfound thrill and turn into reality the fulfillment of fantasies that before this had been available only in my imagination. As I continued my freelance design work of price lists, brochures, package design, and print advertising, my thirst for sexual knowledge and experimentation was being quenched by my surroundings.

After working at the adult merchandise distribution company for about nine months, I was approached by the largest adult merchandiser in Los Angeles to design and lay out the first novelty catalogue consisting of all of the rubber, liquid, and novelty products they stocked. The creation of this catalogue was the first complete presentation of its type showcasing adult sexual enhancement aids, known at this time as marital aids.

Upon the finalization and success of this catalogue, I was recommended to other companies in the adult distribution industry where I created more catalogues and price lists and offered suggestions for new product design. Clients on the East and

West Coasts contacted me about redesigning their standard white 8mm film boxes to display four-color film clip photographs and design new company names and logos.

Since I had been doing all the product photographs for the printed material I had been producing, I had my own camera equipment. When I was asked to photograph the U.S. segment of stills on an upcoming film featuring martial arts action that would be shot using an experimental lens to produce three-dimensional images, I accepted the assignment readily.

The cinematographer who shot the martial arts film contacted me about six months later and asked if I would be interested in being part of his crew for a full-length, big-budget X-rated film to be shot on location in San Francisco; the film, later released as *Cry for Cindy,* turned out to a big success. It was later dubbed in several languages for foreign release. For several years I continued to freelance commercial art and shoot movie stills for the adult industry, until one of the adult novelty manufacturing companies I had been working for was purchased.

From 1977 until today I have been employed by Doc Johnson Enterprises, one of the foremost manufacturers of sexual enhancers and adult toys in the world. Not content with being an art director, I was promoted to the purchasing and shipping divisions, and with constant new ideas and designs I was eventually given complete freedom to design and implement new and different product ideas and directions. This has gained me a reputation for being the most prolific designer of sexual enhancement products in our industry. My fascination with collecting erotic books and art was the impetus for my first design and development of a "Chamber Sword." A drawing from a Victorian book of a dildo with a handle became my first sculpture and sex toy production.

It was during my transition from art director to product designer that I met Ted McIlvenna from the Institute for Advanced Study of Human Sexuality. We worked together on several projects, including an AIDS conference that was held in San Francisco in the early 1990s. Since that time we have continued to work closely in the creation of new and better products and their careful testing for quality and user-friendly attributes. My work has been recognized by the American College of Sexologists. Because of my contribution to the adult industry, the institute awarded me with an honorary doctor of erotology degree. At present, I am continuing my education and hold both Ted McIlvenna and the institute in the highest regard and respect.

I have an extraordinary affinity for my work and admit that I am stimulated by it. I am often asked what my favorite creation is and why. I would have to say that my preference at this point is the "Vac-U-Lock Harness System," patented about four years ago.[2] This has saved many marriages and relationships because of its quality design that really does what it claims. It holds snugly on the hip and the crotch area is open, creating a design that is unisex applicable. With the plug that is attached to the harness, it allows interchangeability of dildo size and design.

---

2. The harness, which can be worn by men or women, uses a unique system in which dildos can be exchanged, alternating sizes and shapes.

My most memorable correspondence came from a male quadriplegic who had had many penile implant operations. Due to extreme scar tissue buildup he was unable to maintain an erection and had lost all sensitivity in his genitals. However, with the use of the Vac-U-Lock Harness System, he was able to maintain his sexual relationship with a long-time partner.

Like the harness, which allows the experience of intercourse to stop only when you want it to stop, many of my designs are used for sexual therapy. Specific pumps are a training device for premature ejaculation, creating blood flow and opening the capillaries that improve the strength of the erection. Vibrators allow one to be exploratory with one's own sexuality. They can also be used during intercourse. Restraint products are becoming more popular because you can use them to learn and teach about trust.

Some of the most artistic adult toys are the high-end vibrators such as the multispeed "Dragon Lady" series with its ribbed shaft and head which rotates a full 360 degrees, advanced integrated circuit chip technology, pearl beads that swirl around for more intense sensations, and the attached clitoral vibrator with its own speed control. The full lines of realistic vaginas, dildos, and vibrator products satisfy fantasies and are great visual assets. These are perhaps the most popular items sold in America and Europe.

I articulate the fantasies of others or my own personal experiences and design products to satisfy those general or requested needs. I view working with the professionals in the sex industry as a positive part of my creativity. This diversification and dedication are the elements that makes me a leading creator, artist, and designer of sexual enhancements, with several patents and over three hundred design copyrights.

I love working with individuals and creating something original for them and myself. Though I am still an avid collector of erotic art, I can now sculpt my own erotic art as part of my work. Several years ago I started using actual body casts in order to create the most "realistic" of sex enhancers. For my doctoral project at the Institute for Advanced Study of Human Sexuality, I chose a retrospective of my casting artistry and this year I donated a special cast for the benefit of the annual meeting of the Society for the Scientific Study of Sexuality (SSSS) in San Francisco.

In developing a series of realistic penises and vulvas I needed to do a lot of research and development on casting and materials to establish set times and detail. To get realistic set times, all of the testing needed to be done on live bodies. Rather than waste a model's time, I started creating a number of erotic art body castings using live models, both male and female, which I displayed at the SSSS meeting in 1995. My sculptures can be called many things—erotic, unique, sexual, but never boring.

My contribution to the world of sex is taking masturbation and exploration with adult toys to an acceptable and enjoyable standard. Many users of the products I have designed have written to me expressing their thanks and praising the products.

With both social and economic globalization, Americans are becoming more candid in their sexual habits and fantasies. We are still more repressed than Europeans, whose requirements have always been for more domination (restraint control), more fantasy, and larger items such as dildos. Asia, however, is even more repressed than the United States. For example, anything phallic is illegal and pornography can be punishable by death in China.

Since sex toys are being accepted as a viable commodity in the 1990s and consumers are looking for higher standards, my next target area is to design more electrical and mechanical products with solid state technology. I also expect to continue student and professional lectures designed to inform and educate about the positive aspects of toys, dispelling the fears of toys replacing the individual. I encourage people to explore and experiment with products designed specifically for them such as clitoral-, vaginal-, anal-stimulation devices, g-spot and products for sexual control during intercourse.

Women seem to me more comfortable and candid in sharing their intimacies and fantasies. I find men not to be as candid about products or product use unless it is truly product specific. Many products designed for men are products dealing with premature ejaculation, performance anxiety impotence, anal stimulation, and penis size.

I will continue to work on research and on new formulations to improve strength, durability, coloration, and odor as well as on seamless production molds, and realistic texture that will produce the highest-quality affordable product. When creating a new product, I give samples to twenty to thirty individuals at the institute (for student testing) and I supply five to ten premier adult video producers with products to use in their films. The feedback that I receive from the groups allows me to finalize the best possible product for the mass market.

Traveling is probably one of the best benefits that come with my vocation. I get to review sexual attitudes and directions of other cultures first hand. Most products are sold worldwide and I particularly enjoy visiting vendor factories in Asia, Europe, and South America to maintain and control production quality and make sure all new design specifications are followed.

Despite twenty-two years of designing products to stimulate and enhance both the sensuous and sexual fantasies of all sexes, I can honestly say that I still have a passion for my work. I welcome candid input by men and women of all sexual preferences for their product fantasy direction. Sex should never be boring, no matter if you are in a long-term relationship or an autoerotic relationship. Sex is an exploratory privilege.

With the repressive climate of the times and the real threat of AIDS and other sexually transmitted diseases, one can be assured that adult toys are the safest of all sexual experiences when used properly. You will not get pregnant or contract a decease as long as you do not share with anyone. And how else could you experience a *menage à trois* without cheating on your partner?

Before selecting sex toys for your partner, it is important to observe and understand some of the major sexual differences between men and women. Here are some of my observations:

1. Men see penis length as a product positive.

2. Women see penis girth as a product positive. Women find more pleasure in pressure established by girth rather than length.

3. Women are more interested in trying restraints and experiencing sexual control by using restraints or a harness with a partner of either sex.

4. Men are starting to find the advantages offered them by introducing a harness in their relationship be it heterosexual or homosexual. Lovemaking can last as long as it is pleasurable, either as the giver or receiver.

As it begins its third decade, Doc Johnson Enterprises has distinguished itself as the world's premier manufacturer of sensual and sexual products. Their catalog offers over one thousand items. Many of the products have been clinically tested and approved by the Institute for Advanced Study of Human Sexuality and the American College of Sexologists. I am proud and honored to be associated with Doc Johnson.

Specific design categories that I have influenced include:

fantasy dildos (sculpted penis shapes)

realistic dildos (cast from live models)

fantasy vaginas (sculpted vulva shapes)

realistic vaginas (cast from live models)

vibrators

penis pumps

restraints

>   beginners lightweight webbing and Velcro, latex whips

>   heavy leather, hoods, whips, cuffs, nipple clamps, cock rings, dildo harness, nipple pumps, clamps

Latex (the first latex garment that needs no powder)

>   Panties, bras, briefs with dildo, cock and ball socks, gloves, stockings, skirts

Vac-u-lock modular system

>   interchangeable penis attachments

>   harness (unisex)

>   harness (deluxe leather) male and female

>   inflatable rocking ball.

Example of Product Development

Doc Johnson wanted to create a realistic vagina sex aid.

1. To add to its marketability, we contracted Savannah, a well-known adult entertainer to be the model for its development.

2. The packaging was designed around Savannah, using her photographs and her name as one of the leading performers in the adult industry.

3. Upon Savannah's arrival, she was put into our "casting" room. For a realistic application of the vagina, it was necessary for the labia and clitoris to be erect.

   Savannah manipulated herself by hand and with a vibrator. Once the lips were fully engorged or as large as possible, casting material, made up of a form of non-toxic alginate, was applied. The material was allowed to set by body temperature for approximately ten minutes.

4. A support casting was placed over it for strength and removed after five more minutes. Once the casting was removed, we backpoured plaster into the impression we just made. The casting impression is a negative from which we create a positive. At this time I had to sculpt out any little bubbles and imperfections.

5. Then we trapped the master in a rubber mold, all applied by hand.

6. Now it was ready for the assembly line where we took the full cast and made it into a production mold that was specifically designed to run on our production line.

7. We had to match the labia color to Savannah's flesh with special permanent dye.

8. Then blonde pubic hairs were individually implanted for realism.

9. The above process was all documented on video, and a copy of the video was enclosed and made a part of the packaging with this product.

   My philosophy is that there are two reasons for sex. One is for "procreation" and the other is for "pleasure." I contribute to *pleasure!*

25

Autobiography of a Feminist Sexual Scientist

Naomi B. McCormick, Ph.D.

Naomi McCormick was a Distinguished Teaching Professor at the State University of New York at Plattsburgh and is now a visiting scholar at the University of Northern Iowa. A past president of the Society for the Scientific Study of Sexuality, she has a special interest in the sexual needs of those with chronic and physical illnesses.

N THE ACADEMY, sex research and women's studies have long been regarded as marginal occupations, in part because both fields are concerned with the perspectives and rights of nondominant groups: lesbian, gay, bisexual, and cross-gendered persons in the case of sex research and women in general, lesbians, ethnic minorities, the physically disabled, and impoverished persons in the case of women's studies. Why, then, have I devoted the past twenty years of my life to two stigmatized areas of scholarly inquiry? I certainly have had little formal academic training in either sexual science or women's studies. And, on numerous occasions, I have been teased and criticized by other academics for doing work that they regarded as intellectually questionable and left of the "respectable" social science mainstream (which feminists like myself sometimes think of as the affluent, heterosexual, white, "male-stream").

Perhaps it is the very lack of political respectability, the academic marginality of my chosen life work, that I find so attractive. I am a Jew and Jews have been outsiders for most of our history. For at least three generations, members of my extended family have been politically liberal and radical social activists, participating in the labor organizing, civil rights, and peace movements. I grew up watching close family members and their friends take stands for what they believed in and being willing to suffer if others judged them badly for their nonconformity and social consciousness. When I was a child, my parents took me to peace marches during the most frozen era of the cold war, a period during which rotten eggs and the taunt "Go back to Russia" were hurled at those who dared to demonstrate against the proliferation of nuclear weapons.

Some of my earliest and most treasured childhood memories are of holding a placard against the proverbial wind of downtown Chicago, accompanying my parents to demonstrations for one cause or another. This family tradition has continued all my adult life. When I was an undergraduate, my mother accompanied me to my first feminist march, a demonstration for women's right to choose abortion in the days before the now-beleaguered *Roe* v. *Wade* decision. Today, at eighty-two, my mother remains an activist in battered women's and Jewish women's organizations, continuing to write articles on her observations as a feminist social worker which I edit and type. So, I have always been an outsider and have been taught by my family to regard that status as a badge of courage. No wonder, then, I was drawn to the exciting but taboo fields of sexual science and women's studies.

How did my professional journey begin? As a child growing up in the Midwest during the 1950s and 1960s, I was exposed to very little in the way of formal sex education. In elementary school, there were the simplified diagrams of human anatomy to memorize, of course, and the field trip to a museum where the class got to peek and giggle at the plastic sex organs of the "invisible" woman and man. This exhibit, however, never attained the popularity of another museum's electric incubator populated by dozens of adorable, wet, newly hatched baby chickens, slowly drying to spirited balls of fluff. Never mind how it was that these baby chickens came to be—that information was to be reserved for high school. But, other than acquiring a vague idea about the shape and location of the organs of reproduction, other than attending that girls-only film in the sixth grade about menstruation and the importance of daily showers and a steady boyfriend after a girl's first menstrual period, I learned little about sexuality from my teachers.

Indeed, I learned quite young that female sexuality was held in contempt. In the sixth and seventh grades, eleven- and twelve-year-old boys delighted in leaving catsup-covered sanitary napkins on top of girls' desks and snapping the elastic backs of our bras in the playground, Robin-Hood style. Lucky me, I still wore an undershirt. What else did I learn then? I learned how conservative and intolerant American culture was of sexual nonconformity and female sexual interest.

Even my politically and socially liberal mother appeared reluctant to discuss sexuality. At age nine, I asked her the long-anticipated question, "How are babies born?" She was attending graduate school in social work at the time. "Let me ask my professor," she said, her voice somewhat shaken. "I'll get back to you soon." "My God," I thought to myself, "she doesn't know!" Two days later, my mother rattled forth the scientific explanation for heterosexual sexuality and reproduction. She obviously was in a hurry. "Oh," I said, "is that all there is to it?" Mom was surprised by what she saw as "my nonchalance" and by what I, in hindsight, like to think of as my "budding scientific attitude." Following this, I became a sex educator of sorts for other children, gleefully informing a friend's younger sister that no, women don't get pregnant simply by taking their clothes off and slowly walking toward their nude husbands, and no, Barbie and Ken are not anatomically correct.

My first adult experience as a sex educator took place when I was an eighteen-year-old counselor to a cabin of ten-year-old girls at a residential summer camp. My sincere but amateur efforts to provide good information about sex came in response to their hysteria after spending the previous night exchanging jokes about trains going through tunnels followed by sexual horror stories about women with three breasts, the third of which was supposedly green (a challenge to lingerie manufacturers), and ghostlike male trespassers who regularly stalked and sexually victimized young girls like themselves who spent their summers in camps in the Wisconsin wilderness. I soon learned that my supervisors did not appreciate my efforts. "Who gave you permission to talk to these girls about sex?" my unit head inquired. "Don't you realize that their parents will be angry about what you told their daughters!" added the camp director.

Later, as a young Ph.D., I had my sexuality classes and public lectures sometimes targeted by Radical Right persons who wrote letters to the editor of our local newspaper (my college is located in a small town in which the local anti-choice protesters have been known to perform exorcisms in front of our community Planned Parenthood clinic). The first such letter, read aloud to my class by one of my undergraduates, protested a talk I had given in defense of the accessibility of safe, legal abortions. "Who is this Naomi McCormick and where does she come from?" the byline of the letter read.

In this same anti-choice community, a Right to Life protester once slammed a colorful poster depicting an allegedly late-term aborted fetus into my husband's and my faces, shouting, "This is what you stand for!" Not long before this incident, I was one of many to testify on behalf of the right of our local Planned Parenthood clinic to offer first-trimester abortions; at the time, there were no abortion providers in our own and a neighboring county. Yes, speaking up on behalf of women's right to choose is risky. But I have learned that it can be just as unpopular to present information on sexual assault and coercion, homosexuality, or AIDS. When I was training crisis hotline volunteers about gay and lesbian issues, a young volunteer blurted out that the only relevant issue to his mind was that "homosexuals are a suicidal lot." I did my best to dispute his negative stereotypes and those unvoiced anti-gay sentiments held by the remaining trainees and staff. I am not sure that I was effective. How can a two- or three-hour education program undo years of anti-gay propaganda?

Prejudiced remarks, however, have been rare through the years. More often, my sex education and feminist programs are simply avoided by those who need them the most. In other words, I find myself "preaching to the choir"; those who show up for programs on sexual orientation, workshops on the prevention of rape and sexual assault, women's health conferences, and AIDS education speeches typically are already well informed and concerned. The trick (and I do not yet have an answer) is how to reach less enlightened individuals.

My research on sex education seems to have been regarded as even more controversial than my teaching and public presentations. When I was a young assistant professor in the late 1970s and early 1980s, my graduate students and I tried our best to gain access to high schools where we could study adolescents' sexual values, knowledge, and contraceptive behaviors. Each day, we drove to a different rural school, spending our first hour building rapport by sympathizing with a principal's busy life and many problems. Following this, we spent the second hour trying to sell our research. During one such visit to a Catholic school, the principal, a man of the cloth, indicated that he was shocked, not by our proposed survey questions about premarital sexual activity, but rather about our inquiry into sexually active students' contraceptive methods. This man was proud to relieve young boys in his charge of the condoms that they carried in their pockets as symbols of manhood. He pulled out one such bit of contraband from his desk drawer as we spoke. "Now, by asking students to answer questions about various methods of birth control," he pointed out, "we don't want to give them ideas, do we?"

Sometimes, our effort to win the hearts of high school administrators worked and we were allowed into a few parochial and public high schools. I still have fond memories of my attempt, via discreet hand signals, to answer a fifteen-year-old girl's questions about withdrawal, one of the birth control methods listed on our survey, while she completed our instrument (questionnaire) along with others in the school's large and noisy gymnasium. Those were the days! Given the current hysteria about sex education and teenage sexuality, I seriously doubt whether I could do this kind of research today in conservative upstate, rural New York, never mind that we always asked for both parents' and students' informed consent.

High school administrators and parents groups have not been the only ones to challenge my sex research efforts; college administrators have been equally confrontational. After a university committee on the protection of human subjects had approved my proposed study of faculty sexual harassment of students, the current college president and two other male administrators asked me to meet with them. The meeting, the sole female administrator of the time informed me, was to be an attempt to stop or at least slow down what they perceived would be a very controversial study that might hurt the college's public relations image. During the meeting, all three men insisted on standing. As each man was at least six feet tall and muscular in build, standing was a symbolic way of pointing out my own inferior status as a young, untenured woman (who was considerably more petite at only five foot four inches). The group of men also showed their dominance by interrupting my speech and touching me whenever they wished to punctuate an opinion. And, the president also demonstrated his authority by puffing on a big, smelly pipe (he knew I hated smoking).

Clearly, the meeting had the purpose of stopping a study, the results of which they feared would be leaked to the local newspaper and television station. I succeeded in calming them down and getting my way only by promising to take "complete responsibility" (read "blame") for the study's methodology and results and mainly to share information about the outcome to various academic journals and scholarly conferences, all safely off campus. Here, as in other interactions I have had with individuals from dominant groups, I have learned that the powers that be would sometimes rather not know about sexuality or sexual exploitation than acquire the information necessary to understand and possibly prevent associated problems.

To the surprise of college administrators, my co-investigators and I received considerable cooperation from faculty, staff, and students alike; our response rate was high. Not surprisingly, we discovered that some sexual harassment did take place on campus (e.g., a student reported that her professor once told her, "If you had bigger breasts, you'd get better grades"). But, the most surprising news was that male students were almost as likely as female to indicate that they had been the recipients of faculty-initiated sociosexual behavior. And faculty members were somewhat more likely to admit that they had engaged in behaviors defined as "sexual harassment" by the majority of members of the campus community than the undergraduates were likely to admit having experienced these behaviors. Important for campus policy makers, we learned that neither faculty nor undergraduates knew much about sexual harassment law and prevention although the faculty had the illusion that they were knowledgeable.

Returning to my own adolescence, a nonstop source of inspiration for my sexological theories, I received the clear message that grownups did not want to discuss sex with teenage girls. A girl doesn't have to be a "rocket scientist" to understand that we live in a sex-negative culture. I came of age in the days when "good" girls were expected to come home at 10:30 P.M. and prove their continued virginity by relating detailed and chronologically meticulous stories about all the respectable things they did on their date with a boy, who was presented to parents to be as innocent and wholesome as a glass of milk and oatmeal cookies. These were the days, too, of chaperones at high school dances, making sure that none of the young couples danced too closely or hugged too eagerly. In this time period in the United States, girls got sent home from school for wearing a short skirt (operationally defined by school administrators as ending above their knees), while boys were sent home for the heinous dress-code crime of allowing their shirts to hang outside their trousers.

When I was a teenager, my mother was employed as a social worker at a home for unwed mothers. "Don't ever let that happen to you!" she remarked on more than one occasion. Her comments were effective, not so much in preventing me from youthful sexual experimentation, but in clarifying that adults, including loving family members, thought that what I desired and what I finally ended up doing was wrong and best kept silent. Clearly, I was on my own sexually, like many adolescent girls today, and then and now, that was a scary thought.

It is no accident, then, that I have chosen to study and publish work on the sexualities and sexual knowledge of high school and college students throughout my career. I want the adolescents and young adults of today to have more adult support for their sexual feelings and questions than did my "baby boomer" generation, for all the phony liberation of our "free-love" days in the late 1960s and early 1970s. The now-nostalgic "make love not war" posters and buttons did not change the fundamental repression of female sexual autonomy and pleasure that characterized the lives of most girls and women. Indeed, ours continues to be a culture that tells youth, especially girls and young women, to be asexual and equates adolescent and young adult sexual activity with danger—disease, single motherhood, and sexual assault. We need a more balanced approach; we should emphasize sexual pleasure and not just danger, female sexual initiative and not just sexual victimization. I agree with Michelle Fine (1992), who explains that what is missing for women and even more so for girls is a discourse of desire. I hope to continue the rest of my career studying, writing about, and teaching a female discourse of desire.

Yes, I am a feminist, but no, this does not mean that I am sex-negative. Like most feminist sexual scientists I know, I endeavor to do sex-positive research without ignoring the shadowy side of sexual experience, sexual abuse and coercion. While most of my research has concerned sexual values, desires, and consensual activities, I have also studied and help shape institutional policies on sexual harassment and public safety.

I am embarrassed to admit that I never saw a textbook, much less a scholarly book, totally devoted to human sexuality until I was a graduate student at the University of California, Los Angeles, when my mentors, Drs. Letitia Anne Peplau and Constance Hammen, were teaching an "experimental," elective, graduate course on sexuality. By this time, I had already chosen sex research as the topic for my dissertation. My chosen research on sexual influence certainly seemed a great deal more interesting than my previous empirical work on childhood creativity and the small-group interactions of psychiatric patients.

In other words, with the exception of my single, ten-week-long graduate course on human sexuality, I am almost entirely self-taught. Almost all of what I know about sexuality has been gleaned from my own independent reading as a graduate student and later as a professional and of course from attending professional meetings.

Fictional discourse on sexuality is also important, as it has the potential to shape readers' or observers' sexual values and expectations substantially more than sex education or the findings of sexual scientists. Growing up, I had limited contact with fictional writing that addressed sexuality. To his credit, my father encouraged me to read novels containing what passed for sexual content in the early 1960s—engrossing, melodramatic, fictional books about adolescents, young adults, and their romantic interactions. I can still remember when my father searched, to no avail, for one such favorite book from his own youth at the public library, only to learn that it was kept under lock and key along with the other "dangerous" works. He had to sign a parental consent statement in order for me to borrow this book, the narrative of which would be very tame indeed by today's standards. Then, of course, there was my own extracurricular reading. I saved up my allowance to secretly purchase what my mother would have considered "trashy" magazines with names like *True Romance* and *True Love*. At night, flashlight in hand, I devoured the contents of these magazines, reading as best I could with my head under my pillow. Here, for the first time, I read about people being nude and other exciting and shocking details of their imagined lives with partners, pretty bland content, again, by today's standards, but an effort on my part to begin understanding my earliest sexual emotions and sensations. Here I am, three books and nearly seventy articles and chapters later, admitting that my sexual scholarship was first inspired by such limited reading materials. Until graduate school and my exposure to the one sex education course in my life and eventually the early edition of *Our Bodies, Ourselves* (Boston Women's Health Book Collective, 1973), women's magazines and romantic novels were my only source of written "information" about sexuality other than the pamphlet that came along with my monthly box of tampons.

It is time to return to earlier memories. At age thirteen, my first boyfriend, a twelve-year-old from another school, taught me about male privilege in heterosexual relationships by being as demanding and possessive as possible, although it was perfectly okay for him to lie and show up late for meetings. When I tried to end the relationship, he insisted on giving me a box of chocolates to persuade me of the economic benefits of remaining in the relationship. After all, an investment is an investment and economic benefits are the foundation of lasting heterosexual relationships, right? Prior to our breakup, Tom and his friends, pubescent swashbuckling types all, eagerly showed off their large pocket knives to other tough boys, supposedly to "protect" us girls on our way home from dances. Fascinated, my young adolescent self was still able to question Tom's hypermasculinity and effort to control me economically. I still wonder about hypermasculinity and its impact on consensual and coercive sexuality but now, of course, I am able to examine these related topics as a serious feminist scholar and sexual scientist.

Additional sexological interests were awakened later in adolescence. Other than review human reproductive anatomy, my health and biology teachers had provided me with absolutely no sex education and certainly no practical information about either my body or sexual intimacy. And, I certainly was not exposed to the writings of the pioneering women who, outside my high school, were awakening the third wave of American feminism—that is, not until I borrowed my mother's copy of Simone de Beauvoir's *The Second Sex* (1978). I did learn a great deal informally, however. Sharon, my best friend, developed an "unusual" illness for several months. She wrote to inform me that I couldn't visit her at "the hospital" but her boyfriend and mother could. I guessed that Sharon might be pregnant but never had the heart to tell her when she returned to high school, presumably after delivering her baby and giving it up for adoption. I didn't want to embarrass her.

Other lessons followed. I became quite active in a youth group which included young people from several high schools and even ran for office. The boy who acted as president of our community center informed me that it was okay for girls like me to run for secretary or vice president but that "we were too emotionally unstable" to qualify as candidates for the presidency. Although his remarks made me angry, that didn't prevent me from developing a crush on him later. This experience was one of many that was the foundation for my interest in feminist work and scholarship. I knew something was wrong and I was motivated to find out what exactly and how it could be fixed. Later, I compensated for this lost opportunity by running for and eventually becoming the twenty-fifth president of the Society for the Scientific Study of Sexuality (SSSS).

Years later, newly graduated with my B.A. degree in psychology, my social consciousness was elevated by a personal traumatic experience in which I learned firsthand about the difficulties faced by women, especially poor women, who "have a bad reputation" and who may, in some cases, be employed in sex work in order to survive. After I had been found guilty (falsely in my opinion) of "obstructing traffic" and being "disorderly" at a student peace march in downtown Chicago, record of my legal appeal was "mysteriously" lost and a deputy sheriff, to the horror of my parents, transported me to Cook County Jail, supposedly to work off my inflated five-hundred-dollar sentence at five dollars a day. I found myself the only white woman there and certainly the only woman well off enough to have all her teeth. It appeared, too, that I may have been one of the few there who did not have a drug or alcohol problem. Our cells were equipped with plastic covered mattresses (in case we got sick or lost bladder control, I guess) and enough vermin to keep me jumpy. Several women around me did appear to be ill, possibly due to their unsupervised withdrawal from addictive drugs. The assumption by my keepers, of course, was that I and all women there must be prostitutes—prostitutes who failed to look after our health! So, like every other new woman prisoner, I was forced to undergo a brutal gynecological exam for sexually transmitted diseases following the humiliating body search that precedes imprisonment. After this, hungry because I had resisted the repulsive institutional food for fifteen hours as well as being shocked and ashamed, I passed out on the hard cement floor. I had no idea how long I was "out," but a kindly African American inmate, not a guard, picked me up off the floor and comforted me. A few hours later, my attorney was able to release me; he eventually succeeded in having the five hundred dollar fine reduced to a token twenty-five dollars, easily paid before my cross-country trip to graduate school in Los Angeles two months later.

No such justice or kindness was granted the other women. This experience made me aware of the privileges I enjoyed as a result of education, middle-class status, and a white skin. It also increased my empathy for women in my country and others who lack my privileges and who, as a result, may face oppression that middle-class, white women cannot even imagine. My living nightmare in Cook County Jail permanently changed my perspective on what social science research should accomplish and who should be studied. All my adult life, I have endeavored to do scholarly work, including sex research, that acknowledges the diversity of women. In my scholarly work and teaching, I note that some women, but not all, face daily hardships and have few choices, economically and sexually. I hope that this attitude is reflected in my book *Sexual Salvation*, especially in my chapter on women sex trade workers and the special burdens faced by poor women, women of color, and immigrant women in the world of commercial sex (McCormick, 1994).

I have just finished my presidency. I must say it was a wonderful year and none of my sister and fellow sexologists seemed overly worried about either my female emotions or feminist ideology. This is not completely true where I work, however. A few weeks ago, a supervising colleague chastised me for providing feminist content to undergraduates enrolled in my classes. "I always get excellent teaching evaluations from students," I said. "Yes, I know," he replied, "I'm sure that those who take your courses have good academic experience. I'm not worried about them; it is the *perception* of you as a feminist given to students who are too conservative to enroll in your courses that concerns me." To make matters worse, my supervisor learned that I actually had been teaching about women and sexuality in mainstream (read "male-stream") courses, not just women's studies and sexuality classes. "I understand that you use a book about women in your undergraduate personality course," he remarked with obvious concern. I noted that this required book was not only about women but also about lesbians, poor persons, and persons of color. Of course, my adoption of a major textbook, which related the personality theories and research of a largely middle class, heterosexual, male group of scientists and clinicians, was never scrutinized.

Even today as a senior sexologist, I am continually reminded that information about sexuality and women is viewed as inherently suspect while excluding such information is regarded as sensible academic practice. It is no accident that an anonymous male colleague returned his survey on sociosexual experiences with students (with the criticism which might be construed by some as sexual harassment): "Only women could have designed a study this stupid!" Apparently, this faculty member's stereotypes about academic women and feminist research were so strong that he failed to notice that one of my main collaborators (and always a valued research colleague and fellow social psychologist at my school) was Dr. William Gaeddert, certainly no woman by any definition.

I first became interested in sexual scripts (socially expected roles in romantic interactions) as a girl of sixteen. More than any other interaction during my adolescence, I hold on to a vivid memory of the following experience, first shared in my book *Sexual Salvation* (McCormick, 1994).

> I was sixteen years old and so was he. We were parked, looking into each other's eyes, talking about nothing in particular. It was a long time ago. I can't vouch for his feelings, but I do remember mine. I was distracted by new emotions, strange and tingling sensations that seemed to pulse forth from the very center of my body. I wanted to touch him, kiss him like I saw in the movies, get closer than I ever had been with anybody. I didn't know the rules so I made them up as I went along. I made the first move and possibly the second and who knows, maybe the third as well. He was flushed and sweaty; he seemed to be in shock; he didn't know what to do. He fell across the steering wheel. Our intimacy evaporated. (p. 15)

As I explained in my book:

This incident actually marked the beginning of my career as a sex researcher. . . .
That night, I began to wonder about things I still wonder about. Why wasn't I
supposed to make the first move? Why was this adolescent boy so startled and anxious? What rules had I broken; what script for proper female behavior had I failed
to follow? (p. 15)

This fascination went on to shape my doctoral dissertation research at the University of California, Los Angeles, completed in 1976. My dissertation research was
eventually published in the article "Come-ons and Put-offs: Unmarried Students'
Strategies for Having and Avoiding Sexual Intercourse" (McCormick, 1979). At
that time, my work suggested that men employ (or at least admit that they employ)
just about any strategy they can think of to influence an attractive heterosexual
partner to have sex whereas women use (or admit using) just about any strategy
available to avoid having sex. So much for the supposed sexual revolution that was
reputed to be in high gear at the time of my initial study!

Two decades later, I continue to enjoy working in this area of research, having
completed naturalistic observational studies of flirtation in bars and sexualized
interactions on the Internet. As my research proceeds, I cannot help but marvel at
the methodological and theoretical breakthroughs made by young scientists since
my early work. The study of flirtation, seduction, and sexual rejection is not just of
passing scientific interest, I believe, but has important political implications for
feminists and anyone else concerned with the balance of power between women and
men. Women and girls, the latest research suggests, sometimes exercise a surprising amount of influence in their sexual interactions (McCormick, 1994). Groups of
young girls checking out the boys in shopping malls and other youthful "hang-
outs," Monica Moore has recently observed (1995), signal sexual interest nonver-
bally but in a more exaggerated manner and with more childlike playfulness than
adult women. Gender shapes sexual scripts more than sexual orientation, since lesbians share many of the same strategies for sexually influencing a partner as do heterosexual women (McCormick, 1994). And sexual scripts seem to be taking on an
increasingly egalitarian direction. I am heartened to read to work of beloved colleagues like E. Sandra Byers and young scientist friends like Lucia O'Sullivan which
suggest that increasing numbers of young women are asserting their sexual desires
with partners, just as I did at sixteen, before this was socially acceptable (Byers and
Heinlein, 1989; O'Sullivan and Byers, 1993).

If sexual influence and courtship have been my major interests in sexology, a
fascination for love and love styles has been almost equally important. This interest
in studying love is closely linked to my interest in women's studies; like many other
aspects of my scholarly work, it was inspired by experiences as an adolescent and
young adult. Challenging me to embrace feminist ideas as an adolescent, my boyfriend during my senior year of high school left me for my best girlfriend, a volup-
tuous young woman with silky blond hair. I became quite depressed. But as I recovered, I came to an important realization. I missed Karen, the girlfriend who jilted

me, far more than Jay, the disloyal boyfriend. I was determined to have women friends my entire life and never abandon them for the sake of "some guy."

More importantly, this incident precipitated my insight into the variety of love experiences individuals may experience and the importance of maintaining friendships, regardless of the status of one's romantic relationship, an insight that has helped to shape my empirical and theoretical work on "love" and my clinical work with individuals and couples struggling to balance love relationships with friendships. Essentially, my recovery from a broken heart taught me something that colleagues and I have since confirmed in research: lovers benefit from being good friends and best friends should not be abandoned for the supposed sake of a lover (McCormick, 1994).

I have, on the whole, had a happy and productive career as a feminist sexuality researcher. I am particularly indebted to my many dear friends in SSSS who have continued to affirm the work I do and have been loving critics of my methodology and theoretical work. There are far, far too many people to thank here and this is most frustrating. Still, I want to single out Professor Betsy Allgeier, the editor of the *Journal of Sex Research* and a psychology professor at Bowling Green State University, for being especially helpful in my career. After reading one of Betsy's journal articles in the late 1970s, I wrote her a fan letter and we have been close colleagues and friends ever since.

It was Betsy who recruited me into SSSS and enthusiastically collaborated with me in preparing the first edited volume of original chapters on gender and sexuality, *Changing Boundaries: Gender Roles and Sexual Behavior* (Allgeier and McCormick, 1983). She encouraged me to become active in the society and run for various offices. It was Betsy, too, who suggested that I combine my newly emerged activism and scholarship on chronically ill persons with my decades-long interest in sexology. At her invitation, I edited a special issue of the *Journal of Sex Research* (1996) on sexuality and chronic illness. My contribution to this special issue came from personal experience, not just scholarship. For the past ten years, I have been partially disabled by interstitial cystitis, an incurable and painful bladder disease that afflicts women significantly more than men and responds suboptimally to conventional medical treatment. The scientist in me adjusted to interstitial cystitis by doing some of the early pilot work on how women cope with this disease sexually and psychologically. Eventually, many wonderful new colleagues in the Interstitial Cystitis Association, a grass-roots advocacy group for patients, their families, and health care providers, came to assist me. Most notable of these new dear colleagues is Dr. Denise Webster, a nursing professor at the University of Colorado who has to my mind done some of the best work to date on the coping, sexuality, and self-care of patients with painful bladder disease.

Although I would never choose to become chronically ill in order to find a new area of research and clinical work, I have been fortunate in learning how to cope with this illness by applying my scientific and clinical skills in order to help others cope. Since 1989, I have had the great privilege of writing a regular column on coping with painful bladder disease for *ICA Update*, the national newsletter of the Interstitial Cystitis Association, in addition to scholarly articles. Most of the time, I confess, I study the health literature, write, and give workshops on my disease, as much to keep up my own sanity as to offer hope and assistance to other patients. Now, thankfully, my concern for the sexual triumphs and losses of the chronically ill and disabled came to full flower in a special issue of the *Journal of Sex Research*, "Bodies Besieged: The Impact of Chronic and Serious Physical Illness on Sexuality, Passion, and Desire" (McCormick, 1996).

No work depends more on friendships and is more collaborative than sex research, especially feminist sex research. There are many people I should be thanking but there is insufficient space in this autobiographical chapter to do so properly. Why, you wonder, do I end this story of my career with an expression of gratitude to many sister and brother sexologists, women's studies scholars, and friends and family? My reason is simple. Good sex research, like a good sexual interaction, is a loving, collaborative process. We are not alone and we do not work best alone. In a society that continues to stigmatize free sexual expression and even the study of human sexuality, to belittle the value of women and minorities, we must stick together to educate one another about and study our sexualities. Whatever small contribution I have made to the field has not been made in isolation but with the encouragement, support, and wisdom of many, many others, including my dear students who continue to be my best scientific co-investigators. With this in mind, I will end my autobiographical narrative by citing the wisdom of two such undergraduates. These young persons explain far better than I what feminist sex research is and should be all about.

> I have learned that feminist research must first and foremost incorporate the voices of the participants. (McCormick, 1995)

> Feminist researchers, and in particular feminist action researchers, attempt to undertake research that will ameliorate the conditions being investigated. This is quite [the] opposite from mainstream [social science] where research is completely removed from action, . . . [where] research is sometimes used as a way to avoid taking action. . . . Feminist researchers believe that it is vital to give something back to society by doing research. Ideally feminists try to establish a give-and-take relationship with those that they are getting information from. . . . This sort of give-and-take relationship resembles . . . friendship whereas in mainstream research, the research-subject relationship is much more hierarchical. (McCormick, 1995)

References

Allgeier, E. R., and N. B. McCormick, eds. 1983. *Changing boundaries: Gender roles and sexual behavior.* Palo Alto, Calif.: Mayfield. Copyright transferred to the authors in 1994.

Boston Women's Health Book Collective. 1973. *Our bodies, ourselves: A book by and for women.* New York: Simon and Schuster.

Byers, E., and L. Heinlein. 1989. Predicting initiations and refusals of sexual activities in married and cohabiting heterosexual couples. *Journal of Sex Research* 26: 210–31.

Beauvoir, Simone de. 1978. *The second sex,* trans. H. M. Parshley. New York: Knopf. (Originally published 1952.)

Fine, M. 1992. Sexuality, schooling, and adolescent females: The missing discourse of desire. In *Disruptive voices: The possibilities of feminist research*, ed. M. Fine, pp. 31–59. Ann Arbor: University of Michigan Press.

McCormick, N. 1979. Come-ons and put-offs: Unmarried students' strategies for having and avoiding sexual intercourse. *Psychology of Women Quarterly* 4: 194–211.

———. 1994. *Sexual salvation: Affirming women's sexual rights and pleasures.* Westport, Conn., and London: Praeger.

———. 1995, November. "Feminist Foremothers, Feminist Future: Women Affirming Sexuality Research in the Twentieth Century." Presidential plenary presented at the 38th annual meeting of the Society for the Scientific Study of Sexuality (SSSS), San Francisco.

———, special issue editor. 1996. Bodies besieged: The impact of chronic and serious physical illness on sexuality, passion, and desire. *Journal of Sex Research* 33: 175–210.

Moore, M. M. 1995. Courtship signaling and adolescents: "Girls just wanna have fun?" *Journal of Sex Research* 32: 319–28

O'Sullivan, L. F., and E. S. Byers. 1993. Eroding stereotypes: College women's attempts to influence reluctant male sexual partners. *Journal of Sex Research* 30: 270–82.

26

The Making of a Sexual Revolutionary

Robert McGinley, Ph.D.

Robert McGinley, a self-styled sexual revolutionary, is a professional promoter of social and recreational sex. Each year he organizes the national Lifestyles Convention which is attended by people from all over the world.

BORN IN 1933 (perhaps prophetically, the year of the great Long Beach earthquake), I like to think that I was destined to shake things up a little, at least in the world of sex. If I have any claim to fame it is that I am the founder and president of the Lifestyles Organization, which some have said has enabled me to do much for the sex lives of thousands of couples.

I am the father of five children (three boys and two girls), have a number of grandchildren and two ex-wives. I am on excellent terms with the second of these, Geri, and work with her at the Lifestyles Organization office on an almost daily basis. I grew up at the end of the hot war and the beginning of the cold war, and my early politics were those typical of an Eisenhower-era right-wing Republican when came what may be called a pivotal point. I worked for a government contractor, the Bendix Corporation, as a senior service engineer in military liaison during the Vietnam War. My area of operations covered the entire Pacific Rim. During my spare time reading (and while I was in the midst of a troubled marriage), I came across a personal advertisement in a magazine from a couple, inviting a personal liaison. They were what would be called swingers.

I answered with a short letter and soon found myself embarking on something of an adventure, much more than I bargained for. The man involved in the ad was an Air Force sergeant stationed at the then home of the top secret SR-71 spy plane. He held all of the government clearances necessary for anyone located at such a sensitive site but, because of his and his wife's lifestyle, he had come under investigation. The government secretly read mail sent to his address, and it was during this time that a sexually explicit letter of mine was intercepted. Holding similar clearances at Edwards Air Force Base, I knew nothing of the events that were soon to shake up my life. Acting swiftly, and without a hearing, the U.S. Department of Defense pulled all my clearances and in effect left me unemployed. The reason? My interest in sex indicated to them that I was probably a security risk.

As a result of this federal foray into my private life I began to question and eventually resist such Big Brother intrusions. In a conversation with the Department of Defense's then head of investigations, a Mr. Cronin, I asked just how many lives had been adversely affected, jobs lost, marriages broken, and suicides committed as a result of the department's unbridled assaults. He did not know but he said the department had investigated some fifty thousand cases, primarily in search of communists. When I asked how many communists had been found, the reply was "we didn't find any . . . but we might have . . ."

After a two-year-long as well as expensive and exhausting battle, I won my case against the government: the officials admitted to acting without cause and making an unwarranted intrusion. By that time, however, my career was gone along with my pension and all company benefits. This experience led me to realize that there were some very bad guys in government and that I could not always trust the system to assure justice. I also began to take a much closer look at what had precipitated the whole tragic affair: S-E-X. I wondered why this single aspect of human nature evoked such emotion, so little reason, and an almost total lack of compassion.

One of the reasons for seeking a liaison is that my own first marriage was a failure. Sex was involved and my meaningful communication was inconceivable just as any meaningful resolution was impossible. Finding myself single and still at a loss as to why society should react to physical passion with such unreasonable repression, I began attending parties sponsored by the American Sexual Freedom League, then located in Hollywood. I soon developed a large enough circle of friends to organize a weekly discussion group. Although the topics were left open, it should come as no surprise that human sexuality became the most frequent theme. This was because the culture itself frustrated biological urges that had evolved over eons, leaving people fixated on what is really among the simplest of needs.

Find a need and then fill it, is a traditional formula for success, and I believed I had found the need—namely, an honest approach to sex. The question was how to fill that need? In 1969 I began inviting a number of guest speakers to address the group on what came naturally to the birds and the bees but to which the answers somehow remained a mystery. Among the speakers was Al Goldstein, publisher of *Screw* magazine and no stranger to government harassment; Dr. Edgar Butler, professor of sociology and department chair at the University of California at Riverside: Dr. Albert Freedman, founder of *Forum* magazine who spoke about his then novel idea of publishing sex letters; and Drs. William Hartman and Marilyn Fithian, directors of the Center for Marital and Sexual Studies. These regularly scheduled meetings went on for more than a decade and finally resulted in the very first Lifestyles Convention.

The weekly group discussions were a factor in my decision to leave engineering and pursue an education in psychology. I eventually earned a doctorate at Newport International University in Southern California.

The Lifestyles Convention, which has become an annual event, is what I have become best known for. It is the largest such gathering of its kind in the world and attracts thousands of couples from almost every state in the union and from dozens of foreign countries. An entire resort hotel is reserved exclusively for this educational, social, and, for those who choose, sexual experience. There are theme dances, costume judging, seminars and workshops, pool parties, an award's luncheon, a sensuous art show, and an erotic emporium. I have spent more than twenty years developing this annual spectacular and it has not been an easy task. A hotel in Palm Springs, California, decided at the last minute not to honor its contract. I found an alternate site, convinced that the "show must go on at all costs," but the actual cost to me was close to a hundred thousand dollars. On another occasion, a hotel in Las Vegas, Nevada—referred to as Sin City only by those who know no better—did their best to dampen spirits and went so far as to propose that local health officials test the pool water for AIDS. Fortunately, it is not that easy (almost impossible, really) to dampen spirits at a Lifestyles Convention.

The sensuous and erotic art exhibition is one of my pet projects. Now in its sixth year, it has attracted the attention of the Save the Art Project of People for the American Way. Contributors include many prominent erotic artists. It has yet to make a profit, but money alone has never been my primary concern. Instead, the show is seen as a means of emphasizing my primary aim, that of making plain to people the fact that sex is an altogether normal and positive aspect of life. It is a topic which should be not only openly discussed but also actively pursued; varied tastes should be encouraged, developed, and sharpened. Why should people exist on meat and potatoes when gourmet dishes from around the world are at hand? Most artists create erotic art but are then forced to keep it from the public because a few individuals see some virtue in stubbornly maintaining a limited perspective.

Just recently, the manager of a Hollywood, California, mall, in an area popular with the gay community, shut down an art gallery where the Lifestyles erotic art exhibition had been displayed. In the two days it had been open to the public, it drew over two thousand people. The act of a single individual, in effect, determined what thousands more could, and in this case could not, see. Meanwhile, a theater in the same complex featured, with complete impunity, sexually explicit homosexual films: this indicated to me that the complaints originated in the gay community and that they were directed at the heterosexual content of the exhibition. Censorship does not always originate on the right. To give an interesting twist, when the magazine *Penthouse* published (January 1996) an illustrated story about this violation of the First Amendment, the article on censorship was itself censored by Canadian authorities.

During my life I have visited many parts of the world and have lived in many places, including a three-year stay in Japan. Following my motto of fulfilling a need which I found to exist, I pioneered the erotic travel business. I found there are many vacation destinations ranging from those for adults who are eager to be children again, to those for others who want to enjoy their fully grown status. Would be vacationers can choose from clothing optional beaches to topless Windjammer cruises to guided tours through some of the world's most exotic ports of call. Such fêtes and forays beyond the border make it clear that human sexuality is subject to enormous variation: the place and the time determine the norm.

I am also founder, and since 1980 president, of the North American Swing Club Association (NASCA), a clearinghouse of news and events that are of interest to the swing community. NASCA is the only such affiliation of its kind in the world, where membership is made up of hundreds of swing clubs and swing publications.

I lecture and speak around the country; I have written hundreds of articles, and have been a guest on dozens of radio and television shows. Often the talk show interviews have been angry and antagonistic. For example, one producer of a program in Florida, who wanted to do a "balanced" piece on the effect that AIDS was having on swinging lifestyles, interviewed me by satellite while showing a cemetery through which a woman reporter walked solemnly from grave to grave in order to emphasize his point.

Through NASCA, and with the assistance of Dr. Edgar Butler, I have conducted research studies on the sexual attitudes and experiences of couples interested or involved in swinging. Because of the opportunity provided by association with NASCA and Club Wide World, a swing club, I have been able to interview about ten thousand couples over the past twenty-five years.

In looking back on my life I find it has given me great rewards. Among the most satisfying is the positive effect that I have had on the sex lives of literally thousands of couples. The letters that arrive on an almost daily basis from almost every part of the world are a very special source of joy. Some couples just say, "Thank you, Dr. McGinley," and sign their names. Others go on for pages telling how their relationships have grown, how their passions have strengthened, and how their lives have expanded as a result of filling a simple need—an honest approach to sex. Many of these couples have referred to me as the King of Swing or the Guru of Sex and have seen me as a kind of guiding light and the leader of some movement. Flattering as this might be, I try to shun such accolades and simply encourage people to "look up to yourself" as a way of life. I am no one's guru.

George Burns once gave as his prescription for a happy life: "Discover what it is that makes you want to get out of bed in the morning and then pursue whatever that may be at all costs." It is the running of the Lifestyles Organization (LSO) that gets me out of bed in the morning and makes me a happy man. I enjoy meeting the new couples who come into the office, and I always find time to sit and chat with old friends who stop by for a visit. The fact that LSO is now involved in so many different projects poses problems, but I find these problems are a never-ending source of mental stimulation and physical excitement, and give me a very definite passion for life.

27

Finding God in Sex

Ted McIlvenna, Ph.D.

> *Ted McIlvenna, a theologian, calls himself a convert to sexology. He was, among other things, the founder of the Institute for Advanced Studies in Human Sexuality, located in San Francisco. In 1995, the Society for the Scientific Study of Sexuality recognized him for his distinguished service to the field of sexology.*

I AM A convert to the field of sexology. I am not on the run, I am not in trouble, nor am I a martyr to a cause. My conversion came through the process of becoming an expert about what people did sexually and how they felt about what they did.

My father was a Methodist minister. When I was a boy in Oregon, our family attended a retreat for ministers and their families in which there was a program of sharing called "Where do you find God?" One minister explained that he found God through communing with nature, walking beside the rushing streams and amidst the tall trees of Oregon. Another minister explained that he found God in his study as he read and prepared for his sermons. A third added that he found God in taking care of those in need and in visiting the poor and the sick. Finally, it was my father's turn; but before he could say anything, my older sister broke in and said, "He finds God by climbing into bed with my mother."

There are many ways to find God. One of the ways you may choose is through the glorious gift of sexuality.

Thirty years ago, the Methodist Church appointed me to study the nature and needs of young adults in San Francisco. One of the areas in which I chose to work was sexual identification in general and homosexuality in particular. I worked within the gay community for two years, and I finally reported back to my guidance committee that you can't understand homosexuality without understanding human sexuality.

Meetings and conferences held among churchmen and foundation persons resulted in my being charged with the task of developing a program on what people in the helping professions need to know about human sexuality. The National Sex Forum was established as part of the Methodist-related Glide Foundation. My job, in essence, was to become a sexologist.

My tasks during the next few years proved relatively easy. I read books, attended conferences and seminars, researched, watched films, and consulted with experts in many disciplines. The problems started when I began to develop programs based on my findings as a sexologist. For I had learned during those first years of study that there were countless people who claimed to be sex experts because of their expertise in other fields, but very few who really knew what they were talking about. Most sex education and counseling consisted of misinformation, advice-giving, and facts concerning reproductive biology. Not only were the people who claimed expertise in the sex field ill-prepared, but the materials available for sex education and counseling were inadequate. We had to create our own sex-education materials, which focused on what people actually do and how they feel about what they do.

The making of a hundred films, many hundreds of video- and audiotapes, and thousands of slides; the endless testing and retesting of educational methodologies; the training of ninety thousand persons in our various courses; the distribution of our materials to more than four thousand counselors and educational institutions throughout the world; and, finally, the establishment of the Institute for Advanced Study of Human Sexuality have brought us to the point of being able to say some things with authority.

It is to the glory of the Methodist Church that at no time has it attempted to censor me or interfere with my special work as a Methodist minister. My personal religious experience and freedom of the pulpit have been treated with the same dignity as if I were preaching from a "tall steeple" church. The Methodist Church nurtured and prepared me for this work with the best possible training in my formative years and then provided me with the opportunity to serve by sending me out to "care ethically for God's action in the historical process." I am now appointed to the nondenominational Exodus Trust, of which the National Sex Forum and the institute are a part.

It is my belief that God is active in the great spiritual movements of our time. One of these is the movement for sexual meaning. The theological question is "How do we use our sexuality?" We use something we value in quite a different way than something we do not value. In order to value our sexuality, we must look with the eyes of reverence on our own bodies and the bodies of others, our own and others' sexual fantasies, the things we all do sexually, and thereby discover whether or not we are celebrating sexuality in our world. I am not talking about selected forms of sexual expressions, but the entire range of behavior in which humans engage. If you look at your own and others' sexuality with the deeper pleasures of understanding and radical humanization, you will find God. Or God will find you.

As we look with the eyes of reverence, a process of sexual-attitude restructuring takes place, which means simply that sex-negative attitudes are changed to sex-positive attitudes, and with those positive attitudes comes sexual health. During the past thirty years we have found that sex-negative attitudes held by an individual are the chief culprit in sexual dysfunction, just as societal sex-negative attitudes create a serious lack of understanding in our social interactions.

If finding God in sex seems strange to you, consider the many different ways in which people look for God: in running, in meditating, in service, in self-abasement, in penitence, in giving, in worship services, in making money, in communing with nature. Why, then, is it strange to think about finding God in the many forms of our sexuality?

I have decided to tell my story about becoming a sexologist by sharing with you some stories of revelation that may have guided me to where I am now.

I was born in Epping, New Hampshire, on March 15, 1932, while my father was studying theology at Boston University. My father chose the mission field, and so I grew up on Indian reservations and in the tough little lumbering towns of the Pacific Northwest.

As the only white child on an Indian reservation in Southern Oregon, I had to ride a horse to school in a neighboring small town. All the other town kids had bikes and, above all else, I wanted a bike. One day my father brought a blessed gift on wheels home from Klamath Falls. Within ten minutes the Indian kids had totally demolished my chariot. An old Indian handyman who lived down by the Indian burial grounds picked up the pieces and several days later invited me to his shack. He told me that he would keep my bike for me and that I could take a short-cut through the burial grounds to the town road but that I must pedal softly and move quickly because I was on holy ground.

MY FIRST REVELATION WAS TO PEDAL SOFTLY AND MOVE QUICKLY FOR I WAS ON HOLY GROUND.

When I was eight we moved to town where I had my first sociosexual experience. I was seduced by an older girl of eleven in the stable in back of a Methodist parsonage. As I recall, my struggles were minimal. This "outrage" occurred several more times before this aggressive young woman, whom I'll call Nancy, abruptly left town. I felt doubly betrayed because she had taught me to like the regular ravishment.

Fifty years later I was doing a television show in a major city when I got a call at the studio from a woman who announced, "Teddy, this is Nancy and I want to see you." Oh, the anticipation and the possibilities as I waited in my hotel room for this fateful rendezvous. At last she arrived and for the next two hours we talked of many things, but mostly about our grandchildren. She had almost as many pictures as I did.

MY SECOND REVELATION WAS THAT ALL SEXUAL SITUATIONS MUST BE FACTORIZED.

My high school days were filled with sports and music. My mother wanted me to be a musician-actor and my father wanted me to be a baseball player. I had a regular best girl whom I parked with at least twice a week and I had a few outside experiences. In other words, "I was a sexually active teenager." I was trying to become a man.

There are many voices crying out from every side about what it means to be a man. Some voices say, "Get money and power," others, "Live fast, die young, and leave a good-looking corpse." Still other voices tell us to gather around us symbols of our masculinity, such as cars and motorcycles—things with sex appeal. Among all these voices we listen for the one that says yes to who we are as sexual beings.

Fat Hal was fat. Not pleasingly plump or overweight, but fat. Hal made the football team, even though he could hardly run the full length of the field, simply because our high school was so small that anyone who went out for the team made it. Running into Hal was like bumping into a marshmallow. Hal was the brunt of many of our jokes, especially in the shower room, where his folds of flesh seemed to hide any evidence of his manhood.

Our team's first road trip in the fall took us to a lumbering town in which there was a house of prostitution. It was customary every year to initiate each of our sophomore players in the "rites of manhood." Since I was the team captain, it was my task to collect the money and handle the negotiations. On the bus trip this particular year everyone was teasing Hal, and I was becoming increasingly anxious about what would happen. Finally the big moment came when I led Hal and the other initiates into the parlor and started my negotiations with the young ladies. Everyone paired off and left for the bedrooms. After several minutes the couples started returning one by one. But no Hal. We waited an hour, and finally Hal ambled down the stairs without saying anything. I turned to the woman who had come out of the bedroom with him and asked, "What happened? Why did it take so long? How did he do?"

She seemed to sense what was going on in our minds, and with a knowing smile she simply answered, "He did just fine."

Hal could have run a hundred yards in eight seconds. He could have pole-vaulted twenty feet. Neither one would have given him as much status and respect as those clear words of loving validation: "He did just fine."

MY THIRD REVELATION WAS THAT SOMEONE SOMEWHERE HAS TO TELL US THAT OUR SEXUAL PERFORMANCE IS "JUST FINE."

College was a time of discovery. There was a great big world out there with things to know and do. I thought sociology was created by God for country boys like myself. I no longer was standing on the rock of ages but was in free fall and free think. Then reality arrived with the dean of the college's reaction to my book report on the first Kinsey volume, *Sexual Behavior in the Human Male*. It was a good report—so good that a special meeting was called for my major professor, the dean, the head of the psychology department, and me to discuss my motivation for writing a report on such a "dirty" book. At the end of the interrogation I was given a choice of taking a "C" for my report since it was obviously not appropriate, or admitting that I had a "problem," and then I would get a "B" and some counseling. I chose the "C" and received my fourth revelation.

IF YOU SERIOUSLY STUDY SEXOLOGY PEOPLE WILL QUESTION YOUR MOTIVATIONS. IF YOU ARE A WOMAN THEY WILL THINK ALL YOU NEED IS A GOOD FUCK. AND I LEARNED THAT MOST SEXUAL PUTDOWNS HAVE TO DO WITH THINGS BEING CONSIDERED NOT APPROPRIATE.

I also learned that schools put this kind of thing on your record. When I transferred from one good Methodist school to another, my new dean (who was a future U.S. senator) used my interest in sex in an attempt to deny me a scholarship I had already won. He said I was an inappropriate candidate. Ironically when I graduated from that university I marched in the graduation procession with another future (and now former) U.S. senator who liked to stick his tongue in women's mouths. As a life-long liberal I now for the first time have respect for that defrocked senator.

Cooler academic heads prevailed; on the basis of my academic and research skills I got the scholarship that allowed me to go to any school anywhere and for any period of time as long as I agreed to come back and work for the Methodist Church for six years.

Theological school was like another world for me. The lighting of candles, the singing of psalms, and the studies were familiar to me, but not the anti-sexual, almost womanless world. I decided that since I had a scholarship I should attempt to lead a celibate life for the year. I managed for almost three months, then found a friendly nurse at the local hospital who shared with me the same eager pleasure two evenings a week. She was a delightful young woman, so much so that often I didn't return to the seminary dormitory till the next morning.

I guess my nocturnal activities bothered some of my fellow inmates because I was summoned to a meeting with the chairman of the school's pastoral counseling department. He noted that while my sexual interests were natural and normal, my acting out of those interests was unworthy of a future man of the cloth and that I might better focus my interest on seeking a helpmate among the young women studying Christian education. (These were the days before women were permitted to enter the ministry.) He further suggested that I might establish a spiritual union that would be far more fulfilling than anything I had ever known.

My fantasies multiplied concerning the sexual possibilities of such a spiritual union, and so I looked anew at the crop of studious, young would-be directors of religious education around me. I finally decided that I liked the way this one woman walked, kind of smooth and slinky. I asked her out to dinner and she accepted. Although she knew I didn't have much money, she insisted on an expensive restaurant and ordered pheasant under glass, which cost exactly what I had budgeted myself to live for a week. I paid gladly, thinking it was going to be worth it.

At the end of the evening we parked in a secluded glen in my borrowed car. I put my arm around the young woman, only to be met with a diatribe about how I could not touch her because even though she would give of her time and conversation, she would not give of her body, for to do so would make her impure. Needless to say, I escorted her home forthwith and headed straight over to stay with my nurse friend.

I learned three lessons quite clearly: think twice before ever taking the sexual advice of an expert on pastoral counseling; a spiritual union with a woman director of religious education doesn't necessarily mean a sexual union; and last and most important, how lovely and warm that friendly nurse was.

MY FIFTH REVELATION WAS THAT A SPIRITUAL UNION DIDN'T MEAN GOOD FUCKING.

The following years were filled with marriage, ordination, more school, internship, and final ordination. At one point I was invited to be a professor of systematic theology and comparative religion, but decided I needed some years of pastoral experience; then almost suddenly I was twenty-eight years old and the senior minister of a big church in a fast-growing suburban area. Senior chaplain of the Masonic Home and co-director of a counseling center with all the chairs of the church waiting on me, I got a call saying that it was time for me to "pay up" for my education and they wanted me to be the director of the Young Adult Project in San Francisco. My wife and I were horrified because we had a new parsonage, a new church, a new car, two young children, and an old dog. They wanted us to move to San Francisco for half the salary and half the housing allowance. But a deal was a deal and off we went.

At last a time to design everything from halfway housing, youth advocacy centers, coffee house ministries, theater in the park, centers for religion and the arts, film festivals, rock bands on flatbed trucks, art shows, and any other experimental ministry I wanted to try. I was in the right job at the right time, and it all turned to gold and glory for a young minister who was soon chosen to direct, with a large Ford grant, the worldwide young adult project experimental ministries out of Nashville, Tennessee. But being surrounded by country music and religious bigots was not for me, so two years later, when a group of foundations asked if I would go back to San Francisco to direct the National Sex and Drug Forum, we headed back to San Francisco.

Sex education courses would have been easier to design, and in general all our work at the institute would have been smooth, except for our insisting at every turn on the sexual rights of gay males. The church, the medical establishment, and the general public spend more time on their anxieties about male homosexuality than anything else.

There occurred on a fateful evening in the mid-1960s an event that changed my life forever. Until then I had had every intention to go back to being a professor of systematic theology and comparative religions. At 11:00 P.M. I was called by one of my friends in the homophile movement to come to room 806 in a Tenderloin hotel. When I got there I found my friend with two young gay men who that evening had had their genitals "kicked in." I immediately demanded that we take the young men to an emergency room and call the police. My friend pointed out that the hospital emergency room would not take them, and that it had been the San Francisco Vice Squad that had done the kicking.

I was horrified by the event, but I was equally horrified by what happened when I reported it. The hospital said that the emergency room doctor had a personal code of ethics that would not allow him to treat "queers." The vice squad explained that the two young men had been caught in a toilet in a local restaurant and that they needed to be taught a lesson. After all, "God hates fags and so should I."

My advisory committee advised me to back off and to be more concerned about the spiritual well-being of the young men; otherwise my intervention might be seen as a projection of my personal interest in the homosexual condition and my future with the church thereby damaged. They resorted once more to that great expression: my response to the situation was "not appropriate."

Perhaps we should quit talking about homosexuality. By way of illustration let me tell you another story.

Many years ago, I was interviewed for a job at the YMCA. During our luncheon meeting, one of the interviewers told that old story, "How do you separate the men from the boys down at the YMCA?" He then answered his own question by saying, "With a crowbar, how else?" It seems that one of my duties was to keep the "queers" out of the steam room. I solved the problem by suggesting to some of the men who were using the facilities for sexual cruising that they limit their activities to the hours that I was on duty and that they pass the word around that they would be left alone if they honored that time structure. Within a few short months, I was known as "the guy who could really handle those damn fairies."

It is my belief that we should look upon homosexuality with the eyes of reverence. Gays have been harassed, misunderstood, discriminated against, and oftentimes physically abused for their sexual preferences. All of this for absolutely no reason, except that they prefer other males as sex partners.

One evening I was asked to take a famous theologian on a tour of the gay community in San Francisco. He asked me not to select or censor for him, but to show him all aspects of gay life. We started off at an elegant gay bar, where he saw hundreds of handsome, well-dressed young men meeting and drinking together. Then we ate at a first-class gay restaurant and visited other gay bars catering to different socioeconomic groups. We also walked along the "meat rack" on Turk Street, where older men (chicken hawks) negotiated with young boys (chickens) for sexual favors, and visited the gay baths. Our last stop, at about 1:00 A.M., was the Embarcadero YMCA, where hundreds of gay males converged as the bars closed for the evening.

For the first couple of hours, my companion didn't say much; but as the evening progressed, he began to theorize, justify, and explain. By the end of the evening he was on a talking jag. At 2:30 A.M. we boarded a bus and headed back to my house. Halfway home, a big black man got on the bus, sat down in front of us, and started to go to sleep. My friend's constant chatter obviously was bothering him, and he turned and said, "Man, you talk too much. Give it up and let it be."

There have been endless books, articles, and theories concerning male homosexuality. Perhaps we should simply "give it up and let it be."

M Y SIXTH REVELATION WAS BIBLICAL: "SO IN THE PRESENT CASE I TELL YOU, KEEP AWAY FROM THESE MEN AND LET THEM ALONE; FOR IF THIS PLAN OR THIS UNDERTAK- ING IS OF MEN IT WILL FAIL; BUT IF IT IS OF GOD, YOU WILL NOT BE ABLE TO OVER- THROW THEM. YOU MIGHT EVEN BE FOUND OPPOSING GOD!" GAMALIEL TO THE SAN- HEDRIN (ACTS 5:38–39)

And so my formal church years were over. I did not know it at the time, but it became obvious when I was no longer asked to speak at church meetings and it was suggested that I should think about leaving the Glide Urban Center and find my own funding. There were some serious grumblings coming from the "Southern bishops." Also, a new San Francisco bishop had been appointed who had a son who was "gay"; he was not emotionally supportive of my work and it might be better if I moved to a status "beyond the connectional system" so that I would not embarrass the church.

Since it was now necessary to find alternate funding, I took a job as a founda- tion president and, along with a group of other professionals, committed myself to a rigorous, systematic, academic study of sexology in order to have a faculty to start the Institute for Advanced Study of Human Sexuality in 1976. An executive com- mittee was named with Dr. Herbert Vandervoort, Dr Loretta Haroian, and myself. Herb was to deal with the academic standards, Loretta was in charge of the cur- riculum, and it was my task to develop an administrative function. The tasks were far more difficult than we could ever have imagined. It seemed that everyone threw road blocks in our way.

The Kinsey Institute refused to help us with materials because what we were doing was "not appropriate."

When Herb and I left the UC medical school program we were called traitors.

When I left the University of Minnesota Program in Human Sexuality the dean of the medical school called our future DHS (doctorate of human sexuality) a doc- tor of horse shit. I can assure you that that medical school dean was an "expert" on horse shit.

Even though an outside academic board was created to oversee things, we were accused of giving ourselves degrees, and when an independent evaluation group was brought in and we were given the highest marks for academic excellence, it was suggested by critics that we had paid someone under the counter. Herb Vandervoort was devastated by the criticism and died before he could take over as our first aca- demic dean. Loretta Haroian, who was certainly the brightest academic sexologist in the world, was attacked from every side for her work with childhood and ado- lescent sexology. In the end her health was broken and she never fully recovered from this onslaught of hatred.

We began in the existing facilities of Glide Methodist Church in San Francisco. We had a faculty, and when we added the eminent sexologist Wardell Pomeroy as dean, and the finest sexological historian in Erwin Haeberle, we had a great mix and a great program. What we needed then was a great crop of students, whom we got. I now understand the term "If you build it they will come."

Those were the difficult years. We raised money by testifying in hundreds of obscenity cases. We also embarked on endless research projects from a variety of sources. In some cases the faculty was not paid, and for materials we had to ask the sex industry for help, which they gave in huge collections of films, videos, and books. Gradually we built the best resource library of sexological material in the world.

Though it was hard for us to understand, we were bad-mouthed not only by the church and medical establishments but also by many of the people who called themselves sexologists or sex therapists. Our own colleagues were becoming the enemy and seemed to glory in the stories of our being the "Hot Tub University," the "Fag and Fag Hag Villa," and the "Faculty Fuck Folly." I guess we did serve a purpose in that other sexological programs could say, "At least we are not as bad as *that institute*."

Of course the majority of criticism came from people who had never been to the institute and knew almost nothing about us. The most persistent story was that the female grad students had to fuck a faculty person if they wanted to graduate. To this Loretta said, "The institute is probably the only graduate school in the country where a woman *can't* get a degree for fucking. The only thing that might happen would be that Ted and Laird Sutton would want to film it if it ever happened."

To all the criticism my answer is to give my basic rules for sexologists:

1. Never defend yourself emotionally.

2. Never put yourself in win/lose situations.

3. Never ally yourself with martyrs.

Above all else, become an expert and not an advocate.

MY SEVENTH REVELATION WAS, ABOVE ALL ELSE BECOME AN EXPERT.

No matter what restrictions—religious, political, economic, or social—are placed upon people, they manage to get together with other people and do sexual things. I am continually amazed at the number of self-proclaimed censors who feel they have been given the task of defining what people should do sexually as well as which people should get together with which other people and on what basis. I am convinced that sexual health is related to how a person feels about what other people are doing sexually. You can either make yourself miserable worrying about how to restrict or regulate other people's sex lives, or you can rejoice in the fact that so many people are enjoying the gift of sexuality.

I am now sixty-five and it is only fair that I tell you about the quest to find God in sex. Since most people seek God for salvation and cosmic security let me close with a story about each.

In American society, many professionals still justify their expertise in the field of sexology based on their professional credentials in other fields. Some years ago I traveled to Sacramento to attend hearings relating to the licensing of sex therapists. Marriage and family-life counselors testified that they were the ones who should be licensed because they were experts on marriage and the family. Psychologists said they should be licensed since they were experts on psychology. Physicians said they should be licensed because they were experts on the functioning of the reproductive system. I was one of the last to testify, and I made the suggestion that people who are licensed as sex therapists should be experts on sex.

It is still the mind-set of many persons that you must have some nonsexual, clinical rationale to justify your interest in sex. You must be "saved" before you can commune. My father often told the story behind his decision to leave one of the most exclusive, conservative Protestant churches to join the Methodist Church. When my parents were first married, they attended a communion service at my father's church. When it came time to go forward, my father took my mother's hand, and they started to move toward the altar. One of the elders barred my mother, saying to her, "Sit back, Lorena, you haven't been saved." My father took my mother's hand and left the church, saying, "If Lorena's not saved, nobody is."

No one has the right to bar you from your interest in sexuality. It is a natural, God-given right, and you never need to sit back. Or, as the preacher says in Ecclesiastes 8:15, "Man has no better thing under the sun than to eat, and to drink and to be merry."

MY EIGHTH REVELATION HAD TO DO WITH THE MEANING OF SALVATION.

My nephew's little boy was looking at a traditional Christmas scene with Mary and Joseph, shepherds, wise men, and all the rest. He became very upset because he could not find God in the scene. (There was a figure of the infant Jesus, but the boy did not confuse that with God.) He finally had to make a figure, put it in the crèche, and call it God. When I was with the board of education of the Methodist Church in Nashville, Tennessee, a layman once asked me, "Where is God in all this sex business?"

My father was appointed minister of a Methodist church in St. Helens, Oregon, when I was nine. The church had no parsonage and required that the minister and his family live in an upstairs apartment in the back of the huge old church building. The church was the biggest in town and was used for all types of special events, funerals, and evangelistic services. During these special services the huge organ pipes next to my room would hiss and moan and make all kinds of strange noises. One stormy night, as the Oregon wind and rain pelted my window on one side and that awful beast of an organ belched and groaned on the other, I became frightened of what other terrors might emerge from down the long, dark hallway outside my room.

Finally the organ stopped hissing, and I crept through the crawlway to peer down the vent at the services below. The sermon for the night dealt with the evil doings in that emerging riverfront town. Beer halls and pool rooms and bowling alleys were springing up. The movie theater showed late movies and planned to be open on Sunday. Worst of all, there was word that a certain establishment had opened up near the waterfront, where girls entertained sailors and mill workers. I listened to all of this with fascination and terror and was just about convinced that the forces of evil had won. Then, when things seemed the worst, my father stopped, came out from behind the pulpit, walked down to the congregation and proclaimed,

"God is here. That is our message to the world. Wherever people congregate, in the midst of all human interaction, God is here. When you are frightened and think all is lost, God is here. Write across your life and the lives of those you know, God is here." I returned to my room and went to sleep, assured that God was there.

Write across your sex life, God is here.

The answer, then, to where God is in all this sex business: God is here.

MY NINTH AND LAST REVELATION IS THAT GOD IS IN ALL THIS SEX BUSINESS.

28

How I Became Interested in Sexology

Earle M. Marsh, M.D.

Earle M. Marsh, who is eighty-five as of this writing, is the oldest contributor. A gynecologist, he worked with the pioneering American physician sexologists Robert Latou Dickinson and Harry Benjamin, thus serving as a contact person with the first American physician sexologists. He also served as a consultant to the Kinsey studies on women.

W HEN I WAS about three or four, I experienced a very sex-negative experience, which later turned out to be very sex-positive.

I was born in Omaha, Nebraska, but had two uncles who were eye, ear, nose, and throat specialists in Sioux Falls, South Dakota. My uncle Ed's wife, Aunt Addie, was sort of the matriarch of the family, and we had gone to visit them. My mother had been very disturbed because I had been playing with my penis, testicles, and thighs, as all children do. She consulted my Aunt Addie, who told her to get some shoe blackening and paint those areas of my body at a time when I was not aware of it. But this was a difficult task to do.

Back in Omaha, several weeks later, my mother noticed that I was examining the genitals of a two-year-old girl who lived on the first floor of our house. It was a bright, sunny day, and my mother was hanging clothes out on the line. Apparently she noticed the goings-on with the neighbor child, and the next thing I knew, my mother was dragging me into the bathroom, screaming and yelling that the blackness that was on my penis and testicles indicated that I was becoming a degenerate. (She had painted me with the shoe blackening during her hysterical outburst, and I had not realized it.) I yelled and screamed along with her, and she said repeatedly, "You are becoming a degenerate, and the blackness that's on you is the degeneracy that is seeping out through your skin. If I can just clean it off and stay ahead of it, you might be saved." So amid tears and yelps and anxious screams, my mother scrubbed and scrubbed and scrubbed until virtually all of the shoe blackening was removed. I was literally terrified and deeply shaken. My mother put her arms around me and stated that she had saved me from degeneracy, and she gave me two pennies to go up to the corner drug store and buy an ice cream cone.

Many years later, after I reached adulthood, I asked my mother about the event—I wanted to know what the blackening was and what had happened. Having undergone a great number of psychological changes herself, she told me the whole story about Aunt Addie, the shoe blackening, and so forth. She apologized and said that she never should have done such a thing, but she had been a young mother and had been hysterical. My mother was a very loving person, and I loved her dearly. I believed what she said and the markedly negative sex experience turned into a positive one because it drew us closer together as mother and son.

This may not be why I became interested in sexology, but there is no question that the event certainly focused my attention on the genitals. It may even be one of the reasons why I became a gynecologist/obstetrician, but I'm not certain.

I was born with the idea that everything that human beings did was perfectly natural. This included sex. As my professional life matured, I became convinced that all forms of sexual activity were physiologically natural. I just didn't understand why there was such an uproar about sexuality. Later I realized that most of the world was in a manmade dilemma concerning the right and wrong of sex. This fact never made sense to me.

My childhood and adolescent years were rather normal, and in the process I developed a reverence for all things human. This happened in spite of another sex-negative event which occurred in my early teens. My father caught me masturbating and became outraged. He told me that masturbation would drive me crazy, that all of my senses—sight, smell, hearing, taste, and touch—would be affected negatively. I was warned never to masturbate again. I remember feeling, as he told me this, that he had somehow been misinformed. It didn't seem to get to me, but I deduced that if I was going to masturbate again, I'd better do it in silence. Yet I was somewhat concerned about going crazy after masturbating. I recall for several years when I was masturbating, I would think to myself, "I wonder if I'm going to go crazy next Tuesday or Wednesday." I would smile at this but as time passed, I realized that my father was incorrect about masturbation. But even this sex-negative experience became a positive one when I realized that my father was not to blame: he was raised the same way by his parents, and was a product of his society at the time.

I was trained in gynecology and obstetrics at the University of California Medical School in San Francisco, and was one of the early diplomates of the American Board of Obstetrics and Gynecology. During my training, I had a few months of psychiatry and liked it because I had a natural interest in human emotions. During World War II, I was admitted to the navy with a specialty rating in obstetrics/gynecology and a specialty rating in psychiatry. I deserved the former, but not the latter. I was pleased but confused. However, the navy had a plan for me, and they sent me to a second residency at the U.S. Naval Medical Center in Bethesda, Maryland; St. Elizabeth's Hospital in Washington, D.C.; and Chestnut Lodge Sanitarium, in

Rockville, Maryland. This was where the renowned Harry Stack Sullivan, M.D., was located and did his teaching, and I was very impressed by him. He and I became close friends, and I appreciated very much what he had to say. To this day, I feel that he was the outstanding psychiatrist of all times.

At the close of World War II, I returned to San Francisco and opened a private practice in obstetrics and gynecology. I had my American boards in obstetrics/gynecology, and though I was board-qualified in psychiatry by this time, I was not permitted to take the psychiatric boards unless I gave up my gynecological boards. (This demand has now been changed, and a physician may have as many diplomatic boards as he or she wishes.)

Gynecology and obstetrics were my primary interests, but I reserved Wednesday evenings and all day Friday for counseling with patients who had psychological problems. This proved to be a very neat and satisfactory combination of my two specialties.

I became interested in marriage counseling and was one of the very early members of the American Association of Marriage Counselors (now known as the American Association of Marriage and Family Therapists). I was national vice-president in 1953 and again in 1968. I had been asked to run for president of the association, but I decided that my plate was far too full.

Because of my interest in the psychological aspects of medicine, I was invited several times to the Menninger Clinic to discuss the psychological aspects of obstetrics and gynecology. In the early 1950s, after a visit with Dr. Emily Mudd, who was the guiding light in the American Association of Marriage and Family Therapists, I spent some time with Robert Latou Dickinson, M.D., the first president of the American Gynecological Association. Bobby Dickinson, as he was affectionately called, was more than a physician; he was also an artist and a sculptor. He produced the models for an atlas which for many years were used by obstetricians to educate their patients.

As Bobby and I were discussing my interest in OB/GYN with its psychological flavoring, he suddenly stood bolt upright and said, "Oh, I've got a man that you must meet." It was agreed that I would meet this individual at nine o'clock the next morning at his hotel, but Bobby ran off to give a lecture to medical students and forgot to tell me the man's name. I was amused but interested so I kept the appointment, and the next morning I met Dr. Alfred Kinsey, affectionately called "Prok." As I was giving my sex history to Prok, the phone rang with a call from Dr. Wardell Pomeroy, the second author of the Kinsey reports. He was flying from Bloomington to New York to continue taking sexual histories in New York City. However, his airplane had been forced to land in Philadelphia because of bad weather, and he explained to Prok that he would not arrive in New York until a day or two later.

When I finished giving Prok my sex history, he and I talked for about a half hour, because his next appointment had phoned and cancelled. He explained that he and Wardell were taking sex histories of the cast of A Streetcar Named Desire and that they were both scheduled to see the performance again that evening. Because Pomeroy had been delayed, Kinsey invited me to join him.

This evening was probably one of the most enlightening of my entire life. After seeing the play, which was marvelous, Kinsey educated me in the sexual life of the underworld. By this time, he was warmly accepted by everyone there because he was so natural and unthreatening. Kinsey introduced me to a variety of male and female prostitutes, drug pushers, and so on, in Times Square. We visited many homosexual bars and bathhouses. Everyone seemed to know Prok and to like him, and we were accepted and not considered threats. There was no sexual activity, but we observed the comings and goings of the patrons of the bathhouses and gay bars. All of this occurred without the interruption of the police. We also spent some time at the toilets at Grand Central Station, where Kinsey pointed out how homosexuals and heterosexuals picked up sexual partners.[1]

Kinsey was exceedingly kind, loving, and tender, and we became fast friends. But his research interests were not about attempting to dissect sexual love, rather, they were in the actual biological sexual behaviors and their variations.

Prok was a taxonomist, absorbed with the variations in behavior among animal species. He made tremendous contributions in comparing the physical and cultural demeanor of gall wasps. He and his son wrote a book on biology for high school students, which I believe is still in use.

Kinsey's interest in sexuality was likewise from a taxonomist's point of view. It centered on the various types of sexual activity in the human species. He discovered that human beings said they did one thing sexually, when actually they did another. This was upsetting to some of the religious institutions, but they had to face the facts.

Because of my background in gynecology, obstetrics, and psychiatry, Kinsey offered me the opportunity to join his faculty, but I had many financial obligations back in San Francisco and unhappily I could not accept. However, he did ask me to become one of the gynecological consultants on the female volume, which I did, and I made many trips to Bloomington.

During the 1940s and early 1950s I had developed a drinking problem; on June 15, 1953, I stopped drinking and have not had a drink or any drugs since that time. But my drinking was a problem in the Kinsey home for a period. I was never criticized or advised, but I could see that I was a bore. On Sunday evenings, Kinsey had a musicale in his living room. He was one of the early owners of hi-fi equipment and his interest in music prompted him to collect an enormous number of records which he displayed at these get-togethers. I would get a little drunk and become somewhat of a disturbance. I recall that when I informed Prok that I had stopped drinking, he sighed a deep sigh of relief and said, "Thank goodness!"

The Kinsey sex library is the greatest in the world. No one but the staff was admitted, but two or three of us "outsiders" were allowed in and we saw many of the films that had been donated to Kinsey by a variety of producers throughout the world. I recall that Kinsey tested the law concerning the admission of explicit sexual films to the United States from other countries. When taken to court, Kinsey won the case because these films were for study and research, not for personal use.

1. Paul Gebhard recounts this in chapter 16.

For some strange reason, I was always intrigued and interested by any new human contact, especially in the sexual field. When a patient or colleague would tell me something about a novel sexual maneuver, my instant reaction was to say "Is that so? Tell me more." And so over the course of years, I became educated by my patients and by some colleagues simply by stating, "Is that so? Tell me more."

As time evolved, my private practice developed to the point where I decided to focus solely on gynecology and drop obstetrics. I was very involved in sexual medicine—from a gynecological as well as a psychological perspective. There are numerous stories I could enumerate from my practice, but a few stand out particularly as my favorites.

One day a beautiful young woman, who seemed very flustered and anxious, was escorted into my consultation room by one of my nurses. She said there were two things: the first was that I had delivered her, and we hadn't met since that day in the delivery room. We both smiled at one another, and I said, "What a beautiful young woman you've grown into; it's nice to meet you once again after all these years."

And second, she said she engaged in an abnormal sexual activity. I said characteristically, "Is that so? Tell me more." She had some trouble bringing herself to tell me the following: "I'm a pianist, and rather frequently when I play certain sonatas, I become sexually aroused and quite frequently come to orgasm." She said she was about to be married, and that she was concerned lest this kind of sexual activity would interfere with her marriage. When I asked her if she had told her husband-to-be about this remarkable phenomenon of hers, she replied that she hadn't. She asked me if I would tell her fiancé myself, and I agreed to do so. It so happened that he was outside in the waiting room, so I had him come in.

He was a very handsome young man, and the two of them made a delightful couple. After I had told bridegroom-to-be what the situation was, he turned to her, bewildered, and said, "Is that so? Can you really do that?" And she shook her head yes as she blushed. The fiancé then looked back at me as if to say "What do we do about this? We're about to be married." I said, "In case you feel this will interfere with your marriage, let me reassure you about this."

And we devised the following plan. She wanted him to have sex with her, and after he orgasmed and ejaculated, she wanted to get up and play the piano. At first he was rather bewildered by this idea, but soon accepted it, and apparently that's exactly what they did. I told her that this kind of sexual activity, though very uncommon, was a perfectly natural phenomenon, and she need not be concerned nor feel guilty. So, when they made love, he would come to orgasm and ejaculate; then he would escort her to the piano and watch her rock in orgastic ecstacy. She would then return to him and fall asleep in his arms. They were very satisfied and able to accept the situational status quo. Over the years, great changes occurred. They were finally able to engage in mutual masturbation, intercourse with her being able to respond as well, oral-genital contact, and a whole variety of other sexual maneuvers which were very rewarding.

Change spontaneously occurred once she had accepted herself as she was and he had accepted her, too. They now have a couple of children, and their sex life is happy and healthy. It so happens she still can have orgasms by playing the piano.

Another patient, the son of one of my gynecological patients, came to me in desperation. Already jailed twice for exposing himself in public, he was frantic and didn't know what to do. I told him that exposing genitals and becoming sexually excited was perfectly natural. In the animal kingdom it happened all the time, but in the human species, for better or worse, it was illegal and meant being jailed if caught. So what to do?

I took a very detailed sexual history and learned that in his fantasy life this young man clearly had a homosexual component. He would experience sucking a penis or being sucked, or having anal intercourse, but he had never explored these behaviors outside of his fantasies. I could readily see that he was predominantly, though perhaps not solely, homosexual. These were the days when the gay baths were open, so I suggested that he go to one in San Francisco that had a good reputation. He went, even though he was a bit anxious. There he met a man with whom he had sex, and it was very rewarding for him. From then on, he enjoyed homosexual contact frequently, and never found it necessary to exhibit himself in public again. He often had the urge, but by this time, he had sufficient homosexual encounters so that the urge to exhibit himself was not very strong. Once he had been able to accept himself as a homosexual, change occurred automatically. He was able to accept the fact that homosexual contact, though looked upon in our society as "immoral," was a natural sexual behavior. I explained to him that I was not there as a moralist, but simply as a scientist who was interested in the biology of sex. After a while, his heterosexual component also became active, and from time to time, he had heterosexual as well as homosexual contact, and seemed to be very satisfied. The urge to exhibit almost vanished.

Then there was my Aunt Edna, who was a Christian Scientist. One day she walked into my office asking to become a patient. I said to her, "But Aunt Edna, you're a Christian Scientist and I'm a doctor." She said "I don't care; I'm changing my mind about the Church, and I want to come to you as my physician." I explained that we didn't like to treat our relatives as patients because our emotions often interfered in caring for them. And she cried and said, "No, I knew you before you were born, so please accept me as a patient." And so I did. I did the routine examination; she was very healthy and I reassured her.

After about seven or eight years, Aunt Edna came to me one day very flustered and red in the face. When I asked her what the trouble was, she stretched her arm way out in front of her and pointed her finger directly to her crotch. She said, "I'm bothered down there! You know, your Uncle Charlie died several years ago, and I'm too old to get a sexual partner, and I'm bothered down there." By this time, she was about eighty or eighty-one. So I reassured her, and acquainted her with masturbation and told her how to do it. She listened intently, and then suddenly frowned and said, "But Earle, isn't that playing with yourself and isn't that *bad*?" I said, "Well, sometimes they use the words 'playing with yourself,' but we call it 'pleasuring yourself,' and it's *not* bad." Her face broke into an enormous grin, and she replied, "Oh, that's different!" She accepted masturbation with great reward to herself. At Christmas or Thanksgiving when the family was together, I would walk up to Aunt Edna and ask how she was. She'd turn to me and give me a great big wink and a smile, and say, "Earle, I'm just fine!" This shows that sexual conversations can occur readily even within the family, and the results are often wonderful.

The next patient was certainly one of my most unusual cases. One day during office hours, the door to my consultation room suddenly opened and in burst a frantic young woman without an appointment. She sat down and said, "I've seen all kinds of doctors, but I just can't get to work on time." I didn't know why she wanted to see me, I was a gynecologist. So I asked what detained her. And she said, "Well, I get up every morning, and I just can't get to work until I've taken several enemas to relax me enough to go to work." And I said, "Is that so? Tell me some more about that." She said, "Well, I've seen all kinds of doctors—psychiatrists, gynecologists, general surgeons, internists, and they all tell me that I'm going to lose my mind, that I'm abnormal, and that something terrible is going to happen to me, and I just can't stop taking the enemas. Most of them have examined me and said that I will hurt myself and injure my rectum. What do you think?" I said, "Well, I've never seen a woman who has taken several enemas every morning for several years. Let's have a look." I put her in the Sims position and inserted a proctoscope. She had a perfectly normal rectum—I must admit it was the cleanest one I ever saw, but it was perfectly normal.

I thought to myself, "What should I say to this remarkable woman?" So I said, "You know, I'm not quite sure what to say to you, but I can tell you this—you have not injured your rectum. It is perfectly normal. I don't know whether this is the right thing to tell you or not, but let me say this: if you derive pleasure from taking some enemas, for goodness sake, go home and take them." She looked at me in dumb amazement: "Is that right?" I replied, "I don't know if it's right or not, but that's the way I look at it." "Oh," she said, "that's wonderful."

I went into my consultation room, expecting that she would come in and talk with me, but she didn't—she walked right through, waved at me, and walked out the door. Well, I thought about this woman for several weeks, but soon this episode disappeared from my memory.

One day about four months later, my nurse called me to the phone to speak to a patient. It was the woman who took the enemas. She said, "After I left your office, I went home—you said if I wanted to take enemas, for goodness sake take them, so I took two weeks off from work and did nothing but take enemas. And I had a wonderful time. Since that time, my need to continue this behavior has lessened more and more, and now I take only one or two enemas in the morning, and sometimes none. And, by the way, I now get to work on time. I wanted to thank you for letting me know that it was all right to take the enemas, because this bothered me. I don't take too many these days, but I have learned to masturbate and do so a couple of times a week." Over the years, this woman has learned all kinds of sexual techniques: she masturbated, and she and a lover engaged in oral-genital contact as well as anal intercourse, which she enjoyed immensely. This is a classic example of a woman who accepted herself exactly as she was, and saw change automatically happen.

I've always been convinced that if people can accept themselves exactly as they are without any demand that changes be made, then nature will automatically bring about change. In other words, all you have to do is live the instant, be who you are at that instant, and forget about change—it will take care of itself. Most people just don't believe that, and work endlessly in therapy and in groups to try to change themselves. If it helps them, that's all right with me, but it's been my experience that it does nothing more than inhibit change. There's no question in my mind that self-acceptance is a greatly liberating and rejuvenating factor in all walks of life. This applies especially to the sexual field.

In addition to my gynecological and counseling activities in my private practice, I also spent several years conducting sex education workshops, which lasted for two and sometimes three days. The results seemed very positive with the majority of the participants feeling very satisfied about the experience.

I also did individual sex therapy, with singles as well as couples, and followed many of the techniques offered by Masters and Johnson. Many of those I worked with felt their relationships were functioning at a more acceptable and accepting level for all concerned, and certainly their ability to communicate with one another about sexual issues improved immeasurably.

In the late 1950s, Kinsey and Pomeroy introduced me to Dr. Harry Benjamin, who was a close friend of theirs. Harry was an internist/endocrinologist with a unique practice. His main practice was in New York City, but in order to avoid the cold winters, he traveled to San Francisco each year for a four-month period.

Harry was deeply interested in both transsexuals and transvestites, and he authored the book *The Transsexual Phenomenon,* the first to be published on this subject. It was difficult in those days for transsexuals to obtain surgery for a sex change. In the interim, Harry administered large doses of the appropriate hormone to bring about a medical transsexual phenomenon. While Harry lived in New York City, I treated his California transsexual and transvestite patients for him in my office. I liked these patients very much: they were in a very difficult social situation and needed some form of empathetic care and understanding. I administered their needs to the best of my ability, and they responded appreciatively.

Even though I stopped caring for Harry's patients in San Francisco in 1970, I always felt very fortunate to have had the valuable opportunity of working with him and his patients. I learned a great deal.

Alfred Auerbach, M.D., professor of psychiatry at the University of California Medical Center and I (also on the faculty of the University of California in San Francisco) arranged a three-day course in Human Sexuality in the mid-1960s. There were many participants, including Wardell Pomeroy from the Kinsey Institute;

Albert Ellis; C. A.Tripp, author of *The Homosexual Matrix*; and others. Bill Masters and Virginia Johnson were also included, and presented a workshop on Managing a Dysfunctional Sexual Function. I arranged for them to get a motel at the beach on the west side of San Francisco, where they stayed for a good number of weeks writing part, at least, of the first draft of their first book. Since those days, Masters and Johnson have shot to international acclaim, almost equal to that of Kinsey. Bill, Ginny, and I had many discussions about sex, and I learned an enormous amount from them. Since they had met Kinsey only once, I was able to fill them in on the Bloomington sexual research institute and the sort of man Kinsey was.

About this time, Dr. Bill Hartman and his colleague, Marilyn Fithian, shone brightly on the sexual research horizon.[2] Bill was professor of sociology in Long Beach, and Marilyn was his associate. I met Bill and Marilyn, and we became very friendly. I had a film business in which I had made a set of films titled *Education for Childbirth,* which I and other obstetricians used in our practice in educating patients. Bill had gotten hold of the films and used several of them in his sociology class. One day he invited me to come to his class to discuss the topic after he had shown the films. In that session, I was asked to describe what "love" was. I remarked that was an enormous, very-difficult-to-answer question. Then I explained that there was such a thing as romantic love, which is appealing and lovely, but usually quite transient. Then comes a period of compassion which can develop between two people. I explained that if one, in a metaphorical sense, can take the little "me" that's inside of himself or herself, and show it to the other person, that the other person will follow and do the same thing. By this exchange back and forth, of getting to know who the individual is and what's inside of him/her, a great bond is set up in which love, compassion, and meaning becomes paramount. Sharing one's feelings at an appropriate time with one's mate is one of the big factors that draw individuals close together and make them realize that fundamentally they are one. By describing love of this sort, the maneuver brought me close to Bill's class, and I've carried that event in my heart ever since that day. I've seen Bill and Marilyn frequently over the years, and we have become fast friends.

In the mid-1960s, Dr. Salvatore P. Lucia, Professor of Medicine, approached me to give the Jake Gimble Sex Lectures in San Francisco, in honor of Jake Gimble, who had left a substantial fund of money with the request that a sex lecturer be picked every few years, either from Stanford or the University of California. I readily accepted.

These lectures came at a fortuitous time because there was an enormous hunger for sex information as well as a quest for sexual liberation following a very conservative era. I recall that Ted McIlvenna, president of the Institute for the Advanced Study of Human Sexuality, made the comment that the information imparted in the Jake Gimble Sex Lectures was like a breath of fresh air.

The lectures were extremely well received and hundreds of people showed up

---

2. See chapters 14 and 20.

to hear them, necessitating the opening of several classrooms where the lecture could be viewed through closed-circuit television.

On six consecutive Wednesday nights, for two hours, I lectured on various aspects of sex. I shared with my audiences what I had learned from Kinsey, Masters and Johnson, Hartman and Fithian, and Harry Benjamin, in addition to my own rather extensive clinical practice.

I used the sex graph, which was based on several elements. One was that all sexual activity, from a biological standpoint, was perfectly natural. After all, who can describe the naturalness of sex as well as the naturalist, and that happens to be the biologist and the scientist. It also compared the biological facts with the moral and legal dilemmas of our culture and drew a clear distinction between sexual freedom and sexual frustration. I saw no reason why the moralists should change their minds; they were entitled to view sex however they pleased. Nevertheless, I felt that they should not obliterate the biologist's view of sex which states that *all* sexual activity is natural, the only restriction being that it be carried on by mutual consent among adults. And that although sexual activity which is forced or coerced is perfectly natural in the animal kingdom, the human animal needs to control and curtail all sexual impulses or behavior that may be harmful to others.

In detail, I described the sexual response cycle and also compared the sexual life of men and women. Research has indicated that males and females are more alike than different. However, men enjoy sexual excitement by a variety of means, but predominantly fantasy. Women enjoy fantasy, too, but enjoy even more touching, holding, whispering, and romance and therein lies the difference between the sexes. However, sex therapy can acquaint men with the fact that it is all right to enjoy romance and touching; and women can enjoy the fact that fantasy is perfectly permissible. Many women have been raised to feel that it is abnormal to fantasize about sex. In recent years, however, this restriction has diminished a great deal.

I emphasized that men reached their sexual peak in the late teens, and women somewhere in their twenties, thirties, and forties. I emphasized that research had revealed that sexual life continues on into the seventies, eighties, and perhaps even nineties.

Following each lecture, there was about an hour of questions and answers. We could have gone on longer except that time would not permit it. The interest in this topic seemed to be enormous.

News of these sex lectures spread quickly to the university systems throughout the United States. Consequently, for several years, I was invited to most American universities to repeat at least part of them. The response was very positive, even in those colleges and universities run by religious orders. Most requested the lectures for their undergraduate students. There was one exception, and that was the Medical College of Georgia, a generic name covering the schools of dentistry, pharmacy, and nursing, as well as medicine. The dental students at the Medical College invited me to give a series of four lectures on their campus. I readily accepted.

While I was there, Dr. William Scoggins, professor of gynecology and obstetrics, made me an offer of a professorship if I would go on leave from the University of California Medical School. Attached was one provision, that I would go to Saigon (as a visiting professor) and lecture at the University of Saigon Medical School and teach the residents obstetrical and gynecological surgical techniques. There was a school of midwives that graduated about 250 midwives per year. Almost all deliveries were carried out by the midwives and my resident staff only interceded when there were serious medical and surgical complications.

When there I was asked by my Vietnamese counterpart, Dr. Hong, to give a lecture on sex to the midwives and medical students which he offered to translate for me. I'm sure that what I had to say was quite a shock to this very sexually conservative area, but they were very kind and patient and listened very attentively.

While in Vietnam, I was invited to visit the medical school in Shiraz, Iran, to give a series of sex lectures to the students. They all spoke English quite well, and I did not need a translator. (This, incidentally, was the time when the shah was the leader of Iran.) I was also invited by the professor of the KK Hospital in Singapore to demonstrate American surgical techniques. He asked me to give a sex lecture to the medical students, nurses, midwives, and staff.

This I did, and the response seemed to be positive.

It seemed to me that the entire world was hungry for sex education.

When Kinsey died, Paul Gebhard was chosen as the director of the Kinsey Institute, and Wardell Pomeroy left to establish a marriage and sexual counseling practice in New York City. After a number of years, he tired of the New York climate and was made an offer by Ted McIlvenna to become the academic dean of the Institute for Advanced Study of Human Sexuality in San Francisco. He accepted and moved to California.

Wardell and I had become very friendly, and several times a year we either met or talked by phone and kept our relationship active. One day while I was in the State of Washington, I called Wardell just to say hello, and he suggested that I consider coming down to become the medical director of the institute. I did this for a couple of years.

The day that I arrived, Wardell and I met for lunch. Afterward, we returned to the institute to soak in a hot tub, talk over old times, and catch up on current news. Suddenly he said, "By the way, we have a student here, Mickey Apter, a bit older than many of the others, but she wishes to talk with you because she is writing her Ph.D. dissertation on the sexual behavior of female alcoholics while drinking and in sobriety." He knew that I was alcoholic, but had not had a drink for a good number of years, and that I was knowledgeable about sex, and had told her about me. She had asked if she should write me in Washington to request that I be on her dissertation committee, but Wardell told her she could ask me in person since I was coming down that week. Mickey worked part-time at the institute while attending classes, so Wardell called the upstairs office and asked her to come down to meet me. Down came this sprightly little gal who took off her clothes, got in the hot tub, and, after appropriate introduction, said to me, "Will you be on my dissertation committee for my Ph.D.?" I looked at this ball of energy and said, "Sweetheart, I'll do better than that—I'll marry you!" This was really a joke, but it so happened that a year or so later, Mickey and I were married, and we've been together for fifteen years in a very delightful, heartwarming, and loving relationship.

Over the course of my professional life, my comments on sexuality have been accepted rather well. There are those hard-nosed colleagues of mine who don't like what I say, but that's their problem, not mine. The horrendous problems of AIDS has now invaded our society and put the brakes on free sexual expression for the present time. In view of the alternative, this seems wise. Hopefully we will soon learn how to effectively treat this terrible epidemic. But sex will continue to be a human behavior, and the best we can do now is to educate consistently and continually about how to have safe sex and be sexual in a responsible way.

I have enjoyed and still enjoy the medical field; I've enjoyed surgery, obstetrics, marriage, and sexual counseling. And now that I am retired, I am enjoying relaxing with my wonderful wife, Mickey, and exploring the many things that we have yet to explore.

29

Pioneer Researcher in Childhood Sexuality

Floyd M. Martinson, Ph.D.

Floyd M. Martinson is a pioneer in the study of childhood sexuality. A rural sociologist, he has taught at Gustavus Adolphus College in Minnesota for over fifty years.

I WAS BORN on November 11, 1916, and spent my childhood and adolescence on a farm in western Minnesota. I played alone much of the time, accompanied only by my dog. There were not many friends my age on neighboring farms. My closest friend didn't have much time for play; he was expected to work all the time.

I attended Buffalo Lake open-country school, with eight grades and one teacher to teach all of them. I got to miss one class because two classes were combined to ease the teacher's load. I always wonder what I missed that year.

When it came time to go to high school, there was a decision to be made. Kerkhoven High School was fifteen miles away, and there were no schoolbuses. Would I go to high school or would I stay home and help on the farm? I wanted to go, but it wasn't my decision to make. These were difficult times on the farm— crops were affected by scorching heat; hot, dry winds; and lack of rainfall. It was also the time of the Great Depression, coupled with the severe drought. I remember the air was filled with dry-as-dust topsoil blowing across the fields, depositing itself like snow drifts along field fences. Great balls of tumbleweeds rolled across the dry, crusty bottom of what had been Buffalo Lake. I remember a day when we were cutting our sparse crops. Dad was riding the tractor, the lugs kicked up clouds of dust, and I was riding the binder, sweat and dust covering me. Grasshoppers, attracted by the salt and sweat, sat on my back and ate holes in my shirt. It was a time that left a lasting impression on a teenager.

The decision was made that I would go to high school. We rented a room (board and room, $15 a month), then began a four-year routine of someone taking me to town on Sunday afternoon and picking me up again on Friday afternoon. I felt lucky, relieved, and scared to be going to high school.

The high school years proved to be pleasant ones. Kerkhoven High was a small school in a small town, giving me a chance to play basketball (once I learned how to dribble), to pitch for the high school kitten ball team, to sing in a male quartet, to be in a couples of school operettas and a couple of class plays, and to spend exciting nights hanging out with friends.

Graduation came as a crushing blow: no more bright lights, no more hanging out with friends, no more walking a favorite girl home. It was back to the farm for me.

The rural economy was still bad, and there was no chance of going to college. I spent the next four years on the farm, all the time dreaming of far-off places and other things to do. I finally obtained a job with the Agricultural Adjustment Administration measuring the compliance of farmers on a government crop program. For that I needed transportation. My father took me to town; we bought a large, used Buick sedan for twenty-five dollars. The dealer threw in enough gas to drive the car home.

Since I'm writing about how I got into the field of sexuality, I might digress and talk about my own sex education in childhood and adolescence. I have heard that farm boys learn all they need to know by watching the farm animals. That would be a pretty crude education in human lovemaking! There were the usual things talked about by the older students in elementary school during recess, the "dirty" stories that farmhands told, and so on. But so far as formal education—I remember finding a book under my pillow which I suspect was placed there by my mother. That was the only "formal" education that I got in elementary school, high school, college, or graduate school.

After four years on the farm, I attended a small, liberal arts college, majoring in economics (because there was no sociology major) and minoring in history. Browsing through the library one day, I came upon an article by a prominent rural sociologist which told about the need for rural sociologists. A rural sociologist—that appealed to me. I did not want to return to the farm, yet rural life seemed pleasant and agreeable. I kept the idea in the back of my mind.

On graduating from college, I applied for and received a social science position in a rural high school. I taught world history, business law, biology, and senior social science, and read every book I could in the school library. The second year I was offered the same course load, plus directing a male chorus and coaching boy's baseball. I had studied music in college and did sing in the college choir, and I had enjoyed playing baseball, but I fell ill-equipped to direct extracurricular activities. Four different course preparations plus two extracurricular activities did not entice me. I entered the University of Minnesota and began to study rural sociology

When I received my degree in sociology and cultural anthropology, there was little indication I would ever come to emphasize sexuality, especially child sexuality.

As a beginning assistant professor at Gustavus Adolphus College, a Lutheran church-related, liberal arts college, I was assigned a standard set of courses: introductory sociology, social problems, rural sociology, and family.

As I looked over the data for my Ph.D. thesis on rural-to-urban migration, with the intention of doing some secondary analysis, I noticed that students who married soon after graduating from high school were those with low scores on social and emotional adjustment. Authors of books on marriage claimed that marriage was for the mature, non-neurotic person, yet it looked to me that marriage was most attractive to younger, less well-adjusted people. I wrote a short article for the *American Sociological Review* titled "Ego Deficiency as a Factor in Marriage" (*American Sociological Review*, April 1955). This was followed by "Ego Deficiency as a Factor in Marriage—A Male Sample" (*Marriage and Family Living*, February 1959). I had written articles before on rural subjects for such magazines as the *Rural Lutheran*, *The Stock and Dairy Farmer*, and an even more professional one in *Rural Sociology*, but they received little attention. The article on "Ego Deficiency" was no sooner published, however, than I got a call from a *New York Times* reporter who wanted to know, among other things, what I had against marriage! I assured her I had nothing against marriage. But what interested me was that here was a topic that excited immediate public interest. What did this mean?

Also, of the courses I taught, the one that seemed to interest students the most was the course on the family. I also found the topic challenging; I studied it and eventually wrote two books, *Marriage and the American Ideal* (1960) and *Family in Society* (1970).

But how did I end up in child sexuality? It was more by accident than plan. The college was experimenting with a plan of teaching called a 4-1-4 plan: one semester of four months, one semester of one month in which a student took only one course, followed by another four-month semester. Faculty members were encouraged to think creatively in designing courses for the one-month term. I proposed a sociology course called "Sex and Society." I found it intriguing to develop a course in sociology and cultural anthropology centering on the theme of sexual culture and sexual socialization in our sex-inhibited society. The students were also interested. I taught the course again during a regular semester, and eventually taught two sections of the course in the fall and two sections in the spring semester.

By this time I was also a member of the board of directors of the Lutheran Social Service, one of the large, private social work agencies in the state. The board and the staff were concerned over the topic of adolescent sexuality: the amount of sexual intercourse among high school students, the number of unwed pregnancies, and so on. As a member of the board, I offered my services as well as those of my undergraduate students who were taking social research methods to work with the Lutheran Social Service in designing and carrying out a project studying adolescent sexual adjustment in Minnesota. I divided the methods class into four teams, trained them in methods of observation and interviewing, developed data-gathering instruments, and sent them out to four communities where we had received permission to work. Some communities were rural, some were urban. The students went out with the general question: "What is it like to grow up in ——— community?" But they also had a more focused question in mind, namely, "What is it like to grow up *sexually* in ———— community?" The students found it difficult, of course, to mingle with high school students during only a couple of weeks in the one-month semester; but they also interviewed school principals, pastors of local churches, the police, librarians, welfare workers, parents, and others to determine how progressive and how organized the community was in thinking about sexual matters. They came back to the campus and wrote a report on each community; one member returned to the communities to check the accuracy of the report. During the summer I also sent a team of students to New York to gather comparable data, and two students to Sweden, a much more open society. At the same time the staff of Lutheran Social Service was interviewing a sample of pregnant adolescent clients. A 373-page report was assembled and published as *Sexual Knowledge, Values and Behavior Patterns: With Especial Reference to Minnesota Youth* (1966). The report was widely covered by the press and resulted in many speaking engagements.

I have dealt with events leading to my emphasis on sexuality, but here is how I came to study child sexuality. It happened this way: I required a term paper of each student enrolled in my classes. Most papers I received were based on library research and dealt with subjects such as mate selection, marriage, divorce, reproduction, and cross-cultural differences. Enrollments were large in these courses, meaning that I read many papers. After a number of years of this routine, I introduced an alternative paper theme that literally changed my professional interest. I suggested to students that they could write on some aspects of their own life experience, which they would describe and analyze utilizing concepts introduced in the course. Many chose this new alternative. To my surprise, many wrote on some sexual experience that had occurred very early in their lives. Given my traditional American background of little education about sexuality at home, in school, in college, or in graduate school, I was unprepared to critique such papers. It called for quick self-education. I read a whole series of texts and studies, and also attended summer institutes on sexuality, one at Dakota Wesleyan University (1947), a second being the first summer session offered by the Kinsey Institute. In subsequent years I spent two leave years in Sweden studying its sex culture and its touted sexuality education system. I joined professional societies such as the National Council on Family Relations (NCFR), the Society for the Scientific Study of Sexuality (SSSS), the Committee on Family Relations, and the International Sociological Association (ISA).

You might ask how colleagues not in the field reacted to me. In a small college there are no others in the field of sexology. I do not recall ever having any difficulty with the faculty, but I do remember moving a course from the experimental January term to a regular semester without asking for faculty approval. I was not sure the faculty would approve. However, I had tenure, was department chairman, a husband and father of five children. This helped establish my status.

My students at one time called me "Dirty Floyd"; yet I never felt the name was derisive, but was used out of curiosity and bemused respect.

I had only one incident with a parent that I remember well. She wrote to tell me that she had heard of the things I was teaching and was thinking of removing her daughter from the college. I read the letter to the class as an example of one of the problems of teaching a course on human sexuality. I had planned to leave it at that, but a student stopped after class and asked me if she could write to the mother. I gave her my permission. Apparently the student did a good job of defending me and what I was doing in the class, for I heard from the mother who became a real friend of sex education in her home community.

I did not feel any rejection by my profession, but I also did not test it. I read and published a number of papers at professional meetings, but always in professional organizations that dealt with sexuality. I was well received in such groups. The SSSS Midwest region awarded me the Kinsey award in 1988 for "pioneering research into child sexuality." I was also voted into regular membership in the International Academy of Sex Research (IASR).

My reception by the church was always a concern, but not a serious handicap. Local pastors from time to time wrote to the college president about me; I was warned but never accused of anything by them, though I realized that the subject matter made me vulnerable. Teaching, even human sexuality, was easier then because the college was not caught up in the hysteria over sexual harassment as it would be later on.

I also had no difficulty with the national church leadership. In fact, I received a research and creativity grant from the Lutheran Church in America (LA) in 1968. I was recognized as an authority on sex, marriage, and family; often spoke to leadership groups; and was elected to membership on the Committee on Marriage with responsibility for helping to write a statement for the church. I was known as a liberal, but not as one too radical to speak to and for the church. I must say that I never compromised my position in my research or in my teaching to conform to any doctrinal position. I felt confident that what I was exposing needed to be exposed.

If I had problems, it was more likely society that gave me grief rather than the church. I wrote two additional books, *Infant and Child Sexuality: A Sociological Perspective* (1973) and *The Quality of Adolescent Sexual Experience* (1974). Only in the case of the first did I make a real effort to have it published. In the end it, I published it myself. I say in the preface that "twenty-nine publishers were offered the privilege of publishing it. All thought that it should be published, but each thought that some other publisher should have the privilege! Why was the book not commercially published? It was favorably received. The only negative reaction came from the warden of the U.S. Medical Center for Federal Prisoners who wrote that the book

> contains material that could encourage sexual relations with children, which is a violation of federal law. This material poses a threat to the good order and discipline of the institution and is, thereby, rejected on these grounds.

Over the years, I received a number of letters from prisoners around the country. Some merely wanted to discuss child sexuality with me, others asked for my help.

By and large, they showed the most understanding of child sexuality of any letters I received. Also, they were the only letters I did not answer. If those letters came today, I could answer them, but at the time, to risk becoming associated with convicted pedophiles and homosexuals was a chance I could not take. Once, while I was in Oslo, Norway, to give a lecture, I received a call from a representative of the local pedophile group. Members of the group wanted to visit with me. I consented, and we met in the hotel lobby. They were a group of young men. Though I do not remember the conversation, I do recall that they explained their organization to me. They empathized with me. I could not empathize with them.

Another rather unpleasant incident occurred in connection with the International Conference on Love and Attraction at University College of Swansea, Wales, in 1977. I convened a symposium on infant and child sexuality. We had no difficulty with the symposium itself or the papers, but the audience that it attracted became a problem. One of the persons who announced his intention of attending was the president of the pedophile organization in England. I did not know at the time that there was a certain hysteria regarding this organization, but it soon became apparent. The union in charge of food services at the university threatened to shut down if this man attended the meeting. Reporters and photographers from both the English and American press were present to note his arrival. He protested that he only wanted to attend the meetings, and he asked me to appear with him on the BBC to explain the situation. I was in a quandary. I had invited speakers for the symposium from the United States, Norway, and Holland and did not want to risk the symposium being canceled. So I declined to appear with him. I never did meet the man, he did not show up at our symposium, and we were allowed to hold our meetings. I don't know if he tried to attend. As a compromise, the audience was monitored by the police.

In 1980, I received a call from a reporter with *Time* magazine. They were doing an article on child sexuality and wanted permission to quote me. The statement was something I had said at Swansea three years before. So *Time* had been at Swansea also. *Time* reporters wrote the following (September 7, 1981):

> Sociologist Floyd Martinson of Minnesota's Gustavus Adolphus College thinks adults involved in affectionate relations with tots should not go to jail. "Intimate human relations are important and precious," he feels. "I'd like to see as few restrictions placed on them as possible."

The quotation appeared in an article titled "Cradle-to-Grave Intimacy: Some Researchers Openly Argue That 'Anything Goes' for Children." The phone rang early the next morning. It was a local woman severely criticizing me for the article, but it was the only telephone call. I did receive a number of letters, generally unfavorable, and the college president received about fifty more. I answered all my letters. The president made out a form letter to send to the others. So far as I know, nothing more came of the incident.

I have now completed fifty years at the college, thirty-seven as professor of sociology and thirteen more as Research Professor of Sociology. I continue to do research and write. In 1992, I decided to make one more attempt, nearly twenty years since the first, to get a book on child sexuality published. After considerable updating to reflect the research that had been done, I published *The Sexual Life of Children*.

Is the climate better today? I don't know. The hysteria over child sexual abuse and sexual harassment at all levels keeps the issue of sexuality a highly emotional one

Selected Bibliography

Martinson, Floyd. 1966. *Sexual Knowledge, Values and Behavior Patterns*. St. Peter, Minn.: Gustavus Adolphus College.

———. *Infant and Child Sexuality*. 1973. St. Peter, Minn.: Gustavus Adolphus College.

———. *The Quality of Adolescent Experiences*. 1974. St. Peter, Minn.: Gustavus Adolphus College.

———. *The Child and the Family*. 1980. Calgary, Alberta: University of Calgary.

———. *The Sexual Life of Children*. 1994. Westport, Conn.: Bergen and Garvey.

30

Serendipities on the Sexological Pathway to Research in Gender Identity and Sex Reassignment[1]

John Money, Ph.D.

Early in his career as a sex researcher, John Money established the term gender *in the language of sexuality and emphasized the difference between sex and gender. His many subsequent studies and his innovative theoretical reasoning mark him as one of the leading sexologists in the world.*

WITH THE KNOWLEDGE of hindsight, some events in one's life have a different significance than when they occurred. And so it is when I look back with the knowledge of hindsight to the day after my fifth birthday on July 8, 1926. That was the day when I first went to school. In New Zealand, where I was born, it was the custom to begin school not at the beginning of the antipodean academic year in February, but immediately after reaching the age of five. Thus I was a stranger in the midst of a group of boys whose power hierarchy was well established. Some of them were the grandsons of Maori warriors, rumored to have been cannibals, who had fiercely defended their lands against the British in the Maori wars of the late nineteenth century. My first-day challenge was to dare to fight these schoolyard warriors and see who would be the victor. I had been taken to school by my girl cousin and to her I ran for protection. I could not have made a worse move, for she was in the girls' play shed, a sanctuary forbidden to boys. My fate was sealed. Having not measured up as a fighter, I was set on the pathway of outwitting other kids by being an intellectual achiever. That was easier for me than for most of them. Here I can see, with the knowledge of hindsight, that a foundation was laid for my becoming interested in gender roles and gender identity. When I was eight, there was another major event that later took on a different and more important significance in my life

1. This account derives from a paper given by John Money in Amsterdam, June 1, 1990, which later appeared in the *Journal of Psychology and Human Sexuality* 4, no. 1 (1991): 101–13. It has been reprinted with the permission of both the author and of Haworth Press, the publishers of the *Journal.*

than when it happened. After a long illness, my father died. His death was not handled very well in our family. Without being told the magnitude of what was happening, I was allowed to say goodbye to him at the gateway when he left on his final trip to the hospital. Everyone else knew he was going away to die.

Three days later I came home from school to find my father's brothers and other relatives assembled with my mother in the living room. There I was told that my father was dead. The comment of my oldest uncle was that now I would have to be the man of the household. That's rather heavy duty for an eight-year-old. It had a great impact on me. Indeed, it was the impact of the whole concept of the responsibilities contingent on gender identity, as I can see now.

Another more or less serendipitous factor that shaped my future career was that I graduated from high school at sixteen, a year too young to be admitted to the Wellington Teachers' Training College. The upshot was a compromise: I was employed as an uncertified teacher in a remote mountain valley where there were only six school-aged children—too few for a certified teacher. It was an important year of becoming a member of a pioneer farming community, and of being geographically liberated in the vast openness of scenically splendid mountains, rivers, and forests.

I elected to go to the teachers' college and train as an elementary school teacher primarily because it paid a small stipend, enough for a student with no family money to live on while at the same time taking university courses at night at Victoria College, now Victoria University of Wellington. University education in New Zealand at that time was free.

Being a part-time student at the university, I was excluded from the daytime laboratory courses in the natural sciences in which I was interested. Therefore, I was directed toward psychology which was taught in the evenings. The discovery of psychology was another serendipitous factor in my career, for at high school the subject had received no mention.

I found psychology immensely influential insofar as it carried potential answers to many personal problems contingent on living with strangers and relatives, some of them quite neurotic people, who joined our household after my father's death. I was being steered toward a career in psychology rather than teaching. The die was cast, again serendipitously, when I was excluded from being a school teacher after I officially became a conscientious objector during World War II.

Psychology still had not been separated from philosophy in the curriculum at the University of New Zealand. That gave me a rather deep interest in basic principles and philosophical matters, as well as in experimental science. I got a good grounding in experimental psychology, insofar as my professor, Thomas Hunter, had trained with E. B. Titchener at Cornell University. Titchener himself had trained in Leipzig with Wilhelm Wundt, founder of the first psychological laboratory.

After graduating with an M.A. in philosophy and psychology, I obtained a second M.A. in education, and then became a junior lecturer in psychology at the southernmost university in New Zealand, Otago University in Dunedin. There I expanded my interest in physiology by auditing the course in the medical school, in which the lectures on neurophysiology were given by John Eccles, a student of Charles Sherrington at Oxford, and later a Nobel Prize winner.

With no doctoral training offered in New Zealand, it was a foregone conclusion that I would go overseas to obtain a Ph.D. At Wellington, I was strongly influenced in favor of American rather than British psychology by Ernest Beaglehole who had trained in cultural anthropology at Yale. Serendipity played its hand again. In 1946 I read in the announcements section of one of the psychiatric journals that the Western State Psychiatric Institute, now part of the University of Pittsburgh, was finally in business after the delays of war, and was offering fellowships to foreign psychologists for advanced training under Saul Rosenzweig, whose postdoctoral research had been with Henry Murray at Harvard. The fellowship included board and lodging in the hospital, as well as a stipend. That enabled me to migrate to the United States, where I arrived in September 1947. It also enabled me to save enough to be able to become a full-time graduate student the next year at the Harvard Psychological Center, in Cambridge, Massachusetts.

Serendipity's next intervention introduced me to what would evolve into a research career. I was enrolled in an elective senior seminar under George Gardner at the Judge Baker Child Guidance Clinic, across the Charles River in Boston. Gardner was on one occasion late for class and not prepared with new material. His backup material was a case of hermaphroditism that would eventually prove to have profound significance for the concept of gender role (then still unnamed) and its counterpart, gender identity.

One knows today that the diagnosis in this case of hermaphroditism would be androgen-insensitivity syndrome, and that the patient should at birth have been assigned as a girl, so that the rearing would have been concordant with the female vulva and the complete feminization of the body at puberty. In this case, the baby had been declared a girl at birth. When, in infancy, a lump was palpated in each groin and declared to be a testis, the parents were instructed to change the baby's name and sex, and to wait until age fourteen when something would be done about the absence of a penis.

At age fourteen, there were no signs of pubertal virilization, since all the cells of the body were incapable of responding to the masculinizing hormone, androgen, secreted by the testes. They had responded instead to the small quantity of estrogen that is also secreted by the testes. The boy had grown completely female-sized breasts and a completely feminized body contour with no facial or body hair, and no deepening of the voice. He was told that he would be better off if he could change to live as a girl. As is still the case today, there was no possibility of masculinizing him with hormonal or any other form of treatment. His response was that he'd spent nearly fifteen years being a boy, and he couldn't change. He couldn't go along with the idea of being a girl.

I was so impressed with this story and its significance for the scientific investigation of sex and sexuality that I put aside a proposed review of early psychoanalytic theories of sexuality and submitted instead a review of the psychology of hermaphroditism, finding as many references as possible in the library of the Massachusetts General Hospital. Hermaphroditism provided an unparalleled opportunity to ascertain how factors of bodily existence and development from prenatal life onward are able to determine a person's sexual orientation compared with social factors contingent on the life experience of growing up in the sex of assignment and rearing.

My next step was to propose hermaphroditism as a Ph.D. dissertation topic. I was able to persuade a slightly balky dissertation committee that there were as many as ten live hermaphrodites in America who were not on display in a circus, and that I would be able to get comprehensive life history data from them, as well as psychological test data. That would constitute one half of the dissertation. The other half would be a review of the English language medical literature from 1895 to 1950, so as to obtain data on behavioral and psychological factors pertaining to sexual orientation and masculinity and femininity of the mind.

I received an excellent reception from Stanley Cobb, chief of the department of psychiatry at the Massachusetts General Hospital. With an appointment in his department, I gained access to all the clinical facilities in the hospital and continuing use of the library as well as the opportunity to consort with a very distinguished faculty. They put me in touch with Lawson Wilkins of Johns Hopkins, who came to Boston to present a workshop at the annual meeting of the American Academy of Pediatrics. Wilkins's specialty was the adrenogenital syndrome, also known as congenital virilizing adrenal hyperplasia (CVAH). When this syndrome occurs in a genetic female, the baby is born as a hermaphrodite with masculinized external genitalia, either a greatly enlarged clitoris or even a complete penis. The masculinization is hormonal in origin. The masculinizing hormone is erroneously secreted by the adrenocortical glands which should be secreting the hormone cortisol instead.

In the 1940s, Lawson Wilkins had set up the world's first pediatric endocrine clinic at the Johns Hopkins Hospital, and so was the first pediatric endocrinologist. He and I got along rather well in the interview I had with him in Boston. I inquired about the possibility of visiting his clinic for a couple of weeks, and of having access to the files of patients who were identified by hospital number in published reports, so that I could retrieve additional data. In the letter I received in reply to my formal request, Wilkins reinterpreted my request to be a visitor and said he would be glad to have me come and work in his clinic, and that he believed he would be able to raise a research grant to get me started. My first visit was for two weeks. The next was for forty years.

One bonus of the first visit was to be able to test and interview a youth with the very rare diagnosis of bilateral true hermaphroditism, the first and only person with this diagnosis whom I have encountered. There was on one side of his body an ovary, and on the other a testis. The ovarian side had feminized, and the testicular side masculinized. The patient had grown up all his life as a boy, and had a very ordinary masculine orientation as a teenaged boy, with no indications of femininity in his personality. His case allowed me to get a greater diversity than I had anticipated of types of hermaphroditism represented among the ten case studies of my dissertation.

One of the facts that enabled me to get along well with Wilkins and other pediatric endocrinologists was that I had already resolved to talk pediatric English and not the psychobabble or Rorschach babble that was much in vogue in the 1950s. Pediatricians, I discovered, genuinely did want the help of psychology, but they wanted it in a language they could understand. My resolve to speak in their language had begun with a letter I had received in response to an inquiry about a very rare case of hermaphroditism in a British girl, whose mother had had a male-hormone-producing ovarian cyst while pregnant.

Quite desperate to find out what had happened to that girl, I wrote to the gynecologist who had published the case. Since he was no longer alive the reply came from his successor who regretted not being able to supply a psychological report, but he could give me his impressions of the child at her last regular checkup. He told me that she wore typical girls' clothing, and that she was carrying a rag doll that she had made herself. These and other details made it perfectly clear that I was getting a story about a little girl and not a little boy. That made me realize the value of ordinary literate English in giving psychological descriptions.

I came to Baltimore in July 1951, and returned to Harvard in February 1952 to take the oral examination on my dissertation and to graduate. I had already committed myself to study all of the endocrine syndromes of childhood to find out about their psychoendocrinology. I knew that I had a special interest in the adrenogenital syndrome, which was also a special interest of Lawson Wilkins. He and his fellow endocrinologists at Massachusetts General had, in January 1950, scored a draw in the race to find the hormone that would suppress the masculinization of the adrenogenital syndrome, namely, the newly synthesized hormone cortisol, more precious than gold since it was not yet on the commercial market.

The new treatment had a very remarkable effect, particularly on older adrenogenital patients whose body habitus was so masculinized that in girlhood they had been called Infant Hercules. They had never menstruated, and had no breasts. Within as soon as three months after beginning treatment with cortisol, they had had a first menstrual bleeding, and had the beginnings of breast development. It was a very rapid change in body and, presumably, in body image. The question was "How much might be changing psychologically, and might there be any serious problems of psychopathology and readjustment?"

It was a major assignment, the study of this adrenogenital group of female hermaphrodites. There were other varieties of hermaphroditism to study also, notably that large conglomerate of different subtypes classified as male hermaphrodites on the criterion of their having only testicular tissue, not ovarian, and not a combination of both.

To study all the endocrine syndromes of childhood put me in the position not only of working in the first pediatric endocrine clinic, but also of being the first pediatric psychoendocrinologist. I give this some emphasis, because people are so absorbed with interest in sex that they lose sight of my work with other syndromes —growth failure and dwarfism in hypopituitarism, for example. Each disorder has its own special interest. For instance, congenital hypothyroidism, if not corrected immediately after birth, leads to irreversible mental retardation. By contrast, in the syndrome of dwarfism secondary to child abuse, mental retardation, and physical and social retardation as well, can be arrested if the child is rescued from abuse, the sooner the better, so far as catch-up growth is concerned. Growth failure in this syndrome is accompanied by failure of the pituitary gland to secrete growth hormone, and resumption of growth after rescue is accompanied by resumption of growth hormone secretion.

Enough of other syndromes—now back to hermaphroditism, and the opportunity it provides to see the interplay between prenatal and primarily hormonal factors, on the one hand, and postnatal social learning and assimilation factors, on the other, in the determination of gender-identity differentiation. The way I like to sum it up briefly is to say that hormone molecules that get into your brain prenatally are no more powerful as determinants of gender-identity differentiation than are light waves and sound waves that get into your brain postnatally through the eyes and the ears, respectively. That's a difficult concept, I've discovered, for many people to comprehend. The general tendency is to want to say that gender identity is either biological or not biological—to which my jocular response is that if it's not biological, then it must be spookological or occult, for there is a biology of learning and remembering, and it does affect the brain, doesn't it?

It was a struggle to write the first papers about the sex of hermaphrodites. Like all of us, I was heir to the assumption of centuries, namely, that sex is a single unity, and that everything can be predicted about being either male or female on the basis of seeing either a penis or vulva on a baby at birth. This assumption didn't apply in the case of hermaphrodites born with a birth defect of the sex organs so that they looked ambiguous. They didn't have a uniform sex, but a multiform sex, differently defined according to the criterion used. It was necessary for me to specify these criteria. The outcome was a list of seven variables of sex: genetic (chromosome counting had not yet been discovered), gonadal, hormonal (prenatal and pubertal), external genital, internal genital, assignment and rearing, and gender role (and identity). The idea of subdividing sex into different variables seems nowadays to have been universal knowledge for a long time. It has even entered the medical dictionary. There was only one kind of sex when I started out, however, and it was either/or sex—male or female.

Either/or sex would not allow me to talk sensibly about the sexuality, the sex lives, of hermaphroditic people. A classic demonstration case is that of a person with a penis and an empty scrotum who has two ovaries and a uterus, who is chromosomally XX (female) and who has been raised as a boy and has the bodily development of a man. The diagnosis is adrenogenital syndrome. Are you going to say that his sex is male or female? It obviously depends on the variable you use. Suppose you use the ovaries as the variable, or the uterus, or the XX chromosomes, then the sex is defined as female. Now, if this person has a sex life with a girlfriend or wife who also has ovaries, a uterus, and XX chromosomes, you are confronted with the conundrum of two people and four ovaries in bed. Is one of them homosexual, or are they both homosexual? The answer is that neither is homosexual. Their situation demonstrates that, even without realizing it, we define sexuality as homosexual or heterosexual on the criterion of the appearance and workability of the external sex organs. We really don't care what the chromosomes are, or the gonads. Provided the body of one partner looks and functions as male, and the body of the other as female, the relationship is defined as heterosexual.

It becomes very confusing to try talking about the sex of a person with two ovaries and raised as a boy, or a person with two testicles and raised as a girl if you are restricted to using the same term, sex, to apply to their gonads and to their rearing, not to mention their genital sexual behavior and their social sexual behavior.

It is equally confusing in the case of a man with virtually only a clitoris, albeit a large clitoris, who has two testicles, and has a history of having been assigned and reared as a boy. He has the body shape of a man, and attempts to have sex as a man with a woman partner. He might declare the attempt to have been a total failure. Genital sexual failure, however, does not define masculinity or femininity. How then does one talk about the all-encompassing concept of sex as masculinity or femininity that includes, but is more comprehensive than, sex as genital performance? This was the question that I struggled with and, in 1955, answered by coining the term *gender role*, which later became *gender identity and role*. In the case of the boy with the clitoridean penis, everything not pertaining to his procreative organs and their performance was masculine. In other words he had a masculine gender role, except as defined by penile performance.

When I first defined and used the term *gender role*, I had hoped that it would be accepted as referring not only to role in the sense that an actor plays a role as a character on stage, but also to the role that the actor assimilates so totally that he *becomes* the character in that role. In other words, the role is internalized and subjective, as well as externalized and manifested before the audience. I had hoped for too much. In popular usage, gender role became defined only as external manifestation, and subjective internalization became defined as gender identity. The two are reunified as gender-identity/role (G-I/R). Gender role is deciphered from body language and vocal language. We usually don't go around smelling or tasting people, or touching them too much, so it is usually the eyes, ears, and to a lesser extent, skin sensors, that give us our evidence of what a person's gender role is. Gender identity is private and introspective, directly accessible only to the self, and known to other people only by inference from the manifestations of gender role.

In 1955 I had no premonition that the term *gender* would be taken up for political use in the women's movement—as in gender gap, which has none of the double entendre of sex gap. In political and popular usage, and in much of social scientific usage also, gender has been conceptually neutered by being divorced from genital and procreative sex. However, it is not scientifically feasible to separate the coital and procreative role of a person from everything else about that person that is masculine, feminine, or androgynous. By contrast, it is feasible to have different components of the gender role and identity: vocational, educational, recreational, and legal, for example, and male/female differentiated fashion, personal adornment, and customary etiquette. The different components are not necessarily concordant with one another, nor with the erotic and copulatory component. Thus there are some gay men and lesbian women whose gender role is orthodoxly masculine or feminine, respectively, except for the erotic and copulatory component. Of such people it is commonly said that they have a homosexual orientation, but a masculine (or feminine) gender identity which is, in fact, erroneous, insofar as it excludes sexual orientation from gender identity. The error is tenacious, perhaps because it rectifies the historical legacy of equating male homosexuality with overall effeminacy and lesbianism with virilism.

Serendipity played its hand yet once again in bringing my work on hermaphroditism into convergence with transsexualism and sex reassignment. The famous case of George, who became Christine, Jorgensen hit the headlines in 1952. A reporter for *Time* magazine phoned Lawson Wilkins, convinced that the case must be one of hermaphroditism, which was not so. In that era, transsexualism was not a word in the dictionary, let alone a diagnostic entity. It was usually diagnosed as transvestism, and the referral was to psychiatry, which the patients abhorred. Their search was for the respectability of a physical diagnosis as, ostensibly, a passport to surgical sex reassignment. Many had read the book *Roberta Cowell's Story*, written by the sex-reassigned fighter-pilot son of a British military surgeon, in which there was an excellent summary chapter on hormones.

As my work on hormones and hermaphroditism became known in the clinics at Johns Hopkins, would-be transsexuals were referred to me for evaluation. Although there was no surgical program for them, sex reassignment had already proved itself a viable procedure for some hermaphroditic patients who had grown up convinced that they had been wrongly sex assigned at birth. Usually they had not been hormonally followed and regulated while growing up and, although they were supposed to live as girls, they had gone through a masculinizing puberty, as boys do. Only two sexes are officially recognized in our society so that, if you feel absolutely wrong in your sex as a girl when you've developed as a boy, the alternative is to conclude, "Maybe I should change over to the other sex and it will be better for me."

The endocrinology of hermaphroditic sex reassignment was under the management of Lawson Wilkins. The surgery was done chiefly by the gynecologist, Howard W. Jones, Jr. (who in retirement now has a second career in IVF [in vitro fertilization] at Eastern Virginia University). He was impressed by the rehabilitative success of sex reassignment for the hermaphroditic patients who needed it. He discussed with me the feasibility of sex reassignment for the people who, after the publication in 1966 of Harry Benjamin's book, *The Transsexual Phenomenon*, would be given a diagnosis of transsexualism.

I had gotten to know Harry Benjamin and attended some of the meetings and clinics held in his offices in New York. He and his associates, Leo Wollman in particular, were very cooperative in getting three patients who had been surgically reassigned, one in Naples, two in Casablanca, to come to Baltimore to be examined by Howard Jones, myself, and others. They were valuable contributors to the decision to begin the transsexual procedure of surgical reassignment at Johns Hopkins.

The first male-to-female operation having been authorized by the court was scheduled for January 1965, but was not carried out by reason of intervention from the department of psychiatry on the basis of philosophical disagreement regarding sex reassignment. Another patient, on referral from Harry Benjamin, was scheduled for male-to-female reassignment, and the surgery was performed on June 1, 1965. It was not until November 21, 1966, that the hospital issued a formal press release, first published in the *New York Times*. Until then, sex reassignment for transsexualism had not been officially recognized or accepted in the United States, although a few cases were said to have been treated surgically by the urologist Elmer Belt in Los Angeles, but not published.

At Johns Hopkins, it turned out that independently of male-to-female surgery under Howard Jones in the operating rooms of the Woman's Clinic, female-to-male reconstructive surgery done in the general operating rooms had come under the purview of the plastic surgeon Milton Edgerton, who subsequently became chief of plastic surgery at the University of Virginia. I remember one patient on whom the surgical house staff requested a consultation from me. She had been admitted and written up as a case of hermaphroditism. It did not take long to recognize that the history of hermaphroditism was a ruse, however, necessitated by prior surgical rejections at other institutions, and that the case was one of straightforward female-to-male transsexualism, for whom the necessary surgery was performed.

It is greatly to the credit of the two surgeons Jones and Edgerton that they realized the legitimacy of reassignment surgery as a rehabilitative procedure to improve the quality of life for people in the transsexual predicament. In 1967 we convened a meeting of all those who had contributed to the care of transsexuals and established both a committee and a clinic. Would the name be Sex Change Committee and Clinic or Transsexual Committee and Clinic? I proposed Gender Identity Committee and Clinic, and that it became. My idea was to have a name that would be consistent with eventually developing a clinic that would encompass all the phenomena of hermaphroditism, transsexualism, and any other phenomena related to the sexology of gender identity.

That was doomed not to happen at Johns Hopkins. In August 1979, the powers that be contrived a press conference in which sex-reassignment surgery at the hospital was disavowed, ostensibly on the basis of efficacy, but actually on the basis of medical morals that affect also controversy over abortion, fetal research, the treatment of sex offenders, and so forth. In the meantime, a gender-identity clinic has become, in general usage, a place restricted all but exclusively to transsexualism and the sex reassignment of transsexuals. Times change, however. With advances in research, the original vision may again become viable.

References

Benjamin, Harry. 1966. *The Transsexual Phenomenon*. New York: The Julian Press.
Cowell, Roberta. 1954. *Roberta Cowell's Story: An Autobiography*. Toronto: William Heinemann.

31

Combining Sex and Medicine

Charles Moser, M.D., Ph.D.

Charles Moser, a physician specializing in sexual medicine, has done significant research into sadomasochism. He practices in San Francisco.

W HEN FIRST ASKED to submit this autobiography, I questioned the purpose of the collection. One of the editors thought I might inspire some bright young student to enter the sex field (or run in terror was my thought). Whether or not this volume will inspire anyone, I do know that the study of sex is important. Sex is so important and many aspects so controversial that sometimes I believe it should not be left to the amateurs. My hope is that even if you do not choose to be a sexologist, you will have an appreciation for the serious issues with which sexologists deal. My purpose is to help the reader understand both what it means to be a sexologist and why I say I am happy and proud to be one.

There are two stories from my preadolescence that are important. First was an incident in the second grade. I remember a discussion with two male friends about where babies come from, with one friend clearly stating that all babies come from doing "it." The other friend felt that if a couple were "really in love," doing "it" could be avoided. I sided with the "really in love" option; I recall how comforting that felt even though I had no idea what "it" was at the time.

I often tell this story to young sexologists who do not want to believe that some politically correct answer cannot be defended by the data. It emphasizes the importance of knowing how the data are flawed and whether they are relevant to the question being asked. Take masturbation: From the Renaissance until the early 1900s, masturbation was either a sin or sickness, but never acceptable behavior. Now most sexologists believe that masturbation is one of the healthiest sex acts in which one can engage. However, there is no study that actually shows masturbation is healthy, just as there is none to show that it is unhealthy.

The second story concerns how I started my journey as a sexologist. I was in the fifth grade, in a discussion with two male friends before class. One announced that a female classmate of ours had just had her first period. At that point in time I thought periods existed only at the end of sentences, although I somehow fathomed that this was not a subject to discuss with one's teacher or mother. The belief that I was missing something led me to the only other resource I had left, the Brooklyn Public Library. There I read anatomy, physiology, good novels, bad novels, psychology, history, and more. I was fascinated to say the least. In later bull sessions with my friends, I developed a reputation for having book knowledge and often the correct answers. This led to more questions and returning to the library for more research. In many ways, that is still what I do.

I grew up in Brooklyn, New York, a subway ride away from the porn shops of West 42nd Street, though all I could do was gaze through the door; the hookers, male, female, and transsexual, on Eighth Avenue; the hippies in Greenwich Village; the foreign art films; and the odd collection of people and media in New York. On the other hand, Brooklyn itself was like a very sheltered small city: mostly residential, family-oriented, and without much overt sexual behavior for a teenager to find. That does not mean that Brooklyn did not have its share teenage pregnancies, or sordid little affairs; you just had to look a little harder for them.

My father was an accountant. My mother was a homemaker, and this was her second marriage. I had an older half-brother and a younger sister. While my upbringing was not perfect, I felt loved and supported. My parents have always been proud of me, though my mother felt she could never brag to the other ladies in the beauty parlor about her son's accomplishments. Somehow, having a sexologist for a son did not quite measure up to Mrs. Goldberg's son the orthodontist who just bought a big house on Long Island. My father keeps copies of my scientific papers, but I don't think he reads them. My brother died of lymphoma, and it was his illness that was partly responsible for my going to medical school. It reminded me that I once enjoyed the hands-on aspects of health care, and that I missed the hard science that goes with medicine. My sister, a computer consultant, lives the stereotypical married life in the suburbs of Atlanta with a husband and child.

When people ask me why I became a sexologist, I often say, because I was a horny teenager. I was always fascinated with sex, both personally and academically. During puberty I wanted to understand what was happening to me. My first struggle to understand the differences between men and women, gay and straight, evolved out of my early observations of the world around me. I remember being a teenager and wondering how to make a living at sex without doing anything illegal, it was that fascinating to me. It seems I finally figured it out.

Several events came together in my freshman year at college, which started me upon the path to sexology with seriousness. I enrolled at the State University of New York at Stony Brook in the fall of 1970 as a physics major, and thought I would eventually get a Ph.D. and have a career as a professor, teaching and doing physics research. I thought I might specialize in biophysics or astrophysics. I did graduate with a B.S. degree in physics and actually came close to embarking on a career in physical science a few times. My approach to problems today has been shaped by my physics training.

Coincident with my entering Stony Brook was the passing of the very liberal New York State abortion law. This created a need on campus for a birth control and abortion counseling service. I was one of seven students who created EROS (Education and Research On Sexuality). I am very proud to know that EROS still exists at Stony Brook, more than twenty years later. It was a mechanism for me to continue studying sex, while still being a physics major. In the early 1970s, to say you wanted to study sex was akin to saying that you wanted to be an astronaut. Yes, those people exist, but there was no clear route to the profession.

Also the year I entered Stony Brook, Dave McWhirter was appointed director of the Student Health Service. Dave, a psychiatrist and a sexologist who became my mentor, is still a dear friend twenty-five years later. He encouraged and helped me in more ways than I can ever hope to repay. It is clear to me that I would not have become a sexologist without Dave's influence and help.

During the summer between my sophomore and junior years, while working as a research assistant for a physics professor, I read *Human Sexual Response* and *Human Sexual Inadequacy* by Masters and Johnson. I read them voraciously, more like novels than scientific texts. I remember being disappointed that there was not more to read. Something else was apparent to me: I loved physics, but I had to work very hard to understand it. Sexology always came easy to me, it made sense. I still had to read and put in the time, but I felt I had a real knack for it. The feeling was clear, sexology was right for me. Despite problems and setbacks that happen to everyone, I have never been sorry that I chose to be a sexologist. It is with pride that I say I am. As part of my opening lecture for new sexology students, we practice introducing ourselves as sexologists. It is surprisingly difficult, but it engenders a wealth of great stories of other people's reactions to this newly identified status.

During college, in a bold move, I decided to begin my sex research career. Obviously, I needed a topic to study. I bought a variety of sex newspapers like *Screw* and similar publications, and read them critically. This technique is actually quite productive; several projects have been initiated using this method. A notice for a sadomasochism organization, The Eulenspiegel Society, with a meeting announcement open to the public, caught my eye. I quickly found that almost nothing had been written on S/M, and thought this was intriguing. Then I worried, what might happen to a naive college student who attended an S/M meeting alone? To say I was frightened is the understatement of all time. I did not know how to proceed at all. Dave McWhirter kindly consented to accompany me. Somehow I knew he would know what to do. Despite that, if the meeting had not been held in a church, I do not think I would have gone. Why I persisted, I am not sure. Why Dave humored me is probably more of a mystery. In retrospect, my fears were unfounded: the lack of anger and aggression at S/M meetings has been confirmed at numerous organizations across the country.

I remember taking a taxi to the Lower West Side of Manhattan. The meeting was located in what I would learn was the first gay church in the United States, the Church of the Beloved Disciple. It was actually little more than a storefront, and crowded with a wide variety of people: women and men, gay and straight, some obviously dominant or submissive, some people in fetish clothes, others in business suits all milling about. There was a lecture, followed by "the circle." The newcomers with some of the leaders gathered their chairs in a circle and went around the room to introduce themselves. The first person to speak was a an attractive blonde woman who said, "My name is Gilda, I'm into heavy pain and humiliation, and I belong to John." The next person who spoke was a young, slim brunette who said, "I'm Ann, and I'm into heavy pain and humiliation, and I belong to John." After that a short, plump, middle-aged African American man just said, "I'm John" with a big toothy grin.

During that first circle, there was a student nurse who was there for a class project, but who admitted that she was really into "it," then blew the smoke of her cigarette directly at John. They made a beeline toward each other at the end of the meeting. There was a lesbian couple, with a very butch dominant and a feminine submissive, the submissive complaining that her partner would not beat her when she misbehaved, and wanting advice on how to elicit the desired behavior. Simply put, I was fascinated. I have been seriously studying S/M ever since that night.

As graduation came closer, I had to decide about my next career move. Several people suggested medicine, though I still needed some prerequisite coursework. Others suggested law, some thought that a Ph.D. in sociology might be the way to go. Still others emphatically indicated that I needed a credential that allowed me to talk to people, either a Ph.D. in clinical psychology or an M.S.W. (master's in social work). I wanted to study sex and thought about the only program open to me, the NYU Human Sexuality Program. I made several decisions in my senior year. First, I proceeded to complete the prerequisites for medical school. Second, I recognized the importance of a counseling credential. I decided to pursue an M.S.W., the best counseling credential I could obtain in a short period of time (two years). I recognized that I had to have solid credentials in a more traditional field, so I regretfully decided to postpone sex to a later date.

I attended the University of Washington School of Social Work in Seattle. I remember this as a very tough time in my life. There I was in a new city without many friends, attempting to learn some very new skills. Without ever having had a psychology course in my life, I was now in a graduate-level counseling program. I had made it through college never having written a formal paper. After two weeks of classes, one of my professors assigned a paper. I really did not know what was expected, so I wrote one only five pages long. The next shortest paper submitted was ten pages and most were in the fifteen-to-twenty-page length. I thought this was going to be a major problem, but the paper was returned with a grade of B–, with the comment "interesting, but very brief." I never had an academic problem after that. Since my goal was to study sex, I tried to make every paper and research project have a sexual focus, often to the amusement of my non-sexologist professors.

As part of my social work curriculum, placement at social service agencies was required. I arranged my first placement at the Seattle Counseling Service for Sexual Minorities (SCSSM). My experience there, being the only heterosexual man on staff, was interesting to say the least. I remember being warned that no straight man had ever survived there more than a couple of weeks. Apparently, the other staff members would make sexual overtures, and the man would feel threatened and leave. Today we might call it sexual harassment, but then it was a way of becoming accepted. I worked there for almost a year and it was where I developed real empathy for the problems that sexual minorities faced. During my placement at SCSSM I socialized and worked in an environment that was devoid of heterosexuals. Nevertheless, I was often subjected to displays of anger about straight society from these people.

Prior to my being placed there, SCSSM had not been an official internship placement. It was seen as too much of a fringe organization for learning social work. Afterward, it became one of the more popular placements through the school of social work. It was an important fight to get SCSSM accepted as a legitimate placement. To hear the more conservative faculty try to find a reason not to accredit the agency and to hear the distrust and isolation emanating from the agency itself were important lessons. This isolation, both conservative and alternative, allows one to stereotype the other's behavior. The success in accrediting the agency taught me that you can educate people if they are willing to listen. It is important that the liberals listen to the fears of the conservatives without just dismissing them out of hand, and vice versa.

It was in social work school that I began to learn how to be a psychotherapist. I remember my first client, who I thought was going to be my last. He was a gay man in his late twenties, whom I saw at SCSSM. I remember taking him into a counseling office and sitting back in a winged chair, feeling as if something momentous were about to happen. I started off with what I thought was an innocent question, "How can I help you today?" My client looked for the words for a few moments and then said, "I'll just have to show you." With that he got up, dropped his pants and underwear, lay on the floor, threw his legs over his head, put several fingers into his rectum and said, "Do you see now?" My only thought was that someone was going to walk in and see this, and my career as a psychotherapist would be over. So I quickly said, "Yes, please get up now." He did and we began to discuss his feeling that he was an inadequate lover because his anus was too tight to allow easy intercourse.

After social work school, I went back to New York, where I spent two years working in state hospitals to complete the experience requirement to become licensed. I also continued doing research on the S/M community in New York. It was obvious that I would go on for a Ph.D., but I was still unsure in what: clinical psychology, social work, sociology? Dave McWhirter called and told me about a program at a brand new school, the Institute for Advanced Study of Human Sexuality (IASHS), in San Francisco.[1] I applied and was accepted. One great feature was you could do the program and still continue to work. The plan was to spend three or four weeks in San Francisco every four months completing papers and doing other work at home.

I remember my father driving me to the airport for my first trimester, when he commented that I seemed sort of sad. We spoke of my great disappointment with not finding others who were interested in the serious study of sex, and my fear that the institute was going to be another letdown. He tried to be encouraging, but it was a difficult time. Most of my professional life was spent being known as that guy who seemed obsessed with sex. More times than I want to remember, I was asked why a bright guy like me wanted to throw his professional life away. There were many of my peers who had embarked on promising careers in the sex field, only to be coaxed away by well-meaning colleagues who made them "better" offers to help them get over their fascination with sex.

Unfortunately, the sex field loses many good people this way. It is notoriously underfunded, which makes it difficult for academics to get promoted on the basis of sex research. It is very rare for an academic department to advertise for a new faculty member with a specialty in sexology. At one time it was common for a department chairperson to assign teaching the human sexuality course to whomever was in his/her doghouse at the moment. This changed only because the course was usually very popular and made a significant contribution to the department's income. It is surprising that given this interest among students, more human sexuality courses were not created, and that this did not lead to the formation of new minors, majors, or even separate departments. In addition, there are several stories of powerful alumni embarrassed by a newspaper account of a sex researcher's discovery, who advocated to get that researcher moved off campus. It is no wonder, then, that many young academics see the field and their future clearly, and choose to specialize in something else.

There were many occasions when people attempted to sabotage the sexual aspect of a course or program. When someone says, you are the expert, discuss what you think best, that usually means they will deny all knowledge of your activities and no one will defend you or what you did. We treat sex differently from other subjects. Can you imagine the dean taking a complaint that one did not like the content of a calculus or sociology course, if it did not meet the preconceived notion of what the student thought should be taught? Yet that is what happens in sex courses all the time. After learning this lesson well, I never taught a course without the administration knowing exactly what I was going to do and say.

Sorry, but I seem to have digressed. Orientation at IASHS was an amazing experience. The institute is located in a nondescript building on the edge of downtown San Francisco, not far from adult bookstores, street corners frequented by

---

1. See chapter 27.

teenage prostitutes of both sexes, and other sex establishments. It is also near some beautiful houses, luxury hotels, and lovely parks. A number of faculty and other new students were already there, everyone was being introduced. I was sitting next to a woman who wore a see-through top without a bra. This by itself was not an issue, but I thought it odd that a new student would wear that to an orientation. As the faculty began giving short introductions and imparting important rules to remember, a door opened. A naked woman came out, toweling herself off, and sat down on the other side of me. No one else seemed to notice anything. It seemed odd, to say the least. The naked woman leaned over and informed me that she hated to get dressed after a hot tub. Later I found out what a hot tub was, but at the time I had no idea. Even today IASHS is known derogatorily as "Hot Tub U," a name it really never deserved. This is what happened though when you put people in a situation where they are given permission and the freedom to experiment. It is the basis of the SAR (Sexual Attitude Restructuring) which was formulated and promoted by IASHS.

After the formal introductions, we all had a crab dinner. Some of my fondest memories of the institute are the crab dinners. During this one we had general discussions with the faculty about sexology. It was an easy and very intellectually stimulating time. It was what I was looking for. The basic lectures and coursework were an opportunity to question and attempt to understand sex. I studied hard. I remember being in the library for hours. It was a great time that seemed to flow too fast.

The IASHS has a reputation for being a very wild place, with everyone experimenting with all forms of sex. Either fortunately or unfortunately, depending on your fantasies, it was pretty much like other graduate schools. The IASHS has also been a victim of the times we live in, and some of the more open attitudes and behaviors once tolerated no longer are. Students and faculty did take hot tubs in the nude and often discussed some sexological concept, but this could be misinterpreted, and now, while not forbidden, it just does not happen any more.

If you are a sexologist, people think you are too obsessed with sex. Talking about your work can embarrass even quite liberal and intelligent listeners. Potential lovers are intimidated by you, believing (incorrectly, unfortunately) that you have special knowledge about what is universally sexually satisfying. It should be pointed out that, at least in my experience, sexual adventurers do not beat a path to your door hoping to find out about this special knowledge. The sad truth is that each of us has our own sexual pattern, probably as unique as our fingerprints, and that pattern makes us an unsuitable sex partners for some and great for others.

My dissertation on S/M was the toughest thing I ever did. I almost gave up one month before I finished. It is so hard to see the forest through the trees. My committee consisted of Loretta Haroian who was one of the great thinkers of the sex field, largely unknown because she was not a writer; Wardell Pomeroy, Kinsey's associate and co-author; and Dave McWhirter.

What does a brand new Ph.D. in sexology do? Pray that s/he finds a job. I was essentially broke when I graduated. My father's graduation gift was paying my typist bill (yes, this was in the days before word processors and the manuscript had to be perfect). I took a job with the Mentally Disordered Sex Offender Unit at Patton State Hospital in San Bernardino, California. While there I made a very important decision. I had toyed with the idea that I would apply to medical school after my Ph.D., but I decided against medical school. I felt that sexology was growing and that if I continued to work hard, I would one day be seen as one of the pioneers of the field. This was 1980, the year Ronald Reagan was elected president and the mood in the country became both conservative and antisexual.

I was able to move back to San Francisco after six months to start a job as the designee of the county mental health director for Contra Costa County. State law required the county mental health director to examine a wide variety of people, the director often designated someone to do those exams, and I was one of those designees. I not only conducted these examinations, but also was involved in a special-alternative-to-probation program for sex offenders which involved my acting as a probation officer as well as doing psychotherapy. It also allowed me to start a private practice, mostly sex therapy, clinical sexology, and marital therapy. IASHS invited me to join the faculty as an instructor. Today I am a professor of sexology and dean of professional studies. This was the time that the institute was attempting to start a clinical program both to train students and to provide care for the community. For many reasons this altruistic endeavor failed, but it was a great, if painful, experience for me.

My research probably has sustained me through my professional life more than anything else. My first research was on sadomasochism. I published a subsequent series of articles on the sexual effects of drugs which was the basis for my later clinical work with substance abusers. I was fortunate to obtain a contract to write a pamphlet for the Board of Medical Quality Assurance (now called the Medical Board of California) on sexual issues in medicine. It turned out to be an a reasonable little booklet, but I do not think it was read by many physicians. I was interviewed in *Forum* magazine in March 1984. I also commented on Elvis Presley's sex life in *Forum*. I contributed to two books on safer sex published through the Institute for Advanced Study of Human Sexuality.

In 1982, the *Journal of Sex Research* published as its feature article the ex-president of the Society for the Scientific Study of Sexuality (SSSS) Ira Reiss's presidential address which took the position that a new discipline of sexology was unnecessary and that the established disciplines (e.g., psychology, sociology, and biology) could more effectively engage in the study of sex. In a response, I laid down the reasons that a new discipline was necessary and would likely be more effective than the established disciplines. This is the only paper I know that argues the justification of sexology as a distinct discipline. Dr. Reiss admits today that sexology is and needs to develop into its own discipline.

In 1984, I joined Martin Weinberg and Colin Williams, two sociologists from Indiana University, in a paper concerning the definition of sadomasochism and its distinction from other phenomena. This led to a long friendship with both these men, their academic interests being closest to mine. While we have not written anything else together, we often critique each other's work and have great discussions whenever we get together.

In 1992, I published my first theoretical piece of research, titled "Lust, Lack of Desire, and Paraphilias: Some Thoughts and Possible Connections." I tend to be very data-oriented, and to write a paper without references was a liberating experience. Hopefully, others will follow in the future.

My major work has concerned S/M or related topics (e.g., nipple piercing). I have said that I am the world's expert on sadomasochism, because I have written more scientific papers than anyone else. It is not clear why just writing papers about S/M makes someone an expert, but I do believe it is important to know what science knows. My work as a whole finds that S/M is not the pit of psychopathology that some have imagined it to be. Rather, most of us have some remnant of S/M as part of our sexuality. In some it is quite pronounced while in others it is just a fleeting fantasy.

In 1986, I was a professor of sexology, had a thriving private practice, was working on several research articles, and was on the board of directors of SSSS. In short my life was going well. Never one to leave well enough alone, however, I decided to give it all up and go to medical school.

My reasons were complicated, but here is part of it. Managed care and other changes in the health care system were coming and I realized that money for the treatment of sexual problems was going to be tight. I also knew that to do quality work required time and care. I realized that soon sex therapists would be bidding to treat people in fewer and fewer sessions. So, I decided to join a better union; quite literally I knew that physicians would be able to marshal resources and political power more effectively than other health care providers. The next reason was that organic/biological causes of both sexual dysfunctions and sexual behavior in general were becoming more important. If I wanted to do more hands-on research and/or use drugs, then I had to go to medical school. The last reason is that I support all my own research. I never apply for grants in the sex field, which is a waste of time, especially when studying the more esoteric areas of sexology.

Medical school was an experience. The lack of original thinking and Herculean feats of memory required astounded me. Medical students rarely ask questions; we were just repositories of information. Surprisingly, there are few textbooks in medical school. You memorize lectures, which you soon forget. but supposedly you retain something. I did not think that I would specialize in internal medicine when I entered medical school or even later. For a long time I floated among specialties, but am happy that I became an internist.

One of my ongoing projects is to create the American College of Sexual Medicine Physicians (ACSMP). This is a group in formation that will identify physicians with special interest and expertise in the medical treatment of sexual problems, including HIV, STDs (sexually transmitted diseases), hormonal treatment (including hormone treatment for transsexuals), medical workup and treatment of sexual dysfunctions, general medical care of sexual minorities, office gynecology, and andrology (the medical care of men). The importance of the formation of this organization is that these physicians will be a resource to others in the treatment of these patients. It will also serve as a source of continued medical education for physicians about these problems.

The future still holds many challenges. I hope to continue my research on S/M as well as other areas that catch my interest. While I admit to not being the captivating teacher I had hoped to be, I will still mentor students and give occasional lectures. My efforts to shape the field into a new discipline will not stop, though it may not be realized in my lifetime. My efforts to help other physicians understand and treat sexual minorities more appropriately will not end either. And most importantly, I promise myself in writing here and now, to enjoy some of the great sex life that I work so hard to ensure in others.

As I write this I am forty-three years old, a middle-aged man. Half of my life is over, and while I have accomplished much, there are many other goals to attain. I hope someone is moved by my story, because we need more help in the sex field. It has been exciting so far, and I think the fun is just beginning. The reader should understand that I am happy that I chose sexology. I doubt that I could be more fulfilled in another field. My vanity license plate says "SEXS FUN." It was a hassle getting it, but it does give my message to the world.

32

"I Wanna Be Good": Sexual Guilt in a Sexologist

Donald L. Mosher, Ph.D., A.B.P.P.

Donald Mosher, a past president of the Society for the Scientific Study of Sexuality, has been a major contributor to the analysis of gender stereotypes. He has also been interested in the public policy issues about sexuality and was the only professional sexologist allowed to testify at Attorney General Meese's hearings on pornography.

DID NOT know that I would become a sexologist; nor did I know that I would be the sexologist that I have become. I believe that understanding my life story requires an understanding of scenes and scripts, but I did not gain this perspective until I had a mid-life mentor, the late Silvan Tomkins, from age forty-five to fifty-five. His affect and script theories guide my theorizing and self-understanding (Tomkins, 1962; 1963; 1991;1992). My purpose here is to describe both some relevant scenes in my early life that formed my personality and the crucial scenes in adulthood that hardened my commitment to sexology. My scientific life is an existential project— a search for meaning that involves excitement, distress, and shame as I try to meet the specific challenges set by my life and personality. As a scientific expert in sexual guilt, I begin by illuminating the aspect of my personality that led me to study guilt. Also, I illustrate some macho themes because that is also a principal area of research interest. Next, I make use of my theory of involvement in sexual scenes to illustrate three paths of involvement in my own life. Finally, I will describe the psychology of commitment to sexology by a clinical psychologist fascinated by personality, sexuality, and gender.

Sexual Guilt in a Sexologist

My personality is succinctly defined by this desire: "I wanna be good."

I am an ordinary heterosexual man living an ordinary life, with ordinary emotions and conflicts. The only thing extraordinary, in an ordinary way, is that I am me, living my life from inside my skin. So I feel the emotions in the scenes of my life, representing each scene in consciousness as it unfolds. I try to make sense of the important (affect-invested) scenes of my life by caring deeply once again about what these families of urgent and related scenes mean. As I respond to the sense that I make of them, I invest fresh affect in these co-assembled scenes and their rules. These are interludes of psychological magnification in which once again I care intensely about what I remember-know-imagine about these somehow related episodes that are so significantly emotional.

Although everyone must make their world predictable, controllable, and meaningful, as a psychologist, within my role as a scientist or theorist, I am interested in my life not only personally but also abstractly. It is only into one life, while trying to know myself, that I have the privilege of the most intimate window—consciousness of the subjectivity of lived experience. From what I understand of myself, I want to be good.

To me, being a good autobiographer means that I should show you, rather than tell you, who I am. To be good is to disclose those scenes that I believe to be important in my becoming the person who is both Don Mosher and a sexologist. For me, being good is mostly about being a moral person, but sometimes it is about being an achieving and contributing person, which in a Calvinist way is being morally good as well.

It is easier for me to be good about disclosing my academic scenes than my sexual scenes because in them sometimes I was bad, or so it seems to me now as I remember and imagine them. Of course, sometimes I believed I was bad then, but now believe I was really good and only believed I was bad because I was scripted to feel guilty over my sexual thoughts, feelings, and acts. However, sometimes I just feel ashamed without being sure whether I was really good or bad while knowing I want to be good now and hoping that I was or wishing that I were good then, too. But mostly, I feel, as the psychologist Harry Stack Sullivan would put it, "simply human." I believe that I am no big deal and that my life, even my sexual sins, are rather ordinary and that all human beings share emotional turbulence about their sexualities.

Born in 1935, I was a good baby. I was a good little boy. The story that I usually tell my graduate students in clinical psychology to illuminate Don, Jr., at five years old is called the "Cat's Tail Tale." It is Halloween and my big sister, Sally, is taking me to a costume party. I am dressed as a black cat with a mask, a tail, whiskers, and everything. Momma made it for me. Sally runs ahead of me—she likes everybody and everybody likes her—while I slowly pass the iris patch, which I used to break to play swords with. It was exciting to play swords, but Momma told me it hurt the flowers. So I never do that now. I like flowers; I don't want to hurt them. Once at the party, I feel like a scaredy cat; I don't know who is behind those masks. The ghosts say boo and the witches cackle something fierce. Already uneasy, I feel quite distressed when a boy-monster pulls my tail. You shouldn't pull a cat's tail, it hurts them. You shouldn't hurt flowers; you shouldn't hurt black cats;

you shouldn't hurt me. By pulling my tail, he hurts my sensitive feelings. I begin to cry and run home. I crawl onto Momma's lap, and she rocks me. Then I go take a nap. I always feel better after a nap, full of energy and excited about playing, at least, when it's not Halloween.

I tell this story to contrast Don, Jr., with me in my role as professor and psychotherapist. Although it was difficult for me, I wanted to become a good therapist; so I persevered until I became one. Although my national reputation is that of a distinguished sexual scientist, my local reputation is for my skill as a psychotherapist, being regarded as a talented healer. This makes me a little scary because I see so much so fast about people that my students fear that I might just see their deepest and most shameful secrets and put them into the words that flow so easily from my tongue. Fearful, because they have not yet discovered my capacity to care. The first self the students see is the self-assured, apparently cocky Dr. Mosher, the persona on stage most of the time in professional scenes. Beneath the mask is shy, sensitive, and scared Don, Jr.

A second story, a major influx of guilt, from age six, is called, "Sister, have you got a dime?" Sally and I get to go to the Saturday movies. We are living in Columbia, Tennessee, the mule capital of the world. We walk about a mile and a half over the Duck River bridge to the theater. Sally has a friend with her. They pay their dimes and get their tickets and run ahead. The usherette stops me. I have been coming to the movies for a while before I turned six. It is free until you are six. She asks me how old I am. I tearfully confess that I am six years old. Sally is already inside, and I don't even know if she's got another dime. I'm going to have to walk home all alone, but I can't just lie and say that I am five. I am a guilty boy now that I am six. The usherette watches the tears role down my freckled cheeks and is merciful, saying, "Go on in, but bring a dime next time."

My mother tells me, and I remember that it is true, that the difference between Sally and me is that Sally will go out and find somebody to play with. If she can't find anyone, then she'll read. But I read until someone comes and asks me to play.

The Boy Scout manual says masturbation is bad for you. I do it anyway. I remember the first time I ejaculated; I was having orgasms that felt real good for some time, but this time I also spurt out this white stuff. It scares me some, but I know better than to confess, because no one talks about sex with their parents. I don't even know it's called cum until the big boys tell me.

Momma teaches me about God and people. I like to talk to her when it is just the two of us. She teaches me that the cavemen were really fallen angels, like Lucifer. Her mother was so special that she had visions from God. But she was killed in a car accident when I was five years old and still living in Columbia. My grandmother, Anna, had gone from Birmingham to Nashville to teach the Bible to a woman's group. She did that a lot. Everybody, and particularly Mom and Dad, treated her like she was a saint or something. But Grandfather Reinhart didn't; he made her ask him for grocery money every week. Of course, the Bible says that the man is the head of the house—even if his wife is a college graduate, can read Greek and Hebrew, and is especially blessed. My parents tell me that I am like my dead and revered grandmother; it makes me messianic.

My dad gets mad when I don't do something he tells me to, like mow the grass when its 106 degrees outside. I say I want to wait until it's cooler, but I really don't want to do it because he said to. Mom is the go-between. She explains me to him and him to me and what his mother did wrong and everything so that I will understand. I wanna understand; maybe that's why I grow up to be a psychologist.

Momma tells me that I can be anything I want to be because I am smart. The teachers say my IQ is real high. Mom and Dad let me alone to do my schoolwork; that is for me to do as I choose. I do real well, but they know I could do better. School is so easy that instead of studying I spend most of my time reading library books. Books are a window to the world and my best friends really.

My mother tells me the parable of the talents. It still haunts me. I know that I am not the son who buried his talents. But I am never sure if I am the one who settled for a modest return or the one who invested them wisely.

At sixteen, I am starting to date. When I am out mowing the grass, Dad comes running out to tease me about the lipstick he found on my handkerchief. I just ignore him. I don't know if that annoys me more than the time he told me not to masturbate because it was a sin and would ruin my mind. I know that it won't ruin my mind or even give me little red hairs on the palm of my hands—like we used to say at scout camp to see who'd look.

Now that I am in high school in Sheffield, Alabama, I go to the library during study hall and read everything. I like to read anything about how people feel and what they want. The librarian brings me her personal copies of five works by Sigmund Freud. When I went back to Sheffield for the first time as an adult twenty years later, I told her that I am now a professor of psychology and reminded her of the Freud. As I am trying to thank her, she asks earnestly, "Don, did I do the right thing?" She believes that it was pretty daring to expose a young and innocent mind to Freud. Maybe I can start a self-help group for adult children exposed to Freud by librarians.

Now to this point in adolescence, I have not had much experience with sex if you don't count "self-abuse." I admit that I am guilty over masturbating. Before I masturbate in the bathroom, I pick up the Bible and thumb it open and put my finger on a verse. If it is odd, I'll jack off, but if it is even, I vow that I will not. But when it's even I always cheat.

My adolescent sex fantasy is that I am a hero who rescues a girl from tigers or evil men. She is so grateful that she lets me have sex with her. I never imagine that she might want it, too, only that she loves me and does it for me. Gosh, I wish a tiger would come along.

One night I am out and learn that some boy has called my father and pretended to be my date's father. He tells my dad that I was too fresh, but that I didn't really hurt her, just scared her. Now I don't like the sound of this at all. Everyone knows my father will come down hard on me. Forewarned is forearmed. I hold off the impending storm by explaining what I have heard. Then I find out who I think it is, and we have a fight. I think my parents know there is going to be a fight, but they don't try to stop it. It is the first fight that I have had since about ten or eleven when I let the big boys talk me into fighting someone for the excitement of it. (I had my last fight at age thirty at Ohio State while playing basketball.) In the middle of that earlier fight I start feeling so guilty that I stop, afraid of being punished by my parents or God for fighting just for the hell of it. But this fight is different, more like a duel to defend one's honor.

My senior year in high school, I am starring in sports and am in the senior play where I am typecast as a fifteen-year-old brat who gets lots of laughs. But I am still a virgin. Finally a girl with a bit of a reputation asks me to go on a hayride with her. She is bad, meaning a nonvirgin; so I must try to be bad with her. One of my friends tells me it will be easy; he knows. I urge her to have sex with me and she reluctantly does, saying, "Is that all you dated me for?" I believe that I have hurt her feelings and feel bad, but I must have her or I am not a man. My condom falls off shortly after she helps me make entry. I am both frustrated and relieved because I feel so uncomfortable.

My buddy sees me in the hall the next day and asks me if I scored. I tell him no, but he makes such a racket—and she is just down the hall—that I say that I did just to shut him up. I am both embarrassed and guilty. We make it a couple more times, but I am so ashamed that everyone will know that I don't ask her to the senior prom. My guilty part believes that I hurt her feelings and that she deserved better than I could give her. At least I am no longer a virgin, but not only do I not brag about it, I am reluctant to admit it because I still wanna be good and having sex is bad.

I am voted the most studious boy in my high school. It puzzles me; I never had to study. I just liked to read. In these most conventional years of the 1950s, I am disappointed that I am not voted to the most popular group. It seems to me throughout my life that I am never really popular, just successful. Some people like me and some don't. I keep my distance, but I am a good friend when people seek me out. I must be close to someone or I am lonely, but I'd rather be lonely than say that I need someone. Of course, as an adult, I would rather speak my mind than be popular (I was once told this would keep me from becoming president of the Society for the Scientific Study of Sexuality [SSSS]). These are perfectly ordinary but manifestly silly rules in my interpersonal scripts.

Still worse are these scripted rules about success. I feel that I can never do enough work, and even after all that I do successfully, often I falsely but steadfastly believe that I am unappreciated. Next, I imagine this is so because people don't like me because my abilities threaten them. Outside of a clinical setting, I have little capacity to hear criticism as valuable feedback, often becoming defensively angry. In general, anger easily replaces my unexpressed distress and shame that I am not as perfect as I imagine myself needing to be in order to be valued and loved. Others' criticisms resonate with my inner voices until in my shame-rage I make everything worse by becoming blindly and senselessly angry. This bathes me in deeper shame and guilt, confusing both me and others, creating turbulence in the wake of my wrath. As the anger fades, I can see myself suddenly—naked, guilty, lonely— until I seek forgiveness and try to make reparation. The most painful of my guilt scripts is this—the guilt over my rage.

My dad has quit the Tennessee Valley Authority and taken a job in Butte, Montana. The night I graduate from high school in June of 1953, my family gets in the car and sets out for our new home. I am so upset that I almost get into a fight with a classmate, but I know that I am more distressed by the move than by him. So I don't fight, good as it might feel to do so. On the drive to Montana I read Freud's (1965/1901) *Psychopathology of Everyday Life*.

Everyone seemed to know everyone else in Sheffield, not counting the blacks who live in Baptist Bottom whom no one really counted as people. I had no exposure to alcohol, much less to drugs or violence, or to life really. I am a conventional and naive all-American WASP fundamentalist boy who wanted to be good in a culture where it seems to me everyone else is also good. And they are, but only if you don't know where to look or choose not to look too deeply to see the bad. And I believed the war between the states was about states' rights and not slavery.

Butte is a bitch. There is drinking, gambling, whoring, and fighting everywhere in this, to me, still wild mining town. I have no friends; I am lonely; I am shocked. So I just read the Bible and pray and read the Bible until I believe that I am called by God to bring these heathen to Jesus. Hallelujah.

My first sermon in Butte, confirming the optimism of the fundamentalist Christian, is titled "In God We Trust." I make one friend that summer. Together we go to the University of Montana as roommates. Bruce also decides to become a minister. Is this my first conversion? But his view of the Methodist Church is more liberal than mine; he doesn't even believe that Jesus literally walked on water. Bruce is like the brother I never had, but his picture of the world is representative of a working-class family from Montana, not Alabama.

In our sophomore year, Bruce or I commute back to Butte on alternate weekends to preach at the Silver Bow Methodist Church that peeks out among the mine derricks on the hill. We also form a formidable debating team, winning several intercollegiate tournaments, including the Northwest Regional.

But my eyes keep getting jarred open. The Montanans accept blacks but hate Native Americans whom I have idolized. In 1954, *Brown* v. *Board of Education* begins to raise my consciousness. During my sophomore year, my Dad loses his job, and my parents move back to Alabama. The first time I visit them by Greyhound bus I see a drunken black man in a white waiting room in Kentucky. Two MPs from Fort Campbell come in and painfully bend his fingers to rouse him from his stupor. Entering the first border state, I witness racial brutality. Of course I have memories from age five of the Ku Klux Klan burning out a family of squatters (Mosher, 1991a). I have to rethink race. Not only that, I have to rethink religion and science and America's ethnocentric political history. I experience what Erik Erikson (1968) described as an identity crisis and its reorganizing effect on personality. Evolutionary theory suggests that so-called cavemen were not necessarily fallen angels.

While a boy preacher I am still interested if untutored in sex. I am alternating preaching in Butte with fumbling efforts at sex with a girl who goes to Methodist Youth Fellowship in Missoula. She tells me that I should suck on her breasts, not just kiss them. She gives me the impression that, although she likes me, she prefers this Korean War veteran who knows more about doing it than I do. My main sexual interest seems to be in whether or not I can just get it in because that means to me that I have made it. If I do, then I am ready to split.

The pinnacle of my success as a boy preacher is also my turning point toward devout disbelief. At a statewide youth retreat, I am preaching on boxing with Jesus. Something like, "Jesus hits me with the left jab of love and the right cross of righteousness, and I am down for the count." All delightfully acted out. The audience stands up and applauds, which is about as appropriate as my metaphor and others that you might think of.

Both elated and embarrassed by my religious rhetoric, I am chagrined and annoyed to learn that a committee of ministers has banished me to my quarters out of fear that I will be sexual with the current apple of my eye. This both overestimates my underdeveloped seductive skills and underestimates her good-girl resistance. These preachers have turned a good scene bad. But it makes me think, a second epiphany that undoes the holy enchantment. I decide three things. First, I am certain that the Bible is not literally true, and I am not even sure that I can believe it as figurative truth. How can a God of love torture souls in hell for an eternity? The punishment seems far worse than my sexual sins. Second, Freud would say that these ministers are projecting their sexuality onto me and are hypocritically punishing me for the sins that I long for and that they only imagine might happen while probably secretly wishing it were them. Third, who am I to pose as a Christlike moral exemplar? When you get down to it, I am definitely not a saint, and although sometimes a fool, I don't covet it as a lifelong preference. Sexual embarrassment just seems to keep happening to me on its own.

Deciding that I had been too conventionally accepting of authority, both religious and parental, I still want to be good. Only now I redefine being good as being a scientific humanist. I flip the polarity by redefining science as good rather than religion and humanism as good rather than spiritualism, but this disenchantment and reversal of polarity was just the lesser variance within a larger messianic project of being good. Instead of waging war on sexual sin, without yet knowing it, I had begun a project of waging war on needless sexual guilt. I was saved from the ministry by Sigmund Freud.

During the summer after my junior year, I spend six weeks at Ft. Lewis, Washington, taking an officer's training course. I am miserable and lonely, but I can do the job. The other guys discover that I am a natural-born leader and keep making me their second-in-command so that I can tell them what to do and how to play these war games. I hate KP. I find myself leading the inspecting officer past my bunk during inspection, subtly beating the system whenever possible. The major who is observing our platoon tells me that when I am placed in the leadership role I excel, but that I never seek out the position. I am impressed by his observation. When we return to Montana in the fall, I am given a medal as the outstanding military cadet for my Ft. Lewis performance. The irony grates on me.

Early Adulthood

Naively, I apply to only one graduate school, Ohio State University, where I am accepted. Arriving at Ohio State I decide to become a scholar, developing the work habits that I had been taught the Mosher name stands for. Also, I decide that, now that I am out of college and have proved my dad wrong about getting married too soon, it is time for me to marry. Because I am guilty over sex and want to be sexual, I must be married. Because I have yet to develop much understanding of my feelings or much ability to communicate them, I push forward with impulsive decisions and actions. Feeling the need both to be sexual and to be married before being sexual, I precipitously propose to a virtual stranger and marry her between winter and spring quarters of my first year of graduate school. When needless sexual guilt restricts personal choices, it can prove catastrophic. My parents are taken aback by this decision, but the Bible tells them to accept it.

I was such a good student at Ohio State that to this day I remain unconvinced that I have lived up to my promise. For my M.A. thesis I turn to the issue of prejudice, which is a thorn in my humanistic side because I so easily accepted segregation and the status of blacks and whites in my youth (Mosher and Scodel, 1960). I complete it rapidly, do some extra research projects, and push up the taking of my various exams to finish the Ph.D. in three years and nine months. I excel during the two-hour oral qualifying exam. For my doctoral dissertation I develop a sentence-completion measure of guilt, beginning the studies of sexual guilt for which I remain best known (Mosher, 1965; 1966; 1979; 1994a, b).

After graduating in 1961, I serve my two years as an army officer as a psychologist at Walter Reed General Hospital. During this time, I am in psychoanalysis four times a week with a psychoanalyst-in-training who works as a psychiatrist at Chestnut Lodge in Rockville, Maryland. After telling him how good I am at doing things and demonstrating this by doing a few dream interpretations, I proceed to lie there silently, with my legs and arms crossed in a class A uniform at 6:30 A.M. each morning for about a year. Most of this resistance is my script about not feeling appreciated and my stubborn refusal to learn from him since how dare he be critical or even insightful when I had rather do it myself? Finally, I learn more about my interpersonal isolation and emotional detachment. In its second year, analysis becomes a good experience for me. I never stop my self-analysis.

As a neophyte psychologist the only thing I am sure of is that I know how to take exams. I discover that I am a skillful diagnostician but a lousy therapist. I begin to progress as a therapist when I can tell the dentist I am treating that his baiting me is "horse shit." Having learned to separate what is therapeutically useful assertion and the need to escape hostility, I begin to do the job of a therapist, but only to the extent that I start moving tentatively in the right directions.

I am saddened by the death of my graduate school advisor, Shepard Liverant, in an auto accident a year after I finish. In a few years I lose two other mentors, Alvin Scodel and George Kelly, to untimely deaths. Julian Rotter, who has always looked after my career, invites me back to Ohio State as a visiting assistant professor, but then he takes a job a the University of Connecticut. At Ohio State I am given unusual opportunities to assume responsibilities in graduate training. After two years there I am given tenure and promoted to associate professor. I become a diplomate in clinical psychology in the minimum time allowed. After receiving eight straight journal rejections, I succeed in publishing several scientific papers at Ohio State. My classic paper on the multitrait-multimethod matrix analysis of three measure of three aspects of guilt is accepted, as is, without any requested revisions (Mosher, 1966). After over a hundred publications, this is still unique in my experience. After only three years at Ohio State, due to the deaths or resignations of others, I find I am becoming the senior professor at age thirty. Although I am learning that accepting professional challenges is a road to growth, I still seem to myself to be too young for such a significant role.

By now, I am an attractive candidate for jobs and select the University of Connecticut from among several offers. Once there, I discover that I am no longer the only and biggest fish in a shrinking pond. It takes several years to reestablish myself, making me wonder about the wisdom of the decision to leave OSU. Although my academic work goes well, and I am quickly given tenure and become a full professor in three years, I still don't feel appreciated, a familiar theme.

A Professional and Personal Identity Crisis

At this time, I make two important career decisions. First, after convincing a panel that I can indeed get in touch with my angry feelings when they start to deny me entrance, I am accepted by the National Training Laboratory (NTL) Institute for Applied Behavior Science for their ten weeks of training as a group facilitator and organizational consultant. In effect, I have entered into the human potential movement with all its seductiveness and promise. The combination of my growing interest in sexuality and human potential catapults me into greater emotional intimacy, self-disclosure, risk-taking, and a series of sexual relationships.

After the NTL experience, I continue to pursue lengthy professional workshops to increase my clinical skills, working with such therapists as James Simkins, Sonia Nevis, Irving Polster, Joseph Zinker, Milton Erickson, Stephen Lankton, Jay Haley, Chloe Madonnes, and Virginia Satir, among others. They teach me a lot. I am not a natural therapist, but my hard work pays off. I discover that I can be a discerning and empathic therapist who will quickly and courageously go to the heart of the matter. Not only that, I am inventive when it comes to techniques. I create much energy in the process of doing therapy, finding that it fulfills rather than drains me. When you wanna be good and you are a good therapist, you feel good taking care of others.

Second, I am invited to do research for the President's Commission on Obscenity and Pornography (Mosher, 1973). This begins to build a commitment to sexology by the process that Tomkins (1965) described as suffering for a cause. The president of the university wants to pretend, hoping to avoid bad press, that there is a conflict of interest between researching pornography and teaching, but he gives in to reason. While doing this pornography research, I have to prove that a woman student with irate parents was adequately forewarned about exposure to sexually explicit films. I produce her signed informed consent. Some of my colleagues prove to be less liberal than I had imagined; they don't like sex research and raise a series of obstacles through the years. These obstacles include a set of special rules and precautions in the research procedures at UConn and require me, at various times, to defend my research against moral and legal paternalism and feminist outrage. These experiences alternately distress me, leaving me in tears, and anger me, vowing to win the fights. I publish position papers and rebuttals (Mosher 1986; 1988a; Mosher and Bond, 1992a; 1992b).

Middle Adulthood

When I see Susan across the room, I am taken with her dark, striking beauty and her charisma which discharges energy in the brightness of her smile and the vivaciousness of her sultry voice. We meet at a nunnery during a workshop conducted by Virginia Satir, a well-known family therapist. She is there with her husband, so I don't approach her. She wonders why I am avoiding her and quite directly asks me the reason. We dance. She is as wild as I, I think. I make indecent proposals which shock her. She is very far from wild, a near-virgin, the good girl I seek. I admire her integrity and determination; she is a tiger who does not need my protection. Rather than my heroically rescuing her, she rescues me from my foolish self. I enjoy her many parts: her passionate and wise woman, her delighted and delightful inner child who plays with me. I discover that I love her.

Believing my first marriage to be a mistake from its onset, I decide to divorce. With some trepidation, I call my parents to tell them that I am seeking a divorce and am now living with Susan. They ask me to put Susan on the telephone. They welcome her to the family. As always, my parents are consistently supportive of me. I discover that they also believe, although they had never said so until now, that my first marriage was a mistake.

When we go to visit them for the first time, my dad announces during the drive to their home that Susan will stay in the guest room and that they have purchased a new couch for me to sleep on. I begin to fume. Susan calms me, saying, that in their house my parents have every right to set the rules that we will follow. Once home, we have a very adult conversation about our sleeping arrangements. It is perhaps the first and best adult-to-adult conversation that I have had with my parents who ordinarily do not talk about such emotional topics. By the time we finish talking about how we each feel, my parents are comfortable with our sleeping together. Not only that, in a shining moment, my father advises me, "Take care of Susan and yourself during this divorce." This is advice that his guilty son needs to hear.

My wife, Dr. Susan Bond, is everything I want and need. I love her desperately. Three years to the day after we meet, we marry on Bastille Day, 1977. We are living one of the great love stories of modern times. Had I known her as a young man, my past would be commensurate with my love for her. I wanna be good with Susan more than with anyone I know. We are romantics who remarry each year on our anniversary.

After Susan and I come together my scientific work is reenergized. She is my muse. In 1979, I entered and won the first Hugo Beigel contest of the Society for the Scientific Study of Sexuality (SSSS) for best scientific paper (Mosher and White, 1980). After attending their annual meeting to receive this award, I was asked to serve on their board of directors, which I did for the next nine years, including a term as president (Mosher, 1989a). Always tending toward introversion, I was never active in a scientific organization until I was asked to come out and play. In SSSS, I found a supportive atmosphere among people who shared the same difficulties that I faced after identifying myself as a sexologist.

I soon discovered that people believe that if you study pornography or rape or S/M or what have you, you must be a card-carrying member or at least a fellow traveler of pornographers, rapists, sadists, and masochists. Not only was I considered weird personally, my science was put down as less respectable than other scientific pursuits by my department head. Despite my appeal to the dean and his sympathy when I published nine papers in a year and received only a moderate merit increase, the departmental decision stood. Colleagues raised so-called ethical or methodological objections to my work that reflected their own legal moralism or legal paternalism. I devoted a lot of energy to defending myself and others who may not defend themselves as well. Knowing more moral philosophy and being able to do sound science proved to be my best defense. I believe that socially disadvantaged sexual minorities deserve my advocacy (Mosher, 1989b, 1994c). I continue to try to overcome my own racism, sexism, and heterosexism. My own sexual history has led me past self-righteous moral judgment of sexual and gender sinners to empathy. I have either been there myself or could have been. Perhaps my best contribution to SSSS was in helping the society take a public role on issues of social policy based upon sexological knowledge (Bullough, 1989). Unfortunately, there are still many miles to go.

The Psychology of a Sexologist

In 1980 (Mosher, 1980), I published a theory of sexual involvement during sexual scenes. It said that orgasms result from optimal stimulation of the sexual skin and depth of involvement, which is a complex of attention to affects invested in the sexual images and action of the moment. In simple terms, this is a deepening emotional intimacy associated with physical and sexual arousal. I sent a copy of this paper to Silvan Tomkins, whose affect theory had influenced me (Tomkins, 1962; 1963). For the next ten years, until his death, Silvan, the only genius I have known, was my mid-life and best mentor (Mosher, 1992). He hypothesized that my sexuality is captured by my theory of three paths of sexual involvement: role enactment is my counteractive subscript; sexual trance is my defensive subscript, and partner engagement is my reparative subscript. What does this mean? (See Tomkins, 1979; 1987; 1991, for an account of script theory.)

Taking the Cat's Tail Tale as a nuclear scene, a script theoretic interpretation posits that I sought comfort by crawling onto women's laps sexually when I was frightened or distressed.

Now a nuclear scene is repeated as a sexual analog first as a celebratory script, by simply repeating the triumphs and tragedies that leave you greedy for more and cowardly about losing the dream of an idealized good scene. For me the idealized loss was my fear that my mother only held me when I asked her to or when I was distressed or frightened, not out of sheer exuberant joy or shared excitement at my very presence, not for appreciating the miracle of my unique self. I believed that I had to be good to be loved. If my distress was that I did not feel loved for myself, then my fear might be that I was somehow missing the juiciness of life, of sexuality itself as a good. Still better, that I feared the loss of meaning from a life without true love.

When the ratio of negative affect predominated over positive affect, whether as a young man desperately seeking sex or as a man trying to become his own person during a second identity crisis, I sank into defensive subscripts. Most of mine are introversive and trancelike: from reading in bed, to sexual fantasy and masturbation, to drinking, to tunnel vision, to macho moving-on when sexual relationships might deepen and threaten me.

To become regnant, my counteractive subscript required an overall balance of positive and negative affect in my life. As I achieved the success of becoming a professor, I felt more attractive and skilled. And I was. I compensated for feeling sexually unattractive or inept in my teens by demonstrating that I was indeed a desirable, seductive stud. Dramatic involvement in roles and sexual power predominated in this path. This is a power script striving to master the maximization of positive affect while minimizing both negative affect and affect inhibition, rather than a script that celebrates positive affect.

Preference for the sexual role-enactment script is correlated with a macho personality constellation, which, in my research (Mosher and Sirkin, 1984; Mosher and

Tomkins, 1988; Mosher, 1991b), is defined by four components: Violence as Necessary, Sex as an Entitlement (or callous sexuality), Danger as Exciting, and Toughness as Self-Control, which are, respectively, means of seeking power over other men, women, nature, and self. I study macho men to understand and free myself from my gender socialization and to protest an unfair gender hierarchy (Mosher, 1994d). Although I was enacting a macho script in many of my sexual encounters, the theme of guilt is more prominent in my own personality than the macho counteractive subscript. Still more prominent is my messianic desire to free sexuality from danger, disgust, guilt, and shame and to restore pleasure and love to sexuality as both naturally human and morally significant.

Thus, I am troubled by cultural feminists who insist that all men are politically motivated rapists and that pornography makes them so. This take-back-the-night strategy both radically oversimplifies the problem of rape and indirectly plays into right-wing biological essentialism. By reversing the polarity of who is good and who is bad within the gender hierarchy, it unfortunately keeps it intact as the dominant, normative, and male-privileged system of gender relations. Gender separatism is offered as a solution for male tyranny to women-identified-women, i.e., lesbian separatists. By maximizing gender differences, rather than minimizing human differences, it demonizes men as sexually rapacious and idealizes women as loving and caring. As a sex-negative and "politically correct" ideology, it equates "compulsory" heterosexuality with danger rather than pleasure. In contrast, the more sex-positive concept of respect for morally autonomous persons embraces sexual and gender diversity (Mosher, 1989b; 1994b).

As my life became still richer in positive affect rather than depleted by negative affect, I enacted my reparative subscript through engagement with a loved partner. My love bond with Susan Bond becomes reparative; she tips the overall balance of positive to negative affect through the excitement and joy that she brings me. I am enriched in scenes in which she shares her gifts of love. She is amazing grace—I once was lost, but now am found, was blind but now I see. She transforms my nuclear scene because she is all women at once, both universal and particular, unity within diversity, simultaneously Wife, Lover, and Friend. In sexual and loving union, we merge as one within a blissful universe in which we promise: only you, forever.

Commitment in a Sexologist

My life has been spent in hot pursuit of three questions. What do I feel? What do I want? What will make my life meaningful? I have pursued answers as an individual who must update his reports minute by minute, hourly, daily, monthly, and yearly. As a psychotherapist and sex therapist, I have helped others pursue their own answers to these questions. As a scientist I have pursued the answers to these same questions writ abstractly: What do people feel? What do they want? What makes a person's life meaningful?

Succinctly, my answer is: I wanna be good. But I feel such lust and anger, and I can be so naive, confused, foolish, and guilty. Yet I know that love and work, as Freud said, give meaning to human lives.

In another autobiographical piece, I wrote, "I study who I am in hopes that I might become who I most want to be" (Mosher, 1991a). I am saying that an analysis of being—honestly looking at who you are now—precedes becoming, reaching toward the ideal image that you have for yourself. And that you use both the windows into self and out into the world to see who you are and what you want to become.

I became a psychologist as part of a polarity flip from boy preacher to scientific humanist during an adolescent identity crisis. Disillusioned with my childlike and therefore unquestioning acceptance of authority, I sought new answers to old questions within the framework of a larger commitment to discovering truth and helping others. Most of all I had to understand guilt rather than sin, the value of affect expression rather than affect inhibition, love rather than lust, and being a person rather than becoming a man.

Like most sexologists, I am both a committed scientist and a committed reformer. Following Tomkins (1965), I believe the psychology of commitment results from a series of scenes which contain a set of triads (+-+) in which positive affect transforms into negative affect that must once again be transformed into positive affect. The scientist is acutely aware of the absence of the longed for and idealized object, permanent truth (or insight into one's self). When things go well the scientist enjoys the fruits of her labor, but it is as brief as it is sweet. According to Tomkins (1965, p. 156):

> Truth is a mistress who never gives herself completely or permanently. She must be wooed and won arduously and painfully in each encounter. With each encounter she deepens both the scientist's suffering and then his reward. It is a love affair which is never entirely and deeply consummated. Immediately following each conquest, the victory is always discovered to have been less than it appeared, and the investigation must now be pursued with more skill and more energy than before.

I know the truth of this depiction from the repeated cycles of seeking truth, finding the imperfections in your methods of search, in the tentativeness of the answer, in the questions that are raised that seem more pressing than those answered, and the subsequent excitement of a new idea that might provide a better answer and so on. I search for truth as both a scientist and as a person who seeks to understand his own life.

As a sex reformer (Mosher, 1991c), I experienced an original resonance to the general idea that human sexuality (and affect itself) is a positive good and necessarily part of human nature. I ventured risk on behalf of those who need to be saved from sexual guilt. More specifically, the decision to do research on pornography was a turning point, being a larger risk than I had expected because it entailed such suffering and punishment from my university and departmental colleagues. This deepened my identification with the oppressed. As a WASP man, by definition the oppressor, I feel guilty over such privilege because I identify with the oppressed and reject my dominant, white, Anglo-Saxon, Protestant male heritage while forever being identified with it by virtue of my birth. Considering pornography, I identify with the lonely and isolated male masturbator who needs pornography to evoke or enhance sexual fantasy so that he can find some form of sexual outlet (Mosher, 1988b; 1994e). But also, more generally, I identify with anyone who is confused, conflicted, and oppressed in the arenas of sexuality and gender. As a sexologist, I experienced personal oppression that further fueled such outraged identification. This led to greater risks, such as being an expert witness in pornography trials, which led to suffering at the hands of prosecutors, who asked questions like, "Is your expertise on group sex based on personal experience or scientific research?" or, "Aren't you being paid for your opinion?" and judges who threatened to hold me in contempt for stating that people are curious about and engage in oral sex in Atlanta, Georgia. So I took more risks and spoke out on behalf of sexual freedom for oppressed sexual minorities. Valuing my own autonomy, I fight against the threat to sexual freedom. The New Right doesn't like what it perceives as threats to its world order from sexual licentiousness and perversion (Mosher, 1986), and some cultural feminists insist that I must hate women and want to incite rape. Excitement alternates with distress until you reach a point of no return, until no other life seems possible than that of sexual scientist who seeks truth, sex reformer who fights irrational sexual guilt and self-righteous hatred of the sexual, and psychotherapist who heals the personally abused and socially oppressed. Such commitments, already shaped by my own pressing, urgent, affect-invested life issues, direct my work as a sexual scientist.

The most interesting part of the question about becoming a sexologist is: what was the original resonance that first attracted me? I have already told you the answer to that in many ways at many levels. I wanna be good yet must deal with my sexual lust and intense anger as I find meaning in life through committed love and work. My values—truth, love, justice—are ardently cherished. They remained the major variance in the midst of a late adolescent identity crisis that was resolved by a polarity shift from right-wing normative to left-wing humanist. Nonetheless, these fundamental values remained regnant and messianically sought. Each life project that I pursue, the study of sexual guilt, of macho personality, of involvement in the sexual scene, echoes a deep affective investment in my own life. Each has entailed a commitment born of deep and fascinated excitement alternating with intense suffering. I study others to know myself. I heal others to heal myself. I reform the world to make it just. I wanna be good.

References

Bullough, V. L. 1989. *The Society for the Scientific Study of Sex: A brief history. A publication of the Foundation for the Scientific Study of Sex.* Lake Mills, Iowa: Graphic Press.

Erikson, E. H. 1968. *Identity: Youth and crisis.* New York: Norton.

Freud, S. 1965/1901. *The psychopathology of everyday life.* New York: Norton.

Mosher, D. L. 1965. The interaction of fear and guilt in inhibiting unacceptable behavior. *Journal of Consulting Psychology* 29: 161–67.

———. 1966. The development and multitrait-multimethod matrix analysis of three measures of three aspects of guilt. *Journal of Consulting Psychology* 30: 25–29.

———. 1973. Sex differences, sex experiences, sex guilt and explicitly sexual films. *Journal of Social Issues* 29: 95–112.

———. 1979. The meaning and measurement of guilt. In *Emotions in personality and psychopathology,* ed. C. E. Izard, pp. 105–29. New York: Plenum Press.

———. 1980. Three dimensions of depth of involvement in human sexual response. *Journal of Sex Research* 16, no. 1: 1–42.

———. 1986. First-Hand Report. *The Meese Commission exposed.* Proceedings of a National Coalition Against Censorship Public Information Briefing on the Attorney General's Commission on Pornography, January 16, 1986, pp. 20–25. New York: National Coalition Against Censorship.

———. 1988a. Balancing the rights of subjects, scientists and society: 10 principles for human subjects committees. *Journal of Sex Research* 24: 378–85.

———. 1988b. Pornography defined: Involvement theory, narrative context, and goodness-of-fit. *Journal of Psychology and Human Sexuality* 1, no. 1: 67–85.

———. 1989a. Advancing sexual science: Strategic analysis and planning. *Journal of Sex Research* 26: 1–14.

———. 1989b. The threat to sexual freedom: Moralistic intolerance instills a spiral of silence. *Journal of Sex Research* 26: 492–509.

———. 1991a. Scared straight: Homosexual threat in a heterosexual therapist. In *Gays, lesbians, and their therapists,* ed. C. Silverstein, pp. 187–200. New York: Norton.

———. 1991b. Macho men, machismo, and sexuality. In J. Bancroft, ed., *Annual Review of Sex Research* 2: 199–247.

———. 1991c. Ideological presuppositions: Rhetoric in sexual science, sexual politics, and sexual morality. *Journal of Psychology and Human Sexuality* 4, no. 4: 7–30.

———. 1992. Tomkins's epilogue: A paean to human freedom. In *Affect, imagery, consciousness,* vol. 4: *Cognition: Duplication and transformation of information,* ed. S. S. Tomkins, pp. 355–72. New York: Springer.

———. 1994a. Guilt: Sex guilt. In *Human Sexuality: An Encyclopedia,* ed. V. L. Bullough and B. Bullough, pp. 237–42. New York: Garland Publishing.

———. 1994b. Guilt. In *Encyclopedia of Human Behavior,* ed. V. S. Ramachandran, 2: 467–75. New York: Academic Press.

———. 1994c. Sex-offenses: Social tolerance or criminalization. In *Handbook of Forensic Sexology,* ed. J. Money and J. J. Krivacska, pp. 369–96. Amherst, N.Y.: Prometheus Books.

———. 1994d. Gender. In *Human Sexuality: An Encyclopedia,* ed. V. L. Bullough and B. Bullough, pp. 232–37. New York: Garland Publishing.

———. 1994e. Pornography. In *Human Sexuality: An Encyclopedia,* ed. V. L. Bullough and B. Bullough, pp. 470–77. New York: Garland Publishing.

Mosher, D. L., and S. B. Bond. 1992a. "Little rapes," specious claims, and moral hubris: A reply to Korn et al. *Ethics & Behavior* 2, no. 2: 109–21.

———. 1992b. Ethics: Perceived or reasoned?: A rejoinder to Korn et al. *Ethics & Behavior* 2, no. 3: 203–14.

Mosher, D. L., and A. Scodel. 1960. Relationships between ethnocentrism in children and the ethnocentrism and authoritarian rearing practices of their mothers. *Child Development* 31: 369–76.

Mosher, D. L., and M. Sirkin. 1984. Measuring a macho personality constellation. *Journal of Research in Personality* 18: 150–63.

Mosher, D. L., and S. S. Tomkins. 1988. Scripting the macho man: Hypermasculine socialization and enculturation. *Journal of Sex Research* 25, no. 1: 60–84.

Mosher, D. L., and B. B. White. 1980. Effects of casual or committed erotic guided imagery on females' subjective sexual arousal and emotional response. *Journal of Sex Research* 16, no. 4: 273–99.

Tomkins, S. S. 1962. *Affect, imagery, consciousness,* vol. 1. New York: Springer Publishing.

———. 1963. *Affect, imagery, consciousness,* vol. 2. New York: Springer Publishing.

———. 1965. The psychology of commitment (Part 1): The constructive role of violence and suffering for the individual and for his society. In *Affect, cognition, and personality,* ed. S. S. Tomkins and C. E. Izard. New York: Springer.

———. 1979. Script theory: Differential magnification of affects. In *Nebraska Symposium on Motivation,* ed. H. E. Howe, Jr., and R. A. Dienstbier, vol. 26. Lincoln: University of Nebraska Press.

———. 1987. Script theory. In *The emergence of personality,* ed. J. Aronoff, A. J. Rubin, and R. A. Zucker. New York: Springer Publishing.

———. 1991. *Affect, imagery, consciousness,* vol. 3. New York: Springer Publishing.

———. 1992. *Affect, imagery, consciousness,* vol. 4. New York: Springer Publishing.

33

Female-to-Male Transsexual: Transsexual Sexologist

Jude Patton

Jude Patton is a female-to-male transsexual who has been active in the gender community. For many years he served as a major resource on radio and television for information about the F/M surgical transformation.

I NEVER PLANNED to become a sexologist. Instead, my childhood dreams were of becoming a veterinarian and, to that end, following high school graduation and brief employment in local small factories, I began to work as an animal health technician for veterinary practices and stayed in this field for seventeen years. In addition to partially fulfilling my childhood fantasies of becoming a veterinarian, this type of employment allowed me the freedom in the late 1950s through early 1970s of dressing casually in men's clothes and reduced the stress/demands from society to be more conventionally "feminine." I had consistently cross-dressed in masculine attire since childhood. As a result I was often ostracized by others.

As a child of eleven I had read of Christine Jorgensen's sex-change surgery but felt this was impossible for me to accomplish. Because of my personal dilemma concerning my sex and gender, from an early age I began to read avidly books and articles related to psychology, sociology, biology, and sexuality. I was largely self-taught following graduation from high school in 1958. Despite my best efforts at self-education, I did not learn until December 1971 that I could seek sex reassignment from female to male. Serendipitously, I became acquainted with a man who had been among the first of six female-to-male transsexuals treated at Johns Hopkins in the late 1960s. He gave me the name of his endocrinologist in Los Angeles, Gerald Leve, a physician who has treated several hundred transsexuals in the past twenty-five years. Dr. Leve evaluated me and referred me for a psychiatric evaluation. The psychiatrist approved me to begin hormone therapy, which was initiated immediately. Later, I contacted Donald Laub, M.D., then at Stanford University, and went

334

through evaluations by Stanford's Gender Dysphoria Program. In September 1972, I underwent the first of four surgeries (the last took place in September 1993) to complete sex reassignment from female to male.

Like most postoperative transsexuals, I never planned or expected to make my transition public. However, I never agreed with the then (and still) prevailing theory that transsexuals must keep absolute secrecy, and that they are deemed by some professionals "unsuccessful" if they do not comply with this recommendation. Also, during and after the transition period itself, I was to meet several professionals who encouraged my involvement in educating other professionals, peers, and the public about transsexualism and gender identity issues. Just before my last surgery in 1993 I received permission from Dr. Laub to attend a biennial meeting of the Harry Benjamin International Gender Dysphoria Association (HBIGDA) in Palo Alto. I was thrilled to be able to see and listen to some of the pioneers in the field, including Dr. Laub, Paul Walker, Richard Green, and John Money. Later, I was elected to serve on the board of HBIGDA for one term, the first transsexual ever to do so. However, this was by a narrow vote margin following much discussion and many negative comments by professionals who treat transsexuals but who feel that to be transsexual is a form of mental illness.

In late 1973, a F/M man who was a friend asked me to replace him as a guest speaker for a sociology class taught by Howard Fradkin at California State University, Fullerton. I agreed, but being very shy, was intimidated by the prospect of speaking to a class of graduate students in sociology. Fortunately, Dr. Fradkin and his students were kind and supportive; that initial experience motivated me to continue efforts in educating others.

In 1974, I enrolled in classes at Santa Ana College as a full-time student, still intent on pursuing my goal to become a veterinarian. Along with all the course work to meet preveterinary medicine requirements I also continued to take all available course work in psychology, sociology, and sexuality. At the beginning of my senior year in 1977, having transferred to the University of California, Irvine, to complete a bachelor's degree, I was told by my faculty advisor that because of my age, it would be next to impossible to gain acceptance to the veterinary medicine program at UC Davis and he recommended that I change my major. I graduated in 1978 with a B.A. in social ecology, then pursued a master's degree in Marriage, Family and Child Counseling at California Family Study Center (now Phillips Graduate Institute) through Azuza Pacific University. Just as I finished this program, I learned of the physician assistant program at the USC School of Medicine. I completed the program in October 1981, and began working as a physician assistant.

All through my college years I continued work in animal health care and for the postal service. Also, during this time I actively continued educating others regarding gender issues. In 1975 I met Sister Mary Elizabeth (then Joanna Clark) and we, along with a friend, began to collaborate in projects to aid the gender community in the greater southern California area. I also began publishing a newsletter, *Renaissance Update*. Most subscribers were transsexuals, along with a few professionals. We also formed Renaissance Gender Identity Services and began an out-reach to extend information and education, interacting with local professionals, educators, and agencies. As in most such efforts, our time and energy was given freely and there were ever greater demands for services, and absolutely no funding sources. We all donated our meager personal resources to continue our outreach.

Between 1973 and 1987 I was a guest speaker at colleges and provided train-ing for professionals in agencies, etc. This became (though largely unpaid) an almost full-time pursuit. In one year alone I spoke to more than two hundred classes and groups. Additionally, following licensure as a Marriage, Family and Child Counselor (MFCC) in 1980, I began a private practice in counseling, specializing in sex therapy. I completed requirements for certification by the American Association of Sex Educators, Counselors and Therapists as both a sex educator and as a sex ther-apist, joined the Society for the Scientific Study of Sexuality (SSSS), and later was approved as a sexologist by the American College of Sexologists and as a diplomate by the American Board of Sexology.

In 1977, I met William Heard, a psychologist in Laguna Beach who was run-ning a small group for pre-operative transsexuals. Dr. Heard allowed me to join the group as a sort of "peer counselor" at first, and later, when I became licensed as an MFCC, as a co-therapist, which I did until 1989. In 1978 I met Tye Roy, an anthro-pologist whose dissertation research was on transvestism. Later, we opened a book-store in Fullerton, which featured books on sexuality, women's studies, and men's studies. Tye organized a group of professionals who met monthly to provide out-reach and publish a newsletter on sexuality and disability. In 1981, I joined Rose-mary Pfuhl, MFCC, in establishing a private practice partnership as therapists.

During the 1970s and early 1980s, during and immediately after the "sexual revolution," there were many professionals in southern California who were (and still are) active researchers and writers. I was fortunate to meet Drs. Vern and Bon-nie Bullough, Drs. Jim and Veronica Elias, Dr. Richard Smith, Dr. Richard Docter, and Dr. Richard MacDonald, all from the faculty of CSU Northridge. About the same time I met Drs. Bill Hartman and Marilyn Fithian at the Center for Marital and Sexual Studies in Long Beach, California. Also, other professional mentors included Mona Coates and Shirley Lampert.

From the mid 1970s to the late 1980s, I participated extensively in aiding other professionals in research projects. There was media involvement too. At first, I was eager to accept any request to appear on radio or television, being totally naive about use of the media to provide education. However, I learned very early on that, for the most part, these media spots were exploitative: instead of educating the pub-lic, television and radio show hosts were largely intent on sensationalizing the sub-ject or being provocative, in an effort to make the show "entertaining." Eventually, I refused to accept radio or TV interviews. Because of time restraints, I also began to limit guest speaking to graduate students or professionals in agencies. Eventu-ally I cut back on all my "public" involvement in sex education. I also began to expand into the field of legal medicine and for several years this was my primary source of income. My private practice in sex therapy was relegated to a part-time pursuit, although I never lost interest and enthusiasm for the field and kept in contact with professional peers.

Formerly I had taken little time for a personal life, but this changed in late 1987 when I met my wife, Carol. We became acquainted through a mutual friend, who arranged for us to meet at a company Christmas party. While Carol had no knowledge at the time of my personal history, she did know I worked as a sex therapist part-time. Although eventually she discovered my "past" before I had a chance to tell her myself, she was able to transcend adverse comments and advice from others who were negative about transsexuals. We were married on November 12, 1988. Following this my formerly "singles" lifestyle changed abruptly. I was an instant stepfather to three teenagers, and my aging mother was also living with us. We all had to learn to adjust to the new "household" and to each other. My training as a marriage and family therapist did not prepare me for all the changes; however, Carol and I persisted, and her love and support has sustained us through some fairly negative circumstances and resultant personal losses in the past few years.

Significantly, it is the losses that have changed our life together now. Fate played an unkind hand in 1992 when, because of vast changes in the California Workers' Compensation System, our once-thriving business writing and editing legal/medical reports for physicians was lost literally "overnight." About six months later our second home in Big Bear Lake, California, was badly damaged in an earthquake. Carol was so frightened, she refused to return to the house. Until then, we had planned to move to Big Bear to live. The value of our primary residence also dropped by over 50 percent in the next year following sweeping changes in California real estate and the general economy. As a result we opted to move to "The Great Northwest," first in Portland, Oregon, for fourteen months, then Seattle in October 1994, struggling to rebuild our careers. Since living in Seattle, our salaries have improved so that Carol now works part-time as a medical coordinator for an attorney, while I've been working part-time as a physician assistant in psychiatry.

Until early 1995, efforts at once again working in private practice were largely not pursued. However, in February of that year I attended the International Congress on Gender, Cross-Dressing and Sex Issues in Van Nuys, California, and while there reestablished contact with former colleagues and met many professionals and peers who had become active in the field of sexology in the last few years. The conference itself brought together a wonderful blend of sexologists, educators, physicians, therapists, researchers and, most importantly, persons who are *living* the experience.

In August 1995, another milestone occurred when the first F/M conference was held in San Francisco, organized and hosted by that city's F/Ms. For the first time in history over four hundred F/M men came together to share support and to educate each other. The conference was a huge success.

Throughout my career as a sexologist, I have believed in, encouraged, and personally learned from dialogue between "professionals" and actual transsexuals. It is impossible to begin to understand the experience until you *share* it, not simply hear about it in a classroom, read about it in a book, or do interventions or give support in a medical office or therapy room. I believe those of us who share a dual role as *both* professional *and* person living the experience can provide new insight and create new paradigms. It becomes then, if we are willing to take the risk, a kind of "obligation" to do so. With those thoughts in mind, I am prepared to continue in the role of both teacher *and* student in the field of sexology, both locally in the Seattle area, but also nationally and internationally via electronic communication.

34

Penology and Sex

William E. Prendergast, Ph.D.

William E. Prendergast spent most of his career working with sex offenders in the criminal justice system and the victims they assaulted or molested. He has been the innovator of many of the techniques now used in such treatment.

WAS BORN on April 2, 1932, into a Slovak-Irish family suffering the results of the Great Depression. Life was hard and the family was dependent on "handouts" and charity for several years. I vividly remember standing in milk and bread lines and being embarrassed that my friends or classmates might see me there. Memories of my parents are also painful; my mother was in and out of hospitals from my earliest memories of her and died when I was only twelve years old; my father and I shared little communication and a combative relationship. Both these factors affected my later years and resulted in an almost obsessive independence.

I was enrolled in a Catholic grammar school operated by an order of nuns so severe and punitive that it was eventually dissolved by the Vatican. My main memories from this time period revolve around the emphasis on anything physical or sexual being evil. It was as if God created man from the head to the navel and then Satan completed the task. I somehow deeply felt that these teachings were wrong and resolved eventually to do something about them.

I also realized that the only way I would ever get out of the ghetto of poverty was through my natural abilities and so I became a serious student. My eighth-grade teacher, noticing my potential, kept me in during recess and cut short my lunch periods to tutor me and prepare me for entrance examinations into Fairfield Preparatory School. Her hard work paid off: I not only was admitted but also was given a scholarship. Maintaining honor-roll status was a condition of my scholarship, and four years later it resulted in a further scholarship to Fairfield University where I majored in education with a minor in psychology.

While a student, I also worked in order to purchase clothes, books, and for travel money (it was a long commute from home to school). All through my grammar and high school, and university years, I had a driving need to help others, especially peers and classmates. Once enrolled in college, I chose the YMCA as a means of earning money to support myself and of working with underprivileged kids like myself, doing all the things for them that no one had ever done for me, replacing many of the lost years of my childhood. Whenever I could help someone, no matter how minimal that help might be, the rewards were tremendous. Becoming a therapist appears to have been preordained and probably resulted from my many years of forced independence coupled with a need, all through my developmental years, of finding someone who would care about me. It was always easier for me to give than to receive and, to an extent, that remains true to this day.

My sex education occurred in the boys' toilets at school and on Boy Scout camping trips and consisted of every possible myth and erroneous "fact" imaginable. Confusion and anxiety resulted and I resolved that "someday" I would uncover the truth. This became a persistent quest throughout my formative years and, even today, I continue to devour all new information that becomes available on the subject.

During my school and college years, there were no sex-education courses offered and no discussion of sex was held except in private and between close male friends. I always felt that this was "stupid" since I viewed sex as a normal human function and something beautiful rather than repulsive and dirty as I was persistently taught. Sex remained important to me and felt natural and positive, in contrast to my strict Catholic teaching that sex was sinful and to be avoided.

At graduation from college, I had not chosen a specific direction for my graduate studies or my life's work. I only knew that I would be a therapist and devote my life to helping others and thereby helping myself. My professional career began in October 1961, when immediately after graduation from the University of Detroit with a master's in clinical psychology, I accepted an internship at the State Home for Boys in Jamesburg, New Jersey.

With no thought of entering the field of sexual crime and abuse, I began to be assigned a large number of boys who had either committed sexual crimes or who were the survivors of sexual assaults, both in the community and in the institution itself. After a short period of time, this became my specialty (since my supervisor and fellow therapists were openly uncomfortable working in this area). I was assigned *all* cases of this type.

My first major surprise and shock was to discover that these boys were repeating the same myths and erroneous facts regarding sex that I had learned some fifteen to twenty years before. I immediately ordered whatever materials I could find (mostly anatomical charts and illustrations) and began teaching sex education to these confused and mixed-up kids.

One case fascinated me and, in retrospect, set the focus for my future career. A twelve-year-old boy was assigned to me following an abrupt loss of his ability to speak (aphonia). The medical department could find nothing wrong physically with his throat or vocal cords and referred him to the "shrinks" (a defamatory name for all psychologists and psychiatrists in correctional settings at that time). The boy who went by the name Robby communicated with me in writing and with drawings. Realizing that he must somehow have been traumatized, I spent hours building up a relationship (rapport) with the boy and gaining his trust. I assured him that nothing that he revealed to me would leave the office without his specific permission (a practice I began then, some thirty-five years ago, and continue today with all my patients, especially abused children and adults).

After a week of daily contacts with no improvement in his speech loss, I received a call from Robby's cottage officer that Robby had to see me and that it was an emergency. I altered my schedule and cleared an hour to spend with him. When Robby arrived, I closed the door to my office and he immediately began to cry and continued to do so for more than ten minutes. I told him it was okay and put my arm around him. (Somehow I instinctively knew for many years that *readiness* to deal with abuse issues could be tested by physical contact. If touch were permitted with no signs of fear, stiffening, or withdrawal, this was an indication that a trust and readiness level had been reached and that the abuse issues could now be approached.) Robby threw his arms around me and continued to weep and shake. He then reached for the pad on the desk and drew a picture of a small, thin, young boy being sodomized by a stronger, older male. He added a balloon coming from the older male's mouth (as in a comic strip) and printed the words: "If you tell anyone about this I'll kill you!" On the little boy's lips, he drew a zipper and a lock. Now Robby's unexplained loss of speech made sense.

I had Robby admitted to the hospital and a sexual-assault examination was performed (mandatory in correctional settings), confirming that he had been brutally sodomized. Since Robby was at the institution on a truancy charge, it was simple to obtain a compassionate parole and Robby was released to his parents directly from the hospital. Naturally and rightfully, the parents sued and won. Several months after his release, Robby and his parents visited the institution and he came to see me at my office. For the first time, I heard Robby speak; his "thank you!" remains a permanent memory that I will cherish.

The satisfaction I received from this experience plus the awareness of the need for therapists to be able to comfortably handle sexual abuse cases immediately decided the focus of my future career.

Upon completing my internship, I transferred to the now-defunct New Jersey State Diagnostic Center, a juvenile, inpatient facility that accepted predelinquent and fully delinquent children and teenagers, ages seven to sixteen, both boys and girls. The center also performed all the court-ordered, post-conviction, presentence examinations on convicted sex offenders under New Jersey's special legislation. Most importantly, the medical director of the institution, the late Dr. Ralph Brancale, was a world-renowned forensic psychiatrist who specialized in sexual offenses and sexual abuse. Dr. Brancale became my mentor and a substitute father as well. I worked under his supervision in both the outpatient department, performing presentence evaluations on convicted sex offenders with a psychiatrist, and in the inpatient department with child and adolescent sex offenders and victims (I prefer the term *survivors*) of sexual abuse where the team consisted of a social worker, a psychologist, and a psychiatrist.

With my experience in the field of sexual deviation and victimization, I was quickly assigned exclusively to the inpatient department and specialized in sexual crime and abuse cases, remaining under Dr. Brancale's tutelage.

Some five years into my career at the center, Dr. Brancale invited me to lunch on a Friday and then to his office for a "chat." (I did not perceive the "come into my parlor, said the spider to the fly" motivation involved). Dr. Brancale sat back in his large judge's chair and asked me the following questions:

"Bill, aren't you tired of seeing the same kids coming back over and over after being abused or for committing new sexual offenses?" "Of course," I answered.

"And aren't you tired of seeing the same sex offenders repeating their crimes again and again and creating new victims?" "Of course," I answered again.

"Well, then, don't you think it's about time somebody did something about these problems?" "Absolutely," I said.

"Great! Then as of Monday, you're assigned to the state prison to open a new treatment unit for sex offenders under the governor's new mandate putting us in charge of this problem."

Note: To this time, convicted sex offenders were housed in the state's mental hospitals with minimal if any treatment, although the law mandated treatment. There had been a major scandal in one of these facilities involving the sex offenders abusing both child and adult patients housed there. Following a Senate investigation the issue became a political one. Demands came from the communities near these facilities to have the sex offenders removed and the governor agreed. Knowing of Dr. Brancale's reputation in the field, the governor made him fully responsible for all of the sex offenders under special legislation and ordered them all removed from the state hospitals in three months.

Shock and disbelief hit me like a ton of bricks but I remained speechless. Dr. Brancale smiled and would hear of no objections to his *coup*. Thus, in May 1967, I was appointed director of the first treatment unit for sex offenders, the Rahway Treatment Unit, located inside the walls of the then Rahway State Prison.

My first months there were a horror. We weren't wanted at the prison by either the staff or the administration and all of them did everything they could to make me quit. First of all we were labeled "baby-fuckers" and I was the head "baby-fucker." Almost no one spoke to me and the correction officers made my life difficult. Each day I was frisked and checked over and over before being allowed entrance to the prison. At each checkpoint, the frisking and checking continued. It took me almost forty-five minutes to get from the front door to 5-Wing (the administration forbid my unit from being called a treatment unit since he feared that the other, "normal" prisoners would resent the "baby-fuckers" ' receiving professional help when they did not).

At lunchtime, when I entered the staff dining room, there was immediate silence; when I sat at a table, whoever was sitting there would get up and leave. It was obvious to all that I was not accepted, even by the prisoners who served in the dining room.

Work supervisors did not want my inmates (a name I was forced to use) working in their area and had to be ordered to allow them entrance. Even then the supervisors treated them like dirt and let them know they were not wanted at Rahway.

Slowly but surely we began to be accepted. My men worked harder and were more reliable than the other prisoners. They were also more gentlemanly and better behaved. We formed sports teams and, when other prison teams would play us, usually won. This gained respect from the general prison population. One by one, staff and officers began to come around and even invited me to sit at their tables for lunch. Since my last name was difficult to pronounce (and I insisted that the Irish form be used), I soon became known as "Mr. P.," "Doc," or just plain "P." Those labels remain to this day.

In 1967, little was known about treating sex offenders. I had to develop specialized techniques since standard psychological methods did not appear to work or to provide any change. Of immense help was a training week sponsored by the Society for the Scientific Study of Sexuality (SSSS) in Palm Springs, California. I met some of the greats in the field, including Drs. William Hartman and Marilyn Fithian, Dr. Wardell Pomeroy, Dr. William Masters and Virginia Johnson, and many, many other learned and wonderful people involved in every aspect of human sexuality.

This was also my first exposure to sexually explicit visuals as treatment aids and to companies like Focus International who provide top-quality visuals that I continue to use. I also quickly discovered how puritanical the eastern United States was (and to a great degree still is, except for New York City) in comparison to California. It was like being on a different planet. I also learned that I was not as "liberal" or "emancipated" as I believed and was in for many shocking learning experiences that I will never forget. That week convinced me that I had made the right specialty choice and, although there will never be another conference like that one, I attend as many professional conferences as I can afford to update my knowledge and to keep in contact with these great thinkers and doers.

I excitedly returned to New Jersey and the Rahway Treatment Unit with a hundred new ideas and a great deal of new knowledge and resources. Convincing the "powers that be" in New Jersey to permit me to use sexually explicit visuals to treat sex offenders was quite a problem, but here again Dr. Brancale and a wonderful board of trustees persisted and forced the prison to allow me their use. They also provided the necessary funds.

For the next seven years, a small staff of consultants and I worked to produce a successful program that boasted a 90 percent success rate. Also, during these seven years, I begged, pleaded, and cajoled the "powers that be" to build a separate facility for the sex offenders, out of the prison control and environment that was hindering necessary treatment modalities and techniques from being implemented.

Finally on February 15, 1976, the Adult Diagnostic and Treatment Center was opened. The ADTC was unique in that while it remained directly under the commissioner of corrections, it was an independent, fully budgeted, and fully staffed facility. In 1976, it was the only one of its kind in the United States.

However, since all my career had been spent in the division of mental health, the commissioner of corrections appointed "one of his own" as superintendent of the new facility and I was made director of professional services. The original population of approximately 110 inmates now rapidly increased until it reached 300 (today I understand that it is over 700!). New staff and new techniques were developed, but the program was never quite the same. Corrections took over and became ever more important and controlling than therapy and the ADTC became more and more of a prison rather than a treatment facility.

In 1980, after working as a script consultant for more than a year, I went to Los Angeles to function as "technical director" for the NBC Movie of the Week *Rage,* starring David Soul and James Whitmore (playing me). The movie was based on one of the many innovative techniques that I had developed, and was loosely based on one of the many offenders whom I had treated with this technique. *Rage* is still used today as a training film by police departments, correctional facilities, and treatment agencies. Where I was concerned, *Rage* produced much jealousy and resentment in my "colleagues" as well as in the administration of ADTC since they felt that their contributions had been ignored and that it was my fault, although I had nothing to do with the content choices of the producers of the film.

Concurrently with prison work with offenders, I maintained a private practice, as a diplomate-certified sex therapist, working with victims. I firmly believe that anyone working in so emotionally charged a field as sexual abuse needs to be involved on both sides of the issue to remain in balance. It is too easy working with offenders to become an offender advocate, and in working only with survivors to be a fanatical survivor advocate.

To follow my own advice, I also treated sex offenders who were on probation with a condition of therapy. I do not charge survivors of sexual abuse for treatment; instead I charge all the offenders in my private practice one and a half times my normal rate to subsidize victim treatment. All potential offender clients are informed of this practice and, surprisingly, none of the offenders has ever objected.

Through all these years, I have conducted tours and presentations at ADTC and conducted seminars all over the United States for prosecutor's staffs, mental health agencies, probation and parole departments, and many other interested citizen groups. I have been a consultant to several mental health facilities as well as many law enforcement agencies; I am a board member of the International Incest and Related Abuse Groups, and have conducted training and lecturing in England and at Scotland Yard. I have also served as a member of the Monmouth County, New Jersey, Commission on Child Sexual Abuse. I consider their "IT HAPPENS TO BOYS TOO!" project to be one of the most important innovations that has occurred in the last several decades in the work of preventing the ritual of recurring sexual molestation and abuse. I have taken this program everywhere I lecture or conduct training, including to different cities and correctional facilities in England.

I will continue to offer training for prospective therapists for sexually molested boys and also for paraprofessionals interested in this project, including prosecutors, detectives, social workers, and others in the field wherever and whenever the need arises.

After retiring from the ADTC in 1991, I wrote three books on my professional experiences and the techniques that I developed and have found to be successful in working with both offenders and the survivors of sexual abuse/assault. The first, *Treating Sex Offenders in Correctional Institutions and Outpatient Clinics: A Guide to Clinical Practice,* deals with sex offenders. The second, *The Merry-Go-Round of Sexual Abuse: Identifying and Treating Survivors,* concentrates on victimology and covers origins, identification, and treatment. Neither of these books would have been possible were it not for the motivating, prodding, and wonderful counsel of my latest mentor, Dr. Nathaniel P. Pallone, who in his own right has published many books on forensic issues and on sexual offenders and the law.

The third book, *Sexual Abuse of Children and Adolescents: A Preventive Guide for Parents, Teachers, and Counselors,* is intended as a manual for parents on how to prevent your child from being sexually abused/molested, how to recognize the signs if your child is being sexually molested, and what to do and what not to do if this turns out to be the case. It also is intended for the survivors themselves so that they might understand why their abuse occurred and how to deal with it, as well as for potential sex offenders, those still in the fantasy stage, so that they will realize the potential damage they can do and that they both need and can find help.

I am presently working on a collaborative book with Dr. Pallone and one of his colleagues on priests and religious leaders involved in the sexual abuse of children in their flocks. It will be a work intended for clerical administrators and those involved in the training of future priests, ministers, and rabbis. The emphasis and focus will be on discovering potential sexual problems during the training process and treating them effectively prior to these individuals being assigned a congregation. It will not be focused on eliminating these individuals from their religious vocations but rather on helping them reach their goals in a healthy and sexually adjusted condition.

I recently completed teaching a graduate course in the Department of Human Sexuality at New York University and hope to continue teaching. The students were wonderful, interesting, bright, and productive. It was truly an experience that bode for hope in our youth and in the future. Teaching is and will remain one of my loves.

Future plans are to teach, lecture, conduct training seminars, to continue with a small private practice, and to find consultation work to "pay the bills." (State retirement is no great benefit and is impossible to live on.)

As long as I am able, I will continue to preach the gospel of *prevention* and, where convicted sex offenders are concerned, *treatment as prevention.* That has been my philosophy since I met my first sex offender and will remain such until I die.

References

William E. Prendergast. 1991. *Treating Sex Offenders in Correctional Institutions and Outpatient Clinics: A Guide to Clinical Practice.* New York: Haworth Press.

———. 1993. *The Merry-Go-Round of Sexual Abuse: Identifying and Treating Survivors.* New York: Haworth Press.

———. 1996. *Sexual Abuse of Children and Adolescents: A Preventive Guide for Parents, Teachers, and Counselors.* New York: Continuum.

35

My Accidental Career

Virginia Prince, Ph.D.

Virginia Prince, a biochemist and a cross-dresser, first entered the sex field by publishing a magazine devoted to cross-dressing. The first large-scale sample of transvestites was drawn from the subscribers to the magazine and marked the beginning of the first serious research into the topic since the writings of Magnus Hirschfeld at the turn of the century. Prince herself has been involved in much of the research and has traveled the world establishing clubs and organizations of cross-dressers.

"A CCIDENTAL" PROBABLY SEEMS a strange adjective to described one's career but when things develop without thought or planning or almost without one's awareness, what else can it be called? It does fit the facts. Probably many contributing to this volume had, by their junior year in college, decided on the field they wanted to enter—sociology, psychology, medicine, or whatever. With that goal in mind they took the appropriate courses and graduated. Most of them went on to graduate degrees and in due course into teaching, research, or counseling in their chosen field. For others their initial career plans provided a jumping-off place for something else. In my case I had career plans, but they were only an unexpected means to something much different.

A word or two about myself personally. I was born November 23, 1912, which makes me, as of this writing, eighty-four years old. My father was a surgeon and my mother a businesswoman involved in real estate and investments. I have one sister four years younger. I have been married twice and twice divorced, the first time because I was a transvestite and the second not because of it, although it played a big part in the court action. I had one son by my first wife. He died of drug-related causes.

I got my B.A. from Pomona College in 1935, with honors in chemistry. I went on to graduate school at the University of California at Berkeley in the department of biochemistry. I found the professor of pharmacology a much more pleasant man to work for and with, and so I transferred to the department of pharmacology at the University of California medical school in San Francisco, obtaining my M.S. in 1937 and Ph.D. in 1939. I then worked as a research chemist with several different companies, none of which had anything to do with my subsequent career. After getting my doctorate I returned to Los Angeles and took a job as a research chemist.

Several years later my professor had received some research grants, so he hired me back as research assistant and lecturer in pharmacology. Being on the faculty I could wear a white coat, look important, and go most anywhere on the medical school campus. One of the places I frequented was the library at the medical school in San Francisco and the Biomed Library in Berkeley to which I commuted by ferry to teach a class in the biochemistry department. My white lab coat got me into the medical library and my education in the fields of sex and gender began.

I didn't learn much about cross-dressing because there was very little in English on the subject besides Havelock Ellis's *Eonism and Other Studies.* That fact alone was a big contributing factor to my subsequent career—finding out all I could about the subject and passing it on in published articles, speeches, and counseling with cross-dressers as well as those who considered themselves to be transsexuals. At this point let me say that although this volume is about "sexologists" and their careers, I don't really consider myself to be a sexologist. Since sex and gender are not the same thing (although they certainly are related), I could more properly be termed a "genderologist" (to coin a new term). I have never been professionally concerned about sexual anatomy, reproductive behaviors, and functions or social attitudes about various forms of sexual activity.

Gender has to do with the various forms of behavior characterizing males and females and the qualities known as masculinity and femininity. All my activities and interests have been in these areas. It is just one more example of the unfortunate tendency to equate sex (anatomical and sociological) with gender (psychological and sociological) that leads people to think that when they are talking about some aspect of sex that gender is automatically included and vice versa.

I had been a transvestite (old term) or a cross-dresser (new term hereinafter abbreviated as "CD") since the age of about twelve. At first I utilized my mother's clothes and by the time I was in high school I had become accustomed to go out of the house, to ride buses or streetcars downtown, go window shopping, eat in restaurants, and go to movies. That is, I had progressed to the point of being a girl in public and passing as such. There were no qualitative changes in this aspect of my life for about the next thirty-five years, only quantitative ones. Although I was able to do most anything while dressed *en femme,* I kept the whole thing a dark secret for fear of what parents, friends, employers, and others would think of me if they found out. There was nothing effeminate or sissy about me in those years. I earned my letter in track in both high school and college, I ran both cross-country and the half mile. I was neither tall, big, nor heavy but I wasn't a pantywaist either.

In late 1939 or early 1940 I had met a girl in a church group that I attended and in 1941 we were married. The day before I had burned all my feminine wardrobe. I wouldn't be needing it any more now that I would have a real live woman around, right? Wrong! Marriage didn't affect my desires at all, it just made it more difficult and risky to satisfy them. Neither has it solved the problem for thousands of others. Yet therapists continue to feel that the dressing is just a substitute for a real woman and presume that marriage will solve it all. It doesn't and it can't because marriage involves an emotional relationship with another person while cross-dressing involves an emotional relationship with oneself. Thus the former does not change the latter.

The marriage took place early on a Saturday afternoon in August; after the ceremony and a reception in the yard we took off on our honeymoon. We drove to Santa Barbara for our first night together and next day, Sunday, we continued to Oakland, looked for and found an apartment, and on Monday I started a new job as a biochemist at the University of California, San Francisco.

I had always wondered about the why of cross-dressing and, being unable to find any books about it, had concluded (like almost all other CDs) that I must be the only such male because if there had been a lot of others there would have been a lot of information available, and in the thirties and forties there wasn't. Just prior to my marriage I thought I had better check it out, so I went to a psychiatrist who decided that since I liked high heels it was "phallic symbolism," which didn't help me a bit. I went to another and he came up with "unresolved Oedipus complex," which also didn't help. So I gave up on psychiatry, got married anyway, and just kept my inclinations a secret.

Having also become part of the medical faculty at the university, I could attend the psychiatric conferences at Langley Porter Clinic, a state mental hospital attached to the medical school. I enjoyed this because I had always been interested in psychology. Much to my amazement, one day they presented a young man who had recently been to court to have his name changed to "Barbara Ann." The court did this on the basis of a urine test which showed a high estrogen titer, a result made possible by the fact he had used a urine sample from his girlfriend. The physicians and judge assumed that he was inherently a female and granted the request. This proved to be the very beginning of my "accidental career" because it turned out that this person had been in my class at Pomona College and lived in the same dorm. He was a CD as was I. We knew each other generally but neither of us knew of the other's interest in feminine attire. The revelations about him were terribly traumatic to me sitting in the audience, because practically everything said by him and about him applied equally to me. Yet he was the first other CD I had ever seen. After the presentation was over it was announced that next week they would present another transvestite. You can bet I was there.

I hung around after the presentation until the person who had reported on the psychometric findings of the case was the last one present. I went up to him, complimented him on his presentation, and said that I found the subject of male cross-dressing fascinating. We walked out to his car still talking and he invited me in to show me a large photo album full of pictures of other CDs. It turned out that he was one himself. With so many pictures it was obvious that I was not alone in my interests. I managed to memorize the address of the girl who had just been presented. She also lived in Berkeley. I made contact with her and visited her, the first real live CD I had ever met. (Please note that it is customary in CD circles to use the feminine pronoun when referring to someone in the feminine mode.) Since I was on the faculty I could not tell her my real name (paranoia was rampant in those days), but I had to have a name I could easily remember. I lived on Prince Street and my father's first name was Charles, so I became Charles Prince. Subsequently, when I was able to meet others, I feminized it to Virginia Prince.

So now the first big, decisive factor in my future life was about to take place. Having tried private psychiatrists with no success because they didn't know enough to deal with me, I resolved to take another chance. The doctors at Langley Porter evidently knew quite a bit about the behavior since they had presented two cross-dressers. I decided, therefore, that I would consult Dr. Karl Bowman, the director of Langley Porter, and who had twice been president of the American Psychiatric Association. With my faculty appointment at risk nobody less than the director himself would do. His secretary couldn't understand why I wouldn't see anyone but Dr. Bowman. And I couldn't tell her but I got my way.

Dr. Bowman was in his fifties or sixties at the time and a very kindly and gentle person. I related the, to me, terrible tale of wanting to wear dresses, heels, and lipstick. He listened quietly and then pulled out the lower drawer of his desk, put his feet up on it, leaned back in his swivel chair, and, with his hands behind his head, took a deep, relaxing breath and said, "So what else is new?" I was upset, almost angry at him. Here I had told him something that was terribly important to me and which I had worried about for many years, and he comes up with a flippant answer like that. However, after a moment he went on to say, "What's so great about that? There are thousands more like you. In fact I have seen dozens of them myself when I was in New York."

Then he said the words that really initiated my career: "You must learn to accept yourself as you are and to relax about it."

Shortly after that I left his office, but I have never forgotten his words. The following year the grant under which I was employed ran out and I went back to southern California for a job as a research chemist. After several changes of job, I found myself associated with a partner in a chemical manufacturing business. In about 1944 I married for the second time. We had gotten into manufacturing grooming products for beauty shops which led to making similar things for grooming dogs.

My wife was crazy about animals, so she took on the selling of the products to pet shops, grooming parlors, and veterinarians. She did very well and everything succeeded for eight or nine years after that. During this time, I began exploring the possibility of a publication for CDs. From various sources I managed to assemble a mailing list of twenty-five people, each of whom was willing to contribute four dollars, and so I started *Transvestia* magazine with a working capital of a hundred dollars. It was the first publication in the country designed specifically for heterosexual CDs, and the first issue appeared in mid-1960. It was digest size and for most of its hundred issues was ninety-six pages long. It contained a balance of fiction, articles, case histories, opinion pieces, biographies, poetry, and two editorials. It grew slowly and survived for twenty years before I retired it and myself. Those twenty years were, in effect, my career. I published the magazine because of Dr. Bowman words to me: "Learn to accept yourself." These were not just for me, because I took them to heart a long time ago, but for my readers and those I counseled.

I have written four books to help in this process. All have been published by the house I established, Chevalier Publications. The first was *The Transvestite and His Wife*, written to help wives understand and thus, to one degree or another, deal with transvestism in their marriages rather than resorting to divorce. The second book, *Understanding Cross-Dressing*, was written to help transvestites themselves deal with the subject. Those who practice the behavior need to understand many aspects of it in order to be able to accept themselves. The third book was titled *How to Be a Woman Though Male*. It is just what the name says, an instruction book for those males who wish to express their feminine side in a public way. There is information about the obvious areas of hairdos, makeup, clothing, and so on. But there are also chapters on public conduct, feminine attitudes, behavior patterns, and legal matters as well as on change of gender and change of sex through surgery. The fourth book has not yet been published but its tentative title is *Everything about Cross-dressing*. It is intended as an explanation of the behavior for the general public.

I long ago realized that because of society's narrow views about CDs, those who practice it have three monkeys on their backs: guilt, shame, and fear of the consequences of discovery. Thus they do not accept themselves. Since I had been through all of those phases myself I wanted to help others to learn to deal with it. Thus the inside front cover of all issues of *Transvestia* said, "The purpose of this magazine is to provide entertainment, education and to help its readers achieve *Understanding, Acceptance, and Peace of Mind*." This has been my life's purpose ever since.

After several issues had appeared, it became apparent that while it was great to have a publication where one's contributions could be printed and other CDs could read and comment upon them, and one could make a public statement by having one's picture printed, it really wasn't sufficient. People needed to be able to meet face to face with others like themselves, to compare notes, pleasures, and problems. So to this end I rented a small room behind a church in Hollywood and sent out invitations to subscribers within driving distance. I asked them to bring two paper bags—one to contain chips, dips, or other edibles and the other a pair of nylons and a pair of heels. I gave no explanation for the latter. Note, this was in 1961. How was I to get twelve men, all of whom were CDs but none of whom knew any of the rest, to relax, accept the others, and let their guard down?

They assembled, sat around in a circle, and gazed curiously at the others. Was that man a policeman? Was the one next to him an FBI agent? Everyone present had something to lose and all were suspicious. They didn't know whether to admit that they were CDs or not. After a time I said, "Well, you have eaten up all the goodies from one set of bags, now it's time to see what is in the other set. So take off your shoes and socks and put on your nylons and high heels."

Each of them did so. The idea was that if that guy you thought might be a cop had a pair of heels that fitted him he was probably one of "us," namely, a CD. So the group came to be known as the Hose and Heels Club. We had three or four congenial meetings and the participants appreciated being able to meet each other. So I decided to go national.

In 1962 I formed an organization known as the Foundation for Full Personality Expression or FPE for short. This referred to the idea of being able to express one's feminine side as well as the daily masculine presentation, this being "full" expression of one's personality. The first chapter of FPE was therefore the "Alpha" chapter in Los Angeles, and it still is. As people heard about the organization and read about it in *Transvestia,* they began to form chapters in many American cities.

I had one bookstore on 42nd Street in New York which sold mainly erotica; evidently tourists and others who visited 42nd Street found that particular store and bought a copy of *Transvestia* to take home with them. Soon I was getting subscriptions from CDs in England, Denmark, Sweden, and even Australia and eventually there were chapters in all those countries. The combined Scandinavian countries still call their group FPE of North Europe and it has a membership of several hundred and subgroups in each of those four countries.

About 75 percent of CDs are married: while many have not told their wives about their interests, many others have either done so or their wives have discovered the activity. The wives' biggest fear was that the husband was either gay or transsexual. To allay such fears, I decided that FPE would not admit homosexuals or transsexuals. The whole idea of the group was to give CDs a place where they could meet others in a safe place and discuss the subject or interact with others in a friendly, nonjudgmental environment. Each person could bring his wife, if she was willing, and wives could meet other men with the same desires as their husbands in order to learn that such individuals were not sick, crazy, homosexual, or about to undergo surgical reassignment surgery (SRS). It was my hope that such experiences would help the wife to deal with her husband's activities and thus would help him to accept and be comfortable with his feminine side.

After I had gotten several chapters of FPE going in various cities, thus proving that there were enough CDs around to support organizations, there were those who started other groups not affiliated with FPE mostly because of its admission policy. We were (and still are) accused of being narrow-minded, biased, homophobic, and bigoted for not being willing to accept all those who cross-dressed. It was simply a recognition that I and FPE couldn't be helpful to everybody so I concentrated our efforts on those whom we could help, namely, those like myself and the first members of the Hose and Heels group, i.e., heterosexual CDs. So over the years FPE grew into many chapters (over thirty as of this writing). Many other non-FPE organizations sprang up, too. Today there are nearly two hundred groups for transgendered persons (including those for transsexuals) in this country alone and fifty or sixty more around the world. All that growth in less than thirty years after my original little Hose and Heels Club. It's amazing.

My life seemed to be proceeding smoothly. My wife and I had built a new home in the Hollywood Hills, I had a magazine and a social group going, and my company was growing. My wife was very accepting of my activities and I frequently went out as Virginia. Then all of a sudden everything blew up. A Los Angeles CD friend had been corresponding with a broad-minded woman in the East who had urged him to speak frankly and tell her all about his interests and activities. When he moved from the city, he gave me her name and address and suggested that I carry on the correspondence with her. I wrote her one letter telling her about myself and my interest in the feminine side of my nature. I said that while I was a sexually normal male it would be great to be able to have sex with a female while I was *en femme* myself. There was no sexy or off-color language in it, just a straightforward description of what I would like to be able to do with her should we ever meet. I wrote only the one letter and never got a reply, so I gradually forgot about her.

Then, about a year later, a postal inspector came to my office and arrested me on a charge of sending obscene letters through the mail. It turned out that the person to whom I wrote, thinking she was a woman, was actually a man. Thus I, a male, had written to another male about a sexual activity. So ipso facto I was a homosexual to the post office. This was in the mid-sixties, when the post office was prosecuting gays and was concerned about pornography; whenever they got a lead on a CD they would search and seize any literature or women's clothing they found. So naturally they took off against me. When shown the letter, I didn't deny writing it because it seemed so innocuous that I didn't see how they could make much of it. But they took me downtown for arraignment. My attorney who bailed me out told me that I must get a lot of letters of recommendation and support for the probation officer. That was very embarrassing because up until then my interest in cross-dressing was known only to fellow CDs and my family, and they were not very happy about it. But I did it and spilled everything to the probation officer. Then came the big explosion that really started my "accidental" career.

I had to go to trial. I pleaded guilty because I had written the letter and because a not guilty plea would probably have lured some reporters to the trial, which would have been very hard on my father, a very prominent surgeon. The trial started with the judge asking the DA to present his case. He hardly mentioned the letter and gave no specific quotations from it; but the charge was mailing obscene matter and he generalized about having to put a stop to such things, make an example, and so on. He ended up requesting the court to order my post box closed and the magazine discontinued. Turning to me, the judge said, "What do you have to say about that?" I replied that I didn't see what point there was in closing the magazine or the post box because the magazine was not in any way obscene or off-color, and that it had prevented several suicides and saved a number of marriages. In the end the judge had no choice but to sentence me since I had pleaded guilty. So I got a sentence of three years in prison and five years of probation. Fortunately, I did not have to serve any jail time.

At that time there was a masquerade ordinance in Los Angeles. I had been accustomed for years to going out shopping, to restaurants, movies, everywhere, as a woman. But when you are on probation you can't break *any* law, even a minor traffic ordinance, on pain of having to serve the original sentence. After the sentence was handed down I was out in the hall simply having a fit, yelling, screaming, jumping up and down, and making a tremendous scene. Because of the probation I was being forced back into the closet, no longer able to live my feminine life out in the world. I was, in effect, being put into a psychological jail and I couldn't stand it. My attorney came up with a solution. "Why don't you give lectures on the subject? I'll fix you up with my local Kiwanis club." In desperation and with much hesitation and fear I agreed because It was the only way that Virginia could have any life at all.

It was a major challenge to figure out how to stand up before thirty or forty ordinary businessmen in a service club, dressed as a woman and trying to explain to them why an otherwise "normal" (that is, heterosexual) male would want to cross-dress. But after happening on the paper by John Money and the Hampsons dealing with pseudo-hermaphrodites I was able to manage it because there was a great definition of gender in their paper and I made this the basis of my talk. The meeting was successful; afterward a man came up to me and said, "That was very interesting. Would you come and speak to our Pasadena Kiwanis Club?" That was the beginning of my "accidental career." It was also a magnificent test of the old saying, "It's an ill wind that blows no good!" The judge's sentence was assuredly a very "ill wind," but it forced me to really examine the phenomenon of cross-dressing so that I could speak about it in public and in general while dressed, rather than just in personal terms and in private. That was the "good" part.

I went on to speak not only to Kiwanians but Rotarians, Optimists, Lions, Sertomans, Knights of Columbus, and a few other less well known men's clubs. When invited to speak to a club, I always asked them to send me a letter formally inviting me to appear and speak at a certain date and location and to do so dressed as a woman. I carried this with me when I went to speak in case I had any traffic run-in with police who might charge me with violating my probation. After several such lectures and the resulting questions I realized that I couldn't possibly cover all aspects of the subject in twenty minutes, so I composed a little pamphlet about it to be passed out on future occasions. My hope was that if they read it and learned more about the subject, they would not so readily condemn someone whom they heard of or read about as being a homosexual or mentally ill. Hopefully if a father in the group were to discover that his own son was a CD he would be better prepared to deal with it than before. Soon I took to going into the police stations of the cities where I spoke and leaving some of the pamphlets with the chief or the head of the vice squad to be passed out to their officers. I did this in the hope that any officer stopping what appeared to be a woman but whose driver's license said "male" would be a bit more understanding and compassionate.

In 1968 I received a long-distance phone call from station WBZ-TV in Boston asking if I would be on a talk show there. They wanted a psychiatrist to accompany me, so I recommended Dr. Leo Wollman of New York who was an associate of Dr. Harry Benjamin, the patron saint of the transgendered community. The program's interviewer began, rather apologetically, "Virginia, I don't want to hurt your feelings, but I think you are a little abnormal." I replied that I wasn't hurt but that I didn't consider myself abnormal. What I was, was "statistically unusual" and proud of it. Every name in history that you can remember was statistically unusual, otherwise you would not remember him or her.

Dr. Wollman brought a woman friend along, Deborah Feinbloom, a sociologist, who became very interested in the subject of cross-dressing. I introduced her to the Boston, or Gamma, chapter of FPE. She worked with them and with what she learned from me and from them, she published a book titled *Transvestites and Transsexuals.*

As with the service club experience, the first successful TV interview led to more radio and television shows. While these shows didn't offer me anything more than transportation, lodging, and food, they paid off by allowing other CDs who might tune in to find me since I had no way of finding them. This resulted in an increased readership for *Transvestia* but, much more importantly, it proved to a great number of otherwise closeted CDs that there were others like themselves out there. Since I always got a chance to mention FPE on the air many such persons joined it. Thus my "career" as friend, counselor, philosopher, and publicist for the CD community got under way.

One of my readers was an attorney in Florida. During the time the post office was harassing any CDs they ran across, he became worried about himself and his reputation should they find out about him. He wrote to a friend who was a former solicitor general for the post office and told him about me and my problems with them. The reply came back to the effect that it was unheard of to prosecute on the first offense. My Florida friend sent me a copy of the letter. So on one of my speaking tours, I resolved to visit the office of the Chief of the Postal Inspection Service.

Before I went into the building I phoned the former solicitor general, introduced myself, and told him what I was about to do. I have forgotten the gist of the conversation, but I do remember that he told me to call him again after I got out of the building. I remember feeling as though his request were a caution that I might not be allowed to come out of the building. It was scary but I screwed up my courage and went in the office—as Virginia, of course. I told him why I was there and showed him various documentation, including a letter from Dr. Harry Benjamin. He told me that I should talk with another man who was in charge of the mailability section. The man came and escorted me to his office where we talked for nearly two hours. I explained the whole behavior pattern to him, with emphasis on the fact that homosexuality didn't enter into it and that neither I nor my readers were gay. I was evidently successful since from that day forward no more of my readers were harassed by postal inspectors.

As for my own situation, after receiving a copy of the solicitor general's letter I went to the chambers of the judge who had sentenced me and asked his secretary if I could see him. She had hardly finished saying that he seldom saw people out-side of court when the judge himself walked in and consented to see me. I had brought a lot of material with me, some of which I had gathered for the probation report. I reminded him of my case and of the DA's statements. Moreover, I told him that I thought the whole thing was a railroad job by the post office on the pre-sumption that I and most of my readers were homosexual. I also showed him the solicitor general's letter. The upshot was that the judge told me to have my attor-ney file an application for termination of probation and that he would sign it. My period in purgatory was finished. I was free to be a woman whenever and wherever I wished as long as I didn't do something illegal. Even the Los Angeles anti-mas-querade ordinance was found illegal later that year on two grounds: (1) it was an unequal application of the law since it was not enforced against females, and (2) a local jurisdiction could not legislate in an area where a higher jurisdiction had already ruled. California had a state ordinance making it illegal to wear "a mask, wig or other regalia or paraphernalia to avoid detection after committing a crime or escaping from custody." So I was home free.

I had sent out questionnaires to all readers of *Transvestia,* all members of FPE, and to any other CDs I could contact. It asked all sorts of questions relative to CDing. When finally compiled there were 504 cases and this was and remains the largest series in the literature on this subject. The first professional presentation of the results were to the American Psychiatric Association convention in Hawaii, which I attended as a woman, my first away-from-home experience. When I had arrived at my room, tipped the bellboy, and was alone, I went out on the balcony overlooking beautiful Waikiki Beach. Suddenly I began to cry very hard. The situation was just too much for me. I never expected to get to Hawaii at all, yet here I was in Honolulu and as a woman, Virginia! And I was committed—I didn't have a stitch of men's clothing with me. It was literally unbelievable. No longer was I a semi-frightened cross-dresser leav-ing my home for a single afternoon/evening adventure. I *was* a woman to the world and I was going to read a paper to an audience of psychiatrists, psychologists, and other professionals on a subject that I knew more about than they did with all their degrees and diplomas. It just couldn't be happening, but here I was.

I had only planned to attend the sessions in Honolulu, read my paper, and go home. But the convention was to continue on Kauai, Maui, and then to the Big Island for sessions in both Hilo and Kona. My paper was well received and I asked several of the doctors whom I knew, including Richard Green and Robert Stoller, what they thought about my attending these other sessions now that my "cover" was blown and it was clear that I was a "wolf in sheep's clothing," or a male woman. They all assured me that it would be fine and urged me to continue the trip. When some of us visited the orchid nursery near Hilo, orchids were passed out to all the women in the group, including me. The custom in Hawaii was to wear the orchid over your right ear if you were a married woman and your left if you were single and "still looking." Since I didn't qualify either way I put mine right in the mid-dle over my forehead which roused a good chuckle from everyone else.

Twenty-five years later my questionnaire was again sent out; this time it resulted in slightly over 1100 responses, which are as of this writing in the process of being computerized and prepared for publication. The study was repeated because the so-called sexual revolution had taken place in the interim and it seemed of interest to see what effect the more open society would have had on the CD community, Apparently little or none, as the responses were about the same as before. About 73 percent of CDs were found to be married and about 70 percent of them were fathers. The educational and economic levels were much higher than the general population. Most reported a normal childhood with no indication of undue favoritism by one parent or the other or of undue neglect or domination by one parent. I regard the collection and publication of both of these surveys as one of the main contributions of my career because the results have pulled the rug out from underneath those who saw some sort of early familial pathology. Another important finding was that there was a lower incidence of homosexuality among CDs than Kinsey had found in the population as a whole. This put to rest the prevalent notion that cross-dressing was only a form of homosexuality.

The convention proved to me that it was possible to pass and be accepted as a woman in social circles, even though this was a specialized professional group and not representative of society at large. I resolved therefore to put myself through some tests to see if I really could be accepted for what I appeared to be—a woman. I would return to Hawaii the next summer and stay at a hotel where I previously stayed, seeing the same desk clerks, chambermaids, waiters, and guests repeatedly over several days. This would seem to be a critical test of my "womanhood." I passed without any problems.

The year after that I took a tour group trip to Alaska. There being a shortage of rooms in Nome, I was assigned one of the other women in the group as a roommate and got my first lessons in woman-to-woman interaction. The experience was valuable because I shared rooms with several other women on subsequent trips. So these "test" experiences satisfied me that I could "be" a woman in ordinary society. (Note that I said "woman"-gender not female-sex)

I increasingly traveled as a woman, even crossing the Canadian border as one, without any interference or even a second look. Jumping ahead a bit, in 1976, I was invited by a psychologist to attend a nude encounter therapy session. By this time, I had taken estrogen and developed B-cup breasts, and I thought it would be the final proof of self-acceptance to go to the encounter where both my female breasts and my male organs would be visible to everyone. It was a deep experience; I broke down and cried my heart out because I had wanted so long to be a girl, and here I was being accepted as one even though my maleness was evident. This added greatly to my self-confidence and self-assurance. In effect I proved to myself that I really was Virginia regardless of what my anatomy said.

I should make it clear at this point that I have not had SRS nor do I wish to. There being no term to describe a male living full time as a woman without surgery, I originally coined the term "transgenderist" to describe myself and others like me.

It was subsequently adopted as a collective term for all people who have modified their general status temporarily or permanently and either anatomically or psychologically. I had conceived the term more narrowly; its subsequent adoption meant there was no longer a term covering the middle ground between transvestism and transsexuality.

My "career" was indeed "accidental" as related above. And, unlike most careers which are generally devoted to teaching students, providing therapy to clients, or possibly in some sort of research, mine has been a bit of all three and almost entirely devoted to one subject, that of cross-dressing. Speaking to student classes in sociology or psychology, to medical groups and professional organizations, and to gatherings of CDs themselves is all teaching. Appearing on radio and television talk shows is also teaching but aimed at the general public in the hope of enlightening them to some degree about a subject that they generally either know nothing about or are heavily biased against out of ignorance of its nature. Writing books, articles, and magazine columns is also teaching.

Counseling or therapy, sometimes in person and frequently in long-distance phone conversations, has taken a great deal of my time. All of it is voluntary and uncompensated. I am not a licensed psychologist so I cannot charge for my time. In any case this is not my living though it has turned out to be my destiny for the last thirty years and more. I have frequently been able to do more for a bewildered CD in a couple of hours for free than his therapist has been able to do for him in several months, or even years in some cases, while being paid well for his time. This is not mentioned either as self-congratulation or as a putdown of psychotherapy. It is simply that having "been there and done that" in the cross-gendered world, I have an inside understanding of their problems and points of view which cannot be learned from books and articles.

My research has been informal and has consisted of finding out about individuals and their problems with self-acceptance or with parents, siblings, friends, or wives. This information and my observations led to generalizations which in turn formed the basis for my efforts in education and counseling. In 1976, the original FPE that I founded merged with a smaller separate organization named "Mamselle," which also dealt with CDs, to form the Society for the Second Self—usually shortened to TRI ESS. It, being the direct descendent of my original FPE, is the oldest and largest organization dealing with cross-dressing in the world. It now has some twelve chapters and nearly 1200 members across the country and publishes a quarterly magazine called the *Femme Mirror.*

My long years of working in, with, and for what is now called the "transgender community" was rewarded in 1987 by having the top award of the International Foundation for Gender Education being named after me as the "Virginia Prince Lifetime Service Award," and I was its first recipient. It has been awarded ten times as of this writing and I have had the pleasure of being the presenter each time. I was further honored in 1994 by being one of four honorees (two of whom were deceased) awarded plaques at the luncheon meeting of the first Cross-dressing, Sex and Gender Convention held in Northridge, California. A further and unplanned mark of respect from my peers in the CD world has been the fact that while there are many Susans, Cathys, Joans, Charlenes, and so on, no one else has taken the name of Virginia (except for a couple of wives who have every right to the name).

An autobiography like this in a volume of such contributions should not be just a list of events of importance in the author's life; I feel that it probably should contain an evaluation of that life even if it is by the author him/herself. I early came to believe that each person should, so to speak, pay his or her way through life. That is, they should leave the world to some degree better than when they came into it. Some Indian guru once said something to the effect that if on his deathbed a man cannot point to some good that he brought to his neighbors, group, or society, his life has been in vain, of no value.

I find myself in the anomalous position of not having started out with any particular goals in mind other than to be a decent human being who would follow the Golden Rule. But I am proud of my accomplishments and feel that I have paid my way and that the world *is* somewhat better as a result of my being here. I am pleased that I have been able to affect the lives of a large number of people positively and to help them achieve some of the same self-acceptance that I strove for all those years. It has been kind of a relay race—Dr. Bowman passed the baton to me when he told me to accept myself and I have fortunately been able to pass on that advice and counsel to a lot of others. And among those there have developed a number of new leaders who have in their own ways passed the baton still farther. The distant goal for all of us, CDs and everyone else, is to hope for a society which recognizes not only that there are all kinds of people but also that there are and should be different ways of living and expressing oneself. It is precisely those differences that make the choice of personal presentation so very fundamental. Everyone should have the right to make and manifest that choice. Male cross-dressers are, in effect, the vanguard of men's liberation since we are breaking free of the bipolarity of gender and seek a wider and deeper expression of ourselves. I am very happy to have had a hand in helping to bring about a better understanding of the separate roles of sex and gender not only for the CDs themselves but for the professionals dealing with them and the public at large.

References

Ellis, Havelock. *Eonism and Other Supplementary Studies.* 1928. Philadelphia: F. A. Davis.

Feinbloom, D. *Transvestites and Transsexual: Mixed Views.* 1976. New York: Delacourte Press.

Money, John, J. G. Hampson, and J. L. Hampson. 1957. "Imprinting and the Establishment of gender Roles." *AMA Archives of Neurology and Psychiatry* 77: 333–36.

Prince, C. V., and P. M. Bentler. 1972. "Survey of 504 cases of Transvestism." *Psychological Reports* 31: 903–17.

36

No Straight Line:
A Scientist's Autobiography

J. M. Reinisch, Ph.D.

Following a career in the music industry, J. M. Reinisch entered the field of sexology to research the influence of biology and prenatal development on gender roles. In 1982 she was made director of the Kinsey Institute, a position from which she retired in 1993. Currently she is a member of the faculty of the SUNY Health Science Center in Brooklyn.

I NEVER STARTED out to be a scientist or, for that matter, a scholar of any kind. I was a dyslexic kid when what we know now as dyslexia was seen as either laziness or stupidity. As a result I hated school (particularly spelling bees and anytime you were forced to read out loud) and looked forward to getting out as soon as and as painlessly as possible. Luckily, my mother was a librarian who despite her "hyper-lexia" didn't think I was lazy or stupid and read to me nonstop until I was fourteen. Her reading of all the children's classics to me left me with a love of books and saved me from the ignorance that can result from not being able to read easily or well.

Since I was from a New York Jewish family, college was considered as necessary as elementary school. No choice was involved. But although I had hated elementary school (except for four years at a private progressive school in Greenwich Village called "City and Country"), detested junior high, and abhorred high school, college turned out to be somewhat less painful and at times fascinating. I loved biology, chemistry, anthropology, sociology, psychology, and non-Western civilization, and with a little planning I could match my lifelong "night-owl" preference and not begin classes until 11:00 A.M. Nevertheless, when my senior year was finally concluded I was so ecstatic to be at long last free of school, that after I finished my last exam, I skipped graduation and headed straight for the airport. I took off for St. Thomas to follow my heart, bask in the sun, sell crystal and china at A. H. Riise, and sky and scuba dive, all with the express goal of never writing another paper or taking another exam. But island life soon paled and after eight months, I returned to New York to follow a number of quite varied career opportunities.

360

These eventually led me to several years in the music industry involved in the flourishing art and business of rock 'n' roll. I assisted the president of a small classical recording company that recorded solo artists, sang in a rock group called "The Seagulls" on Date Records, assisted the producer of the first prime-time rock 'n' roll special called "Popendipity," and managed the Cafe Au Go Go on Bleecker Street in Greenwich Village. Just prior to entering graduate school, I was vice president of promotion and publicity in the company that managed rock artists, including Sly and the Family Stone, for whom I negotiated recording contracts, organized public relations, and handled problems on the road.

Although this might seem to have no relationship to my subsequent career in academia, nothing could be further from the truth. I began graduate school at what was considered in 1969 to be the advanced age of nearly twenty-seven, and there were dire predictions from various friends and "experts" that I'd never be able to catch up with all those who began graduate training at the "appropriate" ages of twenty-one or twenty-two. Quite to the contrary, my experience in contract negotiation, promotion, and business provided much-needed expertise that could be translated into the writing and obtaining of research grants from the government and private foundations. Most of my fellow graduate students had no such business experience to call upon, and were relatively handicapped as a consequence. Much to my pleasure and relief, as a by-product of my seemingly irrelevant and perhaps even unsuitable show business experience, I was able to obtain three grants—one federal and two private—to support my dissertation research.

There were perhaps two moments during my early, seemingly endless years of schooling that may have presaged my entrance into an academic life focused on sex research. Although these incidents were pretty remote in time and it took me ten years of life in academia before I made the connections, I had engaged in one activity and experienced another event early in my schooling that, looking back, appear to have been signposts of my later interests. Both occurred at City and Country School. The first had to do with the "country" part of the school's name. Students at the school, all New York City urbanites, were taken for a week to live on a farm as part of the curriculum. During my agrarian adventure, I was privileged to accidentally view the mating of a bull and cow. To an eight-year-old in the early 1950s, this was a revelation. Sex was not the subject of much public or even private conversation in those days and it was virtually never discussed with or in the presence of children. Yet there were these two enormous animals doing something unusual and about which I felt a vague sense of danger. I wanted to watch, but was afraid of getting caught watching. I somehow understood one wasn't supposed to observe such activity, yet I was fascinated.

I was fortunate and nearly unique in those days to have a mother who, although she had not mentioned sexual behavior in any specific terms, had been answering my many questions with a thorough education in reproduction. (She later reported to me, once I had entered the field of sexology, that my piercing questions about matters reproductive and sexual had begun at age four.) I remember my older cousin asking me one day in the ladies' room when we were eight and nine, respectively, what that metal dispenser on the wall was for. My reply, that I would go to the table in the restaurant and ask my waiting mother, generated a desperate plea that I not say anything or we would be in deep trouble. This naturally stimulated my determined march back to the table—with my cousin slinking behind pulling pleadingly at my sweater—and boldly asking the question. To my cousin's surprise and delight, my mother answered fully, explaining menstruation, a topic about which my cousin had only heard rumors from her thoroughly confused friends. My mother was committed to the idea that I would not be kept in the kind of ignorance she had to bear and which had led to her running home to die the day she got her first period at school. So throughout my childhood and adolescence, I was often the source of the only accurate information available to my peers on reproductive issues. My fortuitous viewing of the bull and cow provided the missing link between my mother's teachings and what I had suspected must precede the meeting of egg and sperm at the beginning of the reproductive process.

The other experience involved the science room at City and Country School. One day in the first grade I discovered six or seven large jars up on the very top shelf near the ceiling. Although they were dimly lit, I had noticed there was something up there. None of the other children seemed to know or care what was there, but for me, a kind of delicious mystery pervaded that shelf. One day when the science room was empty, using a ladder and a modicum of tomboyish agility and fearlessness, I climbed up. What I saw generated a visceral feeling of wonder and excitement. Each of the jars contained tiny naked human forms—from thumb size to almost baby size. (Later I learned they were fetuses donated by students' mothers who had experienced miscarriages.) I was entranced, and made many subsequent surreptitious visits when the science room was vacant. Eventually I began bringing other children from the early grades to visit these miraculous proofs of our lives before birth. I am still fascinated by the era from conception to birth and have dedicated the major part of my academic research career to investigating its mysteries and how what happens there and then affects the rest of one's life. As I broadly interpret the memories of these experiences, it may be that the seeds of my career as sex researcher and sex educator can be discerned in my elementary school life.

When, nearly twenty years later, I considered entering graduate school, it was not with the intention of becoming an academician. Far from it. It was to obtain a master's degree so that one of the leading record companies could hire me as an executive. The company executives told me they needed an explanation for the men who would be working under me as to why they had a women boss. There were few, if any, woman executives in the music business at that time. Those doing the hiring suggested that the way to handle this would be for me to obtain an advanced degree—in anything. Then they could tell the men that I was a vice president because I had this advanced degree and the men didn't. This was before everyone in business had an M.B.A. In those days the graduate business degree was primarily for those who wanted to teach business at the postsecondary school level.

A high school girlfriend was attending Columbia working on a Ph.D. in developmental psychology and I thought, if she could get a Ph.D. then maybe I could attain a master's. So I applied. My plan, if I were admitted, was to go part-time while continuing to work with Sly and then in a couple of years, after I earned the master's degree, take the executive position at the record company. To my complete surprise, on April 1, 1969, a cheery voice woke me on the phone at 8:30 A.M. (the middle of the night for show-biz types) to congratulate me on having been awarded a full-tuition scholarship. My college grades were good, my GREs were reasonable, particularly for a dyslexic, but I later found out that the admissions committee was impressed that I would consider giving up such a "glamorous," high-paying career to return to school. I think they also were about to begin experimenting with "older" students and at nearly twenty-seven, I was considered to be relatively ancient to be starting graduate school. I accompanied Sly and the group to Woodstock and then decided to take the scholarship even though it demanded full-time study. At that rate I could finish the degree in a calendar year, at the end of which I fully expected to return to the music business. I had no way to anticipate how strongly my imagination would be captured by the study of sexual and psychosexual development.

Two events shaped the direction of my professional life. The first was reading a book edited by Eleanor Maccoby. In the fall of 1969, while struggling to return my vocabulary from "rock-talk" to academic speech, relearning how to take notes, and changing my clothes from micro-mini skirts and "go go" boots to more conservative and academically appropriate slacks and jackets, I discovered a book which had a cataclysmic effect on my thinking and opened the door to a world I am still exploring. *The Development of Sex Differences* (1966) was a collection of papers written by the current leading authorities on the topic. Many of the chapters were interesting, but it was the first, which addressed the possible biological factors involved in the development of gender role, that fascinated me. It described the work of John Money with individuals whose genetics or prenatal environment had affected the development of their genitalia and brain. Some of the female subjects mentioned had been exposed to high levels of hormones ordinarily found in such abundance only in males. These girls were found to be more tomboyish in many of their behaviors than girls not so exposed.

Now that I think back on my initial strong reaction to this work, I realize my interest may have derived from personal questions regarding my own development. I had been tomboyish during my childhood, interested in camping, canoeing, and hiking with little enthusiasm for dolls and playing house. I was always getting dirty and was amazed to realize, at the age of thirteen, that my knees were free of scabs for the first time in my memory. In my late teens and twenties I began scuba diving, sky diving, and racing small sports cars and I obtained my pilot's license. My mother, whom I admired greatly, was extremely ladylike in every way. She was always perfectly clean and well-groomed, dainty and feminine, rarely raised her voice, loved dolls as a child, didn't learn to drive until she was forty, and wouldn't think of falling out of an airplane. I had always wanted to be just like her but could never succeed for more than a few minutes. This chapter in the Maccoby volume seemed to hold a clue. Perhaps the prenatal environment during my gestation had somehow affected the development of my brain. Maybe my interests and behavior had been "flavored" by a higher level of androgenic hormones before I was born. I can't be sure whether this is really what fueled my interest, or whether my lifetime fascination with the mysteries of gestation was the spark, but there is no question that the material covered in this chapter captured my imagination.

By the time my master's training was drawing to a close, it was evident to me that regardless of the pleasures and excitement of the music business, I was now hooked on another form of excitement which I still feel today. I had, without consciously intending to, fully embraced the goals and commitments of the scientific enterprise. With some sense of nostalgia, I gave up my plans for reentering the entertainment industry and eagerly sought to further pursuit of my academic and scientific training.

The second pivotal event in my early academic career, meeting John Money, occurred during my second year of graduate school. The chair of my department at Columbia, Brian Sutton-Smith, was a rare academic and researcher who encouraged enthusiasm in his students even when they didn't follow in his footsteps by assisting him directly in his research. After writing several papers on sexual development during my master's year, being accepted into the doctoral program, and being given a predoctoral fellowship to work with Sutton-Smith on his research investigating children's creativity, I tentatively brought up my interest in sexual and psychosexual development with him. Unfazed by my evident desire to work outside his own area, Sutton-Smith offered his support, later giving me an NIMH fellowship to support my doctoral training. It turned out that he was born and raised in New Zealand and he had known Money at university there. He offered to introduce me to him on his next trip to Baltimore.

John Money's brilliance, energy, and creativity are dazzling. Within a few hours of my arrival at his office, he initiated my education by using his teaching technique of "sink or swim"— I found myself in a tiny office, facing a patient with adrenogenital syndrome. This adolescent had been raised in an ambiguous fashion by parents never adequately informed about the condition underlying the ambiguous genitalia with which their genetically female offspring had been born. Having lived life in an ambiguous gender identity/role, neither male or female, with Money's help, he had recently decided to continue from now on as a boy. I was given the assignment of administering a Sentence Completion Test to him. Although I had some limited clinical experience working as an assistant group therapist with "ordinary neurotics," I had never met anyone with such a complicated and difficult sexual and psychosexual developmental history. Somehow the patient and I both survived the experience (as Money undoubtedly knew we would). Next, Money sat me in an office literally filled with erotica from around the world. Here I was to stay for three days conducting my own private SAR (Sexual Attitude Restructuring), until I had pursued everything. Since I had never seen anything remotely similar, except the pictures of naked people in *National Geographic* and *The Family of Man,* I was flooded with images and a deluge of emotions until I habituated, as Money knew I would. His philosophy was that you couldn't talk to and council patients about human sexuality until you knew what it was in all its forms and were comfortable with it. Thus began my many years of tutelage by the extraordinary John Money. I still consider him my mentor today and seek his advice about everything from science to clinical practice, from art to cross-cultural issues, from the history of science to present-day academic politics. After more than twenty-five years of association, I am still amazed at the depth and breadth of his knowledge and understanding and am honored to continue as one of his devoted students.

Money was the outside member of my dissertation committee at Columbia. My research focused on the long-term behavioral effects of prenatal exposure to synthetic progestins. My first paper, published in the *Archives of Sexual Behavior* (Reinisch, 1974), was a literature review of animal and human studies in psychoendocrinology which provided the foundation for this research. The dissertation research revealed, as predicted in this review, that prenatal exposure to synthetic progestins affected the development of personality factors well into childhood, in most instances masculinizing responses (Reinisch, 1977). The study was conducted in Los Angeles with the support of Drs. Seymour and Norma Feshbach of UCLA and the collaboration of William Karow (Reinisch and Karow, 1977) and several other leading OB/GYN reproductive specialists. When it was completed the committee awarded my dissertation the accolade of "with distinction."

As I was finishing my dissertation, I realized that I had really given little thought to what I would do after graduation. In spite of my decision to pursue an advanced degree in psychology, I had on occasion considered the idea that I might still return to show business as a manager, offering my clients both artistic and psychological support. It was late spring 1975 and my NIMH fellowship would end in May. I did have an offer from an old friend of my father, who was now the dean of one of the Police Colleges in New York City, to teach psychology in a new program where the classes would be held at the precincts so that the officers would not have to travel to school after their long shifts. I was giving this interesting idea some consideration as a way of earning a living while I figuring out what to do next. As an afterthought I also made several applications for assistant professor jobs in schools around the New York area, but I understood I was a bit unusual for most positions.

Although I was trained as a developmental psychologist with some clinical training, my research was psychobiological in nature and involved interests in sexual behavior, gender role development, and sexual orientation. Not exactly what every psychology department was looking for in the mid-1970s. Late in May, I received a call from Rutgers University where I had sent an application several months earlier and had received no reply. It seems my application had ended up on the floor under the desk of the search committee chair who wanted to know if I would still be willing to come down and interview. I was told later that thirty new Ph.D.s had been interviewed who all expressed the strong view that both biology and research with laboratory animals had little to inform developmental psychology. The faculty of the Rutgers psychology department was primarily concerned with the study of animal behavior and many investigated the effects of biology on behavior. My dissertation was predicated on the findings from animal research and reflected my understanding that the laboratory animal experiments provide the essential foundation for human psychohormonal studies. The "experiments of nature" and convenient samples available for evaluating the effects of prenatal exposures on development can at best only reveal correlative relationships between the exposure and later behavior, never demonstrate causality. It is the correspondence between the effects produced experimentally in the laboratory, where random assignment of subjects to treatment and control groups is possible, and those derived in correlational studies with human subjects that adds power to any conclusions. Naturally, I began my invited interview lecture with a review of the relevant animal literature. This perspective was understandably viewed in a favorable light by the Rutgers faculty. I was hired.

During my seven years at Rutgers, I was nurtured and supported by the faculty, the department, and the administration, and was successful in garnering several major federal grants to extend my inquiries into the mysteries of prenatal life and their effects on later sexual and psychosexual development. In addition, I had the opportunity to collaborate with Ronald Gandelman in his mouse laboratory on studies of early hormone exposure and aggressive behavior, particularly investigating the effect of contiguity of female and male fetuses in the uterus on the later sex-differentiated aggression and genital development in female mice (Gandelman, Vom Saal, and Reinisch, 1977; McDermott, Gandelman, and Reinisch, 1978). Our studies revealed that placement between two male fetuses in the uterus resulted in masculinization of female behavior and genitalia presumably resulting from exposure to testosterone from surrounding males. We also investigated the effects of early exposure to prednisone (a corticosteroid) on both mice and humans (Reinisch, Simon, and Karow, 1978, 1979; Reinisch, Simon, and Gandelman, 1980) and a virilizing synthetic progestin (Gandelman, Howard, and Reinisch, 1981). Regarding my research on human development, which I had dubbed the Prenatal Development Projects (PDP) (Reinisch, Mortensen, and Sanders, 1993), I continued to refine my methodological strategies and, with Donald Rubin's active collaboration, elaborated and improved the design and analytic techniques necessary for studying the effects of prenatal events on subsequent development. By the early 1980s, we had developed the first generation of a unique computer-generated matching technique. This powerful tool permitted the matching on more than fifteen variables of hormone- or drug-exposed index cases with the most suitable control from a large population of unexposed subjects. Rubin was the chair of statistics at the Educational Testing Service in Princeton, New Jersey, when I first sought out his statistical and methodological advice. During our more than twenty years of collaboration on five major grants, he moved first to the University of Chicago and then to chair the statistics department at Harvard University. I believe that the development of more sophisticated design and statistical methods for conducting sex and psychohormonal research is essential for the growth of our discipline and its acceptance as a respected academic specialty.

My primary colleague in all my research efforts since 1980 has been Stephanie Sanders. She began working with me in 1978 as a graduate student at Rutgers and quickly metamorphosed from student to collaborator to partner. When I left Rutgers and took the directorship of the Kinsey Institute, she joined me in Indiana shortly after I arrived in 1982. There she advanced to associate director and, after I retired in 1993, acted as interim director until John Bancroft arrived to become director in 1995. During these eighteen years, Sanders assisted on my research on synthetic progestins (Reinisch and Karow, 1977; Reinisch, 1981; Sanders and Reinisch, 1985; Reinisch and Sanders, 1987), and collaborated on new investigations of prenatal exposures to diethylstilbestrol (DES) (Reinisch and Sanders, 1992a), and barbiturates (Reinisch and Sanders, 1982; Reinisch, Sanders, Mortensen, et al., 1995); conducted studies of sex differences (Reinisch and Sanders, 1986), high-risk sexual behavior in college students (Reinisch, Hill, Sanders, et al., 1990; Reinisch, Sanders, Hill, et al., 1992; Reinisch, Hill, Sanders, et al., 1995); and initiated a national survey of sexual and reproductive knowledge (Reinisch, Hill Sanders, et al., 1995; Reinisch and Beasley, 1990, 1991, 1994; Sanders, Ziemba-Davis, Hill, et al., 1991; Reinisch, Sanders, Hill, et al., 1991). We've also written several papers on research issues related to AIDS (Reinisch, Sanders, and Ziemba-Davis, 1988; Reinisch, Ziemba-Davis, and Sanders, 1990; Reinisch, Sanders, and Ziemba-Davis, 1995), and sexual and psychosexual development (Reinisch and Sanders, 1983; Reinisch and Sanders, 1984; Reinisch, Ziemba-Davis, Sanders, et al., 1991; Reinisch and Sanders, 1992b). In much of this work we enjoyed the fruitful collaboration of Craig Hill and Mary Ziemba-Davis.

My journey to the directorship of the Kinsey Institute was nearly as serendipitous as my entrance into academia. In 1981 I received a letter that announced I had been nominated as a candidate for the position of the third director of the Institute for Sex Research founded by the legendary Alfred Kinsey at Indiana University in Bloomington. Because of my age and because I did not specialize in the kind of survey research that the institute had been known for, I guessed that I had been nominated to apply because of the very large National Institutes of Health (NIH) grant I had just been awarded. That I was a woman at the time when affirmative action was reaching its zenith and women had to be among any group of individuals considered for any position, probably also helped. Nevertheless, I was honored to be asked and sent in the requested curriculum vitae and list of references.

Several months later I was surprised to be informed that I had been chosen as one of the twelve finalists. Several days later, I received a phone call telling me that the candidates were to be interviewed two at a time until the director was found, and that I was in the first pair. I had just turned thirty-nine and when discovering that the other primary candidate was a male physician ten years my senior, I was now sure I was the affirmative action candidate. The process involved two full days of interviewing and lectures. I spoke to the institute's board of trustees and the search committee. I learned that almost two years before, Indiana University had convened a review committee to assess whether the institute was worth keeping and whether the university should continue to invest in its existence there. The review committee, which was constituted primarily of Indiana University professors with two highly regarded outside members from academic sexology, agreed that the institute should be maintained at the university and that a new director should be sought. When I arrived to be interviewed everyone made it clear that they were looking for a first-class scientist who would expand the institute's research mission into a broader multidisciplinary spectrum, including the biomedical and biological. Someone who would revitalize the institute's physical plant which was housed in cramped decaying quarters under a leaky roof and which hadn't been painted or even had its floors cleaned and waxed in ten years. Much of the art and archival collections was in boxes under plastic to protect it from the drips. I was informed that they also wanted someone who would raise the institute's public profile. Historically, it had purposely assumed a very low profile following the reaction to *Sexual Behavior of the Human Female* in 1953 (Kinsey, Pomeroy, Martin, et al., 1953), which led to attacks on Kinsey by the Congress where a representative had vitriolically opined that anyone (meaning Kinsey) who would study American sexual behavior was paving the way for a communist takeover of the United States. Now, the university administrators made it clear that if they were going to invest in the institute they wanted the world to know where it was and that it was making an educational contribution to the general public.

I left feeling I had done my best and busied myself for the next two weeks with preparations to fly to Denmark and begin the next phase of the Prenatal Development Project. The hundreds of twenty-one- to twenty-three-year-old subjects we would be studying in terms of prenatal events and later life were members of the Danish Perinatal Cohort originally established between 1959 and 1961. The most important task in Copenhagen would be to find and hire a team of Danish psychologists and social workers who would conduct the "hands-on" data collection of the effects of prenatal exposure to progestins, corticosteroids, and later barbiturates. On the morning of the day I was leaving for a month in Copenhagen, my frantic last-minute packing was interrupted by a telephone call from Indiana. I had been chosen as the next director of the Institute for Sex Research. When could I visit Bloomington to discuss the terms? I was surprised, delighted, and thrown off balance. I had never seriously considered actually being hired and hadn't thought about the consequences. I loved Rutgers and teaching large undergraduate courses in general and developmental psychology—each of which had grown to class sizes of 500 to 750 students. In both courses, I had included several lectures on sexual and psychosexual development. And I had great freedom there to teach graduate courses in my area of interest. Flustered, I told the expectant voice on the phone that I couldn't visit for a month since I was establishing my new NIH-funded research project in Denmark. The voice said fine, could I set a date to return for discussions of my views about what the institute needed shortly after I was due to return. We agreed on a three-day period five weeks later.

During my time in Denmark, I found a wonderful group of associates, particularly Dr. Erik Lykke Mortensen (Reinisch, Mortensen, and Sanders, 1993; Reinisch, Sanders, Mortensen, et al., 1995; Mortensen, Reinisch, and Teasdale, 1989; Mortensen, Gade, and Reinisch, 1991), who has coordinated the data collection activities for fifteen years and become the fourth invaluable member of the research team. His theoretical and methodological contributions and dedication to the project have enhanced our efforts immeasurably. Of course, during every spare moment, I was busy mulling over the enormous opportunity that had been offered to me trying to decide whether or not I should take it. What would I want for the institute if I agreed to take this responsibility? What did it need? In what new expanded directions could I guide it that would meet the requirements of its board of trustees, the university administrators, and the review committee; be consistent with the needs of its scholarly constituency and public responsibility; and fit with my own strengths and interests? While I consulted with my colleagues about their vision for the institute's future, many recommended that whatever resources I could garner should be expended only on research and education and that the collections, which were in disarray, should be ignored. But I had spent a day in the archives exploring the library, files, art, artifacts, and ephemera and even in that short period of time, when I could only skim the surface of the holdings, it became clear to me that the collections were precious and had enormous value as educational materials for scholars from a wide range of interests, especially if they were organized, managed, and displayed properly. Against the strong sentiments of some colleagues to the contrary, I made a pledge to myself to do everything possible to conserve, restore, preserve, and protect all these materials.

When I returned to Indiana I had a four-page written contract itemizing what I believed was necessary for the institute's revitalization should I accept the position. Included were requests for a major expansion of space, a complete renovation of the institute with special attention to the library and archives, including the establishment of protected stacks; a greatly enlarged reading room; private offices for the librarians; and temperature and humidity controls. Funds were also requested to triple the library, research, and support staff; update and purchase new equipment, including computers; and, as a means of extending the reach of the institute beyond Indiana University to a broader spectrum of scholars and scientists, convene a series of international multidisciplinary conferences, offer awards in Kinsey's name to reward excellent dissertations in the discipline, and support visiting scholars. In addition, I felt it was essential to have resources to develop private donors and add outside trustees with expertise in fund-raising and skills like law and publishing, and to establish a Science Advisory Board made up of eminent scientists and scholars working in many of the fields that enrich sexuality research.

This board would evaluate and consult on the institute's research and educational efforts. Finally, I wanted to change the name of the institute to honor Alfred Kinsey, its eminent and courageous founder. To my surprise, the university's vice president signed each of the four pages of the contract I had written agreeing to support all my requests. The generosity, enthusiasm, and good will this represented, convinced me to accept. I said a sad farewell to Rutgers, packed up my personal and professional lives, left my friends and family, and moved to Indiana.

Shortly after I arrived, we changed the institute's name to the Kinsey Institute for Research in Sex, Gender and Reproduction to honor our founder and announce the institute's newly expanded focus. The first major decision I was called upon to make derived from the strong suggestion offered by the dean of research and graduate development that, because the pace and focus of life at the Kinsey Institute was about to change dramatically, I should ask the entire staff to resign and begin with a fresh group that would have fewer preconceived notions about how the institute should function. I felt that at least some of these staff members must have valuable contributions to make regarding the institute and its history. Against the dean's advice, I elected to retain the staff, letting them decide whether or not each was comfortable with the major changes in leadership, philosophy, and environment that would inevitably flow from the mandates I had been given. The cost in turmoil, of not taking the dean's advice, was well worth the contributions and years of collaboration I enjoyed with such dedicated and creative staff members as Tom Albright and Ruth Beasley.

In order to fulfill the commitment for a large area of additional space for the institute's growth, the university offered us a new site off-campus which would quickly provide additional space. At first it seemed like a good idea. But the more I considered the move, the clearer seemed to be the importance of keeping the institute nestled in the campus, surrounded by the comparative literature, English, history, and biology departments and the schools of music and education. As a center for the study of human sexuality, still a subject of taboo and controversy in our sexphobic society, I believed the institute's future security well might depend upon its being located in the heart of the university; that its legitimacy, for those who might question its existence, was predicated on its being perceived as an integral and essential part of the academic community. So I lobbied aggressively for the institute to remain in its current home and that additional space be provided in the same building. I believe that my intuition was correct and that its location helped protect it as extremely conservative forces in our society once again began to question its legitimacy and attack its right to exist.

During the first few years of my tenure, as promised, and with the strong support of then Indiana University president, John Ryan, the library and collection's space was more than tripled and completely renovated. The rest of the institute grew to more than twice its previous size with the addition of one and a half new floors, including new research space, a computer facility, offices for the enlarged staff and visiting scholars, and two conference rooms—the larger with an attached audiovisual room, a reception area, and four new bathrooms. The library staff grew from one and a half to three full-time professional librarians and a full-time technical assistant, and we attracted a series of advanced graduate students in fine art who dedicated themselves to the curatorial duties of the art and artifact collections. They began organizing, restoring, conserving, and cataloging these materials as well as presenting lectures and writing about them (Mortensen, Gade, and Reinisch, 1991). The research staff increased from one to eleven, including a full-time computer expert/data analyst. The administrative/support staff expanded from two to seven. The number of student assistants, library patrons, visiting scholars, and visitors multiplied. And for the first time a private fund-raising strategy was initiated and spearheaded by Sherry Hackett, an experienced and energetic outside trustee.

In consultation and collaboration with the members of the Science Advisory Board, we organized five international multidisciplinary symposia: Masculinity/ Femininity (Reinisch, Rosenblum, and Sanders, 1987), Adolescence and Puberty (Bancroft and Reinisch, 1990), Homosexuality/ Heterosexuality: Concepts of sexual orientation (McWhirter, Sanders, and Reinisch, 1990), AIDS and Sex: An integrated biomedical and biobehavioral approach (Voeller, Reinisch, and Gottlieb, 1990), and Sexuality and Disease: Metaphors, perceptions and behavior in the AIDS era. These meetings included psychologists, sociologists, psychiatrists, endocrinologists, medical clinicians, historians, biologists, virologists, anthropologists, urologists, gynecologist/obstetricians, demographers, epidemiologists, pediatricians, and philosophers and were designed to foster maximum interaction. The Kinsey Series of scholarly volumes from Oxford University Press were the well-received and positively reviewed product of these conferences.

Another goal mandated by the trustees and review committee when I was hired was to initiate and then build the institute's educational activities for the general public. My first strategy was to write a syndicated newspaper column that would provide research-based answers to readers' questions about sex, gender, and reproduction in plain language. An additional goal was to provide a public forum in which to present the work of sexologists and other scientists and scholars working in human sexuality. It has always been my strong belief that scientists have a responsibility to share their findings with the public who funds our research. I felt the column would be an efficient way to reach a large number of people. I was fortunate to convince one of the premier syndicators, United Media, to distribute the column which I authored with the strong support of Ruth Beasley and the library staff. The column ran for nine years until I withdrew it just prior to my retirement. The response from the vast majority of the public was enthusiastically positive. I had been warned by the David Hendin, senior vice president of United Media, that based upon his experience with the subject matter, I should expect one out of every two letters to be critical, angry, or derisive. During all the years we produced the column, only one out of every hundred letters from the United States and one out of two hundred from the rest of the world were negative. Most correspondents were very complementary and grateful for the information we provided. *The Kinsey Report* was carried in newspapers across the United States and Canada as well as in Europe, the Middle East, Asia, and South America. Questions were received from nearly equal numbers of women and men, from children as young as ten and readers as old as ninety-six; from heterosexuals, bisexuals, gays, and lesbians; parents and grand-parents; farms, suburbs, and great cities; and many ethnic, racial, and religious groups. The questions from this diverse, widely representative and dispersed read-ership were surprisingly similar. It appeared that many suffered from the same lack of information, the same myths about sexuality; and the same fears, anxieties, and guilt about their sexual behavior, fantasies, and thoughts. It became clear that there was an enormous pool of ignorance with regard to things sexual, that people did not know where or how to obtain the information they needed, and that many harbored false beliefs about human sexuality which caused pain and suffering. Based upon the response to the column, it was decided that we should produce a kind of "friendly encyclopedia" which would answer many of the questions about which we now understood people needed information based upon the most current research avail-able. In collaboration with Ruth Beasley, who had worked in the institute's library for many years before I arrived, and the support of the other librarians, I wrote *The Kinsey Institute New Report on Sex* (Reinisch and Beasley, 1990, 1991, 1994) which answered 650 of the questions the public had repeatedly asked the institute since I became director. Our efforts were rewarded not only by hardcover, trade, and mass-market editions published in the United States, but by publications in France, Spain, Germany, Poland, Taiwan, Mainland China, Japan, Korea, and Britain. All my royalties from the column and books were donated to the institute to support its research and the collections.

Our research efforts flourished as we obtained new grants and mounted studies of high-risk sexual behavior, primarily in college students and lesbians. For exam-ple, we conducted one of the first studies investigating AIDS risk in women reported at the first NIMH/NIH Woman and AIDS Conference: Promoting healthy behaviors research workshop in 1987 (Reinisch, Sanders, and Ziemba-Davis, in press). We conducted a series of surveys on high-risk sexual behavior and attitudes in a midwestern university (Reinisch, Hill, Sanders, et al., 1990; Reinisch, Sanders, and Ziemba-Davis, 1992; Reinisch, Hill, Sanders, et al., 1995) and conducted a national survey of sexual knowledge in collaboration with the Roper Organization for inclusion in *The Kinsey Institute New Report on Sex* (Reinisch and Beasley, 1990, 1991, 1994; Sanders, Ziemba-Davis, Hill, et al., 1991; Reinisch, Sanders, Hill, et al., 1991). In brief: (1) We found that even lesbians were at risk for infection with AIDS, since often, when they did interact with opposite-sex partners, they were friends from their community—that is, gay men. These studies also made clear that there could be a divergence within an individual between his or her sexual orienta-tion identity and actual behavior. From these investigations, we developed the con-cept of behavioral bisexuality as a descriptor of the actual behavior of many women and men who identified themselves as lesbian or gay. Behavioral bisexuality assisted us in rethinking risk in people who label their sexual orientation identity as either exclusively heterosexual or homosexual. (2) We found that among small-town, primarily midwestern college students twenty years old on average who described themselves as politically moderate to conservative, and who reported from six to eight lifetime sexual partners, one out of three young women had been infected with a sexually transmitted disease (STD), and young men who were in nonexclusive sexual relationships at the time of the study had the highest prevalence of STDs. (3) The national survey of sexual knowledge revealed an enormous lack of basic information about sex, gender, and reproduction in the American public aged eighteen to sixty.

The first six of my eleven years at the institute under the aegis of Indiana University President John Ryan were among the happiest and most fulfilling of my life. The last five, despite continued growth and success in research, education, and the development, conservation, and preservation of the collections, were fraught with difficulties I could ill imagine when I accepted the position as director. The detailed story of those last years, filled as it is with anonymous false accusations, wholly and grossly inaccurate newspaper stories, attacks on Kinsey's original research and the institute's mission, is meant for another time and place. Suffice it to say that whatever forces sought to attack me, and, through me, the institute and what it was seeking to accomplish, represented just another version of the venomous assaults which have hounded others in our field in the past (Reinisch and Harter, 1994) and which continue into the present. That the motivation behind these difficulties proceeded from a complex mix of personal animus and the agendas of extreme political and philosophical groups resulted in the curious collaboration of some very strange bedfellows, is also not new. In addition, there has also been, during the last fifteen years, an increasingly virulent, strident, and fraudulent vilification of Alfred Kinsey himself and his research by some very vocal and affluent extremist conservative groups, generously funded individuals, and a congressman from Texas, aided and abetted by the right-wing and tabloid press. I came in the last years of my time as director to appreciate more fully that those who visibly represent the effort to understand and explain the complexities of human sexuality, as has been said in a very different context, can "summons as foes into the field of battle the most violent, mean and malignant passions of the human breast." But in the end, with the unswerving support of a just and courageous institute board of trustees, led by the gallant Gene Eoyang; a brave, committed, and loyal staff; and numerous colleagues throughout the world, Indiana University vigorously and publicly repudiated the baseless accusations against me. I am gratified that my own exoneration was a triumph for the institute as well, which, in the hands of its exceptional new director, John Bancroft, is certain to achieve new heights, built on the firm foundation I helped play a part in creating.

References

Bancroft, J., and J. M. Reinisch, eds. 1990. *Adolescence and puberty.* New York: Oxford University Press.

Gandelman, R., F. Vom Saal, and J. M. Reinisch. 1977. Contiguity to male foetuses affects morphology and behavior of female mice. *Nature* 266: 722–24.

Gandelman, R., S. M. Howard, and J. M. Reinisch. 1981. Prenatal exposure to 19-nor-17 ethynyltestosterone (Norethindrone) influences morphology and aggressive behavior of female mice. *Hormones and Behavior* 15: 405–15.

Kinsey, A. C., W. B. Pomeroy, C. E. Martin, and P. H. Gebhard. 1953. *Sexual behavior in the, human female.* Philadelphia and London: W. B. Saunders Company.

Maccoby, E. E. 1966. *The development of sex differences.* Stanford, Calif: Stanford University Press.

McDermott, N. J., R. Gandelman, and J. M. Reinisch. 1978. Contiguity to male foetuses influences ano-genital distance and time of vaginal opening in mice. *Physiology & Behavior* 20: 661–63.

McWhirter, D. P., S. A. Sanders, and J. M. Reinisch, eds. 1990. *Homosexuality/heterosexuality: Concepts of sexual orientation.* New York: Oxford University Press.

Mortensen, E. L., A. Gade. and J. M. Reinisch. 1991. A critical note on Lezak's "Best Performance Method" in clinical neuropsychology. *Journal of Clinical and Experimental Neuropsychology* 13, no. 2: 361–71.

Mortensen, E. L., J. M. Reinisch, and T. W. Teasdale. 1989. Intelligence as measured by the WAIS and a military draft board test. *Scandinavian Journal of Psychology* 30: 315–18.

Reinisch, J. M. 1974. Fetal hormones, the brain, and human sex differences: A heuristic integrative review of the recent literature. *Archives of Sexual Behavior* 3: 51–90.

———. 1977. Prenatal exposure of human foetuses to synthetic progestin and oestrogen affects personality. *Nature* 266: 561–62.

———. 1981. Prenatal exposure to synthetic progestins increases potential for aggression in humans. *Science* 211: 1171–73.

———. 1993. Preface. In the Kinsey Institute and J. Crump. *George Platt Lynes,* pp. vii–viii. New York and Canada: Bulfinch Press.

Reinisch, J. M., with R. Beasley. 1990, 1991, 1994. *The Kinsey Institute New Report on Sex: What you must know to be sexually literate.* Hardcover, trade, and mass-market editions. New York: St. Martin's Press (updated 1994: new preface, chapter 1); New York: St. Martin's Press and Paperbacks.

Reinisch, J. M., and M. H. Harter. 1994. Alfred C. Kinsey. In *Human Sexuality: An encyclopedia,* ed. V. L. Bullough and B. Bullough, pp. 333–38. New York and London: Garland Publishing.

Reinisch, J. M., C. A. Hill, S. A. Sanders, and M. Ziemba-Davis. 1990. Sexual behaviors among heterosexual college students. *Focus: A Guide to AIDS Research and Counseling* 5, no. 4: 3.

———. 1995. High-risk sexual behavior among heterosexual undergraduates at a midwestern university: A confirmatory survey. *Family Planning Perspectives* 27, no. 2: 79–82.

Reinisch, J. M., and W. G. Karow. 1977. Prenatal exposure to synthetic progestins and estrogens: Effects on human development. *Archives of Sexual Behavior* 6: 257–58.

Reinisch, J. M., E. L. Mortensen, and S. A. Sanders. 1993. The Prenatal Development Project. *Acta Psychiatrica Scandinavica* 370 (Supp.): 54–61. Copenhagen: Munksgaard.

Reinisch, J. M., L. A. Rosenblum, and S. A. Sanders, eds. 1987. *Masculinity/femininity: Basic perspectives.* New York: Oxford University Press.

Reinisch, J. M., and S. A. Sanders. 1982. Early barbiturate exposure: The brain, sexually dimorphic behavior and learning. *Neuroscience and Behavioral Reviews* 6: 311–19.

Reinisch, J. M., and S. A. Sanders. 1983. Hormonal influences on sexual development and behavior. In *Sex and gender—A theological and scientific inquiry,* ed. M. F. Schwartz, A. S. Moraczewski, and J. A. Monteleone. St. Louis, Mo.: The Pope John XXIII Medical-Moral Research and Education Center.

——. 1984. Prenatal gonadal steroidal influences on gender-related behavior. In *Progress in brain research,* ed. G. J. De Vries, J. P. C. DeBruin, H. B. M. Vylings, and M. A. Comer. Vol. 61, *Sex differences in the brain: Relation between structure and function.* Amsterdam: Elsevier, Science Publishers B. V.

——. 1986. A test of sex differences in aggressive response to hypothetical conflict situations. *Journal of Personality and Social Psychology* 50: 1045–49.

——. 1987. Behavioral influences of prenatal hormones. In *Handbook of clinical psychoneuroendocrinology,* ed. C. B. Nemeroff and P. T. Loosen. New York: Guilford Books.

——. 1992a. Effects of prenatal exposure to Diethylstilbestrol (DES) on hemispheric laterality and spatial ability in human males. *Hormones and Behavior* 26: 62–65.

——. 1992b. Prenatal hormonal contributions to sex differences in human cognitive and personality development. In *Handbook of behavioral neurobiology,* ed. H. Moltz, I. L. Ward, and A. A. Gerall. Vol. 11, *Sexual differentiation,* pp. 221–43. New York: Plenum Publishing.

Reinisch, J. M., S. A. Sanders, C. A. Hill, and M. Ziemba-Davis. 1991. Perceptions about sexual behavior: Findings from a national sex knowledge survey—United States, 1989. *Morbidity and Mortality Weekly Report* 40, no. 15: 249–52.

——. 1992. High-risk sexual behavior among heterosexual undergraduates at a midwestern university. *Family Planning Perspectives* 24, no. 3: 116–21.

Reinisch, J. M., S. A. Sanders, E. L. Mortensen, and D. B. Rubin. 1995. In utero exposure to phenobarbital and intelligence deficits in adult men. *Journal of the American Medical Association* 274, no. 19: 1518–25.

Reinisch, J. M., S. A. Sanders, and M. Ziemba-Davis. 1988. The study of sexual behavior in relation to the transmission of human immunodeficiency virus: caveats and recommendations. *The American Psychologist* 43, no. 11: 921–27.

——. 1995. Self-labeled sexual orientation and sexual behavior: Considerations for STD-related biomedical research and education. In *Perspectives on Behavioral Medicine: Proceedings of the 1990 Annual Meeting of the Academy of Behavioral Medicine,* ed. M. Stein and A. Baum, pp. 241–57. New York: Lawrence Erlbaum.

——. In press. Self-labeled sexual orientation. sexual behavior, and knowledge about AIDS: Implications for biomedical research and education programs. In *Women and AIDS: Promoting healthy behaviors.* Monograph: National Technical Information Service.

Reinisch, J. M., N. G. Simon, and R. Gandelman. 1980. Prenatal exposure to prednisone permanently alters fighting behavior of female mice. *Pharmacology, Biochemistry and Behavior* 12: 213–16.

Reinisch, J. M.., N. G. Simon, W. G. Karow, and R. Gandelman. 1978. Prenatal exposure to prednisone in humans and animals retards intrauterine growth. *Science* 202: 436–38.

——. 1979. Prednisone therapy and birth weight (Technical Comments). *Science* 206: 96–97.

Reinisch, J. M., M. Ziemba-Davis, and S. A. Sanders. 1990. Sexual behavior and AIDS: Lessons from art and sex research. In *AIDS and sex: An integrated biomedical and biobehavioral approach,* ed. B. Voeller, J. M. Reinisch, and M. Gottlieb, pp. 37–80. New York: Oxford University Press.

Reinisch, J. M., M. Ziemba-Davis, and S. A. Sanders. 1991. Hormonal contributions to sexually dimorphic behavioral development in humans. *Psychoneuroendocrinology* 16, nos. 1–3: 213–78.

Sanders, S.A.. and J. M. Reinisch. 1985. Behavioral effects on humans of progesterone-related compounds during development and in the adult. In *Current topics of neuroendocrinology,* ed. D. Ganten and D. Pfaff. Vol. 5, *Actions of progesterone on the brain.*

Sanders, S. A., M. Ziemba-Davis, C. A. Hill, and J. M. Reinisch. 1991. Intent and purpose of the Kinsey Institute/Roper Organization national sex knowledge survey: A rejoinder. *Public Opinion Quarterly* 55, no. 3: 458.

Voeller, B., J. M. Reinisch, and M. Gottlieb, eds. 1990. *AIDS and sex: An integrated biomedical and biobehavioral approach.* New York: Oxford University Press.

37

Making a Living in Sex: An Autobiographical Account

Ira L. Reiss, Ph.D.

Ira L. Reiss has recently retired from his position as professor of sociology at the University of Minnesota. He has made major contributions toward establishing the scientific credibility of sociological explanations of sexuality with his pioneering analysis and national study of premarital sexual standards, and later with his writings on extramarital sexuality, cross-cultural sexuality, and on ways of resolving our society's sexual problems. For twenty-seven years he was also director of the university's Family Study Center.

IT STRUCK ME as odd when the editors of this book asked me to write an autobiographical account explaining why I had become so interested in sexuality. It seems to me that *not* having a strong interest in sexuality is much more in need of explanation. But still, each of us does deal with our interest and curiosity in different ways, and we don't all pursue it as a profession. So here, very briefly, is my story as I now see it.

My parents were in a conflict-ridden marriage where verbal arguments were a constant for all sixty years of their marriage. Occasionally outside events would interrupt their quarrels. During the early 1930s, when I was about six years old, and my sister seven, my parents left New York City and took us to Scranton, Pennsylvania. My father's clothing business had gone bankrupt and he wanted to open a new clothing factory in Scranton. These were the Depression years and Scranton appeared to him to offer a chance to start up again.

Scranton was then well known for its lace mills and coal mines. When we first moved into our house, we were warned that we might wake up one morning to find our residence having fallen into a mine shaft—not exactly an enticement to move there. But there was another more interesting industry going on in Scranton—prostitution. Like a number of other cities, Scranton had learned to cope with the Depression by opening up houses of prostitution that attracted people from miles around. The men would come in on the weekend and spend money to eat, sleep, gas up their cars, and such, in addition to paying for sex. So it helped the local economy. In fact, when the houses were finally closed toward the end of the war, the city went into a bad recession.

One of my earliest memories in Scranton is my giving carloads of men coming into the city directions to the houses of prostitution. By the time I was nine or ten I had learned that by standing by one of the key stops on the entry road to the city, I could get nickels and dimes tossed to me by simply pointing in the right direction. The visitors would yell out, "Hey kid, where are the cat houses?" And I would yell back, "Go straight for three blocks and turn right into any alley." Then a coin or two, in gratitude, would be tossed my way. I liked the rewards and so, in my mind, these men were not without some redeeming virtues. The visitors really did not need my directions—they could not miss the houses since there were almost a hundred of them spread out in about twelve of the alleys behind the downtown streets. The houses were painted gaudy colors—purple, yellow, and the most famous of them was called the "Orange Front." It had its own parking lot and over eight "working girls." There was a sign not far from the house that said "Always one dollar." The sign was in a nearby gas station and some said it referred to car washes, but they did not wash cars in that station.

The houses charged sex fees in accord with the acts requested but also according to the skin color of the working girls. White women got double what black women got for each type of trick and in those days it was only a dollar to have intercourse with a white working girl. Such competitive pricing was a clear statement of the relative social value of blacks and whites. Also, the presence of only female prostitution was an obvious statement of which gender had the money and which gender had to do tricks to get some of it.

There was also a political lesson that I learned from observing prostitution. It was illegal but the alleys were patrolled by the police, and it was obvious what was going on even to me as a child. While the police had informal rules about keeping order and keeping kids too young away from the houses, they were casual about enforcement. It was apparent that the local politicians were aware of the houses and were likely part of a protection-for-payment system.

I was thirteen years old when I first visited the houses. I was attending a religious class at night for boys my age, and the leader of the group, a class of about seven or eight, told us he was going to give us an "educational" experience. The leader, David, about eighteen years old, took us down to the Orange Front. It was a weekday night about seven o'clock and business was slow at that hour. We went in and sat down in a room where there were five or six prostitutes in various types of revealing clothing. This was the selection room, where men saw the full array of women available and picked one with whom to go upstairs. We did not have sex. We just sat there and talked to the girls. They were just a few years older than we were—I'd say about sixteen to twenty. They seemed a little ill at ease talking to such young boys. But they knew our leader, David, and so they went along with it, and perhaps they even enjoyed the break from their routine activities.

I went back to the houses during my high school years for sex but also because I wanted to know more about the girls who worked there—they were quite different from the girls in high school who generally played hard to get. They would tell me of their friends and sisters who worked hard for little money in the factories in town. They felt they at least were earning good wages and they planned to leave and open a beauty parlor or some small business when they had enough money. Prostitution was, at least they thought, a path to upward mobility. A few of them did actually follow that path and I saw them in their new businesses years later. Many had married, but I am sure many others got stuck in prostitution longer than they wanted. Some girls moved to bigger cities to work in what they thought would be better-paying houses. While I really don't know what happened to most of these prostitutes, I do know that their friends and sisters who came from the same impoverished neighborhoods also did not have an easy time with their life. Our system of gender inequality offered women a different way out of poverty than men had. In the broader society men had more money and women had the bodies men coveted, and so an exchange in prostitution and in dating and mating was inevitable. I believe some form of exchange of sex for some sort of reward is inevitable in any society but the exact form it takes reflects that society's ideology. In Scranton we had an ideology of racial and gender inequality coupled with a political system willing to perpetuate those beliefs and accommodate some informal exchange arrangements. Scranton's "cat houses" were projecting a vivid picture of the social fabric of that time for anyone who cared to stop and look.

It should be clear that I wasn't spending all my time exploring the cat houses. My early years in Scranton also involved a great deal of religious training. My parents were raised as orthodox Jews and although they did not fully practice their beliefs, they did join an orthodox Jewish synagogue and enroll my sister and me in daily after-school classes in Judaism. Picture the contrast—in a major center of prostitution, every day I am being taught orthodox Jewish views which opposed not only prostitution but all sex before marriage! So there was a major conflict in my sexual socialization.

The religious training did, however, give me a respect for careful scholarship because we examined every word in the first five books of the Old Testament (the Torah). We constantly debated the meaning of each word and every line of the biblical text. I did not know it at the time, but that experience of structured intellectual inquiry offered a model for seeking clarification and resolution of my internal conflicts concerning sexuality. So at the same time as the conflict was being created, I was presented with a possible means of coping. In the years to come that model of scholarship would serve me well both professionally and personally.

To add to my confusion, my parents each had quite different views of sexuality. My mother was more of a hedonist who felt we should get what pleasure we could, while my father was a pragmatist who would only approve those pleasures that were both physically and socially safe. I took parts of both their views and tried to combine them. I had sex but I consistently used condoms with both the prostitutes and with my dates. Imagine that! Safe sex back in the early 1940s. But the moral conflict was not resolved. I was not sure who was right—my religion, my mother, my father, the prostitutes, my friends, or the girls I dated. It was big-time moral conflict that would shape my professional life in the coming years. But it didn't stop me from having sex. In fact, I would justify my sexual experiences as a way of possibly gaining clarification. So the conflict was surely not all pain.

I did get a reasonably clear message from my family on gender equality. My mother was an outspoken and very intelligent woman who did not take second-class treatment from anyone, and woe be to the person who tried! My paternal grandmother was a religious feminist who had argued for women in orthodox Judaism receiving the same training as men. Recall that orthodoxy did not allow women to be "bat-mitvahed" as does conservative and reform Judaism today. My grandmother spoke Hebrew and would argue with the orthodox rabbis. My older sister was a brilliant student who graduated second in her high school class. She pretty much tried to pressure me to do what she wanted. I became free of her dominance only after entering high school.

So I had several models of powerful, talented women in my life. Many of my male friends would belittle women and justify their second-rate status. They had little time for my arguments for fair and equal treatment: women for them were good for just one thing—sex. I was surely into sex, but not because I looked down upon women and just wanted to use them. The prostitutes in the houses liked me because I treated them as people, not just as sex machines. This conflict was different from the internal conflict I had about sexual morality; it was with other men and social customs. That sort of external clash was much easier to cope with than my confusions about how to judge the moral acceptability of sex in my own life.

I was drafted into the army during the last years of World War II and served in the European theater of operation. When I first went in I passed a test for the Armed Services Training Program (ASTP) which would send you to college to be trained for more specialized roles. But since that program was overcrowded, they took thousands of us who had passed and put us into the combat engineers. I was with all the bright people who had passed the ASTP test and we helped each other learn how to survive. I soon noted that these men did not have much background in establishing sexual relationships with women. They were from wealthy homes located in towns without prostitution and they had largely been raised to defer gratification. When they saw that I related easily to women at dances and bars, they asked me for advice. As a result, I started my sex educator role at eighteen. In exchange I learned from them about good literature, good music, and more sophisticated ideas. This experience filled in what had been lacking in my Scranton education. But seeing the major differences in how these men behaved and thought about sex gave me a strong belief in the central role of learning in the sexual area. These men were not different from me physiologically or hormonally, but they differed greatly in sexual experience and in knowing how to achieve what sexual outcomes they wanted.

I went to college after the army, courtesy of the GI Bill and my parents' generosity. I continued my discussions with friends and dates about the need for gender equality in our society and found support among women but not much among men. In the fall of 1948, during my senior year at Syracuse University, I took a philosophy course in which I was asked to write a paper on a controversial area. I wrote on my thoughts about sexual ethics and suggested ways of making "reasonable" choices of sexual behavior and belief. This paper, of course, gave me a chance to try to further resolve my internal conflict about sexual morality. I stressed, even then, a pluralistic approach that relied on evaluating risks and benefits to decide what is right or wrong sexually. I rejected adhering to strict guidelines; I had too much variety in my background to endorse pure orthodox views. My parents, intentionally or not, gave me a great deal of autonomy; they were so often busy arguing with each other that they didn't have time to do otherwise. I now see that 1948 paper as the beginning of my professional work in sexuality and as the spur for my first book, which I started shortly after getting my Ph.D. in 1953. My original working title for the book was *The Basis for Choice in the Problem of Premarital Sexual Intercourse*. My reason for focusing on such a topic should be obvious by now.

I graduated from college in 1949, going summers to get out in three years. I then went to work for my father in his clothing factory, but I soon saw that I did not want to make and sell garments for the rest of my life. I was fortunate enough to have the choice to leave and I took it. One of my close friends, Mort Friedman, suggested to me one day that I might like being a college professor: "You like to argue and analyze and discuss controversial issues—why not get paid for it?" The idea had a powerful appeal to me. Within weeks I had decided to quit working for my father and go back to college to get a Ph.D. I knew I liked psychology and philosophy, but I thought psychology was too morbidly focused on illnesses and philosophy too vague and indecisive. I had never taken sociology in college but another friend, Ralph Forest, told me that he thought that sociology would fit my interests; I decided to major in sociology and minor in philosophy and cultural anthropology. Leaving a secure job was a gamble but now, decades later, I have no doubt that I made the right decision.

Since there were no sex courses in graduate school in the 1950s, I focused on sociological theory, philosophy, and cultural anthropology. I played around with the idea of doing my dissertation on a cross-cultural study of sexuality, but there was so little known and no one to work with. I did come back to that interest years later (Reiss, 1986). I also had in mind doing a book on sexual standards but since I couldn't do that for my dissertation, I did a dissertation on the conflict between the objective and subjective approaches in sociology. I chose that topic because people's intimate feelings were of central concern to me.

In 1953, at the age of twenty-seven, I took my first teaching position at Bowdoin College in Maine. The first course I was asked to teach was on the family. Never having taken such a course myself, I looked over a large number of textbooks and decided that I would judge them by how well they handled the topic of sexuality. I felt I knew something about sex and that would be a good basis for evaluating the textbooks. I had read Kinsey's study on males (1948) and on females (1953). I looked for how this recent research was treated as my basis for judging the family texts. Almost every one ignored most of the research, old or new, and simply presented a moral stance against premarital intercourse. In addition, there was a clear emphasis on female virginity over male virginity, a dogmatic position that offended my sense of scientific and ethical fairness. So I decided that my first articles would be about the bias in the family textbook treatment of sexuality.

My first article (1956) concerned how the double standard for men and women was ignored in our textbooks and elsewhere. I felt that the textbooks had simply taken this as a fact of life and never examined its basis or its impact on men's and women's relationships. My second article (1957) and was a criticism of the overall moral bias against premarital coitus in the family texts. Those texts made it appear as if there was only one type of premarital sex and that was lustful, self-centered, and irresponsible. It took two to three years to get these two journal articles published because they kept getting rejected. I am convinced this happened because they challenged the establishment and its moral premises. Once they did appear, my colleagues' response was overwhelmingly favorable; they were pleased that someone had taken up this battle against moralistic dogma.

Angered by the bias in the family texts and the difficulties in getting my first two articles published, I wanted to write a book that fairly examined sexual standards in our country. The many years of searching for a way to wisely choose a sexual standard had given me a wealth of ideas and I had to get them on paper. In just three weeks in August 1955 I wrote a rough draft of what would become my first book. At this same time I married my wife, Harriet. She was and remains a compassionate, nurturant, intelligent person with her own strong interests. I told her that I would be devoting my career to writing on sexuality and my work could arouse some strong public and private criticisms. Unfazed, she has worked with me on all my books and has been a major source of encouragement and enlightenment. After we married, I took a new position at the College of William and Mary in Williamsburg, Virginia.

I had been talking about sexuality in my family courses at Bowdoin and I increased the emphasis on sexual issues in my classes at William and Mary. Since there were no sex courses, it was in the family area that sexuality discussions best fit. One student complained to the president of the college, a World War II admiral named Alvin Chandler, about the "excessively open" discussion of sexuality. I had been using a short novel as a supplement to the text in my family course, Guy de Maupassant's Une Vie (A Life). It presented a view of the role of women in nineteenth-century France that was not available anywhere else I knew about. The novel, among other things, showed the abusive treatment of a wife by her husband, who was having an affair with the housemaid. President Chandler had been given a copy of that paperback by the student and he had it in his hand when he approached me on the lawn outside of my building.

On the cover of the book was a sketch of a woman in a full-length bathrobe sitting on the edge of a bed. Chandler held up the cover and said to me: "Let's be honest about this, Reiss, isn't this the type of book that you and I used to read behind the barn?" Shocked at his ignorance of de Maupassant and his lack of respect for academic freedom, I responded: "President Chandler, I'm a city boy and I have never even been close to a barn. This is a classic book by a world-renowned author. I think if you read it you will see that it affords excellent insight into women's role in the last century." Looking embarrassed, Chandler smiled weakly at me, said, "Thank you," and left. I never heard another criticism from him.

On rare occasions I had a religious student who would express the view that we shouldn't spend so much time on sex. I would simply respond that in my judgment we needed that much time because we know so little about it. Fortunately for me, my chair, Wayne Kernodle, was a Southern liberal who strongly supported academic freedom. Thanks to him and to the majority of students who liked my coverage, and to my wife and friends and colleagues who encouraged me, I did not hesitate to maintain my focus on sexuality.

Shortly after arriving to William and Mary, I read some of Albert Ellis's books.[1] I liked them but I thought he was wrong in making what I called body-centered sex the equal of person-centered sex. I wrote to him and he responded, beginning a friendship that lasts to this day. But what followed shows some of my timidity about openly presenting myself as a sexologist. After an extensive correspondence Ellis wrote me that he was publishing a new book, *Sex without Guilt,* and that in it he was going to refer to my views about person-centered sex being more worthwhile than body-centered sex. He asked me if I would consent to being mentioned by name. I thought about it briefly and decided that maybe discretion was, after all, the better part of valor. The very fact that Ellis asked me made me think it must be risky in some way. In any case, I told him not to use my name. I am somewhat ashamed of that decision now, but it does say something about the social climate of the mid-1950s that pressured even me, a person who was writing a book about sexuality in America.

However, I did agree to put my name to another of Ellis's projects. He, together with a few others, was seeking to found the Society for the Scientific Study of Sexuality (SSSS). I agreed to publicly support this and become one of the charter members. The "scientific" in the organization's title surely helped me feel comfortable with it. I did want to be scientific in the sense of being fair-minded in my writing because I felt so much of the social science writing was morally biased. Eventually there were forty-seven charter members and in 1957 SSSS was founded.

Ellis became the first president of SSSS but not without a fight. It seems that some members thought he was too extreme and they wanted a more traditional, moderate person to be president. So even in this organization of avant garde sexual scientists, societal pressures were brought to bear. Today SSSS has over 1200 members, a prestigious journal, and is influential in many ways. The societal pressures are different today, but they remain, as I shall discuss shortly.

My experience in obtaining a publisher for my first book also had an influence

---

1. See chapter 13.

on my approach to sexuality. In the summer of 1956 I sent a full draft of it off to some publishers for comments. From the University of Chicago Press I received a response that I was writing a book advocating greater acceptance of premarital sexuality and so I was not using an "objective" scientific approach. I had not thought it necessary to hide my personal preferences in writing this book in order to be "objective." Somehow you are objective only if you are not honest and open about where you stand on the issue being discussed. My belief was that all that was needed was that I should be fair and not distort any research findings or refuse to report findings that contradicted my views. But those were not the rules of the scientific game. So if I wanted to get my book published, I had to move more in that sterile, antiseptic direction. At this same time my colleagues at William and Mary were supporting similar positivistic themes about being value-free. Although I never fully endorsed the value-free perspective on objectivity, I learned how to present myself in that fashion. In more informal academic settings I clearly revealed my personal values and thoughts on sexuality.

The scientific stance implied in this "neutral" and "objective" methodology could serve as protection for researching the intimate domain of sexuality. A sex researcher could state that he or she was just reporting the trends and relationships and not endorsing anything. I did not refrain from writing my personal assumptions in my work for that reason, but I now see that it did serve that purpose. I was to reject the facade of value-free sociology very explicitly as time went on. But for a while, I wore the value-free garb and even accepted some of the beliefs of a more positivistic stance toward sex research.

In 1958, before my first book, *Premarital Sexual Standards in America* (1960), appeared, I began the research that would eventually lead to my second. I led a team of four senior sociology majors at William and Mary on a major research project: a comparison of sexual standards at a white high school and college with a black high school and college. I wanted to test my own idea that a new sexual standard, what I was to call "permissiveness with affection," was growing in America among both women and men and whites and blacks. This research eventually led to my premarital sexual permissiveness scales and to testing them on a representative national sample.

Carrying out a project involving high school sexuality in 1958–1959 Virginia led to some problems. When my four students went to get permission to give out a questionnaire to the white high school they were rebuffed by the principal. So I went instead. When I entered the principal's office, I was struck by his cool demeanor and I knew it was not going to be an easy sell. When the principal told me that he had to deal with parents who wouldn't like their children to fill out questionnaires on their sexual standards, I replied to him: "How many students got pregnant in this high school last year?" He thought for a moment and gave me an estimate. I said to him: "Well what about those girls' parents? What about the parents of all the others who will get pregnant this year and next year and so on? Would you want to be known as the principal who wouldn't help get the knowledge that can show us how to prevent teenage children from getting pregnant?"

I had placed him between two difficult choices. He would now have pressure whichever way he turned. Finally, he said to me, "Okay, but I will not give you the ninth graders; start with the tenth graders." I was pleased and accepted. I was learning the politics of sex research and the need to show people how their own interests lie in the research that we do. Anything less than high-pressure tactics would not have worked.

I also ran into further trouble getting permission at the black high school. Fortunately, my chair, Wayne Kernodle, was a friend of the principal and Wayne took me to talk to him. We started to converse about the Byrd machine in Virginia, and every time I tried to switch the topic to my study, the principal would return to Byrd. Finally, it dawned on me that I was being tested, and I said: "Have you heard the latest about the Byrd machine? They have inbred for so long that they finally have produced an idiot—the governor!" It was the right joke because the governor was not supporting racial integration at the time, and my joke showed where I stood. The principal immediately turned to me and said, "When do you want to give out your questionnaire?" He wanted to be assured, however, that I would not use the results to defame blacks as too accepting of sexuality.

I actually enjoyed such challenges. I felt that I must be doing something important if it was producing resistance. I knew I wasn't the only person in America who was perplexed and confused about sexuality and who would benefit by being more knowledgeable in ways that would enable one to make wiser, more satisfying sexual choices.

One of the main goals of the research was to see if my premarital sexual permissiveness scales would clearly delineate sexual beliefs in all four schools. I recall the excitement of the final calculations to see if the sexual beliefs of the students would fit into the cumulative scale patterns that go with the Guttman scale model I was using. I told John Stephenson, the leader of the four students, to call me when the results were in. Late one evening the phone rang and John was practically screaming into the phone: "They worked, they all worked, on all schools, it's perfect!" I published the scales and the results on the national sample I later obtained in 1964. Those scales have been used in scores of research projects. In 1989 I slightly revised the scales to make it possible to use just four questions to measure premarital sexual permissiveness instead of the much longer scales. The new versions have been tested in America and Sweden and hold up very well.

In 1959 I left William and Mary after and went to Bard College in New York, a small liberal arts college with a six-to-one faculty-student ratio. I felt it would be an ideal setting for me. The students were quite bright and very liberal-minded. But I soon found that the lack of structure led to chaos and goofing off, particularly on the students' part. The school also teetered on the brink of bankruptcy which further alienated me from what I thought was the perfect academic setting. But I wanted to include Bard students as an additional sample in my high school and college research. There was a belief among Bard students that they were all unique and all made their own personal sexual decisions in their own way. But when I gave them my premarital sexual permissiveness scales they came out within a very narrow range, the great majority of them highly acceptant of almost all levels of premarital permissiveness. So much for uniqueness.

At this time I heard from Walter Stokes, a psychiatrist in Washington, D.C., and one of the charter members of SSSS, that the National Institutes of Mental Health (NIMH) had money they were willing to use for sex research projects. I wrote a grant proposal which was to take the data gathered from the four schools in Virginia and analyze it carefully to test out a number of the ideas I would describe in my *Premarital Sexual Standards in America*. Urie Bronfenbrenner, a Cornell University sociologist, was sent by NIMH in late 1959 to interview me about the grant request and to talk to me about my forthcoming book. He seemed favorably inclined and took my description of my book as sufficient without asking to see the manuscript. In June 1960 I received a letter informing me that my grant request to NIMH had been approved by the peer review committee, with the proviso that I remove the word "sexuality" from the proposal's title. This was so that when the Office of Management and Budget (OMB) looked over what grants had been funded, no one would object. Once again, it was clear that even scientific research had to be nonthreatening if it was to be approved. This was true even thirty years later when in the early 1990s the U.S. government refused to fund two sex research projects that were aimed at studying sexual behavior related to HIV/AIDS.

When it was published in 1960, *Premarital Sexual Standards in America* predicted that we would have a major change in our sexual behavior by the end of that decade because we were witnessing significant liberalizing changes in our moral attitudes toward premarital sexuality. I argued that "permissiveness with affection" would become the dominant standard and replace abstinence. I think much of that did happen. The book was translated into several languages, issued in paperback, and kept in print for twenty-five years. Just months after it was published, I was invited to join the faculty at the University of Iowa in Iowa City. Thrilled to escape the false paradise of Bard College, Harriet and I and our two-year-old son, David, headed out to the Midwest.

My research grants multiplied to cover the 1960-to-1964 period. In addition, I received funding to add a representative national sample drawn by the National Opinion Research Center to test my two twelve-item premarital sexual permissiveness scales and see if they would hold up in such a representative national sample. The scales were tested in June of 1963 and they worked beautifully. This ushered in the era of using representative national samples to test our ideas about sexuality. Other national surveys followed in the 1970s, and by the early 1990s we had well over a dozen representative national surveys that contained questions on sexual attitudes and/or behavior.

During the eight years I was at Iowa (1961–1969) I was invited to talk to various campus groups and then to other universities and even appeared on national television and radio. Sexuality in America was changing and by then we all knew it. The sexual revolution was, as I had predicted, underway and America wanted to know more about where we were headed and why. My book *The Social Context of Pre-marital Sexual Permissiveness* (1967) helped fill that gap by reporting on the 1963 national sample and also on the several high school and student samples that I had gathered between 1959 and 1963. The federal government began, a bit more openly, to fund sex research projects. But the atmosphere in the country at large was slow to change. I recall a couple of experiences when I spoke at other universities that made that clear.

In a speech in South Dakota, after I reported on the increased attitudinal accep-tance of premarital coitus among young people, someone in the audience stood up and said: "You have talked to us about sexual trends for forty-five minutes but never once did you mention the name of Jesus Christ. How can we solve our sexual prob-lems without bringing Christ into our dialogue?" I responded: "I had two reasons for not bringing Christ into my talk: First, I am trying to be scientific in my analy-sis and not invoke religious perspectives; and secondly, I am Jewish." That quieted the religious section, at least temporarily. It also got a few laughs. I do believe that humor is a great pacifier in all potentially conflictful situations, including sex.

Another time at a university in Wisconsin, at the end of my talk a man asked me how I would feel if my daughter were to have premarital intercourse. He obvi-ously expected me to feel uncomfortable by that query. I looked at him and said that I would indeed have problems if my daughter had premarital intercourse. He started to smile indicating that he had made his point, but then I added that my daughter was only five years old. These examples illustrate the presence even in uni-versity settings of a strong group of supporters for what I call "compulsory" absti-nence, that is, the belief that abstinence is the only moral standard and therefore we should and must all abide by it. There was a time in my past, given my own ortho-dox religious training, when I myself was inculcated with compulsory abstinence beliefs, but they never fully took hold. I seemed to always be a pluralist, although it took years to figure out just what was acceptable and what was not, even in a broad pluralist setting. I think many Americans retain the remnants of compulsory abstinence in their psyches which has slowed down our ability to develop a plural-ist ethic that can make today's sexual behaviors safer than they are. I dealt with this problem most directly in my book *An End to Shame: Shaping Our Next Sexual Revo-lution* (1990).

After *The Social Context of Premarital Sexual Permissiveness* was published, I was offered many research and other positions. That book utilized the first national sam-ple for a scale measuring sexual permissiveness and it presented seven propositions explaining differences in premarital sexual permissiveness that exist in various sociocultural settings. I put forth my "autonomy theory," which proposed that the greater the autonomy of young people the higher the level of acceptable coitus. That theory has been tested and generally supported in many subsequent research projects. This book has been a major influence on theoretical explanation of sexual-ity and to this day is cited many times by other researchers.

In 1969 I left the University of Iowa to assume my present position as director of the Family Study Center at the University of Minnesota. By then I was serving on U.S. government peer review committees for research projects in the areas of sexuality and family. Money was available for research on teenage pregnancy, divorce, and other projects. Sexuality research of various kinds could be rather easily sandwiched between such projects.

In 1971 I published the first edition of my new textbook on the family. My 1965 article on the universality of the family was one of the cornerstones of this book because it offered a way of seeing what the family does in all societies, not just ours. I also incorporated my first two books on sexuality and the many theoretical ideas that I had developed. The text was very successful and went into four editions between 1971 and 1988 before I got tired of revising it. I believe I have had an influence on subsequent textbooks in this area in that I encouraged others to be bolder in their writings. In 1972 I edited a book of readings to accompany the first edition of the textbook and wrote an article on trends in premarital sexuality for that reader that became one of my most quoted papers.

In 1974 I stepped down as director of the Family Study Center to become a regular member of the sociology department and to have more time to do my own research and writing. I examined some new areas such as explaining contraceptive usage in a study on our campus done by myself and two other colleagues. Theoretical explanation has always excited my interest and it did so here in contraceptive behavior as well. Several followup studies were undertaken by others. I moved on to other challenges, one of which was to develop my autonomy theory to apply to marital and extramarital as well as premarital sexuality. Brent Miller, a Ph.D. student of mine, offered to work with me on this project. In 1973–1974 he examined the retests of my autonomy theory to see how well they fit while I worked on extending the theory to the marital and extramarital areas. We made this project a centerpiece of a two-volume work on family theory that we co-authored (1979).

I took my first sabbatical in 1975–1976. I was interested in studying sexuality and gender in Sweden, so when Jan Trost, a sociologist at Uppsala University who was going on leave, invited me to spend a year there in his position, I jumped at the chance. I thought we in America were heading in the direction where Sweden had moved years earlier but I wanted to see first hand. In the year we lived there, I learned a lot about how similar as well as how different sexuality and gender were in Sweden.

For example, the students at Uppsala University had a difficult time talking about homosexuality. I was one of a few faculty teaching the first graduate-level course in sexuality and this reluctance to discuss homosexuality was clear. Since Swedes have a strong sense of privacy, they feel it is not their business to comment on others and that was part of the explanation. But another part was that homosexuality was not equally accepted and they were just not willing to talk about their negative evaluations. I learned then that although we are more hung up than Sweden, they are not in Valhalla. The Swedes are also more egalitarian than we are, but they still have many problems of gender inequality. One confirmation of the validity of my grasp of Swedish culture came when a few years after my return a well-known Swedish speaker (Ake Dawn) came to our university to speak about sexuality in Sweden. He came to me and said he was using the chapter on Swedish sexuality and gender that I had published in 1980 as the basis for his talk because he could not find anything better written in Swedish!

Even in the late 1970s under President Carter the U.S. government was still hesitant to openly support sex research. To illustrate: In 1977 at the instigation of Jack Wiener of NIMH, a conference of sex experts was organized to discuss methodological and theoretical issues. Each of us composed papers to present and discuss and the proceedings were to be published by the government. But someone who saw the papers just as they were being prepared for publication objected to them as too bold. The government presses were stopped. Only after I, Jack Wiener, and others had written a strong objection did the publication go forward. Finally in 1980, without any notice to interested people, the proceeding appeared in a 500-copy run. Very few people even knew about it. I had the Family Study Center publish my paper in 1980 in one of our technical bulletins. This appeared first and avoided some of the many errors in the government's publication of my paper.

About this same time I worked with two colleagues using four national samples from the National Opinion Research Center to develop a theoretical explanation of extramarital sexual permissiveness. We tested the ideas on the four national samples while I developed a typology of extramarital sexuality and suggested what new measurements we needed. The article won a prestigious award and a few researchers did followup testing of some of our ideas. But like so much in the area of sexuality, this was not theoretically built upon. It seems that many researchers want simply to jump in and check out their ideas without first seeing what else is out there. Many others merely want to present descriptive findings from their survey. It is hard to build cumulative theory in this sort of climate.

The 1980s witnessed the strong antipornography campaigns of radical feminists such as Catherine MacKinnon and Andrea Dworkin. These two advocates twice got the Minneapolis City Council to approve an antipornography bill that would have allowed women to sue, on the basis of civil rights violations, any publisher whose books or magazines might be construed as promoting a sexual offense. The bill was vetoed twice by Mayor Fraser of Minneapolis. In March 1984, during the second attempt to get this legislation passed, I testified before the city council. The proposed legislation seemed to me to be such a clear violation of First Amendment rights that I felt it had to be stopped. I testified at the same session with Ed Donnerstein, a psychologist who had done extensive pornographic experimentation. The feminists felt that Donnerstein would support the view that explicit sexuality produces harm. But on that night, with my prodding, Donnerstein clearly stated that explicit porn without physical violence did *not* produce any aggressive reactions in the experiments.

The radical feminists turned on Donnerstein, but Mayor Fraser once more vetoed the legislation. When Indianapolis passed the MacKinnon/Dworkin bill, the courts declared it unconstitutional. Years later, in 1992, the Canadian courts declared the law constitutional; it now prevails in Canada and has been used against gay and lesbian literature more than anywhere else. So once more we can see that other countries besides the United States demonize sexuality and create laws that produce much more harm than good. Ironically, one of the first books confiscated under the new Canadian laws was a book by Andrea Dworkin herself. No more need be said.

During the early 1980s I decided to examine what we know about sexuality in different types of societies and try to arrive at some unified theoretical explanation. This was, as I noted earlier, one of the projects that in graduate school I thought of doing. It was a most ambitious undertaking but one that was needed. Most of what has been written on sexuality in other societies is descriptive and science requires explanation if its usefulness, both intellectually and practically, is to be maximized. My findings were published in 1986 as *Journey into Sexuality: An Exploratory Voyage.* I refused to accept the prevailing politically correct position that held that societies are all unique and can't really be compared. That position, I believe, is the not an outcome of the desire not to judge one society as better or worse than another, and not the result of any evidence. To accept such a position is to reject any type of scientific analysis. We must be able to compare and generalize if we are to explain and to examine our explanations. Because of my politically incorrect position, this book did not get the attention that I felt it deserved. Now some ten years later it is being cited more by anthropologists and others who are now themselves trying to build a comparative theory of sexuality.

In this book I concluded that there were three major "linkage-areas" in human societies—three parts of society that sexual behavior and attitudes are always intimately related to: (1) *the power system,* particularly in the area of gender power differences; (2) *the ideological system,* particularly in the area of what is considered "abnormal" human behavior; and (3) *the kinship system,* particularly in the area of sexual jealousy in marriage. I called this my PIK linkage theory. While this perspective does not deny many differences in the specific ways that sexuality fits into the power, ideology, and kinship parts of a particular society, it states that sexuality always does fit into those three linkage areas and can best be understood by searching for the particular ways in which those linkages are organized.

Shortly after publishing *Journal into Sexuality* I dedicated myself to writing a book about the new sexual ethic that I felt was developing in our country as well as in the rest of the Western world. My purpose here was to show how the resistance by the traditional compulsory abstinence ethic is one major reason why America leads the Western World in almost all sexual problems, including rape, AIDS, teenage pregnancy, and child sexual abuse. I became interested in doing this book after hearing so many people in the government, religion, and elsewhere say that the way to cope with HIV/AIDS was to "just say no." I viewed that approach are counterproductive and felt I had to speak out. This time, unlike my first book, I made no pretense of being "value-free." The title of this book indicates my approach: *An End to*

Shame: Shaping Our Next Sexual Revolution (1990). I directly and explicitly endorsed what I call HER sexual pluralism as the best hope for our being able both to contain our sexual problems and to develop a sexual ethic to replace compulsory abstinence. HER basically says that love, marriage, age, and gender do not establish the ethical status of a sexual act. Rather, the honest, equal, and responsible negotiation of that act is what gives it its moral stature. This is the new sexual ethic that is being increasingly taken up in the minds of the Western world's citizens. My students tell me that it is the standard they feel the most comfortable with.

An End to Shame was a social criticism and a problem-resolution book, the kind of book I strongly feel we need more of. I strongly affirm the value of fairness and avoidance of bias in our writings. I believe that we must not ignore evidence contrary to our beliefs, or distort what others believe. But we can be fair and even-handed and still make our suggestions for problem resolution. I call this approach postpositivism because it drops the impossible goal of being value-free and instead substitutes the reachable goal of being value-fair. I do not go to the lengths of some antipositivists and reject all science. Instead I make explicit the fact that even though we never will know "ultimate" reality, we still cannot accept a subjective, relativistic view of the world and maintain any sense of right and wrong. So we proceed with caution and modesty in our research and our explanations, but we nevertheless seek to better understand the world in which we live and to better control the sexual problems that impact on us.

In 1992, following an alarming series of rape and child abuse case, Governor Carlson of Minnesota appointed a committee to establish a state institute that would help promote child and adolescent sexual well-being. He asked me to chair the planning committee and I accepted the challenge. The Minnesota Department of Health, which was overseeing the planning committee, organized our opening meeting. Fourteen people from various professional walks of life agreed to serve. Very often these state-appointed committees are just for show and accomplish little that lasts. I wanted something to result and so I came to our first meeting with an agenda: I told the group that I wanted us to focus on defining what we thought was child and adolescent sexual well-being. If we could agree on a definition, then we could agree on what we were seeking and thus be better able to set up an organization to achieve those goals. Some members of the group had other agenda items in mind, such as a specific project to discover what the schools were teaching about sexuality or how effective the sex therapy programs for sex offenders were. But I felt those were objectives that could come later after we had clarified what we were trying to achieve. If we were to form an institute we had first to conceive our shared purpose. The meeting got argumentative, but I ended by asking everyone to come to the next with their ideas of child and adolescent sexual well-being and to give that discussion a chance. Then, if the group did not want to pursue it further, we would discuss an alternative way to proceed.

The Department of Health people were upset by the conflict expressed at our opening meeting. It appeared to me that they wanted consensus more than they wanted to accomplish anything. Three of them asked to meet with me before the next meeting. I began to realize the conformity pressures in a bureaucracy like the Department of Health and to thank my lucky stars that I was not in that type of organization. The three representatives tried to pressure me to let them run the meetings and set the agenda, saying that I could then be one of the discussants; but they would organize the agenda. I told them that if things got too conflicted I would ask them to moderate, but short of that I would not give up my powers to run the meeting. I also mentioned that I had clear ideas of what I thought would promote sexual well-being and that if the group did not end up with those ideas, I would write my own report and give it to the commissioner of health. They asked me if I was threatening them. Imagine that! You express your own ideas and it is taken as a threat. I said: "No, but I have convictions and I have beliefs and I want them to be heard. Haven't you met anyone like that?"

Our second meeting began with a great deal of tension on everyone's part. Would the group continue to fight over what our agenda would be? would they bring in their ideas about sexual well-being? would those ideas be compatible? The result was overwhelming: all fourteen people brought in ideas about sexual well-being that fit with my own thinking about promoting honesty, equality, and responsibility in sexuality. I gave my views last so that I could not be seen as pressuring anyone. The health department people seemed shocked and surprised by the group's cohesiveness, but they yielded and did not complain again. In fact, at the end of our four months we received a written commendation from the commissioner of health and the governor. Our committee reached consensus on our goals, and in the summer of 1993 we legally incorporated an Institute for Child and Adolescent Sexual Health (ICASH). The institute is still in existence and is flourishing. I learned from this experience how stifling a bureaucracy can be and how easy it is for bureaucrats simply to pursue the status quo and take no chances. Since in the area of sexuality this fear of the new and the innovative is even more the case, I encourage all of us to pursue our goals regardless and to challenge the bureaucratic forces of entropy.

As of this writing I am starting on a new book that analyzes the way sexual science has developed in America over the years I have been in the field. It is a personal diagnosis, prognosis, and set of recommendations. My working title is *An Insider's View of Sexual Science*. I will deal with key problematic issues over the past several decades, such as public resistance to sex research, the narrow focus of current sexual science, the lack of theoretical explanation, the hegemony of micro-analyses over macro-analyses, and much more. I will discuss the utility for sexual science of some of my own explanatory schemes, both old and new. I will also comment on the key theoretical and research work done by others. In short, the book will present my personal perspective on the field of sexual science. I have many complaints but I also have great expectations.

Well, in brief form, that's my life so far as a sex worker. But please keep in mind that we are all works in progress. So let's keep tuned to each other as things change.

Bibliography

Reiss, Ira L. 1956. The double standard in premarital sexual intercourse: A neglected concept. *Social Forces* 34 (March): 224–30.

———. 1957. The treatment of premarital coitus in marriage and the family texts. *Social Problems* 4 (April): 334–38.

———. 1960. *Premarital sexual standards in America.* Glencoe, Ill.: The Free Press.

———. 1964. The scaling of premarital sexual permissiveness. *Journal of Marriage and the Family* 26 (May): 188–98.

———. 1965. The universality of the family: A conceptual analysis. *Journal of Marriage and the Family* 27 (November): 443–53.

———. 1967. *The social context of premarital sexual permissiveness.* New York: Holt, Rinehart and Winston.

———. *Family systems in America.* 1971, 1976, 1980, 1988. New York: Holt, Rinehart and Winston. (1988 ed. co-authored by Gary R. Lee.)

———. 1972. Premarital sexuality: Past, present and future. In *Readings on the family system,* ed. Ira L. Reiss, pp. 167–89. New York: Holt, Rinehart and Winston.

———. 1980. Sexual customs and gender roles in Sweden and America: An analysis and interpretation. In *Research on the interweave of social roles: Women and men,* ed. Helena Lopata, pp. 191–220. Greenwich, Conn.: JAI Press.

———. 1986. *Journey into sexuality: An exploratory voyage.* New York: Prentice-Hall.

———. 1989. Is this my scale? *Journal of Marriage and the Family* 51 (November): 1079–80.

———. 1989. Society and sexuality: A sociological explanation. In *Human sexuality: The societal and interpersonal context,* ed. Kathleen McKinney and Susan Sprecher, pp. 3–29. Norwood, N.J.: Ablex Pub.

———. 1990. *An end to shame: Shaping our next sexual revolution.* Amherst, N.Y.: Prometheus Books.

———. 1993. The future of sex research and the meaning of science. *Journal of Sex Research* 40 (February): 3–11.

Reiss, Ira L., R. Anderson, and G. C. Sponaugle. 1980. A multivariate model of the determinants of extramarital sexual permissiveness. *Journal of Marriage and the Family* 42 (May): 395–411.

Reiss, Ira L., Albert Banwart, and Harry Foreman. 1975. Premarital contraceptive usage: A study and some theoretical explanations. *Journal of Marriage and the Family* 37 (August): 619–30.

Reiss, Ira L., and Robert K. Leik. 1989. Evaluating strategies to avoid AIDS: Number of partners vs. use of condoms. *Journal of Sex Research* 26 (November): 411–33.

Reiss, Ira L., and Brent C. Miller. 1979. Heterosexual permissiveness: A theoretical analysis. In *Theories about the family: Research based theories,* ed. W. Burr, R. Hill, I. Nye, and I. L. Reiss, vol. 1, pp. 57–100. New York: The Free Press.

Reiss, Ira L, R. Walsh, M. Zey-Ferrell, W. Tolone, and O. Pocs. 1980. *A guide for researching heterosexual relationships.* Technical Report No. 4, University of Minnesota, Family Study Center.

38

The Sex Surrogate

Barbara Roberts

Barbara Roberts was a Los Angeles sex therapist who professionalized the use of sexual surrogates and for a time served as a surrogate herself.

J AY WAS DIVORCED. He'd been dating but hadn't found anyone with whom he wanted to spend a lot of time. He'd had sex with some of the women he'd dated but found it not very satisfying. In fact, he was having trouble with coming too fast. Sometimes he came just at the point of penetration. It was with the women he liked the best, the ones who were pretty and sexy, that he had the most trouble. He decided to find out if sex therapy would help.

When Jay and I first talked, he told me that he was divorced and had settled on living the rest of his life as a bachelor. Although he wasn't interested in getting married again, he did want to have a normal and satisfying sex life. All he wanted was to learn how to hold back his ejaculation long enough for both him and a part-ner to come to orgasm. Jay asked me if there was any solution to his problem. There was, I replied, but he would need to have a partner to practice with. Jay didn't know anyone he would feel comfortable asking to do that, it was too embarrassing. I then asked Jay what he thought about working with a surrogate partner.

Jay knew that I used surrogates to assist with the sex therapy—that's why he had chosen me as a therapist—but he had many questions. What if he were not turned on to the surrogate? Since she was the expert, if he learned how to perform with her, how could he be sure that he would be able to function with other women?

From my experience, if Jay learned the things he needed to learn with a surro-gate, it was almost guaranteed that he could do the same later with other partners of his choice. I explained that he would learn that the magic wasn't in the surrogate but within himself. One of the causes of sexual problems is the belief that it's the other person who is responsible for one's arousal and satisfaction. At first he would just have to take my word for it and find out for himself as the therapy progressed.

I matched Jay with Ann, an experienced surrogate a couple of years older than he, attractive but not what society would call a raving beauty. Although Jay wasn't thrilled with my choice, he agreed to give it a try. During the feedback times with me after Jay and Ann had been alone doing touch exercises, Ann had to do most of the talking. She said that Jay followed my instructions very closely but that he didn't share much of how he was feeling about it all. Nor could I get him to talk about it. All he would say was that it was "okay." He seemed to be unusually reticent.

Ann, on the other hand, told me and Jay how much she enjoyed his touch and how comfortable she felt with him, but that she wished he would share some of his feelings with her. She was feeling "left out" and didn't know if he was enjoying himself, even a little bit. I, too, wondered what was behind his silent facade.

During a subsequent session, Ann and Jay ended early, urgently wanting to talk to me. Ann had been giving Jay a face caress, silently and slowly exploring every line and contour. Suddenly Jay grasped her hands with his as he tried to choke back the tears that were welling up in his eyes. In that moment Jay realized that what he really wanted was a close, intimate relationship with a woman, not just the ability to perform sexually. He had felt a tenderness and involvement with Ann which he had not thought possible. After all, she was only his surrogate, someone who would never see him again when the therapy sessions ended. Now, at last, Jay was really beginning to believe that Ann did care for him. The fact that she was not his ideal type just seemed to fade away.

Ann told Jay that she was relieved and complimented that he had finally shared some of his inner self with her. She explained that, yes, she did care for him and wanted him to be able to live his dreams. And, equally important, she was able to thoroughly enjoy the touching exercises because not only did his touching feel good, but during her surrogate training, she had also learned how to enjoy the experience of touching others. Thus she was not totally dependent upon another's skills and responses to make her feel good.

This was a breakthrough! It was now clear that Jay's silence was a coverup for his fears about getting close. Now the unresolved issues surrounding Jay's divorce and the denial of his need for emotional closeness could be addressed constructively in therapy. Concurrently, Jay and Ann would continue in their client/surrogate relationship working to improve both Jay's sexual capacities and his capacity for intimacy.

Privately Jay confided to me that he was getting to like Ann a lot but did not know what to do about it. I encouraged Jay to tell her just how he was feeling, reminding him that there would be no chance to do that after the therapy was over. He needed to make the most of his opportunity.

I would be there in our joint therapy sessions to help Jay and Ann end their relationship when that time came. Both I and Ann knew that when Jay had developed more confidence in being able to relate intimately to a woman, both sexually and emotionally, separation could take place without undue pain.

❊   ❊   ❊

When I first established the Center for Social and Sensory Learning, a Los Angeles sex therapy clinic specializing in the use of surrogate partners for single men and women, in the early 1970s, my focus was intimacy in sexual relationships, not just the reversal of sexual problems. My view was that even a one-night stand could be intimate. It all had to do with having a positive view of sexuality, self-esteem, and respect for one's partner. I was excited about the prospect of using surrogates as a part of sex therapy because only through the trial and error of experience have people been able to learn about sexuality. As with any other physical skill, book learning isn't enough. But this was the first time that experimental learning in the sexual realm had the chance of becoming a socially acceptable model.

Masters and Johnson shocked the world with the publication of *Human Sexual Inadequacy,* in which they wrote of their successful use of a new experimental therapy called *sensate focus.* With this method, couples were able to overcome sexual problems far more successfully than with talk therapy alone.

When these successes became known, many single men expected to be able to use similar methods for their problems. To Masters and Johnson the only solution was to provide surrogate partners. In explaining his reason for so doing, Dr. Masters stated: single dysfunctional males are "societal cripples. . . . If they are not treated, it is discrimination of one segment of society over another" (*Time,* May 25, 1970, p. 49).

At that time, providing sex therapy partners was both controversial and courageous. Dr. Masters was not, however, courageous enough to offer single women the same opportunity as men. He felt that both the professional community and the public at large would not accept that radical breach of what seemed to be the prevailing morality. But Masters and Johnson's first step had opened the door for surrogates subsequently to be used with anyone who had a sexual problem: men, women, gay, straight, couples, the disabled, sex offenders—even teenagers!

Following Masters and Johnson's example, a handful of therapists began specializing in sex therapy using the new sensate focus approach, and here and there therapists started to use surrogate partners to assist in the therapy. This was the wave of the future, and I decided to get in on the ground floor.

I had been a psychotherapist for over ten years, but being a staunch believer in experience as the best teacher, I decided that I needed to work as a surrogate myself before I could train and supervise others as surrogates. Therefore, I participated in the first surrogate training program ever conducted, a weekend of sensate focus exercises, held in San Bernardino, California. Rudimentary as it was, it was a great start. Thereafter, I offered my services as a surrogate to several therapists in the Los Angeles area. While there was a good deal of theoretical information available about human sexuality, how to use this information to help clients working with surrogate partners had not yet been developed. In the beginning it was necessary for surrogates and therapists to work closely together to establish the standards for this new type of therapy.

My first client was a man with multiple sclerosis. At age thirty-two he had never ever touched or been touched by a woman in an affectionate way. This was to be my ultimate test. First I had to teach Bill to wipe the drool from his chin. My second task was to protect myself, in the midst of a close embrace, from the spastic flailing of Bills arms, hands, head, and legs. Interestingly Bill's spastic reactions were less frequent and less intense once I had begun a body caress. I was also surprised, and delighted, that he was able to learn enough about pleasing a woman that there was a good chance he would be able to relate sexually to other women of his choice.

Working as a surrogate with my second client turned out to be a great privilege. The therapist had only told me that this fifty-eight-year-old man was "inexperienced." Seeing Neil once a week for a month, I followed all of the therapist's instructions for teaching the ABCs of sex. Then Neil said he had a secret he could no longer keep.

Neil was a Roman Catholic priest. He told me of the agony he had gone through making the decision to go to a sex therapist and asking to work with a surrogate. For many years he had counseled couples regarding their marital and sexual relationships. He felt that he was a compassionate and understanding person and he had been specially trained for this work. Yet, not knowing what an intimate sexual relationship was like from his own personal experience, he had always felt inadequate in his counseling.

With me Neil was breaking his vow of celibacy. He had very consciously chosen to do this and was glad that he had done so. However, he did not know whether he should reveal this fact in confession.

Neil's rationale was that this experience with me was a necessary part of his education, not just a personal sexual adventure. Only under the supervision of a qualified sex therapist would he allow himself to do this. I certainly was not one to judge his decision, nor had the therapist who also had been taken into Neil's confidence. Even if Neil's motive had been pure lust rather than education, I would have felt that a great honor had been bestowed upon me for being chosen to share in this momentous event.

After working as a surrogate with several other clients who had various problems, including premature ejaculation, impotence, delayed orgasm, and lack of desire, I felt ready to open my own sex therapy clinic. While Masters and Johnson had shown that using surrogates was much more successful than just talking about sex, it was still far from being an accepted professional practice. After all, wasn't it providing sex for money? And wasn't that the same as prostitution? Didn't that make me a madam? I often had to answer these accusations. I was continually being bombarded with requests for interviews and TV appearances, but I took on all comers in order to have the opportunity to explain what surrogate-assisted sex therapy was really all about.

There are several major differences between what a surrogate does and what we typically think of a prostitute doing. Frequently a prostitute provides only the sexual experiences that are asked of her. In many cases her job is simply to provide instant gratification. She may never see the client again.

A surrogate's main purpose, rather than to just provide sexual pleasure, is to educate the client in how to reverse specific sexual problems. And it is the therapist, not the surrogate or the client, who decides what activities are appropriate in view of the overall therapy. A course of therapy is likely to take several months or more. And, in most cases, sex (defined as genital stimulation and orgasm) is the least of it.

The fact that money is paid—for the services of a prostitute, a surrogate, or a sex therapist—is not the issue. We live in a society where monetary exchange for goods and services is the rule. The intent of those who insist upon comparing surrogate-assisted sex therapy with prostitution is to demean and discredit both. It is a reflection of our basically repressive culture regarding sexuality.

As to my being a madam, I was so confident that my use of surrogate partners was therapeutically advantageous that I didn't give it a second thought. Only after twelve years of practice did we have a minor crisis at the center. Following several talk sessions with me, I assigned a young man to work with a surrogate in hopes of reversing his problem of reduced sexual desire. In the middle of his first session with the surrogate, the man burst into my office to tell me that he was on the vice squad and that he needed to ward off a planned raid on the center. During just the first half hour with the surrogate, he had become convinced that we were a legitimate sex therapy clinic, not a front for anything against the law. That was the end of that.

Being thought of as a madam was so far-fetched that it really was not a problem for me at all. Nevertheless, some people were convinced that being a sex therapist automatically implied having prurient interests. For me it was not uncommon at social gatherings for people to hold me at arm's length because they were intimidated by my expertise. Sometimes I would be "hit on" in hopes of getting a free lesson on sexuality. Then there were the inevitable snide sexual jokes, which showed that my companions, many of them professionals, were not always that comfortable in confronting the subject of sexuality in a candid manner.

None of these things daunted my determination to become the very best sex therapist I possibly could. Helping people accept and respect their sexual urges as a natural part of life and helping them to have satisfying sex lives was compelling for me. As a child I'd had several sexual experiences initiated by adult men. There had been no violence or threats of violence. Yet I was sworn to secrecy and knew, from an uneasy place deep inside, that this was not socially acceptable behavior. The most traumatic part, however, was that I was blamed for being seductive and made to feel guilty.

From that time on, I searched for understanding about this most powerful of human drives: sex. I observed, asked questions, read everything I could get my hands on, and experimented wherever I could. In order to learn even more I talked my husband into having an open relationship for a short while, in which either of us could, by mutual agreement, have other sexual partners. From all my searching

I could only conclude there was something radically wrong with the attitude toward sex in our culture. The most important thing I discovered was that, despite the fact that we are continually being bombarded by sexual images and sexual innuendos, our society basically denies the value and beauty of sexuality. Therefore, we are taught very little about it, being left to discover what little we can, through a great deal of fumbling and bumbling and embarrassment.

What masquerades as sexual freedom is often only a rebellion against the lies, secrecy, hypocrisy, and ignorance about sex that our culture imposes upon us. We have been given the message that our sexual urges and attractions are bad. They are not. They are natural and beautiful. However, in our ignorance, how we act upon those urges is often what turns the sublime into the horrific.

Sex therapy utilizing experimental methods and surrogate partners became for me a way of making sex right both for myself and for my clients. I also hoped my work might have a redeeming influence upon some of the negative sexual attitudes in our society.

39

How I Became Interested in Sexology: A Personal Journey

Herbert Samuels, Ph.D.

Herbert Samuels is one of the few African Americans active in the sexology field. His becoming a sex educator and researcher resulted in a denial of tenure at one of the campuses of the City University of New York. Ultimately, however, following arbitration, he was reinstated and again allowed to teach classes in human sexuality.

I WAS BORN February 17, 1950, in a small town in Kentucky, one of the first black children born in the "white" hospital because my mother needed a cesarean section. My parents were working-class people: my father for most of his life was a janitor and my mother a domestic.

Growing up in the South in the 1950s, I can remember the "whites only" signs that designated restrooms and drinking fountains, movie theaters where blacks had to sit in the balcony, and restaurants where we could not sit at all. I attended a segregated school until eighth grade. The transition to an integrated school system went relatively smoothly, or at least from my thirteen-year-old vantage point it did. However, I did spend an inordinate amount of time in the principal's office for reasons I truly did not understand. The principal, a black man, told me that I should not become overly friendly with the white girls in my class because the town was not ready for "race mixing." I was perplexed by his reaction. I was only trying to find out what homework was due that day.

My parents were always open and honest when it came to sex; they invariably answered my questions without embarrassment or hesitation. As a result of their openness, I became the neighborhood sex expert. I described where babies come from to anyone who would listen. This would often cause problems for my parents when their less open, more inhibited friends would complain. Since that time, I have been totally fascinated with sex. What follows is my attempt to identify what influences led me to become a sexologist.

As an only child I received a good deal of attention, but I also spent much of my time alone, lost in fantasy with my toys. Two had great significance during my early childhood. My teddy bear (Boo Boo) was my favorite playmate when I was very young (between two and four). One of the games we played quite often was barber shop. I would be the barber and Boo Boo was the customer. Another favorite toy I had at that time was my Charlie McCarthy dummy. I would pretend that I was Edgar Bergen and perform for my audience—Boo Boo—to whom I would explain the facts of life.

I am sure that I was the only boy in Kentucky who had an electric stove and tea set. Why I wanted those particular items escapes me now; however, I do remember making an effort to bake pies and cakes in the oven. The stove was a toy but it did actually work by using an electric light bulb as its heat source. After baking some goodies I would have Boo Boo and Charlie over for tea and cake and converse with them, frequently about sex, as though they were real. My mother once told me that she received many negative comments from her friends in regard to my playing with dolls and tea sets; but she would explain that this was something I wanted and that she could see no harm in my having them. My mother was well ahead of her time. I had a relatively androgynous upbringing before anyone knew what androgyny was.

Clothing played a major role in my fantasy life, in particular, theme costumes. Depending my mood I would put on one of the outfits and play, usually alone, but sometimes with my cousin or a boy down the street. If we were playing cowboys and Indians I would wear my Wild Bill Hickok outfit. This consisted of a fake buckskin jacket, cowboy hat, two guns, and boots. We would chase the Indians on our stick horses so as to make the West safe for the settlers. When we played explorers I wore my Davy Crockett suit: a coonskin cap, buckskin shirt and pants, and a pair of moccasins. Superman was my favorite. I had the tights and cape and played superhero often, that is, until I jumped off the roof one day and found out how super I really was. Then I would imagine that I was saving a girl from some fate worse than death. My reward would be a kiss. I can remember my body tingling.

My earliest recognition of differences between the sexes was observing my parents nude when I was about four years old. I remember trying to peek under the bathroom door while my mother was bathing. On one such occasion my mother realized what I was trying to do, so she opened the door to let me see what she looked like. I noticed her breasts as well as her pubic region. I believe that I asked her why she did not have a penis. She told me that only boys have penises and girls have vaginas. I assume that must have satisfied my curiosity, for I never peeked under the door again.

The first time that I can remember being sexually aroused by someone of the opposite sex was in the first grade. I always wanted to touch the little girls in my class. Whenever I thought about it I would get an erection and I thought about it often. The first one-to-one experience I remember was in the sixth grade when I was the stage manager for the seventh-grade class play. After a rehearsal a girl asked me if I wanted to kiss her. This was the first time someone put her tongue in my mouth. I thought that I would die! I could not believe how soft her mouth and tongue felt on my lips. By eighth grade, I was totally captivated by sex. There were several girls in my class who were developed well beyond their years. One girl I remember vividly: at age thirteen she was 34-22-36! I stared at her every chance I got. I would take the same classes she took just so that I could be close to her. Words cannot express how totally obsessed I was. Eventually, she "allowed" me to touch her ass. I thought that I had died and gone to heaven. However, my "groping" was the extent of our physical contact.

From eighth grade to the end of high school my ability to discuss sexual topics got me a good deal of attention. But I was all talk and no action. I could talk about sex with ease at the drop of a hat. But I was too shy ever to ask anyone to have sex with me! Thus, I escaped high school with my virginity intact.

College started out very much the same way that high school ended. I was very free-talking about sex to the point where some people would want to talk to me about their sexual problems, whereas others thought I was crazy. I began to realize that most people responded to me differently. Things I said would have resulted in a slapped face if said by someone else, but I could get away with it. In response to my casual comments, people, usually women, would describe to me, in some detail, their sexual desires and experiences. While listening to their stories I would wonder, why are they telling me this stuff?

It has subsequently occurred to me that I was a very nonjudgmental person. I was never shocked by what anyone said to me nor did I condemn anyone's behavior. As far as I can remember I have always been that way. My parents never put people down for what they did. The best way to describe my attitude is by analogy with the first Polaroid cameras which were introduced in the 1950s. After you took a photograph you had to brush on a chemical fixative to ensure that the picture would not fade. As I grew up, I was never rubbed with a judgmental fixative.

I loved shocking people. The more outrageous I was, the more attention I received. The more attention I received, the more outrageous I became. Among some of my friends I was known as "Herbert the pervert," which I took as a compliment. But I was still all talk and no action.

The first time I had intercourse I was nineteen years old. The girl was a nineteen-year-old prostitute named Rosemary (I never knew her last name), who was introduced to me by an acquaintance from work. She did me for free! This was one of the most incredible nights of my life. Besides being the first time getting laid, this was the first time I ever touched a real, live naked girl! I acted very nonchalant, but I had a circus going on inside my head. I could not believe that I was actually going to have sex with another person in the room. Panic! What do I do? Do I become completely naked? Or do I leave something on? Well, the so-called sex expert wore his underwear all night. The next morning my underwear was so stiff it was as though it had been starched. But at least I was no longer a virgin. Amen.

My first year of college also marked the beginning of sex, drugs, and rock 'n' roll. Several weeks after my tryst with Rosemary, I had my second sexual experience—group sex! One of the few classes that I attended during my freshmen year was a sociology class taught by Professor James DeBurger, who later became a good friend. A woman named Sally quite often came to class wearing a fishnet top with her nipples thrusting through. I could not take my eyes off them. One day she saw me staring at her and asked me if I liked what I saw. I replied that I thought that her nipples were exquisite, and would she like to go out sometime? To my astonishment she said yes and invited me to her house for dinner. I also found out that she was twenty-eight years old—my first "older" woman. Arriving at her apartment with thoughts of lust on my mind, I rang the bell. No answer. I knocked on the door. No answer. Finally I turned the doorknob, the door was open; I walked in and called "hello." I heard Sally's voice say, "Come in, we're in here." At that moment I thought that my night of lust had been replaced with dinner with some of her friends. I walked forward expecting to see the dining room. What I saw instead was five naked people lying on a bed. Sally said, "Come join us." It took me about a second to decide what I should do. It was one of the most extraordinary nights of my life! To that point I do not think that I had ever even thought about group sex, let alone participated in it. This was an eye-opening experience.

Over the next two or three years, I married and divorced, did my share of drugs, had more than my share of sex, and was on academic probation until I graduated some seven years after I had started college. As poor a student as I was, Professor DeBurger always said that I had the potential to do whatever I wanted. Knowing about my drug taking and sexual habits, one day he asked me, "Why are you doing what you're doing?" I did not have a clue what he was talking about nor, for that matter, the answer to his question. When I replied, "I don't know," he said, "Why don't you find out?" and gave me a reading list of books that he knew would pique my interest. One was a novel by Robert Rimmer called *Proposition 31,* which describes alternative lifestyles and living arrangements that I had never heard of or thought about. I became fascinated with the ideas expressed in Rimmer's work. It was a revelation. I was surprised to find that so many people had written about sex in such a serious way. I discovered Kinsey, Masters and Johnson, Havelock Ellis, and many others. Although I did not know it at the time, this was the beginning of a career.

I finally graduated from college with a B.A. in psychology. If it were not for my girlfriend/second wife, Joan, I would have never finished. She gave me the support and encouragement I needed to complete my undergraduate work.

I had been working as a drug counselor at a therapeutic community and I continued at that job after I graduated. I was thrilled to have a B.A., and the work that I was doing was meaningful. Nevertheless, it did not provide me with enough emotional or intellectual satisfaction. There was something missing. Then two new employees were hired, both of whom had just received master's degrees in psychology. It did not take me long to determine that they were making twice as much money as I was and that they knew about half as much about drugs. Entirely from an economic standpoint, I embarked upon a quest for a master's program.

My undergraduate transcript was an embarrassment. But with letters of recommendation and affirmative action, I was admitted to a social work program. I had no particular calling to become a social worker, I just wanted a master's degree. At first I was intimidated at the thought of being in graduate school. I felt like an impostor who would soon be discovered as someone who lacked the skills necessary to succeed. But as time went by, I realized that I could hold my own; in fact, I did quite well.

All students were required to take field placements. Mine was in the education department of Planned Parenthood where my main responsibility was to conduct birth control lectures for adolescents seeking contraception. Subsequently, I began to do birth control lectures for area junior and senior high schools. The questions that many students had were more about sexual behavior than about contraception. The more sexual questions the students asked, the more uncomfortable their teachers became. I knew that I had found my calling, talking about sex and getting paid for it! What could be better? My field placement led to a full-time position after I received my master's in social work.

Working at Planned Parenthood was a very good experience. I learned a great deal about conducting training groups from my boss, Howard Mason, a very skilled and talented educator. I eventually became the adult program coordinator, which included curriculum development. I had been working at Planned Parenthood for about a year when I found myself becoming more and more restless. At the age of twenty-seven, I was thinking, "Is this all there is?" I had never been out of Kentucky for more than a week. Until I was twenty-five, I had never been on a plane! I wanted more, but I did not know what.

Deus ex machina! I received a telephone call from one of my former social work professors who knew of my interest in sexuality and had recently spoken to someone who had received his Ph.D. in human sexuality from New York University. I never knew that such a thing existed. The more I learned about the NYU program, the more intrigued I became. It seemed as though someone had looked into my psyche and designed a program especially for me.

I had to get into this program. It was not only my way out of Kentucky, it was a Ph.D.—in sex! It does not get any better than this. I had my interview with the late Deryck Calderwood, the director of NYU's human sexuality program, at the Bristol Bar & Grill in Louisville, Kentucky. I had never before met any one like Deryck. He was a middle-aged white male with white hair and a white beard, wearing an earring in his left ear and dressed in a blue jumpsuit—very unusual attire for Kentucky in 1978. The interview went well. I started the NYU human sexuality program that summer as part of a group that would be spending the summer in Nairobi, Kenya. For someone who had scarcely been out of Kentucky, I was overwhelmed. Many of the participants had gone on previous NYU excursions; therefore, they had developed a natural bond of closeness and comfort with each other. Fortunately, there were several individuals who, like me, were new to NYU. We gravitated toward each other.

My second day in New York City, the group went on a field trip to Plato's

Retreat, the premier on-premises swing club in the country. Wall-to-wall naked people having sex! I had found a home! The next day we were on a plane to Kenya.

My years in the NYU human sexuality program were some of the most gratifying of my life. I was surrounded by people who could at least discuss sexual topics without apologizing for it. And then there was Deryck Calderwood, one of the most unique, creative, and misunderstood persons I have ever known.

Deryck's approach to sexuality education, in part, was to provide you with an opportunity to confront your prejudices. He would challenge you to go beyond preconceived notions about atypical sexual behavior and those who engaged in them. It was his philosophy that if you have not had the experience yourself, you should at least talk with someone who has. To this day I am continually surprised by colleagues who write about a variety of sexual behaviors without having spoken to anyone who has engaged in those behaviors.

While I was pursuing my doctorate, I began to do adjunct teaching at some area colleges. This led to a full-time position within the City University of New York (CUNY) system. In my health education courses I began to develop topics on human sexuality, drugs, and behavior. While presenting the proposal for the sexuality course to the college-wide curriculum committee, I was surprised by the sophomoric attitude of many of my colleagues. These were people with advanced degrees giggling at the mention of sex. Of the many comments made at the meeting, two stand out in my mind. First, someone wanted to know if there was going to be a lab component to the course; second, someone alleged that the content of the course might be too controversial for our student body. There was definitely an air of discomfort in the room that day. Nevertheless, my proposal was approved.

From the reaction of a few of the members of the curriculum committee, I knew that teaching sexuality in the manner that I had proposed was going to disturb some of my colleagues. However, I was not going to change my teaching methodology to make a few people more comfortable. As the years went by, I would periodically hear from students and friends about how controversial other faculty considered my sexuality course to be. They not only thought it was scandalous but also that I was the devil incarnate. I was mostly amused by these observations until October 19, 1985, ten minutes before the start of my human sexuality class. I was informed by the acting department chair that the Departmental Personnel and Budget (P&B) Committee had voted to deny me tenure. I was stunned. My own department voted against me. How I managed to teach my sexuality class after hearing the news escapes me.

I followed the appeal process within the college and every time I was denied, it reopened the wound. I always felt that if I could have a fair hearing, my case would be sustained, but that would be several years away. August 31, 1985, was my last official day at the college.

To a certain extent I had been very naive in regard to the tenure process. But, as I was subsequently informed by a few colleagues who supported me, the issues surrounding my case had more to do with the fact that I taught sexuality at all than with how well or poorly I taught it. It seemed that some members of the P&B committee were troubled by the fact that I provided sex counseling for students and that I wore an earring.

On December 31, 1988, I was informed by my union representative that my case had gone to arbitration and that I had won by a unanimous decision. By September 1989, I returned to the college, with tenure, to resume my teaching responsibilities. Although this was a painful episode in my life, initially being denied tenure afforded me with experiences and opportunities that I would otherwise not have had; and I became more sophisticated in navigating through the political eddies of academe. It also reaffirmed my commitment to teach sexuality at CUNY by applying the same methodological principles and theoretical assumptions that I had learned at NYU. However, the most rewarding aspects of this whole affair were the letters and phone calls of support I received from former students. It was a most humbling experience being told by students that I had made a difference in their lives, and it helped to sustain me through this difficult time.

It has been more than twenty years since my initial involvement with sexuality education. It still remains a source of controversy and those who enter the field are still viewed with opprobrium. Like many of my colleagues I did not plan to become a sexologist, I more or less stumbled into it. Nevertheless, I cannot imagine doing anything else. I have had the privilege of teaching and interacting with more than 15,000 students from twenty-six different countries. I have learned just as much, if not more, from them as they have from me. I do not believe that sexologists or sexology will ever be accepted as a mainstream, esteemed profession. The erotophobes will see to that. But if you can stand the heat, the kitchen can be a warm, life-enhancing place.

40

A Leader Grows in Brooklyn

Patricia Schiller, Ph.D.

Pat Schiller started as a lawyer, but became interested in sexuality through her service with the Legal Aid Society. She founded the American Association of Sex Educators and Counselors (AASEC) in 1967, the name of which was soon changed to include Therapists (AASECT). It was the first professional organization of sex educators and therapists to establish national standards for training and certification. It also established a code of ethics for its members.

I WAS BORN and spent the first twenty-eight years of my life in Brooklyn, when Brooklyn was a considerably different kind of place than it is today. My background was that of the nonpracticing, but deeply idealistic Jew, with a passion for the betterment of the human condition. My mother encouraged me to think for myself, and to be myself. And she helped me to make the fullest possible use of the cultural riches of Brooklyn and Manhattan—their museums, their concerts, their theater, their parks. Under this kind of encouragement, I thrived and matured. I was told by others that I was bright child and I was a tall child, physically. This helped me assume a leadership role among my peers at an early age. Thus developed patterns of relating to people and causes that have stood me in good stead throughout my career.

At the age of ten, I started the first course of nature talks for children, by children, at the Children's Museum, a section of the Brooklyn Museum. At school, I was usually the one who was placed in charge of the class when the teacher found it necessary to leave the room. I developed a love of teaching that has stayed with me throughout my career. I was a Girl Scout leader by the time I was nineteen, where I developed a reputation for insisting that scouting should prepare a girl for womanhood, and that nature walks were not the only aspect of life that should be of concern to those who were working with maturing girls. By the time I was twenty-one, I was one of the youngest head counselors at coed children's summer camps. Here, again, my interest in innovation, and in education, came quickly to the fore. Not only did I develop programs for the children and youth who were campers, but I organized counselor-in-training programs as well, teaching the older children to work with the younger ones.

Meantime, I had been making my own career choice. This had not been easy for me. My widowed mother urged me to become a teacher. This seemed a logical choice, in view of my fascination with all aspects of the teacher-learner situation; moreover, it fitted nicely with the prevailing attitude that teaching was somehow the kind of thing a woman ought to do. Besides, the Depression was worsening, and a woman needed to be trained at something that would enable her to work if she needed to. And "there would always be a need for teachers." But I had become fascinated with the study of law. This seemed to be the best instrument and process to change social evils. I stuck to my determination that I would be a lawyer. I was keenly aware of the problems of poverty and human need brought on by the Depression, and I saw the law as a defender of the underdog.

This decision proved to be a crucial one in many ways. My father died when I was eight, and my mother and siblings took a united stand: they would help me financially with my education if I would prepare to become a school teacher, but that assistance would not extend to the study of law. Thus, to decide for the law meant a significant step in the direction of psychological and financial independence. Yet, after a year spent in trying to follow my family's advice, I decided I had been right all along. I withdrew from my full-time teacher-training program and enrolled in a pre-law course as a part-time student. The decision did not result in a sharp break with my family. They did not waiver in their mutual respect and love, and I continued to live at home throughout the rest of my educational career. It did become necessary for me to find work to pay my college expenses, however, so I got a job at sixteen years at Macy's, where I became the youngest part-time section manager Macy's had ever employed. I felt grown up, good, and on my way.

I continued, after pre-law studies, on to law school, working part-time. I was having my first experience of competing in class with a group of my intellectual peers, yet of being one of only three women enrolled in the class. Here, as might well not have been the case had I chosen teaching, I became aware of sexist stereotyping and of the difficulty with which a woman could obtain the right to stand on her own feet, as a person, and be accepted for what she was and what she could do.

It was, however, a time of almost boundless opportunity for young lawyers. Franklin Roosevelt's New Deal, with its proliferating governmental agencies, together with the sense it provided of really getting things done for those who needed help the most, made Washington a magnet for the idealist. During the law school period, in spite of a 9:00 A.M.-to-2:00 A.M. schedule of work, study, and school, I did volunteer work for the Women's Trade Union League, League against War and Fascism, and League to Abolish Capital Punishment. After passing my bar examination, I worked for a time as a labor lawyer in New York City.

But in May 1941, I went to Washington, where I began a series of governmental legal jobs with the Bureau of Indian Affairs; with the Office of Tax Certification for the new aircraft industries; and with the Office of Price Administration, where I gained experience as a litigator against industries in price violations. It was there, also, that I began to sense the significance of an interdisciplinary approach to human problems: economic, legal, social, and psychological.

Meantime, I had met and married Irving Schiller, himself an outstanding lawyer with the Securities and Exchange Commission, and a husband who was always to prove supportive of my determination to make the fullest possible use of my many abilities, both within my home and outside of it. The first three years of our marriage found us separated by World War II. I resigned my job to mother two children in a one-parent home. The needs of a young family claimed my first attention. However, by mid-1947 with a returned husband, the urge for a career had reasserted itself, and my interest in working part-time, because of my desire to be with my children, made my decide to become a teacher after all. I completed my teacher preparation, passed my District of Columbia license examination, and, on a part-time basis for two years, I taught English and history in a neighbor junior high school. But in 1951 the Korean War broke out. Suddenly, there was a great need for those with legal experience in governmental agencies, and I did litigation and appellate work for the Wage Stabilization Board, a position I held until 1954.

Uncertain as to what I wanted to do next, but urged by my husband and friends to make more direct use of my legal training, I made a first step by volunteering for service with the Legal Aid Society. This proved to be one of those steps—taken utterly without foresight or intention—that turned out to be the greatest significance, for me personally, and for the sex education, counseling, and therapy movement. For half of the people who came to the Legal Aid society for help came with problems in family law. For some time, it had been apparent in the society that the legal approach to such problems was not adequate. The adversary stance is not designed to deal with people and viable marriages. The result was that many poor clients with marriages that, given the right kind of help, might have been saved, simply did not get the kind of help they needed.

Efforts had been made to refer these clients to family agencies in the district, but this approach had proven to be less than satisfactory. Such referrals frequently involved a delay of several weeks before an initial appointment could be made, during which time a deteriorating situation had deteriorated further. Clients were angered at being told they must contact another agency, having already worked up their courage to the point where they would seek help from one. Lawyers had no understanding of the marriage counseling process, or of its changes in helping a marriage. Frequently, the lawyers themselves (all volunteer, it should be remembered) had so little knowledge of marriage counseling that they failed adequately to structure the referral they were attempting to make.

Convinced of the significant contribution that marriage counseling could make, I proposed that the solution was a marriage and sex counseling service within the Legal Aid Society. When it was then suggested that I undertake such a service, I consulted with Dr. Walter Stokes, psychiatrist and marriage counselor and president of the American Association of Marriage Counselors, and Robert A. Harper,

Ph.D., formerly head of training of the Merrill-Palmer Institute in Detroit, two prominent, pioneering marriage and sex counselors in the D.C. area. With their backing, encouragement, and supervision, I began such a service on a part-time, volunteer basis, beginning in 1955, while enrolling at the same time in a doctoral program in clinical psychology at American University. In 1958, I was offered the full-time directorship of what was to become the first formally established marriage counseling service within a Legal Aid Society. In 1960, I received my M.A. in clinical psychology and was invited by American University to become its first director of guidance and and counseling in a office I was asked to organize. The services would include sex and marriage counseling in addition to the usual testing and personal counseling.

When viewed from the perspective of the 1990s, the range of problems was perhaps not startling: emotional immaturity on the part of one, or both, partners; lack of sex knowledge; distorted social and personal values; failure to develop goals in marriage; inadequate social relations outside of marriage; and absence of any cohesive family life. (It is of passing interest to notice how early, and in what a variety of ways, the awareness of interpersonal relationships—which Masters and Johnson were to explore so creatively and fruitfully—emerged as one of the key components in dealing with problems of human sexuality.) Exposure to such problems in the context of personal awareness, and the rapid growth of the social and behavioral sciences, especially in the areas of family living and human sexuality, combined with my basic interest in helping personal and my first conviction that life can be improved, to bring a new focus to my efforts. At heart, I am a rebel with a cause of some sort, yet with an awareness of the personal dimension in all human problems. At the same time, my growing experience in this new field meant that I was increasingly called upon for help by parent, school, church, and youth groups. So many, and so varied, were these demands on my time and experience, that I left the Legal Aid Society in 1962 to devote myself entirely to the burgeoning field of sex education and sex counseling.

Meantime, a chronological look at my major activities from 1956 will serve as an overview of the breadth and scope of the field as a whole, and as a sketch of the matrix out of which AASECT was to emerge.

In 1956, because of my growing reputation as a sex and marriage and family life counselor with the Legal Aid Society, I was invited to develop a sex education course for teachers at the D.C. Teacher's College. This was one of the first interdisciplinary courses to be offered in the country.

In 1962, working with the wives of the president's cabinet, at the invitation of Mrs. Dorothy Goldberg, wife of the former Supreme Court justice Arthur Goldberg, I directed a program for Widening Horizons, an organization concerned with providing vocational opportunities for inner city youth in the D.C. area. In turn, this opened up a new area of exploration, for it brought me in contact with pregnant teenagers who—as was the style at the time—were forced to drop out of school. It became clear that these girls, now homebound because of their pregnancies, needed schooling in the normal school subjects. Even more, they needed training in "mothering" as well as education in all aspects of sexuality if they were not simply to keep producing a series of out-of-wedlock children.

Thus, in 1963, I became the research and clinical psychologist and sex counselor at the Webster School—a pioneer public school for pregnant girls founded by Mrs. Elizabeth Goodman, a leader in special education, funded for four years as a demonstration project by the federal Children's Bureau and supervised by the Board of Education of the District of Columbia. After the initial four-year period, the school operated as a part of the district public school system and became the model throughout the country for providing sex education, personal and family counseling, continuing education, medical and nursing care, and nutrition education for pregnant junior-high-school-age girls. I developed the group-centered sex and family life education program as well as sex pretests and projective tests as well as peer group counseling programs.

In 1965–1966, I participated in a series of summer workshops in sex education at the University of Maryland, under the sponsorship of the National Association of Independent Schools. And in 1967–1970, at the urging of District Superintendent of Schools Carl Hansen, I developed an interdisciplinary program under Title III ESEA for the training of counselors, teachers, nurses, social workers, and students in public, private, and parochial schools so that they might begin to provide sex education and counseling at an early age in a school setting. This program introduced group-centered decisionmaking approaches, peer counseling, and parent education to the field of primary and junior and senior high school programs. An interdisciplinary team approach was built into the process. The project received the Pacesetters Award as the most innovative and experimental project by the federal Health, Education, and Welfare (HEW) Office of Education. These programs helped me gain insight into the need for training standards.

In 1966, Dr. Paul Cornely, professor of community medicine at the Howard University College of Medicine, and an active participant in various community sex education and counseling projects with which I was also involved, introduced me to Dr. John F. J. Clark, chairman of the department of obstetrics and gynecology. He appointed me special lecturer and, later, assistant professor at the College of Medicine, where I developed a pioneering program for the training of medical students in human sexuality and marital counseling. This was the only four-year program offered in any medical school in the United States.

It was clear by this time that a growing need existed to establish professional standards and training in a chaotic field. Throughout the country there were wide variations in the aim and content of courses in sex education, depending to a considerable extent on the background of the teacher: home economics, nursing, medicine, social work. Sometimes sex education was felt to be the province of the biology teacher, sometimes it was looked upon as a part of the program of physical education. There was similar chaos in the field of sex counseling. Some had come to it from a background of marriage counseling, law, medicine, teaching, or clinical psychology. Some who called themselves sex counselors had virtually no training worthy of the name, and there were some who were out-and-out charlatans. I was by inclination an idealist who believed profoundly that the human condition could be improved, a teacher and leader, and one who by training and experience was an organizer and administrator, as well as a sex educator and counselor.

In September 1967, I became the unpaid founder-executive director of the American Association of Sex Educators and Counselors (AASEC), eventually to become the American Association of Sex Educators, Counselors and Therapists (AASECT). With the full support of my husband, I devoted three rooms in my house to office space for the fledgling organization, and loaned it $1,000 from my personal savings to make it operational. A gift of $500 from Philip Stern, a Washington philanthropist, paid for a mailing announcing the first annual meeting in April 1968. Closely associated with me in these efforts was Rosalie Blasky, my good friend who came to AASECT on a part-time basis at its inception, and who remained as my part-time aide until April 1980. Warren Johnson, Ed.D., served as its first president. Working together, the board set standards, training programs, and certification which came to be nationally and internationally recognized. Over five thousand professionals have been members.

In retrospect, the guiding principles upon which AASECT was founded seem to have been inevitable. But by their enunciation, they have worked a powerful influence on the sex education, counseling, and therapy movement in this country, helping to establish it as a separate profession distinct from marriage and family counseling, psychiatry, social work, nursing, and so on, and thus giving it an indispensable foundation on which to grow and develop.

41

Timing Is Everything: From the Sexual Revolution to Sex Research

Pepper Schwartz, Ph.D.

Pepper Schwartz's research into couples had the distinction of being denounced by Senators William Proxmire and Jesse Helms. In part because of this she became a media celebrity, and since that time she has been able to do serious and scholarly research as well as write for popular publications such as Glamour *magazine. She is a past president of the Society for the Scientific Study of Sexuality and a professor of sociology at the University of Washington.*

HOW DOES SOMEONE end up as a sex researcher? As this book spins out story after story, it becomes apparent that there are many routes to this destination. My own is improbably stereotypical. Most lay people assume that people study sex because of some personal problem, issue, or obsession. Most sex researchers protest and say it ain't so—and many are telling the truth. But I would have to say, in all candor, that I was certainly drawn to the study of sex by an inordinate interest in the topic—not all of it academic. In some ways, I was destined—if anyone is destined for anything—to study this subject.

I say that because my first research and study group began when I was about ten years old. My mother (who would be in her mid-eighties now if she were still alive) was ahead of her generation and wanted me to be free of fears and myths about human sexual reproduction and functioning. I remember she had volumes of Kinsey and Havelock Ellis on the shelf and a huge drawing of a woman, nude to the midsection, on the stairway wall that led up to the second floor of our house. The picture was the subject of much snickering by my grade-school friends, but no matter, I bought my mother's judgment that the picture was "art" and that only barbarians would laugh at such a graceful representation. So I would sanctimoniously inform my friends of their lesser nature and defend the picture. I felt from the first, as my mother said, that sex was a good and beautiful and healthy part of life and that snickerers were the worse for their nasty turn of mind.

My mother was an unlikely champion of this subject. Born in 1911, she was desperately poor until she married my dad, and her high spirits had to be contained

413

in the most proper package if she was to make a "good marriage." She would not have dreamed of actually having premarital sex and she married an almost puritanical man; still, somewhere along the line, she developed the utmost compassion and tolerance for all kinds of people—homosexual or wildly heterosexual; she did not exact the same standards or behaviors from others that she expected from herself. She would have died before having an extramarital affair; she would never have forgiven my father if she believed he had strayed; yet she knew people who did all these things—and loved and accepted them as friends and neighbors.

When I was ten—and already showing a preternatural interest in sex—she decided that some kind of kindly intervention was necessary. A few years before she had had a wake-up call when one of my teachers not so gently called her up and said she had to do something about her daughter who was, perhaps unconsciously but nonetheless prodigiously, masturbating in class. My mother called me in and supportively told me that the teacher said I was squeezing my legs rather rhythmically together and that this was behavior that really should happen only in the privacy of my room. I knew instantly what she was referring to—but somehow I had thought it was my own private, and quite unnoticeable, little pleasure, and so felt quite mortified. But because of the way she told me that I had not chosen the wrong behavior, only the wrong place, I continued my behavior in a new venue.

Still, my mother knew that she had a child who, as she used to say, might need birth control "way ahead of schedule." So, at the age of ten, as puberty no longer seemed purely theoretical, she bought me a bunch of sex education books and told me that they would be in the linen closet any time I wanted them.

Now imagine what a nice sensation it is to go into the linen closet with all its white sheets and sweetly smelling towels and reach for a sex education pamphlet. And what pamphlets they were! *You and Your Menstruation, How the Sperm Finds the Egg, Myths about Masturbation.* No teen books in 1955 had explicit pictures of intercourse or hints about sexual pleasure. But, believe me, this was hot stuff, and I knew it.

So I decided to share it with all my friends. I started a club that met in my parents' knotty pine basement. Once a week eight girls sat around in a circle and read from my books and talked about the facts of life. We passed around a sanitary napkin and debated the possible destructiveness of tampons on our future. We talked about cramps—and how we would bear them. We argued about whether or not there was really such a thing as French kissing, which sounded too yucky to really be true. I published a newsletter—for five cents apiece—with bulletins about the latest discoveries about sex, such as what I read in the tampons box instructions, and little bits of information from our readings.

The essential confirming experience happened somewhere in our eleventh year. I was home when a close girlfriend of mine called me up in a near-hysterical state. She had to see me, something terrible had happened. Of course, I said come right over, and waited nervously to see what could be so terribly wrong. When she got to my house her face was tear streaked and she was seriously upset. Her mother, she sobbed, had found her touching herself and had screamed at her and told her that she was going to go crazy and go to hell because she was masturbating. Was that true?

A thrill of knowledge coursed through me. I can remember the feeling that moment so long ago. I *knew* that Francie's mother (an adult!) was wrong. I knew I *could* help Francie. I went to the appropriate pamphlet and together we read the sections that talked about going crazy from masturbation as "old wives' tales" (these pamphlets, admittedly, left something to be desired from a post-women's movement perspective) and read all about how masturbation was a normal and healthy expression of sexuality and that it was just ignorance that made people so scared of it. I told her that I masturbated all the time, my mother *knew* about it, and didn't think it was a bad thing. I told her, triumphantly, that maybe her mother grew up with all this bad information, but that *she* didn't have to. She could be saved by knowledge—as I had been.

My life in sex research went quiescent after this brief year or so of stardom, but the dormancy did not extend to my personal life. I was, as my mother feared, sexually precocious and because I was also smart, I understood very quickly that sex could get me entrance to places where nothing else could. The difficulty was, of course, figuring out how to stay on the "good girl" side of the line since it was also clear that being "easy" would ultimately lose you power even if it gave you a few early advantages.

My compromise was not to "go all the way" until later in high school, when I had a boyfriend who loved me, but to do "everything but" and see if I couldn't stretch my power over men—even adults!—more than current mores really allowed.

So I had a series of adventures that would have landed several men in jail for a long, long time in today's sexual climate. I will mention two. I was thirteen and my parents were at a resort. I caught the eye of a young doctor there (in my memory I think he was a gynecologist—but this may be my mind gilding the lily). We flirted—and ended up necking and petting in the archery hut. He was thirty-two. I tremble to think what would have happened to him even then if my father had caught him or I had squealed on him. Lucky man. I had no doubts about being every bit as thrilled—and culpable—as he was.

A later "conquest" was of a similar nature. I was fifteen and had gone to see a musical comedy show in my home town of Chicago. I started flirting with one of the male stars from the audience. I was sure he was returning my looks, and I wanted to meet him. Since my dad knew the man who owned the theater, I asked the owner if I could interview his actors for a class project. No problem. So I met Tom and—this part escapes my memory—somehow started seeing him. He was thirty. We ultimately ended up doing "everything but" in his apartment—crazy man, crazy me. But he respected my rules—and we had a great time. We stayed friends for the next fifteen years or so. I remember visiting Tom when he worked on "Dragnet" in Los Angeles.

Sex as a hobby as well as a vocation may not be in everyone's vita, but I found it gave me both interest and insight into my subject as it became clear that sex was to become one of the main things I wanted to know more about intellectually as well as physically.

However, I have to admit that for quite a while it seemed that it was going to be sport rather than science. Since sex wasn't really something you signed up for as a career, I was thinking about acting, law school, journalism, and, later in high school, sociology. I attended the University of Washington in St. Louis as an undergraduate studying sociology and medieval Japanese history, never really thinking about sex as more than a great part of my life.

When I applied to graduate school at Yale, it never occurred to me that picking that school was really going to shape my career interests. I was fascinated by the Ivy League patina, the challenge of an elite school with ambitious students, and the program of sociology and law. I was torn between going to law school and continuing with sociology, so Yale, which had a program that combined both, seemed the place to be.

And it proved the place for me to be, but for different reasons. I went to Yale right at the regeneration of the women's movement—and what better place to see contradictions between men's and women's liberty than at a traditionally all-male school. And what better moment to be there, during the debate and subsequent transition to coeducation. The tension over the "fall" of tradition and the excitement of coeducation was palpable. I became more interested in gender and gender issues, among them sexuality, than about the law, which seemed, in the late sixties, seriously beside—and in the way of—the point. I attended "consciousness-raising sessions" and women's groups, and read tracts on the inequity of gender roles as presently constituted. I got angry and got active. I reconsidered the "rules" and found them not only problematic but ridiculous. I, along with other women at Yale, started making up new rules more to our liking—though not necessarily always successfully or mutually agreed upon by men.

I became much closer friends with a woman I had known at Washington University named Janet Lever. We were both kids in a candy store—the male-to-female ratio at Yale was something that women in places like Washington, D.C., can only dream about—and we also found graduate school less compelling than the human drama swirling around us. We were both iconoclasts and, to some extent, sybarites (although I will admit to being somewhat the leader in this arena). We were also both feminists and interested in feminist scholarship before that term had been concretized (and before it embraced some ideologies which neither of us would have been comfortable with, such as some of the current stands on explicit sexual materials). We found the culture of Yale—and the gender division it engendered—so astoundingly sexist that we thought it might rupture when the first women arrived as full citizens. So we decided to research this phenomenon and, in order to experience most fully the conflicts and issues of the gender wars that might ensue, to enter as much as possible into the undergraduate experience.

And here's where sex gets academic. At this time Phil and Lorna Sarrel were putting together one of the first two large sex education courses for undergraduates in the country (the other was at Stanford). Phil was a professor in the medical school, Lorna a social worker who had a university appointment, and together they set up the course, student counseling, and eventually a small student advisory group. We asked if we could be part of that effort and if we could also participate as discussion leaders for the class. We were graciously allowed to be part of the group which was an eye-opening experience for me.

My first shock was the readings. Sarrel assigned what was available—and what was available was mostly pretty bad. Sometimes it was bad simply because it didn't handle what were, to my mind, central questions of interest to women. Sometimes I was sure that opinion was being passed off as fact. And sometimes the material was just downright sexist. Phil and Lorna, to their great credit, saw most of this as I did, and the discussion groups were allowed to be critical of much of the material. But I started reading as much as I could about sex, particularly about female sexuality. When I read the then wildly popular *Everything You Wanted to Know about Sex, But Were Afraid to Ask,* it confirmed my worst fears of popular literature. This book was prima facie evidence of research ineptitude and ignorance and contempt for women. I decided, as I'm sure many women across the country were deciding at that time, that it was my job in life to provide better information than what was being passed off as such.

I didn't worry too much about it as a career move at the time. This was the end of the 1960s and the beginning of the 1970s, when nothing seemed too outrageous. And unlike students of today, we seemed to have few job worries. Jobs were plentiful in the beginning of the new decade and the women's movement had finally found a crack in the employment market. Guilty departments were looking for a few women to hire as soon as possible—which of course didn't last forever, but was very much the case when we started to look to our professional future. So I didn't think much about the fact that my interest in sex might not be a high prestige area of study. And in truth, I was interested not just in sex, but in family and gender. My Ph.D. thesis was on courtship and its effect on gender norms and self-image; sex was only one part of the dissertation. Even an early book I co-authored had only one chapter on sex. Still, that was one chapter more than most books of the time had devoted to the subject; it helped me be identified by—and identify with—other people who were studying this brave new subject.

I was hired right out of graduate school, with my thesis still incomplete and without an interview, by the University of Washington. Coming west was not really my first choice. But my first husband was from San Francisco and deeply loathed the East Coast. So I promised him that if I got a job offer on the West Coast, I would take it. The offer sealed my fate, and having glimpsed Seattle and found it beautiful, I conceded a West Coast venue. Twenty-three years later I am still here and still in love with the place. Lucky me. Lucky that I had happened into a place that could provide me support, instead of scorn, for the kind of work I wanted to do. And, most incredibly lucky of all, another person to write with, who would change my life for the next twenty years.

I came in the summer when most of the faculty was elsewhere. But there was a going-away banquet for Otto Larson who was leaving (it turned out to be for quite a while) to work at the American Sociological Association and National Institutes. So I was looking forward to meeting a few colleagues. I immediately noticed that one young man had very long straight hair and an earring—and thought this might be a soulmate. I got behind him in the cafeteria line and asked him his name. He seemed most suspicious of me, but that didn't last long. His name was Philip Blumstein, and he was to be my collaborator and dearest of friends until the day he died on March 15, 1991. I changed his life—and he changed mine—forever. Both of us, I think, were pioneers in sex research. We knew it and it excited us.

Philip was gay, but, amazingly, not "out" at the time I first met him. I assumed he was gay immediately—he was stunned that I did so. Philip and I began to hang out together and to talk about gender, desire, homosexuality, heterosexuality, assumptions, presumptions, past research, and studies that had to be done. The first major study we did together stemmed from our mutual interest in sexual identity and desire. It was such a "black box." How did people decide they were gay or straight? Was Kinsey's catalogue of sexual behavior linked up to sexual identity? Was it complex enough? If most people were either heterosexual or homosexual— how did some incorporate both men and women in their sexual repertoire? And what did that make them? We had a million questions—some from the concerns of the new gay rights movement, some from the women's movement, others personal or purely intellectual. We interviewed 150 men and women who had had sexual experience with both men and women and did almost ten papers on the nature of sexual identity. It was the beginning not only of a productive partnership but also of exciting discourse every day for twenty years. It soon made my marriage a residual category—not because I was having an affair of the body with Phil, but because I was having an affair of the mind, soul, and heart. I loved Phil; I loved being with him and talking with him and writing and thinking with him. Although it didn't eliminate my need for other men in my life, it made it quite impossible for me to be married at that time.

After that project and some small other ones, Philip and I engaged in a research project that would take the next ten years of our lives: the American Couples project.

I have gone into the etiology of that project elsewhere (Berger, *Authors of Their Own Lives*) and so won't go into much detail here. In brief, this was a large study comparing homosexual and heterosexual (both married and cohabiting) couples, ultimately about twelve thousand in all receiving a forty-four-page questionnaire, about six hundred having two- to three-hour face-to-face interviews, and a couple thousand getting two-year-followup, brief questionnaires. The study looked at the impact of gender and status on a variety of relationship issues and behaviors, not the least of which was the couple's emotional and sexual life.

Because it was funded by the National Science Foundation, it caught the attention of Senator William Proxmire and the laughable, but canny and powerful, Jesse Helms. The study was denounced on the floor of Congress for using taxpayer funds to study homosexuals. However, our grant was not revoked. Later, other researchers would be less fortunate.

American Couples made a public splash—in both the public and academic world. Irrespective of its scientific worth, its public relations' worth was significant: it was the first large study that systematically compared homosexuals and heterosexuals without posing homosexuals as a deviant case, and that saw the heuristic value in showing how same-sex couples illuminated heterosexual couples and vice versa.

Doing that study required becoming acquainted with a wide variety of gay community leaders and gay communities. Philip had some entrée of course, but not as much as heterosexual people might suppose. Gays and lesbians exist in different classes, subcultures, and value systems. Finding homosexual plumbers as well as stay-at-home lesbian moms turned into quite a challenge.

In the end, however, it was a fascinating journey and forever made me a staunch believer in gay civil liberties. After personally interviewing about eighty couples (about half of whom were gay or lesbian) and reading the transcripts of three hundred, I was struck most by how little their sexuality actually ultimately mattered and how much I ranked them by their humanity. There were many gay communities but few defined people day to day—there were successful and unsuccessful families, there was nobility as well as delusion.

For about a decade after the book was published in 1983, our data were really the best to be had on couple sexuality and also couple attitudes and behaviors. Philip and I became "experts" on a national and even global scale. What this means in practical terms is that both scholarly and media needs present themselves almost daily. At the height of it, I must have received four or five media interview or fact-checking needs a day. Even now, I get an average of one or two media or reference-type calls or e-mails daily. It is very flattering to be asked to pontificate on all manner of questions relating to gay or heterosexual couples' lives: but it is also dangerously easy to go beyond what you think you know into what neither you know you nor anyone else has a firm grasp on. Writers who call or visit have a job to do: they need to give readers answers. Researchers have to distinguish themselves from advocates or writers: they need either to have the facts or to show the logic of their hypotheses and emphasize that this is a hypothesis, not a fact.

But as one's work filters down into a more public area of debate it is hard to be pure. I found myself doing an enormous amount of expert testimony in areas both central to my area of research (gay custody cases) and a good deal more peripheral (the psychic impact of a man's inability to have sex ever again because of a personal injury situation). In the latter case, it doesn't take a Ph.D. to conclude that if a twenty-two-year-old sailor is rendered impotent because of faulty navy equipment, he will be angry, depressed, and run a whole gamut of negative emotions; and that this injury will complicate his future emotional commitments. But once you are an "expert," such things are asked of you and you try to apply some research, along with common sense and compassion, to the circumstances. There, is of course, the danger of becoming a "hired gun," particularly when you have given your expertise on a topic and then get called by lawyers all over the country to replicate that performance. Suddenly the expert is seen as a "professional witness," which means that the opposition will try to derail your credibility by trying to put that explanation to your testimony rather than the truer fact that your research happens to have made you very valuable to one side of a case. If the stakes are high (as they have been for the plaintiff in a number of HIV blood-transfusion cases I have been involved in), the tactics get nasty. The defendant's legal team tries to make you feel it just isn't worth it to be involved. They can make a pretty persuasive argument; but ultimately it would be too awful not to stand your ground and stick up for your perspective and the persons it will benefit.

Other pitfalls and opportunities came my way as Philip and I recovered from American Couples hoopla. Philip, always the more private person, rededicated himself to research a second book we were working on at the time. I did the same, but also got more intense about everything I was doing, which included popular writing and TV. This also has its perils and payoffs. Sometimes the payoffs are financial, although, unfortunately, not as grand as the lay observer might think; mostly they are the ego gratification of being recognized and thanked, and the legitimate feeling of doing good when speaking to a very large audience. I have done this now for a solid thirteen years in my columns in *American Baby* and *Glamour* (with Janet Lever), or on my local television station, KIRO, answering questions from viewers and calming their fears or giving them strategies for their lives that hopefully are well based in what I and other researchers have found about sex and relationships from the various studies and reviews of studies over our professional lives. Nowadays there are not many social scientists who do this on television—and far too many who do it on radio. Of the radio advice givers, only a few strike me as giving a damn about the people they talk to or of ever having picked up a book or a journal article. I am appalled at the kind of response I hear given over syndicated shows of various kinds. As I have realized how much trust I have been given—and how easily led many people are—I have come to believe that the proliferation of expert status is a dangerous thing. I have truly tried not to abuse this trust.

This combined academic-media identity has made me somewhat an odd duck among sociologists, although somewhat less among sexologists. The latter are always being asked to put what they have to say in plain language and to help people to understand how it will affect their life. Sociologists are considered suspect by most of their peers for trying to combine both rigorous research and the dissemination of information to the widest possible audience.

Philip, basic researcher that he was, saw this need of mine to take information to the masses as a character flaw but tolerated it. He was such a strong influence on me that it was only after he was gone that I became more serious about my media involvements. Philip, the traditionalist, would have thought much of it unworthy. But I disagreed then and even more so now. There is so much completely fabricated, mean-spirited prognostication going around that it needs an antidote, is so much news to be digested that it needs a context. And there is a public that often misunderstands and resents sex and sex research. Social science needs interpreters and defenders; otherwise, as history clearly shows, the voices of reason and research will be silenced.

Most of my research on sex concerns its practice in the context of close relationships. I have also studied some aspects of AIDS but I have not had the heart to concentrate all my work on it. Watching Philip and his lover, and my dear friend, Gerry, die was easily the grimmest thing I have ever witnessed. I have tried to help by joining the AIDS foundation board for a while, being charitable, and helping to fight for the civil rights of the afflicted. But too many losses have made me shy away from doing even more research on this topic. Just a year or so ago I and the world lost one of the most talented men ever to grace academia with his presence, or to grace my life as a friend, John Boswell, past chair of the history department at Yale and extraordinary scholar. I feel guilty that I have not dedicated more of my life to the study of AIDS, but I haven't the guts for it. I am so grateful for those seeing someone's disdain or amusement at my field of study written arrogantly all over his or her face; but these don't add up to much. What is privileged is to be able to spend the time writing and researching, speaking and disseminating information about a topic that people really want to know about, that really can make a difference in their lives. I am grateful to all the media outlets that have given me this opportunity. I feel I have picked a career that has helped me make a contribution; that has kept me fascinated, entertained, challenged, and happy. My husband is never bored when I bring home my work; even my kids are interested. If I have suffered from my choice of career, it hasn't been in any significant way. I hope this trend continues.

References

Berger, Bennett. 1990. *Authors of Their Own Lives: Intellectual Autobiographies by Twenty American Sociologists*. Berkeley and Los Angeles: University of California Press.

Blumenstein, Philip, and Pepper Schwartz. 1983. *American Couples: Money, Work, Sex*. New York: William Morrow.

Schwartz, Pepper.1993. *Love between Equals: How Peer Marriage Really Works*. New York: Free Press.

42

Sex: The Spiritual Catalyst

Kenneth Ray Stubbs, Ph.D.

Kenneth Ray Stubbs established the field of erotic massage. He is a publisher as well as a writer in the field, particularly in what he calls the spiritual aspects of sexuality.

EVELYN AND I were high school sweethearts. These were pre-pill teen years, a time when good girls *didn't*. What we did do was kissing, lips to lips, and necking. Fragrances of Old Spice and Shalimar lace memories of humid summer evenings while we parked in my mother's car, a green '53 Ford Club Coupe, in Bryan Park.

I wanted to go all the way. She probably did, too. But the puritanical mores and the bar of pregnancy kept us kissing for hours and hours, slow dancing to Johnny Mathis: "It's heavenly, heavenly / each time our lips touch / breathlessly." Kissing for hours on our first date, a water-skiing trip down on the river, I could feel the sun burning my back the whole afternoon. I didn't care. Evelyn's lips were full, moist with red lipstick, more like Marilyn Monroe's smiling invitation than Brigitte Bardot's erotic pout.

When I was thirteen, while hormones ushered in new urges, the basic skills of kissing began. I started playing the trumpet. The secret is in the embouchure, holding the lips tightly together while forced air from the diaphragm vibrates the lip membranes. Add the ta ta ta ta, the ta-ca ta-ca, and the ta-de-ca ta-de-ca of the tongue, and you have the agility and endurance for hours of kissing. Evelyn always smiled when she said her lips were tired.

Before the trumpet, before Evelyn, was Spin the Bottle and other games. My first erotic kiss came at about nine, playing Hide and Seek. Somehow a girl and I ended up in the same dark closet. One thing led to another. That kiss, and it was only a kiss, elicited a strange, new, swelling sensation in my pelvis. It was wonderful, and I didn't know why or what.

Not for another eleven hormone-wacky years, until I was twenty, would I have what we think of as "the real thing"—sexual intercourse. In the meanwhile, I participated in the age-old ritual known as *frottage*. Fully clothed, my date and I would rub our chests, abdomens, pelvises, and thighs together, almost to the point of friction burns. Always accompanying this was a fiery passion play of only lips and tongues probing, thrusting, circling, sucking, tasting. This ritual ensured virginity and prevented pregnancy, was frantically frustrating, but better than nothing.

When I finally went all the way, it was disappointing. All the years of hoping, fantasizing, and making out had set high expectations. Disappointment, however, didn't deter me from trying again. Hormone-driven desires, like tornadoes, find few obstacles.

Then I met Shannon. By now I was teaching sociology in a small northeastern college. The Beatles had progressed from "I Want to Hold Your Hand" to "Why Don't We Do It in the Road." Bob Dylan was shifting from the social protest of "Blowin' in the Wind" to lyrics about liberated women: "She's an artist / She don't look back."

The first evening we met, Shannon invited me to go to bed. Finally fantasy emerged as reality: the woman was the sexual initiator. In a daze, I could barely stutter out, "But I don't know you." Two hours later I recanted. Twenty-four hours later, without any disappointments, I waddled home, bowlegged and sore and very sexually satisfied. It was the beginning of three years of loving, kissing, cuddling, licking, sucking, and balling, the popular descriptive term of the day. Fully clothed frottage was now a part of the play, no longer a Victorian substitute. All across the country, traveling in our VW van, at any frequent flareup of passion, we would pull over, close the drapes, and proclaim the bumper sticker slogan: "If this van is rockin', don't bother knockin'."

The love and the sex were good to the very end. But we had evolved in different directions, and it was time to follow separate paths. Shannon went back East to become a poet. I headed to Mexico to study Spanish.

My career as a sexologist probably began in 1965, the beginning of my senior year as a sociology undergrad at Indiana University. I handed to one of my major professors my summer diary, written while I had been a civil rights worker in Alabama and Virginia with Martin Luther King's organization. But the diary included more than encounters with the Ku Klux Klan, tear gassing, and sometimes sleeping with a rifle by my bed. My personal life, including my sexual experiences, was there right along with all the other details. The first thing my professor suggested was to show the diary to the Kinsey Institute, only a few buildings away on campus. It turned out the institute was preparing a study of college students. After reading my diary, a couple of the Kinsey researchers asked me to come in for an interview. I had often fantasized about being one of the sex statistics at the famous institute. Now I had the honor of being specifically invited.

Only a few months later, in the course The Community, taught by one of the Kinsey researchers, we began studying the homosexual community, one of the few times human sexuality was discussed in any depth during all of my sociology undergraduate and graduate years. This was the mid-sixties. Homosexual acts were illegal in most places; psychiatry still classified homosexuality as an illness; and sociology was only beginning to move away from the "deviant behavior" label.

In the midst of this, Allen Ginsberg appeared as a guest speaker in my community course. Ginsberg, the famed Beat poet, was touring the country on a Guggenheim Fellowship, writing (speaking into a tape recorder) and reading his poetry. Accompanying Ginsberg was his lover Peter, a tall, handsome man with a blond ponytail down to his waist. Peter began the class reading his own poetry with exclamations of men loving men, of phallic-to-phallic sex, of sweat and muscular male physiques.

My rural roots paled innocent and naive under the feet of these modern troubadours from an urbane, intellectual-outlaw band (though innocent and naive I was not). Ginsberg and Peter were out of the closet before it became a concept. They were artists breaking the cultural embargo with messages from the muses. They were heralding a possible eve of destruction: the Vietnam War. These two Village people were the seeds of Queer Nation: I'm gay, it's good, and I'm singing it loud. But their songs were more than hymns to bearded queens. Here was an incarnation of Blake and Whitman, celebrating the flesh of the godbody and proclaiming the birthright of sexual freedom. It began to become clearer to me: sexual acts *are* political acts.

But the single most important development of the sixties might well have been the birth control pill. While every woman did not use the pill, it, along with several other forms of reproductive control, became the catalyst for a paradigm shift: the female gender need no longer be a reproduction factory. Millennia of programming changed almost overnight. Technology had broken the lock on the chastity belt, and popes and senators could only pontificate while the *people* fucked their brains out all night long!

Technology, however, without education, legal and financial accessibility, and personal commitment, can be useless, as I discovered a couple of years later when my friend Dorothy phoned from Chicago. She was visiting her South Side, storefront-preacher grandfather, and she was pregnant by her boyfriend back home in Louisiana. At the time I was a grad student with a research assistantship at the University of Wisconsin. Dorothy and I had become close friends the previous summer in Kentucky while I was a staff member and she an attendee at an educational camp for teens from diverse socioeconomic, ethnic, and religious backgrounds. After we talked on the phone for several hours, I borrowed a car from a fellow grad student. On a very humid summer day, I headed off a hundred miles with the hope of finding a doctor who allegedly performed abortions in Gary, Indiana, a steel-mill town on the southern tip of Lake Michigan.

This was a time when abortion was still a serious crime in the United States. Even on such a politically radical campus as the University of Wisconsin and with all my liberal friends, I had found it very difficult to obtain quickly the name of a willing doctor. A back-alley abortion was out of the question, and I never learned of any local women's underground abortion-support groups.

When I arrived at the doctor's, he immediately asked for my driver's license. I guess a wallet with no badge made me less suspect. I was anxious; he was vague. How could I convince him I was not undercover vice? He was taking a major risk: prison and loss of all those years in medical school. Eventually I heard an approximate cost and some general details. '

In a daze I drove back past the bellowing smokestacks of that steel town. Where could I raise the money? The price was not excessive, though more than Dorothy or I could afford. How could we get away from her grandfather's suspicious eyes for a whole day or more? What if medical complications arose in the procedure? Money, time, and indecision decided the outcome. Dorothy headed back to her rural Deep South county pregnant, seventeen, unmarried, and poor. Eventually, I later learned, everything was to turn out okay. She had an enduring spirit and a bright intellect. But when she left to go back home, I felt helpless. I was angry. Again it rang out: Sex acts are political acts.

As in my civil-rights-worker days, I needed to try to do something to change "the system." The next summer I became a summer intern at Planned Parenthood of Chicago. My role was as outreach worker to the many different ethnic communities of America's then-second largest city. Soon I was to be reminded I was living most of my life in an academic ivory tower. To some of the European immigrants who were Catholic sex "only for procreation" was the rule. To some rural Southern whites, having babies was a way of life. To some blacks, birth control was just another genocide scheme (even though most of the top administrative positions at Chicago's Planned Parenthood were held by blacks).

Those ten weeks in the Windy City were like beating my head against a wall. Neither the top nor the bottom of "the system" seemed to want to change. During many of the interims waiting for the community meetings, though, I availed myself of Planned Parenthood's sex education library of films and literature. It was my own private Human Sexuality 101 before such college courses were to become available. The basic teachings were sex is good, get information, make responsible choices.

After my summer internship ended, I began my third year of graduate school as usual, intensely plunging into my studies. But within a month I was to leave. An inner voice said, "Go." Something inside had changed, almost overnight it seemed. For eighteen continuous years, school and college had been my home. I loved academic learning, but now it was time to follow a different path. Within a week I handed in the final version of my master's thesis on demographic factors and civil rights workers' experiences, sold my motorcycle, and reread Herman Hesse's *Siddhartha,* a novel about the Buddha. My first stop was a retreat at a nearby Trappist monastery. After three days, a monk gave me a ride to a freeway entrance to begin my hitchhiking journey. When he let me out of the car, I noticed a discarded handwritten sign on the ground. It read, "Anywhere."

In the next three months I went ten thousand miles on 150 dollars. In Mexico,

I swam naked in tropical mountain rivers and slept on cardboard on earthen floors with workmen building a new village plaza. In San Francisco I meditated cross-legged in silence at a Zen Buddhist center, chanted "Om" with several hundred hippies while their university professor-turned-guru blew into a ram's horn, and celebrated Shabbas with young countercultural Hassidic Jews.

I had begun my spiritual quest.

The Vietnam War and the draft, however, were still a frightening reality, and with one more draftable year to go, I received a draft deferment to teach junior high on St. Thomas in the U.S. Virgin Islands. Then I accepted a position at a small Northeastern college teaching sociology 101, race and minority relations, and research methodology. Wanting students in the 101 course to somehow know the worlds I had learned about outside the ivory tower, I selected as additional reading Lenny Bruce's *How to Talk Dirty and Influence People.* In the late sixties, Lenny Bruce was one of the first nationally known comedians to use *fuck* to wake people up to the cultural bullshit. His mantra was "didyacome, didyacome, didyacome?"

My second additional reading was Carlos Castañeda's then recently published *Teachings of Don Juan.* While doing research as an anthropology graduate student, Castañeda met don Juan, a Yaqui Indian *brujo,* or shaman, in the Southwest. Something was profoundly touched within Castañeda, and he began to seek out don Juan, eventually "going native" and becoming an apprentice.

In the midst of this academic year there arrived an earthy, lusty poet, the sexually liberated Shannon described earlier. It was passionate chemistry all the way, at the drop of a hat. This was to be my first cohabitation relationship. When the school year ended, we traveled through America and Mexico, eventually making a living as migrant workers. We were going back to nature, living in a northern California cabin; picking cherries in Montana, fir tree cones in Oregon, apples and pears in Washington; and planting trees for the Forest Service in the Idaho Saw-tooth Mountains.

We had been on the road together for two years when we decided to part. It had been intense, a special exploration for each of us, my body and heart bathed in the touch of love. Single again, I headed deep into Mexico once more, secretly hoping to discover Castañeda's don Juan in Oaxaca. Up in the Chiapas Mountains I journeyed by horse to an Indian village inaccessible by car. Near the Yucatan I picked and ate hallucinogenic psilocybin mushrooms. I was still searching for God. In the travels with Shannon, I had read several of Carl Jung's tomes while recording my dreams almost daily. But in Mexico I was able to feel the spiritual in the earth, not only in my dreams.

With about two hundred dollars left in my savings, just after Christmas 1972, 1 headed my VW van back north to San Francisco. This was to become my University of Life, a classroom without grades. Immediately I started taking classes in t'ai chi ch'uan, massage, and biofeedback. I was able to begin analysis at a greatly reduced fee at the Jungian Institute. Equally as educational was my $2.25-an-hour, minimum-wage job selling tickets at a high-class porn theater.

After a few months I had enough money saved to enter massage school and to be Rolfed, a form of deep connective tissue "massage." Jung's writings, with his transcultural *archetype* and *collective unconscious,* had guided me into a nonreligious spiritual realm.

In massage and especially in Rolfing, I found I could neither run nor hide from my emotional armoring. Masturbating the evening after an intense Rolfing session on my inner thighs, sacrum, and lower back, I experienced my first full-body orgasm, a powerful surge of energy rushing from my feet up to the top of my head and back down to my feet.

After massage school and certification, I began giving massage professionally and teaching a few weekend seminars. Though genitals were considered off limits, I knew, based on experience, that many people adapted and used massage techniques in personal lovemaking. Why not publicly teach a nurturing massage that included the genitals as a part of the human body? I considered this for several months. Learning massage had definitely made me a much better lover.

There were no erotic massage training manuals, so I had to invent my own. "Will you pull down your pants, and let me play with you, and tell me if it feels good?" I began to ask some of my friends. Sometimes the asking was embarrassing, sometimes thrilling. This was the beginning of a fifteen-year adventure, teaching erotic massage throughout North America and Europe. Most of the classes were for the public. Usually heterosexual couples attended. Quite a few of the weekends were for gay men, some for bisexuals. I had the honor to teach a few all-women classes. Once there was also a benefit for COYOTE, the San Francisco sexworkers' organization. All the students were "working women," with several of my male friends paying to be the recipients in the practice sessions. Sex acts are political acts, and I was having fun.

Then in 1976 came an invitation to be on the adjunct faculty of the newly founded Institute for the Advanced Study of Human Sexuality, a graduate school in San Francisco. Because, I guess, of my unique academic and practical background, I was asked to develop and teach an experiential course in sexological body approaches. It was an exciting opportunity for me. I loved to teach, and now, to keep up with my students, I *had* to study this developing field of sexology. Eventually I wrote a manual based on my course. A literary agent was having no luck in getting it published when the managing editor of the German edition of *Penthouse* saw the manuscript and invited me to write a monthly column for his magazine. After several issues, a major German publisher saw the column and asked me to double the number of chapters so they could bring it out as a book. Shortly after I finished the manuscript I sold the French rights. However, I still couldn't find a publisher in the United States. These were the Reagan-Bush years and the rise of the Religious Right. Many of the freedoms won in the late sixties and seventies were under heavy attack.

So with loans from my former students, I decided to publish it myself. In 1986 Secret Garden Publishing was born with *Romantic Interludes,* my how-to book on massage, bathing, feeding, and other sensual experiences for lovers. Next I wrote and published *Erotic Massage: The Touch of Love,* the first massage book to illustrate explicitly female and male genital massage. The *Erotic Massage Video* followed. For my next book, about oral lovemaking between men and women, I chose a provocative title, *Clitoral Kiss.*

Book titles do mean sales. For example, even though *Erotic Massage* would be more accurately titled "meditative massage," many New Age bookstores were unreceptive to this popular manual. Changing the title to *Tantric Massage* for another printing, putting on an "Eastern" cover, and writing a new introduction, I finally reached this audience. It is my best-seller to that audience, along with *Sensual Ceremony and Sacred Orgasms.*

Most recently, *Women of the Light: The New Sacred Prostitute* presents the lives of nine sexual visionaries. These stories of women reclaiming their personal and sexual power is an inspiration for all of us who seek a deeper meaning to our sexuality. Now with over 400,000 self-published copies of my books and videos in people's hands, I feel I have learned to take "sex acts are political acts" to a positive place, one that can enrich our lives.

My evolution as a teacher and writer of erotic massage, sensual ceremonies, and other pleasuring techniques is only half of what happened after I arrived in San Francisco from the mountains of Mexico in 1972. I was still on my spiritual search, a path that seemed to parallel my sexual path. As I pursued my spiritual quest through reading, meditation, and studying with various "gurus," it all began to come together for me. The common essential element in good lovemaking, good massage, and effective meditation is mindfulness—the willingness and ability to be present in our sensations. This was to become the underlying theme in my erotic massage classes and the how-to books that followed. Most of my writings actually are Buddhist meditation methods disguised as sensuality-sexuality techniques. My two paths, the spiritual and the sexual, were beginning to cross more often.

Soon I began to study the Chinese Taoist tradition. I practiced ejaculation control and retrograde ejaculation techniques. Though I am not certain of the physical health claims, I did find ejaculation retention greatly affecting my sexual patterns. Learning to build and ride higher sexual waves, I could also deepen my awareness of my sexual energy as well as a partner's pleasure.

Several years later I discovered another system of spiritual sexuality teachings called Quodoushka, a Native American tradition that had gone underground after the Europeans arrived in the Americas. It offered a whole spiritual context with sexual energy as the dynamic core. Finally someone was laying out in front of me an integrated cosmology with sex at the center of it all! Our spiritual essence, our spiritual power, the sacred flame is already *within* us. Orgasm can teach us that—this is what I began to realize with the orgasmic experiences during the Quodoushka course and the events that followed as my book *Sacred Orgasm* began to unfold in my daily life. In that book was evident that the term orgasm had evolved for me to include a wide range of energetic experience (though not all energetic experiences are orgasms. Some of my orgasms were explosions, some were subtle waves of pi without a peak. Some occurred in conjunction with sex and pelvic floor contractions with ejaculation. Sometimes after my usual sexual orgasm, I would go into an energetic orgasm as a partner orgasmed sexually.

Western science and sexology were no longer a context that could hold my world. The shamanistic path, as I loosely termed my unfolding, was calling. San Francisco was sex mecca for me, I had learned so much; but now, like the last days of graduate school in Wisconsin, it was time to follow my heart. I was ready to live in the desert. I arrived back in my San Francisco Bay Area apartment, eager to finish my book on sacred orgasms so I could make my desert move.

On an unusually hot September afternoon, with the drapes closed to block the intense rays of the sun from my writing desk, I finished the final draft. The book was at last complete. About two minutes after finishing, I felt a familiar "shivering up the spine" coming on. This gentle energy rush and other nonorgasmic energetic experiences had become commonplace while writing the book: Sometimes as I become "aware" of an idea to include, an accompanying energy "wall" or field would slam into me. I decided to sit back in my chair for this "shivering." Next I remember an intense white light in the center of my head, similar to what I call the sacred-earth orgasm.

"Wow," I thought as I came back to my everyday consciousness, "that was a very intense orgasm!"

Then I realized I was lying face down on the floor. It was a struggle to try to lift my left arm toward my face. After a few moments it became obvious my body from my lower shoulders down was paralyzed. I lived alone, so I yelled for help, hoping the neighbors in the two adjoining apartments would hear. The closed drapes muffled my calls into the common yard as well. Fifty hours later, a passerby near the patio finally heard my calls.

After being helicoptered to a regional hospital specializing in spinal cord injuries, the doctors informed me the ligament between my fifth and sixth vertebrae had come loose, allowing my spine there to compress the spinal cord. A physician told a close friend that the only other times they had seen injuries like this was from high-impact car accidents, but none of those people had lived to talk about it. Was my injury a deteriorating spine accident waiting to happen? Or had I, in my passionate quest to be at one with God, flown too close to the sun? This was a question I would consider occasionally during my next seven months in the hospital.

There were more pressing issues, however. My spinal cord injury was "incomplete," meaning everything to nothing could return. Slowly some motor functions and sensations began to reappear. Now, four and a half years later, I am not a typical quadriplegic. Much of the muscular ability in my torso and arms has returned. I can walk enough in a walker for exercise purposes. I have some bladder control, and my bowel movement abilities continue to improve slowly. If it were not for my hands remaining so contracted, I might be able to live without frequent attendant assistance. Fortunately, my arms can move my hands enough so my thumbs can dial telephones, turn book pages, and type on a computer. I can still be creative through my writing.

Sexually, at least 50 percent of my penis sensations have returned. Erections are easy. (When I first arrived home from the hospital, erections seemed almost as spontaneous as my early puberty years.) Sexual orgasms and ejaculations are similar to prior to the injury, though I feel only about a quarter of the sensations. What is significantly different in lovemaking is my hands. If I had gained mastery in anything in my life, it was my ability to touch and massage others. With my penis I had sex, with my hands I made love. Now with a greatly limited physicality, sexual energy still remains my spiritual catalyst.

Recently I have occasionally been able to consciously initiate mutual energetic orgasms with others simply by focusing on an energetic area near my navel and "connecting" to another's nearby energetic body. This, however, has been only with others who have also devoted much of their lives to the practice of tantric, shamanistic, or other spiritual teachings with sexuality at the center.

Where this will lead I have no certainty. Ironically, by losing much of my motor ability and sensation, especially in my hands, I have even more impetus to seek the light of the orgasm—within myself, with others, with nature, with God.

Much of my life I have vaguely sensed a meaningful connection between what we label the sexual and the spiritual. As I began to give and teach massage and reconnect with my body, I could *feel* that connection within me. Not by conscious design, but by fortunate circumstance I evolved into the academic field of sexology. What I have learned from the students and faculty at the Institute for the Advanced Study of Human Sexuality as well as many other sexologists has been of immense impact and value for me. I am honored my colleagues have invited me to share in this chapter my evolution into this provocative interdisciplinary field.

If I had to label my view, I would probably say it was political and mystical. Our sexuality and our orgasm are our birthright. The academic discipline of sexology offers a liberation from oppressive belief systems. The study and teaching of sexuality cannot *not* be a political act. Our sexuality and our orgasm are also, potentially, our most sacred of teachers. For me, my sexuality is far from being the great schism between myself and God, or what I term *Source*. My sexuality and my orgasm are my most direct route to God. As human beings, we cannot *not* be sexual. Neither can we not *not* be spiritual. We are inherently both. They, the sexual and the spiritual, are inherently One.

43

The Naive Priest

Harry Walsh, Ed.D.

Harry Walsh is an Irish-born Catholic priest who came to this country in his late thirties to take a parish in Minnesota. Since he entered the seminary at an early age, he found out he knew very little about sex, and has spent considerable effort in recent years to gain a better understanding of the varieties of human sexual expression.

TWO PRISON INMATES had had differing opinions about oral sex. At my weekly sexuality program, they argued the issue back and forth. One considered oral sex "the best way to pleasure your woman." The other was opposed mightily, calling oral sex "perverse" and "against God and nature." God, the latter argued, had "invented" sexual intercourse, thus making penovaginal intercourse the only sexual activity to receive the stamp of divine approval. "C'mon, man," he pleaded. "You gotta stick with God and nature. Oral sex don't show no respect for God or nature. That ain't no place for your face, man!"

I tried to stay connected to the two debaters, my head swiveling back and forth like someone watching a tennis match, but my mind started to drift. Stockpiled memories invaded my consciousness, ghosts of Christmases past, some precious, some painful, all strands of the fabric of my life's story now, for better or worse. Settling an argument about oral sex—if, indeed, it could be settled—seemed unimportant, and the arguing voices retreated from my consciousness until they became little more than the distant drone of clustered bees on a summer's evening.

I was a mix of sadness and exhilaration: sadness that, since becoming a sexologist, the church had no place for my face; yet, exhilaration at the challenge of reconciling two forces that had not been on speaking terms for centuries—the spiritual and the sexual. I was excited at the prospect of seizing truths that, within twenty years, have reduced former beliefs and practices to obsolescence.

Since mysteries are meant to be relished rather than dissected, I bowed before the mystery of how a sexually illiterate lad from Tipperary, Ireland, who used to

pick wild primroses and rhododendrons for the Virgin's shrine, had ended up facil-
itating a discussion about oral sex in a Midwestern jail, especially since, as a Roman
Catholic priest, my specialty was Matthew, Mark, Luke, and John, not Masters,
Johnson, Hartman, and Fithian.

The memory of presenting the bouquet of wild flowers to my mother for the Virgin's shrine reminded me that, buried among my memorabilia, was a picture of myself
as a child. For whatever reason, this old photograph rose up now before my vacant eyes.
I determined to rummage for this old photograph as soon as I returned home.

I snapped out of my reverie when an inmate waved his hand like a magic wand
in front of my face. They took my lapse of consciousness in good humor. The dis-
putants had not budged from their respective positions on oral sex.

As soon as I got home, I went down to the basement, opened the abused Sam-
sonite that served as a safety deposit box for my memorabilia, and found the photograph of myself, at age three. It was one that my father had stuffed away in an old
shoe box years before. The week before I left Ireland for the United States (1963),
my father, probably a bit melancholy over my leaving, though careful not to show
it, retrieved this photograph from his treasure trove of family artifacts. It was a picture of a cute three-year-old with a cherubic, pudgy face under a massive shock of
convoluted, blond curls, It was the kind of angelic face you'd associate with religious paintings of the Italian Renaissance. Curious to see if my mother remembered
what I looked like at age three, I showed her the photograph. She became irate.
Mother never screamed or yelled when angry. Instead, words tumbled out, tripping
over each other, a mix of King's English and ancient Gaelic. "I told your father to
destroy that photograph years ago," she snapped. I was taken aback. In the name of
all the saints of Ireland, what was wrong with the photograph? Mother pointed at
my crotch. "That rigout your father bought for you in Dublin," she stammered,
"was the most vulgar thing I ever saw in my whole life."

I was dressed in a child's one-piece, cotton suit that fitted like an overall, complete with shoulder straps and frontal pockets; had I held a carrot between my teeth,
I would have passed for a Bugs Bunny look-alike. Following the direction of my
mother's extended forefinger, I noticed that the cotton suit was snug enough in the
crotch area to reveal a tiny bulge where my three-year-old penis was located. That
was Mother's problem.

Lips pursed and bloodless, muttering something about the sorry state of morals
in the world, she reached into her sewing basket, took out a pair of scissors, and cut
the photograph in two. She handed me back my torso and threw my crotch into the
turf fire. I watched it sizzle, turn brown, and fold over on itself like someone having a bilious attack. Not sure whether to cry from rage or sadness, I stared in disbelief at the disintegrating picture of my young self, consumed, like Joan of Arc, in
the flames of orthodoxy. I knew, at that point, that my sexual script had been written for me years before. My parents' horoscope read: This one shall be crotchless.
This one shall be a priest.

❋   ❋   ❋

Throughout my prepubertal years, every effort was made to keep me focused on the script. Mother had a litany of one-liners that were as familiar to me as the words of the latest folk song: "women are trouble"; "I should have been a nun"; "priests are God's favorites"; "priests are so lucky not to be married." Statues and pictures of the Virgin Mary were positioned in strategic places throughout the house. Priests were our only visitors. We were a strict "Members Only" family in which every behavior was dictated by what the church said, and judged by what the neighbors said. When my father whipped us with the sally-rod, it was because of something we did that might lead others to suspect that we were not the perfect family after all.

At the age of twelve and a half, I was checked into a monastic boarding school for boys, a cement fortress surrounded by high walls laced with shards of broken glass, and a commanding sign inside the front door with one word etched on it: ENCLOSURE. The windows were of corrugated glass to ensure that, literally, we had no window on the world. Down to the last detail, the structure was designed to keep out the three great enemies of the soul—the world, the flesh, and the devil. For the longest time I had trouble figuring out the difference between the three until, eventually, I quit trying. From what our spiritual directors were saying, world, flesh, and devil came together in one word: sex. Across the street was a boarding school for five hundred adolescent girls. Through contact with "the fortune five hundred" was totally outlawed, at least they provided grist for my fantasy mill during those years of confinement. Removed from all contact with "members of the opposite sex," it soon became clear that the one remaining fortress of sexual expression that needed to be conquered and leveled was "the solitary vice of self-abuse."

Thirteen years of isolation followed. For the first five, we were allowed home for a week at Christmas and for three weeks in the summer. While at home, I was obliged to check in weekly with the local parish priest to assure him that I was not socializing with "members of the opposite sex," and to tell him what movies I had seen (he cautioned me against Bette Davis, whom he referred to as "the bride of Satan"). When I reached age seventeen, Christmas and summer breaks at home were terminated. The few photographs of parents, siblings, and friends in my possession were confiscated because good monks, I was told, must remove themselves, not only from family and friends, but even from memories. The work of spiritual formation had begun in deadly earnest.

The spiritual direction of the next eight years behind closed doors built on the work of the previous five. The two primary emphases were subordination and castration. Subordination went by the name "blind obedience," which meant surrendering one's mind and will to those of the superior who, supposedly, was the authentic interpreter of God's mind and will in our regard. "Having no mind or will of your own," was how spiritual writers put it. Although I couldn't put words on my instincts at the time, something inside told me that "blind obedience" was cultist, that it was absolute power masquerading as spirituality. Several rituals practiced us in "blind obedience" as, for instance, the requirement to make three crosses with the tongue on the ground where the superior had walked. Sometimes the superior would have just walked in from the monastery farm, so you got matter on your tongue that humans do not put in their mouths. My anger and sense of humiliation at this practice was enormous, especially when I recalled how Moses was invited simply to take off his sandals in the presence of God, but was not obliged to lick the mountain top. The whole idea was to see the superior as God walking among us, something I found very difficult because I couldn't imagine God bonking me with a fist on the side of the head, mimicking the way I talked, wrongly blaming me to test my degree of submission, calling me stupid, or urinating on the toilet floor followed by instructions to mop it up. Many years later, I unloaded my warehoused anger on a colleague. His comment was: "The principle of blind obedience still operates in churches, my friend. We've just gotten more sophisticated in how to demand it."

The other goal of the spiritual formation program was castration—sexual, of course, not testicular, although we were reminded of how Saint Eusebius lavished praise on theologian Origen (d. 254) for his act of physical self-castration. To rid ourselves of what were called "venereal inclinations," a special bell had been installed outside the monk's quarters. Should slumbering hormones awaken, we were to ring that bell and a monk would come running from the monastery to exorcise us of our impure stirrings.

We were supplied with several weapons for the fight against world, flesh, and devil. One was the cilice (pronounced sill-iss). The cilice—actually there were three: one for the back, one for the leg, and one for the arm—was a bracelet made of barbed wire with the hooks turned inward. The cilice was worn for about four hours, long enough for the teeth to become embedded in your flesh. When you took it off, pieces of your flesh came with it, and the holes it left itched like crazy.

Another aid to self-castration was the "discipline," a whip of knotted thongs with which to lacerate your bare posterior, preferably to the point of blood. Those with blood on their cell walls were seen as occupying a high rung on the spiritual ladder. When studying for my doctorate in human sexuality, I asked a specialist in sadomasochism if the whip, supposedly designed to render us asexual, might not, in fact, be a left-handed way of stimulating the nerve highway that runs between the buttocks and the genitals so that, for some, self-flagellation might be a sexual experience. "Could be," he said, unwilling to commit further.

Reflecting on the thirteen years of spiritual formation, one thing surprises me more than anything: I was being prepared for a life of celibacy, yet spiritual directors rarely mentioned it. There was plenty about sexual abstinence, practically nothing about celibacy. It seems that celibacy and sexual abstinence had become identified in the minds of formation directors, so much so, they operated on the presumption that celibacy would take care of itself once sexual abstinence had been mastered. Consequently, no direction was given in how to deal with the human need for intimacy.

A further reductionism was evidenced in how sexuality was treated. Since shared sex was presumed out of the question, all that remained to be tamed was masturbation. Spiritual directors made every effort to dispel any false notion we might have about "the solitary vice" being less evil because of its solitary nature. God, we were reminded, was all-seeing and all-knowing, so he could see and keep track of every masturbator between Tipperary and Taiwan. I remember being very relieved when a retreat master told us that masturbation offended "our blessed mother" (the Virgin Mary) more that it offended God himself, and that she pulled the veil over her face in sadness when she saw an individual self-abusing. I was sorry to make her sad, but I appreciated the privacy.

Sex, more than faith, hope, or love, was the litmus test of one's standing in the sight of God. The rise to holiness, or the fall from grace, was determined by the rise and fall of the penis. To a young man with testosterone oozing out his ears, the mountain seemed so high, and those in authority were not qualified to attend to my sexual development. A spiritual director, whom I consulted about my sexual confusion, spoke for the whole system of formation when he said: "Son, there's only one way to attain to holiness; keep your Bible open and your fly closed." Such zipper spirituality was of little support.

Fortunately, there was one voice of reason inside the ENCLOSURE—our professor of moral theology. The bishops of Ireland invited him to address this question at their annual meeting: should a young man who masturbated be admitted to ordination? (How they planned to check this out, I don't know.) When he returned from the bishops' conference, we pressed him to give us a capsule version of the paper he had delivered. "I kept it very simple and practical," he said. "I just reminded the bishops that, if they made masturbation an impediment to ordination, then none of them should have been ordained."

"Adsum" (Here I am), I answered when called forward by the bishop for ordination to priesthood. The luminous glow on the faces of my parents assured me that I had secured their love by realizing their dream. Any time I had felt like pulling out, it was fear of losing their love and shattering their dream that got me back on track. Spiritual directors added the fear of eternal damnation to the fear of losing my parents' love. The words of monk renowned for holiness had been pounded into my head: "Should any young man fail to follow his calling, I will accuse him personally before the Tribunal of God on the Last Day." With God's love, my parents' love, and eternal damnation hanging in the balance, I learned to banish any consideration of options as temptations of Satan. "Adsum!"

However, there was all that unresolved, sexual confusion. Ironically, it was the bishop himself who summed up my sexual state of soul with a blooper in his address to the candidates for ordination. "My dear young men," the bishop said, "bear in mind that those who dedicate themselves to a life of perfect chastity will be exhausted . . . I mean . . . exalted."

Napoleon Bonaparte, his eye on conquest in the New World, is reported to have said: "This Old World wearies me." The Old World of subordination, castration, and realizing the dreams of others had wearied me. What would it be like, I wondered, just for once, to exercise stewardship over my own humanity? I had surrendered that power into the hands of others in the mistaken belief that God wanted it so. Little did I realize at the time that it would take me twenty-five years to reclaim the power of stewardship over my own humanity. Hoping that a change of environment would facilitate the work of reclamation, I boarded a ship traveling between Bremerhaven and New York. The year was 1963.

"You sound like you just got off the boat." The waitress was right. I just had. With a few days to see the sights of New York before checking in with church authorities in Chicago, I walked the blistering sidewalks of a city in the grip of a heatwave. It was on one such stroll that I came to my first sexual enlightenment in the New World. Stepping into a bookstore to get some relief from the heat, I felt as though I had stepped into Nero's palace. Before my eyes were rows and rows of glossy magazines displaying a bonanza of bare breasts which, in an instant, made a mockery of the whips and chains that were supposed to banish world, flesh, and devil for all time. When the attendant appeared more interested in getting his cigar stump lit than in the customers, I opened a magazine not wrapped in cellophane. A naked female was sprawled the full length of the two center pages with nothing but a staple in her navel. I stared in disbelief, replaced the magazine, and left the store on wobbly legs. At age twenty-eight, I had made a startling discovery: a woman had pubic hair.

I had carried my sexual ignorance and struggles across the Atlantic. Nonetheless, I ministered with enthusiasm. I enjoyed being a carrier of hope and discovered that I held inside a special affinity for the marginalized and the alienated. When ritual changes were introduced after Vatican Council 2, I put my creative foot forward and experimented with new ways for people to experience God in their lives. Ministry energized me. And I energized ministry. The albatross, the missing part, was sexual health.

For a long time, I attempted to master my sexual confusion by clinging to negative messages that I had been given during the years of formation. One in particular became my raft in the rapids: what right do I have to complain when I compare my insignificant sufferings with the excruciating sufferings of Christ on the cross? I also sought opportunities to discuss my struggles with colleagues in ministry, hoping to find one who could enlighten me on why my soul was as divided as the photograph scissored by my mother. Why, inside, was I a man sexually divided against himself? Some were very black and white in their response, reducing my struggle to a simplistic Hamlet formula: "to screw or not to screw, that is the question." That was not the question. Opportunities to screw abounded. The question was intimacy, intimacy with myself especially, or how to reclaim the sawed-off, sexual half of my soul, the half that I had surrendered into the hands of people who threw it in the fire. I sought counsel from those who appeared to be well adjusted to celibacy and sexual abstinence, hoping they would share the secret of their success with me. It became clear, however, that what worked for them was not going to work for me. Some appeared unable to travel the eighteen inches from head to heart. Because of their commitment to rationalization as the solution to all problems, they had as much warm blood as a prosthesis. Then there were those committed to the premise that the sexual and the spiritual would remain locked in deadly combat until the end of time, with final victory to the spiritual assured. Applied to my struggle, I was being told that I needed some spiritual vitamins, that there was a serious deficiency in my spiritual diet. This sounded too much like what confessors had told me in the past: "Say three Hail Marys and the bad thought will go away." Then there were those I consulted who were so committed to defending the ideology of the institution that all they dished up were pious platitudes, or sermonettes on the church triumphant.

By now I had tired of the old clichés: "God's grace is sufficient for you," or "God will not allow you to be tempted beyond your strength." These nuggets of wisdom supported Christians in times of persecution and, apparently, there were some who perceived sexual instincts as persecution directed at them by the world, the flesh, and the devil. On my part, however, I never thought of sexuality as an opportunity for martyrdom. I suspect that a church giant like Saint Jerome would have beaten his chest with rocks even more vigorously had he known what I was thinking. But, then again, Jerome had Paulina.

My boat was stuck on a sand bar. I was not successful in exercising stewardship over my own humanity, even though I knew that it was my birthright to do so. That began to change, however, with guidance from an excellent sexologist. He led me to understand that, what I had considered sexual confusion, was, in fact, incarcerated sexual truth screaming for liberation. Slowly, painfully, I began to tear away the walls of that prison. My hand was in the fire searching for the truncated part of myself. With the swiftness of a falling star, the thought of becoming a sexologist flashed across my mental horizon. I began to feel that I had a torch to pass along.

I came to realize that the sex-sin connection had been imbedded resolutely in my mind like a tick in a dog's back, yet, all along, some inner voice kept telling me that there had to be a sex-grace connection over and above sex-for-procreation which the Church Fathers considered the only redeeming feature of sex. Though I hadn't dwelt on it that much, I had wondered from time to time why Jesus and Paul never mentioned procreation when speaking of sexuality, and how they had emphasized the unitive purpose of sex, sex as soulful copulation. It was only logical to ask: Whose idea was it, anyhow, to make sexual abstinence synonymous with grace, sexual activity synonymous with disgrace? Who built the holiness pyramid that positioned perpetual virginity as the high road to holiness, sex for procreation as the low road, and sex for sex the road to perdition? I began to question where divine revelation left off and human manipulation began. I continued to be vexed by the suspicion that sex had become more important than faith, hope, and love in the Christian economy. The more I pulled back the lid off the can, the more worms popped out. My mind was like a beehive under glass. I remembered my father's admonition: "Little boats should stay close to the shore." But, I had hauled anchor. The tide of curiosity was carrying me into deep and dangerous waters.

Christmas 1988 holds a special significance for me. A priest friend who goes into depression at Christmastime called on Christmas Eve to ventilate his frustration at the excessive consumerism surrounding the religious celebration. Bells didn't jingle for me at Christmas either and, like my friend, I attributed this to the frustration of trying to maintain the religious character of the season in the face of vulgar consumerism. On Christmas Day, however, I came to realize that there was more to it.

The church emptied after the last service and I set about locking the church doors. The air was heavy with body odors, colognes, aftershaves, and incense. Just a short time before, this sacred space had rocked to the lusty singing of "Angels We Have Heard On High." Now, all was silent. So silent, you could hear a sin drop. I flopped down in the last pew to give my plantar's wart some relief, stared at the bunch of church keys in my fist, and wondered if God might some day raise up a Bishop of Rome who would open church doors to optional celibacy. I banished the thought as foolish since God never raised up a Bishop of Rome to impose celibacy in the first place. I stood up, walked over to the crib, and leaned in to switch off the blue light. For a moment I contemplated the three main characters in the Christmas drama. These three were connected. That's when it dawned on me that consumerism was not the principal reason for my annual bout of Christmas depression. Lack of connectedness was. God had connected with humans through human flesh. Christmas was a celebration of connectedness. My sexuality, the created energy that drives us to seek connectedness and avoid loneliness, had been assaulted.

The picture was coming into sharper focus. To achieve its celibate purpose, the thirteen years of formation needed to strike at the very heart of sexuality—the drive for connectedness. No wonder I had been removed from the family table and glasshoused, even before the onset of puberty. No wonder so-called particular friendships were forbidden. No wonder my photographs were confiscated. No wonder I was expected to surrender my mind and will, lick floors, mop up urine, puncture and lacerate my body. All this training in how to disconnect from self and others was designed to strike at sexuality's center.

Many years ago, an old Irishman, referring to his penis, said to me: "If it weren't for my masher, I'd be a saint today." There was a time when I also thought that to screw or not to screw was the question. But, on this Christmas morning, I came to understand that my "masher" was not the center of my sexuality. The created drive for connectedness was. And I had never been able to pull the plug on that created energy. "Spiritual relationships," the only kind allowed, never came close to satisfying my need for connectedness. The irony was that I had been trained so assiduously to disconnect, yet, my responsibility that Christmas Day was to lead several congregations in a celebration of connectedness. It felt as though I had been given swimming lessons on dry land. Although my experience in sex therapy had led me to flirt with the idea of becoming a sexologist, this Christmas reflection moved me from flirtation to going steady.

When I came down with a dose of the flu, I expected no more than the usual runny nose and aching joints. Having little ambition to do anything constructive, I stretched out on the couch and tuned into the Phil Donahue show. An Irish bishop who had impregnated an American divorcee was the topic of a heated discussion, some excusing the bishop on grounds of human frailty, others condemning him to eternal flames forever and ever, amen. An Irish woman from the Boston area called in with her angry, uncomplicated assessment of the situation: "The bishop knew bloody well what he was doing." That single remark made me still more determined to explore the mystery of human sexuality, and the church's attitude to it, in greater depth.

For one thing, the remark angered me because it appeared to reduce human sexuality to nothing more than an act of the will. It reminded me of Saint Augustine's nonsensical advice to married couples: that they should have sex with as little passion as possible so as to protect the integrity of the will. Augustine had enough sex in his lifetime to know that sex without passion is all froth and no beer. Indeed, as individuals raised to be sexually submissive can testify, sexual activity for which they feel no passion is like rape. The woman from Boston fingered a truth, however: churches are suspicious, even fearful, of sexual passion. They take comfort from Augustine's enthronement of the human will as the master switch that controls all human behavior, irrespective of the findings of other sciences. "He knew bloody well what he was doing" was a neat package, a convenient moral yardstick that bypassed the complexities of human sexuality and kept in place the traditional opposition of will power and passion power which considers the former as noble, therefore, of God, the latter ignoble, therefore, a consequence of fallen human nature. For many years, I had preached that human passions were the "animal" side of us. This made sex an animal act performed by humans who were destined by God to rise above animality through the power of the will. The woman's judgment on the bishop lit a fire under me because it represented an uncompromising will-sex-sin theology and allowed no space for a passion-sex-grace theology. It said nothing of love.

The Bostonian's remark pushed another button. Throughout our formative years we were reminded that self-castration was possible if we employed a technique called sublimation. As explained to us, sublimation meant that we could translate our sexual energy into service to the church and into charity toward others. Applied: the Irish bishop should have sublimated, not copulated. I had tried sublimation for years, and even became a workaholic trying. The promised charity payoff of sublimation became highly questionable to me when I was assigned to serve under pastors who were the crankiest, meanest sublimators this side of Suez. I finally decided that human energies cannot be moved around. Charity is its own energy. Sexuality is its own energy. How do you change nuclear power into gasoline?

"He knew bloody well what he was doing." The remark appeared to absolve the institution and its system of formation of all responsibility. Since this bishop had been formed and fashioned in much the same system as I, he must have been as poorly prepared as I was to deal with his sexuality and, especially, with the intricacies of human relationships. He, too, was the product of a system that relied on sex-negative conditioning, person-degrading rituals, and misogynist propaganda to prepare its clergy for a life of celibacy and sexual abstinence. The woman's remark carried no hint of corporate responsibility. She seemed to represent a church that said: "We are innocent of the blood of this man."

The debate over the philandering bishop was the final push I needed to follow a dream that had been rising up in my heart for some time. I would become a sexologist, for my own sake first, then, in the hope that I might be of service to others. However, dreams can be expensive. Church authorities said that my age was against me, that established policy favored investing in younger men. I had always believed in angels, though I had ceased to be influenced by the angelic imagery that decorates the walls and stained-glass windows of churches and cathedrals. Rather, I had come to think of angels as humans who flit in and out of our lives bringing support and good counsel. When I took my leap into the unknown, the skies opened and angels descended bringing gifts: an offer of tuition, a home to live in, travel costs to and from school. Thanks to the ministrations of angels, the dream became an attainable reality.

However, all was not peaceful in paradise. Some found the idea of a priest specializing in sexuality as incompatible as holy water in a satanic ritual. A priest friend of many years felt that I had slipped into temporary insanity, and prayed that it would be temporary. Another remarked with exquisite sarcasm: "Well, have fun at the porn shop." An older brother was concerned about the family reputation—how explain to the neighbors that his priest-brother was specializing in sex? "Couldn't you specialize in scripture or something?" he pleaded. A nun suggested that I avoid the title "sexologist" since this might scandalize some of the faithful. There was no shortage of vinegar remarks at social gatherings: "I hear you're into sex in a big way, Father," and, "Making up for lost time, Father?"

Here in the Midwest, they give us this piece of advice for winter driving: if you skid on ice, don't hit the brakes because this makes the skid worse. At first, I was slamming on the brakes, defensively, in the face of criticism and cynicism, coming up with cutsie responses like: "You don't have to commit homicide to be on the vice squad." It was an attempt to insulate myself from self-doubt because, more than once, I felt as though I were trucking behind the Magi, finding the star, losing it, finding it again, at times with nothing to follow but the camel prints in the sand. For one thing, there was no priest-sexologist model to work with. Added to that, a chasm so wide separated spirituality and sexuality that, in the eyes of many, my becoming a sexologist was equivalent to sleeping with the enemy. It became patently clear to me that I needed to validate myself, not sit around and hope others would. Having conquered this last peak, I enrolled in the doctoral program at the Institute for the Advanced Study of Human Sexuality, San Francisco.[1]

---

1. See chapter 23.

I thought that my first day at the institute would be my last. For forty-five minutes, I was exposed to a montage of sexually explicit images, enough to cross the eyes of a saint. A Roman Catholic student from Mexico turned to me at the end of the presentation and asked: "Did we sin by watching this?" I was in no condition to give him spiritual direction. I was concerned about my deceased mother laying a curse on my head, an Irish one at that, the worst kind. The institute staff challenged me to revisit the sexual attitudes that had been my meat and potatoes since childhood. As I researched my doctoral dissertation, several questions tormented me immensely: Who influenced Christian sexual attitudes more—Jesus or men? Where did divine revelation leave off and human manipulation begin? Had sexual abstinence become more important than faith, hope, and love? Had the trauma of troubled relationships, Augustine with his meddling mother, Jerome with Paulina, influenced these men to abandon their robust sex lives and set about turning everyone else against sex? Had the church given the sexual teachings of these men the authority of divine revelation?

Thanks to many angels, I completed my doctoral studies and moved a long way toward reconnecting with the sawed-off part of my sexual self. Angels continue to enter my life and provide a place for my face. The great moments of life are provided for me by people seeking counsel on how to reconcile their spiritual and sexual needs. Understandably, when those people are fellow priests, life takes on meaning to the fullest. The whip that I had used to control my "venereal inclinations," somewhat yellowed with age, hangs on a nail in my bathroom. The photograph that my mother scissored is now framed. Mixed on my shelves, deliberately, are books dealing with theology, scripture, and sexuality. On my refrigerator door are the words of fellow Irishman George Bernard Shaw: "Do not follow where the path may lead. Go, instead, where there is no path and leave a trail."

44

You Didn't Know about Me

Martin S. Weinberg, Ph.D.

Martin Weinberg was a borderline student before college. Encouraged by his parents and his high school counselor, he entered college and ended up a Phi Beta Kappa. During his college years, he was a jazz musician, and for a while was strung out on drugs. Yet in college he discovered sociology, and from sociology he moved into sexology, becoming one of the more significant researchers in the field.

T HE TRUTH OF the matter is that I wanted to be a jazz musician. Music was the first endeavor that filled my head with dreams. It taught me that I could work hard at becoming more proficient at something, and enjoy it immensely at the same time. I loved playing with other musicians, the connecting, the being part of a larger whole, the musical communication. I loved playing for audiences and moving them to listen, to dance, or to pause in reflection.

Although I didn't continue on as a musician, as I look back, it did wind up playing a significant part in my experiential and intellectual growth, and did indeed help launch me toward becoming the sociologist and sexologist I am today.

There wouldn't seem to be much of a link among jazz, sociology, and sexology. But then again, the word "jazz" was a slang term referring to sex, long before it became attached to a particular genre of music. I think playing jazz is an experience that is a lot like sex. In addition, the social groups that surround the world of jazz are of wide sociological interest. And while some think of jazz, sociology, *and* sexology as *each* involving overly complicated intellectual exercises for rather eccentric people, these pursuits really *move* their aficionados. Perhaps the connection among these areas does make sense after all.

I was born in 1939 in a lower-middle-class neighborhood of two-family flats in Albany, New York. My first memories begin vaguely at age three and more clearly at age four, when I entered kindergarten early. My mother, often ill, was hospitalized frequently, hence my early enrollment. Believe me, it didn't have anything to do with any advanced scholarship on my part.

It was a pleasant mile walk to school. And while there are always blustery, cold days to suffer in Albany, I learned my share of diversions, such as catching forbidden rides by hanging on to the backs of buses and sliding dangerously through the city streets covered with ice and snow. I remember begging, urchinlike, for coins outside the corner store, so that I could buy penny candy. I remember our family huddled around the radio, listening to the news about the war in Europe and the Pacific, the concern about uncles who were in the service. I can hear the sirens and recall the blackouts, the neighborhood air raid warden, the rationing stamps, the toy soldiers, playing war, and watching the Western Union boy deliver bad news. I remember, too, the joy of the victory celebrations and the warmth of the neighborhood bonfire when peace finally arrived. It all takes on more drama now.

I didn't really understand, either, the significance of the illness plaguing my mother, Pearl Cohen Weinberg. I trusted that she loved me and that she tried to be there for me. Things felt stable, and normal, despite being a year younger than my classmates and despite my problems learning to read. I didn't see myself as different from any other kid until my mother died from her high blood pressure, soon after I started second grade.

The road got a little rougher after that, though I don't recall feeling sorry for myself. My father, Fred Weinberg, still had to organize a life for himself. I was passed around, never for too long, to a housekeeper, various relatives, to places for children in predicaments such as mine, and to a stepmother who didn't keep her title too long. I didn't see much of my father, a man who was very depressed and obstinate when the chips were down (but had a kindness and great sense of humor when they weren't). There was a time when our somewhat independent struggles for survival merged more: just after his second marriage, just the two of us. I'd spend my time after school downtown, hanging out in the Five and Dime, watching the goings on, hanging out on the street. Dad had a one-man, one-secretary bill collection agency. When he'd finish work, we'd go for dinner at a diner, cafeteria, or other inexpensive restaurant. We'd walk around, watch that marvelous new technology, television, through the appliance store window, and then go back to our little rented bedroom to sleep in our double bed.

The freedom made me streetwise at a fairly early age. I smoked and pushed boundaries. My grades were poor and, likewise, my overall attitude. Dad shipped me to relatives in Pennsylvania for my sixth-grade year. My behavior improved so much that my relatives wanted to adopt me and keep me in a stable environment. The bond with my father was too great for me to do that, however. And, as much as he played the role of the distant father, I think he missed me, too.

We enjoyed another beginning when, in the spring of 1950, he met Edith Lupatkin, a single woman, thirty-one, who in every way was quite a catch for a man of fifty-five. That summer he moved to the Bronx with her, living in her father and stepmother's apartment. I joined them and in September of that year they married. I borrowed a camera for the wedding celebration, launching an interest in photography I continue to this day.

It didn't take my dad long to become so enamored of this fresh new start that he decided to continue it in Florida. We found a one-room furnished apartment to rent in Miami Beach. It was closer to my middle school than the mile-long walk in Albany, and best of all, no blizzards. I got a job selling newspapers after school, the *Miami Herald*, if I recall accurately. My dad found work with a company that sold sheets and pillow cases to hotels. Edith stayed home, the first time in her adult life that she didn't have a job.

I was now eleven years old, and more important, I was starting to become interested in things other than survival skills and my own entertainment. My new mother had attended Hunter College during the Great Depression and began teaching me about socialism, communism, agnosticism, atheism, and euthanasia. A loquacious woman who loved people, whose own hunger for knowledge had never slackened, she introduced me to the worlds of literature, art, and ballet.

To give you an idea of her attitudes, in my seventh-grade class we had a session on sex education—a movie on reproduction—which I described in detail to my parents. My mother was disappointed with the lesson: they hadn't taught anything about contraception, she fumed. My parents were very sex-positive and inclined to cut through the air of mystery that always seemed to pervade discussions about sex. They always gave me straight information about sexuality. And they were also very egalitarian: their attitudes toward social class, gender, ethnicity, and race were, indeed, politically correct far ahead of their time.

We all loved the weather and we spent a lot of time being entertained by my father's twin brothers, Phil and Jerry Weinberg, Runyonesque characters who worked in the always colorful prizefighting business. They were always joking around, and they took us to shows and celebrity parties. Times couldn't have been much better, except that my father wasn't making any sales and I sure wasn't making much. Also, my new mother's asthma started becoming more acute as the oppressive, humid south Florida summer wore on.

Reluctantly, we moved back to Albany, where my father rejuvenated his bill collection business. My mother worked at the office with him. I was in a stable environment again, surrounded in the eighth grade by working-class kids and feeling comfortable being there. I was impressed by my schoolmates' friendliness, knowledge of machinery, the blue-collar ethos—and I have continued to keep in touch with many of my old friends. These boys, most at least a year or two older than I because of my early entry into kindergarten, also helped open up the world of sexuality to me. One classmate was sixteen, very tall and long past puberty. I was twelve, very short, and curious, more than anything. He would show me photographs of himself and different women engaging in sex. This gave me my first visual images of sexual acts. Later, I would look back with interest at the social class differences in the age at which boys became sexually active.

For whatever reasons, I didn't find junior or senior high school to be very interesting. My new mother had by now formally adopted me; she didn't like the distance between us implied by the title "stepmother." Despite the intellectual direction she had given me, I still wasn't ready, or in the right environment to blossom. I did, however, really want to play a musical instrument, and I had enough chutzpah to march into the band room in high school and offer myself up as a candidate. They knew immediately what to do with my unspecific request: they suggested string bass or tuba, the perennial Rodney Dangerfields of school bands and orchestras. I knew I didn't want to play tuba; I couldn't think of anyone or anything cool associated with a tuba. So I chose the bass, and it proved to be a good choice after all. I played in the orchestra, the concert band, and the school dance band. I took to the instrument and to practicing like I'd never taken to anything before. Soon I was playing in Tony Toscino's "Blue Dreamers" Friday and Saturday nights at school canteens in outlying areas. Our repertoire included such classics of the fifties as "Teach Me Tonight" and "Earth Angel." Indeed, I began forming a self-identity as a musician. I still picked up any type of work I could for after school, on weekends, and in the summer, but I always looked forward to the band gigs we played on weekend evenings.

A friend and fellow bassist named Mike Fuda would have a big influence on me. A lover of Miles Davis, Teddy Charles, Sonny Rollins, and Thelonius Monk, among many others, he was the person most responsible for getting me interested in jazz, and the expansive attitude that would later make me say "Why not?" when "opening up your mind" meant more than just musical improvisation.

I still didn't especially like school, though. I got caught skipping several times, once sneaking into a theater to see a nudist movie with a friend. I got into fights, despite, or perhaps partly because of, the fact that I wasn't very big. I did always keep in mind the advice bestowed on me at a very early age by my biological mother's Aunt Jenny: "If someone bullies you, you better not just walk away." I learned, through hard-earned experience, that there were times it was best to walk away. I wasn't that cocksure. But as a result of her indoctrination, I probably fought more than anyone else my size.

Ironically, the resulting school suspensions actually played a role in my future academic career: My parents saw enough of Mr. Lincoln, the assistant principal at my school, to get to know him well. And when they asked him if he thought I could go to college, he said "yes," surprisingly enough. Turned out he liked me. And he told my parents that, despite my occasional unruliness, I was different from other students who got into trouble. (His saying that meant a great deal to me and I would keep in touch with him for many years.)

Mr. Lincoln said I had potential, and when my parents asked him what college I should apply to, he suggested St. Lawrence University in Canton, New York. I don't know how he picked that school. We thought it might be a Catholic institution with a lot of discipline, but it turned out to be a nonreligious upper-class school, prompting more questions as to why a kid like me would go there. I was accepted, and that's where my academic interests began to flow. In the meantime, though, my appearance, demeanor, and sexuality were still being molded more by the blue-collar than the white-collar of that time. (The social-class contrasts in sex-

uality which I would come to document in my later work have decreased in recent
years; see Weinberg et al., "Social Class Background, Sexual Attitudes, and Sexual
Behavior in a University Undergraduate Sample," forthcoming.)

That year people who would especially influence me in terms of my future
would include David Pierce, a jazz fan who provided me with some very hip intellectual thoughts and proposed I start keeping a diary. I would also go with a young
woman by the name of Charlotte Sackman, whose father was an attorney for the
state and who wrote law books. He used to sit at an imposing, important-looking
wooden desk at home and Charlotte would sharpen a big bunch of pencils for him
to do his drafts on a legal pad. I once told Charlotte that I was going to write a book
myself one day, and, indeed, I would copy her father's writing technique up until
the fall semester of 1995, when I finally embraced the personal computer and the
luxuries of WordPerfect. But the painstaking diligence of Charlotte's father provides me inspiration still.

I anticipated that college would be a new and different experience, but I didn't
expect the culture shock I felt immediately upon arriving at St. Lawrence University.
Most of the students were from prep schools. I looked like a public school hood, with
my greasy long hair and pegged pants, tight around the ankle. I felt like one, too,
surrounded by the well-dressed and affluent preppies. "I'm going home," I told my
parents. "Try it for two months," they insisted, "then if you want to, come home."

Conscious of the social-class differences, I looked around for people like me,
and found some in the dormitory cafeteria: athletes. They were more like me, but
much different in other ways. Then it occurred to me: musicians. I heard that there
were jazz types at the Sigma Chi house, of all places. I walked over one Sunday afternoon and could barely believe my eyes. There was a jam session going on, right on
the fraternity lawn. "Yeah, I play," I mentioned. The next thing I knew, someone
had borrowed a bass for me from the music department. Flushed with enthusiasm,
a group of us quickly formed "The Quartet," consisting of piano, vibes, bass, and
drums. Within a week a group of us embarked on the eleven-hour road trip to
Albany and back, to get my bass from home.

That bass wound up teaching me a lot about life. Our vibes player booked our
band at preppy teen parties in his upper-class hometown of Greenwich, Connecticut, on school breaks. It was my off-campus introduction to that culture, and while
it turned me on and off at the same time, it did fascinate me to learn that I could
fit in and develop real friendships with people who were born with more money
than I might ever hope to earn. I still respected my roots and blue-collar loyalties,
but at the same time, I enjoyed feeling a bit more worldly.

The classroom also held surprises. Consider this letter, written early in my first
semester and saved by my mother. "Dear Mom and Dad: When you go to class, this
guy comes in the room and gives a great speech. In philosophy class, I'm learning
about the 'creation of religion,' my sociology professor is pointing out 'social patterns,' I'm reading poetry in English, and I'm doing a report on Freud. . . ."

It was almost like someone threw a switch in my mind. I earned As and Bs my first semester, surprising even the most optimistic observers, including myself. And I followed up on that 3.3 first half with a slam dunk the second, a perfect 4.0. My self-doubts about college vanished. From then on, I couldn't imagine not earning all As. You just had to apply yourself.

There was a little matter of military service to consider, however. I read an article in *Life* magazine, I believe, about how the National Guard and Army Reserves were rackets—no one ever received any active training, the article pointed out. Damn journalists. The government moved quickly to close the loophole, mandating six months active training for both groups. I snuck in under the wire, joining the local military police unit of the Army Reserve a day before the rule changed. I also took two years of ROTC at St. Lawrence because it counted off my reserve time. Despite my efforts my initial assumptions proved true: the military was not my cup of tea. I didn't like being a grunt, and neither did I want to be an officer, my lower-class identification recoiling at the notion of having officer's privileges. And, to be perfectly honest, I was stoned a lot. At the time of my discharge, I had still failed to earn even a single stripe.

My personal social education continued on quite nicely, however. The summer after my freshman year, I was back in Albany pounding the pavement selling encyclopedias during the week and playing music in a bar on weekends. The encyclopedia job was a con game—my new associates not only admitted as much but reveled in the stories they could tell. We started at 4:30 in the afternoon, traveling to areas outside Albany and working the neighborhoods until 10:00 at night. After work, we'd rendezvous in bars that attracted people like us, sitting and drinking and sharing stories of past and present cons. One of our field managers even got caught that summer conning the company by forging sale contracts. He skipped out quickly on a tip that his managers were coming after him. And then he found out that his girlfriend had been conning him, running up thousands of dollars of purchases on his credit before going on the lam herself, one step ahead of him. I took all of it in with the clear vision of an eighteen-year-old. I began to conceptualize the American economy as an ecology of con games.

I also got involved with Dottie Seaborn, an African American woman, that summer, so much so that after a while I began to spend all my free time with her. The African American community was providing most of the support and appreciation of jazz at that time and it was a delight to be involved with a woman who loved jazz and the night life. I learned a lot about the African American community in the six months the relationship lasted. I loved my girlfriend's family and friends and they treated me warmly, to the point of bringing me into their social organizations and activities. Naturally, I became interested in racial issues more than ever, and these interests would in turn combine with my interests in social class and deviant social worlds, pointing me, fairly clearly, toward sociology.

My old Albany pal Mike Fuda and I still hung out in the jazz clubs whenever we could. And drugs were already as endemic to that scene as they would become, almost a decade later, to American college campuses. We did a lot of speed, pot, bottles of cough medicine with codeine, and, of course, alcohol. Fuda and I both got to know and play with Nick Brignola and J. F. Monterose, the major jazz figures living and performing in the Albany area. To this day, that association remains a valued memory and enriching part of both our lives.

Despite the maelstrom of my extracurricular life, my I.Q. score rose quite a bit during my college years, demonstrating the tests' social-class bias that I truly believe exists. My physics professor asked me to major in physics, but philosophy was the subject I was most in love with. Sociology ran second, at least in my mind, because I didn't fully realize that my primary interest in philosophy was "social constructionism" (the social creation of reality), and that professors in other classes would start remarking on the sociological cast of my papers in literature and art history, for example.

My experiences outside of school continued to push me toward the sociologist and sexologist I became. The summer after my sophomore year, I played in a band in a scuzzy white bar in Massena, New York. When we weren't playing dance music, the entertainment consisted of a stripper and a comedian. This association with strippers helped educate me initially about people in sex-related work. Having a woman undress and be nude around me didn't prove arousing, much to my initial surprise. I learned that friendship with a stripper was possible, and that the friendship didn't have to point in a sexual direction. I learned, in my role as one of the guys in the band, that many strippers (as well as other sex workers) were monogamous in their private lives—something I would document and study in my later work. I realized that except for their occupation, these people weren't essentially different from other, more conventional persons.

I also tested, fairly successfully, my theory, first realized the previous summer, that scams make the world go round. The local musicians' union wanted us to list our "stage names" when we joined. Roger Rossito, the piano player, became Roger Rossi, and suggested that I answer to the nom de plume of Marty Darté. French Canadians would ask me if my name was French. When I said "oui," there would be expressions of camaraderie and free drinks. When Italians would ask me if my name was Italian, I'd say, "si," and again, the drinks flowed free. For better or worse, most people never considered that with a name like Marty Darté I might be Jewish, and that gave me a window to anti-Semitic talk I didn't realize was so prevalent. These events had a profound effect on me that deepened my thoughts about ethnicity and anti-Semitism. Having had a black girlfriend had done that with regard to race. Back at school I would contemplate these experiences sociologically.

Three of the band moved on from our seedy club to a major hotel in Massena. The show was classier, the demands greater, and the subculture different. I had become accustomed to the jazz culture, but this subculture was very white even though it included some black male entertainers (because their significant others were always white). I also encountered my first gigolos. Talk about a con. All of this would combine to enrich my conception of society as an ecology of games. I realized it all went beyond mere con games; people used a variety of sets of rules that intertwined to organize the game of life.

I palled around with Bobbie Ephram, a black tap dancer, who thought like a jazz drummer when he danced. I also became involved with Nickie, a thirty-one-year-old married waitress at the hotel, a beautiful half-French, half-Spanish woman who told everyone I was her "chicken." (I was still just nineteen.) After her construction worker husband showed up unannounced one night at the hotel, suspicious, I decided I was too young, too interested in self-preservation, to continue down that road.

Not that I was turned off to intrigue: I then got involved with a customer of the nightclub who called herself Helena, the "Queen of Massena." And she wanted to be my patron. She liked to present me as her "man," an elevation, I thought, from being a woman's "chicken." She publicly gave me money. And we had fun, continuing our relationship well into the school year.

Major changes had occurred in the philosophy department when I returned to St. Lawrence my junior year. It seemed that a large number of parents complained that their sons and daughters had returned home as agnostics or atheists. The two faculty members who made up the department were gone. And I contemplated leaving as well, until I realized that sociology was probably a better fit for me, anyway. My life experiences and academic interests in sociology, philosophy, literature, religion, art, and music were all pulling together into a framework of social constructionism. I made my own attempts at art, poetry, and short stories, but in none did my efforts meet my expectations for myself any better than music.

Fate was still grooming me for the future, however, in ways I would only fully realize years later. I was back in Albany one weekend that fall and, greatly to my surprise, a songwriter/pimp friend mentioned to me that Shirley, a black prostitute, wanted me to join her for a drink at the bar. I had become acquainted with Shirley in the jazz clubs through my former girlfriend and thought the woman hated me, primarily because Shirley was known to be bisexual and fond of my girlfriend. I thought wrong. Shirley liked me so much, in fact, that she wanted me to be her man, not her john. And the longer we saw each other, the more jealous and possessive she became.

I did not realize at the time that prostitutes, off the job, yearned for the same monogamy and security that most people want in relationships. She always knew, instinctively when I'd be with another woman. I'd complain, "You have sex with other men every night," and she'd answer, "That's different." And she was consistent. Again, I recognized that her take on life had different rules, but rules nonetheless. I would one day, because of my association with Shirley, her friends, and others living the "sporting life," finally undertake a research project (forthcoming) on the lifestyle and social constructions of females, transgenders, and males engaged in prostitution.

For better or worse, however, there were aspects of living in that realm of society that began taking its toll. I was getting pretty strung out on the drugs that always seemed to be around. I lost weight and suffered from fatigue and depression. I dropped out of school, despite the fact that I'd been waiting a long time to get into several senior level classes. I sold my bass, stopped listening to music, stopped hanging around the jazz clubs. It was soul-searching time indeed, and it didn't take a therapist to point out to me that I wasn't a good enough musician to ever be great, that drugs and booze had become more a vocation than avocation, and that most of my friends were traveling in the same rut. In relative terms, it didn't take me long to straighten out. I felt that I was a good student, I thoroughly enjoyed academics, and I concluded that a peaceful, thoughtful life fit my ultimate desires more than the merry-go-round I was riding.

I'll spare you the term "born again." I returned to St. Lawrence for my senior year, determined to cram a year and a half of work into one year. Under the inspiration and guidance of Professor Donald Newman, I did an independent study paper, expanding on Edwin H. Sutherland's differential association theory, from insights through my own life experiences. It would link into a system of thinking that would underlie my work for the rest of my life, focusing more on the subjective meanings attached to social contacts than the objective characteristics of these contacts as the key to understanding social influence. For my research methods course with Professor Donald Auster, I did an analysis of the Kinsey reports, my first venture into sex studies. (Actually, Kinsey's work, e.g., on social-class differences in sexual patterns, got me more directly interested in sociology than sex research.)

Amid all of this focused academic activity, I also met Barbara Lee Appleman, who quickly became the most stabilizing and important person in my life. This was early 1960. We've been together ever since. She is, indeed, the sunshine of my life. (Nowadays, I jokingly say that *she's* the "envy of Bloomington," which always makes her and everyone else laugh.)

That spring, I received a phone call from my freshman physics professor, a pleasant enough surprise in its own right, made more enjoyable by his news that I had been elected to Phi Beta Kappa. I also received word that I had been admitted to the philosophy and sociology honorary societies. This made me take stock of myself in new ways. Despite the good grades I had been making, I never considered myself one to be singled out for scholastic honors or held up as a (positive) example. I was still fairly rough and greasy, something my parents were beginning to harp on ("Stop walking like that!"). I knew that Barbara had never dated someone like me, and she was striving already to reconcile the guy on the outside with the guy on the inside.

I graduated on time and with honors. Barbara was there and met my parents. It was a great day to celebrate, until Professor Auster pulled my folks aside and told them, "Make sure Martin goes to graduate school." That started more than a little bit of trouble. Despite all of the success I found at the undergraduate level, I hadn't really given any thought to graduate school. Maybe it was my background. Part of it, though, was the absence of graduate students at my small, liberal arts school. It just wasn't something I thought about. Plus, my aspirations weren't all that high. I still just wanted to work in a record store.

My mother continued to provide a shining example, however. While I had been in college, she went on to law school, finished her degree, and put it to work in my father's collection agency. I helped her enough to know I wasn't interested in law—their new hope for my future. My mother suggested that I take some interest, aptitude, and achievement tests to help me choose a career. The counselor recommended that I apply to Harvard Business School. Confronted with that possibility, I started to check out Ph.D. programs in sociology. The University of Massachusetts was just a few hours away, and while it only offered a master's program at the time, it just so happened that the graduate assistant for their large courses in introductory sociology and criminology had gotten drafted and they wanted me to take his position, beginning that fall. I balked (because I wanted to wait a year). They raised their stipend offer. I balked and they raised it again. Suddenly, it was a deal I couldn't refuse, and cemented when Barbara said she'd transfer schools so that we could be together.

If I was on a cloud in undergraduate school (don't say in more ways than one), in graduate school I was in heaven. I especially loved my social theory courses the first year. In fact, I loved everything so much that the Ph.D. didn't seem to be even a question of choice—of course I would be continuing my studies. Barbara and I both felt that a change of region would be good for us. The Midwest seemed like a good possibility and Northwestern University certainly was a good school. So I finished my M.A. during the summer. Barbara again transferred schools. And off we headed to Evanston, Illinois.

Everything about the new environment was exciting, ranging from the amenities of Chicago to the relatively less structured nature of the Northwestern program. There were no bibliographies for the Ph.D. qualifying exams. We were just expected to know everything important, and this provided a great excuse for reading all the sociology I could. Faculty member Aaron Cicourel was just beginning to mold an ethnomethodological perspective (i.e., one using ethnology as an anthropological method), but, alas, he would leave Northwestern for the University of California before I arrived. Graduate students, such as my friend James Wilkins, would pass some of Cicourel's teachings on to me, as would faculty member John Kitsuse, who co-authored with Cicourel. And Kitsuse, who was on leave my first two years at Northwestern, would chair my dissertation committee after he returned. I think, though, that many of these people were disappointed that I also found great interest in less ethnomethodological studies, such as Raymond Mack's. Ray was interested in a variety of sociological foci, and the choice of the method suited best for any one particular research question. Donald Campbell, Richard Schwartz, Robert Winch, and Scott Greer also influenced me a great deal in the use of multiple methods.

I read a great deal of sociology during my years at Northwestern and thought a great deal about the logic of social inquiry. I was aware of the great interpretive leaps we make in social science as in all human thinking, and that different types of sociological work involved greater and lesser degrees of inference. But I knew I wasn't simply interested in the restricted topics I would be able to study from what I saw as the safest epistemological approach—that of ethnomethodology. Rather, I used its teachings to be more careful in my use of a variety of approaches, being eclectic, and using multiple methods to investigate all the topics I would study. I was greatly interested in the study of meanings (perceptions, interpretations, constructions), and with this in mind I ended up embarking on a study of nudism for my doctoral dissertation. This was my first sex research.

How does one come to study nudism? It wasn't, as one might expect, an idea dreamed up as a male teenager. A fellow graduate student and his wife came over for dinner one night. She was angry at him because she had found some nudist magazines hidden in his dresser. It wasn't the principle as much as the money: they were graduate students, and the magazines weren't cheap. Still, she had already thrown them out. I retrieved the magazines from her apartment building's trash. And I was fascinated with these "official nudist publications." On the back of the cover, it read, for example, that "nudism was a sociological experiment." It was clear from the family pictures and the text that nudism represented nudity differently than did clothed society. I then found that the publisher's address was right around the corner from my attic apartment in a Polish Evanston neighborhood.

When I met with John Kitsuse about pursuing this topic for my dissertation, he was enthusiastic. In fact, he got right on the phone and called the publisher, who invited us to come over and meet with her. This woman, not a nudist herself, agreed they "needed studying." She got in touch with Alois Knapp, a nudist leader and owner of the largest nudist camp in the area, who phoned me and insisted I visit the camp as his guest the forthcoming weekend. I was nervous about going (imagine that!), and said I would attend if my dissertation chair, John Kitsuse, could attend with me. I then got my first insight into strategies that were used to control the definition of the situation in the nudist camp. "We don't allow sole men to come to camp with one another," Knapp explained. So I went alone.

I spent the weekends throughout the summer doing fieldwork at this and two other camps within easy traveling distance from Evanston. I found the study of nudism from the sociological perspective I was interested in to be a fascinating one. I realized, however, that fieldwork was not sufficient as a method for documenting what I was imputing to the participants, so I asked them if I could interview them more systematically off-season in their homes. Nearly all agreed, which surprised me, because many of the people seemed to conceal their personal identity and to be concerned about being stigmatized if other people found out they were "nudists." It was clear that I was trusted and that people wanted to talk to me; I learned early on that sex-related interviews can be something people *want to do* when they trust and are comfortable with the researcher. Even after doing one hundred in-depth interviews, however, I still wanted additional assurance about the generalizability of my findings. So, when the National Nudist Council offered to send and cover the costs of mailing a questionnaire to their membership, located throughout the United States and Canada, I was pleased. The resulting triangulation of a period of intensive fieldwork, private in-depth interviews (with a considerable number of people), and questionnaire tabulations (with a larger number of people) became a model for much of my future work.

Barbara and I had decided to wait to get married until she had finished her undergraduate degree and I had completed my preliminary doctoral examinations. We were able to get married that winter. We moved into a Swedish neighborhood in Evanston, where Barbara taught second grade in an adjacent suburb and I worked on my dissertation.

In the summer we traveled for three months throughout Western Europe on the shoestring budget of "five dollars a day." I found the trip to be the next major experience of my life. It became clear how culture-bound a social scientist could be if not widely traveled. While domestic travel and learning about different cultures within the United States had been a major interest up until then, extending this to the world would become a passion of ours. The European trip fed into my work in providing an opportunity for fieldwork on nudism and on contrasts in "modesty" in a number of countries, and this material was incorporated into my dissertation. My interest in different social worlds would come to take on a more cross-cultural character.

I finished writing my dissertation at the end of the fall semester and defended it in January. I then started working on articles to publish from the dissertation. I would present the first of these articles, a paper entitled, "Sexual Modesty, Social Meanings, and the Nudist Camp," at the Midwest Sociological Society meetings that spring. I also obtained an appointment in the department of sociology at Rutgers University to begin that fall. Since I had been on fellowships the whole time I was at Northwestern University, I had no teaching experience, so that summer I taught introductory sociology to police officers in a special course at Northwestern. I discovered fortunately, that I enjoyed teaching. And I was eager to move on to Rutgers.

Faculty Life

Barbara and I moved into a new interracial apartment complex in New Brunswick, New Jersey, only a half hour from midtown Manhattan. Barbara found a second-grade teaching position.

We were close to both our families. Our respective relationships with our parents had become more like friendships than anything else. My father-in-law treated me like a dear, but junior, friend. He relished the opportunity to teach me to enjoy the best in cigars, liquor, and restaurants. His best friend, a boyhood chum who will go unnamed here, taught me a lot that I didn't know about the world of organized crime, and extended his friendship to us in ways I'll never forget.

This bliss would prove to be temporary. My mother would soon die at the tender age of forty-six, from a heart attack caused by severe asthma attacks. And after twelve months of difficult, debilitating grieving, my father also would also succumb. I wrestled with grief, self-pity, and sadness. Moving on with my life seemed disrespectful, somehow.

I wanted to run away from the East Coast, although I enjoyed Rutgers and being so close to New York City. At the time, I was concentrating in my work less on the study of sex and more on the labeling of people and situations as deviant, and the problems and consequences of these definitions. I also was teaching courses related to these topics, and since there wasn't much in the way of books available to use, I co-authored two books that my colleague Earl Rubington and I had started thinking about during my final semester at Northwestern: *Deviance: The Interactionist Perspective* (1972), now in its sixth edition, and *The Study of Social Problems: Seven Perspectives* (1971), now in its fifth edition. I was also doing research on the problems of anti-Semitism and the social predicament of physically impaired people such as midgets and dwarfs.

Despite the sad emotions from my personal life, I felt exhilarated by my research and my opportunities to look into areas that hadn't been examined sociologically. It wasn't just work.

But as open-minded and understanding as I perceived myself to be, I can look back with some chagrin, by today's standards, at the revelation that would shoot me straight toward sex research. It was a guest lecture by a member of the Mattachine Society to our fairly large class of male students, at a time when it was uncommon for gays to be "out," and not politically correct to treat them politely. I was afraid of the worst. But instead this man held the class spellbound with his stories of the gay world and life as a homosexual: he was a regular guy, from the prospective of the potentially homophobic viewer. He was confident and well-spoken. I took him out to lunch and asked, tactfully, I hope, what he thought the factors were that seemed to affect how well homosexuals adapted to the stigmatization of homosexuality in society. He didn't have much in the way of answers, but he respected the questions, and suggested I visit the Mattachine Society in New York, where he could take me around the gay subculture to talk to men who had adjusted to greater or lesser degrees. It was like any trip into any culture that is new to you—if you have a guide who knows his way around, you can avoid a lot of wasted time and get down to the nitty-gritty more efficiently. From this and other fact-finding missions, I wrote a grant proposal that was approved and funded by the National Institutes of Mental Health (NIMH). I began a study of approximately 2,500 men in the United States, the Netherlands, and Denmark which led to the book *Male Homosexuals: Their Problems and Adaptations*, and my being asked to come aboard at the Institute for Sex Research at Indiana University (the Kinsey Institute).

Though researchers across the country and the world were beginning to delve into the forbidden topics of human sexuality, the Kinsey Institute, through Alfred Kinsey's controversial findings, had become the lightning rod for public attention. Still, it was through the legwork of research that I connected with the institute. I had developed a method of sampling of gay bars, one of them, a bar in San Francisco, where I happened to hand a questionnaire to Alan Bell, an Indiana University psychologist who was doing preliminary fieldwork for institute studies that I would soon join in. This is how Alan and I met. John Gagnon and Bill Simon, he told me, were planning to leave as the senior research sociologists at the institute and they needed a sociologist to co-direct these studies. Paul Gebhard, the director of the Kinsey Institute, then contacted me when I returned to New Jersey, and he and Alan Bell met with me in New York City to discuss the opportunities they had in mind.

They invited me to present a colloquium to the sociology department and look over the institute and Indiana University. But despite the institute's reputation, I still had significant trepidation about how cosmopolitan the environment would be in southern Indiana. I told my wife I was just going out of curiosity, and she made me promise this was the case. We were getting used to New York City, the art, entertainment, and restaurants. We liked the regular contact with her family, which had become an important part of our lives. Frankly, moving to Indiana sounded like a long shot.

But from the moment I arrived, I loved Bloomington and Indiana University. The campus was as beautiful as the verdant hills and rugged limestone topography surrounding it. The endless plains and cornfields that typify most of the Midwest, I came to learn, stopped about twenty miles north of the city, where the great glaciers ended. The music school was fabulous—huge, well-funded, and with a surprising mix of esteemed educators, former opera stars, and career musicians on the faculty. Live entertainment was abundant—every night of the week—and dirt cheap. I had gotten back into listening to jazz, and professors such as David Baker were turning out young lions. The people in Bloomington also seemed more casual and relaxed than in New Jersey. Everything seemed less formal. It looked more like the rich and contemplative life I envisioned that academic work could provide. And they met all my "What would it take to get you here?" requirements.

My only hesitation now was to what extent I wanted to become a "sexologist." The institute emphasized interdisciplinary work, and I didn't want to dilute the sociological character of my research. I was given a lot of assurances in this regard. I also would become a full member of the department of sociology, where I would receive a promotion to associate professor.

Barbara, not having the benefit of my enchanting visit, wasn't thrilled. She had already done enough compromising on my behalf to earn sainthood in some religious denominations. But after hearing my earnest descriptions of Bloomington, the university, the Kinsey Institute, the sociology department, and what was involved in the offer, she lost much of the fire of her reluctance, if not her initial premise. She had just given birth to the first of our two daughters (Ellana Fayth and Marion Debra, who would lead me profoundly to understand the difference between "sex" and "gender"), and, fortunately, now that she was no longer employed, the increase in salary and perks came at a perfect time.

One of the things I had requested from the institute was that they also hire Colin Williams, who was completing his doctorate with me at Rutgers. I wanted to be sure I had another sociologist to work with who was interested in the same type of sociology that I was. Colin had been my assistant on the previously mentioned anti-Semitism study, and was now working with me on an offshoot of the homosexual problems/adaptations study, a study of persons being labeled homosexual in the U.S. military and given a "less than honorable discharge." While at the Kinsey Institute, Colin and I would complete and co-author two books from the problems/adaptations studies: The *Male Homosexuals* book and *Homosexuals in the Military: A Study of Less Than Honorable Discharge*.

I would also begin work on the ten-year institute study that I was hired to co-direct with Alan Bell. It would result in three books: *Homosexuality: An Annotated Bibliography*, *Homosexualities: A Study of Diversity among Men and Women*, and *Sexual Preference: Its Development in Men and Women*. The first book resulted from the review of the literature for the study. It catalogues and describes each of the scholarly articles and books on homosexuality published in English between 1940 and 1968.

The second and third books are based on the extensive interviews we did in the San Francisco area in 1969–1970 with approximately 1,500 people. *Homosexualities* presents the theme that, just as we don't consider heterosexuals to be very similar to one another (a unitary type), we must also think of homosexuals as a plurality. We can't talk about *the homosexual* but must think in terms of *homosexualities*. Thus, in this study we look at differences between homosexual *men* and *women* and among *five types of homosexual* that we empirically delineate within each gender. We also show that how homosexuals compare with heterosexuals, e.g., in terms of adjustment, depends on the *type* of homosexual being used in the comparison.

Sexual Preference has as its third co-author the second outstanding graduate student to study with me, Sue Kiefer Hammersmith. This part of the study tested the most popular psychological and sociological theories of the development of sexual preference/orientation and found no support for them. We concluded with the point that the configuration of the data from the exclusive homosexuals (Kinsey 6's) was not *inconsistent* with biological theory. Since we did not have biological data, we could not test this. We never concluded that biology *was* a cause—as many people say we did.

These books cited were published in separate editions in Britain and Australia, and translated into Dutch, Norwegian, French, German, Italian, Spanish, Portuguese, and Chinese. Meanwhile, Colin Williams began working on another institute project, but we were still able to do an ethnographic study of gay baths (*Social Problems*, 1975), and to get to a study I had been looking forward to for a long time: a new examination of sex and social class (*American Sociological Review*, 1980).

In May 1980, Alan Bell, Colin Williams, and I would leave our joint appointments with the Kinsey Institute. Due to financial strains, administrative changes had greatly decreased the rewards and increased the costs of a joint appointment with a university department and a research institute. Next, Paul Gebhard would retire as director of the institute and June Reinisch would be brought in to replace him.[1] She

---

1. See chapter 36.

would bring a more biological and reproductive focus to its work and change its name to the Kinsey Institute for the Study of Sex, Gender, and Reproduction. John Bancroft, the current director, has continued this expanded focus. Before I left, I published a history of the institute and a survey of its work up until 1976 (*Sex Research: Studies from the Kinsey Institute*).

Nothing at all changed in the sex-related character of my work after I left. By then I was thinking of myself as a *sexologist* as well as a *sociologist,* having learned a lot about the sexual perspectives of other disciplines during my time at the institute. The institute summer programs, which I began in 1970, brought in people representing the gamut of sexology, and this experience would play a role in this new self-concept (as would Wardell Pomeroy, who had been discussing this with me for a while, and Ted McIlvenna and others associated with the Institute for Advanced Study of Human Sexuality in San Francisco who helped broaden my knowledge in the area of sexology).

Since leaving the institute, my studies, if anything, have become even more sexual *per se*, but still with a strong sociological perspective. I have worked on studies on female sexuality (*Social Problems*, 1983); sadomasochism (*Social Problems*, 1984); establishing and developing models of premarital coitus (*Social Psychology Quarterly*, 1984); black sexuality (*Journal of Sex Research*, 1988); a sex information switchboard (*Journal of Contemporary Ethnography*, 1988); sex, alcohol, and gender in Finland (*Nordisk Sexologi*, 1990); reactions to pornography (*Sex Roles*, 1993); and homosexual foot fetishism (*Archives of Sexual Behavior*, 1994; *Journal of Sex Research*, 1995).

After numerous trips to Scandinavia, I became convinced that the popular views of rampant premarital sexuality in Sweden were false, and started a study of various aspects of the sexual behavior of Swedish and U.S. heterosexual college youth (*Archives of Sexual Behavior*, 1995; *Journal of Sex Research*, 1996). The Swedish articles have been done primarily with Ilsa Lottes from the University of Maryland at Baltimore County, and we are submitting for publication papers on the social determinants of differences between Swedish and American sexuality, and a comparison of Swedish and U.S. students' prevention measures with respect to AIDS.

In 1983, while on sabbatical in San Francisco, I had started a study of bisexuality with Colin Williams and Douglas Pryor (another outstanding graduate student of mine). This ten-year study was published as a book in 1994 (*Dual Attraction: Understanding Bisexuality*, Oxford University Press). We are continuing this study of the characteristics of bisexuality, how they have been highlighted by the AIDS crisis, how our subjects have changed since the 1980s in their attempts to avoid AIDS, and how the above is all linked to the social environment. I am also involved in a large study of prostitution with Frances Shaver at Concordia University in Montreal.

The Society for the Scientific Study of Sexuality awarded me a Distinguished Scientific Achievement Award in 1995. This recognition means a lot to me. I started out unsure that I would ever see the inside of a college, and I've never left the college world. What a ball! I love my research. I love my teaching. And I find it extremely gratifying to have been able to play a political role in disseminating knowledge and helping to change society. I've given testimony to the U.S. Congress and Senate and in legislatures throughout the world, as well as in federal and state judiciaries, to try and make it easier for people to live their sexual lives without erotophobia creating hardship. Sexology is a fascinating field, and I can't help but relish my own journey of discovery. Today, my work, my family, and my life as a whole area are all very fulfilling.

I want to express my appreciation to those people, named and not named, who have affected my life by influencing me to be the sociologist, sexologist, and the person I am, flawed as that may be, and who gave me love or support in the process.

Would I be pushing it if I said that writing this chapter has provided me with "A Sentimental Journey"? It has. My thanks to the editors for asking me to do it! By the way, the title that I decided on for this chapter, "You Didn't Know about Me," is a play on the song title, "I Didn't Know about You." You didn't know all this about me, did you?

References

Weinberg, Martin. 1976. *Sexual Research: Studies from the Kinsey Institute.* New York: Oxford University Press.

Weinberg, Martin, and Alan Bell. 1979. *Homosexualities: A Study of Diversity among Men and Women.* New York: Simon and Schuster.

———. 1972. *Homosexuality: An Annotated Bibliography.* New York: Harper & Row.

———. 1981. *Sexual Preference: Its Development in Men and Women.* Bloomington: Indiana University Press.

Weinberg, Martin, and Earl Rubington. 1972. *Deviance: The Interactionist Perspective.* New York: Macmillan; 6th ed. Needham Heights, Mass.: Allyn & Bacon, Inc.

———. 1971. *The Study of Social Problems: Seven Perspectives.* New York: Oxford University Press, 5th ed.

Weinberg, Martin, and Colin Williams. 1971. *Homosexuals in the Military: A Study of Less Than Honorable Discharge.* New York: Harper & Row.

———. 1974. *Male Homosexuals: Their Problems and Adaptation.* New York: Oxford University Press.

Weinberg, Martin, et al. Forthcoming. Social class background, sexual attitudes, and sexual behavior in a university undergraduate sample.

45

Love Child:
My Career as a
Sexologist Pioneer,
Prover, and Critic

James D. Weinrich, Ph.D.

James D. Weinrich began as an evolutionary biologist but, like most in the sexuality field, had to acquire expertise in other disciplines. He is in the forefront of current research in what has been called neurobehavioral biology.

> *Love child—never quite as good.*
> *Love child—misunderstood.*
> —The Supremes, "Love Child"

The repressions of suburbia have produced {Sandra} Bernhard, Madonna and me. Half of us is a nice suburban girl; the other half is a raving pornographic maniac, the beast buried in the cellar.
> —Camille Paglia (1992, p. D-2)

'M A BASTARD. Growing up, no one ever told me this. I had to figure the awful truth out all by myself.

More precisely, I'm an intellectual bastard. My mother discipline and my father discipline have a lot in common, but they don't seem to get along very well. I don't think their fights and petty jealousies are very important, because I use what each of them taught me every single day. Accordingly, I don't really have an intellectual home. But what's a poor bastard to do?

My Mother

My mother discipline is evolutionary biology. I learned it at a hotbed of evolutionary thinking, Harvard University, where I had originally wanted to be a mathematical biologist, using computers and equations to describe the life-and-death processes of populations. But that first year as a graduate student I fell in love with evolution and behavior after taking a course taught by the rising young (and still reigning) star evolutionist, Robert Trivers. By the end of my first year he was my thesis advisor.

It's not as if other disciplines hadn't tried to seduce me. Students with nubile, undecided brains are fed "lines" designed to snatch those soggy circuits from the clutches of other disciplines. Such as:

- "Do you really want to decapitate rats for the rest of your life?"

- "Historian of science? Are you crazy? Do you want to *do* science or do you want to *watch* science?"

- "Well, you know the Ph.D. is really the higher degree. An M.D. is just a trades-man's union card."

- "*Why* would something evolve? I can't understand . . . [trails off] That's just such a pointless question. That's the way it is, that's all. That's the only thing you can prove."

- "Well, of course, you know that that's all just speculation. They can't prove a thing."

I liked studying behavior, because it was real. I loved learning about evolution, because it involved a lot of logic and deduction. (More on this later.) The sixties were over chronologically, but their better aspects weren't over politically, socially, or academically. Change was normal. In particular, biologists were getting ready to announce to the world (rightly or wrongly) that evolutionary thinking was the key to understanding not only the physical structure of organisms but also their mental structure—including the human psyche, morality, and the best and worst of human nature. It was thrilling to be part it all.

For my Ph.D. thesis, all I had to do was to marry my theoretical training—evolution—with a specific topic, which turned out to be sex. Mom—meet Dad.

My Father

My father discipline was the rowdy one. A bit disreputable, perhaps, but trying to reform. Old enough to have some experience under his belt (ahem), but ready to settle down and become a bit more respectable. This was sexology in the 1970s.

One summer I did field work in Knock Knees, Texas (certain details have been changed to protect the guilty), out in the middle of nowhere, just a few feet above sea level. I was studying Texas scrub jays. I tossed bits of peanut between two jays from neighboring territories to see where the territorial boundaries were, then marked them on a map. My advisor had thought it advisable that I see how much I liked field work.

The answer: not much. When the jays headed back to their nests, I headed back to the dorm. There, I observed the mating rituals of two human beings: she twisted her wedding ring at the dinner table while talking about how awful her husband was, and he sat across the table pretending that he was no more or less interested in this subject than any other heterosexual male in the room. I was so innocent back then that it took me most of the summer before I stumbled across him sneaking out of her room late at night. They hadn't just met each other there; both had specifically arranged to be stranded.

In the middle of that summer, I took a break for several days and flew to Bloomington, Indiana, where I attended the summer program in human sexuality and sex education at the Kinsey Institute, then called the Institute for Sex Research. Paul Gebhard (Kinsey's successor as director), Richard Green, Martin Weinberg, Alan Bell . . . so many people whose work I'd read were there, catching us up with what amounted to a course in Sexology 101.

I had gotten interested in sex research the summer before, which I spent reading at my parents' home in Michigan. On a whim, I took the Kinsey *Male* and *Female* volumes off the shelf of my local library. Soon I had read both of them from cover to cover, and was particularly entranced by the *Male* volume's chapter on social-class differences in sexual behavior. And thankful to the librarian who had firmly opposed putting any books under lock and key.

Kinsey described two very different patterns of erotic development in what I will simplistically refer to as "working-class men" and "middle-upper men." Working-class men acted as if they valued coitus (penovaginal intercourse) above all other acts; petting was short or nonexistent, deep kissing considered filthy, masturbation shameful and resorted to only by boys who couldn't get laid. Middle-upper men apparently valued petting, foreplay, deep kissing, masturbation, and a wide variety of noncoital acts much more highly, relatively speaking. Of course they valued coitus, too, but tended to begin it at much later ages than the working-class men did.

Wow! I thought. Those are different reproductive strategies, and I've learned a lot about reproductive strategies! If those two types of men had been animals from two different species, evolutionary biologists would have been all over those data, trying to understand what factors in the environment had contributed to the evolution of those different reproductive patterns. The working-class strategy seemed to favor standardizing the roles of husband and wife, proceeding as quickly as possible to coitus and reproduction—as if Mother Nature were equipping them for an uncertain world in which quick reproduction is most adaptive and change of partners is fairly likely, sooner or later. The middle-upper strategy seemed to favor wife and husband taking more time to find a spouse who complemented their own strengths and weaknesses—as if Mother Nature were equipping them for a relatively predictable world in which slower, more optimized reproduction is most adaptive, and in which nonreproductive sexual acts (like petting) would function to strengthen the pair bond. Kinsey had suggested that these two different patterns went back centuries, at least, in humans.

Of course, these two social groups are absolutely *not* two different species. But I was still surprised that no one had tried to understand which aspects of the environment would have made these two strategies adaptive. (For my solution to the problem, see Weinrich, 1977.) Even in that early stage of my graduate training, I knew that a biological model need not be a genetically deterministic model. It was entirely possible that these two kinds of men had the same genes for reproductive behaviors, but that one or the other set of behaviors would be wired into the brain according to their environmental circumstances growing up. Or that men could switch freely from one set of values to the other as the environment changed, much as genes dictate that our skins darken when exposed to the UV light of the sun, and fade to lighter shades under less sunny conditions. Kinsey showed that neither social group was very knowledgeable about the other's erotic habits, and that *boys and young men who grew up in one social class but ended up in the other showed the pattern of their acquired class before they made the move!* This was the pattern—still news to a great many sexologists even today, alas—which got me thinking that mere socialization and reinforcement theories were probably not enough to explain human sexuality in all its complexity and wonder.

So there I was at the Kinsey Institute, talking to the people who knew these data backward and forward. I was hooked. Colleges everywhere were beginning to teach courses in human sexuality. The past century's freeze on sex research seemed to be permanently thawing. Kinsey had been a biologist (trained at the Bussey Institute, a Harvard component just across the quadrangle from my graduate student office), but I was surprised to observe that he had applied little modern evolutionary thinking to his data. Sociologists, psychologists, therapists, historians, anthropologists—all were exploiting the fact that sex now seemed a wide-open field, with lots of previously tabooed but important questions now available for study. I was trained in a more modern and aggressively explanatory theory of evolution than Kinsey had been. Why not become an evolutionary sexologist?

Present at the Wedding

As I discovered sexology through its journals and meetings, I found that sexologists were often more willing to consider biological factors than many other social or psychological academics were. I already knew that biologists were more likely than most academics to consider sexual matters a legitimate topic; after all, sex is the means by which genes are passed from one generation to the next, and evolution is (by definition, actually) what takes place when some genes become more or less frequent from generation to generation. And so I thought, why don't these two disciplines—these two intellectual parents—get together?

By the end of my graduate career, I had started to discover the advantages and disadvantages of being the product of this type of mixed marriage. For one thing, I was bilingual, speaking the language of transsexualism and paraphilia, as well as that of reproductive strategies and inclusive fitness. That meant that I had two disciplines' worth of papers and books to read, which doubled my chances of curling up with a good journal on a Saturday night!

And I noticed that, in spite of my best efforts, Mom and Dad were flirting with new partners. My dad was flirting with biologists with names like Frank Beach and Robert Goy; my mom with smooth sexual operators like Donald Symons and Lionel Tiger. And although Mom and Dad could certainly have done worse, they could also have done better. To be perfectly frank, Beach's knowledge of evolution was about that of Kinsey's: accurate enough for many purposes, but limited and out of date. And Symons and Tiger, while brilliant and original in their own ways, didn't know enough about the human sexuality that sexologists knew to bring their theories sexologically up to date. All these famous men had tried hard to be interdisciplinary, but succeeded only in part.

So what's a poor bastard child to do? If I didn't watch out, I'd spend my entire life sitting on the edge of my chair, scheming and waiting for the day when Mom and Dad would get married—and feeling like a victim of their choices in the meantime.

Well, if life hands you a lemon, make lemonade. I realized that most sexologists who gave short shrift to my ideas were not mean-spirited. They were not out to "get" me; they barely knew me. They were not out to "get" evolutionary biology (with a few notable exceptions) or sexology; they just didn't know enough about them. And after all, no one can be expected to know everything. But I could understand both disciplines. I could come up with ideas neither Mom nor Dad could come up with by themselves. And as I watched their papers skid past each other, I learned some things as a participant-observer about how scientists work.

How scientists *really* work, I mean. I didn't see the pristine, bias-free investigation of all the logical possibilities that junior high school teachers propagandize. Neither did I see the underhanded, culturally ignorant, or prejudiced pursuit of pseudo-truth that yesterday's radicals and today's social constructionists would have you believe is part and parcel of any scientist's life. What I saw was much more complicated and intellectually interesting than either of those caricatures.

Only in the past three years have I been able to make out patterns in all this. Once I did so, I realized that I had been, and probably always would be, a particular kind of scientist. I was predestined, by ability and personality, to be this type, whereas others were predestined for corresponding reasons to resist people like me. I began to understand much better why my ideas were slow to be accepted in the academic world I loved so dearly.

Pioneers, Provers, and Critics

Just about every scientist I know is a mixture of three ideal types, which I call Pioneers, Provers, and Critics. Also, just about every scientist I know is predominantly *only one* of these three types. Here are the definitions:

- *Pioneers* are the first ones to come up with a new idea that eventually will replace an older idea. They lead a revolution.

- *Provers* are the first ones to prove to skeptics that the idea is true. They implement a revolution.

- *Critics* are the last honest ones to hold on to the older idea. They preserve a previous revolution.

The following table lists other characteristics of the three types. All good scientists need to be able to operate in all three modes. I don't view any of them as generally superior or inferior to the others; each type has its own strengths and weaknesses.

	Pioneers	Provers	Critics
Key definition	Lead a revolution	Implement a revolution	Preserve a revolution
When evidence is incomplete	Enjoy playing with incomplete evidence	Enjoy completing evidence	Use incomplete evidence as a weapon
Attitude toward criticism	Criticism is a blow to the ego	Criticism is a sign of interest	Criticism is their goal
Jigsaw puzzle activity 1	Start a puzzle	Fill in a puzzle	Find holes in a puzzle
Jigsaw puzzle activity 2	Find edges, determine broad outline	Lock in as many pieces as possible	Point out other arrangements
Begin to lose interest when . . .	. . . they know the answer	. . . they've proved the answer	Never lose interest
Worst epithets	That doesn't make sense. That's impossible	That's not scientific. That's just speculation	There is still insufficient solid, replicable evidence that . . .
Major weaknesses	Undisciplined; can shade into pseudoscience	Can spend too much time nailing down trivialities	Become pathetic if others decide they will never change
Famous examples	Albert Einstein, Charles Darwin, Alfred Kinsey	James D. Watson, Anke Ehrhardt	Peter Duesberg
Traits of the famous	Historically important	Most respected in their time	"No one ever erected a statue to a critic"

More important are the emotional traits associated with these types. Scientists' skills and personalities tend to channel their careers predominantly into one of these three directions. Since each type has different values, and since scientists consciously are of the belief that science has only one set of values, misunderstandings and controversies can easily arise, especially between individuals from two different categories.

One useful analogy is with police and crime. Pioneers—like police detectives—are comfortable with incomplete and partially contradictory information, and excel in establishing the first rough outline of what will turn out to be the truth. Provers—like prosecuting attorneys—excel in producing much stronger evidence which will convince nearly anyone—even fairly dense people such as judges and juries(!). Critics—like defense attorneys—excel in challenging Provers to come up with evidence to support supposedly obvious deductions.

As any fan of cop stories and courtroom dramas knows, these three types attract different personalities and require different skills. Each type frequently complains about the other two, but all three are necessary to arrive at a just conclusion.

In my case, I'm a Pioneer with Prover tendencies, plus a touch of the Critic. Let's discuss the three types in more detail, and I'll show you how these insights fit into my experience.

Pioneers are the first ones in a new territory. Some say they're the ones most likely to have arrows in their backs. Scientifically, they enjoy playing with incomplete or even contradictory evidence—and the best ones are amazingly good at figuring out, or intuiting, which of several options will turn out to be right. They start a puzzle, decide on a strategy ("Let's find the edge pieces first"), and determine the broad outlines of the results ("These red pieces are probably a barn"). Typically, they lose interest once they're pretty sure they know the answer—at which point the Provers move in.

Pioneers tend to be theoreticians, not experimentalists, with good powers of deduction. Their attitude is, if an experiment contradicts a theory, then the experimenter probably didn't set things up properly or interpret the results correctly. (Emphasis here is on the *probably*, because sometimes theories are disproved by experiment.) For example, Einstein barely performed any experiments in his lifetime, but had amazing powers of deduction. He certainly never proved that the speed of light is always a constant, but he saw that *if* it is constant then many intriguing consequences follow. Darwin knew that his theory of evolution would have grave difficulties explaining nonreproductive castes in ants, bees, and wasps— but he knew so clearly that everything else about his theory must be correct that he specifically refused to propose an explanation, wisely leaving this problem to future generations. (This contradiction was resolved with the theory of kin selection in the mid-1960s.) A Prover or a Critic would go nuts with contradictions like these.

I have found throughout my life, no matter what I get involved in, that I am likely to want to do something that no one has ever done before. Luckily for me, I can usually look at a field in an entirely novel way. When I got interested in origami (the Japanese art of paperfolding), I didn't want to fold flowers and birds; I wanted to invent folds for a Parthenon, a fire hydrant, a checkerboard with recessed spaces. The part of me occupied by Paglia's "raving pornographic maniac" of course thought of folding human figures which included genitalia. I lost interest once I found out a couple of other people had already figured out how to do that quite well.

One of the things that Pioneers like me do is observe other scientists to see what metascientific "rules" they follow as they come up with hypotheses which (later) turn out to be true. My thesis advisor liked to give a rule he attributed to the naturalist William Drury, and which he therefore termed "Drury's First Law of Animal Behavior": *An animal is assumed smart until proven dumb.* Drury's Second Law? *The student of behavior is assumed dumb until proven smart.* These "laws" reflect plenty of experience in understanding animal behavior, and it's easy to see how they might apply to human behavior. Drury's First Law asserts that most behavior exists for a reason; it doesn't just "happen" and probably does not constitute a "mistake" of any kind. Right there, one has a profound contradiction with most biomedical approaches (which assume that behaviors are either "normal" or "abnormal"), and with "stage" theories of development (e.g., Kohlberg's stages of moral development) which presume a single path of maturation. (For more on this point, see Weinrich, 1995a or 1995b.)

A primary guide used by Pioneers to evaluate a new theory or idea is whether or not it *makes sense* in the light of such grander principles. Accordingly, one of the stronger epithets Pioneers can use if they don't like a particular theory is that it just doesn't make sense. Because figuring out what's the truth is so important to Pioneers, claims that they are wrong, or other attacks on their ideas, are likely to be hurtful rather than stimulating. At least they were to me.

Obviously, a high degree of creativity is necessary to be a good Pioneer, but that very trait can lead to problems. Pioneers tend toward being undisciplined, and in extreme cases Pioneers can veer off into pseudoscience. What are we to think when the mind that gave us the double helix of DNA also tells us that life's origins were not on earth? When an effective proponent of scientific exploration of the planets spends time raising tons of money to listen for signs of extraterrestrial life?

The most famous scientists in history are usually Pioneers—Einstein, Pasteur, Kinsey, Masters and Johnson. Darwin was a rare beast: an excellent Pioneer who was also an excellent Prover. It is common, but not inevitable, that Pioneers were not famous or highly esteemed at the time they made their contributions.

Provers settle new territory, rather than discover it. Scientifically, they are good at tossing a hypothesis around in their heads and in deducing consequences of the idea which can be tested. They fill in a puzzle ("Okay, I've got this corner done"), implement a strategy, and work out contradictions ("I think these red pieces must be a painting, not a barn"). Typically, they lose interest once they've answered all of the objections to a hypothesis which they deem to be reasonable.

Provers tend to be experimentalists, not theoreticians. Their attitude is that an experimental result always takes precedence over a theory contradicting it. In fact, contradictions irritate the hell out of them. One of the most subtle things I had to learn about Provers is how to interpret criticism coming from them. After I would explain my nifty theory to someone at some conference or other, it hurt my pride to hear people criticize it; challenging my theory seemed emotionally almost the same as challenging my powers of deduction and my intelligence.

This is precisely the wrong reaction to have, however, because criticism of a theory by a Prover is a compliment—especially if the theory is new. It's a sign that the Prover is challenged enough by a theory to spend time and research funds to test it. It is in the nature of Pioneering that Provers will object. After all, there was a lot of evidence which previously led the Provers to a conclusion different from the one a Pioneer is espousing; what else would one expect? Even though I consider myself mostly a Pioneer, I have also found as I mature that my Proving is getting better.

Provers' most common epithets are "That's not scientific" and "That's just speculation"—either of which can be accompanied by a dismissive wave of the hand. Stringent standards, perseverance, an attention to detail, and a dash of rigidity of thought are necessary to be a good Prover. On the minus side, Provers (if they're not careful) can spend too much time nailing down trivialities. And if they don't have the good sense to ally themselves with a good Pioneer, they can spend their careers testing alternatives which have no chance of yielding significant results. Likewise, a Pioneer who doesn't ally with a Prover, or develop Prover capacities, will be intellectually lonely.

Proving is the type of science most respected by the general public and the media at the time the work is being done. This kind of work is what gets someone a Nobel Prize, or into *Scientific American*. (Einstein never won a Nobel for his work on relativity.) Provers are most likely to be esteemed by colleagues during their lifetimes. If Crick is the Pioneer of DNA structure, then Watson is the Prover. If John Money is a Pioneer of sexology, then Anke Ehrhardt is a Prover. (Again, keep in mind that none of these scientists mentioned is just one of the three types.)

Critics are scientists who support the previous revolution. Therefore they are doomed, since a new revolution is always coming from somewhere. Scientifically they cannot abide contradictory evidence, and enjoy bringing such contradictions to light. They are very uncomfortable with incomplete evidence, and use it as a weapon. Even after a puzzle is mostly assembled, they're checking every detail to make sure that no piece has been jammed into an incorrect spot.

Critics are not theoreticians. Many are experimentalists, although they need not be; all a Critic really needs is a clever mind with a contrarian bent. Most scientists (myself included) are Critics when it comes to disciplines other than their own, and one of the first things graduate students learn is why every other discipline is full of nonsense.

Critics rarely if ever lose interest in defending against the new idea. The hallmark of Critics is their use of the phrase, "As yet, there is still insufficient evidence that. . . ." Soon, the phrase will become "As yet, there is still insufficient *direct* evidence that. . . ." Next, it's "As yet, there is still insufficient direct, *replicated* evidence that. . . ." And so on, perhaps forever. Another favorite phrase: "That paper could *never* get published in a well-refereed journal in ————."

Critics, like Pioneers and Provers, can become pathetic if they go too far. Creationism is a good example. Critics do so when their iconoclasm becomes too obvious, and others realize that they will never change their minds, no matter how strong the pattern of evidence. Over-the-edge Critics are rarely critical of their own alternate explanations.

Creativity and cleverness are not necessary to be a Critic, although some Critics are very creative and/or clever. Accordingly, as someone else said, no one ever erected a statue to a critic (with the possible exception of Edmund Wilson), and it is very difficult to come up with examples of historically famous Critics. Who remembers those who said that Mozart's music was just noise? That E does not equal mc^2?

Nevertheless, there are always famous Critics in any era. Peter Duesberg, the molecular biologist who believes that HIV is not the cause of AIDS (Duesberg, 1994), is a well-known critic today.

Sexology as a Multidisciplinary Science

Sexology is by nature an interdisciplinary science. Although each of us has her or his own mother discipline, in order to be good sexologists we must also acquire one or more father disciplines. If I want to understand why some people grow up to be heterosexual and others homosexual, I'd be foolish to look only at biology. In fact, from my coursework as a graduate student to the journals I read today, I make sure I read widely and in depth. For my thesis work on social-class differences in heterosexual behavior, I had to delve into sociology, psychology, and demography. For the other half of my thesis (on evolutionary models of homosexuality and transsexualism), I had to learn about psychology, anthropology, endocrinology, and history.

A paper explaining why males are (or are not) more promiscuous than females might be published in a journal of evolutionary biology, economics, social psychology, sociology, psychiatry, family therapy, or even psychoendocrinology. But it is doubtful that any paper on this topic published in a journal in one of those disciplines would meet the critical standards of any journal from a different discipline.

So to be a good sexologist you must both stand by and reject the point of view of your original discipline. One technique I use to reveal these points of view is to examine what practitioners consider to be null hypotheses, and what standards of proof they are expected to meet before receiving acceptance in that discipline of their work. For example, consider this question: are there genes which predispose people to perform or enjoy a particular kind of sexual behavior—say, heterosexual versus homosexual?

The standard of proof in many social sciences is that genetics and biology are explanations of last resort. If a socially mediated explanation can be devised—even one with no direct experimental support—then the biological model is rejected, graduate students are directed into other lines of investigation, and no definitive tests are funded.

From the perspective of evolutionary biology, this sequence of events is premature at best, and just plain wrong at worst. Evolutionists in the past fifty years or so performed experiments in animals and in humans in which the variance in a behavior could be definitively divided between genetic and environmental sources. They noticed that

- most behaviors in nonhuman animals had a strong heritable component;

- essentially all animal reproductive behaviors had a genetic component;

- the small number of human studies of behavior and genetics (for example, the adoption studies by Kety and Schulsinger in Scandinavia) were completely consistent with the animal studies;

- those human studies showed that sometimes the environmental component was unmeasurably small; and

- there can be no doubt that human behavioral tendencies evolved under the action of natural selection in a hunter-gatherer environment.

It follows that nearly every animal behavior (including most human behavior) must have functioned adaptively in the environment in which that species spent most of its time evolving its behavior, and probably had a genetic basis. Observations plus logic yield deductions; it's as simple as that.

But what about the things that make us uniquely human? Well, there is no reason for all these genetically influenced behavioral predispositions to have suddenly gone away when humans developed language and culture. Those evolutionarily recent additions to our repertoire would have to coexist with, and not supersede, the preexisting tendencies of the organism.

This reasoning applies with special clarity in the realm of sexual behavior. No cultural or linguistic factors have progressed to the point that would permit human beings to bring their sexual arousal under the direct control of their motor cortex. We can will ourselves to reach out and pick up a sandwich, but we cannot will our vaginas to lubricate or our penises to become erect. Those crucial organs remain completely under the control of our autonomic nervous system. We can do things which we hope will indirectly influence these arousal processes, but we cannot control them directly. We have more direct control over our breathing than we do over our sexual arousal.

This underscores the point that the ascendance of culture and language has only gone so far. Whenever a definitive test is performed to divide the variance in a behavior between genetic and environmental causes (the adoption studies, the back-crossing breeding experiments in animals, etc.), the genetic side never turns out to be zero, and the environmental side sometimes does. Evolutionists thus propose in their null hypothesis that any human or animal sexual arousal-related phenomenon must have a non-zero genetic contribution, and that it is the duty of the social scientists to prove otherwise beyond a reasonable doubt. We evolutionists deduced that this must be the case; otherwise the data just *don't make sense*—a classic Pioneer evaluation.

Twenty years ago, I was proposing a series of models which could explain why a trait that lowered reproductive success could spread in a human population under the action of natural selection, and many other evolutionists were asked similar questions about other behaviors under study. We were often asked if we were being premature in doing so in the absence of direct evidence that "homosexuality genes" or "heterosexuality genes" existed.

The answer is no, not by the standards of Pioneers; and yes, if judged by the standards of Provers and Critics. Now that molecular biology has the ability to provide direct evidence of genetic influence on behavior—for example, Dean Hamer's work on a genetic marker for homosexuality on the X chromosome (Hamer, Hu, Magnuson, et al., 1993)—the Provers are getting busy, and some great science is getting done. Assuming that this work will be replicated by other researchers (Hamer's group has already replicated it themselves: Hu, Pattatucci, Patterson, et al., 1995), were we just lucky twenty years ago? Did I risk being proved wrong and thus wasting my time writing half or all of my thesis?

No. It is important to stress that the idea that there are genes which influence human sexual behaviors and fantasies was a *deduction*, not a lucky guess or hypothesis. It is always gratifying, and useful, to have direct evidence supporting a deduction. But if you're smart enough, and courageous enough, you should be willing to risk relying on your own powers of deduction, as I did beginning as a graduate student.

That said, I am aware that deductions can be incorrect. (I have some amazing examples of very subtle logical traps scientists have fallen into, but no space to describe them here.) As a Pioneer first and foremost, I make it my business to perform reality checks on my theoretical outlook. I read the results of Provers' experiments, and I change my mind. I am intensely interested in fallacious reasoning, especially fallacious reasoning I have engaged in myself.

Sometimes I wonder why I am more willing to grant deduction higher priority than many other scientists do. I suspect that it has something to do with my having been a math major as an undergraduate. After all, mathematicians claim to be able to prove—*prove!*—interesting and important things with no experimental data at all.

On Becoming a Sexologist

Note that so far in this chapter, I have given absolutely no evidence in favor of my typology of Pioneers, Provers, and Critics aside from a few personal anecdotes. Nor will any such evidence be presented in the next few lines. So how can I be so insufferable as to assert that I'm right? I'll bet that your own reactions to this exercise fell predominantly into one of my three categories. If you don't watch out you'll start becoming data in favor of my new theory!

If you see the previous paragraph as cheeky but on the right track, you're probably a Pioneer, mostly. If you see it as a nice story and nothing more, then you're a Prover. If you're already hot and bothered about it, ready to give me hell, then you're mostly a Critic.

For decades if not centuries, scientific inquiries into sex have been frozen in taboo. To choose to be a sexologist—underfunded, misunderstood, supposedly unscientific, supposedly immoral—is to choose to be not just a Pioneer, but at least a bit of a rebel. Now that the sexological Ice Age seems to be thawing, it is inevitable that the Provers will be moving in and taking over. The Critics are already here. As I've faced the difficulties of my career, I have only recently come to understand which problems were my own fault, and which just came with the territory. Reaching this understanding helps one's mental health immeasurably, reduces the tendency to see oneself as a victim, and gives strength for the future. To the new settlers here, I say: Welcome! Now let's see if what you're proposing . . . makes sense.

References

Duesberg, Peter. 1994. Infectious AIDS—stretching the germ theory beyond its limits. *International Archives of Allergy and Immunology* 103: 118–27.

Hamer, Dean H., Stella Hu, Victoria L. Magnuson, Nan Hu, and Angela M. L. Pattatucci. 1993. A linkage between DNA markers on the X chromosome and male sexual orientation. *Science* 261: 321–27.

Hu, Stella, Angela M. Pattatucci, C. Patterson, L. Li, D. W. Fulker, S. S. Cherny, L. Kruglyak, and Dean H. Hamer. 1995. Linkage between sexual orientation and chromosome Xq28 in males but not in females. *Nature Genetics* 11: 248–56.

Paglia, Camille. 1992. Sans bitterness, a more confident Bernhard emerges. *San Francisco Examiner,* December 6, p. D-2.

Weinrich, James D. 1977. Human sociobiology: Pair-bonding and resource predictability (Effects of social class and race). *Behavioral Ecology and Sociobiology* 2: 91–118.

———. 1995a. Biological research on sexual orientation: A critique of the critics. *Journal of Homosexuality* 28: 197–213.

———. 1995b. Biological research on sexual orientation: A critique of the critics. In *Sex, cells, and same-sex desire: The biology of sexual preference*, ed. John P. De Cecco and David Allen Parker, pp. 197–213. Binghamton, N.Y.: Haworth Press.

46

How I Became Interested in Sexology

Beverly Whipple, R.N., Ph.D.

Beverly Whipple, a nurse and neurophysiologist, came to public attention when she rediscovered and named the Grafenberg spot (G spot) and the phenomenon of female ejaculation. In order to conduct more basic research into the physiology of sexual response, she went back to graduate school to obtain a Ph.D., and has become one of the leaders in the profession.

AS WITH MOST of us my age in the field of sexology, I did not set out to become a sexologist; in fact, I had never even heard the term. As a woman growing up in the 1940s and 1950s, there were basically two career choices: teaching or nursing. Since my mother was a nurse and I saw more opportunities in nursing, I chose that. Although I was a good student, I did not see myself as having any unusual ability, but I did want a college degree. I was not encouraged to do any more than graduate from college, so I entered Wagner College and majored in nursing.

Wagner was a Lutheran college and we belonged to a Lutheran church. However, our pastor was quite upset with me because it was not a Missouri Synod college. And here I thought I was being a "good girl" by attending a Lutheran-affiliated school, which just happened to have a very highly rated nursing program. I was third in my nursing class and missed graduating *cum laude* by 0.01 of a point. I knew in college that I wanted to teach nursing, believing that I would have more influence on the health care system by teaching than by working in an institution. Little did I know just what kind of an influence I would have.

I grew up in northern New Jersey, in a suburb of New York City. My father, a vice president at Bankers Trust in New York, was a quiet but friendly man who was liked by everyone. He was interested in all I did, and I am sorry that he died before my research was published and I began appearing on television. I think he would have been proud of me. He and my mother paid the tuition for my first master's degree, so they supported my desire for more education.

My closest relative was my mother's sister, Ethel, who was always very supportive and encouraging. She lived with us when I was having problems with my second pregnancy and was always available when I needed someone to talk with. She died last year after having dementia for a few years. I miss her.

Looking back, I realize how extremely naive I was regarding sexuality. I remember when I learned about menstruation from a film in junior high school. I came home all excited and told my mother what I had learned. Her response was, "that's what's wrong with your Aunt Ethel, she bleeds all the time." Great introduction to menstruation.

Although I dated some in high school, I thought it was because of my long blond hair, not my personality or looks. My mother gave me very negative messages about sex and sexuality. In fact, I was forbidden to go into our local ice cream parlor because the girls there "kissed and let boys touch their bodies." When this took place or how my mother knew about it, I never did know. I did go there a few times with a girlfriend in high school and saw none of the behavior that my mother described, but being the "good girl" that I was, my guilt feelings did not allow me to continue joining my friends at the ice cream parlor after school.

I dated a lot in college. I had one steady boy friend for quite a while, but my mother did not like him, and again forbid me to continue seeing him. To describe how naive I was, I remember studying for an anatomy exam and trying to understand how there could be two testicles and only one scrotum. I asked my boyfriend to explain this to me. We could talk, but limited our sexual activities to kissing and petting.

I remember the summer I had my psychiatric affiliation and learned that one of the teenage girls on the women's ward masturbated. I had no idea what she did, but as far as I knew masturbation was something boys did, not girls. I assumed it was something to do with her mental illness. Yes, we still had those myths in 1961.

Jim, my husband, and I met in 1958, during the summer before I started college. We dated off and on throughout my college years and were married in September 1962, after I graduated. We were both virgins and knew very little about sex. Although I loved to read, I had just never put it all together and I couldn't ask anyone. I did not talk about sex with my friends in college and I certainly couldn't talk with my mother. It took Jim and me a long time to learn about sexuality, which may be one reason I am out there disseminating information, so others don't have to go through the long process of learning that we did. We have been married now for thirty-four years and feel we have a loving and supportive relationship.

Another example of how naive and insensitive I was concerning sexuality involves a story I have told only once before, and that was at a sexuality workshop at Thornfield a few years ago. By the time this incident occurred in the early 1970s, I had obtained a master's degree in counseling and was involved with counseling students in the program where I was teaching nursing. One of my students told me that she was a lesbian and my response to her was that she couldn't be, she was too pretty. Believe it or not, she helped me in many ways to learn about and accept alternative lifestyles, and we are still good friends today. I don't know if I could have told this here if it weren't for Brian McNaught's response to this story at Thornfield. At the time I told this story, I was pretty well known in the field. Brian (author of *On Being Gay*) felt that my sharing my insensitivity was a wonderful example for new people entering the field. I still feel awful about my response, but that was how I was brought up and how naive I was at this time.

Shortly after that, another of my students asked me what a man could do sexually after he had a heart attack. I said I did not know but it was a good question. (Here we were talking about a heterosexual man, so maybe that's why I responded positively.) This led to the faculty hiring a consultant and incorporating sexuality into the curriculum. However, at this particular school the hospital board had to approve our curriculum, and they did not give their approval for us to teach such things.

This may have been the beginning of my risk taking. To me, it was a tremendous risk to leave that job and go to somewhere else. But I did it. I felt I could not continue teaching in a program that had such control over the curriculum and such a sex-negative attitude.

I began teaching nursing at Gloucester County College in Maryland and decided I wanted to learn more about sexuality. I took two of the American Association of Sex Educators, Counselors and Therapists (AASECT) courses, one at Hofstra with Michael Carrera and the other at American University with Bill Stayton. What an eye opener these courses were!

I was also surprised when Bill Stayton invited me and my colleague from Gloucester County College, Ray Gick, to visit him and see his office and SAR (Sexual Attitude Restructuring) room. I asked Ray why Bill would have invited us. Ray said, maybe he liked us or thought we had something to offer to the field. Well, Bill and I have been close friends and colleagues ever since and I value his friendship and our professional relationship.

I also had an opportunity to meet a woman from Hahnemann Medical School in Philadelphia at a workshop at the National Audio Visual Center in Atlanta, Georgia. She invited me to lead a small group during an SAR at Hahnemann. I then went to a conference in Philadelphia devoted to sexuality, where I met many of the well-known people in the field, such as Wardell Pomeroy, Alex Comfort, and Alan Warbeck. One of the people I also met was Bob Francoeur, who invited me to lead small groups during the SAR portion of his human sexuality course at Fairleigh Dickinson University.

I also joined AASECT and the Society for the Scientific Study of Sexuality (SSSS) in the mid-1970s and I took a course with Masters and Johnson. Around this time, Ray Gick and I started the first human sexuality course at our college, which was extremely well received. One of the classes I remember being the most fun was showing *Ripple in Time*, a film about aging and sexuality. Ed Brecker, one of the persons in the film, walked into the class when it ended. I found people in the field to be extremely supportive and generous with their time and knowledge.

Around 1979, I was still teaching nursing along with the human sexuality course with no plans to do anything further in the field. At an AASECT meeting that year I responded to a posted sign about "female ejaculation" and met people interested in this phenomenon. I also met John Perry from Vermont. He had developed an electronic perineometer which I thought would be great for women with urinary stress incontinence. John and I unexpectedly met again in the summer of 1979 when we were both taking an AASECT course at Amherst with Hap Copeland. We talked about ideas and found many of our interests overlapped. Our interest in the phenomenon of female ejaculation, urinary stress incontinence, and John's ability to measure muscle strength and teach Kegel exercises with biofeedback led to our studying the pelvic muscle strength of women who claimed to ejaculate and those who did not. We also rediscovered a sensitive area that is felt through the anterior vaginal wall, which we named the Grafenberg spot, after Ernst Grafenberg, M.D., who wrote about it and the phenomenon of orgasmic expulsion of fluid from the urethra in 1950. John and I presented our preliminary findings at AASECT and SSSS meetings and published our results in two articles in the *Journal of Sex Research*.

What followed next was probably the most difficult and the most exciting part of my professional career. Alice and Harold Ladas were beginning to write a book about our research. George Bach wanted me to write a book about it also and introduced me to his literary agent. So the Ladases and I joined together and agreed on a book contract that my agent (thanks to George Bach) negotiated with Holt, Rinehart and Winston. John Perry joined us and Harold, ill with cancer, stepped down as a co-author. *The G Spot and Other Recent Discoveries about Human Sexuality* came out with a great deal of media hype. It received some excellent reviews, others that were devastating, and it was selected by five book clubs. Professionally, I was called upon by colleagues and medical professionals to defend writing a book for the general public. How could a nurse without a doctorate conduct research and rediscover something that the medical profession did not know about? And I was asked to defend receiving an advance for the book. It was one of the most difficult times in my life. Since then, over thirty research publications have supported most of our findings, although a few have not. I believe that we may have allowed the Grafenberg spot and female ejaculation to be linked together when they may or may not be related. I have since published on this concept, with supporting data.

It was also an exciting time because I had the opportunity to talk with people all over the United States, Canada, France, and England; appear on television and radio; and disseminate the message that women can respond sexually in many different ways. And I was able to interview many women and listen to their stories.

The information we disseminated about female ejaculation helped women to avoid having surgery for something that is a natural phenomenon. Many women said they had stopped having orgasm because they felt something was wrong with them. Talking about this information helped to free these women to enjoy their sexual responses. To have helped prevent surgery and have more women feel good about themselves and their sexual response made all the difficult times worthwhile.

I do believe that the publication of *The G Spot* helped to affirm the experiences of women who did not fit into a monolithic pattern of sexual response. I believe that it helped educators, therapists, and researchers to understand that each woman is a unique individual and as such has the capacity to respond in various ways. These findings have led us to learn more about female sexuality and female sexual response.

At an SSSS meeting in Philadelphia, Betsy Allgeier and Vern Bullough had a long talk with me and strongly encouraged me to obtain a Ph.D. I wanted to study for a doctorate and learn more about research and now two well-known professionals whom I admired and respected believed in me, so I began investigating doctoral programs. In February 1986, I received a Ph.D. in psychobiology, with an emphasis in neurophysiology. Thanks to another colleague from the field, Sharon Johnson Brown, who provided a room nearby, I was able to be a full-time graduate student at Rutgers University. Jim Ramey, from Bowman-Grey Medical College in Winston-Salem, North Carolina, and author of a number of sexuality books, served as an outside member of my dissertation committee.

With my advisor, Barry Komisaruk, I investigated the natural significance of the Grafenberg spot, and found that stimulation of the vagina produces a strong analgesia effect, which has been demonstrated across species. We also conducted studies that demonstrated that this natural analgesic effect occurs during labor in women and during birth in rats (at that time we did not study women giving birth). Our further studies demonstrated that sexual stimulation that is pleasurable and not forceful also produces an analgesic effect.

One observation I made when I was teaching OB nursing was that Spanish-speaking women had a harder time during labor, which I told my students was probably cultural; that is, they felt more comfortable expressing their pain. However, when Barry and others discovered that neonatal rats injected with capsaicin do not get the natural pain-blocking effect from vaginal stimulation when they are adults, I began to wonder if the two observations were related. The Spanish-speaking women had diets high in chili peppers. We then investigated the effects of the ingestion of capsaicin, the main pungent ingredient in hot chili pepper, on pain thresholds. We found that women in Mexico who eat a diet high in chili peppers do not have the same natural analgesic effect from vaginal self-stimulation as do Mexican women who eat a moderate amount of or no chili peppers in their diet. We are now investigating the effect of diet on pain during labor.

While finishing my doctorate, I began a second master's degree in nursing so I could join the faculty at Rutgers College of Nursing. I have been teaching at Rutgers since 1987. When I came, I received funding to create a human physiology laboratory in which I could continue my research program. In addition to my faculty position in the College of Nursing, I am also an associate at the Institute of Animal Behavior and the Molecular and Behavioral Neuroscience Center at Rutgers.

In the late 1980s, Gina Ogden and I co-authored *Safe Encounters: How Women Can Say Yes to Pleasure and No to Unsafe Sex.* I believe that our book came out prematurely, because in 1989 society was not ready to believe that women could be at risk for HIV infection and AIDS. And the media certainly did not want to talk about the risk to women. This was a gay male and IV drug user disease, how could heterosexual men and lesbian women be transmitting the infection to their partners? Our information on safer sex is still important today, but, alas, the book is no longer in print. *The G Spot,* however, which was an international best-seller, is now being translated into its nineteenth language. To me, both books offer valuable information about sexual pleasure, but safer sex and outercourse just don't sell.

I have continued my research in the area of women and HIV infection and AIDS and also conducted a study on older adults and HIV infection, which Kathy Scura and I published in 1990. I am continuing to function as a co-investigator on a number of projects concerning women and HIV infection with Loretta Sweet-Jemmott and Suzanne Smeltzer.

During the writing of *Safe Encounters,* Gina and I often discussed the findings from her dissertation with easily orgasmic women. She found that 64 percent of her sample reported that they could have orgasm by imagery alone, without touching their bodies. I felt we needed to document this in the laboratory; therefore, Gina Ogden, Barry Komisaruk, and I investigated imagery-induced orgasm. We were able to document that there is no difference in the significant elevations in blood pressure, heart rate, pupil diameter, or pain thresholds from genital self-stimulated orgasm compared to those that result from imagery-induced orgasm.

Barry Komisaruk and I are currently documenting orgasm in women with complete spinal cord injury. We have identified a nerve pathway in rats that bypasses the spinal cord and goes directly to the brain. We are currently conducting PET (positron emission tomography) scans of the brain in women with spinal cord injury to determine if this same pathway is involved in their report of orgasm (with concomitant elevations in autonomic responses and pain thresholds) from genital self-stimulation. These are women who have been told, based on literature, that they could not experience orgasm or if they did, it was labeled a "phantom orgasm."

My research has been supported by intramural and extramural grant funding. I have been principal investigator, co-principal investigator, or co-investigator on fifteen funded grants totaling almost two million dollars.

Throughout the years I have co-authored two books and authored or co-authored over sixty journal articles and book chapters. I have delivered over three hundred professional talks internationally and have been on over one hundred fifty international television and radio programs. I have received a number of honors, including the Hugo G. Beigel Research award for the best article published in the *Journal of Sex Research* and the New Jersey State Nurses' Association Award for Excellence in Nursing Research. Two colleagues from nursing and sexuality, Bonnie Bullough and Jackie Hott, nominated me for fellowship in the American Academy of Nursing. I was elected a fellow in the American Academy of Nursing and also a fellow of the SSSS. I am extremely proud to have been so honored by both professions. And my mother, who has always asked me to please do something she can tell her friends about, finally told me for the first time in fifty-odd years that she was proud of me. When I asked her why, she said it was because I was in *Reader's*

Digest and she showed it to all of her friends. I guess we just have to learn the proper criteria.

The reactions of others to my research in sexuality has been very mixed. My husband and our adult offspring, however, have always been extremely supportive, even back when *The G Spot* came out. Our son Allen said it got him a lot of dates in college. Our daughter Susan and her friends helped with *Safe Encounters* by writing some of the lines men use to get women to have unsafe sex, and the responses women can use. Allen and Sue also helped with library research.

Most of my colleagues in nursing think of sexuality as my thing; some have said that they don't believe that the studies I conduct are real research, or at least not nursing research. Others have been extremely supportive and many have conducted research and published with me. Since I have received tenure at both Gloucester County College and Rutgers, some colleagues must believe my research and publications are valid and contribute to a body of knowledge.

I have been elected to serve two separate terms as treasurer of SSSS and three years as the Eastern Regional representative to its board of directors. In addition, I have been elected to serve for four years as the director-at-large on the Board of Directors of AASECT and served for six years on the board of directors of the Foundation for SSSS. I have edited every issue of AASECT's publication, *Contemporary Sexuality,* since its inception. I have been elected to the International Academy of Sex Research and am a member of the Sex Information and Education Council of the United States (SIECUS). I serve as a reviewer or on the editorial board of a number of professional journals. I feel that by serving the sexuality organizations in whatever capacity I am able is helping to contribute to the advancement of the field.

The reaction of the profession to my research has usually been extremely positive. I have had sexuality colleagues say that they come to hear me present at professional meetings because they are always interested in my new discoveries, whatever they are. Internationally, I have met many colleagues who have replicated our studies. Karl Stifter drove from Vienna, Austria, to Italy, where I was speaking at a conference on pain and reproduction, to talk about each of our findings with the analysis of the fluid expelled during female ejaculation. He has written a book on the subject in German.

I had my first experience crossing the iron curtain in 1986 when Jim and I traveled to meet Dr. Milan Zavicac in what was then Czechoslovakia. When the Czech border guards took Jim's and my passports, left the bus with them, and then called us off the bus, we didn't know what would happen. We were asked to change a certain amount of money and later allowed to reboard the bus with our passports. That experience produced quite some anxiety. Milan and his family were waiting for us at the bus station in Bratislava and we had a wonderful visit with them. Dr. Zavicac is a pathologist who has conducted a number of immunohistochemical studies concerning female ejaculation. We have since published together and have received an award from the Slovak Sexology Society for exceptional research publications.

I was invited to give three talks at the Third Asian Conference on Sexology in

New Delhi, India, in 1994. My husband, who came with me, was very impressed by all the presentations by people from Asian countries on or relating to the G spot. One researcher from India has found references to this sensitive area in Sanskrit and in the *Kama Sutra*. Another from Malaysia has extended our work with the G spot to helping women with problems of decreased vaginal lubrication. I felt as if I had given birth and my children were presenting. I thoroughly enjoyed and continue to enjoy exchanging ideas with colleagues worldwide. Chua Chee Ann from Malaysia came to Singapore to meet with Jim and me a few months ago so that I could help him rewrite his research papers for publication. He also served as an excellent tour guide, since his family was from Singapore.

I have been very fortunate to have been invited to speak about my research all over the world, well, at least in over twenty countries north of the equator. I just crossed the equator for the first time a few months ago to speak in Jakarta, Indonesia. I am so thrilled and honored that there is worldwide interest in female sexuality and research concerning female sexual response, and that people are inviting a female sexuality researcher to speak about her research.

I have also had the opportunity to talk with teens and young adults worldwide about sexuality and safer sex. I am always amazed at how interested and receptive young people are from Russia to Hong Kong to Guatemala. It is so rewarding knowing that you may have saved a life by helping them through the intricacies of safer sex.

In all my talks and in many of my publications I try to emphasize the concept of pleasure-oriented in contrast to goal-directed sexual expression. The most common view is goal-directed, which I describe as being analogous to climbing a flight of stairs. The first step is touch, the next step kissing, the next steps are caressing, then vagina/penis contact, which leads to intercourse and then to the top step of orgasm. There is a goal that both or one partner has in mind, and that goal is orgasm. If the sexual experience does not lead to the achievement of that goal, then the couple or the person who is goal-oriented does not feel good about all that they have experienced.

Pleasure-directed expression I conceptualize as a circle, with each expression the perimeter of the circle considered an end in itself. Whether the experience is kissing, oral sex, holding, or whatever, each is an end in itself and each is satisfying to the couple or the individual. There is no need to have this form of expression lead to anything else.

As I report my findings, I try to incorporate the concept of pleasure-oriented sexual expression. When we wrote *The G Spot* we stated that "sex is for pleasure, and when it becomes goal-oriented, the pleasure is often diminished. The facts we have presented indicate that there are many dimensions to the way people experience sexual orgasm" (p. 170). I hope that all of our findings concerning the G spot, female ejaculation, vaginal orgasm, imagery-induced orgasm, and so on, will not be set up as a goal that someone has to achieve. I hope that people will focus on the process of sexual interactions rather than a goal.

480 "HOW I GOT INTO SEX"

I probably sound as if I have been on a soap box. But it is so important to me to have people feel good about themselves as sexual beings and not be so goal-oriented in terms of their sexual responses. I feel that I have come a long way in my own personal and professional development and I want to share the best of what I have learned with others.

I continue to teach nursing, although I now teach mostly graduate courses. I have Ph.D. students working with me in my laboratory and I continue to publish and speak about sexuality. I alluded earlier to being a risk taker. I believe everyone in the field of sexuality is a risk taker. We are teaching, counseling, and conducting research in an area that among some people is still stigmatized as not being quite a legitimate profession. Society is comfortable talking about and supporting research on pain, but still uncomfortable talking about and providing support for the study of pleasure. And I, for óne, believe that we have to change this.

I feel very blessed to have had the opportunity to learn about sexuality and to have contributed some to the field. And I thank you for giving me this opportunity to tell you about my life as a sexologist.

References

Ladas, Alice, Harold Ladas, and Beverly Whipple. 1982. *The G Spot and Other Recent Discoveries about Human Sexuality.* New York: Holt, Rinehart and Winston.

Ogden, Gina, and Beverly Whipple. 1990. *Safe Encounters: How Women Can Say Yes to Pleasure and No to Unsafe Sex.* New York: McGraw Hill.